PRINCIPLES OF INTERNATIONAL TRADE LAW

including

The World Trade Organization, Technology Transfers, and Import/Export/Customs Law

Second Edition

Ralph H. Folsom

Professor of Law
University of San Diego School of Law
A.B. Princeton University, JD Yale Law School
LLM London School of Economics

CONCISE HORNBOOK SERIES™

WEST
ACADEMIC
PUBLISHING

© 2014 LEG, Inc. d/b/a West Academic
© 2018 LEG, Inc. d/b/a West Academic
          444 Cedar Street, Suite 700
          St. Paul, MN 55101
          1-877-888-1330

Printed in the United States of America

ISBN: 978-1-64020-140-8

Preface

Principles of International Trade Law is part of West Academic Publishing's Concise Hornbook series. Its coverage commences in Part One with the World Trade Organization, followed by Part Two on Customs and Import Law, Part Three on Export Law, and Part Four on Technology Transfers across Borders.

Principles of International Trade Law can be used in connection with **any** international trade or international business transactions course book. It can also be used on its own as a course book or treatise, notably in conjunction with the documents appended at the end of various chapters and at the end of the text.

Your feedback and suggestions are most welcome.

Ralph H. Folsom
Professor of Law,
University of San Diego
rfolsom@sandiego.edu

August 2017

About the Author

Ralph H. Folsom has been a Professor at the University of San Diego School of Law since 1975. A graduate of Princeton University, Yale Law School and the London School of Economics (LLM), Professor Folsom teaches, writes and consults extensively in the field of international business law.

Folsom has been a Senior Fulbright resident scholar in Singapore and a Visiting Professor at the University of Hong Kong, University of Aix-Marseille, University of Brest, University of Paris, University of Toulouse, University of Puerto Rico, Monash University in Australia and Tecnológico de Monterrey in México.

Professor Folsom's has co-authored course books with West Academic Publishing. These include: *International Business Transactions*; *IBT: International Trade and Economic Relations*; *IBT: Foreign Investment Law; and IBT: Contracting Across Borders*.

He is the author of a number of West Academic Nutshells, including: *International Trade and Economic Relations; NAFTA Re-Negotiated and Its Business Implications* (forthcoming)*; European Union Law including BREXIT; Foreign Investment Law; and International Business Transactions* (co-authored).

Professor Folsom has also written in the West Concise Hornbook Series: *Principles of International Litigation and Arbitration; Principles of European Union Law including BREXIT; Principles of Free Trade Agreements* (forthcoming), *and Principles of International Business Transactions* (co-authored).

He is the author of a two-volume *Practitioner Treatise on International Business Transactions* and is revising the nine-volume Eckstrom treatise on *International Joint Ventures,* both published by Thomson Reuters and available on Westlaw.

Summary of Contents

Table of Contents

PART THREE. EXPORT LAW

PRINCIPLES OF INTERNATIONAL TRADE LAW

including

The World Trade Organization, Technology Transfers, and Import/Export/Customs Law

Second Edition

Part One

WORLD TRADE LAW

Chapter 1

THE ESSENTIALS OF INTERNATIONAL TRADE LAW/THE WTO

Table of Sections

NOTE: A Directory of coverage in this book of the World Trade Organization (WTO) agreements is presented in Section 1.3 below.

Selected provisions of the GATT 1947 and 1994, various WTO agreements, and the WTO Dispute Settlement Understanding (DSU) are appended at the end of this book.

---

§ 1.0   Introduction to International Trade and Trade Treaties

International trade law has a long and controversial history. Many nations, especially in their early stages of development, are fearful of trade across borders. International trade is a competitive force, one that typically shakes up domestic economic interests, creating larger markets focused on greater specialization, lower costs, higher and lower incomes, and overall a bigger global economic pie. As such international trade is a powerful engine of change, creating winners and losers in its path. It is now certain, for example, that China's admission to the WTO in 2001 contributed to a large negative impact on U.S. manufacturing jobs and wages in the Midwest, but also shipment to China of 60% of all U.S. exports of soya beans. Simultaneously, WTO membership helped to lift many millions of Chinese out of poverty, but also caused the laying off of millions of state-owned enterprise employees.

At the same time, Wal-Mart's heavy importation of inexpensive Chinese goods notably reduced U.S. consumer costs, particularly for lower income and displaced Americans. That said, President Trump's America First election revealed deep resentment of the consequences of trade, especially the resulting U.S. trade deficits with China, Japan, Mexico and Germany. Forgotten in the political dialogue were the U.S. trade surpluses with Hong Kong, the United Kingdom and Singapore.

But there is a need to "unpack" trade deficit data. For example, roughly 65% of the value of iPhones shipped from China originates in the U.S., yet their full value appears in U.S.-China trade data. Roughly 40% of the value *all* Mexican goods crossing into the United States is American in origin. Furthermore, U.S. trade deficit numbers tend to be portrayed in goods only, omitting trade surpluses in services, and not considering foreign investment capital flows.

The United States in its early years sheltered "infant" agricultural and industrial sectors behind protective tariffs and regulatory restraints. When the Great Depression of the 1930s arrived, the United States enacted highly protective tariffs under the Smoot-Hawley Tariff Act of 1930 intended to wall off its economy from foreign competition, in theory "saving American jobs for American citizens". Other nations around the world retreated from international trade through similarly protective laws. Fear of foreign trade (and foreigners) reached a zenith that most economists agree deepened and prolonged the Great Depression. World War II rescued the United States from the Depression, but did nothing to remove the

Smoot-Hawley tariffs and encourage other nations to do likewise. International trade law was at a crossroads.

Despite its economic power and leadership in the development of the WTO and modern trade law, the United States retains, notably under the Trump administration (*see* Chapter 16), some of its early fear and concerns about international commerce and multilateral trade agreements. This is particularly apparent when U.S. free trade agreements are debated and undertaken (*see* Section 2.4), but also when the U.S. invokes "trade remedies" (*see* Chapters 4, 5 and 6) and controls exports of goods and technology (*see* Chapter 10). Little wonder then that developing nations, many not much more than 50 years old and created out of colonial empires, hesitate to embrace the panoply of modern international trade law.

Unlike the United States, some developed nations are unusually dependent on international trade in goods and services. The Netherlands, for example, depend on exports for over 75% of their Gross Domestic product (GDP). Roughly 50% of the GDPs of Sweden, Germany and Switzerland derive from exports. Canada, New Zealand, France and Britain come in at about 25%, with the United States at approximately 12%.

The need to balance the protection of local industries from harm by foreign competitors and the encouragement of trade across national borders is a recurrent theme in the law of international business transactions. There has been a shift in recent years toward freer international trade reflected notably in diminished restrictions on imported goods and services. However, problems associated with imports and exports across borders still arise because of restrictive laws and practices which impede or distort trade. In most countries, "trade adjustment assistance" (*see* Chapter 5) to adversely damaged workers has been insufficient economically and politically.

The law of international trade, for better or worse, shapes the scope and direction of the disruptive force of international trade. Common protective devices include tariff barriers (e.g., normal import and export duties, and special antidumping and subsidy countervailing duties), as well as nontariff trade barriers (NTBs) such as quotas, import and export licensing procedures, safety, environmental, health and other regulatory standards, complex customs procedures, and government procurement policies. For example, France once required that all video recorders entering France had to do so through a small customs post at Poitiers and carry documentation written in French. Product distribution practices have been an effective NTB in Japan. The United States has a host of NTB restraints, reviewed in Chapter 7, and the Trump administration has suggested invocation of protective trade remedies and rules for six "core industries"—steel, aluminum, vehicles, aircraft, shipbuilding and semiconductors. *See* Chapter 16.

Lastly, not all trade inhibiting barriers are government-made. Private sector cartel restraints can also keep international trade from reaching its full potential. See R. Folsom et al, *Principles of International Business Transactions.*

Trade Treaties

Early efforts by countries to limit disruptive trade practices were traditionally found in bilateral treaties of Friendship, Commerce and Navigation (FCN), some of which remain in force. Such treaties opened the territory of each signatory to greater imports, at times controversially under "unequal treaty" terms favoring European nations and the United States in Asia, for example. Bilateral FCN treaty clauses were usually linked to other preferential trade agreements. Such linkage was most often accomplished through a reciprocal "most favored nation" (MFN) clause. In a MFN clause, both parties agree not to extend to any other nation trade arrangements which are more favorable than available under the bilateral treaty, unless the more favorable trade arrangements are immediately *also* available to the other FCN signatory. FCN treaties also focused on promoting foreign investment across borders, shipping and basic trade and investment principles of "national treatment". . . . the right to be taxed, regulated and generally treated in the same legal manner as domestic businesses.

At this point, the United States has moved beyond many of its FCN treaties to bilateral Trade and Investment Framework Agreements (TIFAs), Free Trade Agreements (FTAs) and Bilateral Investment Treaties (BITs). All three can be found at www.ustr.gov. FCN trade and investment law principles, notably MFN and national treatment, carry over into these agreements. TIFAs are centered on dialogue about trade and investment issues. They often precede the more advanced legal regimes of U.S. FTAs and BITs.

The United States has numerous TIFAs with individual countries and regional economic groups. The U.S. has TIFAs with Angola, Ghana, Liberia, Mauritius, Mozambique, Nigeria, Rwanda, South Africa and the Common Market for Eastern and Southern Africa (COMESA), the East African Community, the West African Economic and monetary Union (WAEMU) and the South African Customs Union (titled as a Trade, Investment and Development Agreement). The U.S. also has TIFAs with Algeria, Bahrain, the Caribbean Common Market (CARICOM), Egypt, the Gulf Cooperation Council, Georgia, Iceland, Iraq, Kuwait, Lebanon, Libya, Oman, Qatar, Saudi Arabia, Switzerland, Tunisia, Turkey, Ukraine, the United Arab Emirates, Uruguay and Yemen. Additional TIFAs have been concluded with Afghanistan, collectively with five Central Asian nations, the Maldives, Nepal, Pakistan, Sri Lanka, the ASEAN group (Association of South East Asian Nations), Brunei, Cambodia, Indonesia, Malaysia, New Zealand, the Philippines, Thailand and Vietnam.

In various parts of the world, two or more countries have joined in customs unions or free trade areas in order to facilitate trade between those countries, and to acquire increased bargaining power in trade negotiations. The European Union and NAFTA are prime examples. *See* R. Folsom, *Principles of European Union Law including BREXIT* (2017) and R. Folsom and W. D. Folsom, *NAFTA Re-Negotiated and Its Business Implications* (forthcoming). Hundreds of bilateral and multilateral free trade agreements now lattice the globe, many replacing older FCN treaties. The free trade agreements of the United States are reviewed in Chapter 2.

But the most dramatic and far reaching trade agreements in modern times originate from the General Agreement on Tariffs and Trade (GATT, 1947) and its successor, the World Trade Organization (WTO). Commencing in 1995, the WTO package of international trade agreements establishes a rules-based legal baseline for some 165 member states. *See* Section 1.3 for a list of the WTO agreements and directions as to their coverage in this book.

In the materials that follow, we move first to a review of the GATT (1947). The GATT was an international arrangement with over one hundred countries as Contracting States which regularly held multilateral trade negotiations (MTN) seeking ways of making international trade more open. These periodic negotiations cumulatively reduced tariff barriers by an average of up to eighty percent below those existing in the Great Depression. For example, after the most recent multilateral negotiations completed in 1994, average tariff rates of developed countries on dutiable manufactured imports were cut from 6.3 percent to 3.9 percent. In addition, considerable international trade now crosses borders duty free. *See* R. Folsom, *Principles of Free Trade Agreements* (forthcoming).

Tariff reductions and eliminations are one of the success stories of GATT (1947). *See* Section 1.2. That said, as the Trump administration has noted, there are presently significant differences on key products such as autos, generally subject to a 2.5% tariff entering the USA, a 10% tariff entering the EU, and a 25% tariff entering China.

Not all nations participated in the GATT 1947 or are members of its replacement, the WTO. By the 1970s, nontariff trade barriers

(NTBs) began to be addressed by the GATT, including agreements designed to lessen NTBs such as complex customs valuation procedures, import licensing systems, product standards, subsidies and countervailing duties, and dumping practices. The GATT 1947 NTB agreements were optional, however, and most of the developing world membership opted out. When the 1990s arrived, international trade law was once again at a crossroad.

§ 1.1   The General Agreement on Tariffs and Trade (1947), Core MFN and National Treatment Principles

United States, British and other participants in the 1994 Bretton Woods, New Hampshire meetings recognized a post-War need to reduce trade obstacles in order to foster freer trade. They envisioned the creation of an International Trade Organization (ITO) to achieve the desired result. Fifty-three countries met in Havana in 1948 to complete drafting the Charter of an ITO that would be the international organizational umbrella underneath which negotiations could occur periodically to deal with tariff reductions and a wide range of trade law matters. A framework for such negotiations had already been staked out in Geneva in 1947, in what was expected to be only a transitional document, the General Agreement on Tariffs and Trade (GATT 1947) in goods.

Twenty-three nations participated in that first GATT session, India, Chile, Cuba and Brazil representing the developing world. China participated; Japan and West Germany did not. Stringent trading rules for goods (and only goods) were adopted only where there were no special interests of major participants to alter them. The developing nations objected to many of the strict rules, arguing for special treatment justified on development needs, but they achieved few successes in drafting GATT 1947. Some commenters believe GATT 1947 was in essence a deal struck between the United States and Europe, especially Britain.

The ITO Charter was never ratified. The United States Congress in the late 1940s was unwilling to join more new international organizations. Thus U.S. ratification of the ITO Charter could not be secured. Nonetheless, moving by way of the President Truman's power to make executive agreements, the United States did join twenty-one other countries, as Contracting Parties, in signing a Protocol of Provisional Application of the General Agreement on Tariffs and Trade (61 Stat.Pts. 5, 6) (popularly called the "GATT 1947 Agreement").

One notable feature of this protocol was the exemption of existing trade restraints of the Contracting States. Because of the failure to create the ITO, the GATT 1947 Agreement evolved from its "provisional" status into the premier international trade body, GATT the **organization** based in Geneva. It was through this organization that tariffs were steadily reduced over decades by means of increased membership and GATT negotiating Rounds. Today, the GATT 1947 Agreement has been replaced by the substantially similar GATT 1994 Agreement, part of the World Trade Organization "package" of trade agreements that took effect in 1995. *See* Section 1.3. The United States, having denied the creation of the ITO in the late 1940s, had to wait more that forty years for a second bite at the apple. When that opportunity finally came, the U.S. was among the strongest proponents of the WTO.

Trade in Goods: MFN Treatment

One of the central features of GATT 1947 and 1994 is Article I, which makes a general commitment to "most favored nation treatment" (MFN) by requiring each Contracting Party to accord unconditional MFN status to goods from all other Contracting Parties. Thus, any privilege or tariff granted by a Contracting Party to products imported from any other country (not necessarily a WTO member) must also be "immediately and unconditionally" granted to any "like product" imported from any Contracting Parties. Article 1 of the GATT (1947) and (1994) spells out the golden rules of MFN trading:

> With respect to customs duties and charges of any kind imposed on or in connection with importation or exportation or imposed on the international transfer of payments for imports or exports, and with respect to the method of levying such duties and charges, and with respect to all rules and formalities in connection with importation and exportation, and with respect to all matters referred to in paragraphs 2 and 4 of Article III, <u>any advantage, favor, privilege or immunity granted by any contracting party to any product originating in or destined for any other country shall be accorded immediately and unconditionally to the like product originating in or destined for the territories of all other contracting parties</u>. (*emphasis added*).

MFN principles essentially ban de jure and de facto tariff and trade discrimination, tit-for-tat trade wars a la the 1930s, and encourage agreements by ensuring that subsequent deals do not undercut MFN tariff levels. MFN has generally benefited latecomers (such as China in 2001) by providing them the benefits of prior GATT/WTO negotiating rounds, such as the zero MFN tariff status on U.S. imports of steel. This reduces the range of concessions the United States and other founding GATT/WTO members can offer applicant countries and has led to disparate tariffs on similar goods. China, for example, tariffs steel at 4 to 5% and autos at 25%, and the EU tariffs autos at 10% whereas the United States generally collects a 2.5% tariff on automobiles. For leading WTO Appellate Body decisions on the application of MFN rules, see EC—Bananas, WT/DS27/AB/R (1997), Canada—Autos, WT/DS139/AB/R (2000).

There are two major exceptions to the MFN obligation of Article I: Free trade areas and customs unions (see R. *Folsom, Principles of Free Trade Agreements* (forthcoming)) and differential and more favorable treatment of goods from developing countries (see Section 1.2). General exceptions contained in GATT Article XX and XXI (below) may also apply.

One unprecedented MFN issue is how Britain and the European Union will be treated after BREXIT. The EU negotiates GATT MFN tariffs and GATS trade in services commitments as a group. Britain, despite being a founding GATT 1947 member, may have to "rectify" (adjust under GATT Article 28 and GATS Article 25) or re-negotiate its EU-derived MFN tariff schedule and GATS commitments. Likewise, the EU may need to rectify or re-negotiate its MFN schedule and GATS commitments minus the UK, a less powerful bargaining position. Both BREXIT parties would be subsequently open to WTO complaints from other member states about such rectifications. *See* Section 16.2.

Trade in Goods: National Treatment

GATT Article III incorporates the practice of according "national treatment" to imported goods by providing, with enumerated exceptions, that they shall receive the same tax and regulatory treatment as domestic goods. In this context, national treatment requires that "like products" of the exporting GATT Contracting State be treated no less favorably than domestic products of the importing State under its laws and regulations concerning sale, internal resale, purchase, transportation and use. Physical properties, consumer perspectives and tariff classifications all contribute to evaluating the "likeness" of products. See EC—Asbestos, WT/DS 135/AB/R (2001). In addition to film distribution quotas (Article IV), two major exceptions apply to Article III: Government procurement policies (see Section 1.13), and authorized subsidization of domestic industries (see Chapter 5).

The core text of Article III provides:

> The contracting parties recognize that internal taxes and other internal charges, and laws, regulations and requirements affecting the internal sale, offering for sale, purchase, transportation, distribution or use of products,

and internal quantitative regulations requiring the mixture, processing or use of products in specified amounts or proportions, should not be applied to imported or domestic products so as to afford protection to domestic production.

The products of the territory of any contracting party imported into the territory of any other contracting party shall not be subject, directly or indirectly, to internal taxes or other internal charges of any kind in excess of those applied, directly or indirectly, to like domestic products. Moreover, no contracting party shall otherwise apply internal taxes or other internal charges to imported or domestic products in a manner contrary to the principles set forth in paragraph 1. * * *

The products of the territory of any contracting party imported into the territory of any other contracting party shall be accorded treatment no less favorable than that accorded to like products of national origin in respect of all laws, regulations and requirements affecting their internal sale, offering for sale, purchase, transportation, distribution or use. The provisions of this paragraph shall not prevent the application of differential internal transportation charges which are based exclusively on the economic operation of the means of transport and not on the nationality of the product.

Where GATT does permit non-discriminatory "duties, taxes and other charges," the powers of a Contracting Party are limited even as to these devices. First, GATT Article X requires that notice be given of any new or changed national regulations which affect international trade, by requiring the prompt publication of those "laws, regulations, judicial decisions and administrative rulings of general application." Second, the Contracting Parties commit themselves "from time to time" to a continuing series of multilateral tariff negotiations (MTN) to seek further reductions in tariff levels and other barriers to international trade. Such negotiations are to be "on a reciprocal and mutually advantageous basis." GATT negotiated tariff rates (called "concessions" or "bindings"), which are listed in the "Tariff Schedules", are deposited with GATT by each participating country. These concessions must be granted to imports from any Contracting Party, both because of the GATT requires MFN treatment, and also because Article II specifically requires use of the negotiated rates.

The 1947 GATT Agreement and its subsequent multinational negotiating rounds were quite successful in reducing tariff duty levels on trade in goods. *See* Section 1.2 below. This was its original purpose, and the mechanism was well-adapted to accomplishing that purpose. However, its effectiveness was also limited to trade in goods, and primarily to reduction of tariffs in such trade. It was not designed to affect trade in services, trade-related intellectual property rights or trade-related investment measures. As tariff duty rates declined, the trade-distorting effects of these other issues became more important.

Trade in Goods: General Exceptions

Even within "trade in goods," the 1947 GATT had limitations. It included a Protocol of Provisional Application which allowed numerous grandfathered exceptions to Members' obligations under the GATT Agreement. The Protocol exempted from GATT disciplines the national laws of Member States which were already enacted and in force at the time of adoption of the Protocol. This "grandfather clause" no longer applies under GATT 1994.

Framers of GATT 1947 were well aware that a commitment to freer trade could cause serious, adverse economic consequences from time to time within part or all of a country's domestic economy, particularly its labor sector. The GATT 1947 and 1994 contains at least seven safety valves (in nine clauses of the Agreement) to permit a country, in appropriate circumstances, to respond to domestic pressures while remaining a participant in GATT. Two safety valves deal with antidumping duties and countervailing government subsidies. *See* Chapters 4 and 5. Another important safety valve concerns "safeguard procedures." *See* Chapter 6.

General omnibus exceptions to the GATT are established in Chapter XX, notably for measures "necessary" to protect public morals, and human, animal and plant life or health. Australia's plain packaging requirements on tobacco products, a regulatory approach increasingly copied elsewhere, was deemed by a 2017 WTO panel a legitimate public health measure. *See also* U.S.-Shrimp, WT/DS 58/AB/R (1998) (protection of endangered sea turtles). Evaluating whether measures are "necessary" requires consideration of reasonably available alternative approaches to achieve public policy goals. *See* Brazil—Tires, WT/DS332/AB/R (2007) (ban on imports of retreaded tires upheld) and EC—Asbestos, WT/DS/AB/R (2001) (ban on asbestos imports upheld).

Another general exception concerns measures "relating to" the conservation of exhaustible natural resources. *See* China—Raw Materials, WT/DS 394, 395, 398 (Panel, 2011) (export quota on bauxite and export duty on fluorspar did not relate to conservation). Other general exceptions concern trade in gold and silver, prison labor, protection of national treasures, commodity agreements, government stabilization plans and products in general or local short supply.

All of these general exceptions are subject to the qualifying language of the Article XX "chapeau": They may not be applied in an arbitrary or unjustifiably discriminatory manner, or constitute a disguised restriction on international trade. *See* U.S.—Shrimp, 21.5, WT/DS58/AB/RW (2001) (unjustifiable and arbitrary discrimination found in U.S. shrimp import restraints intended to conserve endangered sea turtles). For additional examples of the application of these exceptions and its chapeau, see Sections 1.7, 7.4 and 7.5.

Chapter XXI of the GATT preserves the right of member states to act in ways it considers necessary for the protection of its essential security interests, a little used but potentially very disruptive provision that the Trump administration and other nations are focusing upon. WTO members, in accordance with GATT Articles XII, XV and XVIII, may also generally undertake trade and monetary exchange restraints necessary to deal with their balance of payments needs.

§ 1.2   The GATT 1947 Multinational Trade Negotiations (Rounds)

Under the auspices of GATT 1947 Article XXVIII, the Contracting Parties committed themselves to hold periodic multinational trade negotiations (MTN or "Rounds"). They completed eight such Rounds with the GATT membership steadily increasing:

Geneva (1947) with 19 countries

Annecy (1948) with 27 countries

Torquay (1950) with 33 countries

"Dillon Round" Geneva (1960–62) with 36 countries

"Kennedy Round" Geneva (1964–67) with 74 countries

"Tokyo Round" Geneva (1973–79) with 85 countries

"Uruguay Round" Geneva (1986–94) with 128 countries

The WTO Doha Round (2001–) with 164 countries is marginally ongoing.

The largest exporters by volume of particular goods generally take the lead on tariff reduction negotiations. While the first five Rounds concentrated on item by item tariff reductions, the "Kennedy Round" (1964–1967) was noted for its achievement of across-the-board tariff reductions. In 1961, GATT began to consider how to approach the increasing trade disparity with the developing world. In 1964, GATT adopted Part IV, which introduced a principle of "diminished expectations of reciprocity". Reciprocity remained a goal, but developed nations would not expect concessions from developing nations which were inconsistent with developmental needs. For the developing nations, non-reciprocity meant freedom to protect domestic markets from import competition. Import substitution was a major focus of developmental theory in the 1960s, and developing nations saw keeping their markets closed as a way to save these domestic industries. Part IV of GATT 1947 resulted in a substantial growth in developing nation Contracting Parties.

Although they also sought preferential treatment of their exports, that was a demand which would remain unsatisfied for another decade and longer. *See* Sections 2.10–2.16 covering GATT approved "generalized tariff preference" (GSP) schemes.

The "Tokyo Round" (1973–1979) engendered agreements about several areas of nontariff barrier (NTB) trade restraints. Nearly a dozen major agreements on nontariff barrier issues were produced in the Tokyo Round. In the early 1970s, national and regional generalized preference schemes (GSP) developed to favor the exports of developing nations. The foreign debt payment problems of the developing nations suggest that they need to generate revenue to pay these debts, and that developmental theory must shift from import substitution to export promotion.

In 1986, the "Uruguay Round" of multilateral trade negotiations began at a Special Session of the GATT Contracting States. This Uruguay Round included separate negotiations on trade in goods and on trade in services, with separate groups of negotiators dealing with each topic. Subtopics for negotiation by subgroups included nontariff barriers, agriculture, subsidies and countervailing duties, intellectual property rights and counterfeit goods, safeguards, tropical products, textiles, investment policies, and dispute resolution. The negotiating sessions were extraordinarily complex, but were able to achieve a successful conclusion at the end of 1993, giving birth to the World Trade organization in 1995.

WTO Negotiating Rounds

In 1999 an attempt at launching a "Seattle Round" led by President Clinton failed with violence in the streets. Two years later, the "Doha Round" was successfully launched in Qatar covering all existing WTO fields as well as E-commerce, trade and the environment, debt and finance, and special and differential treatment and assistance for developing countries. Developed WTO countries have been pushing foreign investment, competition policy, transparency in procurement, state-owned enterprise rules, and trade facilitation topics. At Cancun in 2003, the WTO developing nations rejected these topics, focusing on agricultural trade barriers to their exports. In 2017, India threatened to bring the WTO to a halt unless international investment facilitation discussions were terminated, which they were.

Scheduled for completion in 2005, the Doha Round of WTO negotiations collapsed in July 2008 after marathon sessions. India and China, in particular, insisted upon Special Safeguard Mechanisms against surges in agricultural imports, provisions the U.S. and EU did not accept. The members were in agreement on nearly all other areas of the Doha Round negotiations. In 2013, WTO members agreed on a "Bali Package" concerning trade facilitation focused on customs law and procedure that finally took effect in 2017. At this writing, the Doha Round remains on life support, which has caused many nations to accelerate their participation in bilateral and regional free trade agreements.

§ 1.3 The World Trade Organization (WTO): Directory of Agreements, Admission/ Withdrawal

The WTO is the product of the Uruguay Round of GATT negotiations, which was successfully completed in 1994. The Uruguay Round produced a package of agreements, the Agreement Establishing the World Trade Organization and its Annexes, which include the General Agreement on Tariffs and Trade 1994 (GATT 1994) and a series of Multilateral Trade Agreements (the Covered Agreements).[1] These agreements extend way beyond trade in goods to trade in services, trade-related intellectual property rights, trade-related investment measures, and a binding system of dispute settlement. All of the Covered Agreements are non-negotiable; they are mandatory. Four Plurilateral Trade Agreements are optional, though two of these Agreements (Dairy and Bovine Meat) have been rescinded.

GATT 1947 and GATT 1994 are two distinct agreements. GATT 1994 incorporates the provisions of GATT 1947, except for the Protocol of Provisional Application, which is expressly excluded. Thus, the problems created by exempting the existing national laws at the time of the adoption of the Protocol have been avoided by this exclusion. Otherwise, in cases involving a conflict between GATT 1947 and GATT 1994, GATT 1947 controls. The WTO will be guided by the decisions, procedures and customary practices under GATT.

---

[1]   *See* 33 Int. Legal Mat. 1130 (1994).

The WTO package of agreements are routinely construed in light of the Vienna Convention on the Interpretation of Treaties. *See, e.g.,* EC—Chicken, WT/DS269/AB/R (2005).

Annexed to the WTO Agreement are several Multilateral Trade Agreements. As to trade in goods, they include Agreements on Agriculture, Textiles, Antidumping, Subsidies and Countervailing Measures, Safeguards, Technical Barriers to Trade, Sanitary and Phytosanitary Measures, Pre-shipment Inspection, Rules of Origin, and Import License Procedures. In addition to trade in goods, they include a General Agreement on Trade in Services and Agreements on Trade-Related Aspects of Intellectual Property Rights and Trade-Related Investment Measures.

Affecting all of these agreements is the Understanding on Rules and Procedures Governing the Settlement of Disputes (DSU). All of the Multilateral Trade Agreements are generally binding on all members of the World Trade Organization. Moreover, should a conflict arise between GATT 1994 and one of these Agreements, the latter prevails. Hence in WTO dispute proceedings where a conflict may exist, panels are required to first examine the specific Multilateral Agreement before taking up the GATT 1994 issue. *See* EC—Sardines, WTO/DS231/AB/R (2002) and U.S.—Internet Gambling, WT/DS 285/AB/R (2005).

Existing WTO members may declare "non-application" of all these Agreements vis-a-vis new members, thus opting out of their application to them. The United States, for example, declared non-application of the WTO Agreements to Armenia, Moldova, Georgia, Mongolia and the Kyrgyz Republic when those nations joined the WTO, although these declarations were subsequently revoked for all but Moldova.

In addition to the Multilateral Trade Agreements, there are also Plurilateral Trade Agreements, which are annexed to the WTO Agreement. These agreements, however, are not binding on all WTO members, and states can choose to adhere to them or not. They include Agreements on Government Procurement, Trade in Civil Aircraft, International Dairy (rescinded), and an Arrangement Regarding Bovine Meat (rescinded). Member states which do not join the plurilateral trade agreements do not receive reciprocal benefits under them. Participating members agree to utilize the DSU to settle Plurilateral Trade Agreement disputes.

WORLD TRADE ORGANIZATION AGREEMENTS

AGREEMENT ESTABLISHING THE WORLD TRADE ORGANIZATION

ANNEX 1A: AGREEMENTS ON TRADE IN GOODS

1   General Agreement on Tariffs and Trade 1994

   (a)   Understanding on the Interpretation of Article II:1(b) (tariff concessions)

   (b)   Understanding on the Interpretation of Article XVII (state trading enterprises)

   (c)   Understanding on Balance-of-Payments Provisions

   (d)   Understanding on the Interpretation of Article XXIV (free trade areas and customs unions) **See R. Folsom, *Principles of Free Trade Agreements* (forthcoming).**

   (e)   Understanding on the Interpretation of Article XXV (waivers)

   (f)   Understanding on the Interpretation of Article XXVIII (modification of tariff schedules)

   (g)   Understanding on the Interpretation of Article XXXV (non-application of GATT)

2   GATT 1994 **(See Section 1.3)**

3   Agreement on Agriculture **(See Section 1.8)**

4   Agreement on Sanitary and Phytosanitary Measures (SPS) **(See Section 1.7)**

5   Agreement on Textiles and Clothing **(See Section 1.6)**

6   Agreement on Technical Barriers to Trade (TBT) **(See Section 1.7)**

7   Agreement on Trade-Related Investment Measures **(See Section 1.12)**

8   Agreement on Implementation of Article VI (antidumping and countervailing duties) **See Chapters 4 and 5.**

9   Agreement on Implementation of Article VII (customs valuation) **See Chapter 3.**

10   Agreement on Preshipment Inspection

11   Agreement on Rules of Origin **(See Section 1.10)**

12   Agreement on Import Licensing Procedures **(See Section 1.6)**

13   Agreement on Subsidies and Countervailing Measures **(See Chapter 5)**

14   Agreement on Safeguards **(See Chapter 6)**

ANNEX 1B: General Agreement on Trade in Services and Annexes (GATS) **(See Section 1.9)**

ANNEX 1C: Agreement on Trade-Related Aspects of Intellectual Property Rights, Including Trade in Counterfeit Goods (TRIPs) **(See Section 1.11)**

ANNEX 2:   Understanding on Rules and Procedures Governing the Settlement of Disputes (DSU) **(See Sections 1.14 and 1.15)**

ANNEX 3:   Trade Policy Review Mechanism **(See Section 1.4)**

ANNEX 4:   Plurilateral Trade Agreements

ANNEX 4(a) Agreement on Trade in Civil Aircraft

ANNEX 4(b) Agreement on Government Procurement **(See Section 1.13)**

ANNEX 4(c) International Dairy Arrangement (rescinded)

ANNEX 4(d) Arrangement Regarding Bovine Meat (rescinded)

In addition, Accession Agreements undertaken by new members may add to or subtract from the WTO package of mandatory multilateral agreements. China, for example, agreed to the application of special "safeguard" rules against its exports for a limited period of time after its WTO admission in 2001. *See* Section 6.12.

The duties of the World Trade Organization are to facilitate the implementation, administer the operations and further the objectives of all these agreements. Its duties also include the resolution of disputes under the agreements, reviews of trade policy and cooperation with the International Monetary Fund (IMF) and the World Bank. To achieve these goals, the WTO Agreement provides a charter for the new organization, but for only minimalist institutional and procedural capabilities, and no substantive competence. Thus, there is a unified administration of pre-existing and new obligations under all agreements concerning trade in goods, including the Uruguay Round Agreements. In addition, the administration of the new obligations on trade in services, intellectual property and foreign investment were brought under the same roof.

The WTO as an institution has no power to bring actions on its own initiative. Under the provisions of the WTO Agreement, only the members of WTO can initiate actions under the Dispute Settlement Understanding. Enforcement of WTO obligations is primarily through permitting members to retaliate or cross retaliate against other members, rather than by execution of WTO institutional orders. *See* Section 1.6 below. As Article 3.2 of the DSU suggests, many panel and Appellate Body decisions utilize the Vienna Convention on Interpretation of Treaties to clarify the meaning of the WTO package of agreements.

Admission to the WTO

The existing 130 or so members of GATT 1947 became the WTO's founding members Admission is open to nation states and customs territories (such as Hong Kong). Admission to the World Trade Organization is in common practice by "consensus." In theory, this gives each member a veto over applicant countries, though a formal two-thirds affirmative vote could be employed. In reality, no nation wishing to join has ever formally been vetoed, though many have been long delayed. Iran's desire to join has basically been frustrated by U.S. refusal to negotiate on WTO entry. It took, for example, well over a decade to negotiate acceptable terms of entry for the People's Republic of China and Chinese Taipei (Taiwan) in 2001, Vietnam in 2007 and Russia in 2012.

Such negotiations are handled individually by member states, not by the WTO as an organization. United States negotiations with China were particularly lengthy and difficult, one principal issue being whether China should be admitted as a developing or developed nation, which is normally a self-selected choice. The issue was fudged, with China treated differently within the WTO mandatory package of agreements.

Essentially, applicant counties make an offer of trade liberalization commitments and compliance with the mandatory Covered Agreements to join the WTO. This offer is renegotiated with interested member states, some 40 nations regarding China, including the European Union which negotiates as a unit (NAFTA does not). Regarding China, the last member to reach agreement on WTO admission was Mexico, which extracted stiff promises against the dumping of Chinese goods. The various trade commitments made by the applicant in these bilateral negotiations are consolidated into a final accession protocol, which is then approved by "consensus."

Withdrawal

As of 2017, there are approximately 165 WTO member states and customs territories. Any member may withdraw with six months' notice, something that has never happened, but could conceivably become an issue under the administration of U.S. President Donald Trump.

§ 1.4 WTO Decision-Making

The World Trade Organization is structured in three tiers. One tier is the Ministerial Conference, which meets biennially and is composed of representatives of all WTO members. Each member state has an equal voting weight. This is unlike the representation in the IMF and World Bank where there is weighted voting, and financially powerful states have more power over the decision-making process. The Ministerial Conference is responsible for all WTO functions, and is able to make any decisions necessary. It has the power to authorize new multilateral negotiations and to adopt the results of such negotiations. The Ministerial Conference, by a three-fourths vote, is authorized to grant waivers of obligations to members in exceptional circumstances. It also has the power to adopt interpretations of Covered Agreements. When the Ministerial Conference is in recess, its functions are performed by the General Council.

The second tier is the General Council which has executive authority over the day to day operations and functions of the WTO. It is composed of representatives of all WTO Members, and each member has an equal voting weight. It meets whenever it is appropriate. The General Council also has the power to adopt interpretations of Covered Agreements.

The third tier comprises the councils, bodies and committees which are accountable to the Ministerial Conference or General Council. Ministerial Conference committees include Committees on Trade and Development, Balance of Payment Restrictions, Budget, Finance and Administration. General Council bodies include the Dispute Settlement Body, the Trade Policy Review Body, and Councils for Trade in Goods, Trade in Services and Trade-Related Intellectual Property Rights. The Councils are all created by the WTO Agreement and are open to representatives of all member states. The Councils also have the authority to create subordinate organizations. Other committees, such as the Committee on Subsidies and Countervailing Measures are created by specific individual agreements.

Trade Policy Review Mechanism

Of the General Council bodies, the two which are most important are the Dispute Settlement Body (DSB) and the Trade Policy Review Body (TPRB). The DSB is a special meeting of the General Council, and therefore includes all WTO members. It has responsibility for resolution of disputes under all the Covered Agreements, discussed in more detail in Section 1.14 under Dispute Resolution.

The purpose of the Trade Policy Review Mechanism (TPRM) is to improve adherence to the WTO agreements and obligations, and to obtain greater transparency. In that regard, the TPRM supplements the general trade law transparency requirements of Chapter X of the GATT. Individual Members of WTO each prepare a "Country Report" on their trade policies and perceived adherence to the WTO Covered Agreements. The WTO Secretariat also prepares a report on each Member, but from the perspective of the Secretariat.

The Trade Policy Review Body (TPRB) then reviews the trade policies of each member based on these two reports. At the end of the review, the TPRB issues its own report concerning the adherence of the member's trade policy to the WTO Covered Agreements. The TPRB has no enforcement capability, but the report is sent to the next meeting of the WTO Ministerial Conference. It is then up to the Ministerial Conference to evaluate the trade practices and policies of the member.

Consensus Rules

The process of decision-making in the WTO Ministerial Conference and General Council relies upon "consensus" as the norm, just as it did for decision-making under GATT 1947. "Consensus", in this context means that no member formally objects to a proposed decision. Thus, consensus is not obtained if any one member formally objects, and has often been very difficult to obtain, which proved to be a weakness in the operation of GATT. However, there are many exceptions to the consensus formula under WTO, and some new concepts (such as "inverted consensus") which are designed to ease the process of decision-making under WTO.

Article IX (1) of the WTO Agreement first provides that "the practice of decision-making by consensus" followed under GATT shall be continued. The next sentence of that provision, however, states that "where a decision cannot be arrived at by consensus, the matter at issue shall be decided by voting", except where otherwise provided. The ultimate resolution of the conflict between these two sentences is not completely clear.

There are a number of exceptions to the requirement for consensus that are expressly created under the WTO Agreement. One such exception is decisions by the Dispute Settlement Body, which has its own rules (see Section 1.14). Another set of exceptions concerns decisions on waivers, interpretations and amendments of the Covered Agreements. Waivers of obligations may be granted and amendments adopted to Covered Agreements only by the Ministerial Conference. Amendments of Multilateral Trade Agreements usually require a consensus, but where a decision on a proposed amendment cannot obtain consensus, the decision on that amendment is to be made in certain circumstances by a two-thirds majority vote. In "exceptional circumstances", the Ministerial Conference is authorized to grant waivers of obligations under a Covered Agreement by a three-fourths vote. Another exception to the consensus requirement allows procedural rules in both the Ministerial Conference and the General Council to be decided by a majority vote of the members, unless otherwise provided.

Operationally speaking, the WTO membership rarely meets in its entirety. Alliances and groups within the membership meet to undertake WTO decisions. For example, the "Cairns Group" of 18 member-states has focused on agricultural trade issues and endured as a group for some time. Groups and alliances often shift depending upon the subject matter.

§ 1.5   WTO Agreements and U.S. Law

The WTO Covered Agreements concern not only trade in goods, but also trade in services (GATS), trade-related aspects of intellectual property (TRIPS) and trade-related investment measures (TRIMs). The basic MFN and national treatment concepts that GATT 1947 applied to trade in goods (see Section 1.1) are now applied to these areas through GATS and TRIPS. The basic concepts of GATT 1947 and its associated agreements are elaborated and clarified through interpretive "understandings". In addition, there is an attempt to transform all protectionist measures relating to agriculture (such as import bans and quotas, etc.) into only tariff barriers, which can then be lowered in subsequent MTN Rounds (a process known as "tariffication"). Some of the WTO provisions, particularly those concerning trade in goods, are discussed in more detail below in relation to United States trade law.

The United States enacted legislation to implement WTO and the Covered Agreements on December 3, 1994. The implementing legislation was submitted to Congress under the "fast track" procedures of 19 U.S.C.A. § 2112. The statutory authority for "fast track" procedures also required that the President give 90 days' notice of his intention to enter into such an agreement. Fast track required that the WTO Agreements be considered by Congress as negotiated by the President, with no Congressional amendments via the implementing legislation. Nevertheless, the Uruguay Round Agreements Act of 1994 was adopted with relatively little controversy. Similar fast track procedures were in place for the Doha Round of WTO negotiations under the Trade Promotion Authority Act of 2002, but expired in July of 2007.

GATT 1947, GATT 1994, the WTO Agreement and the other Covered Agreements have not been ratified as treaties. They therefore comprise international obligations of the United States only to the extent that they are incorporated in United States' implementing legislation. GATT 1947 was not considered controlling by the courts of the United States, which have always held themselves bound only to the U.S. legislation actually enacted.[2]

§ 1.6   Textiles and Clothing, Import/Export Quotas and Licensing

One critical reason why developing nations opted into the WTO package is the Agreement on Textiles. It eliminated as of 2005 the quotas long maintained under the Multi-Fiber Arrangement (MFA). The demise of MFA textile quotas in 2005, as widely expected, dramatically accelerated Chinese and other Asian textile exports to the United States. Responding to domestic pressures, the United States repeatedly invoked special safeguard protections against textile and clothing imports during the ten-year phase-out period that ended in 2005. Since then the average U.S. bound and applied tariff on textile products has been around 8 percent, and consumers must search very hard to find Made-in-the-USA clothing.

In addition to requiring MFN and national treatment, GATT 1947 and 1994 prohibits use of certain kinds of quantitative restrictions. Subject to exceptions such as balance of payment crises, Article XI prohibits "prohibitions or restrictions" on imports and it specifically prohibits the use of "quotas, import or export licenses or other measures" to restrict imports from a Contracting Party. Quotas include voluntary export restrain agreements. See Japan-Semiconductors, GATT Panel Report (1988). If utilized, Article XIII requires non-discrimination in quantitative trade restrictions, by barring an importing Contracting State from applying any prohibition or restriction to the products of another Contracting

---

[2]   *See, e.g., Suramerica de Aleaciones Laminadas, C.A. v. United States,* 966 F.2d 660 (Fed.Cir.1992).

State, "unless the importation of the like product of *all* third countries. . . is similarly prohibited or restricted." (*emphasis added*).

The WTO has significantly reduced the number of trade quotas. Voluntary export restraints (quotas) are severely limited by the Safeguards Agreement. *See* Section 6.3. In addition, the WTO removes trade quotas by advancing "tariffication," replacing quotas with tariffs—sometimes even at extraordinarily high tariff rates. Tariffication is the approach adopted in the WTO Agricultural Agreement. *See* Section 1.9.

Quantity restrictions, such as numerical quotas on the importation or exportation of goods continue to exist, despite GATT Article XI which calls for their elimination, subject to a number of broadly worded exceptions to relieve critical shortages, to ensure domestic price controls, and to remediate short supply conditions. "Tariff-rate quotas" admit a specified quantity of goods at a preferential rate of duty. Once imports reach that quantity, tariffs are normally increased. WTO disputes concerning quotas have resulted in a number of panel and Appellate Body decisions that largely treat import rules that can create de facto quantitative restraint effects as prohibited by Article XI. For example, in *India— Autos* (WTO/DS16/AB/R (2002) "trade balancing" rules requiring producers to export in order to import were held to breach Article XI.

Import (but not export) licensing schemes are allowed when quotas are permitted. On export licensing, see Section 1.6. International concern about delays which result from cumbersome import licensing procedures was manifested in the 1979 Tokyo Round MTN Import Licensing Code (which most developing countries refused to sign). The United States adhered to this Code, as did a reasonable number of other developed nations. The Uruguay Round made the Agreement on Import Licensing Procedures (1994) binding on all World Trade Organization members. The Agreement's objectives include facilitating the simplification and harmonization of import licensing and licensing renewal procedures, ensuring adequate publication of rules governing licensing procedures, and reducing the practice of refusing importation because of minor variations in quantity, value or weight of the import item under license.

§ 1.7   GATT/WTO Nontariff Trade Barrier Codes, TBT and SPS Codes

There are numerous nontariff trade barriers applicable to imports. Many of these barriers arise out of safety and health regulations. Others concern the environment, consumer protection, product standards and government procurement. Many of the relevant rules were created for legitimate consumer and public protection reasons. They were often created without extensive consideration of their international impact as potential nontariff trade barriers. Nevertheless, the practical impact of legislation of this type is to ban the importation of nonconforming products. Thus, unlike tariffs which can always be paid, and unlike quotas which permit a certain amount of goods to enter the market, nontariff trade barriers have the potential to totally exclude foreign exports.

Multilateral GATT negotiations since the end of World War II have led to a significant decline in world tariff levels, particularly on trade with developed nations. As steadily as tariff barriers have disappeared, nontariff trade barriers (NTBs) have emerged. Health and safety regulations, environmental laws, rules regulating products standards, procurement legislation and customs procedures are often said to present NTB problems.

Negotiations over nontariff trade barriers dominated the Tokyo Round of the GATT negotiations during the late 1970s. A number of optional NTB "codes" (sometimes called "side agreements") emerged from the Tokyo Round. These concerned subsidies, dumping, government procurement, technical barriers (products standards), customs valuation and import licensing. In addition, specific agreements regarding trade in bovine meats, dairy products and civil aircraft, as well as government procurement, were also reached. The United States accepted all of these NTB codes and agreements except the one on dairy products. Most of the necessary implementation of these agreements was accomplished in the Trade Agreements Act of 1979. Nearly all of the developing members of GATT opted out of these NTB codes.

Additional NTB codes were agreed upon under the Uruguay Round ending in late 1994 and became part of the WTO legal regime. All of the NTB areas covered by the Tokyo Round Codes were revisited, and new codes created for sanitary and phyto-sanitary measures (SPS), trade-related investment measures (TRIMs), pre-shipment inspection, rules of origin, escape clause safeguards and trade-related intellectual property rights (TRIPs). Unlike the Tokyo Round Codes, the WTO nontariff barrier codes (save a few plurilateral codes) are **mandatory** for all members. The United States Congress approved and implemented these Codes, along with the optional WTO Procurement Code, in December of 1994 under the Uruguay Round Agreements Act.

One problem with nontariff trade barriers is that they are so numerous. Intergovernmental negotiation intended to reduce their trade restricting impact is both tedious and difficult. There are continuing attempts through the World Trade Organization to come to grips with additional specific NTB problems. Furthermore, various trade agreements of the United States have been undertaken in this field. For example, the Canada-United States Free Trade Area Agreement and the NAFTA built upon the existing GATT agreements in attempting to further reduce NTB problems between the United States, Canada and Mexico.

SPS Code

The SPS Code strongly encourages the use of international SPS standards, such as the Codex Alimentarius Commission. But member states may proceed to enact their own nondiscriminatory SPS rules, subject to the Code's mandates, notably that they be based upon risk assessments and scientific evidence. There is some suggestion in the decisions of the WTO Appellate Body that SPS measures must be "proportional" to the risks involved. See *Japan-Apples*, WT/DS245/AB/R (2003).

Some of the difficulties of these NTBs are illustrated in the *EU Beef Hormones* case (WT/DS 26/AB/R (1998). The Sanitary and Phytosanitary Code (SPS Code) basically requires adherence to international food standards, or a scientific basis for regulatory rules governing food products. The EU, adhering to "precautionary principles," banned imports of growth-enhancing hormone-treated beef from the U.S. and Canada as a health hazard. The Appellate Body ruled in 1997 under the SPS Code that, since the ban was stricter than international standards, the EU needed scientific evidence to back it up. The Appellate Body noted the EU had failed to undertake a scientific risk assessment, and the EU's scientific reports did not provide any rational basis to uphold the ban. In fact, the primary EU study had found no evidence of harm to humans from the growth-enhancing-hormones. If the "relevant scientific evidence is insufficient", there is limited recognition of precautionary principles in Article 5.7 of the SPS Code.

The Appellate Body concluded that the ban violated the EU's SPS obligations, and required the EU to produce scientific evidence to justify the ban within a reasonable time, or to revoke the ban. Arbitrators later determined that 15 months was a reasonable time. But the EU failed to produce such evidence and the U.S. retaliated (as authorized) by imposing substantial tariffs on EU imports. Late in 2004, the EU commenced WTO proceedings asserting that new scientific studies and precaution justified its ban and required removal of U.S. retaliation. This WTO proceeding also went against the EU, again in the absence of adequate proof of scientific basis. *See* U.S.-Continued Suspension in EC—Hormones, WT/320/AB/R (2008). Finally, in 2009, a phased four year settlement of the *Beef Hormones* dispute was reached. The U.S. got a higher quota to export hormone-free beef to the EU in return for phasing out its retaliatory tariffs on EU goods.

TBT Code

Widespread use of "standards" requirements as NTB import restraints resulted in 1979 in the GATT Agreement on Technical Barriers to Trade (called the "Standards Code"). This Code was made operative in the United States by the Trade Agreements Act of 1979, and was followed by a reasonable number of other developed nations.

Its successor is the WTO Agreement on Technical Barriers to Trade (1994) (TBT Code). By explicit provision in Article 1.5 of the TBT Code, the SPS Code takes precedence over the TBT Code. The Appellate Body has held that both Codes take precedence over GATT 1994 issues. The TBT Code is binding on all WTO members. It strongly favors conforming use of international product standards, such as those of the International Standards Organization. See EC— Sardines, WT/DS231/AB/R (2002) (EC marketing rule not based on Codex Alimentarius standard). In general, the TBT Code deals with the problem of manipulation of product standards and labels, product testing procedures, and product certifications in order to slow or stop imported goods. To this end, the TBT Code requires NTBs to be not more trade restrictive than necessary to effectuate legitimate governmental objectives.

The TBT Code provides, in part and subject to some exceptions, that imported products shall be accorded treatment (including testing treatment and certification) no less favorable than that accorded to like products of national origin or those originating in any other country. It also requires that WTO members establish a central office for standards inquiries, publish advance and reasonable notice of requirements that are applicable to imported goods, and provide an opportunity for commentary by those who may be affected adversely. The TBT Code establishes an international committee to deal with alleged instances of noncompliance. For U.S. implementation of the TBT Code, see Section 7.4.

Various United States TBT, notably dolphin-safe and imported meat origin labels as well as flavored cigarette standards, have been challenged in WTO dispute settlement proceedings. *See* Section 7.5.

§ 1.8   The WTO Agreement on Agriculture

Agricultural issues played a central role in the Uruguay Round negotiations and are critical to the Doha Round as well. More than any other issue, they delayed completion of the Uruguay Round from 1990 to 1993. The agreement reached in December of 1993 is a trade liberalizing, market-oriented effort. Each country has made a number of commitments on market access, reduced domestic agricultural support levels and export subsidies. The United States Congress approved these commitments in December of 1994 by adopting the Uruguay Round Agreements Act.

Broadly speaking nontariff barriers (NTBs) to international agricultural trade are replaced by tariffs that provide substantially the same level of protection. This is known as "tariffication." It applies to virtually all NTBs, including variable levies, import bans, voluntary export restraints and import quotas. *See* Chile—Price Band System, WT/DS207/AB/R (2002). Tariffication applies specifically to U.S. agricultural quotas adopted under Section 22 of the Agricultural Adjustment Act. All agricultural tariffs, including those converted from NTBs, are to be reduced by 36 and 24 percent by developed and developing countries, respectively, over 6 and 10 year periods. Certain minimum access tariff quotas apply when imports amount to less than 3 to 5 percent of domestic consumption. An escape clause exists for tariffed imports at low prices or upon a surge of importation depending upon the existing degree of import penetration.

Regarding domestic support for agriculture, some programs with minimal impact on trade are exempt from change. These programs are known as "green box policies." They include governmental support for agricultural research, disease control, infrastructure and food security. Green box policies were also exempt from GATT/WTO challenge or countervailing duties for 9 years. Direct payments to producers that are not linked to production are also generally exempt. This will include income support, adjustment assistance, and environmental and regional assistance payments. Furthermore, direct payments to support crop reductions and *de minimis* payments are exempted in most cases.

After removing all of the exempted domestic agricultural support programs, the agreement on agriculture arrives at a calculation known as the Total Aggregate Measurement of Support (Total AMS). This measure is the basis for agricultural support reductions under the agreement. Developed nations reduced their Total AMS by 20 percent over 6 years, developing nations by 13.3 percent over 10 years. United States reductions undertaken in 1985 and 1990 meant that little or no U.S. action was required to meet this obligation. Agricultural export subsidies of developed nations were reduced by 36 percent below 1986–1990 levels over 6 years and the quantity of subsidized agricultural exports by 21 percent. Developing nations had corresponding 24 and 14 percent reductions over 10 years.

All conforming tariffications, reductions in domestic support for agriculture and export subsidy alterations were essentially exempt from challenge for 9 years within the GATT/WTO on grounds such as serious prejudice in export markets or nullification and impairment of agreement benefits. However, countervailing duties could be levied against all unlawfully subsidized exports of agricultural goods except for subsidies derived from so-called national "green box policies" (discussed in Chapter 5). In *U.S.—Upland Cotton* (WTO/DS267/AB/R (2005), the Appellate Body affirmed that member states must not only conform to the Agreement on Agriculture, but also the SCM Agreement. In that decision, U.S. compliance with the Agriculture Agreement was acknowledged, but its "Step-2" payments to cotton users favoring domestic over imported cotton (local content subsidies) were held to violate the SCM Agreement.

§ 1.9   The General Agreement on Trade in Services (GATS)

Because protectionist barriers to international trade in services were stifling, the United States and other developed countries insisted that there should be a General Agreement on Trade in Services (GATS). In the United States, services account for over two-thirds of the Nation's GDP and provide jobs for nearly two-thirds of the work force. Services account for almost one-third of U.S. exports in sectors such as tourism, education, construction, telecommunications, transport and health. In contrast, most developing nations are minimal exporters of services, save by means of exporting their people. . . . but migration was not included as a subject under the GATS.

Market access for services is a major focus of the General Agreement on Trade in Services (GATS), a product of the Uruguay Round of Negotiations. The GATS defines the supply of services broadly to include providing services across borders or inside member states with or without a commercial presence therein. Apart from ensuring transparency of national regulatory controls over services, the core GATS Article XVII commitment is to afford most-favored-nation treatment to service providers, subject to country-specific, preferential trade agreement or labor market integration agreement exemptions, such as audio-visual services in the EU.

In addition, each WTO member state made under GATS XVI specific schedule of commitments (concessions) on opening up their markets in services' sectors negotiated using the WTO Services Sectoral Classification List. They further agreed under Article XVI to provide national treatment to their services' commitment schedule. For example, to what degree may foreign banks or foreign economic consultants provide services, and are they entitled to national treatment? The answers to those questions will be found in the GATS specific commitments of each member. Much to its consternation, the United States was found to have failed to exclude Internet gambling services under its GATS commitments' schedule. This caused Antigua-Barbuda to prevail in a dispute that alleged U.S. gambling laws discriminatorily prohibited its right to export such services to the U.S. market. *See* U.S.—Gambling, WT/DS285/AB/R (2007). The United States also lost the argument that its Internet gambling services' restraints were justifiable on public morals' grounds. This argument failed as discriminatory under the "chapeau" of the GATS Article XIV general exceptions (similar to GATT Article XX general exceptions discussed in Section 1.1).

Special "GATS Rules" govern use of safeguards against surges of services' imports, subsidies applicable to services' exports, and government procurement of services. General GATS exceptions apply (for example, government supplied services), as do national security GATS exceptions.

National laws that restrict the number of firms in a market, that are dependent upon local "needs tests", or that mandate local incorporation are regulated by the GATS. Various "transparency" rules require disclosure of all relevant laws and regulations, and these must be administered reasonably, objectively and impartially. Specific service market access and national treatment commitments are made by various governments in schedules attached to the agreement. These commitments may be modified or withdrawn after 3 years, subject to a right of compensation that can be arbitrated. Certain mutual recognition of education and training for service-sector licensing occurs. State monopolies or exclusive service providers may continue, but must not abuse their positions. Detailed rules are created in annexes to the GATS on financial, telecommunications and air transport services. Under the Telecommunications Reference Paper (TRP), for example, the United States successfully argued that Telmex had abused its monopoly position in Mexico by charging discriminatory, non-cost-oriented connection fees for foreign calls. *See* Mexico—Telecoms, WT/DS204/AB/R (2004).

The U.S. Congress approved and implemented the GATS agreement in December of 1994 under the Uruguay Round Agreements Act. Subsequently, early in 1995, the United States refused to extend most-favored-nation treatment to financial services. The European Union, Japan and other GATS nations then entered into an interim 2-year agreement which operated on MFN principles. Financial services were revisited in 1996–97 with further negotiations aimed at bringing the United States into the fold. These negotiations bore fruit late in 1997 with 70 nations (including the United States) joining in an agreement that covers 95 percent of trade in banking, insurance, securities and financial information. This agreement took effect March 1, 1999.

The GATS has reduced unilateral U.S. action under Section 301 to gain access to foreign markets for U.S. service providers. This reduction flows from U.S. adherence to the Dispute Settlement Understanding (DSU) that accompanies the WTO accords. The DSU obligates its signatories to follow streamlined dispute settlement procedures under which unilateral retaliation is restrained until the offending nation has failed to conform to a World Trade Organization ruling.

GATS Disputes

GATS, and the 1996 Protocol on Telecommunications and 1997 Protocol on Financial Services, have generated only a handful of WTO disputes. Here is a sampling of them:

1. EC—Regime for the Importation, Sale and Distribution of Bananas, WT/DS27/AB/R (1997) (traders of goods may also be traders of services, such as wholesaling or retailing, GATS Articles II and XVII apply to de jure and de facto discrimination).

2. Canada—Certain Measures Concerning Periodicals, WT/DS31/AB/R (1997) (GATT and GATS co-exist, no override).

3. Canada—Certain Measures Affecting The Automotive Industry, WT/DS139,142/R (2000) (coverage under GATS must be determined before assessment of consistency with GATS obligations).

4. Mexico—Measures Affecting Telecommunication Services WT/DS204/R (2004) (Mexican cross-border interconnection rates not cost-oriented and unreasonable in breach of Telecoms Annex, failure to allow access to private leased-circuits also violated commitments) (settled with rate reductions and increased access).

5. United States—Measures Affecting The Cross-Border Supply of Gambling and Betting Services, WT/DS 285/AB/R (2005) (gambling included in U.S. recreational services' commitments, U.S. import ban amounted to "zero quota" in breach of GATS Article XVI, necessary to protect public morals under Article XIV defense but discriminatory

enforcement regarding Interstate Horseracing Act fails to meet "chapeau" requirements) (U.S. pays compensation to all GATS signatories except Antigua and Barbuda, the complaining party. . . . $21 million retaliation authorized in 2008).

6.   China—Certain Measures Affecting Electronic payment Systems, WT/DS413/R (2012) (discriminatory restraints on foreign electronics payment services' suppliers violate GATS commitments).

§ 1.10   The WTO and Rules of Origin

The Uruguay Round accord on rules of origin is, in reality, an agreement to agree. A negotiations schedule was established along with a WTO Committee to work with the Customs Cooperation Council on harmonized rules of origin. Certain broad guiding principles for the negotiations are given and considered binding until agreement is reached. These principles are:

- Rules of origin applied to foreign trade must not be more stringent than applied to domestic goods.

- Rules of origin must be administered consistently, uniformly, impartially and reasonably.

- Origin assessments must be issued within 150 days of a request and remain valid for three years.

- New or modified rules or origin may not be applied retroactively.

- Strict confidentiality rules apply to information submitted confidentially for rule of origin determinations.

To date, no WTO agreement on rules of origin has been reached.

§ 1.11   The WTO TRIPs Agreement, International Intellectual Property Law

The Uruguay Round accords of late 1993 include an agreement on trade-related intellectual property rights (TRIPs). This agreement is binding upon the roughly 165 nations that are members of the World Trade Organization. In the United States, the TRIPs agreement has been ratified and implemented by Congress under the Uruguay Round Agreements Act. There is a general requirement of national and most-favored-nation treatment among the parties.

Many developed nations had been trying unsuccessfully to promote expanded intellectual property rights through the U.N.-

created World Intellectual Property Rights Organization (WIPO). WIPO agreements are not mandatory, and much of the developing world had declined to opt into their terms. Much to the benefit of private parties in the developed world, the TRIPs Code covers the gamut of intellectual property. **It has de facto become a near-global IP Code.**

On *copyrights*, there is protection for computer programs and databases, rental authorization controls for owners of computer software and sound recordings, a 50-year motion picture and sound recording copyright term, and a general obligation to comply with the Berne Convention (1971 version)(except for its provisions on moral rights). The Berne Convention is discussed in Chapter 15.

On *patents*, the Paris Convention (1967 version, discussed in Chapter15) prevails, 20-year product and process patents are available "in all fields of technology", including pharmaceuticals and agricultural chemicals. However, patents can be denied when necessary to protect public morals or order, to protect human, animal or plant life or health, and to avoid serious environmental prejudice. The TRIPs provisions did not stop the Indian Supreme Court in 2013 from denying Novartis a patent on its cancer drug, Gleevac. The court took the view that Novartis was engaged in "evergreening", i.e., making small, inconsequential changes to existing patents and that Indian law could require proof of "improved therapeutic efficacy" before a patent grant.

Article 31 of the TRIPs permits compulsory licensing of patents in national emergencies or other circumstances of extreme urgency, subject to a duty to reasonably compensate the patent owner. Thailand has issued compulsory licenses on a range of cancer, heart disease and AIDS drugs. There is considerable controversy over pharmaceutical patents based on traditional medicines of indigenous peoples, which some see as bio-piracy. Proposals have been made to amend TRIPs to require disclosure of the origins of bio-patents, obtain informed consent from the indigenous communities involved, and share the benefits of such patents.

For *trademarks,* the Paris Convention (Chapter 15) controls, service marks become registrable, internationally prominent marks receive enhanced protection, the linking of local marks with foreign trademarks is prohibited, and compulsory licensing is banned. Geographical indicators of origin (Feta cheese, Parma ham) are protected unless they have become generic terms (California champagne anyone? Perhaps with a U.S. parmesan on ciabatta?). Gray market trading and related IP issues are explicitly not covered by TRIPs, allowing each WTO member state to differ on such law. *See* Chapter 9.

Note that by incorporating the Berne and Paris conventions, TRIPs and the WTO DSU (Section 1.14 below) become an enforcement mechanism for those longstanding treaties.

In addition, *trade secret* protection is assisted by TRIPs rules enabling owners to prevent unauthorized use or disclosure. These rules closely parallel those of NAFTA. Integrated circuits are covered by rules intended to improve upon the Washington Treaty. Lastly, protection of industrial designs and selected geographic indicators of product origin (e.g., Canadian Whiskey) are also part of the TRIPs regime.

Mandatory IP infringement and anti-counterfeiting remedies are included in the TRIPs, for both domestic and international trade protection. There are specific provisions governing injunctions, damages, judicial and customs seizures, and discovery of evidence. Willful trademark counterfeiting and copyright piracy on a commercial scale must be criminalized. Counterfeit goods may not be re-exported by customs authorities in an unaltered state. See generally Chapter 8.

The Medicines Agreement

Late in 2001, the Doha Round of WTO negotiations were launched. These negotiations have reconsidered the TRIPs agreement, particularly as it applies to developing nations. Their compliance deadline for the TRIP's rules on patents for pharmaceuticals was extended to 2016, thereby allowing a continuation of cheaper, local generics. In addition, a Declaration on the TRIPs Agreement and Public Health was issued at the Qatar Ministerial Conference. This 20001 Declaration includes the following statement:

> We agree that the TRIPs Agreement does not prevent Members from taking measures to protect public health. Accordingly, while reiterating our commitment to the TRIPs Agreement, we affirm that the Agreement can and should be interpreted and implemented in a manner supportive of WTO Members' right to protect public health and, in particular, to promote access to medicines for all.

A "Medicines Agreement" waiver (2003) and amendment to TRIPs (2005) implement this Declaration. Compulsory licensing and/or importation of generic copies of patented medicines needed to address developing nation public health problems are authorized. Such activities may not pursue industrial or commercial policy objectives, and different packaging and labeling must be used in an effort at minimizing the risk of diversion of the generics to developed country markets. Under pressure from the United States, a number of more advanced developing nations (such as Mexico, Singapore and Qatar) agreed not to employ compulsory licensing except in situations of national emergency or extreme urgency. Canada, China, the EU, India, South Korea and other members, on the other hand, have licensed production of drugs for nations incapable of pharmaceutical production.

Special 301—Prioritization of U.S. Intellectual Property Rights Disputes

The Special 301 procedures established by the 1988 Omnibus Trade and Competitiveness Act are permanent features of United States trade legislation. These procedures are located in Section 182 of the Trade Act of 1974.[3] Under these procedures the United States Trade Representative is required to identify foreign countries that deny adequate and effective protection of intellectual property rights, or deny fair and equitable access to United States persons that rely upon intellectual property protection. The USTR is given discretion to determine whether to designate certain of these countries to be "priority countries."

If so designated, a mandatory Section 301 investigation (see Section 14.4) must follow in the absence of a determination that this would be detrimental to U.S. economic interests or a negotiated settlement of the intellectual property dispute. Once designated, Special 301 investigations and retaliations against priority countries must ordinarily be decided within 6 months by the USTR. Whether to retaliate or not is discretionary with the USTR, but retaliation is not authorized if the country in question enters into good faith negotiations or makes "significant progress" in bilateral or multilateral negotiations towards increased protection for intellectual property rights. Many commentators have observed that unilateral use of Section 301 prior to creation of the WTO helped push the U.S. agenda in the TRIPs negotiations. Since 1994, if the dispute is covered by the WTO TRIPs agreement, the United States must avoid using unilateral Section 301 trade sanctions and pursue WTO dispute settlement. *See* Section 1.14.

In identifying priority foreign countries in the intellectual property field, Section 182 indicates that the USTR is to prioritize only those countries that have the most "onerous or egregious" practices, whose practices have the greatest adverse impact on United States products, and are not entering into good faith negotiations bilaterally or multilaterally to provide adequate and effective protection of intellectual property rights.[4] For these

---

[3]   19 U.S.C.A. § 2242.

[4]   19 U.S.C.A. § 2422(b).

purposes, the term "persons that rely on intellectual protection" covers those involved in copyrighted works of authorship or those involved in the manufacture of products that are patented or subject to process patents.[5] Interestingly, this definition does not include those who rely on United States trademarks.

However, the relevant definitions include trademarks in connection with the denial by foreign countries of adequate and effective protection of intellectual property rights. The definition of practices that deny fair and equitable market access in connection with intellectual property rights appear to be limited to copyrights and patents. This denial must constitute a violation of provisions of international law or international agreements to which both the United States and that country are parties or otherwise constitute a discriminatory nontariff trade barrier.[6]

Regular reports to Congress are required of the USTR by Section 182. The USTR has chiefly placed foreign country intellectual property practices on watch lists rather than formally designating priority countries. These watch lists are divided as between "priority watch lists" and "secondary watch lists." Many nations have been listed by the USTR since 1989 in this fashion. This has the practical effect of placing pressure on those nations to enter negotiations with the United States that will improve their protection of intellectual property rights.

The use of these lists gives the USTR more room to negotiate settlements with the countries concerned. For example, the USTR formally named China, India and Thailand as the first "priority countries" for Special 301 purposes. The formal process of negotiation backed up by a mandatory Section 301 investigation and potential sanctions was begun. Thailand was cited for its failure to enforce copyrights and for the absence of patent protection for pharmaceuticals. India was named because its patent laws are deficient from the U.S. perspective, particularly on compulsory licensing and the absence of pharmaceutical protection. Extensive book, video, sound recording and computer software piracy in India was also cited.

United States Special 301 investigations and watch lists, now including "Out-of-Cycle Reviews of Notorious Markets", have continued relentlessly in spite of the WTO TRIPs agreement. The USTR has filed numerous TRIPs complaints with the WTO. *See* Section 1.15. Filings have been made, for example, against Denmark,

---

[5]   19 U.S.C.A. § 2242(d).

[6]   *Id.*

Sweden, Ireland, Ecuador, Greece, Portugal, India, Russia, Pakistan, Turkey and, not surprisingly, China.

TRIPs Disputes

Dozens of TRIPs complaints have been initiated under WTO dispute settlement procedures. Most have been settled, but a few have resulted in WTO Panel and Appellate Body Reports. Here is a sampling of those disputes:

  1. India—Patent Protection for Pharmaceutical and Agricultural Chemical Products, WT/DS50/AB/R (1998) ("mailbox rule" patent applications for subjects not patentable in India until 2005 inadequate, denial of exclusive marketing rights in breach of TRIPs Article 70.9).

  2. Canada—Term of Patent Protection, WT/DS170/AB/R (2000) (pre-TRIPs Canadian patents must receive 20 year term).

  3. U.S.—Section 110 (5) Copyright Act, WT/DS160/R (2000) (copyright exemption for "homestyle" dramatic musical works consistent with Berne Convention, "business use" exemption inconsistent with Berne and therefore in breach of TRIPs) (settled by payment).

  4. Canada—Pharmaceutical Patents, WT/DS114/R (2000) (Canadian generic pharmaceutical regulatory review and stockpiling patent rights' exceptions not sufficiently "limited").

  5. U.S.—Section 211 Appropriations Act, WT/DS176/AB/R (2002) (prohibition against registering marks confiscated by Cuban government, e.g. HAVANA CLUB rum, without original owner's consent violates Paris Convention and TRIPs, trade names covered by TRIPs).

  6. EC—Trademarks and Geographical Indications WT/DS 174,290/R (2005) (EC regulation violates national treatment and most-favored treatment obligations to non-EC nationals, procedural violations also found).

  7. China—Measures Affecting The Protection and Enforcement of Intellectual Property Rights, WT/DS362/R (2009) (China's implementation of TRIPs upheld as to criminal law thresholds and disposal of confiscated, infringing goods by customs authorities, rejected as to denial of copyright protection for works not authorized for release in China).

8.   China—Measures Affecting Trading Rights and
Distribution Services for Certain Publications and
Audiovisuals Entertainment Products, WT/DS363/AB/R
(2009) (China's ADV restrictions limited to state-owned or
approved channels violate WTO Accession Protocol, GATT
1994 and GATS; Restraints not necessary to protect public
morals).

9.   European Communities—Information Technology
Tariffs, WT/DS375–377 (2010) (EU tariffs on cable
converter boxes with Net capacity, flat panel computer
screens and printers that also scan, fax or copy violated
1996 Information Technology Agreement zero tariff rules).

§ 1.12 Trade-Related Investment Measures (TRIMs)

The WTO package of mandatory agreements includes TRIMs,
Trade-Related Investment Measures. This is the only WTO
agreement concerning foreign investment law, an area which is
almost devoid of common international rules. The WTO is a trade law
organization, hence its coverage of foreign investment is only "trade-
related". In practice, this means that TRIMs is almost exclusively
concerned with "performance requirements", i.e. national rules
requiring designated performances by foreign investors. There are 14
performance requirements enumerated in and broadly prohibited by
TRIMs. They fall into three general categories: (1) Local content
rules; (2) Trade balancing rules; and (3) Export requirements.

Regarding performance requirements, TRIMs tracks the GATT
Article III rule of "national treatment" and Article XI proscription
against quotas. But member states may "deviate temporarily" from
these principles, thus undermining their impact. Trade-related
investment practices which are deemed inconsistent with TRIMs are
listed illustratively in an Annex. These include minimum domestic
content rules (say 50% of the value of the foreign investor's products
must be sourced locally), limitations on imports used in production,
the linkage of allowable imports to export requirements, export
quotas or percentage of production requirements, and restrictions on
foreign exchange designed to limit imports.

Perhaps because of their limited scope and soft prohibition,
there have been relatively few TRIMs disputes, all centered on local
content rules. For example, the United States and others succeeded
in challenging Indonesia's local content requirements for autos. See
Indonesia—Certain Measures Affecting the Automobile Industry,
WT/DS/AB/R 54, 55, 59 & 64 (1998). In 2014, Ontario's local content
rules for its green energy program were also struck down under

TRIMs. In 2016, the U.S. prevailed before the WTO concerning India's local content mandates on solar cells and modules (WT/DS456/AB/R (2016), which caused India to file a WTO claim against the United States for similar mandates on solar units subject to U.S. tax preferences.

§ 1.13   The Optional WTO Public Procurement Code

Where public procurement is involved, and the taxpayer's money is at issue, virtually every nation has some form of legislation or tradition that favors buying from domestic suppliers. The Tokyo Round GATT Procurement Code was not particularly successful at opening up government purchasing. Relatively few GATT members and the United States adhered to that Procurement Code. This was also partly the result of the 1979 Code's many exceptions. For example, the Code did not apply to contracts below its threshold amount of $150,000 SDR (about $171,000 since 1988), service contracts, and procurement by entities on each country's reserve list (including most national defense items). Because procurement in the European Union and Japan is often decentralized, many contracts fell below the SDR threshold and were therefore GATT exempt. By dividing up procurement into smaller contracts national preferences were retained. United States government procurement tends to be more centralized and thus more likely to be covered by the GATT Code. This pattern may help explain why Congress restrictively amended the Buy American Act in 1988.

The Uruguay Round WTO Procurement Code took effect in 1995 and replaced the 1979 Tokyo Round GATT Procurement Code. The WTO Code expanded the coverage of the prior GATT Code to include procurement of services, construction, government-owned utilities, and some state and local (sub-central) contracts. The U.S. and the European Union applied the new Code's provisions on government-owned utilities and sub-central contracts as early as April 15, 1994. Other participants include Armenia, Aruba, Chinese Taipei (Taiwan), Iceland, Japan, Korea, Israel, Lichtenstein, Norway, Singapore and Switzerland. Nearly all developing nations have opted out of the WTO Procurement Code, though China has expressed interest in it.

Various improvements to the procedural rules surrounding procurement practices and dispute settlement under the WTO Code attempt to reduce tensions in this difficult area. For example, an elaborate system for bid protests is established. Bidders who believe the Code's procedural rules have been abused will be able to lodge, litigate and appeal their protests. The WTO Procurement Code became part of U.S. law in December of 1994 under the Uruguay Round Agreements Act. The United States has made, with few exceptions, all procurement by executive agencies subject to the Federal Acquisition Regulations under the Code's coverage (i.e., to suspend application of the normal Buy American preferences to such procurement). Thirteen U.S. states have not ratified the WTO Procurement Code. The economic stimulus and auto bail-out legislation of the Obama administration raised questions of U.S. compliance with the Code.

Chapter 13 of the North American Free Trade Area Agreement opened government procurement to U.S., Canadian and Mexican suppliers on contracts as small as $25,000. However, the goods supplied must have at least 50 percent North American content. These special procurement rules effectively created an exception to the GATT Procurement Code which otherwise applied. The thresholds are $50,000 for goods and services provided to federal agencies and $250,000 for government-owned enterprises (notably PEMEX and CFE). These regulations are particularly important because Mexico, unlike Canada, has not traditionally joined in GATT/WTO procurement codes. In 2011 Canada-U.S. procurement provisions were incorporated in a long awaited agreement to expand the WTO Procurement Code. This expansion selectively brings more types of procurement contracts, notable service contracts, and more sub-central government entities within the Code's coverage. Contract value thresholds are also selectively lowered.

§ 1.14 WTO Dispute Settlement

GATT 1947 did not have an institutional charter, and was not intended to become an international organization on trade. It did later develop institutional structures and acquired quasi-organizational status, but there was always a lack of structure. This lack was most often perceived in the somewhat over-stated inability of GATT to resolve disputes which were brought to it. Indeed, GATT 1947 members could block the formation of a panel to hear a dispute. Moreover, GATT panel decisions could be blocked by the losing state! Hence most GATT 1947 dispute settlement panel reports were un-adopted, and as such "the GATT acquis" is said to merely provide guidance in the context of WTO dispute settlement. *See* Japan-Alcoholic Beverages II, WTO/DS/R 8, 10, 11 (1996).

The WTO provides a unified, mandatory, and exclusive intergovernmental system for settling trade disputes governed by WTO law through the Dispute Settlement Understanding (DSU) using the Dispute Settlement Body (DSB). There are no private remedies, though private sector interests are often motivating elements. In the United States, private parties and their attorneys can attempt to trigger WTO dispute settlement proceedings by filing complaints with the U.S. Trade Representative (USTR), a presidential appointee. Whether to pursue WTO trade law complaints is entirely discretionary for the USTR. Under the terms of the DSU, the USTR can pursue complaints of breach of WTO agreement obligations, or nullification or impairment of benefits accruing under WTO agreements.

Assuming the WTO has subject matter jurisdiction, WTO dispute settlement procedures can be invoked by the United States or any its free trade partners, including Mexico and Canada. See R. Folsom, *Principles of Free Trade Agreements* (forthcoming).

The DSB is a special assembly of the WTO General Council, and includes all WTO members. There are six stages in the resolution of disputes under WTO: 1) Consultation; 2) Panel establishment, investigation and report; 3) Appellate review of the panel report; 4) Adoption of the panel and appellate decision; 5) Implementation of the decision adopted, and 6) Authorized retaliation. There is also a parallel process for binding arbitration, if both parties agree to submit this dispute to arbitration, rather than to a DSB panel. In addition, the party subject to an adverse decision may seek arbitration as a matter of right on issues of compliance and authorized retaliation.

Although the DSU offers a unified dispute resolution system that is applicable across all sectors and all WTO Covered Agreements, there are many specialized rules for disputes which arise under them. Such specialized rules appear in the Agreements on Textiles, Antidumping, Subsidies and Countervailing Measures, Technical Barriers to Trade, Sanitary and Phytosanitary Measures, Customs Valuation, General Agreement on Trade in Services, Financial Services and Air Transport Services. The special provisions in these individual Covered Agreements govern, where applicable, and prevail in any conflict with the general provisions of the DSU.

Under WTO, unlike under GATT 1947, the DSU practically assures that panels will be established upon request by a member state. Further, under WTO, unlike GATT 1947, the DSU virtually ensures the adoption of unmodified panel and appellate body decisions. It accomplishes this by requiring the DSB to adopt panel reports and appellate body decisions automatically and without amendment unless they are rejected by a consensus of all members. This "inverted consensus" requires that all members of the DSB, including the state that prevailed in the dispute, decide to reject the dispute resolution decision. Not surprisingly, this has never happened because if any member formally favors that decision (the winner in the dispute for example), it becomes binding. This inverted consensus requirement is imposed on both the adoption of panel reports or appellate body decisions and also on the decision to establish a panel.

The potential resolutions of a dispute under DSU range from a "mutually satisfactory solution" agreed to by the parties under the first, or consultation phase, to authorized retaliation under the last, or implementation phase. The preferred solution is always any resolution that is mutually satisfactory to the parties. After a panel decision, there are three types of remedies available to the prevailing party, if a mutually satisfactory solution cannot be obtained. One is for the respondent to bring the measure found to violate a Covered Agreement into conformity with the Agreement. A second is for the prevailing Member to receive compensation from the respondent which both parties agree is sufficient to compensate for any injury caused by the measure found to violate a Covered Agreement.

Finally, if no such agreement can be reached, a prevailing party can be authorized to suspend some of its concessions under the Covered Agreements to the respondent. These suspended concessions, called "retaliation," can be authorized within the same trade sector and agreement; or, if that will not create sufficient compensation, can be authorized across trade sectors and agreements.

The entire WTO dispute resolution process, from filing a complaint to authorized retaliation, can take roughly three years. Roughly, one-third of all WTO disputes concern antidumping or unlawful subsidy disputes. *See* Chapters 4 and 5. One perspective on WTO dispute settlement seeks a rule-oriented use of the "rule of law". The other seeks a power-oriented use of diplomacy. The United States and less developed countries have traditionally sought to develop a rule-oriented approach to international trade disputes.

The European Union and Japan have traditionally sought to use the GATT/WTO primarily as a forum for diplomatic negotiations, although the EU now ranks second in number of WTO dispute proceedings. These different views created part of the conflict at the December 1999 Seattle WTO meeting (which failed to launch the Millennium Round). If the DSB is a court, its proceedings should be open and "transparent." However, if it is just another form of government-to-government diplomacy, that has always been held in secret.

Viewed either way, the WTO dispute settlement process has clearly reduced uncertainty and friction in international trade. By

2017, dozens of trade disputes were being processed yearly through the WTO.

Phase 1, Consultation

Any WTO Member who believes that the Measures of another Member are not in conformity with the Covered Agreements may call for consultations on those measures. The respondent has ten days to reply and must agree to enter into consultation within 30 days. If the respondent does not enter into consultations within the 30 day period, the party seeking consultations can immediately request the establishment of a panel under DSU, which puts the dispute into Phase 2.

Once consultations begin, the parties have 60 days to achieve a settlement. The goal is to seek a positive solution to the dispute, and the preferred resolution is to reach whatever solution is mutually satisfactory to the parties. If such a settlement cannot be obtained after 60 days, the party seeking consultations may request the establishment of a panel under DSU, which moves the dispute into Phase 2.

WTO member third parties with an interest in the subject-matter of the consultations may seek to be included in them. If such inclusion is rejected, they may seek their own consultations with the other member state. Alternatives to consultations may be provided through the use of conciliation, mediation or good offices, where all parties agree to use the alternative process. Any party can terminate the use of conciliation, mediation or good offices and then seek the establishment of a panel under DSU, which also will move the dispute into Phase 2.

Phase 2, Panel Establishment, Investigation and Report

If consultations between the parties fail, the party seeking the consultations (the complainant) may request the DSB to establish a panel to investigate, report and resolve the dispute. The DSB must establish such a panel upon request, unless the DSB expressly decides by consensus not to establish the panel. Since an "inverted consensus" is required to reject the establishment of the panel and the complainant member must be part of that consensus, it is almost guaranteed that a panel will be established. Roughly 100 panels were established in the first five years of operation of the DSU, and many more since then.

Almost any WTO member state may intervene in the dispute. No specific legal or trade interest in the dispute is required since every WTO member has a legal interest in seeing that WTO rules are observed. Hence, for example, the United States intervened in the

Bananas dispute between Latin American exporters and the European Union. One measure of the significance of the dispute is how many and which WTO members join either side of the dispute. . . . resulting in say seven states against ten.

The WTO Secretariat maintains a list of well-qualified persons who are available to serve as panelists, mainly international trade law specialists drawn from the world of law practice, the academe and government service. The panels are usually composed of three individuals from that list who are not citizens of either party. If the parties agree, a panel can be composed of five such individuals. The parties can also agree to appoint citizens of a party to a panel. Panelists may be either nongovernmental individuals or governmental officials, but they are to be selected so as to ensure their independence. Thus, there is a bias towards independent individuals who are not citizens of any party. If a citizen of a party is appointed, his government may not instruct that citizen how to vote, for the panelist must be independent. By the same reasoning, a governmental official of a non-party member state who is subject to instructions from his or her government would not seem to fit the profile of an independent panelist.

The WTO Secretariat proposes nominations of the panelists. Parties may not normally oppose the nominations, except for "compelling reasons." The parties are given twenty days to agree on the panelists and the composition of the panel. If such agreement is not forthcoming, the WTO Director-General is authorized to appoint the panelists, in consultation with other persons in the Secretariat.

Complaints brought to DSB panels can involve either violations of Covered Agreements, or non-violation nullification and impairment of benefits under the Covered Agreements. A prima facie case of nullification impairment arises when one member infringes upon the "obligations assumed under a Covered Agreement." Such infringement creates a presumption against the infringing member, but the presumption can be rebutted by a showing that the complaining member state has suffered no adverse effect from the infringement. A classic nullification and impairment complaint concerns use of government subsidies after tariff reductions cause increased imports. See the *Australian Subsidy* case, 2 GATT Panel B.I.S.D. 188 (1950).

The panels receive pleadings and rebuttals and hear oral arguments. Panels can also engage in fact development from sources outside those presented by the parties. Thus, the procedure has aspects familiar to civil law courts. A panel can, on its own initiative, request information, including from experts selected by the panel. It can also obtain confidential information in some circumstances from an administrative body which is part of the government of a member state, without any prior consent from that state. A panel can establish its own group of experts to provide reports on factual or scientific issues. In a series of rulings commencing with the *Shrimp-Turtles* decision in 1998, the WTO Appellate Body has affirmed the right of panels and itself to elect to receive unsolicited informational and argumentative briefs or letters from non-governmental organizations (NGOs), business groups and law firms representing persons interested in the dispute.

A panel is obligated to produce two objectively assessed written reports—an interim and a final report. These reports are normally drafted by the WTO Secretariat, subject to review by the panelists. A panel is supposed to submit a final written report to the DSB within six months of its establishment. The report will contain its findings of fact, findings of law, a decision and the rationale for its decision. Before the final report is issued, the panel is supposed to provide an interim report to the parties. The purpose of this interim report is to apprize the parties of the panel's current analysis of the issues and to permit the parties to comment on that analysis. The final report of the panel need not change any of the findings or conclusions in its interim report, unless the panel is persuaded to do so by a party's comments. However, if it is not so persuaded, it is obligated to explain in its final report why not. At this writing, well over 200 WTO panel reports have been issued.

The decisions in panel reports are final as to issues of fact. The decisions in panel reports are not necessarily final as to issues of law. Panel decisions on issues of law are subject to review by the Appellate Body, which is Phase 3, and explained below. Any party can appeal a panel report, and appeals are usually taken.

Phase 3, Appellate Review of the Panel Report

Appellate review of panel reports is available at the request of any party, unless the DSB rejects that request by an "inverted consensus." There is no threshold requirement for an appellant to present a substantial substantive legal issue. Thus, most panel decisions are appealed as a matter of course. However, the Appellate Body can only review the panel reports on questions of law or legal interpretation.

The Appellate Body is a new institution in the international trade organization and its process. GATT 1947 had nothing comparable to it. The Appellate Body is composed of seven members (or judges) who are appointed by the DSB to four-year terms. Each judge may be reappointed, but only once, to a second four-year term. Each judge is to be a recognized authority on international trade law and the Covered Agreements. To date, Appellate Body members have been drawn mostly from the academe and retired justices. They have come from Germany, Japan, Egypt, India, New Zealand, the Philippines, Argentina, China, the United States and other WTO member nations.

The review of any panel decision is performed by three judges out of the seven. The parties do not, however, have any influence over which judges are selected to review a particular panel report. There is a schedule, created by the Appellate Body, for the rotation for sitting of each of the judges. Thus, a party might try to appear before a favored judge by timing the start of the dispute settlement process to arrive at the Appellate Body at the right moment on the rotation schedule, but this limited approach has major difficulties.

The Appellate Body receives written submissions from the parties and has 60, or in some cases 90, days in which to render its decision. The Appellate Body review is limited to issues of law and legal interpretation. The panel decision may be upheld, modified, or reversed by the Appellate Body decision. Appellate Body decisions are anonymous, and ex parte communications are not permitted. Appellate Body decisions do not represent binding precedent. That said, many have observed a desire on the part of the Appellate Body to achieve consistency and a willingness to discuss its prior rulings when rendering decisions.

Phase 4, Adoption of the Panel or Appellate Body Decision

Appellate Body determinations are submitted to the DSB. Panel decisions which are not appealed are also submitted to the DSB. Once either type of decision is submitted, the DSB must automatically adopt them without modification or amendment at its next meeting unless the decision is rejected by all members of the DSB acting by "inverted consensus", which has never happened.

An alternative to Phases 2 through 4 is arbitration, if both parties agree. The arbitration must be binding on the parties, and there is no appeal from the arbitral tribunal's decision to the DSB or Appellate Body.

Phase 5, Implementation of the Decision Adopted

Once a panel or Appellate Body decision is adopted by the DSB, implementation is a three-step process. In the first step, the member found to have a measure which violates its WTO obligations has "a reasonable time" (usually 15 months) to bring those measures into conformity with its WTO obligations. That remedy is the preferred one, and this form of implementation is the principal goal of the WTO dispute settlement system. To date, most disputes have resulted in compliance in this manner. If the adequacy of compliance is disputed, such disputes typically return to the WTO panel that rendered decision on the merits. The panel then determines, acting as an arbitrator, the amount (if any) of authorized retaliation. The retaliation process is discussed below.

Compensation

If the violating measures are not brought into conformity within a reasonable time, the parties proceed to the second step. In that second step, the parties negotiate to reach an agreement upon a form of compensation which will be granted by the party in violation to the injured party. Such compensation will usually comprise trade concessions by the violating party to the injured party, which are over and above those already available under the WTO and Covered Agreements. The nature, scope, amount and duration of these additional concessions is at the negotiating parties' discretion, but each side must agree that the final compensation package is fair and is properly related to the injury caused by the violating measures. Presumably, any such concessions need not be extended under MFN principles to all WTO members.

Few such compensation agreements have ever been achieved, though the United States compensated most of the membership after losing a dispute to Antigua about whether it had "reserved" (excepted) Internet gambling from coverage under the GATS. See Section 1.9. The United States also compensated the EU in a copyright dispute involving small business use of music, and Brazil after losing a subsidies dispute concerning cotton.

Phase 6, Authorized Retaliation

Both "compensation" and "retaliation" provide only for indirect enforcement of DSB decisions. There is no mechanism for direct enforcement by the WTO of its decisions through WTO orders to suspend trade obligations. Commentators differ on whether retaliation will be an effective implementation device. The division represented by these conflicting views represents two different approaches to the nature of both international law and international trade law.

If the parties cannot agree on an appropriate amount of compensation within twenty days, the complainant may proceed to the third step. In the third step, the party injured by the violating measures seeks authority from the DSB to retaliate against the party whose measures violated its WTO obligations. Thus complainant seeks authority to suspend some of its WTO obligations in regard to the respondent. The retaliation must ordinarily be within the same sector and agreement as the violating measure. "Sector" is sometimes broadly defined, as all trade in goods, and sometimes narrowly defined, as in individual services in the Services Sectoral Classification List. "Agreement" is also broadly defined. All the agreements listed in Annex IA to the WTO Agreement are considered a single agreement. If retaliation within the sector and agreement of the violating measure is considered insufficient compensation, the complainant may seek suspension of its obligations across sectors and agreements. This is known as "cross-sector retaliation."

The DSB must grant the complainant's request to retaliate within 30 days unless all WTO members reject it through an "inverted consensus." (Article 22.6, D.S.U.) However, the respondent may object to the level or scope of the retaliation. The issues raised by the objection will be examined by either the Appellate Body or by an arbitrator. The respondent has a right, even if arbitration was not used in Phases 2 through 4, to have an arbitrator review in Phase 5 the appropriateness of the complainant's proposed level and scope of retaliation. The arbitrator will also examine whether the proper procedures and criteria to establish retaliation have been followed. The Phase 5 arbitration is final and binding, and the arbitrator's decision is not subject to DSB review.

In addition to objecting to the level of authorized retaliation, the responding WTO member may simultaneously challenge the assertion of noncompliance (Article 21.5, D.S.U.). This challenge will ordinarily be heard by the original panel and must be resolved within 90 days. Thus the request for authorized retaliation and objections thereto could conceivably be accomplished before noncompliance is formally determined. In practice, WTO dispute settlement has melded these conflicting procedures such that compliance and retaliation issues are decided together, typically by the original panel.

Retaliation in Action

Retaliation has rarely been authorized and even less rarely imposed. The amount of a U.S. retaliation permitted against the EU after the WTO *Bananas* and *Beef Hormones* decisions were not implemented by the EU was contested. The arbitration tribunals for this issue were the original WTO panels, which did not allow the entire amount of the almost $700 million in retaliatory tariffs proposed by the United States. The U.S. was authorized and levied retaliatory tariffs amounting to about $300 million against European goods because of the EU failure to implement those WTO decisions.

Since 2000, Congress has authorized rotating WTO retaliatory tariffs in "carousel" fashion upon different goods. The threat of carousel retaliation contributed to an April 2001 settlement of the

Bananas dispute. In 2009, a four year settlement of the *Beef Hormones* dispute was reached. The U.S. obtained a higher quota to export hormone-free beef to the EU in return for phasing out its retaliatory tariffs on EU goods. The U.S. threat of carousel sanctions was again instrumental to this settlement.

Perhaps the most dramatic use of retaliation occurred in a tax subsidy dispute. The amount of EU retaliation permissible after the U.S. lost (for the second time) under WTO subsidy rules concerning Internal Revenue Code extraterritorial export tax preferences (FISCs) was disputed. A WTO panel, serving as an arbitrator, authorized approximately $4 *billion* in EU retaliation against U.S. exports. This retaliation commenced in March of 2004 and escalated monthly until the U.S. capitulated by amending the I.R.C. late in 2004.

Cross-Sector Retaliation

In a landmark ruling, a WTO panel acting as an arbitrator authorized Ecuador to remove protection of intellectual property rights regarding geographical indicators, copyrights and industrial designs on European Union goods for sale in Ecuador. This authorization was part of Ecuador's $200 million compensation in the *Bananas* dispute. The WTO panel acknowledged that Ecuador imports mostly capital goods and raw materials from the European Union and that imposing retaliatory tariffs on them would adversely harm its manufacturing industries. This risk supported "cross-retaliation" under Article 22.3 of the DSU outside the sector of the EU trade violation.

Allowance of cross-sector IP retaliation was probably the most critical driver behind the 2001 settlement of the *Bananas* dispute. Cross-sector retaliation was also authorized against the U.S. after losing a GATS dispute to Antigua on Internet gambling restraints. The United States settled this dispute with nearly all WTO members save Antigua via compensation. At this writing, Antigua is still debating whether and how to retaliate.

§ 1.15 U.S. Involvement in WTO Dispute Resolution

The WTO dispute resolution process has been invoked more frequently than many expected. The United States has been a complainant or a respondent in hundreds of disputes since 1995. It has won about 86% of the disputes when filing complaints, and lost about 75% when responding, with both percentages better than overall WTO DSU averages. The U.S. and the EU have been involved as the complainant or respondent in roughly 80% of all WTO

disputes. The sampling of disputes summarized below illustrates the
WTO dispute settlement process in action.

United States WTO Disputes

The United States lost a dispute initiated by Venezuela and
Brazil concerning U.S. standards for reformulated and conventional
gasoline. The offending U.S. law was amended to conform to the WTO
ruling. It won on a complaint initiated jointly with Canada and the
European Union regarding Japanese taxes on alcoholic beverages.
Japan subsequently changed its law. When Costa Rica complained
about U.S. restraints on imports of underwear, the U.S. let the
restraints expire prior to any formal DSB ruling at the WTO. Similar
results were reached when India complained of U.S. restraints on
wool shirts and blouses. The United States won a major dispute with
Canada concerning trade and subsidies for periodicals This
celebrated *Sports Illustrated* dispute proved that WTO remedies can
be used to avoid Canada's cultural industries exclusion under
NAFTA. See R. Folsom and W.D. Folsom, *NAFTA Re-Negotiated and
Its Business Implications* (forthcoming).

In the longstanding *Bananas* dispute noted above, the United
States joined Ecuador, Guatemala, Honduras and Mexico in
successfully challenging EU import restraints against so-called
"dollar bananas." The EU failed to comply with the Appellate Body's
ruling, and retaliatory measures were authorized and imposed. . . .
tariffs on EU goods by the United States and cross-sector IP
retaliation by Ecuador and others. In April 2001, the *Bananas*
dispute was settled on terms that generally converted EU quotas to
tariffs by 2006, though limited preferential quotas for ACP exporters
were retained. A patent law complaint by the U.S. against India
prevailed in the DSB and ultimately brought changes in Indian law
regarding pharmaceuticals and agricultural chemicals.

In *Beef Hormones,* also noted above, the European Union lost
twice before the Appellate Body for want of proof of a "scientific basis"
for its ban on hormone beef. It refused to alter its import restraints
and absorbed $200 million in retaliatory tariffs on selected exports to
Canada and the United States. In 2009, an arguably pro-European
settlement was reached. The U.S. effectively got a higher quota to
export hormone-free beef to the EU, in return for phasing out over
four years its retaliatory tariffs on EU goods. The U.S. threat of
carousel sanctions, i.e. rotating goods subject to retaliation, was
instrumental to this settlement. Meanwhile, because the U.S. beef
industry failed to timely ask for a continuation of the retaliatory
tariffs, the Federal Circuit ruled in 2010 that they expired in 2007.
Refunds were given to importers of EU products who paid those
tariffs.

The United States prevailed against Argentina regarding tariffs and taxes on footwear, textiles and apparel. It lost a challenge (strongly supported by Kodak) to Japan's distribution rules regarding photo film and paper. In this dispute the U.S. elected *not* to appeal the adverse WTO panel ruling to the Appellate Body. In contrast, the European Union took an appeal which reversed an adverse panel ruling on its customs classification of computer equipment. The U.S. had commenced this proceeding. Opponents in many disputes, Japan, the United States and the European Union united to complain that Indonesia's National Car Program was discriminatory and in breach of several WTO agreements. They prevailed and Indonesia altered its program.

India, Malaysia, Pakistan and Thailand teamed up to challenge U.S. shrimp import restraints enacted to protect endangered sea turtles. The WTO Appellate Body generally upheld their complaint and the U.S. has moved to comply. The adequacy of U.S. compliance is being challenged by Malaysia. The European Union and the United States jointly opposed Korea's discriminatory taxes on alcoholic beverages. This challenge was successful and Korea now imposes flat non-discriminatory taxes. The United States also complained of Japan's quarantine, testing and other agricultural import rules. The U.S. won at the WTO and Japan has changed its procedures.

In a semiconductor dumping dispute, Korea successfully argued that the U.S. was not in compliance with the WTO Antidumping Agreement. The United States amended its law, but Korea has instituted further proceedings alleging that these amendments are inadequate. The United States did likewise after Australia lost a subsidies dispute relating to auto leather. The reconvened WTO panel ruled that Australia had indeed failed to conform to the original adverse DSB decision. A U.S. challenge concerning India's quotas on imports of agricultural, textile and industrial products was upheld. India and the United States subsequently reached agreement on a timeline for removal of these restraints.

Closer to home, New Zealand and the United States complained of Canada's import/export rules regarding milk. Losing at the WTO, Canada agreed to a phased removal of the offending measures. The United States also won against Mexico in an antidumping dispute involving corn syrup, but lost a "big one" when the Appellate Body determined that export tax preferences granted to "Foreign Sales Corporations" of U.S. companies were illegal. Another "big one" went in favor of the United States. The European Union challenged the validity under the DSU of unilateral retaliation under Section 301 of the Trade Act of 1974. Section 301 has been something of a bete noire in U.S. trade law (see Chapter 14), but the WTO panel affirmed its legality in light of Presidential undertakings to administer it in accordance with U.S. obligations to adhere to multilateral WTO dispute settlement.

U.S. involvement in WTO dispute settlement continues to be extensive. The Appellate Body ruled that U.S. countervailing duties against British steel based upon pre-privatization subsidies were unlawful. The European Union prevailed before a WTO panel in its challenge of the U.S. Antidumping Act of 1916, since repealed. U.S. complaints against Korean beef import restraints and procurement practices were upheld. Canada's patent protection term was also invalidated by the WTO under a U.S. complaint. European Union complaints concerning U.S. wheat gluten quotas and the royalty free small business provisions of the Fairness in Music Licensing Act of 1998 have been sustained. The *Wheat Gluten* dispute questions the legality of U.S. "causation" rules in escape clause proceedings under Section 201 of the Trade Act of 1974.

A WTO Panel ruled in 2002 that the Byrd Amendment violates the WTO antidumping and subsidy codes. The Byrd Amendment (Continued Dumping and Subsidy Act of 2000) authorizes the Customs Service to forward AD and CVD duties to affected domestic producers for qualified expenses. Eleven WTO members including the EU, Canada and Mexico challenged the Amendment. This ruling was affirmed by the WTO Appellate Body and retaliation was authorized. Late in 2005, the U.S. repealed the Byrd Amendment, subject to a contested two-year phase out. The Appellate Body also ruled against Section 211 of the Omnibus Appropriations Act of 1998 denying trademark protection in connection with confiscated assets (the "HAVANA CLUB" dispute). U.S. compliance with these rulings has been slow in forthcoming. The United States and other complainants prevailed in a 2002 WTO proceeding against Indian local content and trade balancing requirements for foreign auto manufacturers. These requirements violated the TRIMs agreement.

In March of 2004, the European Union commenced raising tariffs against U.S. goods under the WTO retaliation authorized out of the FSC/export tax subsidy dispute. Monthly increments were planned until either the U.S. complied or the EU reached the maximum of roughly $4 billion annually it was authorized to retaliate. In the Fall of 2004, the United States repealed the extraterritorial income exclusion and the EU subsequently removed its retaliatory tariffs. In 2004, also, Antigua-Barbuda won a WTO panel ruling under the GATS against certain U.S. Internet gambling restraints. Retaliation was authorized, and the U.S. settled with nearly all members by offering compensation. The U.S. won a panel decision against Mexico's exorbitant telecom interconnection rates, but lost a 2004 cotton subsidy challenge by Brazil. Retaliation by Brazil was authorized.

The United States also lost a second dispute with the EU about pre-privatization countervailable subsidies, in particular the legality of the U.S. "same person" methodology. The U.S. won a SPS dispute against Japanese quarantine of U.S. apples, while losing an important softwood lumber "zeroing" methodology complaint brought by Canada. In 2006, the Mexico-United States "sugar war" came to a head before the Appellate Body. Mexico's 20% soft drink tax on beverages not using cane sugar, its 20% distribution tax on those beverages, and related bookkeeping requirements were found to violate GATT Article III and not exempt under Article XX(d). Subsequently, the two countries settled their dispute by agreeing, effective in 2008, to free trade in sugar and high fructose corn syrup. Further in 2006, the U.S. failed to persuade the Appellate Body to require the European Union under GATT Article X (3) to undertake a major overhaul of its customs law system targeting inconsistencies therein among the 28 member states.

In 2010, the United States agreed to pay $147 million annually to provide technical assistance to Brazilian cotton farmers. In return, Brazil has suspended retaliatory tariffs and cross-sector IP sanctions authorized by the WTO because of U.S. cotton subsidy violations. In 2009, a WTO panel ruled that Airbus had received $20 billion in illegal EU "launch" subsidies. By 2010, that same panel found Boeing the recipient of $5 billion in federal research contract subsidies that violated the WTO Subsidies Code. Appeals taken in both disputes resulted in affirmations by the WTO Appellate Body.

The United States has also settled a number of disputes prior to WTO panel decisions, and remains in consultation on other disputes that may be decided by a WTO panel. For the latest summary of all WTO disputes, including many not involving the United States, see www.wto.org.

§ 1.16 China Involvement in WTO Disputes

China, a member since 2001, is involved in a growing number of WTO disputes. China has lost nearly all the complaints filed against it, and won relatively few WTO disputes it has filed. Here is a sampling of those disputes.

Canada, the European Union and the United States complained against Chinese duties on imported auto parts (10 percent) that rose to those on complete autos (25 percent) if the imported parts exceeded a fixed percentage of the final vehicle content or price, or if specific combinations of imported auto parts were used in the final vehicle.

In addition, extensive record keeping, reporting and verification requirements were imposed when Chinese auto companies used imported parts. In July of 2008, a WTO panel ruled that these "internal charges" violated Articles III (2) and III (4) of the GATT and China's accession commitments. The core Panel ruling, affirmed by the Appellate Body, found China's auto parts measures discriminatory in favor of domestic producers, a violation of the national treatment standard for taxes and regulations. This ruling marked the first time since China's admission in 2001 that it was held in breach of its WTO commitments and obligations.

Less than one month after losing this dispute, China enacted a clever "green tax" on gas-guzzling autos, most of which just happen to be imported. The sales tax on cars with engine capacities over 4.1 litres has been doubled to 40%. Autos with engines between 3 and 4.1 litres are taxed at 25%, up from 15%. Most Chinese-made cars have engines with 2.5 litres or less. Autos with engines between 1 and 3 litres remain taxed at 8% and 10%. The smallest cars with engines below 1 litre have their sales tax reduced from 3 to 1 percent. This green tax could achieve protective results similar to China's Auto Parts tariff structure and could be challenged under GATT Article III.

Other disputes challenging China's compliance with WTO law are pending. They concern China's auto export subsidies and CVDs on auto imports, protection and enforcement of intellectual property rights (2009 WTO panel ruled against China), trade and distribution of publications and audiovisual entertainment products and services (2009 Appellate Body ruled against China), commodity export tariffs and restrictions (2012 WTO Appellate Body ruled against China), application of Chinese AD to U.S. grain-oriented flat rolled steel (GOES) (2012 WTO Appellate Body ruled against China), discriminatory treatment of foreign electronic payment services (2012 WTO panel ruled against China) and rare earth export restraints (2014 WTO Panel ruled against China). The United States is a complaining party to all of these disputes.

China, in turn, has challenged U.S. safeguard measures applied to Chinese steel exports (2010 WTO Panel rejected challenge) and tires (2011 WTO Panel rejected challenge). It has challenged U.S. antidumping and countervailing duties on paper products from China (2011 WTO Panel ruled against U.S. dual assessment of AD and CVD duties), as well as U.S. AD on Chinese solar panels. China has also applied AD duties to U.S. exports, e.g. chicken.

China challenged in 2017 continued U.S. and EU application of nonmarket economy rules in antidumping disputes. *See* Chapter 4. The United States is challenging Chinese export restrictions on raw materials and alleged unlawful subsidization of aluminum, rice, wheat and corn.

Part Two

CUSTOMS AND IMPORT LAW

Chapter 2

UNITED STATES TRADE
AND TARIFF LAW

Table of Sections

PART A

U.S. TRADE LEGISLATION AND ADMINISTRATIVE AUTHORITIES

U.S. international trade law is primarily found in the frequently amended Tariff Act of 1930 and the Trade Act of 1974. Much of the content of these statutes is derived from World Trade Organization principles. Additional statutes of note include the NAFTA Implementation Act of 1993, the Uruguay Round Agreements Act of 1994, the Export Administration Act of 1979, the Foreign Corrupt Practices Act of 1977, and the Caribbean Basin Economic Recovery Act of 1983.

The international trade of the United States is regulated by a number of different governmental bodies. The International Trade Administration is part of the Commerce Department, which in turn is part of the Executive Branch of the federal government. The Commerce Department also contains the Office of Export Licensing and the Office of Anti-boycott Compliance. The International Trade Commission is an independent federal government agency, and the Court of International Trade is part of the Judicial Branch of the United States government. Lastly, the Office of the United States Trade Representative works directly under the President.

The international trade of the United States is regulated by a number of different governmental bodies. The International Trade Administration is part of the Commerce Department, which in turn is part of the Executive Branch of the federal government. The Commerce Department also contains the Office of Export Licensing and the Office of Anti-boycott Compliance. The International Trade Commission is an independent federal government agency, and the Court of International Trade is part of the Judicial Branch of the United States government. Lastly, the Office of the United States Trade Representative works directly under the President.

§ 2.1 U.S. International Trade Administration (ITA)

The Commerce Department's International Trade Administration (ITA) is an administrative agency. In broadest terms, the ITA is to foster, promote and develop world trade, and to bring U.S. companies into the business of selling overseas. At a practical level, the ITA is designed to be helpful to the individual business by providing it with information concerning the "what, where, how and when" of imports and exports, such as information sources, requirements for a particular trade license, forms for an international license agreement or procedures to start a business in a foreign country. The ITA provides business data and educational programs to United States businesses.

In addition to these duties, the ITA also decides whether there are subsidies in countervailing duty (CVD)[1] cases, or sales at less than fair value in antidumping duty (AD) cases.[2] Prior to 1980, such decisions were made by the Treasury Department. The ITA is not, however, involved in decision-making in escape clause (Section 201), market disruption (Section 406) and unfair import practices (Section 337) proceedings.

§ 2.2   U.S. International Trade Commission (ITC)

The United States International Trade Commission (ITC) is an independent bipartisan agency created in 1916 by an act of Congress. The ITC is the successor to the United States Tariff Commission. In 1974, the name was changed and the ITC was given additional authority, powers and responsibilities. The Commission's present powers and duties include preparing reports pertaining to international economics and foreign trade for the Executive Branch, the Congress, other government agencies and the public. To carry out this responsibility, the ITC conducts investigations which entail extensive research, specialized studies and a high degree of expertise in all matters relating to the commercial and international trade policies of the United States.

Statutory investigations conducted by the ITC include unfair import trade practice determinations (Section 337 proceedings),[3] domestic industry injury determinations in antidumping and countervailing duty cases,[4] and safeguard and market disruption import relief recommendations.[5] The ITC also advises the President about probable economic effects on domestic industries and consumers of modifications on duties and other trade barriers incident to proposed trade agreements with foreign countries.

The ITC is intended to be a quasi-judicial, bipartisan, independent agency providing trade expertise to both Congress and the Executive. Congress went to great lengths to create a bipartisan body to conduct international trade studies and provide reliable expert information. The six Commissioners of the ITC are appointed by the President and confirmed by the United States Senate for nine year terms, unless appointed to fill an unexpired term. The presence

---

[1]   *See* Chapter 5.
[2]   *See* Chapter 4.
[3]   *See* Chapter 8.
[4]   *See* Chapters 4 and 5.
[5]   *See* Chapter 6.

of entrenched points of view is inhibited because a Commissioner who has served for more than five years is not eligible for reappointment. Not more than three Commissioners may be members of the same political party.

The Chairman and Vice-Chairman are designated by the President for two year terms. No Chairman may be of the same political party as the preceding Chairman, nor may the President designate two Commissioners of the same political party as Chairman and Vice-Chairman. Congress further guaranteed the independence of the ITC from the Executive Branch by having its budget submitted directly to the Congress. This means that its budget is not subject to review by the Office of Management and Budget.

§ 2.3   U.S. Court of International Trade (CIT)

The United States Court of International Trade (CIT) is an Article III court under the United States Constitution for judicial review of civil actions arising out of import transactions and certain federal statutes affecting international trade. It grew out of the Board of General Appraisers (a quasi-judicial administrative unit within the Treasury Department which reviewed decisions by United States Customs officials concerning the amount of duties to be paid on imports in actions arising under the tariff acts) and the United States Customs Court which had essentially the same jurisdiction and powers. The President, with the advice and consent of the Senate, appoints the nine judges who constitute the Court of International Trade. Not more than five of the nine judges may belong to any one political party.

The geographical jurisdiction of the Court of International Trade extends throughout the United States, and it is also authorized to hold hearings in foreign countries. The court has exclusive subject-matter jurisdiction to decide any civil action commenced against the United States, its agencies or its officers arising from any law pertaining to revenue from imports, tariffs, duties or embargoes or enforcement of these and other customs regulations. This includes disputes regarding trade embargoes, quotas, customs classification and valuation, country of origin determinations and denials of protests by the U.S. Customs Service.

The court's exclusive jurisdiction also includes any civil action commenced by the United States that arises out of an import transaction, and authority to review final agency decisions concerning antidumping and countervailing duty matters, the eligibility of workers, firms and communities who are economically harmed by foreign imports for trade adjustment assistance, disputes concerning the release of confidential business information, and decisions to deny, revoke or suspend the licenses of customs brokers. However, the CIT does *not* have jurisdiction over disputes involving restrictions on imported merchandise where public safety or health issues are raised. This limitation on CIT jurisdiction arises because such issues involving domestic goods would be determined by other regulatory bodies, and only referral to United States District Courts can ensure uniform treatment of both imports and domestically produced goods.

The standard for the judicial review exercised by the CIT varies from case to case. In some instances, such as confidentiality orders, a *de novo* trial is undertaken. In others, notably antidumping and countervailing duty cases, the standard is one of substantial evidence, or arbitrary, capricious or unlawful action, or an abuse of discretion. In trade adjustment assistance litigation, the administrative determinations are considered conclusive absent substantial evidentiary support in the record with the CIT empowered to order the taking of further evidence. Unless otherwise specified by statute, the Administrative Procedure Act governs the judicial review by the CIT of U.S. international trade law.

The CIT possesses all the remedial powers, legal and equitable, of a United States District Court, including authority to enter money judgments for or against the United States, but with three limitations. First, in an action challenging a trade adjustment ruling, the court may not issue an injunction or writ of mandamus. Second, the CIT may order disclosure of confidential information only as specified in Section 777(c)(2) of the Tariff Act of 1930. Third, the CIT may order only declaratory relief for suits brought under the provision allowing the court accelerated review because of a showing of irreparable harm.

The CIT must ordinarily give due deference to Customs Service regulations under *Chevron* rules[6] even when undertaking *de novo* review.[7] However, the Supreme Court has ruled that *Chevron* does not apply to product classification decisions by the Customs Service.[8] CIT decisions are first appealed to the Court of Appeals for the Federal Circuit (formerly to the Court of Customs and Patent Appeals), and ultimately to the United States Supreme Court.

---

[6]   *Chevron, U.S.A., Inc. v. Natural Resources Defense Council, Inc.*, 467 U.S. 837, 104 S.Ct. 2778, 81 L.Ed.2d 694 (1984).

[7]   *United States v. Haggar Apparel Co.*, 526 U.S. 380, 119 S.Ct. 1392, 143 L.Ed.2d 480 (1999).

[8]   *United States v. Mead Corp.*, 533 U.S. 218 (2001). *See* Section 3.1.

§ 2.4   The USTR, Free Trade Agreements and U.S. Fast Track Negotiations

Removing trade barriers is usually done on a reciprocal basis, and requires lengthy bargaining and negotiations between the sovereigns. Congress is not adapted to carry on such negotiations, so it routinely delegates limited authority to the President to negotiate agreements reducing trade restrictions. Recent efforts to reduce trade restrictions have been multilateral, bilateral and trilateral. Congress has intermittently given quite broad authority to the President, or his representative, to reduce or eliminate United States tariffs on a reciprocal "fast track" basis, discussed below.

The USTR

In response to Section 1104 of the Trade Agreements Act of 1979,[9] the President reviewed the structure of the international trade functions of the Executive Branch. Although this did not lead to the establishment of a new Department of International Trade and Investment, it did lead to enhancement of the Office of the Special Representative for Trade Negotiations,[10] which has since been renamed the United States Trade Representative (USTR). The powers of the USTR were expanded and its authority given a legislative foundation. The USTR is appointed by the President, with the advice and consent of the Senate.[11] The Office of the USTR has been the principal vehicle through which tariff and trade negotiations have been conducted on behalf of the United States. Among other things, the USTR has had continuing responsibility in connection with implementation of the WTO Agreements and U.S. free trade agreements. The USTR is the contact point for persons who desire an investigation of instances of noncompliance with any trade agreement.

In 1988, the duties of the USTR were significantly expanded in conjunction with an overhaul of Section 301 of the Trade Act of 1974. *See* Chapter 14. Section 301 creates a controversial unilateral trade remedy which principally has been used to obtain foreign market access for U.S. exports. Prior to 1988, the President directly administered Section 301. Thereafter, as amended by the Omnibus Trade and Competitiveness Act, the USTR assumed this role along with new duties governing the Super 301 and Special 301 procedures created in 1988. Moreover, since the 1988 Act expanded the coverage of Section 301 and introduced mandatory (not discretionary) remedies, the USTR became involved in many domestic industry

---

9   Public Law 96–39.

10   The office had been established by an Executive Order in 1963.

11   19 U.S.C.A. § 2171.

complaints about foreign governments. Such complaints can reach breaches of international agreements as well as unjustifiable, unreasonable or discriminatory foreign country practices. *See* Chapter 14.

Free Trade Agreements

The USTR has negotiated about 20 free trade agreements for the United States (see below). Hundreds of free trade agreements (FTAs) lattice the world, including for example between the European Union and South Africa, Canada and Costa Rica, China and Chile, Japan and Singapore. Mexico has dozens of bilateral free trade agreements. A variety of factors help explain why free trade has become the leading edge of international trade law and policy. Difficulties encountered in the Uruguay, "Seattle" and Doha Rounds of multilateral trade negotiations are certainly crucial. *See* Section 1.2. GATT/WTO regulatory failures regarding free trade and customs union agreements have also fueled this reality. Yet these "negatives" do not fully explain the global feeding frenzy of free trade agreements.

A range of attractions are also at work. For example, free trade agreements often extend to subject matters beyond WTO competence. Foreign investment law is a prime example, and many FTAs serve as investment magnets. Government procurement, optional at the WTO level, is often included in free trade agreements. Competition policy, labor and environmental matters absent from the WTO are sometimes covered as well. In addition, free trade agreements can reach beyond the scope of existing WTO agreements. Services are one "WTO-plus" area where this is clearly true. Intellectual property rights are also being "WTO-plussed" in bilateral free trade agreements. Whether this amounts to competitive trade liberalization or competitive trade imperialism is a provocative question.

For much more extensive coverage, see R. Folsom, *Principles of Free Trade* (forthcoming).

"Fast Track" U.S. Trade Negotiations

Fast track originated as a compromise after Congress refused to ratify two major components of the Kennedy Round of GATT negotiations. When in place, fast track requires Congress to vote within 90 legislative days up or down, without amendments, on U.S. trade agreements. In return, Congress receives substantial notice and opportunity to influence U.S. trade negotiations conducted by the USTR. Congress also sets nonbinding trade negotiation objectives under fast track enabling legislation.

NAFTA and the Uruguay Round WTO agreements were negotiated and implemented under fast track procedures in place from 1991–1996. The bipartisan Trade Act of 2002 (P.L. 107–210) authorized President George W. Bush to negotiate international trade agreements on a fast track basis for five years. *See* 19 U.S.C. § 3801 et seq. President Bush and the USTR quickly completed, and Congress quickly approved, free trade agreements (FTAs) with Chile and Singapore. Thereafter U.S. FTAs with Morocco, Australia, Central America/Dominican Republic (CAFTA), Peru, Jordan, Oman, and Bahrain followed. Just prior to the expiration of fast track authority in July of 2007, President Bush signed FTA agreements with Colombia, Panama and Korea. Several years later these agreements were implemented by Congress under the Obama administration.

Congress granted fast track trade promotion authority to President Obama in the summer of 2015 under the Trade Preferences Extension Act. This authority lasts through June 2018 of the Trump administration. Recognizing that China is a rapidly developing economic superstar, the United States under the Obama administration pursued what resembled a "containment" strategy by promoting a "Trans-Pacific Partnership (TPP)." This strategy sought to bring the U.S., Australia, New Zealand, Chile, Peru, Malaysia, Brunei, Singapore and notably Vietnam into a broad trade, technology and investment alliance. Mexico, Canada and Japan also notably joined these negotiations. Nevertheless, President Trump withdrew from the TPP agreement early in 2017.

With all three NAFTA nations participating in the Trans-Pacific Partnership (TPP) agreement, NAFTA could have effectively been updated via the TPP. Instead, President Trump notified Congress in 2017 of his intent to re-negotiate NAFTA with Mexico and Canada under fast track procedures. See Section 16.1. In addition, the USTR under President Obama commenced negotiations with the European Union on a "Transatlantic Trade and Investment Partnership (TTIP)" agreement. The intent of the Trump administration regarding the TTIP remains unclear, particularly because of BREXIT. *See* Section 16.2.

For U.S. free trade partners, fast track suggests that once they reach a deal with the USTR Congress cannot alter it. That said, in recent years Congress has effectively tacked on additional requirements via letters of intent, notably regarding labor and the environment.

PART B

UNITED STATES TARIFFS

§ 2.5   Overview of U.S. Tariffs and Duty Free Entry

The sections that follow focus on United States tariffs under the Harmonized Tariff Schedule (HTS). Column 1 tariffs, known as most-favored-nation (MFN) tariffs, are the lower and most likely to be applicable. Column 2 tariffs, originating in the Smoot-Hawley Tariff Act of 1930, are the higher and least likely to be applicable. United States tariffs generally take one of three forms. The most common is an ad valorem rate. Such tariffs are assessed in proportion to the value of the article. Tariffs may also be assessed at specific rates or compound rates. Specific rates may be measured by the pound or other weight. A compound rate is a mixture of an ad valorem and specific rate tariff. Tariff rate quotas involve limitations on imports at a specific tariff up to a certain amount. Imports in excess of that amount are not prohibited, but are subject to a higher rate of tariff. Thus tariff rate quotas tend to restrict imports that are in excess of the specified quota for the lower tariff level.

Duty Free Entry

Some goods may enter the United States at less than most-favored-nation tariff levels or duty free. This occurs because of special tariff preferences incorporated into United States law (outlined below). It is important to realize that these preferences create valuable trading opportunities for U.S. importers and exporters located in qualified nations. These people are the clients for whom lawyers work to secure duty free entry into the United States market. Duty free entry is, of course, the ultimate goal of all exporters and importers involved in United States trade. Various free trade and customs union agreements (including NAFTA and other FTAs of the United States) achieving duty free outcomes are discussed in Section 2.4.

Perhaps the widest of the U.S. duty free programs is known as the Generalized System of Preferences (GSP) adopted through the GATT. The GSP is a complex system of duty free tariff preferences benefiting selected goods originating in developing nations and intended to foster their economic improvement. A second program is the Caribbean Basin Economic Recovery Act of 1983 (also known as the Caribbean Basin Initiative), which permits certain goods to enter the United States market duty free. To a significant degree, the CBI duty free program was duplicated in the Andean Trade Preference

Act of 1991 initially benefiting Colombian, Ecuadorian, Bolivian and Peruvian goods. Another important "duty free" category allows fabricated U.S.-made components shipped abroad for assembly to return to the U.S. without tariffs on the value of the components. Authorization for this importation is found in Section 9802.00.80 of the Harmonized Tariff Schedule. Goods of this type are subject to a United States Customs duty limited in amount to the value added by foreign assembly operations. This provision is perhaps best known in connection with Latin American maquiladoras.

The least restrictive rules of origin for duty free entry of goods into the United States apply to its insular possessions. These include American Samoa, Guam, Johnson Island, Kingman Reef, Midway Islands, Puerto Rico, the U.S. Virgin Islands and Wake Island. Generally speaking, goods from such possessions may contain up to 70 percent foreign value and still be admitted duty free.

Some of these duty free programs overlap and effectively compete with each other. It might be helpful to think of them in terms of concentric geographic circles. The widest circle is Section 9802.00.80 which applies to the entire globe. The next circle represents the GSP system and most developing nations. Inside that circle is the Caribbean Basin Initiative, the Andean Initiative, and U.S. insular possessions followed by NAFTA and other U.S. free trade agreements. A manufacturer based in the Caribbean may seek duty free entry into the United States market under Section 9802.00.80, the GSP program or the CBI, but not U.S. free trade agreements, save the Dominican Republic. To most developing nations, these are selectively discriminatory duty free programs that undermine their GSP benefits.

Unusual trade opportunities can arise by linking U.S. duty free entry programs with those of the European Union (EU). For example, the Union has its own complicated and different GSP program, its equivalent of Section 9802.00.80, and two selective duty free programs for developing nations. The latter are known as its Mediterranean Policy and Cotonou Conventions. A producer in Israel can quite possibly gain duty free access to the EU (under its Mediterranean Policy) and to the United States (under the Israeli-U.S. FTA). A producer in Jamaica might achieve similar results under the Cotonou Conventions, the CBI and/or the GSP programs of the EU and the United States.

§ 2.6   The Origins of United States Tariffs

Article I, Section 8, of the United States Constitution authorizes Congress to levy uniform tariffs on imports. Tariff legislation must originate in the House of Representatives. Although tariffs were primarily viewed as revenue-raising measures at the founding of the nation, it was not long before tariffs became used for openly protectionist purposes. The Tariff Act of 1816 initiated this change in outlook. During much of the Nineteenth Century, the United States legislated heavy protective tariffs. These were justified as necessary to protect the country's infant industries and to force the South to engage in more trade with the North (not with Europe). Exceptions were made to the high level of tariffs for selected United States imports under conditional most-favored-nation reciprocity treaties. The first of these treaties involved Canada (1854) and Hawaii (1875).

As the United States moved into the 20th Century, additional tariffs in excess of the already high level of protection were authorized. "Countervailing duty" tariffs were created in 1890 to combat export subsidies of European nations, particularly Germany. After 1916, additional duties could also be assessed if "dumping practices" were involved. Early American dumping legislation was largely a reaction to marketplace competition from foreign cartels. Throughout all of these years the constitutionality of protective tariffs was never clearly resolved.

In 1928, however, the United States Supreme Court firmly ruled that the enactment of protective tariffs was constitutional.[12] This decision, followed by the crash of the stock market in 1929, led to the enactment of the Smoot-Hawley Tariff Act of 1930. The Act set some of the highest rates of tariff duties in the history of the United States. It represents the last piece of tariff legislation that Congress passed without international negotiations. These tariffs remain part of United States law and are generally referred to as "Column 2 tariffs" under the Harmonized Tariff Schedule (HTS).

Since 1930, changes in the levels of tariffs applicable to goods entering the United States have chiefly been achieved through international trade agreements negotiated by the President and affirmed by Congress. During the 1930s and 40s, the Smoot-Hawley tariffs generally applied unless altered through bilateral trade agreements. The Reciprocal Trade Agreements Act of 1934[13] gives the President the authority to enter into such agreements, and under various extensions this authority remains in effect today. An early agreement of this type was the Canadian Reciprocal Trade Agreement of 1935.

---

[12]   *J.W. Hampton, Jr. & Co. v. United States*, 276 U.S. 394, 48 S.Ct. 348, 72 L.Ed. 624 (1928).

[13]   48 Stat. 943 (1934).

§ 2.7　Column 1 U.S. Tariffs and the GATT/WTO

The Trade Agreements Extension Act of 1945 authorized the President to conduct multilateral negotiations in the trade field. It was out of this authority that the General Agreement on Tariffs and Trade (GATT) was negotiated. The GATT became effective on January 1, 1948 and was implemented in the United States by executive order. Indeed, despite its wide-ranging impact on United States tariff levels since 1948, the GATT was never ratified by the United States Congress. Nevertheless, it is the source of the principal tariffs assessed today on imports into the United States. These duties, known as most-favored-nation (MFN) tariffs or "Column 1 tariffs," have been dramatically reduced over the years through successive rounds of trade negotiations. See the sample U.S. tariff schedule excerpted in Section 3.4. They are unconditional MFN tariffs, meaning that reciprocity is not required in order for them to apply. Multilateral tariff agreements have predominated over bilateral negotiations since 1948.

The term "most-favored-nation" is misleading in its suggestion of special tariff arrangements. It is more appropriate and since 1998 officially correct to think of MFN tariffs as the "normal" level of U.S. tariffs, to which there are exceptions resulting in the application of higher or lower tariffs. After the Tokyo Round of GATT negotiations in 1978, the average MFN tariff applied to manufactured imports into the United States was approximately 5.6 percent. Reductions in this level to approximately 3.5 percent have been accomplished under the Uruguay Round of 1994. That said, unusually high Column 1 tariffs apply selectively: 10% to certain shoes and 25% to certain trucks, for example.

Telecommunications and Technology Tariffs

In 1997, agreement on liberalizing trade and reducing tariffs on basic telecommunications equipment was reached by 69 nations. This agreement took effect Feb. 5, 1998. World trade in office machines and telecom equipment is significant—$626 billion in 1996, or about 12.2 per cent of world merchandise trade. The agreement covers six main categories: computers, telecom equipment, semiconductors, semiconductor manufacturing equipment, software and scientific instruments. It does not currently cover consumer electronic goods.

Tariff cuts on a wide range of information technology (IT) products were agreed to late in 1996 by a "coalition of the willing." The United States, the European Union and most of East Asia agreed to abolish tariffs on computers, electrical capacitors, calculators, ATM's, fax and answering machines, digital copiers and video cameras, computer diskettes, CD-ROM drives, computer software, fiber optical cables and hundreds of other items by 2000. In its time, this agreement covered more than 90 percent of all IT trade. In 2010, a WTO Panel ruled against EU information technology tariffs on cable converter boxes with Net capacity, flat-panel computer screens and printers that also scan, fax or copy. The EU elected not to appeal this ruling. Zero tariffs should apply.

The 1996 agreement aged as new information technology products emerged: Videogames, GPS devices, pre-paid cards, printer-ink cartridges, advanced semiconductors, and medical devices (MRIs for example). Late in 2014, with China and the United States in the lead, an updated information technology agreement that embraces these new generation products and covers roughly 97 percent of all IT exports, amounting to more than $1 trillion annually among 78 countries, was obtained.

§ 2.8   Column 2 U.S. Tariffs

Between 1948 and 1951 the United States granted Column 1 most-favored-nation tariff treatment to goods originating from virtually every part of the world. Commencing in 1951, goods originating in nations controlled by communists were withdrawn from such tariff treatment. This had, and to some degree continues to have, the effect of treating the importation of goods from communist nations under Column 2 United States tariff headings. See the sample U.S. tariff schedule excerpted in Section 3.4. As a practical matter, very few such imports can overcome the high Smoot-Hawley tariffs embodied in Column 2.

The designation of which nations are "communist" for these purposes has varied over time. Yugoslavia was generally not treated as a communist country and its goods therefore entered under Column 1 MFN tariffs. Goods from the Balkans presently do so as well. Central and Eastern European nations were sometimes treated as communist countries, particularly during the 1950s and 1960s. This is no longer the case, and at this point nearly every European and Baltic nation has been granted MFN status under United States tariff law. Belarus, Kazakhstan, Turkmenistan, Georgia, Azerbaijan, Tajikistan, Moldova, Kyrgyzstan, Armenia, Uzbekistan, the Russian Federation and Ukraine are also MFN beneficiaries.

It is perhaps more useful, therefore, to indicate those nations that do not presently benefit from most-favored-nation tariff treatment. These include Cuba and North Korea. Goods from some of these nations are totally embargoed as a matter of national security; the law in this area is covered in Chapter 11. The most current listing of those nations whose products are subject to Column 2 tariffs can be found in General Headnote 3(b) to the HTS.

§ 2.9   The Jackson-Vanik Amendment

Section 402 of the 1974 Trade Act governs American grants of most-favored-nation tariff status.[14] This is commonly known as the "Jackson-Vanik Amendment." Under its terms, no products from a nonmarket economy nation may receive MFN treatment, nor may that country participate in U.S. financial credit or guaranty programs, whenever the President determines that it denies its citizens the right or opportunity to emigrate, imposes more than nominal taxes on visas or other emigration documents, or imposes more than nominal charges on its citizens as a result of their desire to leave.

These statutory conditions are widely thought to have been the product of United States desires to have the Soviet Union permit greater exodus of its Jewish population during the early 1970s. However, the passage of the Jackson-Vanik Amendment was an important factor in the Soviet decision to withdraw from a broad trade agreement with the United States at that time, and led to sharply curtailed Jewish emigration from the Soviet Union.

The application of Jackson-Vanik by the President is subject to a waiver by executive order whenever the President determines that such a waiver will substantially promote the objectives of freedom of emigration and the President has received assurances that the emigration practices of a particular nonmarket economy nation will lead substantially to the achievement of those objectives. If the President decides to exercise this waiver authority, the waiver must be renewed annually and reported to Congress. These reports and the exercise of presidential waivers have over the years been contentious.

Congressional Veto

At one point Congress had the power to veto presidential waivers under the Jackson-Vanik Amendment. However, a 1983 decision of the United States Supreme Court strongly suggested that these veto powers were unconstitutional.[15] The Customs and Trade Act of 1990 amended the Trade Act of 1974 so as to permit Congress to jointly resolve against presidential Jackson-Vanik waivers. These resolutions can be vetoed by the President, and the President's veto can in turn by overridden by Congress. It is thought that these amendments resolved the constitutional problems associated with Congressional vetoes of presidential action.

---

[14]   19 U.S.C.A. § 2432.

[15]   *See Immigration and Naturalization Service v. Chadha,* 462 U.S. 919, 103 S.Ct. 2764, 77 L.Ed.2d 317 (1983).

Congress and the President disagreed significantly over the renewal of most-favored-nation treatment for Chinese goods. Questions surrounding China's emigration policies, and its general human rights record, were downplayed by U.S. authorities for many years prior to Tiananmen Square. As internal discord within China increased, especially in Tibet and more generally in connection with the Democracy Movement, the Jackson-Vanik amendment came to the forefront of Sino-American trade relations. President Bush's renewal of China's most favored nation status in 1990, 1991 and 1992 was heavily criticized.

China and Jackson-Vanik

Jackson-Vanik became the political fulcrum of Sino-American trade relations. Congress threatened but did not achieve a veto of the President's renewal of MFN tariffs for Chinese goods. Early in 1992, Congress adopted the United States-China Act of 1991. This law would have prohibited the President from recommending further extensions of MFN status to China unless he reported that the PRC had accounted for citizens detained or accused in connection with Tiananmen Square and had made significant progress in achieving specified objectives on human rights, trade and weapons proliferation. President Bush Sr. vetoed the Act and the Congress was unable to override that veto.

In 1993, President Clinton renewed China's MFN status subject to some general human-rights conditions, including "significant progress" in releasing political prisoners, allowing international groups access to prisons and respect for human rights in Tibet. This seemed to pacify Congress for the moment. But it engendered hostility and resistance in China. Less publicly, the United States business community opposed the linkage of human rights to MFN tariffs as its PRC trade and investment commitments and opportunities were endangered. China, meanwhile, had developed the world's fastest growing economy and it decided to force the issue. If anything, abuse of human rights in the PRC actually increased early in 1994, notably prior to a well-publicized visit of the U.S. Secretary of State.

With Congress increasingly split on the issue, President Clinton made an historic reversal in policy. In June of 1994, he renewed China's MFN tariff status without human rights conditions, limiting its coverage only as regards Chinese-made ammunition and guns. President Clinton renewed China's MFN tariff status each year after 1994. Congress did not seek to override these decisions. In 1998, for the first time, President Clinton waived the Jackson-Vanik requirements for Vietnam. President George W. Bush did likewise. This waiver survived Congressional scrutiny. It opened the door to

EXIMBANK and OPIC programs, as well as Column 1 MFN tariffs on Vietnamese goods entering the United States.

WTO members like China since 2001, Vietnam since 2007 and Russia since 2012 receive MFN tariff status automatically and unconditionally. Hence the Jackson-Vanik amendment no longer has significant application.

§ 2.10   U.S. Generalized System of Tariff Preferences (GSP)—Statutory Authorization

The Generalized System of Preferences (GSP) originated in United Nations dialogues between the developed and the developing world. The third world successfully argued that it needed special access to industrial markets in order to improve and advance their economies. One problem with this approach is that it is contrary to the unconditional most-favored-nation principle contained in the GATT. Nevertheless, in 1971 the GATT authorized its parties to establish generalized systems of tariff preferences for developing nations. The European Union, Japan and nearly all other developed nations adopted GSP systems before the United States. Although similar in purpose, each of these systems is governed by a unique body of law of the "donor" country.

It was not until the Trade Act of 1974 that a GSP system was incorporated into United States tariff law. The Trade Act authorized GSP tariff preferences for ten years. The program was renewed in the Trade Act of 1984 for an additional nine years ending in July 1993. Incremental extensions have since been made pending a program review. The Trade Promotion Authority-Trade Adjustment Assistance Act of 2002 (TPA-TAA) renewed the GSP program through 2006 retroactive to its expiration on Sept. 30, 2001. Various GSP renewals have followed. At this point, tens of billions worth of goods enter the U.S. market duty free under the GSP program, but it is estimated that more imports could achieve this status if traders better understood the GSP.

Title V of the Trade Act of 1974 contains the provisions authorizing the United States GSP program.[16] The United States GSP system, as presently operated, designates certain nations as "beneficiary developing countries." Unless a country is so designated, none of its imports can enter duty free under the GSP program. In addition, only selected goods are designated "eligible articles" for purposes of the GSP program. Thus, for duty free entry under the

---

[16]   19 U.S.C.A. §§ 501–506.

GSP program to occur, the goods must originate from a beneficiary nation and qualify as eligible articles.

§ 2.11   U.S. GSP—USTR Petition Procedures

Any United States producer of an article that competes with GSP imports can file a petition with the United States Trade Representative (USTR) to have a country or particular products withdrawn from the program. This petitioning procedure can also be used in the reverse by importers and exporters to obtain product or beneficiary country status under the United States GSP program. The President is given broad authority to withdraw, suspend or limit the application of duty free entry under the GSP system.[17] Specific products from specific countries may be excluded from GSP benefits. In one case, for example, the President's decision to withdraw GSP benefits for "buffalo leather and goat and kid leather (not fancy)" from India was affirmed.[18] In another decision, the President's discretionary authority to deny GSP benefits to cut flowers from Colombia was similarly upheld.[19]

The President is required to take into consideration the impact of duty free entry on U.S. producers of like or directly competitive products. There is a set of regulations, codified at 15 C.F.R. Part 2007, which details the petitioning procedures used in connection with the certification of GSP eligible products or countries. These regulations require the domestic competitor to cite injury caused by duty free GSP imports. Within 6 months after the petition is filed, and a review by the United States Trade Representative (USTR) acting with the advice of the International Trade Commission (ITC) has been undertaken, a decision on the petition will be rendered by the USTR.

§ 2.12   U.S. GSP—Competitive Need Limitations

There are two statutory limitations on the applicability of duty free GSP entry. These are known as the "competitive need" limitations. They are found in Section 504 of the Trade Act of 1974, codified at 19 U.S.C.A. § 2464(c). The first statutory limitation focuses upon dollar volumes. Duty free entry is not permitted to any eligible product from a beneficiary country if during the preceding year that country exported to the United States more than a designated dollar volume of the article in question. There is a statutory formula for establishing this dollar volume limitation. In recent years, the maximum dollar volume limitation has ranged

---

[17]   *See* 19 U.S.C.A. § 2464(a).

[18]   *Florsheim Shoe Co. v. United States*, 744 F.2d 787 (Fed.Cir.1984).

[19]   *Sunburst Farms, Inc. v. United States*, 797 F.2d 973 (Fed.Cir.1986).

between 75 and 80 million dollars. The second statutory limitation on duty free GSP entry is framed in terms of percentages. Duty free entry is denied to products if during the preceding year the beneficiary country exported to the United States 50 percent or more of the total U.S. imports of that particular product.[20]

A complex system of waivers applies to the competitive need formulae. These are administered by the USTR and the President acting on advice of the International Trade Commission.[21] Basically, there are five possibilities for waivers of the competitive need limitations. The first can occur if the President decides that there is no like or directly competitive article produced in the United States and the imported product is exempt from the percentage but not the dollar value competitive need limitation. The second can occur under circumstances where the President determines that the imports in question are *de minimis*.

The third possibility involves imports from the least developed developing nations, after notice to Congress. A list of these countries can be found in HTS General Note 3(c)(ii)(B). A fourth opportunity for a competitive need waiver exists when there has been an historical preferential trade relationship between the United States and the source country, and there is a trade agreement between that country and the United States, and the source country does not discriminate against or otherwise impose unjustifiable or unreasonable barriers to United States commerce.

Lastly, the President is authorized to waive the competitive need requirements of the GSP program if the International Trade Commission decides that the imports in question are not likely to have an adverse effect on the United States industry with which they compete, and the President determines that such a waiver is in the national economic interest.[22] In making waiver determinations, the President must consider generally the extent to which the beneficiary country has assured the United States that it will provide equitable and reasonable access to its markets and basic commodity resources. The President must also consider the extent to which the country provides adequate and effective means for foreigners to secure and exercise intellectual property rights.

Once a waiver of the competitive need limitations is granted, it remains in effect until circumstances change and the President decides that it is no longer justified. Attorneys can play a useful role

---

[20]   *See West Bend Co. v. United States*, 10 C.I.T. 146 (1986) (competitive impact still must be proven).

[21]   *See* 19 U.S.C.A. § 2464(c).

[22]   *See* 19 U.S.C.A. § 2464(c)(3)(A).

in monitoring Department of Commerce trade statistics to determine how close imports are coming under the competitive need formulae to restriction. By shifting to purchases of similar goods from another country, importers can preserve duty free entry and avoid the effects of these statutory restraints.

§ 2.13 U.S. GSP—Country Eligibility

Thousands of products from over one hundred countries benefit from duty free GSP entry into the United States.[23] A list of GSP qualified nations and territories is presented in HTS General Note 3(c)(ii). Goods from insular possessions of the United States (e.g., American Samoa and the U.S. Virgin Islands) ordinarily receive duty free GSP entry "no less favorable" than allowed GSP beneficiary nations.[24]

The President's power over the list of eligible countries and eligible products is wide and politically sensitive. For example, the President is required to evaluate, in determining whether a country is eligible under the U.S. GSP program, if it is upholding "internationally recognized workers' rights." Such rights include the right of association, the right to organize and bargain collectively, a prohibition against forced or compulsory labor, a minimum age for employment of children, and acceptable working conditions (minimum wages, hours of work, and occupational safety and health.)[25] In 2002, the definition of "core worker rights" for GSP country eligibility purposes was updated to include the ILO prohibition on the worst forms of child labor. The President must report annually to the Congress on the status of internationally recognized workers' rights in every GSP beneficiary country, but the issue is not open to private challenge.[26]

The President must also consider whether the foreign country is adequately protecting United States owners of intellectual property, (compliance with TRIPs is not necessarily sufficient), and whether its investment laws adversely affect U.S. exports. In addition, when designating GSP beneficiary nations, the Trade Act requires the President to take into account various factors which amount to a U.S. agenda on international economic relations:

(1)   The desires of the country;

---

[23]   *See* Executive Order 11888 (Nov. 24, 1975, 40 F.R. 55276, extensively amended, for a detailed listing of eligible products and countries).

[24]   19 U.S.C.A. § 2462(d).

[25]   19 U.S.C.A. § 2462(a).

[26]   *See International Labor Rights Education & Research Fund v. Bush*, 752 F.Supp. 495 (D.D.C.1990), *affirmed* 954 F.2d 745 (D.C.Cir.1992).

(2)   Its level of economic development;

(3)   Whether the EU, Japan or others extend GSP treatment to it;

(4)   The extent to which the country provides equitable and reasonable access to its markets and its basic commodity resources, and the extent to which it will refrain from unreasonable export practices;

(5)   The extent to which it provides adequate and effective intellectual property rights; and

(6)   The extent to which it has taken action to reduce trade distorting investment practices (including export performance requirements) and reduced barriers to trade in services.[27]

No communist nations and no oil restraining OPEC nations (Indonesia, Ecuador and Venezuela are excepted) may benefit from the GSP program. Furthermore, the President must not designate countries that grant trade preferences to other *developed* nations. The President must also consider, in making GSP decisions, whether beneficiary countries are cooperative on drug enforcement, whether they are expropriators of U.S. property interests, whether they offer assistance to terrorists, and whether they are willing to recognize international arbitration awards. The President may waive the expropriation requirement if it is determined that the country in question has paid prompt, adequate and effective compensation or entered into good faith negotiations or arbitration with the intent to do so.

The statutory bar against communist, oil restricting OPEC and preferentially trading countries as GSP beneficiaries is absolute. The bar against expropriating, drug dealing, denials of arbitration award enforcement, terrorist aiding and workers' rights non-recognition beneficiaries is discretionary with the President. The goods of such nations may still qualify if the President determines that GSP duty free entry would be in the national economic interest of the United States.[28]

In applying these country eligibility criteria, past Presidents have disqualified a variety of nations from the U.S. GSP program. For example, Romania, Nicaragua, Paraguay, Chile, Burma, the Central African Republic and Liberia have all been disqualified in the past for failure to meet the workers' rights standards. Argentina and Honduras have lost GSP benefits for perceived failures to

---

[27]   19 U.S.C.A. § 2462(c).
[28]   19 U.S.C.A. § 2462(b).

adequately protect U.S. pharmaceutical patents. Panama under General Noriega was rendered ineligible because of the failure to cooperate on narcotics. Intellectual property piracy led to the suspension of Ukraine's country eligibility in the GSP program. Argentina in 2012 was suspended for failure to pay international arbitration awards.

The President's review of a country's eligibility under the GSP program is ongoing. This led to the reinstatement of GSP beneficiary nations. Russia was made a GSP beneficiary by President Clinton. Any country designated as a beneficiary nation under the GSP program that is subsequently disqualified by exercise of Presidential discretion, or graduated, must receive 60 days' notice from the President with an explanation of this decision.[29] This, in effect, presents the opportunity to reply and negotiate.

Since the GSP program originated within the GATT/WTO nearly all the beneficiary countries are members of that organization. It is not, however, mandatory for a developing nation to be a member of the WTO in order to receive GSP trade benefits from the United States. China is a WTO member, but for other reasons its goods do not qualify for GSP duty free entry. Other nations whose goods are not eligible are specifically listed in the Trade Act: Australia, Austria, Canada, European Union States, Finland, Iceland, Japan, Monaco, New Zealand, Norway, Republic of South Africa, Sweden, and Switzerland.[30]

§ 2.14 U.S. GSP—Product Eligibility

For each designated GSP beneficiary country, the President also issues a list of products from that country eligible for duty free entry into the United States. The statutory authorization for the United States GSP program generally excludes leather products, textiles and apparel,[31] watches,[32] selected electronics and, certain steel, footwear and categories of glass from being designated as eligible articles.[33] All these goods are thought to involve particular "import sensitivity."

The UNCTAD Certificate of Origin Form A is ordinarily required of the foreign exporter when GSP eligible merchandise is

---

[29]   19 U.S.C.A. § 2462(a).

[30]   19 U.S.C.A. § 2462(b).

[31]   *See Luggage and Leather Goods Mfrs. of America, Inc. v. United States*, 588 F.Supp. 1413 (C.I.T.1984) (man-made fiber flat goods are textile and apparel articles).

[32]   *See North American Foreign Trading Corp. v. United States*, 600 F.Supp. 226 (C.I.T.1984), *affirmed* 783 F.2d 1031 (Fed.Cir.1986) (exemption for watches includes solid-state digital watches).

[33]   19 U.S.C.A. § 2463(c).

involved. Complex "rules of origin" determine where goods are from for purposes of the United States GSP program. Basically, for goods to originate in a beneficiary country, at least 35 percent of the appraised value of those goods must be added in that nation.[34] The statutory rules of origin for GSP eligible goods are found in 19 U.S.C.A. § 2463(b).[35]

A federal Circuit Court of Appeals has ruled that a "two-stage" substantial transformation process must also occur in order to qualify goods for GSP purposes.[36] Thus, the value of U.S.-grown corn did not count towards meeting the 35 percent requirement because the intermediate products into which it was turned did not qualify as Mexican in origin for lack of substantial transformation into a new and different article of commerce.[37] But the assembly of integrated circuits in Taiwan from slices containing many integrated circuit chips, gold wire, lead frame strips, molding compound and epoxy (all of which were U.S. in origin) did constitute a substantial transformation of such items into a new article of commerce. Thus

---

[34]   See *Madison Galleries, Ltd. v. United States*, 870 F.2d 627 (Fed.Cir.1989).

[35]   19 U.S.C.A. § 2463(b). Eligible articles qualifying for duty-free treatment:

(b)(1) The duty-free treatment provided under section 501 shall apply to any eligible article which is the growth, product, or manufacture of a beneficiary developing country if—

(A) that article is imported directly from a beneficiary developing country into the customs territory of the United States; and

(B) the sum of (i) the cost or value of the materials produced in the beneficiary developing country or any 2 or more countries which are members of the same association of countries which is treated as one country under section 502(a)(3), plus (ii) the direct costs of processing operations performed in such beneficiary developing country or such member countries is not less than 35 percent of the appraised value of such article at the time of its entry into the customs territory of the United States.

(2) The Secretary of the Treasury, after consulting with the United States Trade Representative, shall prescribe such regulations as may be necessary to carry out this subsection, including, but not limited to, regulations providing that, in order to be eligible for duty-free treatment under this title, an article must be wholly the growth, product, or manufacture of a beneficiary developing country, or must be a new or different article of commerce which has been grown, produced, or manufactured in the beneficiary developing country; but no article or material of a beneficiary developing country shall be eligible for such treatment by virtue of having merely undergone—

(A) simple combining or packaging operations, or

(B) mere dilution with water or mere dilution with another substance that does not materially alter the characteristics of the article.

[36]   See *Torrington Company v. United States*, 764 F.2d 1563 (Fed.Cir.1985). *See generally* Cutler, United States Generalized System of Preferences: the Problem of Substantial Transformation, 5 North Carolina Journal of International Law & Commercial Regulation, 393 (1980).

[37]   *Azteca Mill. Co. v. United States*, 890 F.2d 1150 (Fed.Cir.1989).

the circuits could be deemed from Taiwan for purposes of the 35 percent value added GSP rule.[38]

One unusual feature of the rules of origin for the United States GSP program is that which favors selected regional economic groups. Goods made in the ANDEAN pact, ASEAN or CARICOM may be designated as "one country" for purposes of origin. So too may goods produced in the East African Community, the West African Economic and Monetary Union and the Southern African Development Community. This means that the value added requirement as applied in these regions is met if 35 percent of the value added has been created inside each group as opposed to inside any one nation of the group. It is notable that many other third world regional economic groups are not similarly treated, e.g. MERCOSUR, and the Gulf Council of the Middle East.

§ 2.15   U.S. GSP—Graduation

As nations develop, U.S. law either bars their participation in the GSP program absolutely or vests discretion in the President to remove nations or products from its scope. Developing nations with a per capita gross national product in excess of $8,500 are totally ineligible for GSP duty free entry. The Bahamas, Bahrain, Brunei, Israel, Nauru and Bermuda have been disqualified under this rule. In addition, the President has a broad authority to "graduate" countries from the United States GSP program. The basic concept here is that certain nations are sufficiently developed so as to not need the benefits of duty free entry into the United States market. Discretionary graduation is based on an assessment of the economic development level of the beneficiary country, the competitive position of the imports and the overall national economic interests of the United States.[39]

In recent years, Presidents have been graduating more and more products from countries like India and Brazil. In January of 1989, President Reagan graduated all products from Hong Kong, Singapore, South Korea and Taiwan. At that time, these countries were the source of about 60 percent of all goods benefiting from the United States GSP program. Mexico then emerged as the chief beneficiary country under the program until late in 1993 when all of its products were removed from the GSP treatment in anticipation of the North American Free Trade Agreement. In 1997, President

---

[38]   *Texas Instruments Inc. v. United States*, 681 F.2d 778 (C.C.P.A.1982). *See Madison Galleries, Ltd. v. United States*, 688 F.Supp. 1544 (C.I.T.1988) (blank porcelain from Taiwan substantially transformed when painted and fired in Hong Kong).

[39]   *See* 47 Fed.Reg. 31,099, 31,000 (July 16, 1982).

Clinton graduated Malaysia entirely from the GSP program. President Obama graduated Russia in 2014. U.S. free trade partners, such as Jordan, Morocco and Peru, have also been eliminated as beneficiary countries. *See* Section 2.4.

§ 2.16 U.S. GSP—Judicial and Administrative Remedies

Legal challenges to presidential revocations of duty free GSP treatment were originally filed with the U.S. Customs Court. This was the case despite contentions of inadequate legal remedies in that court and the fact that plaintiff could not pursue class action relief except in federal district court.[40] Litigation involving the GSP program is now commenced in the U.S. Court of International Trade.

The goods entering the United States duty free through the GSP program remain subject to the possibility of escape clause relief under Section 201 of the Trade Act of 1974.[41] Moreover, such goods may also be restrained pursuant to Section 232 of the Trade Expansion Act of 1962 in the name of the national security of the United States.[42]

§ 2.17 U.S. Caribbean Basin Initiative (CBI)

The European Union has had for many years a policy which grants substantial duty free entry into its market for goods originating in Mediterranean Basin countries. The United States has duplicated this approach for the Caribbean Basin. This is accomplished through the Caribbean Basin Economic Recovery Act of 1983 (19 U.S.C. §§ 2701–2707). For these purposes, the Caribbean Basin is broadly defined to include nearly all of the islands in that Sea, and a significant number of Central and South American nations bordering the Caribbean. So defined, there are 28 nations which could qualify for purposes of the United States Caribbean Basin Initiative.

As with the GSP program, the Caribbean Basin Initiative (CBI) involves presidential determinations to confer beneficiary status upon any of these eligible countries. However, unlike the GSP, there are no presidential determinations as to which specific products of these countries shall be allowed into the United States on a duty free basis. All Caribbean products except those excluded by statute are eligible. Moreover, there is no "competitive need" or annual per capita income limits under the CBI. Lastly, unlike the GSP program which

---

[40] *Barclay Industries, Inc. v. Carter*, 494 F.Supp. 912 (D.D.C.1980).

[41] *See* 19 U.S.C.A. § 2251 and Chapter 15.

[42] *See* 19 U.S.C.A. § 2463(c)(2).

must be renewed periodically, the Caribbean Basin Initiative is a permanent part of the U.S. tariff system.

The United States has maintained a steady trade surplus with Caribbean Basin countries. Leading export items under the CBI are typically beef, raw cane sugar, medical instruments, cigars, fruits and rum. The leading source countries have often been the Dominican Republic, Costa Rica and Guatemala, now all U.S. free trade partners. The value of all CBI duty free imports now exceeds $1 billion annually, but CBI countries fear a diversion of trade and investment to Mexico and Central America as the North American Free Trade Agreement (NAFTA) and the Central American Free Trade Agreement (CAFTA) mature.

§ 2.18 CBI Country Eligibility

The President is forbidden from designating Caribbean Basin Initiative beneficiaries if they are communist, have engaged in expropriation activities, nullified contracts or intellectual property rights of the U.S. citizens, failed to recognize and enforce arbitral awards, given preferential treatment to products of another developed nation, broadcast through a government-owned entity United States copyrighted material without consent, failed to sign a treaty or other agreement regarding extradition of United States citizens, failed to cooperate on narcotics enforcement, or failed to afford internationally recognized workers' rights. For these purposes, the definition of workers' rights enacted in connection with the GSP program applies.[43] Since 2000, CBI countries must also show a commitment to implementing WTO pledges.

These prohibitions notwithstanding, the President can still designate a Caribbean Basin country as a beneficiary if he or she determines that this will be in the national economic or security interest of the United States. However, this can be done only in connection with countries that are disqualified as being communist, expropriators, contract or intellectual property nullifiers, non-enforcers of arbitral awards, unauthorized broadcasters, or those who fail to provide for internationally recognized workers' rights. Thus, if a Caribbean nation is disqualified because it grants preferential trade treatment to products of another developed nation or refuses to sign an extradition treaty with the United States, there is no possibility of its designation as a beneficiary nation under the Caribbean Basin Initiative. As with the GSP statutory requirements, if the basis for the disqualification is expropriation or nullification of benefits, the President may override this disqualification if that nation is engaged in payment of prompt, adequate and effective

---

[43] See § 10.9, supra.

compensation or good faith negotiations intended to lead to such compensation.

In addition, the President is required to take various factors into account in designating beneficiary countries under the Caribbean Basin Initiative. These include:

(1) The desire of that country to participate;

(2) The economic conditions and living standards of that nation;

(3) The extent to which the country has promised to provide equitable and reasonable access to its markets and basic commodity resources;

(4) The degree to which it follows accepted GATT rules on international trade;

(5) The degree to which it uses export subsidies or imposes export performance requirements or local content requirements which distort international trade;

(6) The degree to which its trade policies help revitalize the region;

(7) The degree to which it is undertaking self-help measures to promote its own economic development;

(8) Whether it has taken steps to provide internationally recognized workers' rights;

(9) The extent to which it provides adequate and effective means for foreigners to secure and enforce exclusive intellectual property rights;

(10) The extent to which the country prohibits unauthorized broadcasts of copyrighted material belonging to U.S. owners; and

(11) The extent to which the country is prepared to cooperate with the United States in connection with the Caribbean Basin Initiative, particularly by signing a tax information exchange agreement.

Under these criteria, the President has designated a large number of the 28 eligible nations as beneficiary countries under the Caribbean Basin Initiative. These include Antigua and Barbuda, Aruba, the Bahamas, Barbados, Belize, the British Virgin Islands, Costa Rica, Dominica, the Dominican Republic, El Salvador, Grenada, Guatemala, Guinea, Haiti, Honduras, Jamaica, Monserrat, the Netherlands Antilles, Nicaragua, Panama, St. Christopher-Nevis, St. Lucia, St. Vincent and the Grenadines, and Trinidad and

Tobago. Cuba is not even listed among the nations eligible for consideration in connection with the Caribbean Basin Initiative. Some of these countries are now U.S. free trade partners and therefore no longer CBI eligible. *See* Section 2.4.

U.S. Presidents have typically required of each potential beneficiary a concise written presentation of its policies and practices directly related to the issues raised by the country designation criteria listed in the Caribbean Basin Economic Recovery Act. Wherever measures were in effect which were inconsistent with the objectives of these criteria, U.S. presidents have sought assurances that such measures would be progressively eliminated or modified. For example, the Dominican Republic promised to take steps to reduce the degree of book piracy and the Jamaican and Bahamian governments promised to stop the unauthorized broadcast of U.S. films and television programs.[44]

§ 2.19 CBI Product Eligibility

Unless specifically excluded, all products of Caribbean Basin nations are eligible for duty free entry into the United States market. Certain goods are absolutely excluded from such treatment.[45] These include footwear, canned tuna, petroleum and petroleum derivatives, watches, and certain leather products. It should be noted that this listing of "import sensitive" products is different from but overlaps with that used in connection with the United States GSP program. Since 2000, products ineligible for CBI benefits enter at reduced tariff levels corresponding to Mexican goods under NAFTA. . . so-called "NAFTA parity".

One of the most critical of the products that may enter the United States on a duty free basis is sugar. But the President is given the authority to suspend duty free treatment for both sugar and beef products originating in the Caribbean Basin or to impose quotas in order to protect United States domestic price support programs for these products.[46] Sugar exports have traditionally been critical to many Caribbean Basin economies. Nevertheless, sugar import quotas into the United States from the Caribbean have been steadily reduced in recent years. For example, by 1988 the sugar quota allocations for some CBI countries reached a low of 25 percent of their 1983 pre-Caribbean Basin Initiative allocations.[47] Many consider the

---

[44]   19 U.S.C.A. § 2702.
[45]   *See* 19 U.S.C.A. § 2703(b).
[46]   19 U.S.C.A. § 2073(c) and (d).
[47]   *See* Fox, Interaction of the Caribbean Basin Initiative and U.S. Domestic Sugar Price Support: A Political Contradiction, 8 Mississippi College Law Review 197 (1988).

few duty free import benefits obtained under the Initiative to be more than counterbalanced by the loss in sugar exports to the United States market.

The rules of origin for determining product eligibility in connection with the Caribbean Basin Initiative are virtually the same as discussed previously under the GSP.[48] As a general rule, a substantial transformation must occur and a 35 percent value added requirement is imposed (but 15 percent may come from the United States). This percentage is calculated by adding the sum of the cost or value of the materials produced in the beneficiary country or two or more beneficiary countries plus the direct cost of processing operations performed in those countries.[49] It should be noted that this approach effectively treats all of the CBI-eligible nations as a regional beneficiary since the 35 percent required value can be cumulated among them.

As under the GSP program, the President is given broad powers to suspend duty free treatment with reference to any eligible product or any designated beneficiary country.[50] Import injury relief under Section 201 of the Trade Act of 1974 can be invoked in connection with Caribbean Basin imports. And the equivalent of that relief is authorized specifically for agricultural imports upon similar determinations by the Secretary of Agriculture.[51] The effects of these protective proceedings may be diminished in the context of Caribbean Basin imports.

Whenever the International Trade Commission is studying whether increased imports are a substantial cause of serious injury to a domestic industry under Section 201 or its agricultural equivalent, the ITC is required to break out the Caribbean Basin beneficiary countries. The President is given the discretion if he or she decides to impose escape clause relief to suspend that relief relative to Caribbean Basin imports. A similar discretion is granted to the President in connection with national security import restraints under Section 232 of the Trade Expansion Act of 1962. However, these discretionary provisions relate only to those goods that are eligible for duty free entry under the Caribbean Basin Initiative.[52]

In 1986, President Reagan initiated a special program for textiles produced in the Caribbean. Essentially, this program

---

[48]   *See* HTS General Note 3(c)(v).

[49]   19 U.S.C.A. § 2703(a).

[50]   19 U.S.C.A. § 2702(e).

[51]   19 U.S.C.A. § 2703(f).

[52]   *See* 29 U.S.C.A. § 2703(e).

increases the opportunity to sell Caribbean textile products when the fabric involved has been previously formed and cut in the United States. If this is the case, there are minimum guaranteed access levels. This program is run in conjunction with Section 9802.00.80 of the Harmonized Tariff Schedule of the United States.[53] *See* Section 2.21.

The U.S.-Caribbean Basin Trade Partnership Act of 2000 grants duty-free and quota-free access to the U.S. market for apparel made from U.S. fabric and yarn. Apparel made from CBI fabric is capped for duty free into the United States. CBI textiles and apparel are subject to market surge safeguards comparable to those under NAFTA. Late in 2006, duty free treatment of Haitian apparel products was expanded under the HOPE Act. In certain cases, Haiti may utilize third country fabrics and still ship apparel duty free into the United States.

§ 2.20 U.S. Andean Trade Preferences

The Andean Trade Preference Act (ATPA) of 1991[54] authorizes the President to grant duty free treatment to imports of eligible articles from Colombia, Peru, Bolivia and Ecuador. Venezuela is not included as a beneficiary country under this Act. The Andean Trade Preference Act is patterned after the Caribbean Basin Economic Recovery Act of 1983. Goods that ordinarily enter duty free into the United States from Caribbean Basin nations will also enter duty free from these four Andean countries. The same exceptions and exclusions discussed above in connection with the Caribbean Basin Initiative generally apply. However, while the CBI is a permanent part of United States Customs law, the ATPA was only authorized initially for a period of ten years. Furthermore, the guaranteed access levels for Caribbean Basin textile products, separate cumulation rules for antidumping and countervailing duty investigations, and the waiver of the Buy American Act for procurement purposes are not authorized by the ATPA.

The Andean Trade Preference Act was renewed by the TPA-TAA through February 2006 retroactive to its expiry Dec. 4, 2001. Periodic renewals have followed. Textile and apparel products, and most other products previously excluded, are now included under the ATPA. Country eligibility for enhanced benefits includes consideration of steps taken to comply with WTO obligations, the protection of worker rights and combating corruption. Broadly speaking, the passage of the ATPA represents fulfillment of the elder President Bush's commitment to assist these nations economically in return for their

---

[53]   *See* 51 Fed.Reg. 21,208 (June 11, 1986).

[54]   Public Law 102–82, 19 U.S.C.A. § 3201 et seq.

help in containing narcotics. Peru and Colombia are now U.S. free partners, a status that removes ATPA benefits. Free trade negotiations with Ecuador and Bolivia have not succeeded, leaving their Andean benefits uncertain. Ecuador has renounced ATPA benefits, and the Act expired July 31, 2013.

§ 2.21   U.S. African Trade Preferences

The Africa Growth and Opportunity Act of 2000[55] granted duty-free and quota-free access to the U.S. market for apparel made from U.S. fabric and yarn. Apparel made from African fabric is capped for duty free entry. The least developed sub-Saharan countries enjoy duty-free and quota-free apparel access regardless of the origin of the fabric. In 2008, the so-called "abundant supply" provision of AGOA was repealed, thus assuring least-developed country textile exports to the United States. U.S. imports of AGOA textiles using third country fabrics have also been liberalized.

The Act also altered U.S. GSP rules to admit certain previously excluded African products on a duty-free basis, including petroleum, watches and flat goods. Sub-Saharan countries can export almost all products duty-free to the United States. These countries are encouraged to create a free trade area with U.S. support. African exports are subject to import surge (escape clause) protection and stringent rules against transshipments between countries for purposes of taking advantage of U.S. trade benefits.

AGOA was renewed in 2015 subject to eligibility rules concerning market-based economies, poverty reduction, rule of law, and anti-corruption and human rights efforts, including internationally recognized workers' rights.

§ 2.22   Section 9802.00.80 of the USHTS

Section 9802.00.80 of the Harmonized Tariff Schedule of the United States (formerly Section 807.00 of the Tariff Schedule of the United States) is an unusual "duty free" provision.[56] This section

---

[55]   Public Law No. 106–200, 114 Stat. 252.

[56]   Harmonized Tariff Schedule of the United States (2013) (edited):

9802.00.80 Articles, except goods of heading 9802.00.90 and goods imported under provisions of subchapter XIX of this chapter and goods imported under provisions of subchapter XX, assembled abroad in whole or in part of fabricated components, the product of the United States, which (a) were exported in condition ready for assembly without further fabrication, (b) have not lost their physical identity in such articles by change in form, shape or otherwise, and (c) have not been advanced in value or improved in condition abroad except by being assembled and except by operations incidental to the assembly process such as cleaning, lubricating and painting. . .

A duty upon he full value of A duty upon value of the imported the full value of the imported article, the imported article, less the article, less the less the cost allows for the duty free importation of United States fabricated components that were exported ready for assembly abroad. If qualified, goods assembled abroad containing U.S. components are subject only to a duty upon the value added through foreign assembly operations regardless of where assembled.

In order for this to be the case, Section 9802.00.80 requires that the components be fabricated and a product of the United States, that they be exported in a condition ready for assembly without further fabrication, that they not lose their physical identity by change in form, shape or otherwise, and that they not be advanced in value or improved in condition abroad except by being assembled and except by operations incidental to the assembly process such as cleaning, lubricating and painting.

The regulations issued in connection with Section 9802.00.80 indicate that there are other incidental operations which will not disqualify components from duty free re-entry into the United States. These include removing rust, grease, paint or other preservative coatings, the application of similar preservative coatings, the trimming or other removal of small amounts of excess material, adjustments in the shape or form of a component required by the assembly that is being undertaken, the cutting to length of wire, thread, tape, foil or similar products, the separation by cutting of finished components (such as integrated circuits exported in strips), and the calibration, testing, marking, sorting, pressing and folding and assembly of the final product.[57]

In contrast, the regulations also provide examples of operations that are not considered incidental to assembly for these purposes. These examples include the melting of ingots to produce cast metal parts, the cutting of garments according to patterns, painting which is intended to enhance the appearance or impart distinctive features to the product, chemical treatment so as to realize new characteristics (such as moisture-proofing), and the machining, polishing or other treatment of metals which create significant new characteristics or qualities.[58]

If all of the Section 9802.00.80 criteria are met, the tariff that will be assessed upon the imported assembled product will be limited to a duty upon the full value of that product less the cost or value of U.S. made components that have been incorporated into it.[59] Those who seek to take advantage of Section 9802.00.80 must provide the

---

or cost or value of cost or value of such products value of such of the United such products of States.

[57]   19 C.F.R. § 10.16(b).

[58]   19 C.F.R. § 10.16(c).

[59]   *See generally* 19 C.F.R. § 10.14 et seq.

United States Customs Service with a Foreign Assembler's Declaration and Certification. This is known as Form 3317. The assembly plant operator certifies that the requirements of Section 9802.00.80 are met, and the importer declares that this certification is correct.

Billions of dollars of ordinarily tariffed value have been excluded as a result of this Customs law provision. Motor vehicles, semiconductors, office machines, textiles and apparel, and furniture are good examples of the kinds of products assembled abroad with fabricated U.S. components so as to meet the requirements of Section 9802.00.80. Historically, many of these products have been assembled in Japan, Germany or Canada. In more recent times, the assembly operations to which Section 9802.00.80 frequently applies have more commonly been found in the developing world.

§ 2.23 Maquiladoras

Section 9802.00.80 is applicable to goods imported into the United States from anywhere in the world. However, it is most frequently associated with maquiladoras. Maquiladoras are "in-bond" assembly plants that often take advantage of the duty free potential of Section 9802.00.80. Maquiladoras enjoyed a phenomenal popularity after 1982 when the Mexican peso was dramatically devalued. This had the practical effect of rendering Mexican labor costs lower than those of Taiwan, Hong Kong, Singapore and South Korea. These Asian nations were traditionally low-cost assembly plant centers. In 1995, Mexican labor costs were dramatically lowered when the peso crashed once again.

Since 1982, thousands of maquiladoras have been established in Tijuana, Ciudad Juarez, Nuevo Laredo and other border cities. They provide Mexico with hundreds of thousands of jobs and are a major source of foreign currency earnings. Electronics, apparel, toys, medical supplies, transport equipment, furniture and sporting goods are examples of the types of industries that have been attracted south of the border. United States components, when assembled in maquiladoras and qualifying under Section 9802.00.80, are exported and then reimported on a duty free basis. Maquiladoras have been developed throughout the Caribbean Basin and Central America. Much to the frustration of organized labor, such offshore assembly operations exemplify the internalization of the United States manufacturing sector.

The maquiladora industry enjoyed explosive growth before and in the early years of NAFTA. Mexican law, like Section 9802.00.80, supported this growth. Various decrees permit goods to enter Mexico on a duty free basis *under bond* for purposes of assembly in maquiladoras. Mexican law permits duty free importation of equipment, technology and components for six months. At the end of that period the goods must be exported from Mexico, typically back to the United States. Except with special permission, which has been increasingly granted by the authorities, maquiladora-assembled goods may not enter the Mexican market. Investors may own maquiladoras, typically using 30-year land trusts (fideicomiso) and Mexican subsidiaries. Alternatively, they may lease assembly plant space from a Mexican company and operate a maquiladora from that space. The simplest way to enter into maquiladora operations is to contract with a company to assemble the goods in question ("shelter operations").

Until late in 1993, there was also a link between the United States System of Generalized Preferences (GSP) and Mexican maquiladoras. Under the rules of origin that govern the GSP program, if at least 35 percent of the value of a maquiladora product was of Mexican origin, it could qualify entirely for duty free entry into the United States. The possibility of this result caused many users of maquiladoras to seek out Mexican suppliers in order to try to meet the 35 percent rule of origin. This incentive was enhanced by the fact that South Korea, Singapore, Taiwan and Hong Kong were all graduated from the United States GSP program in 1989. Mexico was the largest source of GSP qualified goods entering the United States market prior to December, 1993 when all of its products were removed from the GSP program as a result of NAFTA.

The net result of the United States and foreign laws like that of Mexico in this area is to create an interdependent legal framework mutually supportive of maquiladora operations. Many have characterized this legal framework as a "co-production" or "production sharing" arrangement between the two countries. However, utilization of maquiladoras is not limited to U.S. firms or United States' components. Japanese and Korean companies have become major investors in maquiladora industries. To the extent that they utilize U.S. components, they may benefit from the duty free entry provisions of Section 9802.00.80.

In 1998, Mexico's Ministry of Commerce and Industry Development (SECOFI) published an amended Maquiladora Decree. The revised Decree streamlines regulation of maquiladoras in Mexico, notably reducing SECOFI's discretion to deny, suspend or cancel maquiladora programs. A translation of the Decree can be found at www.natlaw.com. Mexico was responding, in part, to increased assembly plant competition from Asia, especially China after its 2001 admission to the WTO. At this stage, some firms have moved their plants to Asia where lower labor costs often prevail.

Nevertheless, rising Chinese labor and shipping costs have actually caused some assembly plants to migrate back to Mexico.

The North American Free Trade Area incorporating Mexico, Canada and the United States creates an incentive to invest in Mexico. Nearly all Mexican-made goods are able to enter the United States market on a duty free basis. NAFTA phased out over seven years the duty free entry Section 9802.00.80 benefits applied to Mexican maquiladoras, but not as regards goods assembled with United States components elsewhere in the Americas.

There seems to be an evolutionary cycle in assembly plants-from cheap raw labor to more skill-oriented operations to capital-intensive manufacturing. One of the most interesting comparative questions is whether there is also an evolutionary process in the applicable laws of these countries. In other words, what legal regimes do developing nations have to adopt in order to first attract assembly operations and do they evolve from extremely accommodating to more demanding as the cycle reaches completion? Or, does the manufacturer's ability to go elsewhere to even cheaper labor markets (e.g., from Mexico to Guatemala to Haiti, or from Hong Kong to the People's Republic of China to Vietnam) constantly temper the legal regimes regulating assembly plants?

§ 2.24   Section 9802.00.80 Case Law

There is a surprisingly large body of case law interpreting Section 9802.00.80. Much of it was developed when this provision was formally known as Section 807 of the Tariff Schedule of the United States.

One issue is whether the United States components have been advanced in value or improved in condition abroad. If this is the case, duty free re-entry into the United States is prohibited. An early decision of the Court of Customs and Patent Appeals held that the export of U.S. fish hooks, which were assembled abroad into individually packaged assortments so as to meet the requirements of retail purchasers in the United States, were not advanced in value or improved in condition so as to be disqualified.[60] In another decision, U.S. revolvers were re-chambered in Canada such that they no longer fired with accuracy .38 caliber bullets as originally designed. This change in condition caused the revolvers to be disqualified under Section 9802.00.80.[61] United States tomatoes shipped to Canada in bulk and sorted, graded as to color and size, and repackaged in

---

[60]   *United States v. John V. Carr & Son, Inc.*, 496 F.2d 1225 (C.C.P.A.1974).

[61]   *A.D. Deringer, Inc. v. United States*, 386 F.Supp. 518, 73 Cust.Ct. 144 (1974).

smaller cartons were not changed, advanced in value or improved in condition so as to be disqualified from duty free re-entry.[62]

The buttonholing in Mexico of U.S. shirt components (cuffs and collar-bands) did not advance them in value nor improve their condition as a result of this incidental operation.[63] But polyester fabric exported from the United States to Canada where it was dyed and processed, and then exported back to the United States as finished fabric did advance in value and changing of the condition of the U.S. component so as to disqualify it from duty free entry.[64] Similarly, glass pieces produced in annealled form in the United States which were sent to Canada for heat treatment and returned for use as pieces of tempered glass were not capable of benefiting from duty free entry.[65] Terminal pins of U.S. origin were shipped to Mexico and incorporated into header assemblies and relays. This operation constituted an assembly which did not advance the value of the terminals nor improve their condition.[66]

Another requirement of Section 9802.00.80 is that the United States component be fabricated and ready for assembly without further fabrication. Circuit boards for computers made in the United States from foreign and U.S. parts qualify as fabricated components for these purposes.[67] In this case, the programmable read only memory (PROM) was programmed in the United States causing it to undergo a substantial transformation and become a United States product. Aluminum foil, tabs, tape, paper and Mylar made in the United States and shipped to Taiwan in role form where they were used together with other articles of U.S. origin to produce aluminum electrolytic capacitors were not eligible for duty free entry because they were not "fabricated components" upon departure from the United States to Taiwan.[68] The fact that gold wire made in the United States was not cut until used for transistors assembled in Taiwan did not make it a U.S. component that was not ready for assembly abroad without further fabrication. The cutting of the gold wire was an

---

[62]   *Border Brokerage Co., Inc. v. United States*, 314 F.Supp. 788, 65 Cust.Ct. 50 (1970).

[63]   *United States v. Oxford Industries, Inc.*, 668 F.2d 507 (C.C.P.A.1981). *See United States v. Mast Industries, Inc.*, 668 F.2d 501 (C.C.P.A.1981) (buttonholing and pocket slitting operations incidental to assembly process do not lead to duty free entry disqualification.)

[64]   *Dolliff & Co., Inc. v. United States*, 455 F.Supp. 618 (Cust.Ct.1978), *affirmed* 599 F.2d 1015 (C.C.P.A.1979).

[65]   *Guardian Industries Corp. v. United States*, 3 C.I.T. 9 (1982).

[66]   *Sigma Instruments, Inc. v. United States*, 565 F.Supp. 1036 (C.I.T.), *affirmed* 724 F.2d 930 (Fed.Cir.1983).

[67]   *Data General Corp. v. United States*, 4 C.I.T. 182 (1982).

[68]   *General Instrument Corp. v. United States*, 67 Cust.Ct. 127 (1971).

incident of the assembly process.[69] But the assembly in Ecuador of flattened cylinders and ends into tuna fish cans which were then packed with tuna and shipped back to the United States did not qualify under Section 9802.00.80.[70]

The failure to lock knitting loops to keep the knitting from unraveling in the United States meant that knitted glove shelves were not exported in a condition ready for assembly without further fabrication. The importer of those gloves was not entitled to duty free entry for the value of the shelves.[71] On the other hand, pantyhose tubes made in the United States were fully constructed and secured from un-raveling by stitches. A closing operation did not create a new toe portion and the goods were permitted the benefits of Section 9802.00.80.[72] Likewise the joinder of molten plastic to the upper portion of a shoe abroad did not prevent the shoe vamp from duty free entry upon return to the United States. This operation did not constitute further fabrication of the vamp.[73]

The scoring and breaking of silicon slices along designated "streets" was an incidental operation to the assembly of transistors and therefore the slices were entitled to duty free entry into the United States.[74] Magnet and lead wire made in the U.S. and exported to Taiwan where it was wound into coils and cable harness put into television deflection yolks were entitled to duty free entry.[75] The two-step assembly process in this case did not defeat the application of Section 9802.00.80. The burning of slots and holes in steel Z-beams in order to incorporate them into railroad cars was an operation incidental to the assembly process and therefore the beams were not dutiable.[76]

For Section 9802.00.80 to apply the components must be assembled abroad. It has been held that a needling operation causing fibers to be entwined with exported fabric in order to create papermaker's felts constituted an assembly abroad for these purposes.[77] Likewise the adhesion of Canadian chemicals to sheets of the United States polyester involved an assembly.[78]

---

[69]   *General Instrument Corp. v. United States*, 462 F.2d 1156 (C.C.P.A.1972).

[70]   *Van Camp Sea Food Co. v. United States*, 73 Cust.Ct. 35 (1974).

[71]   *Zwicker Knitting Mills v. United States*, 613 F.2d 295 (C.C.P.A.1980).

[72]   *L'Eggs Products, Inc. v. United States*, 704 F.Supp. 1127 (C.I.T.1989).

[73]   *Carter Footwear, Inc. v. United States*, 669 F.Supp. 439 (C.I.T.1987).

[74]   *United States v. Texas Instruments, Inc.*, 545 F.2d 739 (C.C.P.A.1976).

[75]   *General Instrument Corp. v. United States*, 499 F.2d 1318 (C.C.P.A.1974).

[76]   *Miles v. United States*, 567 F.2d 979 (C.C.P.A.1978).

[77]   *E. Dillingham, Inc. v. United States*, 470 F.2d 629 (C.C.P.A.1972).

[78]   *C.J. Tower & Sons of Buffalo, Inc. v. United States*, 304 F.Supp. 1187 (Cust.Ct.1969).

Another requirement of Section 9802.00.80 is that the components not lose their physical identity by change in form, shape or otherwise. Fabric components used to make papermaker's felts which were needled abroad and thus perforated with holes and changed in width did not lose their physical identity and therefore continued to qualify for duty free re-entry.[79] The absence of a loss of physical identity was apparently included as a requirement of Section 9802.00.80 in order to exclude U.S. components that are chemical products, food ingredients, liquids, gases, powders and the like. These products would presumably lose their physical identity when "assembled" abroad.[80]

§ 2.25 U.S. Antidumping, Countervailing and Other Special Tariffs

In addition to its GATT/WTO negotiated MFN tariffs, the United States and other WTO member states are authorized in appropriate circumstances to assess special tariffs. President Nixon closed the gold exchange window for the U.S. dollar and in the name of "national security" imposed a 10% tariff surcharge on imports in order to reach new currency exchange rate parities with other countries (especially Japan). Presidents Nixon and later George W. Bush imposed special tariffs on steel imports, an industry that always seems to be seeking protection from foreign competition.

Antidumping duties are authorized to counteract dumping practices (sales of goods abroad at prices below those in the country of export). *See* Chapter 4. Countervailing tariffs are authorized in response to selected foreign government subsidies that benefit their exports. *See* Chapter 5. Occasionally, as well, additional tariffs may be assessed under escape clause (safeguard) proceedings when imports surge. *See* Chapter 6.

---

[79]   *E. Dillingham, Inc. v. United States*, 470 F.2d 629 (C.C.P.A.1972).

[80]   *See United States v. Baylis Bros., Co.*, 451 F.2d 643 (C.C.P.A.1971).

Chapter 3

CUSTOMS CLASSIFICATION, VALUATION AND ORIGIN*

Table of Sections

---

* I am indebted to Prof. Andy Spanogle for his work on a prior version of this chapter.

3.24   Valuation—Value When Other Methods Are Not Effective.

PART A

CLEARING U.S. CUSTOMS

Suppose you wish to import goods into the United States. U.S. customs must be cleared. The following material summarizes the issues and actors most likely to be encountered.

Many disputes in the customs area arise over the classification of imported goods under the Column 1 customs schedule. The rate of duty depends upon such classification, and substantial amounts may depend upon the outcome. The classifications are enunciated in abstract terms, so that overlap is possible; and, where such overlap exists, the importer wants to choose the classification with the least duty. Other disputes concern the place of origin of the goods. The country of origin may determine whether the goods enter under Column 1 or Column 2 tariffs, or perhaps duty free.

§ 3.1   Entry Formalities

The formalities of entry of imported goods are usually handled by a customs broker, but as an attorney you need to understand them for the same reasons that you need to understand other parts of the transaction. Customs brokers are licensed and regulated by federal law as administered by the U.S. Customs Service. The consignee, or an agent such as a customs broker, will file an "entry" form with the United States Customs Service and also documents sufficient to enable the customs officer to determine whether to release goods or not. At the same time, or within ten days, the consignee or agent must file an "entry summary" form. This form will be used by the customs officers to determine duties, collect aggregate statistics, and determine conformity of merchandise with United States domestic health and safety legal requirements. Alternatively, the consignee or agent may file only the "entry summary" form and its required documents as a substitute for both "entry" and "entry summary" forms. Estimated customs duties are also to be deposited at the time of filing either entry documentation or entry summary documentation.

The customs entry procedure was significantly streamlined in 1978 to allow immediate release of the imported goods after filing of entry documentation only, without posting of a bond to cover customs duties, and with no requirement of deposit of estimated duties until the entry summary is filed subsequently (within ten days). The customs service sends importers consolidated periodic statements for all entries made during a billing period, rather than requiring settlement on an entry-by-entry basis. Further streamlining, including a national electronic customs automation program, was implemented by the Customs Modernization Act of 1993.[1]

§ 3.2   The U.S. Customs Service

The United States Customs Service, as part of the Department of the Treasury, administers the entry of goods into the Customs Territory of the United States, which includes the fifty states, the District of Columbia, and Puerto Rico.[2] This process allows Customs officials to detain and examine goods to determine compliance with all laws and regulations. Title 19 of the Code of Federal Regulations contains extensive regulations governing such entry.[3]

An importable item must "pass customs". Usually, the passage through customs and physical entry into a country occur simultaneously. When goods arrive at the United States border, the consignee (or an agent, such as a customs broker) files both "entry" and "entry summary" forms which are used to determine the classification, valuation, origin and conformity to product standards of the imported goods. At the same time, a deposit of the amount of estimated customs duties is made with customs officials. A procedure for immediate release of imported goods is available, as is the use of consolidated periodic statements for all entries made during a billing period.

Because the entry process requires the importer to classify and value goods, a Customs Service official must determine the correctness of the documentation presented by the importer. If the Customs official rejects the importer's documentation, the decision may be appealed to the District Director (Regional Commissioner if for the port of New York), and to the Commissioner of Customs.[4]

---

[1]   Public Law 103–182 (Title VI).

[2]   19 U.S.C.A. § 1500, granting Customs authority to appraise, classify and liquidate merchandise entering the United States.

[3]   Title 19 of the C.F.R. is divided into three chapters. Chapter I includes parts 1–199 entitles United States Customs Service, Department of the Treasury. Chapter II and Chapter III include parts 200 to the end and are entitled United States International Trade Commission, and International Trade Administration, Department of Commerce, respectively.

[4]   19 C.F.R. §§ 173–174. There is a process for omitting the review by the district director in certain instances, by application for "further review." *See* 19 C.F.R. § 174.23–174.27.

Customs' decisions may be reviewed by the judiciary.[5] Specifically, the United States Court of International Trade (CIT),[6] which has exclusive jurisdiction.[7] Appeals from the CIT may be made to the Court of Appeals for the Federal Circuit (CAFC).[8] From these specialized courts, appeals are ultimately made to the United States Supreme Court. In *United States v. Mead Corp.,* the U.S. Supreme Court held Customs Service classification rulings are **not** entitled to full administrative deference. Rather, such rulings are entitled to limited deference depending on their "thoroughness, logic and expertness, fit with prior interpretations, and any other sources of weight."[9]

§ 3.3   The Customs Cooperation Council (CCC)

International actors are also involved in the law of clearing U.S. customs, and play an important role.

The Customs Cooperation Council (CCC) is a Brussels-based organization formed under the Convention on the Commodity Description and Coding System (the Convention) as an administrative entity. Since 1970, the CCC has sought to develop an internationally accepted "Harmonized Commodity Coding and Description System." This system, called the Customs Cooperation Council Nomenclature (CCCN), gives nations a domestic law for classifying goods for all purposes, including the application of tariffs and gathering statistics. It was formerly known as the Brussels Tariff Nomenclature (BTN). The CCCN evolved into the Harmonized Tariff Schedule (HTS), which is the system in currently used by the United States.

The Customs Cooperation Council (CCC) is composed of four committees. These committees have worked closely with the HTS, however, only one remains active today, the Harmonized System Committee.

§ 3.4   Customs Documentation and Liability

The documentation required by the customs service is an entry form (Customs Form 3641), a commercial invoice, a packing list, and other evidence of the right to make entry—such as a bill of lading. In most transactions, the bill of lading requirement is satisfied by a

---

[5]   *See Dell Products v. U.S.,* 642 F.3d 1055 (Fed. Cir. 2011) (affirming an appeal from importer regarding Customs and Border Protection decision under Harmonized Tariff Schedule of the United States).

[6]   19 C.F.R. § 176.

[7]   The CIT is the successor to the Customs Court.

[8]   The CAFC is the successor to the Court of Customs and Patent Appeals.

[9]   533 U.S. 218, 121 S.Ct. 2164, 150 L.Ed.2d 292 (2001).

"carrier's certificate," a certified statement by the importing carrier that a designated person or firm is the owner or consignee for customs purposes. Other documents may be needed for a particular type of shipment—*e.g.*, export country documents for importation of certain textiles under bilateral textile agreements, meat products, steel shipments over $10,000, etc.

Careful attention must be paid to preparation and presentation of the necessary customs documents. Harsh civil penalties apply to false and material statements, acts and omissions.[10] Such penalties may be assessed for mis-descriptions of goods, under-valuations and false claims of tariff exemption whether intentionally or negligently caused.[11] Only clerical errors will be excused. Pre-penalty notice to the importer must be given by the Customs Service. After a reply period, the penalty may be assessed. The importer may appeal all such customs penalties to the Court of International Trade (CIT) for *de novo* review.

The Customs Service has stepped up its compliance audits which can now be undertaken with the assistance of the Internal Revenue Service. The importer's duty to show reasonable care is sanctionable by substantial civil penalties, as are record keeping and false statement requirements. These changes follow the Customs Modernization Act of 1993, Public Law No. 103–182.

The Customs Service normally examines at least one package per invoice and at least ten percent of the packages of merchandise. However, the Customs Service may examine either more or less than this. It has the authority to examine every package, if that is believed necessary. On the other hand, it may open only one package where the goods are uniform; and, at designated ports, the district director has discretion to release designated merchandise without any examination. The purpose of customs examinations is to determine, first, whether the goods are accurately invoiced as to description and quantity; then second, the dutiable status of the goods and the proper amount of customs duty owed. In addition, the examination is to determine whether the required "country of origin" markings appear, and whether the packages contain any prohibited articles.

The importer is liable for all import duties. It is liable even if the Customs Service releases the goods in error without payment, or if

---

[10]   *See* 19 U.S.C.A. § 1592. But foreign companies cannot be held negligently liable for aiding and abetting customs negligence of another party. They can be held liable for knowingly doing so. *See United States v. Hitachi America, Ltd.*, 172 F.3d 1319 (Fed.Cir.1999).

[11]   *See, e.g., United States v. Ven-Fuel*, Inc., 758 F.2d 741 (1st Cir.1985) (importer liability for negligently filed false statement); *United States v. Frowein*, 727 F.2d 227 (2d Cir.1984) (omissions' liability).

the importer pays its agent the customs broker, but the customs broker fails to pay the United States Customs Service. The liability for customs duty constitutes a "lien" on the goods, and the government's claim for unpaid duties takes priority over other creditors in bankruptcy. If goods are reimported, they are dutiable on each successive importation unless they are personal or household effects, tools of the trade or professional books, automobiles taken abroad for non-commercial use, goods sent abroad for repair (although dutiable for the value of the repair) and domestic animals sent abroad for pasturage for eight months.

A nonresident may enter imported goods, but it must post a bond provided by a resident corporate surety. A foreign corporation entering imported goods must have a resident agent. That agent may be a corporate officer, regular employee, or customs broker, as long as they have a proper power of attorney, are a resident of the United States, and are authorized to accept service of process on behalf of the importer.

Since the consignee did not ship or load the goods, the consignee cannot declare of his or her own knowledge that the goods conform to the bill of lading. Thus, the "consignee's declaration" merely requires a declaration that, to the best of its knowledge, the goods are what the invoice says they are. Where the named consignee is not the actual owner of the imported goods and wishes to be relieved of liability for increased and additional customs duties, an actual owner's declaration may be filed, stating that the consignee is not the actual owner and furnishing the name and address of the actual owner. If the entry is made by a customs broker or other agent, a customs power of attorney must be executed by the consignee or owner. An agent must file this power of attorney with the customs district office, but a customs broker need only keep it in its own files, available for inspection.

The requirements for "informal entries" and "mail entries" are somewhat less elaborate. The informal entry is available for shipments having a value of less than $250, including installments of less than $250 (if the other installments arrive at different times), and for shipments of personal and household effects and books for libraries. The informal entry requires no customs invoice, but a commercial invoice is needed for goods purchased for import or intended for resale in the United States. Mail entry is also available where the imported goods are sent by sealed letters or parcel post. In such entries, the duties on parcels with a value under $250 can be collected by the postal carrier, and there is no need to clear these mailed shipments personally. It should be noted, however, that mailed imports are still subject to customs inspection. Parcel post packages must have attached to them a customs declaration form provided by a foreign post office giving an accurate description and the value of the contents. Customs officers may open for examination mail which appears to contain matter other than correspondence, if they have "reasonable cause to suspect" the presence of either merchandise or contraband.[12]

There are, however, classes of transactions in which the importer need not pay any duty—or at least not pay duty at that time. These transactions involve goods which are entered into a bonded warehouse or a foreign trade zone. In these transactions, the duty is not due on the imported goods until they are withdrawn from the warehouse or foreign trade zone, and they may be so withdrawn only by the importer or actual owner. In warehouses and foreign trade zones, the goods may be cleaned, sorted, repacked, or even undergo manufacturing operations (car parts to finished automobile), including smelting or refining—or they may simply be stored, awaiting better market conditions or awaiting their turn to be admitted under an import quota program.

PART B

U.S. CUSTOMS CLASSIFICATION

Prospective rulings on U.S. customs classification issues may be obtained.[13] An importer may request a ruling from the Commissioner of Customs on the proper classification of goods whose importation is merely contemplated, and which have not arrived in the United States. Such a request, if properly presented, will be answered by a "ruling letter," which is binding on all Customs Service personnel; but only if the actual import transaction corresponds with the transaction described in the letter requesting the ruling.

The initial product and origin classification of the imported goods is made by the importer, consignee, or broker.[14] But this classification is subject to disapproval by the District Director. If an improper classification is found, the District Director notifies the importer of the proposed change of rate and amount of tariff duty.[15] The importer then normally has 20 days to pay the increase in the duty or seek further administrative review before the imported goods will be "liquidated" (sold) to cover the unmet charges.

---

[12] *United States v. Ramsey*, 431 U.S. 606, 97 S.Ct. 1972, 52 L.Ed.2d 617 (1977).

[13] 19 C.F.R. § 177.

[14] 19 C.F.R. § 141.90.

[15] 19 C.F.R. § 152.2.

If the importer seeks a review of the Customs classification, the importer bears the burden of proof that Customs is wrong.[16] The importer's protest will be reviewed first by the District Director, and then may be reviewed by the Regional Commissioner or the Commissioner of Customs, especially in cases of first impression.[17] If Customs denies the protest, the importer may seek judicial review in the Court of International Trade.[18] Customs Service classification decisions are entitled to limited judicial deference.[19]

The classification problem may be illustrated as follows: Are parts of a wooden picture frame, imported piece by piece in separate packages for later assembly within a country, to be assessed duties prescribed for wood picture frames or for strips of wood molding? Is "wood picture frame" even an appropriate nomenclature, or should what is commonly known to be a wood picture frame have a tariff nomenclature of "art object" or "forest product" or simply "personal belonging?"

For decades, most of the countries in the world, except the United States and Canada, classified imports according to the Brussels Tariff Nomenclature (BTN), which identifies items along a progression from raw materials to finished products. The United States had its own system of classification set out in the Tariff Schedule of the United States (TSUS). However, beginning in 1982, the United States initiated steps to convert the TSUS into a Harmonized Commodity, Description and Coding System (HS) of classification, in common with the classification system used by most other countries and developed by the Customs Cooperation Council in Brussels. The United States adopted the Harmonized System as the Harmonized Tariff Schedule (HTS) for classification of all imports by enactment of the Omnibus Trade and Competitiveness Act of 1988, with an effective date of Jan. 1, 1989. Many nations have adopted HS and use it for exports bound for the United States.

§ 3.5   Calculating U.S. Customs

To calculate import duties, you must first determine the classification, country of origin and the customs valuation of goods. In other words, what is it, where is it from, and what is its customs value? U.S. customs officials classify, value and identify the origin of imported merchandise. In some cases, the importer (and the

---

[16]   *Corning Glass Works v. United States*, 448 F.Supp. 262 (Cust.Ct.1977), reversed on other grounds 586 F.2d 822 (Cust. & Pat.App.1978).

[17]   19 C.F.R. §§ 173, 174.

[18]   19 C.F.R. § 175.

[19]   *United States v. Mead Corp.*, 533 U.S. 218, 121 S.Ct. 2164, 150 L.Ed.2d 292 (2001). *See* discussion at § 9:23.

exporter) may disagree with those conclusions reached by the official regarding the classification of the merchandise, its country of origin, and its valuation. This chapter concentrates on the customs process, those who play a role in the process, and some of the difficulties that may arise.

There are trillions of dollars of annual imports into the United States each year. To calculate import duties, you must first determine the classification, country of origin and the customs valuation of goods. In other words, what is it, where is it from, and what is its customs value? U.S. customs officials make these decisions routinely and in large volume. In some cases, the importer (and the exporter) may disagree with those decisions. This chapter concentrates on the customs process, those who play a role in the process, and some of the difficulties that may arise.

All foreign goods entering the United States must be identified in a process called classification. Classification takes two forms, determining the nature of the product, and the product's country of origin. The first classification looks to the nature of a product, such as whether an imported doll wig made from human hair should be classified as a wig of human hair, part of a doll, or as a toy.[20] Fortunately, there is a set of widely used Harmonized Tariff System (HTS) rules governing the classification of goods. The second looks at the country or countries where a product was made. For example, if the doll wig was made in Argentina from human hair from Cuba, is the doll wig a product of Argentina or Cuba? This form of classification by country will likely involve national rules of origin.

Knowing the nature of the product allows Customs to determine the proper tariff within the HTS system. But because tariffs differ from nation to nation, knowing the country of origin informs Customs which tariff "column" to use. For example, different U.S. tariffs apply to countries granted most favored nation (MFN) status, countries denied such status, or countries with preferential or duty free tariff levels such as Canada and Mexico under the North American Free Trade Agreement (NAFTA), Caribbean Basin beneficiaries under the Caribbean Basin Economic Recovery Act, or other such agreements noted in Chapter 2. Additionally, identification of the country of origin informs Customs of products that cannot be imported at all, such as by reason of the United States embargo of Cuba.

---

[20]   A hypothetical problem involving imported doll wigs and the process of classification and valuation was included in R. Folsom, M. Gordon & J. Spanogle, International Business Transactions: A Problem Oriented Coursebook 276 (2d ed. 1991). The hypothetical in the latest edition of this book involves classifying peanut butter-jelly swirl.

But even when the product and its source of origin have been identified, Customs must know the value of the product before the tariff can be determined. Assigning a value to an import is called valuation. Customs officials must be able to determine a value in order to calculate the appropriate import tariff, usually calculated as a percentage of the value. The task is easier if the product is entitled to duty free entry. In such case the valuation is not needed for purposes of collecting a tariff. But valuation remains useful for gathering information regarding the value of various classes of imports for statistical purposes.

§ 3.6   International Sources of Law on Classification of Goods and Valuation

The process of classification (of the item and the country of origin) and valuation requires us to turn to separate rules. Classification of products or materials requires use of the Harmonized Tariff Schedule, adopted by the enactment of the Omnibus Trade and Competitiveness Act of 1988. Classification of the country of origin tends to focus on theory developed in U.S. cases (see Sections 3.12 and 3.13), whereas the process of valuation utilizes provisions in the Tariff Act of 1930, which generally follow the GATT/WTO Customs Valuation Code. The statutory development of classification of products and valuation follows.

Classification of Goods

Although most nations used the internationally accepted Brussels Tariff Nomenclature (BTN), the United States refused to participate in the system. Instead, the United States used its own system of classification, found within the Tariff Schedule of the United States (TSUS). These two systems created very different classifications for United States exports destined to a nation using the BTN, and those classifications of products entering the United States from other nations. What might be very narrowly defined in one system, might be very broadly defined in another. It made achieving fairness in lower tariffs for certain products quite difficult. What was called a widget in the foreign nation, might be a gadget in the United States.

As a result of using a separate system, the United States became increasingly isolated, and it became apparent that the United States TSUS would have to give way to the BTN. In 1982, after much urging from other major trading partners, the United States began converting to the HTS, the effective successor to the BTN. The HTS is administered by the World Customs Organization (WCO) in Brussels. This conversion was completed by adoption of the HTS for all imports in the Omnibus Trade and Competitiveness Act of 1988, effective January 1, 1989.[21] Most United States exports enter other nations under the HTS, and now the same is true for products of those other nations entering the United States.

The HTS "nomenclature" has twenty sections, the majority of which group articles from similar branches of industry or commerce. For example, Section I covers live animals and animal products, Section II vegetable products, Section III animal or vegetable fats, Section IV prepared foodstuffs, and Section V mineral products. The twenty sections are subdivided into 99 chapters, which in total list approximately 5,000 article descriptions in the heading and sub-heading format. These provisions apply to all goods entering the customs territory of the United States. Most problems arise when it is possible to classify imported goods under more than one heading.

Valuation of Goods

For many years the United States used the American Selling Price (ASP) system to determine the value of an imported good. This system valued an imported good at the level of the usual wholesale price that the same product was offered for sale if manufactured and sold in the United States. Thus, the valuation had no relation to the cost of production in the foreign nation, which caused the system to be much criticized abroad.[22] Many other nations, especially in Europe, used a system based on the 1950 convention that established the Brussels Definition of Value. To many, the Brussels Definition was too general, and was not adopted by either the United States or Canada.

Harmonization of customs valuation became one of the most important topics at the 1979 GATT Tokyo Round, which produced the GATT Customs Valuation Code.[23] The United States abandoned the ASP when it adopted the GATT Customs Valuation Code in the Trade Agreements Act of 1979.[24] The GATT's approach to valuation differs significantly from the ASP because it values goods based on "positive" rather than "normative" economic principles. In other words, the Code values goods based on the transaction price (price paid or payable) and not what the value of the good should be. If the

---

[21]   Public Law 100–418, title I, §§ 1202–1217, Aug. 23, 1988, 102 Stat. 1107. The HTS is not published in the U.S. Code. The United States International Trade Commission maintains the current version.

[22]   Such criticism was quite expected since United States domestic producers could indirectly control the valuation applied to foreign competitors' imports.

[23]   Its importance is reflected by its adoption by the European Union, Canada and the United States, plus such major trading nations as Australia, Japan, Spain (prior to joining the EU) and Sweden, and even important developing nations such as Argentina, Brazil, and India.

[24]   19 U.S.C.A. § 1401a.

transaction price cannot be determined, several fallback methods in a descending order of applicability may be used.

Because the United States replaced the TSUS with the HTS for the classification of imports, and the ASP with the GATT Customs Valuation Code for valuation of imports, its classification and valuation systems obtained greater harmony with its major trading partners.

The Uruguay Round of negotiations ushered in the next stage of development of customs valuation. The World Trade Organization replaced the GATT, and incorporated customs valuation provisions rather than having them exist as a separate external code. The three principal amendments to the Customs Valuation Code are discussed below. The provisions, which allow pre-shipment inspection, are of considerable importance to customs procedures.[25] These provisions attempt to balance the interests of some nations in contracting with outside companies to determine whether imports were fairly valued in the invoice, with the interest of exporting nations to reduce or remove impediments to trade, not to increase them.

§ 3.7   Classification of Goods—Sample Provisions of the U.S. Harmonized Tariff System

In any classification dispute, two issues must be resolved: (1) under what category or categories is it proper to classify the goods; and, (2) if there are several permissible classifications, which one takes priority over the others? Although the HTS updates every five years to account for new products, obsolete products, and provide more thorough classifications, multiple classifications can still result.[26]

As to the first question, no provisions in the United States HTS (HTSUS) "General Rules of Interpretation" (GRI) purport to limit the categorization of a product to a single categorization. In other words, the General Rule of Interpretation 2 (GRI 2) is inclusive, not exclusory, and the GRI 3 assumes that multiple categorizations will occur. See Section 3.11.

To solve the issue of multiple classifications, the GRIs provide priorities among competing categories, and the GRI 3(c) provides a "last resort" provision for cases where all else fails. However, even

---

[25]   *See* Creskoff, Pre-Shipment Inspection Programs: The Myth of Inconsistency with GATT Customs Valuation Provisions, 35 Fed.Bar News & J. 83 (1988).

[26]   For example, since 2012, Chapter 3, covering "Fish and crustaceans, mollusks, and other aquatic invertebrates," has a new heading for aquatic invertebrates (i.e. sea urchin and jellyfish), which had previously been classified only under "Other" or "Not Elsewhere Included." *See* Harmonized Tariff Schedule of the U.S., Annotated for Statistical Reporting Purposes (USITC Publ. 4299).

within the GRI, interesting ambiguities exist. For example, even though an international treaty produced the HTS and attempts to avoid the now-repealed TSUS system, a U.S. court may consult prior U.S. cases under the TSUS to interpret GRI 3(a)'s preference for "the most specific description."[27]

In addition to the GRI, the U.S. has included "Additional U.S. Rules of Interpretation," and "General Notes" in the HTS. These allow any determined attorney to create additional interpretations, and have particular importance because it is unclear whether the General Notes prevail over the GRIs and the Additional U.S. Rules, or vice versa. The best example of these possible conflicts arises when one tries to determine the priority between competing classifications. Should one first attempt to use the provisions of GRI 3, including the "last resort" provision in GRI 3(c)? Or, should one first attempt to apply the General Notes, especially Note 3(f)? And, what is the role of the Additional U.S. Notes to the Chapter Headnotes?

Below is a small portion of the extensive classification schedule of the United States.[28] The illustration shows the schedule of tariffs in the various columns. New products that fall between the cracks of the HTS system are frequently invented. Does "Peanut Butter Jelly Swirl", saving many American parents lunch box labor, fall under classification 2007 (jams, fruit jellies) or 2008.11.05 (peanut butter)? What should be its HTS classification?

Peanuts are subject to duty free quota controls under U.S. tariff law. For additional information, research U.S. Additional Note 5 accompanying the Chapter 20 Notes in the HTSUS.

---

[27]   *See Mitsui Petrochemicals v. U.S.*, 21 C.I.T. 882, 887 (1997) (citing *United States v. Siemens America, Inc.*, 653 F.2d 471 (C.C.P.A. 1981) (applying the "relative specificity" test under the Tariff Schedules of the United States)).

[28]   *See* Harmonized Tariff Schedule of the U.S., Annotated for Statistical Reporting Purposes (USITC Publ. 4299).

HARMONIZED TARIFF SCHEDULE of the United States (2011)

Heading/ Subheading	Stat. Suf- fix	Article Description	Units of Quantity	Rates of Duty		
				1		2
				General*	Special*	**
2007		Jams, fruit jellies, marmalades, fruit or nut pureé and fruit or nut pastes, obtained by cooking, whether or not containing added sugar or other sweetening matter:				
2007.10.00	00	Homogenized preparations	kg......	12%	Free (A+, BH, CA, D, E, IL, J, JO, MX, P, PE, SG) 4.8% (MA) 4.8% (OM) 7.2% (AU) See 9911.96.71–9911.96.75 (CL)	35%
		* * *				
		Fruit jellies:				
2007.99.70	00	Currant and berry	kg......	1.4%	Free (A+, AU, BH, CA, CL, D, E, IL, J, JO, MA, MX, OM, P, PE, SG)	35%
2007.99.75	00	Other	kg.......	3.2%	Free (A, AU, BH, CA, CL, E, IL, J, JO, MA, MX, OM, P, PE, SG)	35%
2008		Fruit, nuts and other edible parts of plants, otherwise prepared or preserved, whether or not containing added sugar or other sweetening matter or spirit, not else- where specified or included:				
		Nuts, peanuts (ground-nuts) and oth- er seeds, whether or not mixed togeth- er.				
2008.11		Peanuts (ground-nuts):				
		Peanut butter and paste:				
2008.11.02	00	Described in general note 16 of the tariff schedule and entered pursuant to its provisions...........	kg......	Free		15¢/kg
2008.11.05	00	Described in additional U.S. note 5 to this chap- ter and entered pursuant to its provisions	kg......	Free		15¢/kg
2008.11.15	00	Other	kg......	131.8%	Free (JO, MX) 43.9% (CL) 79% (P) 105.4% (PE) See 9910.12.05, 9910.12.20 (SG) See 9912.12.05, 9912.12.20 (MA) See 9913.12.05, 9913.12.20 (AU) See 9914.12.05, 9914.12.20 (BH) See 9915.20.05–9915.20.20 (P+) See 9916.12.05, 9916.12.20 (OM)	155%

*   Column 1 **General** Tariffs are "normal" or "MFN" tariffs as negotiated in the GATT/WTO. See the prior problem in this chapter.

*   Column 1 **Special** Tariffs refer primarily to preferential or duty free trade agreements and programs of the United States.

**   Column 2 Tariffs date principally from the Smoot Hawley Tariff Act of 1930. At this point, they apply only to Cuba and North Korea.

§ 3.8 Classification of Goods—Headings in the USHTS

The heading in the excerpt above is used under the General Rules of Interpretation to determine classification of products. Customs must apply the rule of relative specificity in the classification process, which requires that goods be classified under the provision that most specifically describes it. Here, false eyelashes made of human hair, for human adult use, appear to fall under Chapter 67 because it is an article of human hair. However, it seems that this commodity may fit under more than one heading. This potential problem will be discussed in the next section.

§ 3.9 Classification of Goods—Notes in the USHTS

The notes at the beginning of chapters in the HTS provide a useful tool in classification. They are to be used in addition to the terms of the headings, under the General Rules of Interpretation. For example, Note 1 in Chapter 67 states footwear cannot be classified under Chapter 67, but is the subject of Chapter 64. These "chapter notes" should not be confused with the Explanatory Notes to the Harmonized System, or the General Notes to the HTS.

§ 3.10 Classification of Goods—Columns in the USHTS

After looking through the applicable chapter notes, the next step is to look at the columns. The United States HTS utilizes a combined number system, including the six digits used internationally, and adding further digits for more subdivisions and statistical use. As seen in the above excerpt the first column, titled "Heading/Subheading", has eight digits. The first six are the heart of the HTS, and must be adopted by all contracting nations. The first two (67 in the excerpt) repeat the chapter. The second two designate the heading (03 for Human hair, etc., 04 for Wigs, etc., in the excerpt). The next two are subheadings. The additional two numbers provide further sub-subheadings (.30 for Human hair and .60 for Other in the excerpt),[29] and the columns titled "Stat. Suf. & cd" help maintain records for statistical purposes.

The three-column section entitled "Rates of Duty" discloses the rate of duty for the particular article. The Column 1 rates apply to nations that receive most favored nation (MFN) status. MFN tariffs

---

[29] The use of an additional four digits is permitted by the Convention and other nations have adopted their own form of using these additional digits. Such use will lead to some lessening of the uniformity of the system.

are set by GATT/WTO negotiations and are now referred to officially as "normal" tariffs. The "General" column applies to most MFN nations. The "Special" column applies to nations that have tariff preferences, making these nations even more favored than the most favored. The tariffs may be commodities, which enter duty free or with less than the general MFN rate. The capital letters denote different special preferential tariff programs.

For example, A means nations qualifying under the Generalized System of Preferences (GSP),[30] B means commodities under the Automotive Products Trade Act, C means products under the Agreement on Trade in Civil Aircraft, CA means commodities under the Canada-United States Free Trade Agreement, E means commodities under the Caribbean Basin Economic Recovery Act,[31] IL means commodities under the United States-Israel Free Trade Area, and NA means commodities under the North American Free Trade Agreement.

Column 2 applies to all nations, which are not entitled to Column 1 rates of duty. These countries are listed in General Note 3(b). They include principally nations under communist or socialist rule. Essentially these counties are "least" favored nations, although that term perhaps ought to be saved for those nations, which are excluded from trading with the United States altogether.

While it might seem the HTS offers a fairly easy resolution to classification, it does so only when a commodity clearly fits into one chapter, one heading, and if present one sub-heading. Fortunately, that is often the case, but many commodities are not clearly allocated within the system, and multiple possibilities for their classification may exist. This is the subject of much of the remainder of this chapter.

§ 3.11 Classification of Goods—Applying the HTS General Rules of Interpretation

While the Customs Service classifies goods, the importer (also the foreign exporter) has an obvious interest in the classification, because when the goods are classified at a high rate of duty applicable, the transaction may not go forward. Thus, the United States importer may consider the classification themselves. If the importer's conclusion is not the same as the Customs Service (meaning undoubtedly that the latter will be a classification at a higher rate of duty), the importer may (1) decide not to import the

---

[30] An A* appears if a country is specifically ineligible.

[31] The symbol E* appears if a country is ineligible.

goods, (2) pay the higher duty, or (3) challenge the Customs' determination.

The process of determination, whether conducted by Customs or the importer, must use the rules of interpretation of the United States (e.g. the General Rules of Interpretation and the Additional U.S. Rules of Interpretation).[32] A walk through those rules illustrates how difficult the classification process can be.

---

[32]   Harmonized Tariff Schedule of the United States (2010)

GENERAL RULES OF INTERPRETATION:

Classification of goods in the tariff schedule shall be governed by the following principles:

1.   The table of contents, alphabetical index, and titles of sections, chapters and sub-chapters are provided for ease of reference only; for legal purposes, classification shall be determined according to the terms of the headings and any relative section or chapter notes and, provided such headings or notes do not otherwise require, according to the following provisions:

2. (a)   Any reference in a heading to an article shall be taken to include a reference to that article incomplete or unfinished, provided that, as entered, the incomplete or unfinished article has the essential character of the complete or finished article. It shall also include a reference to that article complete or finished (or falling to be classified as complete or finished by virtue of this rule), entered unassembled or disassembled.

    (b)   Any reference in a heading to a material or substance shall be taken to include a reference to mixtures or combinations of that material or substance with other materials or substances. Any reference to goods of a given material or substance shall be taken to include a reference to goods consisting wholly or partly of such material or substance. The classification of goods consisting of more than one material or substance shall be according to the principles of rule 3.

3.   When, by application of rule 2(b) or for any other reason, goods are, *prima facie*, classifiable under two or more headings, classification shall be effected as follows:

    (a)   The heading which provides the most specific description shall be preferred to headings providing a more general description. However, when two or more headings each refer to part only of the materials or substances contained in mixed or composite goods or to part only of the items in a set put up for retail sale, those headings are to be regarded as equally specific in relation to those goods, even if one of them gives a more complete or precise description of the goods.

    (b)   Mixtures, composite goods consisting of different materials or made up of different components, and goods put up in sets for retail sale, which cannot be classified by reference to 3(a), shall be classified as if they consisted of the material or component which gives them their essential character, insofar as this criterion is applicable.

    (c)   When goods cannot be classified by reference to 3(a) or 3(b), they shall be classified under the heading which occurs last in numerical order among those which equally merit consideration.

4.   Goods which cannot be classified in accordance with the above rules shall be classified under the heading appropriate to the goods to which they are most akin.

5.   In addition to the foregoing provisions, the following rules shall apply in respect of the goods referred to therein:

    (a)   Camera cases, musical instrument cases, gun cases, drawing instrument cases, necklace cases and similar containers, specially shaped or fitted to contain

Headings and Relevant Section or Chapter Notes (Rule 1)

The legal classification of a good is determined according to (1) the terms of the *headings*; (2) any relative *section*; and (3) *chapter notes*.[33] This means the section, chapter and sub-headings are subordinated to the headings in importance. If the headings and notes do not otherwise require, one turns to the additional provisions of the General Rules,[34] and also to the Additional U.S. Rules of Interpretation.[35] The General Rules specifically note that the "table of contents, alphabetical index, and titles of sections, chapters and sub-chapters" are only for reference, not legal classification.[36]

Heading References to Articles (Rule 2(a))

When any reference in a heading is to an *article,* as opposed to a material or substance, the reference is to be understood to include that article in an incomplete or unfinished state as long as it "has the essential character" of the complete or finished article.[37] The reference also includes that article unassembled or disassembled.[38] This emphasis on the *material* as well as on the *function* of the good replaces emphasis on how the goods were used under the TSUS.

Heading References to a Material or Substance (Rule 2(b))

If the reference heading describes a *material* or *substance,* as opposed to an article, it should be understood to refer to mixtures or combinations of that material or substance with other materials or

---

a specific article or set of articles, suitable for long-term use and entered with the articles for which they are intended, shall be classified with such articles when of a kind normally sold therewith. This rule does not, however, apply to containers which give the whole its essential character;

(b)   Subject to the provisions of rule 5(a) above, packing materials and packing containers entered with the goods therein shall be classified with the goods if they are of a kind normally used for packing such goods. However, this provision is not binding when such packing materials or packing containers are clearly suitable for repetitive use.

6.   For legal purposes, the classification of goods in the subheadings of a heading shall be determined according to the terms of those subheadings and any related subheading notes and, *mutatis mutandis*, to the above rules, on the understanding that only subheadings at the same level are comparable. For the purposes of this rule, the relative section, chapter and subchapter notes also apply, unless the context otherwise requires.

[33]   General Rules of Interpretation 1.

[34]   *Id.*

[35]   The Additional U.S. Rules of Interpretation are found immediately following the General Rules in the HTS, as adopted in the United States. These additional rules often include methods of interpretation used under the prior classification system in the United States. *See* Section 3.9.

[36]   General Rules of Interpretation 1.

[37]   General Rules 2(a).

[38]   *Id.* Rule 2 generally follows the previous position under the TSUS.

substances.[39] Also, any reference to goods of a given material or substance should include a reference to goods consisting wholly or partly of such material or substance. The obvious problem with this is that when the goods are only partly of a material or substance, the other party may have its own classification. This can also occur when there are mixtures or combinations. The Rules acknowledge this and require one to move on to Rule 3.

Classification under Two or More Headings—Most Specific Description (Rule 3(a))

When goods may be classified under two or more headings,[40] the most specific description is preferred over the *more general description*.[41] This rule parallels the long used "rule of relative specificity," and decisions under that rule may continue to be of some use.[42] However, if each possible heading refers only to a *part* of the material or substances in mixed or composite goods, or of the items in a set for retail sale,[43] the headings must be considered equally specific. This is so even if one heading provides a more complete or precise description of the goods.[44] If this occurs, one must move to Rule 3(b).

Classification under Two or More Headings—Essential Character (Rule 3(b))

If an item cannot be classified under the most specific description test in Rule 3(a), then it must be classified with regard the material or component that gives the items their *essential character*.[45] While no similar provision existed in the TSUS[46] and the HTS does not strictly define "essential character," it has some parallel under the TSUS definition of the term "almost wholly of." Even some United States cases hold "almost wholly of" may be used while defining "essential character." However, the determination is fact-intensive[47] and should still be made on a case-by-case basis.

---

[39]   General Rules 2(b).

[40]   This applies to Rule 2(b) discussed above and to any other situation where two or more headings seem possibly applicable.

[41]   General Rules 3(a).

[42]   That includes the doctrine that an *eo nomine* description prevails over headings having only general or functional descriptions.

[43]   In April 2011, the Federal Circuit held that "goods put up in sets for retail sale" include goods that are packaged together in a certain manner at the time they enter the United States, and does not include secondary materials that the customer must purchase separately. *Dell Prod. LP v. U.S.*, 642 F.3d 1055, 1060 (Fed. Cir. 2011).

[44]   General Rules 3(a).

[45]   General Rules 3(b).

[46]   A "chief value" determination applied, no less capable of exact determination.

[47]   *CamelBak Prod. LLC v. United States*, 649 F.3d 1361, 1369 (Fed. Cir. 2011).

Classification under Two or More Headings—Last in Numerical Order (Rule 3(c))

If classification is not possible using either the most specific description or essential character tests, the rules move from a substantive classification method to one based simply on location. More specifically, the proper classification is the one heading, which occurs last in numerical order among those which might be applicable.[48]

Goods Unclassifiable Under Rules 1–3—"Most Akin" (Rule 4)

When no headings appear directly applicable, the goods should be classified under the heading the goods are most akin. While this test has been used very infrequently, it is essentially a "do the best the headings allow" test, and may result in two or more headings being equally "most akin." In such case one should try to find which is "more" akin. However, if uncertainty still results, move on to Rule 5.

Specially Shaped or Fitted Cases for Goods—Classed with Their Contents (Rule 5(a))

Containers, such as camera cases, musical instrument cases, gun cases, drawing instrument cases, and necklace cases, which are "specially shaped or fitted" are classified with the goods they serve, if they enter with those goods and are suitable for long term.[49]

However, the rule does not apply if the containers give the whole its essential character. For example, expensive carved tea caddies containing tea would not be classified as tea, because the container is not shaped to fit the tea (as is a musical instrument case) and the container gives the whole (tea plus caddy) the essential character.

Packing Materials and Containers—Classed with Their Contents (Rule 5(b))

Subject to the provisions of Rule 5(a), packing materials and containers that enter with goods are classified as the goods if they are the normal kind used in packaging or containers.[50] However, this is not true when the materials or containers are suitable for repetitive use.

Rules 5(a) and (b) are specific and apply only in limited situations. In fact, in most cases when a clear classification cannot be determined after using Rule 4, it will be necessary to go on to the final General Rule 6 for additional guidance.

---

[48]   General Rules 3(c).

[49]   General Rules 5(a).

[50]   General Rule 5(b).

Subheadings and Subheading Notes (Rule 6)

The subheadings, found in the first "Heading/Subheading" column of each chapter in the tariff schedules define goods more specifically than the heading. When subheadings or subheading notes are used, and two or more subheadings on the same level seem applicable, the process follows the outline in the rules discussed above.[51]

§ 3.12   Classification of Goods—Additional U.S. Rules of Interpretation

The six General Rules of Interpretation make up the classification system provided by the HTS. However, when the United States adopted this system, it added its own rules, called the "Additional U.S. Rules of Interpretation."[52] In addition to applying the General Rules, these rules must also be examined to determine whether a use is (1) consistent with the General Rules; (2) helpful where the General Rules do not lead to a satisfactory conclusion; or (3) in conflict with the conclusion reached under the General Rules.

Classification Controlled by Use Other than Actual Use (U.S. Rule 1(a))

If a classification is controlled by use other than actual use, and there is no special language or context mandating otherwise, it must be the use in the United States. . . . more specifically, the use in the United States at, or immediately prior to, the time of importation. Furthermore, the controlling use must be the *principal* use (which exceeds any other single use).[53] This requirement steps away from the Rule's past reference to chief use (which exceeds all other uses).

---

[51]   General Rules 6.

[52]   **ADDITIONAL U.S. RULES OF INTERPRETATION**

1.   In the absence of special language or context which otherwise requires—

(a)   a tariff classification controlled by use (other than actual use) is to be determined in accordance with the use in the United States at, or immediately prior to, the date of importation, of goods of that class or kind to which the imported goods belong, and the controlling use is the principal use;

(b)   a tariff classification controlled by the actual use to which the imported goods are put in the United States is satisfied only if such use is intended at the time of importation, the goods are so used and proof thereof is furnished within 3 years after the date the goods are entered;

(c)   a provision for parts of an article covers products solely or principally used as a part of such articles but a provision for "parts" or "parts and accessories" shall not prevail over a specific provision for such part or accessory; and

(d)   the principles of section XI regarding mixtures of two or more textile materials shall apply to the classification of goods in any provision in which a textile material is named.

[53]   U.S. Rules 1(a).

Classification Controlled by Actual Use (U.S. Rule 1(b))

This rule is similar to that above. However, to satisfy this provision, the imported goods must, (1) be the use intended at the time of importation, (2) the goods are so used, and (3) proof thereof is furnished within three years after the date the goods are entered.[54]

Parts and Accessories—General v. Specific (U.S. Rule 1(c))

Where a provision specifically describes a part or accessory, it must be used over a general "parts and accessories" provision.[55] Thus, the import of bicycle chains would be classified as bicycle chains if described specifically, and not under a "catch-all" "other parts and accessories" category. This rule provides consistency with the General Rules' preference for specificity, even though the General Rules do not specifically contain a rule for parts.[56]

Textile Materials (U.S. Rule 1(d))

The principles of section XI, which govern mixtures of two or more *textile* materials, apply to any goods in any provision where textile materials are named.[57] Textiles have their own mystique, and are subject to special trading rules throughout the world. These provisions assure the special rules of classification for textile materials are applied throughout the tariff schedules wherever textile material is mentioned.

Conflicts between General Rules and Additional U.S. Rules

When a conflict arises between the application of the General Rules and the Additional U.S. Rules, no guidance exists within the rules to handle that situation. However, it seems likely that the Additional U.S. Rules would supplant as well as supplement the General Rules. But, the likelihood for such conflict is slim because the Additional U.S. Rules were not intended to set forth views where the United States differs with the HTS. Instead, the Rules provide a necessary supplement.

Fair and accurate application of the above rules is not an easy task, and certainly does not mean that all reasonable minds (including those found in the Customs Service) will reach the same conclusion. However, another important source should be considered while classifying products, the "United States Customs Service, Guidance for Interpretation of Harmonized System."

---

[54]   U.S. Rules 1(b).
[55]   U.S. Rules 1(c).
[56]   However, individual chapter and section notes sometimes include parts rules.
[57]   U.S. Rules 1(d).

§ 3.13 Classification of Goods—United States Customs Service, Guidance for Interpretation of Harmonized System

When the HTS was adopted in 1989, some questions existed as to how Customs would classify some of the materials developed over the years. Of specific concern was the use of the Explanatory Notes to the Harmonized System, and reports of the Nomenclature Committee, which administered the Customs Cooperation Council (CCC) Nomenclature. Additionally, how letters from the Secretariat of the CCC would be used was unclear, and rulings and regulations from the customs administrations of other nations. The United States Customs Service soon issued the *Guidance for Interpretation of Harmonized System*.[58] The guide makes several points quite clear.

The United States Customs Service does not seek uniformity of interpretation with other nations. While the Harmonized System Committee (HSC) under Article 7 of the Convention functions to provide uniformity, the United States Customs Service does not. To illustrate, the United States does not to alter "sections, chapters, headings or subheadings" of the HTS, and will consider background documents to avoid such alterations. However, the Customs Service will not purposely make its interpretations of the HTS consistent with the interpretations of other HTS member nations. If serious inconsistencies in interpretation result, the HTS will likely be modified to minimize the inconsistency, such as by further refining the classification.

Use of Explanatory Notes to the Harmonized System. These notes are the official interpretation of the Harmonized System created by the Customs Cooperation Council. According to the Custom Service, Customs should use the notes as a useful tool, providing guidance, but should not treat them as dispositive.[59] Further, because the Explanatory Notes are amended from time to time and reflect changes in interpretation, they should be consulted periodically as changes are adopted. The only other documents given this status by Congress are the "similar publications of the Council," which essentially refers to the Compendium of Classification Opinions (below) because it is the only similar publication.

Use of the Compendium of Classification Opinions. The Harmonized System Committee (HSC) writes these opinions on the classification of different products. They are the result of requests presented to the HSC, and have the same weight as Explanatory

---

[58]   54 Fed.Reg. 35127 (1989).
[59]   *See* Conf.Rep. No. 100–576, 100th Cong., 2d Sess. 549 (1988).

Notes. Additionally, the Opinions are the official interpretation of the HSC on the particular issue decided.

Harmonized System Committee Reports. In addition to opinions, the HSC periodically issues reports on various subjects. While they do not have the same weight as the Explanatory Notes or Compendium of Classification Opinions, they may be helpful in determining the intention of the HSC. However, the reports of committees within the HSC, such as the Nomenclature Committee, carry virtually no weight, but may nevertheless be of some assistance in interpretation. Of even less use are the "working documents" of the Nomenclature and Classification Directorate of the CCC. They are the basis of discussions in HSC sessions, but they may not necessarily reflect the intent of the HSC.

Rulings of Other Countries. Because other nations that have adopted the HTS use the same General Rules of Interpretation, Section and Chapter Notes, and first six digits in the classification tables, their customs administration decisions are sometimes presented to the United States Customs Service. In general, U.S. Customs does not follow other nations' rulings because their decisions "may have been subject to political realities or domestic regulations which are different from our own." The meaning of this has not been further defined, but illustrates that there may be political pressure to classify goods so as to more readily admit them to, or more readily exclude them from, the United States. In any event, these foreign rulings are considered "merely instructive of how others" classify imports.

Position Papers. Before a session of the HSC, U.S. Customs, the International Trade Commission, and the Bureau of Census prepare position papers for the session. These papers do not reflect Customs' position in the interpretation of the HTS and are considered to have no value, although they are occasionally circulated and obtained by importers or their counsel.

These notes, opinions, reports, rulings and papers all add to the process of interpretation, a layer which did not exist before the adoption of the HTS by the United States. Awareness of their use by the Customs Service may be helpful to United States counsel, but should not expect to be given weight beyond that announced by the Customs Service as described above.

§ 3.14   Classification of Goods—U.S. Court Decisions

While it may seem strange to suggest that decisions of United States courts may not be applicable in interpreting the HTS, which may be correct for decisions interpreting the prior TSUS.[60] Interpretations of the United States HTS must follow the procedure outlined above. Certainly decisions rendered subsequent to the adoption of the HTS in 1988, which interpret the HTS, will be useful. But in many cases decisions have little usefulness because they apply to a narrow set of issues affecting specific goods where two or more classification possibilities exist. Although the HTS has a different process, the approach used in the past may find use in the future.

Thus, some earlier decisions may be useful to understand the analytical process used by the courts.[61] For example, prior United States decisions applying the rule of relative specificity may be used in interpreting General Rule of Interpretation Rule 3(a), which uses a kind of "rule of relative specificity" under the wording "most specific description."[62]

Customs classifications can apparently be gamed. In 2017, for example, Ford won its argument that vehicles made it Turkey were passenger vehicles (2.5% tariff) not cargo vans (25% tariff). The vehicles entered the U.S. with second row seats and additional footwells and windows. Shortly after clearing U.S. Customs, Ford removed all these features and sold the vehicles as cargo vans. The Court of International Trade ruled in Decision No. 13–00291 that the proper classification was to be determined as of the moment of entry into the USA.

PART C

RULES OF ORIGIN

When a country's tariff schedules provide that duties on an imported item may vary depending upon the country from which the item comes, certain "rules of origin" may come into play. Two common situations raising questions of origin are when a product is shipped to the United States from Country "X" but has been manufactured in fact in Country "Y", and when a product is shipped to the United States from Country "X", in which the product was made, but certain component parts of the product have originated in Country "Y".

A statutory U.S. "rule of origin" is provided in the Trade Agreements Act of 1979.[63] This general "substantial transformation"

---

[60]   *See JVC Company of America v. United States*, 234 F.3d 1348 (Fed.Cir.2000).

[61]   For example, the *Mattel, Inc. v. United States decision*, 287 F.Supp. 999 (Cust.Ct.1968), might be used when the issue involves priority of one classification over another.

[62]   *See, e.g., Great Western Sugar Co. v. United States*, 452 F.2d 1394 (C.C.P.A.1972).

[63]   19 U.S.C.A. § 2518(4)(B): "An article is a product of a country . . . only if . . . it is wholly the growth, product, or manufacture of that country . . . , or . . . in the case of

rule of origin reflects longstanding Customs Service regulations[64] and is relevant in determining the rate at which customs duty is charged (MFN or not). It also has deep roots in the jurisprudence of the Supreme Court,[65] and principally asks whether the product has changed in name, character or use. In most cases, this approach applies for purposes of United States country of origin marking requirements and determination of the origin of goods subject to U.S. import quotas.[66] Variations on the substantial transformation theme occur for goods subject to voluntary trade restraints (VERs),[67] economic sanctions,[68] country of origin marking requirements,[69] antidumping and countervailing duty circumvention law,[70] customs duty drawback (refunds or waivers),[71] and government procurement preferences.[72]

Different more quantitative (value-added) rules of origin usually apply for goods from developing nations seeking duty free entry into the United States.[73] The Canada-United States Free Trade Agreement and the NAFTA generally replace the substantial transformation test with origin criteria emphasizing changes in HTS tariff classifications along with regional value content which are treated as the equivalent of a substantial transformation.[74] Product specific rules of origin have been created for textiles,[75] motor vehicles,[76] electronics and other goods.

---

an article which consists in whole or in part of materials from another country . . . it has been substantially transformed into a new and different article of commerce with a name, character, or use distinct from that of the article or articles from which it was so transformed."

[64]   *See* 19 C.F.R. § 134.1(b).

[65]   *See Anheuser-Busch Brewing Ass'n v. United States*, 207 U.S. 556, 28 S.Ct. 204, 52 L.Ed. 336 (1908).

[66]   *See* Chapter 7.

[67]   *See Superior Wire v. United States*, 669 F.Supp. 472 (C.I.T.1987), affirmed 867 F.2d 1409 (Fed.Cir.1989).

[68]   Re Marking of Felt Manufactured from South African Wool, 24 Customs Serv. Dec. 30 (Jan. 17, 1990).

[69]   *See Uniroyal v. United States*, 542 F.Supp. 1026 (C.I.T.1982), affirmed 702 F.2d 1022 (Fed.Cir.1983).

[70]   *See* 19 U.S.C. § 1677j.

[71]   *See Anheuser-Busch Brewing Ass'n v. United States*, 207 U.S. 556, 28 S.Ct. 204, 52 L.Ed. 336 (1908).

[72]   *See* 19 U.S.C.A. § 2518(4)(b); 19 C.F.R. Part 177. For example, steel slabs imported into the U.S. and made into steel coils in the USA via modern "slab converters" are not substantially transformed for purposes of the Buy American Act.

[73]   *See* Chapter 2.

[74]   *See* R. Folsom, *Principles of Free Trade Law* (forthcoming).

[75]   *See* 19 C.F.R. § 12.130; *Mast Industries, Inc. v. United States*, 652 F.Supp. 1531 (C.I.T.1987), affirmed 822 F.2d 1069 (Fed.Cir.1987).

[76]   *See* 19 C.F.R. § 10.84.

One thoughtful commentator has concluded that the substantial transformation test of origin is inherently ambiguous, complex and difficult to apply consistently. He notes that in determining whether merchandise has emerged from a manufacturing process with a new name, character or use, the courts consider the following factors:

(1)   The value added to the merchandise at each stage of manufacture;

(2)   The degree and type of processing that occurred in each country;

(3)   The effect of processing on the article;

(4)   The markets in which the article was sold at each stage of production;

(5)   The capital costs of the processing;

(6)   The manner in which the article was used before and after processing;

(7)   The durability of the article before and after processing;

(8)   The lines of distribution in which the article was sold;

(9)   The article's name or identity in commerce before and after processing; and

(10) The tariff classification of the merchandise before and after processing.[77]

§ 3.15   Determining Origin Under U.S. Rules

A second form of classification determines the country of origin of the items to be imported. Unlike, the determination of the proper classification discussed above, the country of origin determination discloses whether Column 1 or Column 2 rates of duty apply. If Column 1 rates of duty apply, the goods may qualify for preferential or duty free treatment, if from a country of origin that qualifies under "Special" in Column 1. The Court of International Trade requires importers seeking preferential tariff treatment to verify the country of origin of their goods. "Reasonable care" must be exercised, not just

---

[77]   Maxwell, Formulating Rules of Origin for Imported Merchandise: Transforming the Substantial Transformation Test, 23 Geo.Wash.J.Int'l L. & Econ. 669, 673 (1990).

simple reliance on the exporter's assertions of origin. Failures in this regard can result in collection of lost duties and penalties.[78]

Additionally, knowing the country of origin uncovers more general prohibitions of trade with that country, because the United States nearly always has several nations with which it does not trade by legislative or presidential declaration.[79] The United States may also put limits on products entering from a specific foreign nation. This limitation may be the result of a formal quota,[80] or an informal voluntary restraint agreement (VRA). VRAs have in the past covered a wide range of products (e.g., steel, vehicles, electronics), and have been a device adopted by the United States (and other areas such as the European Union) as executive policy in order to discourage legislative action to establish mandatory and involuntary quotas to reduce trade imbalances.[81] VRAs are now generally prohibited under the WTO Safeguards Agreement (1995).

Counsel representing an importer must know the framework for determining the country of origin of articles.[82] Eligibility of entry often depends on country of origin determination.[83] Country of origin law does not have as consolidated a framework as for classification of the goods discussed above. Although the classification is dealt with exclusively in the HTS, working within that system is not a simple matter. Determination of the country of origin requires using rules that may apply in a spectrum of different areas. While there are several references to various aspects of the rule of origin in different sources of law, the *substantial transformation* test (treated below) in its various costumes, has traditionally been *the* test.

§ 3.16 U.S. Rules of Origin—Sources of Law

Trade Agreements Act of 1979

Section 308 of the Trade Agreements Act provides various definitions, including the rule of origin for eligible products.[84] The

---

[78]   *United States v. Golden Ship Trading Co.*, 2001 WL 65751 (C.I.T.2001) (T-shirts imported from Dominican Republic under Caribbean Basin Act were from China).

[79]   These prohibitions may extend to both exports and imports, but may have certain exceptions, such as medical supplies.

[80]   Quotas are regulated by the Customs Service. *See* 19 C.F.R. Part 132.

[81]   *See, e.g.*, Note, Voluntary Restraint Agreements: Effects and Implications of the Steel and Auto Cases, 11 N.C.J. Int'l L. & Com.Reg. 101 (1986).

[82]   Counsel may wish to obtain a ruling from Customs in advance of importation. *See* 19 C.F.R. §§ 177.1–177.11.

[83]   The United States must know whether the country of origin is one entitled to most favored nation treatment.

[84]   19 U.S.C.A. § 2518.

definition focuses on the concept of substantial transformation,[85] leaving the courts to interpret the meaning of substantial transformation. This is the fallback or general U.S. rule of origin for goods for purposes of tariff collection, absent more specific legislative rules. For example, all U.S. free trade agreements, the GSP, and the CBI have their own rules of origin. *See* Chapters 2 and 16.

Code of Federal Regulations, Country of Origin Marking

Part 134 of 19 C.F.R. provides rules governing the country of origin *marking,* which on occasion may be different from a product's origin for purposes of assessing tariffs. The regulations define articles subject to the marking, with special rules for articles repacked or manipulated, and ones usually combined with another article.[86] Rules also specify how containers or holders must be marked,[87] exceptions to the marking requirements,[88] method and location of marking,[89] and the consequences of finding articles not legally marked.[90] Essentially, the consequences for not properly marking a good are (1) properly mark the goods; (2) return the goods to the foreign nation; or (3) destroy the goods.[91]

Generally, a single country of origin must be determined for labeling purposes, even though the product may have been made in several countries. The country of origin, as determined by Customs, may not disclose other nations that may have participated in the process. While this may be important to the United States consumer, who may not wish to purchase products from a country substantially benefiting from the sale, it is not important to the determination of the official country of origin for marking purposes.

Special Rules—The North American Free Trade Agreement (NAFTA)

In drafting the NAFTA, as with drafting the earlier Canada-United States Free Trade Agreement, there was considerable concern that products entering the United States, as products of Canada or Mexico, actually had little fabrication or processing in those countries. To prevent this, special, complex NAFTA rules of origin

---

[85]   "An article is a product of a country or instrumentality only if (i) it is wholly the growth, product, or manufacture of that country or instrumentality, or (ii) in the case of an article which consists in whole or in part of materials from another country or instrumentality, it has been substantially transformed into a new and different article of commerce with a name, character, or use distinct from that of the article or articles from which it was so transformed." 19 U.S.C.A. § 2518(4)(B).

[86]   19 C.F.R. §§ 134.13–134.14.

[87]   19 C.F.R. §§ 134.21–134.26.

[88]   19 C.F.R. §§ 134.31–134.36.

[89]   19 C.F.R. §§ 134.41–134.47.

[90]   19 C.F.R. §§ 134.51–134.55.

[91]   19 C.F.R. § 134.51(a).

were adopted, which rely principally on changes in tariff classifications and regional value content to determine which goods may freely be traded. *See* R. Folsom and W.D. Folsom, *NAFTA Re-Negotiated and Its Business Implications* (forthcoming). These provisions include articles governing customs procedures for the certification of origin.

The procedures create a North American "Certificate of Origin" and require extensive verification provisions. The exporter provides the Certificate of Origin when the importer tries to claim the duty free tariff treatment offered by the NAFTA.[92] However, a Certificate of Origin is not required for goods valuing $1,000 or less, or where a member state has waived their use.[93] A member state may conduct verification through written questionnaires, visits to the premises exporter/producer, or other procedures the member states agree.[94] Verification is of considerable concern to the United States because it does not want Mexico to be used as a base for transshipping products from outside the NAFTA area, especially from Asia. The Court of International Trade requires importers seeking preferential tariff treatment to verify the country of origin of their goods. "Reasonable care" must be exercised, which requires more than simple reliance on the exporter's assertions of origin. Failure to do so can result in collection of lost duties and penalties.[95]

Decisions of United States Courts

There are several areas where Customs is required to determine the country of origin. However, the determinations sometimes lead to problems. For example, products from countries that the United States does not trade may be transshipped through a country that the United States does trade. Products from countries subject to high rates of duty in Column 2 may be transshipped through countries subject to lower rates of duty in Column 1. Products with most favored nation status, Column 1 rates of duty, may be transshipped through a country with special access, such as a Caribbean nation. Exporters from a nation that has agreed to a voluntary restraint agreement may try to exceed the agreed upon numbers by having the products transshipped through a nation without such a quota. As the United States enters into free trade agreements such as NAFTA, other nations may attempt to take advantage of that relationship by

---

[92]   NAFTA Art. 501.

[93]   NAFTA Art. 503.

[94]   NAFTA Art. 506.

[95]   *United States v. Golden Ship Trading Co.*, 2001 WL 65751 (Ct. Intl' Trade 2001) (T-shirts imported from Dominican Republic under Caribbean Basin Act were from China).

having goods transshipped through Canada or Mexico into the United States.

Fortunately, some case law has evolved, addressing the country of origin issue. Those cases, which involve one specific area, may be helpful in addressing another. For example, a case that has identified the country of origin may be useful in determining whether the agreed amount under a voluntary restraint agreement has been exceeded.[96] Or it may be helpful where products are allegedly violating the rules of the generalized system of preferences. Thus, when dealing with a country of origin issue, cases outside the scope of the form of entry (i.e., GSP, NAFTA, etc.) must be consulted.[97]

§ 3.17 Rules of Origin—U.S. Substantial Transformation Test

While some consistency in the identification of the country of origin exists, the process requires more than simply reading the label, which states the country of origin. Because a nation may do little more to an item than sew on the country of origin label, the product itself must be measured.

Substantial Transformation Test

The principal focus in a U.S. country of origin determination examines whether the product was substantially transformed in the country claiming the country of origin status.[98] One of the bedrock cases defining substantial transformation in the United States, an early United States Supreme Court decision, involves drawbacks.[99] The Court held substantial transformation occurs when a product is transformed into a new and different article "having a distinctive *name, character or use.*"[100] However, while this case provides a standard, it has been applied in many different ways.[101] For example, while a name change alone would not always be sufficient, such as from "wire" to "wire rod,"[102] a court held that changing heat-treated

---

[96] *See, e.g., Superior Wire, A Div. of Superior Products Co. v. United States,* 669 F.Supp. 472 (C.I.T.1987), *affirmed* 867 F.2d 1409 (Fed.Cir.1989).

[97] *See Ferrostaal Metals Corp. v. United States,* 664 F.Supp. 535, 538 (C.I.T.1987) (case law does not suggest that the court should depart from "policy-neutral rules governing substantial transformation in order to achieve wider import restrictions in particular cases.").

[98] This test is in the Trade Agreements Act of 1979. *See* 19 U.S.C.A. § 2518(4)(B).

[99] *Anheuser-Busch Brewing Ass'n v. United States,* 207 U.S. 556, 28 S.Ct. 204, 52 L.Ed. 336 (1908).

[100] *Id.* at 562, 28 S.Ct. at 206.

[101] But it is applied by the courts. *See, e.g., Texas Instruments Inc. v. United States,* 681 F.2d 778, 782 (C.C.P.A.1982).

[102] *See Superior Wire, A Div. of Superior Products Co. v. United States,* 669 F.Supp. 472 (C.I.T.1987) (the court noted that in recent years the focus was on a change in use or character).

steel to galvanized steel was sufficient. More specifically, because the annealing process involved substantial manufacturing, which ultimate strengthened the steel and made it resistant to corrosion, it caused a substantial transformation to occur.[103]

Courts tend to concentrate on changes in *character* or *use* rather than in the name of the product. Also, they often develop subtests appropriate for a particular kind of article. For example, whether a *significant value* was added, or *additional costs* were incurred. But each test leads to some subjective evaluation, which provides a sort of sense of whether the product is really from the state country. While the substantial transformation test has been criticized,[104] it remains the generally applicable U.S. law.

However a U.S. court reaches a decision on a substantial transformation question, in this author's experience it is likely to have considered most of the following changes:

1.   Change in name (and change in tariff classification);

2.   Change in physical appearance;

3.   Change in material substance (at each stage of manufacture);

4.   Change in apparent use;

5.   Change in value of item in the mind of the consumer;

6.   Additional capital vested in article;

7.   Additional labor vested in article;

8.   Type of processing;

9.   Effect of processing; and

10.   Change in method of distribution.

There is no secret formula for determining which factor, if any, plays the most significant role. Little wonder Canada, Mexico and other U.S. partners insisted on creating different rules of origin when agreeing to free trade.

In 2008, the Bureau of Customs and Border Protection proposed shifting to a single uniform approach to determine the origin of

---

[103]   *Ferrostaal Metals Corp. v. United States*, 664 F.Supp. 535 (C.I.T.1987) (there was a "significant altering" of the "mechanical properties and chemical composition of the steel").

[104]   Maxwell, Formulating Rules of Origin for Imported Merchandise: Transforming the Substantial Transformation Test, 23 J. Int'l L. & Econ. 669 (1990).

imported goods.[105] Although Customs and Border Protection withdrew the proposal, if adopted, it would have abandoned the historic test for the "substantial transformation" of foreign goods. The proposal elicited so many responses that the time for public comment on the proposal was extended twice. Most of the responses opposed the proposal because the rule could have substantially impacted the cost of entry into the United States, place undue burdens on those in the trading community, and cause the importation process to become more complex.[106] Eventually, in 2010 the Bureau of Customs and Border Protection abandoned the proposal.

PART D

CUSTOMS VALUATION

Even though an imported item may be classified and have a known rate of duty, expressed as a percentage of the item's value, difficulty may still arise in getting the importer and customs authorities to agree upon the item's value. For decades, United States Customs valuation of an imported item was gauged by the American Selling Price (ASP) of the item—i.e. the usual wholesale price at which the same item manufactured in the United States was offered for sale.

However, Article VII of GATT requires that "value for customs purposes. . . should not be based on the value of merchandise of national origin or on arbitrary or fictitious values." The 1979 Tokyo Round produced the Customs Valuation Code, which established the details of an approach which was quite different from ASP. The GATT approach was incorporated into the U.S. Trade Agreements Act of 1979. United States Customs valuation is now calculated by the "transaction value" of the imported item and, if that cannot be determined, by certain fallback methods which are, in descending order of eligibility for use, the transaction value of identical merchandise, the transaction value of similar merchandise, the resale price of the merchandise with allowances for certain factors (deducted value) or the cost of producing the imported item (computed value). "Transaction value" is "the price actually paid or payable for the merchandise when sold for exportation to the United States" plus certain amounts reflecting packing costs, commissions paid by buyer, any assist, royalty or license fee paid by buyer, and any resale, disposal or use proceeds that accrue to seller.

---

[105] *Uniform Rules of Origin for Imported merchandise, Notice of Proposed Rulemaking*, 73 FR 43,385 (2008).

[106] Vivian C. Jones and Michael F. Martin, INTERNATIONAL TRADE: RULES OF ORIGIN, Cong. Res. Serv., RL 34524 at 2 (January 5, 2012).

§ 3.18   Valuation—The Law of the GATT/WTO

Of the several codes adopted by the GATT in the Tokyo Round and renewed in the Uruguay WTO Round, the Agreement on the Implementation of Article VII of the General Agreement on Tariffs and Trade (GATT Customs Valuation Code) is of considerable importance to the United States.[107] While Article VII of the GATT 1947, titled "Valuation for Customs Purposes," established a form of transaction value, it was not until the Customs Valuation Code was adopted that the form of valuation by a descending order of tests was introduced. This form of valuation was incorporated into the United States law in 1979, and is the source of law one must consider for valuation of U.S. imports.

§ 3.19   Valuation—United States Law

The law applicable to valuation can be found in the United States Tariff Act of 1930, as amended. However, the United States' commitment to the GATT Customs Valuation Code, and the successor World Trade Organization must be considered.

For the most part, the United States Tariff Act of 1930 incorporates the GATT Customs Valuation Code of 1979.[108] However, because the United States adopted that GATT Code in 1979 amendments to the Tariff Act of 1930, some of the prior methods of interpretation of valuation may continue to be considered by courts.[109]

§ 3.20   Valuation—Appraisal of Imported Merchandise

Imports of merchandise are valued according to a series of alternative methods,[110] but not alternative methods in the sense that Customs may use any method it chooses. Nor may Customs reject information provided if based on the use of generally accepted accounting procedures.[111] The methods of valuation are set forth in

---

[107]   Geneve, 1979, GATT, 26th Supp. BISD 116 (1980). *See* Davey, Customs Valuation: Commentary on the GATT Customs Valuation Code (1989).

[108]   19 U.S.C.A. § 1401a. *See* Sherman, Reflections on the New Customs Valuation Code, 12 Law & Pol'y Int'l Bus. 119 (1980).

[109]   The same is true of other areas with pre-Code established procedures. *See* Snyder, Customs Valuation in the European Economic Community, 11 Georgia J. Int'l & Comp.L. 79 (1981).

[110]   Merchandise is defined as of the same class or kind as other merchandise if within a group or range which is produced by a particular industry or industrial sector. 19 U.S.C.A. § 1401a(e)(2).

[111]   19 U.S.C.A. § 1401a(g)(3).

the order of use. Most valuations never go beyond the first, the transaction value.

§ 3.21 Valuation—Transaction Value

All merchandise imported into the United States must be appraised. First, Customs considers the transaction value of the merchandise.[112] The transaction value is often referred to as the *invoice value* because in the absence of over or under invoicing, it would be the value of the transaction. The statute describes the transaction value as the *price actually paid or payable.*[113] In other words, it is the price when sold for exportation to the United States, also known as the wholesale price.[114] This may be confusing where there are several contracts, in addition to the actual contract between the buyer-seller. This situation can occur as between a party to the sale and the party's parent entity,[115] or between a foreign seller and United States company acquiring items purchased by the foreign seller from a foreign manufacturer.[116]

Also, the transaction value may include some elements that create doubt as to application of duties. For example, quota charges clearly separated on the invoice are nevertheless includable.[117] Rebates to the price actually paid or payable made after the merchandise has entered the United States are disregarded in determining the transaction value.[118] However, dividing the assembly (service) price from the consumer (sale of goods) price for made-to measure clothing does not relieve the importer from duty on the former portion, the full cost is subject to duty.[119]

---

[112]   19 U.S.C.A. § 1401a(a)(1)(A).

[113]   19 U.S.C.A. § 1401a(b)(1). Price actually paid or payable is defined in 19 U.S.C.A. § 1401a(b)(4). Disbursements by the buyer for the benefit of the seller are included, as when the buyer disburses some funds to the agent's seller who assists in bringing about the sale. *Moss Mfg. Co., Inc. v. United States,* 714 F.Supp. 1223 (C.I.T.1989), *affirmed* 896 F.2d 535 (Fed.Cir.1990). The price payable may be determined by a clear, definite and agreed pre-importation formula. *Del Monte Corp. v. United States,* 730 F.3d 1352 (Fed. Cir. 2013).

[114]   As of January 1, 2011, Customs and Border Protection.

[115]   *Nissho Iwai American Corp. v. United States,* 786 F.Supp. 1002 (C.I.T.1992), *aff'd in part, rev'd in part* 982 F.2d 505 (Fed.Cir.1992) (holding the master contract between the buyer and seller controls, rather than the contract price paid by the seller's Japanese company's parent to primary manufacturer).

[116]   *See Brosterhous, Coleman & Co. v. United States,* 737 F.Supp. 1197 (C.I.T.1990)

[117]   *Generra Sportswear Co. v. United States,* 905 F.2d 377 (Fed.Cir.1990).

[118]   19 U.S.C.A. § 1401a(b)(4)(B). *See Allied Int'l v. United States,* 795 F.Supp. 449 (C.I.T.1992) (importer has the burden of showing that the rebate occurred on or before date of entry).

[119]   *E.C. McAfee Co. v. United States,* 842 F.2d 314 (Fed.Cir.1988).

Transaction Value: Associated Costs

Five other categories of associated costs must be also added to the transaction value. Some are costs, which may be part of the price paid or payable, but some are costs, which, if not subject to tariffs, could be split off from the price of the goods and paid separately, thus avoiding or evading proper duty.[120] These additional costs subject to duty are:

　　1.   Packing costs incurred by the buyer.[121] If incurred by the seller they would be part of the price paid for the merchandise, probably buried in the price of the goods.

　　2.   All selling commission incurred by the buyer with respect to the imported merchandise.[122]

　　3.   The value of any assist, apportioned as appropriate.[123] An assist includes a very broad range of benefits, and is the subject of an extensive definitional provision.[124]

　　4.   Any royalty or license fee related to the goods, which the buyer pays directly or indirectly as a condition of the sale.[125] This can be a difficult provision to interpret. However, if a buyer pays a flat fee per year directly to the designer of the goods, no matter how many are sold, the buyer may escape duty. But, any payment related to the number sold seems subject to duty.

　　5.   Any direct or indirect accrual to the seller from the subsequent resale, disposal, or use of the goods.[126] This prevents the sale at a low base price, with the buyer required to pass on a percentage to the seller after the goods are resold.

---

[120]   *See All Channel Products v. United States*, 787 F.Supp. 1457 (C.I.T.1992), *judgment affirmed* 982 F.2d 513 (Fed.Cir.1992) (inland freight charges separately invoiced properly included in transaction value); *United States v. Arnold Pickle & Olive Co.*, 659 F.2d 1049, 68 C.C.P.A. 85 (1981) (inspection costs).

[121]   19 U.S.C.A. § 1401a(b)(1)(A).

[122]   19 U.S.C.A. § 1401a(b)(1)(B). *See Jay-Arr Slimwear Inc. v. United States*, 681 F.Supp. 875 (C.I.T.1988).

[123]   19 U.S.C.A. § 1401a(b)(1)(C).

[124]   19 U.S.C.A. § 1401a(h)(1). *See, e.g., Texas Apparel Co. v. United States*, 883 F.2d 66 (Fed.Cir.1989), *cert. denied* 493 U.S. 1024, 110 S.Ct. 728, 107 L.Ed.2d 747 (1990) (sewing machine costs constitute an assist in manufacturing jeans). *See* Collins, The Concept of Assist as Applied to Customs Valuation of Imported Merchandise, 1991 Detroit Col.L.R. 239.

[125]   19 U.S.C.A. § 1401a(b)(1)(D).

[126]   19 U.S.C.A. § 1401a(b)(1)(E).

The price paid or payable shall be increased by any of the above five additions, if it can be shown that they have not already been included in the price paid or payable by "sufficient" information.[127] The statute defines sufficient information as that which "establishes the accuracy of such amount, difference, or adjustment."[128] Where sufficient information is not available, and it seems like one or more of the five additional amounts exist, the transaction value is not determinable, and one must move to the next section in the chronology of applicable provisions.[129]

Appraised Value

Where the transaction value is determinable, as discussed above, it will be considered the *appraised* value only if certain further conditions exist. The first of these conditions requires the buyer to dispose of or use the goods without restriction, except restrictions that (1) are required by law, (2) limit resale to a geographical area, or (3) do not substantially affect the value.[130]

The second condition requires that there may not be any condition or consideration affecting the sale of or the price paid or payable where the value of the condition or consideration cannot be determined.[131]

The third states that no part of the proceeds from the use or resale may accrue directly or indirectly to the seller, unless that amount is calculable under the provisions noted above.[132]

The fourth requires the buyer and seller to be either unrelated, or if related that the transaction is acceptable.[133] Because buyers and sellers are often related through a parent and subsidiary relationship, the statute sets forth special rules. Often the prices reflected in transfers within an organization do not truly reflect arm's length prices because they want to avoid taxes, avoid tariff duties, or for other purposes.[134] The transaction value in such a transaction will be the appraised value, as long as (1) the circumstances of the sale do not suggest the relationship influenced the price, and (2) the transaction value approximates the transaction value in an

---

[127]   19 U.S.C.A. § 1401a(b)(1).

[128]   19 U.S.C.A. § 1401a(b)(5).

[129]   *Id.*

[130]   19 U.S.C.A. § 1401a(b)(2)(A)(i).

[131]   19 U.S.C.A. § 1401a(b)(2)(A)(ii).

[132]   19 U.S.C.A. § 1401a(b)(2)(A)(iii). The above provision is 19 U.S.C.A. § 1401a(b)(1)(E).

[133]   19 U.S.C.A. § 1401a(b)(2)(A)(iv).

[134]   Known generally as "transfer pricing".

unrelated parties' transaction, the deductive value, or computed value for identical or similar merchandise.[135]

This exception introduces the concepts of *deductive* value and *computed* value, both alternative valuations methods discussed below. The exception also requires defining both *identical* merchandise and *similar* merchandise.[136] The comparison values referred to above must be values for merchandise entering the United States on or around the same time as the merchandise in question.

The values used for comparison purposes usually consists of identical or similar goods,[137] however, varying method of sales may distort the comparison between the goods. Consequently, the values used must consider these differences, if based on sufficient information, in commercial levels, quantity levels and any costs, commissions, values, fees and proceeds in § 1401a(b)(1), discussed above.[138]

Items Not Included in Transaction Value

While the above identifies provisions designating the composition of the transaction value, specific items should not be included in the transaction value, including:

First, transaction value should not include any reasonable cost or charge for either: (1) construction, erection, assembly, or maintenance of, or technical assistance to the merchandise after importation or (2) transportation after importation.[139]

Second, transaction value should not include the customs duties or other federal taxes imposed upon importation, nor federal excise tax.[140]

Transaction Value of Identical and Similar Merchandise

This material largely draws from the material above applicable to transaction value. The identical merchandise value method is used when the transaction value cannot be determined or used. When the identical merchandise value cannot be used, the similar merchandise value should be used.[141] Where the transaction value has been determined above for identical merchandise or for similar

---

[135]   19 U.S.C.A. § 1401a(b)(2)(B).

[136]   19 U.S.C.A. § 1401a(h)(2) & (4).

[137]   *See Walter Holm & Co. v. United States*, 3 C.I.T. 119 (1982) (use of value of exports of cantaloupes through Laredo, Texas, to determine value of same items through Nogales, Arizona).

[138]   19 U.S.C.A. § 1401a(b)(2)(C).

[139]   19 U.S.C.A. § 1401a(b)(3)(A). International transportation is separately excluded in 19 U.S.C.A. § 1401a(b)(4)(A).

[140]   19 U.S.C.A. § 1401a(b)(3)(B).

[141]   19 U.S.C.A. § 1401a(a)(1)(B) & (C).

merchandise, as defined in the statute,[142] it must be adjusted. This adjustment requires consideration of all different commercial level or quantity level of sales for identical or similar merchandise.[143] It must also be based on sufficient information. Where two or more comparison transactions exist, the appraisal of the imported merchandise will be based on the lower or lowest of the comparison values.[144]

§ 3.22 Valuation—Deductive Value

The most important question is when will the deductive method of valuation be used? Deductive value should be used when the above transaction value does not lead to an acceptable determination to Customs.[145] However, the importer may request that the computed value discussed below be used in place of the deductive value.[146] If computed value does not prove possible, the deductive value must be used next.[147]

Deductive value may be applied to the merchandise being appraised, or to either identical or similar merchandise.[148] The deductive value focuses on unit value,[149] and constitutes the most appropriate value as determined in one of three ways.

The first method applies when the merchandise imported is sold (1) in the condition as imported, and (2) at or about the date of importation. The deductive value is the unit price at which the merchandise is sold in the greatest quantity.[150]

The second method applies when the merchandise imported is sold in the condition as imported, but not at or about the date of importation. The deductive value in this case is the unit price at which the merchandise is sold in the greatest quantity, but within 90 days after importation.[151]

The third method is where the merchandise is neither sold in the condition imported nor within 90 days after importation. The

---

[142] 19 U.S.C.A. § 1401a(h)(2) & (4).

[143] 19 U.S.C.A. § 1401a(c)(2).

[144] *Id.*

[145] 19 U.S.C.A. § 1401a(a)(1)(D).

[146] 19 U.S.C.A. § 1401a(a)(2).

[147] *Id.*

[148] 19 U.S.C.A. § 1401a(d)(1).

[149] Unit value is the price the merchandise is sold (1) in the greatest aggregate quantity, (2) to unrelated persons, (3) at the first commercial level after importation (at level i and ii discussed below), or after further processing (at level iii discussed below), (4) in a total volume which is both greater than the total volume sold at any other unit price, and sufficient to establish the unit price. 19 U.S.C.A. § 1401a(d)(2)(B).

[150] 19 U.S.C.A. § 1401a(d)(2)(A)(i).

[151] 19 U.S.C.A. § 1401a(d)(2)(A)(ii).

deductive value is the unit price at which the merchandise, after further processing, is sold in the greatest quantity within 180 days of importation.[152] This third method only applies at the election of the importer and upon notification to the customs officer.[153]

If the deductive method applies, some reductions from the unit price may result, including commissions, additions for profit and expenses, costs of domestic and international transportation, customs duties and other federal taxes on the merchandise. If the third method of deductive value is used, the costs of additional processing may reduce the unit price.[154] However, deductions for profits and expenses must be consistent with profits and expenses in the United States for similar merchandise, and any state or local taxes on the importer relating to the sale of the merchandise is considered an expense.[155]

There may also be an increase to the unit price, if such costs have not already been included, amounting to the packing costs incurred by the importer or buyer.[156]

A final provision requires one to disregard any sale to a person who supplies an assist for use in connection with the merchandise.[157]

Where deductive value is inapplicable, or where the importer has chosen to pass over deductive value, the next method is computed value.

§ 3.23 Valuation—Computed Value

Computed value should be used when transaction and deductive value methods do not provide an appropriate result. However, the importer may skip over the deductive value tests and go straight to the computed value test.[158] The computed value determination consists of the sum of four parts.[159]

---

[152]   19 U.S.C.A. § 1401a(d)(2)(A)(iii).

[153]   *Id.*

[154]   19 U.S.C.A. § 1401a(d)(3)(A).

[155]   19 U.S.C.A. § 1401a(d)(3)(B).

[156]   19 U.S.C.A. § 1401a(d)(3)(C).

[157]   19 U.S.C.A. § 1401a(d)(3)(D).

[158]   19 U.S.C.A. § 1401a(a).

[159]   19 U.S.C.A. § 1401a(e)(1). For cases which have used the constructed value approach, *see Campbell Soup Co., Inc. v. United States*, 107 F.3d 1556 (Fed. Cir. 1997) (calculating the computed value of transported tomato paste from Mexico to United States); *New York Credit Men's Adjustment Bureau, Inc. v. United States*, 314 F.Supp. 1246 (Cust.Ct.1970), *affirmed* 342 F.Supp. 745 (Cust.Ct.1972).

First, computed value considers the cost or value of materials and fabrication or processing,[160] but it does not include any internal tax by the exporting country if the tax is remitted upon exportation.[161]

Second, compute value considers the profit and expenses of the amount usually associated with the same kind of merchandise.[162] They are based on producer's profits and expenses, unless inconsistent with those for sales of the same class or kind of merchandise by producers in the country exporting to the United States, in which case there is a calculation of such profits and expenses using the "sufficient information" procedure.[163] For example, freight costs incurred through the shipment of tomato paste from Mexico to the United States should be included in the computed value.[164] Also, the costs of a warranty for aircraft should be included as profit, less expenditures the manufacturer-seller establishes as incurred by the warranty obligations in curing defects.[165]

Third, computed value includes any assist if not already included in the amount above.[166] Computing the value of jeans would allow the addition of the cost or value of the sewing machines used to produce the jeans.[167] Finally, packing costs are included in the computed value.[168]

§ 3.24   Valuation—Value When Other Methods Are Not Effective

If the value cannot be determined under the above-discussed methods, there is a final method for calculating value. It is to derive a value using the methods set forth above, and then adjusting them to the extent necessary to achieve a reasonable result.[169] But in

---

[160] 19 U.S.C.A. § 1401a(e)(1)(A). *See Texas Apparel Co. v. United States*, 698 F.Supp. 932 (C.I.T.1988), *affirmed* 883 F.2d 66 (Fed.Cir.1989), *cert. denied* 493 U.S. 1024, 110 S.Ct. 728, 107 L.Ed.2d 747 (1990).

[161] 19 U.S.C.A. § 1401a(e)(2)(A).

[162] 19 U.S.C.A. § 1401a(e)(1)(B). *See Braniff Airways, Inc. v. United States*, 2 C.I.T. 26 (1981).

[163] 19 U.S.C.A. § 1401a(e)(2)(B).

[164] *Campbell Soup Co., Inc. v. United States*, 107 F.3d 1556 (Fed. Cir. 1997).

[165] *Braniff Airways, Inc. v. United States*, 2 C.I.T. 26 (1981).

[166] 19 U.S.C.A. § 1401a(e)(1)(C).

[167] *Texas Apparel Co. v. United States*, 698 F.Supp. 932 (C.I.T.1988), *affirmed* 883 F.2d 66 (Fed.Cir.1989), *cert. denied* 493 U.S. 1024, 110 S.Ct. 728, 107 L.Ed.2d 747 (1990).

[168] 19 U.S.C.A. § 1401a(e)(1)(D).

[169] 19 U.S.C.A. § 1401a(f)(1).

making such an appraisal, the statute prohibits using any of seven items:[170]

(1) United States selling price of United States produced merchandise,

(2) Any system using the higher of two alternatives,

(3) Domestic market price in country of exportation,

(4) Cost of production for identical or similar merchandise which differs from such cost of production determined under the computed value method,

(5) Price for export to a country other than the United States,

(6) Minimum values, or

(7) Arbitrary or fictitious values.

As first noted, transaction value expressed in the invoice is used in the vast majority of cases. However, when challenges to transaction value appear, the procedure may become more complex. While any of the determinations of Customs may be challenged, the cost of such challenge for all but the largest importers will often result in paying the Customs determined value, or not importing the goods. Counsel should calculate the possible rates of duty under all the possible alternatives and should only import the products if the rate of duty is acceptable and does not cause the price for resale to be either excessive, or more than would result from using United States products which may cost more to produce, but do not have added duty.

---

[170]   19 U.S.C.A. § 1401a(f)(2).

Chapter 4

ANTIDUMPING DUTIES

Table of Sections

§ 4.0   Antidumping and Countervailing Duties

The core of the GATT (1947) and (1994) agreements is the principle of binding tariffs applied equally to all WTO member states, the most-favored-nation (MFN) principle. These tariffs, negotiated in the various GATT/WTO Rounds, are commonly referred to as MFN tariffs. The national tariff levels of the WTO member states reflect these negotiated MFN tariffs. In the United States tariff code, MFN tariffs are referenced as Column 1 tariffs. *See* Chapter 2.

The GATT/WTO system allows, however, certain exceptions to MFN tariff levels. The two most important are "antidumping duties" (ADs) and "countervailing duties" (CVDs). Such duties are intended to "remedy" what the GATT/WTO has agreed are unfair international trade practices. Think of them as special tariffs which, in authorized circumstances, are additional to MFN tariffs. This Chapter will analyze antidumping duties; Chapter 5 will examine the subject of governmental subsidies and the response of countervailing duties.[1]

Antidumping duties are a permissible trade response where an enterprise prices its goods for sale in the country of importation at a level that is less than that charged for comparable sales in the home country (*i.e.*, at "less than fair value" (LTFV)). Hence AD generally counteract private sector discriminatory pricing. Countervailing duties are a permissible response to certain "subsidies" given in another country that favor its exports in the international marketplace. Hence CVD counteract governmental subsidies. See Chapter 5.

AD and CVD cannot simultaneously be applied. *See* U.S.-AD and CVD Duties (China), WT/DS 379/AB/R (2011).

§ 4.1   WTO Authorized Trade Remedies

The WTO system recognizes and permits both antidumping duties and countervailing duties, providing of course the respective requirements are satisfied. Each "trade remedy" also is governed by a separate Agreement ("Code") that provides more detail on the circumstances under which member states may impose these exceptional duties. Because the AD and CVD Codes are mandatory in the WTO system, they provide the foundation for a reasonably uniform body of legal rules for trade remedies among the roughly 160 WTO member states.

---

[1]   Chapter 6 examines a third allowed response to import competition: temporary "safeguard" (or "escape clause") measures. This form of governmental protection against import competition is substantially less common and not based upon the premise that unfair international trade practices have occurred.

Under the WTO Antidumping Agreement (AD Code) and the WTO Subsidies and Countervailing Measures Agreement (CVD Code), a country may impose a special duty on products of another WTO member state only if two requirements are met. First, the country must find sufficient evidence of an unfair trade practice, either dumping (sales at less than fair value) or prohibited or actionable subsidies. Second, the practice must cause a sufficiently significant injury to a domestic industry. In the case of dumping or subsidies, this requires proof that the practice has caused or threatens to cause "material injury" to a domestic industry, or that it has "materially retarded" the establishment of such an industry. Thus, the substantive grounds for the determination of the existence of "dumping" and of a "countervailable (actionable) subsidy" are different, but the domestic injury standard is essentially the same.

Neither of these trade remedies in favor of domestic producers is based on any notion of reciprocity. That is, neither arises because another country has restricted the importation of U.S. goods into its markets. Antidumping and countervailing duties instead address unfair selling prices of dutiable imported goods. WTO data indicates that goods from China and the EU are most frequently subject to ADs, while India, the U.S., the EU and Argentina are the most frequent jurisdictions imposing ADs. By 2017, the United States had over 400 trade remedy orders.

§ 4.2   Dumping—What Is It and Why Is It Done?

Dumping involves an exporter selling goods abroad at a price that is less than the price charged for the same goods in the home market (the "normal" or *"fair"* value). This alone is not sufficient however. Antidumping duties are allowed as a trade response only if the practice causes or threatens to cause a material injury to an industry in the export market. Dumping is recognized by most of the trading world as an unfair practice (akin to price discrimination as an antitrust offense). As noted, dumping is the subject of a special WTO Code that defines when dumping occurs, what constitutes a material injury, and the rules for the calculation of an allowed antidumping duty response.

The economics of dumping arise from a producer's opportunity to compartmentalize the overall market for its product, thus permitting it to offer the product for sale at different prices in different geographic areas. Only if trade barriers or other factors insulate each market sector from others is there opportunity to vary substantially the product's price in different sectors of the global market. For example, a producer can securely "dump" products in an overseas market at cheap prices and at high volume only if it can be sure that the product market in its home country is immune from (return) penetration by these products. The objectives of dumping include increasing marginal revenues, ruining a competitor's market position, and developing a new market on an expeditious basis.

On the other hand, a sale at less than the home price may not necessarily represent an unfair trade practice. It may instead merely result from a short-term need to introduce new products, sell off excess inventory, or conduct a distress sale in difficult financial circumstances. Indeed, "dumping" products in order to establish a foothold in a new foreign market or to raise brand awareness in an existing market may make sense as a marketing technique. Consumers, at least in the short term, are typically enthusiastic about obtaining goods at "dumped" prices.

Hence there is considerable debate about the economic rationality of categorizing dumping an unfair trade practice. In addition, some commentators assert that large global firms "game the system" by filing antidumping complaints when foreign rivals cut prices to gain market share. Such filings or the threat thereof may raise consumer prices. Nevertheless, a substantial body of international trade law seeks to identify dumping and counteract it through AD tariffs.

§ 4.3   The WTO Antidumping Agreement (1994)

The law regarding dumping has repeatedly been the subject of discussion in the various rounds of negotiations under GATT and (later) the WTO. A technical area, antidumping remedies were for many years principally used by developed nations to protect against competition from developing country imports. Then, in a remarkable transfer of legal technology, the principles endorsed by various GATT antidumping agreements took hold in newly developing countries. Today, antidumping duties are as likely to be imposed on U.S. exports by Mexico, India or China, as vice-versa. Antidumping proceedings remain the preferred trade remedy of domestic producers. India, the European Union, the United States and Argentina are the most frequent users of antidumping remedies, with products from China and EU states by far the top target of antidumping duties.

Late in 1993, the Uruguay Round of GATT negotiations came to a successful conclusion and President Clinton notified Congress of his intent to sign the many "covered agreements" that resulted from those negotiations. One of those agreements is yet another attempt at a codification of antidumping law. As a basic matter Article VI of the longstanding GATT grants WTO member states the right to impose antidumping duties. But the more detailed standards for such duties are set forth in a separate WTO Agreement, "The Agreement on Implementation of Article VI of GATT 1994."

The WTO Antidumping Agreement, adapted from the earlier Tokyo Round GATT "Antidumping Code," focuses upon dumping determinations (particularly criteria for allocating costs) and material injury determinations (particularly causation). The WTO Antidumping Agreement provides that dumping occurs with respect to a product if its export price is less than the "normal value." It defines the "normal value" of a good as the comparable price, in the ordinary course of trade, for the same or a similar product "when destined for consumption in the exporting country." Thus, in evaluating whether an export price constitutes dumping, the best baseline for comparison is the domestic sales price of comparable goods in the exporting country (*i.e.*, the home country).

However, such comparable sales may not be available, either because comparable products are not sold domestically or because the usual retail transaction there is not comparable (*e.g.*, leasing rather than a sale). In that situation, the WTO Antidumping Agreement provides a hierarchy of alternative computation methods to achieve an approximate evaluation. Among these alternatives, the preferred one uses the *price* for the same or a similar product in the ordinary course of trade for export to a third country. The next preferred alternative is to calculate the *cost* of production of the exported goods in the country of origin, plus a reasonable amount for profits and for administrative, selling and any other general costs. In either case, the value thus determined is then compared against the price charged on the export price to the import country.

The WTO Agreement has detailed rules that permit a member state to impose an antidumping duty only if a sale at less than fair value has caused a sufficient injury to a domestic industry.

Because the United States has agreed to abide by the WTO Antidumping Agreement, each of these requirements is reflected in conforming provisions of the U.S. Tariff Act of 1930. The remaining Sections of this Chapter will examine in detail these rules of antidumping law.

The WTO Antidumping Agreement also has a few special rules that are worthy of emphasis. First, it forbids duties for *de minimis* dumping, defined as less than two percent of the product's export price; in such cases member states must terminate any antidumping investigations immediately. Second, the Agreement permits "cumulation" of imports—*i.e.*, imports of the same goods from more than one country—if the dumping from each is more than *de minimis* and this is otherwise appropriate under the circumstances. Third, it recognizes, but does not expressly allow or disallow, antidumping petitions by employees and their union representatives. Fourth, the Agreement obligates member states to notify the WTO of any changes to their domestic antidumping laws as well as any related administrative actions. More generally, a special WTO "Committee on Anti-Dumping Practices" oversees implementation of the Agreement by member states.

Finally, when another member state challenges the imposition of antidumping duties before the WTO, the Dispute Settlement Body (DSB) panel may rely on the facts developed in the domestic administrative proceedings and must accept those facts if the domestic evaluation "was unbiased and objective, even if the panel might have reached a different conclusion." The WTO Agreement also expressly allows for "competing, reasonable interpretations" of its obligations under the domestic law of its member states.

§ 4.4   The Evolution of U.S. Antidumping Law

The United States was an early advocate of the perspective that dumping constitutes an unfair trade practice. Indeed, complaints about dumping were recorded as the subject of a protest by Secretary of the Treasury Alexander Hamilton in 1791. In general, U.S. antidumping statutes compare the price at which articles are imported or sold within the United States with their price in the country of production at the time of their export to the United States. This approach was first established by the Antidumping Act of 1916, a rarely-invoked criminal statute prohibiting "predatorily low price levels."[2] This statute, which also created a private remedy for treble damages, required proof of an intent to seriously injure or destroy a U.S. industry. The European Union, Japan, and other states successfully challenged this 1916 Act in WTO dispute settlement proceedings as inconsistent with the Antidumping Agreement. The pressure of the adverse rulings by the WTO's DSB ultimately led the United States to repeal the Act in 2004.

The modern U.S. rules and procedures governing antidumping duties are set forth in a statute that is still known as the Tariff Act of 1930.[3] Congress has enacted amendments to this statute numerous times. The most important of these for present purposes came through the Uruguay Round Agreements Act of 1994 (URAA),[4] by which Congress amended the Tariff Act to implement the numerous Uruguay Round WTO agreements, including the Antidumping Agreement. Finally, the Code of Federal Regulations

---

[2]   15 U.S.C. §§ 71–77.

[3]   Codified at 19 U.S.C. §§ 1671–1677g.

[4]   Public Law No. 103–465, 108 Stat. 4809.

contains more detailed rules on the requirements for, calculation of, and process for assessing antidumping duties.[5]

U.S. law places authority for administering antidumping law in two different governmental agencies.[6] Generally, the Secretary of Commerce (which in turn has delegated specific authority to its International Trade Administration (ITA)) is the "Administering Authority."[7] The ITA is responsible for all administration determinations except those relating to injury to a domestic industry. Injury determinations are the responsibility of the International Trade Commission (ITC).[8] To provide guidance on the application of the applicable statutory and regulatory rules, the International Trade Administration publishes an "Antidumping Manual," the most recent version of which is from 2009.[9]

Sections 12.5 through 12.19 below will examine in detail the substantive rules of U.S. law on antidumping determinations. In brief, and in conformity with the WTO Antidumping Agreement, the fundamental determination under U.S. law is whether a sale is at "less than fair value" (LTFV).[10] This requires a comparison of the U.S. price of imported goods with their "normal value." "Normal value" is usually determined by the price charged for the goods in the exporter's *domestic* market (the home market) in the ordinary course of business.[11] The ITA then compares this value with the price of the goods for export to the United States.[12] As noted, the ITC separately makes determinations on injury and causation in antidumping proceedings. In order to impose antidumping duties, the Tariff Act requires an affirmative determination by the ITC that a challenged practice presents an actual or threatened "material injury" to a domestic industry, or that it has "materially retarded" the establishment of such an industry.[13]

If sales are both at LTFV and cause or threaten "material injury" to a domestic industry, then the Tariff Act declares that an

---

[5]   The principal U.S. antidumping regulations are found in 19 C.F.R. Part 351.

[6]   For more on the administrative processes governing antidumping duties *see* Sections 4.22 through 4.25.

[7]   19 U.S.C. § 1677(1). Prior to 1980, the Treasury Department was the "administering authority", but the Secretary of Commerce was so designated in 1980. *See President's Reorganization Plan No. 3 of 1979*, 44 Fed. Reg. 69,273 (1979), and Executive Order 12188, 45 Fed. Reg. 989 (1980).

[8]   19 U.S.C. §§ 1673(2) and 1677(2).

[9]   Import Administration Antidumping Manual (2009), available at http://ia.ita.doc.gov/admanual/index.html.

[10]   19 U.S.C. § 1673(1).

[11]   19 U.S.C. §§ 1673(1), 1677b. *See also* Sections 4.6–4.9.

[12]   19 U.S.C. §§ 1673(1), 1677a. *See also* Section 4.10.

[13]   19 U.S.C. § 1673(2). *See also* Sections 4.12–4.18.

antidumping duty "shall be imposed."[14] Thus, antidumping duties are a statutory remedy, one which the President cannot veto or affect (except by the extraordinary act of negotiating an international trade agreement).

§ 4.5 The Basic U.S. Dumping Determination

The ITA determines whether foreign merchandise[15] is, or is likely to be, sold in the United States at less than fair value (LTFV) by comparing the foreign market value (the "normal value") of the goods to the price charged for export to the United States. If the former exceeds the latter, dumping has occurred. Much turns, therefore, on the definitions of these two central concepts. Sections 12.6 through 12.9 below will examine the calculation of the foreign market value. Section 12.10 below will then analyze the appropriate comparison price regarding the export of the goods to the United States.

If a sale is at LTFV and meets the statutory material injury requirement, then the Tariff Act provides that an antidumping duty "shall be imposed."[16] The amount of the duty will correspond to the "dumping margin." The ITA normally compares the "weighted-average" foreign market value with the "weighted-average" U.S. price for the dumped product.[17] The term "weighted average dumping margin" is a percentage that is determined with reference to the "aggregate dumping margins" of the exporter or producer for the type of products at issue.[18] For large capital goods, however, the ITA will typically use the actual normal value and the U.S. price on a transaction-to-transaction basis.[19] Whichever calculation method is used, the "dumping margin"—and thus the amount of the antidumping duty—corresponds to the amount by which the foreign market "normal value" of the goods exceeds the price charged in the export to the United States.[20] The dumping margin may be different for similar merchandise from different foreign states, and may also be different for different manufacturers from the same foreign state.

§ 4.6 Foreign Market Value ("Normal Value")

The first step in the analysis is to determine the appropriate value of the allegedly dumped goods in a relevant foreign market.

---

[14] 19 U.S.C. § 1673.

[15] Antidumping law generally does not apply to services, but also is not limited to "cash-only sales." *See U.S. v. Eurodif S. A.*, 555 U.S. 305 (2009).

[16] 19 U.S.C. § 1673.

[17] 19 U.S.C. § 1677(35)(B).

[18] *Id.*

[19] 19 U.S.C. § 1677(35)(A).

[20] *Id.*

The Tariff Act refers to this value as the "normal value."[21] It recognizes three different measures for this normal value:

Home Market Price. The standard measure of the "normal value" is the price at which the foreign merchandise is first sold for consumption—in usual quantities, in the ordinary course of trade, and preferably at the same level of trade—in the exporting country ("home market price").[22]

Third Country Price. If, however, sales in the home market are nonexistent or too small to form an adequate basis for comparison (usually, less than five percent of the U.S. total), then export sales to other countries may be used ("third country price").[23] Sales intended to establish fictitious markets in the source country, however, cannot be considered.[24]

Constructed Value. If comparable merchandise is not offered for sale either in the home market or for export to other countries, the ITA is authorized to calculate a "constructed" value.[25] In such a case, the ITA will build a figure using one of three methodologies: (1) the producer's actual costs and profit for the specific product under investigation; (2) the producer's actual costs and profit for similar products; *or* (3) a weighted average of other producers' actual costs and profit for the category of products under investigation.[26] If the foreign producer is in a non-market economy, then the ITA will construct an appropriate value based either on various "factors of production" or on "surrogate country prices."[27]

The time and place for determining the normal value is often crucial. The Tariff Act requires that the relevant time for measuring the sales in the foreign country must "reasonably correspond]" to the time used to calculate the comparison export price to the United States.[28] That is the time when the product is "first sold (or agreed to be sold) before the date of importation by the producer or exporter of

---

21   19 U.S.C. § 1677b.
22   19 U.S.C. § 1677b(a)(1)(B)(i). Section 504 of the 2015 Trade Preferences Extension Act expanded the authority to disregard home market prices when "a particular market situation" indicates those prices do not "accurately reflect the cost of production in the ordinary course of trade". This provision can be used concerning market economy goods.
23   19 U.S.C. § 1677b(a)(1)(B)(ii).
24   19 U.S.C. § 1677b(a)(2).
25   19 U.S.C. § 1677b(a)(4), (e).
26   19 U.S.C. § 1677b(e).
27   19 U.S.C. § 1677b(c). For more detail on this issue *see* Section 4.9.
28   19 U.S.C. § 1677b(a)(1)(A).

the subject merchandise outside of the United States to an unaffiliated purchaser in the United States."[29] That is also the date for determining the appropriate exchange rate for converting prices in foreign currency into U.S. dollars.[30]

In determining foreign market value, the ITA may use averaging and generally recognized sampling techniques whenever there is a significant volume of sales or number of adjustments.[31] The authority to select averages and statistical sampling "rests exclusively" with the Secretary of Commerce (and thus the ITA).[32]

When the goods are manufactured in one country and then shipped to another, from which they are exported to the United States, a question arises as to which foreign country is the relevant one. The Act provides a partial answer. Generally, the price in country of transshipment (the "intermediate country") is the correct one *unless*:

(A) The producer knew at the time of the sale that the subject merchandise was destined for exportation;

(B) The goods are merely transshipped through the intermediate country;

(C) Sales of the goods in the intermediate country are too small to form an adequate basis for comparison; or

(D) The goods are not produced in the intermediate country.[33]

Other issues relating to the determination of foreign market value are discussed below. These problems include issues arising out of sales at less than the costs of production; constructed values; imports from nonmarket economy countries; special rules for multinational corporations; and adjustments necessary to ensure a proper comparison of value with price.

§ 4.7   Sales Below Cost Disregarded

The central question in most antidumping proceedings is whether and to what degree the foreign producer or exporter is selling its goods in the home market below the cost of production. Sales are below cost if they do not recover total costs, both fixed and variable, over a commercially reasonable period. Thus, a significant volume of sales by a foreign producer at prices that cover only its

---

[29]   19 U.S.C. § 1677a(a).

[30]   *See* 19 U.S.C. § 1677b–1.

[31]   19 U.S.C. § 1677f–1.

[32]   19 U.S.C. § 1677f–1(a).

[33]   19 U.S.C. § 1677(a)(3).

variable costs can be disregarded by the ITA in its calculation of the foreign market value of the goods. The Tariff Act explicitly authorizes the ITA to disregard sales at less than the cost of production when it makes its "normal value" determinations.[34]

The ITA will investigate this issue whenever it "has reasonable grounds to believe or suspect" that sales of the goods under investigation "have been made at prices which represent less than the cost of production." If the ITA determines that such sales (a) have occurred "within an extended period of time in substantial quantities," and (b) "were not at prices which permit recovery of all costs within a reasonable period of time," then it "may" disregard the sales in determining the "normal value."[35] Thus, recovery of start-up costs may be prorated over commercially reasonable periods. A decision to disregard sales below cost from the normal value calculation naturally raises the average cost and thus increases the potential to find dumping. A decision to include such sales has the opposite effect.

If the ITA disregards sales as below the cost of production, it will make its "normal value" determination based on the remaining sales of the goods "in the ordinary course of trade."[36] And if no sales are made in the ordinary course of trade, the ITA must instead use the "constructed value" of the goods.[37]

§ 4.8   Nonmarket Economy Constructed Values, Surrogate Countries

The ITA will always use the "constructed value" to determine the foreign market value of imports from nonmarket economy countries.[38] The actual prices used in the exporter's (home) foreign market are deemed irrelevant because they are assumed to be determined bureaucratically and not by market forces. That is, they are not sufficiently subject to the forces of competition to form an accurate standard for comparison.

The Tariff Act delegates to the ITA the authority to determine when imports are from a "nonmarket economy country,"[39] and then insulates that administrative determination from judicial review.[40] The Act nonetheless gives the ITA a basic definition—whether the country's economy operates on "market principles" so that home

---

[34]   19 U.S.C. § 1677b(b).

[35]   *Id.*

[36]   *Id.*

[37]   *See* Section 4.9.

[38]   19 U.S.C. § 1677b(c).

[39]   19 U.S.C. § 1677(18)(A), (C).

[40]   19 U.S.C. § 1677(18)(D).

market sales reflect "fair value." It then provides five factors to consider.[41] The factors include the convertibility of the foreign country's currency, the extent to which wages and prices are determined by government action or free bargaining, the extent of government ownership of the means of production, and the receptivity to private foreign investment.[42]

Although the Act speaks in terms of a country by country decision, the ITA has more often analyzed the particular industrial segment involved, for example with allegedly dumped exports from China. Many WTO members have recognized China as a market economy, and the accession provision allowing treatment of China as a nonmarket economy arguably expired in 2016. One of the major issues pending in WTO dispute proceedings is whether China is now to be considered a market economy, thus escaping constructed value determinations that are more likely to result in antidumping duties. The same issue will emerge in 2018 concerning Vietnam.

If the imports are from a nonmarket economy (NME) country, the Act directs the ITA to "construct" a foreign market value by determining the factors of production (labor, materials, energy, capital, etc.) actually used by the NME to produce the imported goods.[43] The ITA then determines a value for each of those factors of production according to the prices or costs in a market economy that is appropriate under the circumstances. Surrogate countries are appropriate if they are "at a level of economic development comparable to that of the nonmarket economy country" and also are "significant producers of comparable merchandise."[44]

The Act then directs the ITA to add to the cost of production— again, as constructed based on the factors of production—appropriate amounts for general expenses, profits, and the packaging of the goods for shipment to the United States. The amounts for general expenses and profits are to be derived from sales of the same class or kind of merchandise in the "country of exportation,"[45] but this term simply means an "appropriate" market economy country.

In recognition of some of the difficulties with a "cost of production" approach, the Act provides an exception to the constructed value method outlined above, by allowing the use of a different method of constructing a foreign market value for imports from a NME. The ITA may use this alternative method if it finds that

---

[41]   19 U.S.C. § 1677(18)(B).
[42]   *Id.*
[43]   19 U.S.C. § 1677b(c)(1).
[44]   19 U.S.C. § 1677b(c)(4).
[45]   19 U.S.C. § 1677b(e)(1)(B).

the best available information on the factors of production is not adequate. In such cases, the ITA will find a "surrogate" market economy country that produces the goods that are the same as or similar to the merchandise imported from the NME, and base the foreign market value on the price of the goods imported from the surrogate country.[46] Such a construction methodology does not require the ITA to break the pricing of the goods into factors of production.

Several problems arise in the application of this scheme. First, "appropriate" market economy countries may be limited or unavailable. Second, the surrogate market economy countries selected may be obviously inappropriate, when compared to the level of economic development of the NME. Third, producers in such countries may not furnish the necessary information, even though the ITA is authorized to use the "best available information."[47] Fourth, there is no necessary relationship between the price so constructed by the ITA and any price that the NME producer may decide to charge. This leaves the NME producer or exporter always open to antidumping duties, and there is no pre-transaction analytical path for avoiding such duties.

§ 4.9   Market Economy Constructed Values

The ITA may use constructed values not only for imports from NME countries, but in other circumstances as well. It is directed to construct a foreign market value whenever merchandise comparable to the imported merchandise is not offered for sale either in the home market of the foreign producer or exporter or for export from that home market to other countries.[48] A constructed foreign market value is also to be used when so many sales in the home market are below cost of production, and therefore are disregarded, such that the remaining sales provide an inadequate basis for determining foreign market value.[49]

In such a case, the ITA will calculate the foreign market value based on one of three methodologies: (1) the producer's actual costs, plus sales, general, and administrative expenses, and plus a profit for the specific product under investigation; *or* (2) the producer's actual costs and profit for the products in the same category as those under investigation; or (3) a weighted average of other producers'

---

[46]   19 U.S.C. § 1677b(c)(2).
[47]   19 U.S.C. § 1677b(c)(1).
[48]   19 U.S.C. § 1677b(a)(2).
[49]   19 U.S.C. § 1677b(b).

actual costs and profit for the category of products under
investigation.[50]

The Act also has a special rule for determining the foreign
market value of merchandise produced by a corporation with
production facilities in two or more countries. This "special rule for
certain multinational corporations" applies when there are
insufficient sales by that producer in its home market on which to
base a comparison of its export sales to the United States.[51] If the
foreign market value of the goods produced in the country of
exportation is less than the price of the goods produced in the
corporation's facilities in another country, the ITA "shall" construct
a foreign market value which reflects the price of the goods produced
in the non-exporting country.

§ 4.10 United States Price

To determine whether dumping exists, the ITA will compare the
foreign market value ("normal value") of the goods with the price
charged for export to the United States. The Tariff Act recognizes two
different methods for calculating this price:

Export Price

The ITA generally uses the "export price" for the price of the
goods for exportation to the United States. This is the price at which
the goods are first sold *outside* of the United States to an unaffiliated
person before the goods are imported into the United States.[52] The
standard example of this is when a foreign producer or exporter
contacts an unaffiliated U.S. business in order to distribute a foreign
product in the United States and the parties agree on the sale terms
(price, quantity, delivery, etc.).

Constructed Export Price

If, however, the foreign exporter first sells the goods to an
affiliated person outside the United States—such that this "export"
price is not a reliable one—, then the ITA may use the "constructed
export price."[53] This is the price at which the goods are first sold to
an unaffiliated person *in* the United States irrespective of whether it
occurs before or after importation. This typically occurs when a
foreign exporter or producer first sells to a U.S. subsidiary, and in
that case the relevant price is that charged by the subsidiary to the
first unaffiliated U.S. buyer.

---

[50]   19 U.S.C. § 1677b(e)

[51]   19 U.S.C. § 1677b(d).

[52]   19 U.S.C. § 1677a(a).

[53]   19 U.S.C. § 1677a(b).

§ 4.11 "Foreign Like Product" Determinations and Required Adjustments

All of the U.S. price analysis above depends upon a comparison of the prices of a "foreign like product,"[54] a concept also relevant in injury determinations by the ITC.[55] Because merchandise sold in foreign markets is often different, due to cultural, technical or legal constraints, the determination of comparability of merchandise sold in the foreign market to the imported merchandise is often a crucial one. The Act provides a definition, with a hierarchy of criteria.[56] Thus, merchandise that is identical in physical characteristics, and produced in the same country by the same person as the imported merchandise, is to be categorized as a "foreign like product."[57]

If such identical merchandise is not available, the ITA next looks for merchandise that is (a) produced in the same country by the same person, (b) has similar component materials, and (c) is approximately equal in value to the imported merchandise.[58]

If none of these reference points is available, the ITA is to look at merchandise that (a) is produced in the same country by the same person, (b) is of "the same general class or kind as the subject merchandise," and (c) in the judgment of the ITA "may reasonably be compared with" the imported merchandise.[59] In practice, the ITA considers similarities in the physical characteristics, use and expectations of ultimate purchasers, including advertising of the product, and distribution channels.

A considerable number of adjustments are necessary to obtain comparable prices for goods sold in home markets and for export to the United States. To determine the United States price, packing costs and container costs are added to the purchase price or exporter's sales price, if they are not already included in that price.[60] If generally applicable taxes are either not collected or are rebated by the exporting government, these also may be included in the determining United States price.

Adjustments deducted from the purchase price or exporter's sales price include any expenses, such as freight or insurance, included in that price and attributable to the costs of bringing the goods from the country of export to the United States and most export

---

[54]   19 U.S.C. § 1677b(a)(1)(A), (B).

[55]   *See* Section 4.13.

[56]   19 U.S.C. § 1677(16).

[57]   19 U.S.C. § 1677(16)(A).

[58]   19 U.S.C. § 1677(16)(B).

[59]   19 U.S.C. § 1677(16)(C).

[60]   19 U.S.C. § 1677a(d)(1).

taxes of the exporting country.[61] Deductions also are appropriate for any commissions and other expenses for selling in the United States and for the costs of additional processing or assembly in the United States after importation and before sale.[62] However, the additional cost of U.S. product liability insurance is not a permitted adjustment.[63]

Adjustments and exchange rate conversions are also made to determine the foreign market value of the goods. Exchange rate conversions are required whenever the foreign market price or the United States price is not in U.S. dollars. The rates for the relevant sales period as determined quarterly by the Federal Reserve Bank of New York are ordinarily used except when those rates are fluctuating rapidly. In such cases, the ITA will test whether the dumping margin remains if the rates from the prior quarter are used. If the margin disappears, the dumping is attributed to exchange rate fluctuations and the ITA may determine that no dumping occurred.

To obtain an equivalent of the United States price, the ITA will add to the foreign market value an amount equal to the packing costs and container costs for shipment to the United States.[64] Allowances may be made for sales at different trade levels (wholesale versus retail), quantity or production cost discounts, differences in the circumstances of sale, and physical differences in the merchandise.[65] Differences in the circumstances of the sale include credit terms, warranties, servicing, technical assistance, and advertising allowances. Adjustments for cost differences in the circumstances of sale are allowed even if they do not give rise to comparable price increases in the foreign market. This is true even if they involve rebates or discounts not made available to all purchasers.[66] These decisions reflect the substantial deference the courts give to the ITA on the important issue of adjustments to its price and value calculations.

§ 4.12 The U.S. Injury Determination

Antidumping proceedings in the United States are conducted in two stages. In the second stage, the International Trade Commission (ITC) must determine whether the dumping has caused material

---

[61] 19 U.S.C. § 1677a(d)(2).

[62] 19 U.S.C. § 1677a(e).

[63] *See Carlisle Tire & Rubber Co. v. United States*, 622 F. Supp. 1071 (C.I.T. 1985).

[64] 19 U.S.C. § 1677b(a)(1), last paragraph.

[65] 19 U.S.C. § 1677b(a)(b).

[66] *See Zenith Radio Corp. v. United States*, 783 F.2d 184 (Fed.Cir.1986).

injury to concerned domestic industries.[67] The following sections review the material injury determination under U.S. law, including market definition, injury factors, and causation.

The injury determination by the ITC involves three separate inquiries:

> (1)   First, the ITC must define the relevant "domestic like product" and relevant domestic industry;

> (2)   Second, the ITC must determine whether that industry is suffering or threatened with a sufficiently serious injury; and

> (3)   Third, the ITC must determine whether a causal link exists between the injury and the sale at LTFV (*i.e.*, the dumping).

The most import of these steps is the determination of whether a domestic industry is suffering a sufficient injury due to a dumping practice. The Tariff Act provides that an affirmative injury determination is required when an industry in the United States is materially injured or is threatened with material injury by reason of dumped imports, or the establishment of an industry in the United States is materially retarded.[68] Both the "material injury"[69] and the "threat of material injury"[70] standards apply to established industries, and substantial overlap exists between the two. Nonetheless, the Act makes clear that they are independent grounds for a sufficient injury to justify antidumping duties.[71]

§ 4.13   The "Like Product" and Relevant Domestic Industry Determinations

In order to assess "material injury," the ITC and the ITA must first identify the relevant products and relevant domestic industry affected by an alleged dumping practice. The ITA necessarily focuses on which foreign products are like those alleged to be dumped in the United States. For its part, the ITC must define the relevant domestic industry that produces like products in order to make its injury determinations.

The term "domestic like product" is defined by the Tariff Act as one that is "like, or in the absence of like, most similar in characteristics and uses with" to the foreign product under

---

[67]   19 U.S.C. § 1673(2).

[68]   *Id.*

[69]   19 U.S.C. § 1677(7).

[70]   19 U.S.C. § 1677(7)(F).

[71]   19 U.S.C. § 1673(2).

investigation. WTO Appellate Body rulings suggest that products are "like" when they are "directly competitive or substitutable". *See* Korea-Alcoholic Beverages, WT/DS75/AB/R (1999). The "like product" determination is a factual issue for which the ITC weighs six relevant factors: "(1) physical characteristics and uses; (2) common manufacturing facilities and production employees; (3) interchangeability; (4) customer perceptions; (5) channels of distribution; and, where appropriate, (6) price."[72]

Separately, the ITA and the ITC must define the relevant domestic industry potentially affected by dumped products. The Tariff Act defines the relevant "domestic industry" as those domestic producers, "as a whole," of a "domestic like product" or as those producers "whose collective output of a domestic like product constitutes a major proportion" of the total domestic production.[73] Although these definitions apply to both the ITA and the ITC, they do not always agree on the outcome. The ITA and ITC may assess injury on a geographically regional basis if local producers sell most of their production in the regional market, and the demand in the regional market is not supplied by other U.S. producers outside that region.[74]

The determination of domestic "like products" and the relevant domestic industry can be decisive for ITA dumping determinations, but especially for ITC injury determinations. Some early cases on the subject, which have paved the way for later determinations, illustrate the point. In one early case, for example, the ITC excluded large screen TVs from the U.S. domestic industry definition. This had the effect of giving Japanese TV exports a much larger market share in the United States, thus supporting an affirmative injury determination.[75] In another early decision, the ITC narrowly defined the relevant U.S. industry as the canned mushrooms industry, noting that fresh and canned mushrooms were not always interchangeable. This narrow market definition again supported a preliminary injury determination.[76]

Variations on the theme of defining "domestic like products" can occur if the ITC decides it is appropriate to exclude domestic companies that also import the allegedly dumped goods or are related to the importer or foreign producer.[77] The ITC may also define the

---

[72]   *Cleo Inc. v. U.S.*, 501 F.3d 1291, 1295 (Fed. Cir. 2007).

[73]   19 U.S.C. § 1677(4)(A).

[74]   19 U.S.C. § 1677(4)(C).

[75]   *See Television Sets from Japan*, U.S.I.T.C. Publ. No. 367 (March 1971).

[76]   Canned Mushrooms from the People's Republic of China, U.S.I.T.C. Publ. No. 1324 (Dec. 1982).

[77]   19 U.S.C. § 1677(4)(B).

domestic industry regionally in situations where this reflects market realities.[78] Thus, which U.S. firms the ITC chooses to include or exclude in its "domestic like product" definition is an important threshold issue in material injury analysis.

§ 4.14 Material Domestic U.S. Injury

There are two potential perspectives on the appropriate meaning of "material" to U.S. industries. The first is that the term means any economic harm that is more than trivial, inconsequential, or *de minimis*. The second is that it contemplates a higher threshold, something not quite as hurtful as the "serious injury" required for safeguard relief,[79] but yet still serious in the ordinary sense of that word. The consensus view is that the spirit of Article VI of the GATT embraces the higher standard.

The Tariff Act defines material injury as "harm which is not inconsequential, immaterial, or unimportant."[80] (The same standard applies in CVD proceedings[81] and much of the law in the area is therefore interchangeable.) In assessing this essential "material injury" standard, the Act *requires* the ITC to consider three factors:

(1) The volume of imports of the merchandise subject to investigation;

(2) The effect of these imports on prices in the United States for like products; and

(3) The impact of these imports on domestic producers of like products, but only in the context of domestic U.S. production operations.[82]

The Act also *permits* the ITC to consider "such other economic factors as are relevant to the determination regarding whether there is material injury by reason of imports."[83]

The ITC is required to explain its analysis of each factor considered and the relevance of each to its determination.[84] The Tariff Act nonetheless provides that the "presence or absence" of any of the three mandatory factors should "not necessarily give decisive guidance" to the ITC in its material injury determination, and the

---

[78]   19 U.S.C. § 1677(4)(C).

[79]   *See* Chapter 6.

[80]   19 U.S.C. § 1677(7)(A).

[81]   *See* Chapter 5.

[82]   19 U.S.C. § 1677(7)(B)(i). *See also Angus Chemical Co. v. United States*, 140 F.3d 1478 (Fed. Cir. 1998)(holding that consideration of these three factors is mandatory).

[83]   19 U.S.C. § 1677(7)(B)(ii).

[84]   19 U.S.C. § 1677(7)(B).

ITC is not required to give any particular weight to any one factor.[85] The factors are examined through extensive statistical analyses. This analysis occurs on industry-wide basis and not on a company-by-company basis. The ITC may select whatever time period best represents the business cycle, best captures the competitive conditions in the industry, and most reasonably allows it to determine whether an injury exists.[86]

The Tariff Act also gives detailed guidance for the ITC's assessment of each of the three mandatory considerations for a material injury determination:

Volume of Imports

The Tariff Act requires the ITC to consider the absolute volume of imports or any increase in volume of imports in evaluating the volume of imports subject to investigation. This assessment may be made in relation to production or consumption in the United States. The standard in this evaluation is whether the volume of imports, viewed in any of the above ways, is significant.[87]

Data relating to the volume of imports are an important factor in the ITC's injury determinations. In particular, the ITC is more concerned with the dynamics of the market share, such as a significant increase in market penetration, than it is with the size of market share. It is also primarily concerned with the effects that market share changes might have on profits and lost sales. Injury can be found when an a specific producer has a small market share, but imports from its home country as a whole are increasing rapidly, such that the U.S. domestic industry must reduce its prices in response. On the other hand, a large market share for the importer, coupled with increases in production, domestic shipments, exports, employment and profits of the domestic industry, may indicate that no material injury is occurring.

Price Effects

While price issues are obviously crucial to any determination of dumping margins, they have no strict correlation to injury determinations. However, under the Tariff Act, the ITC may consider the effect of the dumped imports upon prices for like products in the domestic market. This is done to the extent that such a consideration assists in evaluating whether (1) there is significant "price underselling" in the imported merchandise as compared with the

---

[85]   19 U.S.C. § 1677(7)(E)(ii).

[86]   19 U.S.C. § 1677(7)(C).

[87]   19 U.S.C. § 1677(7)(C)(i).

price of like products of the United States;[88] and (2) the effect of the imported merchandise is otherwise to depress domestic prices to a significant degree or to prevent price increases that otherwise would occur.[89]

If there is no price underselling, but instead the exporters cut their U.S. prices to effectively meet price competition from U.S. producers, this is traditionally considered only "technical dumping" and precludes a finding of material injury. The rationale for this approach focuses upon the purposes behind antidumping law, *i.e.*, to prevent unfair dumping not to protect against pro-competitive trade practices. Thus, technical dumping constitutes a defense to U.S. material injury determinations.

Price underselling is not a *per se* basis for a finding of injury. For example, if the demand for the product is not price sensitive, price underselling will not be a central consideration. Price underselling in fact may be irrelevant, even if domestic producers are losing sales in the United States, if their inability to sell goods is not attributable to dumped imports. For example, the industry's decline may have been caused by its failure to develop, produce, and market a competitive product. (The next Section will analyze causation issues in more detail.)

Substantial underselling, on the other hand, will lead to an affirmative injury finding where the market is price sensitive. The ITC looks for a pervasive pattern of underselling. If the ITC finds that demand for a specific product is price sensitive and importers are engaging in price underselling, it will then examine whether domestic producers are being forced into price suppression[90] or actual price cutting.[91] Because price suppression can be as severe a burden to domestic producers as can an actual price cutting, the ITC will find an injury if it determines that, in order to respond to dumping practices, domestic producers have lowered or have been unable to raise their prices to accommodate rising costs.

Domestic Industry Impact

The impact on a domestic industry of an allegedly dumped product commonly is the most important consideration in the ITC's injury analysis. Because of this, the Tariff Act provides supplemental factors for the ITC to consider. These include (1) actual and potential

---

[88]   19 U.S.C. § 1677(7)(C)(ii)(I).

[89]   19 U.S.C. § 1677(7)(C)(ii)(II).

[90]   Price suppression arises when the domestic industry can affect smaller price increases on those articles directly competitive with dumped imports than it can on those articles that directly compete with non-dumped imports.

[91]   Price cutting arises when the domestic industry is compelled to lower its prices to meet the prices of dumped imports in an attempt to protect its market share.

decline in "output, sales, market share, profits, productivity, return on investments, and utilization of capacity," (2) impact on domestic prices, (3) actual and potential "negative effects on cash flow, inventories, employment, wages, growth, ability to raise capital, and investment," (4) actual and potential negative effects "on the existing development and production efforts of the domestic industry," and (5) in specific cases, the magnitude of the margin of dumping.[92]

The ITC must evaluate all these relevant economic factors within the context of the business cycle and conditions of competition in the affected industry.[93] But the ITC traditionally relies primarily on two of the factors in making this determination. First, the industry must be in a distressed or a stagnant condition. Second, the low domestic price levels must be a factor in the industry's difficulties (*e.g.*, high unemployment or low capacity utilization rate), and these low prices must be having a serious negative effect on profits.

The ITC will often base an affirmative determination of material injury on severe downward trends in profitability among domestic producers. In one early case, the ITC found that a drop in the ratio of net profit to sales from 5.55 percent to 1.05 percent over a three year period, coupled with a 75 percent decline in the aggregate profit in the relevant industry in the same period, justified an affirmative determination of material injury.[94] Thus, it is not necessary that an industry suffer an actual loss as a prerequisite to a finding of material injury. On the other hand, simply because an industry is experiencing a decline in profitability does not require a finding of material injury due to dumping. Other factors unrelated to dumping, such as general economic conditions and industry over expansion, may be the cause.

The effect of dumped imports on employment in the relevant domestic industry often is a significant factor. Employment data are not dispositive, because decreases in the level or rate of employment may be due to a broad spectrum of economic factors unrelated to dumping. The economic downturn that commenced in 2008 provides ample proof of this point. Nonetheless, sudden changes in domestic employment during the period of dumping can be an important signal for the ITC that dumping is causing a material injury. For example, in one early case the ITC found that a thirty-five percent drop in employment during the period of dumping was a reasonable indication of material injury.[95] On the other hand, an increase in

---

[92]   19 U.S.C. § 1677(7)(C)(iii).

[93]   19 U.S.C. § 1677(7)(C), last paragraph.

[94]   Sugars and Syrups from Canada, 46 Fed. Reg. 51,086 (1981).

[95]   Montan Wax from the German Democratic Republic, 45 Fed. Reg. 73,821 (1980).

employment levels and hours worked can be a strong indication that
dumping did not cause a material injury to the relevant industry.

Finally, the utilization of plant capacity can be a significant
factor in material injury determinations. Again, however, such
capacity utilization data commonly is affected by a variety of factors.
For example, the ITC found a reasonable indication of material injury
from the fact that capacity utilization in the affected industry fell
from 88 percent to 77 percent in two years.[96] In contrast, the ITC
found no material injury in a case where capacity utilization
similarly dropped from 85 to 77 percent, because in that instance
frequent equipment breakdowns and quality control disruptions
were the actual cause of the decline.[97]

§ 4.15   Threat of Material Domestic U.S. Injury

The ITC may also make an affirmative determination of injury
if it finds that dumped imports represent a "threat of material injury"
to a domestic industry. The Tariff Act lists a variety of "economic
factors" that the ITC "shall consider" in making such a determination
in an antidumping proceeding:

(1) Any "unused production capacity or imminent,
substantial increase in production capacity in the exporting
country. . .indicating   the   likelihood   of   substantially
increased imports" into the United States;

(2) "A significant rate of increase of the volume or
market penetration of imports. . .indicating the likelihood
of substantially increased imports":

(3) Whether imports are coming to the U.S. "at prices
that are likely to have a significant depressing or
suppressing effect on domestic prices, and are likely to
increase demand for further imports";

(4) The existing inventories of the imported products;

(5) The potential that the low prices for the imports
will cause other production facilities in the foreign country
to switch to the products at issue;

(6) "The actual and potential negative effects on the
existing development and production efforts" of the
industry in the United States.[98]

---

[96]   Carbon Steel Wire Rod from Brazil, Belgium, France, and Venezuela, 47 Fed.
Reg. 13,927 (1982).

[97]   Crystal from Austria and Italy, 45 Fed. Reg. 31,830 (1980).

[98]   19 U.S.C. § 1677(7)(F)(i).

Beyond these, the Tariff Act requires the ITC to consider "any other demonstrable adverse trends that indicate the probability" of a material injury to a domestic industry.[99]

The Tariff Act obligates the ITC to consider these factors "as a whole" in making a determination of a threat of material injury. Therefore, the presence or absence of any one factor is not determinative. In any event, the determination "may not be made on the basis of mere conjecture or supposition."[100]

The case of *Rhone Poulenc, S.A. v. United States* represents a good example of the analysis of the *threat* of material injury standard.[101] That case involved the shipment of package anhydrous sodium metasilicate from France to the United States. The U.S. industry comprised four companies, only one of which was demonstrably injured. *Rhone Poulenc* was an appeal to the U.S. Court of International Trade (CIT) from an ITC decision concerning the "threat of material injury" standard. The court first rejected the importers' argument that the market penetration by imports is the crucial fact in determining whether such a threat exists. Instead, the court found that it is proper for the ITC to consider, in determining the likelihood of future injury, the developing trends in all the indicators used to determine whether an actual injury has occurred. These indicators of actual injury include the volume of imports, the effect of imports on prices, and the impact of the imports on the domestic industry. The court also held that the ITC also may look at likely future conduct of the producers or exporters of the dumped products.

§ 4.16 Material Retardation of a U.S. Industry

The Tariff Act recognizes as an independent ground for an affirmative injury determination by the ITC that a dumped import product has "materially retarded" the establishment of an industry in the United States. The standard for "material retardation" is applied to new industries, *i.e.*, those that have made a substantial commitment to begin production, or have recently begun production.[102] As the ITA notes in its Antidumping Manual, however, this ground "has rarely been asserted by a petitioner in an antidumping duty investigation. Nearly all antidumping

---

[99] *Id.*

[100] 19 U.S.C. § 1677(7)(F)(ii).

[101] 592 F. Supp. 1318 (C.I.T. 1984).

[102] For a rare analysis of this standard *see BMT Commodity Corp. v. United States*, 667 F. Supp. 880 (C.I.T. 1987), *affirmed* 852 F.2d 1285 (Fed. Cir.1988), *cert. denied*, 489 U.S. 1012 (1989).

investigations have been initiated on the basis of petitions by established manufacturers of the domestic like product."[103]

§ 4.17   Causation

Causation of material injury by dumping is a required element in addition to, and independent of, the finding of material injury, threat of material injury or the material retardation of the establishment of a domestic industry. As a practical matter, however, the two separate inquiries (injury and causation) are closely linked. As a result, when it has found a material injury from a dumping practice the ITC has tended to make an affirmative injury determination without a lengthy analysis of the causal link between them. In a negative injury determination, on the other hand, the ITC may engage in a rather detailed analysis of causation.

The Tariff Act requires a simple causation element: that the material injury to a domestic industry is "by reason of" the dumped imports.[104] Again, the same standard applies in CVD proceedings and the law in this area is largely interchangeable.[105] The causation requirement is not a high one. Imports need only be *a* cause material injury, and need not be the most substantial or primary cause of injury suffered by domestic industry.[106] The "by reason of" standard nonetheless "mandates a showing of causal—not merely temporal—connection between the LTFV goods and the material injury."[107] The Tariff Act does not require that the ITC use any particular methodology in making such a determination, and it "need not isolate the injury caused by other factors from injury caused by unfair imports."[108] Nonetheless, the Federal Circuit has made clear that "causation is not shown if the subject imports contributed only 'minimally or tangentially to the material harm.' "[109]

In short, the causation element of an affirmative injury determination can be satisfied if the dumped products contribute in any noteworthy way to the conditions of the domestic injury.[110] Under

---

[103]   Antidumping Manual, *supra* footnote 9, Ch. 18, I, § III.D.

[104]   19 U.S.C. § 1673(2).

[105]   *See* Section 5.18.

[106]   *See Nippon Steel Corp. v. Int'l Trade Comm'n*, 345 F.3d 1379, 1381 (Fed. Cir. 2003) (observing that " 'dumping' need not be the sole or principal cause of injury").

[107]   *Gerald Metals, Inc. v. United States*, 132 F.3d 716, 720 (Fed. Cir. 1997).

[108]   *Bratsk Aluminium Smelter v. U.S.*, 444 F.3d 1369, 1373 (Fed. Cir. 2006)(quoting *Taiwan Semiconductors Industry Ass'n v. Int'l Trade Comm'n*, 266 F.3d 1339, 1345 (Fed. Cir. 2001)).

[109]   *Id.*, 444 F.3d at 1373 (*quoting Gerald Metals, Inc. v. U.S.*, 132 F.3d 716, 722 (Fed. Cir. 1997)).

[110]   Antidumping Manual, *supra* footnote 9, Ch. 18, I, § III.F (observing that:[t]he courts have held that this causation standard is satisfied if the dumped imports

this "contributing cause" standard, causation of injuries may be found despite the absence of correlation between dumped imports and the alleged injuries if there is substantial evidence that the volume of dumped imports was a contributing factor to the price depression experienced by the domestic injury.

In examining the causal link between the dumped imports and the material injury, the ITC must consider other causal factors that might be responsible for the alleged injury. The Federal Circuit has observed that, for example, "the increase in volume of subject imports priced below domestic products and the decline in the domestic market share are not in and of themselves sufficient to establish causation."[111] On this reasoning, the Federal Circuit has held that the ITC must consider "fairly traded imports" of non-dumped products as a relevant "other economic factor" for causation inquiries.[112] Thus, the ITC may uncover other major causes for the problems of the domestic industry. These may include huge unnecessary expenses, chronic excess capacity, inefficiency, poor quality, price sensitivity or increased domestic competition. Nonetheless, the presence of such major alternative causes of injury does not foreclose the possibility that imports have been *a* contributing cause of the industry's problems.[113]

The ITC may, but is not required to, consider the margin of dumping when evaluating causation. In practice the margin of dumping is an important factor in the ITC's causation analysis. If the dumping margin is slight or substantially lower than the margin of underselling, this may indicate that the injury was not caused by the dumped imports. The imports will still be able to undersell domestic producers, even if the prices of the imports are raised to their fair values. If, on the other hand, the dumping margin is higher than the margin of underselling, thereby enabling the foreign exporters to undersell domestic producers, the dumping can be the cause of the material injury because the foreign exporters may be able to undersell only because of the higher dumping margin.

§ 4.18 Cumulative Causation

Can "material injury" be caused by imports from exporters from more than one country through the cumulative effect of many small

---

contribute, more than minimally or tangentially, to the injured condition of the domestic industry").

[111] *See Bratsk Aluminium Smelter v. U.S.*, 444 F.3d 1369, 1374 (Fed. Cir. 2006).

[112] *See, e.g., Gerald Metals, Inc. v. United States*, 132 F.3d 716, 723 (Fed.Cir.1997).

[113] *See, e.g., Iwatsu Electric Co., Ltd. v. United States*, 758 F. Supp. 1506 (C.I.T.1991) (regarding small telephone systems); *United Engineering & Forging v. United States*, 779 F. Supp. 1375 (C.I.T.1991), *opinion after remand* 14 ITRD 1748 (C.I.T.1992)(regarding crankshafts).

injuries? There are arguments against cumulating each source of dumping to determine whether it is a cause of injury. For example, cumulation could penalize small suppliers who would not have caused injury if their dumping had been examined in isolation. Nevertheless, the WTO Antidumping Agreement expressly permits cumulation.[114]

In turn, the Tariff Act requires that the ITC cumulatively assess the impact of reasonably coincident dumped imports from two or more countries if the imports compete with like U.S. products. In specific, the Act requires the ITC to "cumulatively assess the volume and price effects of imports of the subject merchandise from all countries" with respect to which antidumping petitions were initiated on the same day, "if such imports compete with each other and with domestic like products in the United States market."[115] An exception exists, however, for imports from beneficiary countries of the Caribbean Basin Initiative.[116] The injury to a domestic industry is measured by the cumulated results of dumping on the ground that an injury caused by "many nibbles" is just as harmful as one caused by "one large bite." Cumulation also provides administrative ease, since the ITC is not required to allocate the amount of injury caused by each individual exporter.

The CIT has observed that to support a cumulation decision, the ITC "must find a reasonable overlap of competition between imports from the subject countries and the domestic like product."[117] In applying this "reasonable overlap" test, the ITC traditionally has applied a "four factor" test: "(1) fungibility; (2) sales or offers in the same geographic markets; (3) common or similar channels of distribution; and (4) simultaneous presence."[118]

§ 4.19 Negligible Dumping

The Tariff Act requires that an investigation be terminated with a negative injury determination if imports of the subject merchandise are negligible. The Act defines imports as "negligible" if they "account for less than 3 percent of the volume of all such merchandise imported into the United States" during a defined twelve-month period."[119] In the case of cumulated imports from a number of

---

[114] *See* Antidumping Agreement, art. 3.3.

[115] 19 U.S.C. § 1677(7)(G)(i). *See also Hosiden Corp. v. Advanced Display Mfrs. of America,* 85 F.3d 1561 (Fed. Cir. 1996).

[116] 19 U.S.C. § 1677(7)(G)(ii)(III).

[117] *Nucor Corp. v. U.S.,* 594 F. Supp. 2d 1320, 1347 (C.I.T. 2008)(*quoting Noviant OY v. United States,* 451 F. Supp. 2d 1367, 1379 (C.I.T. 2006), *aff'd, Nucor Corp. v. U.S.,* 601 F.3d 1291 (Fed. Cir. 2010).

[118] *Nucor Corp. v. U.S.,* 594 F. Supp. 2d 1320, 1347 (C.I.T. 2008).

[119] 19 U.S.C. § 1677(24)(A)(i).

countries,[120] however, the "negligible threshold rises to seven percent.[121] In computing import volumes for these purposes, the ITC "may make reasonable estimates on the basis of available statistics."[122]

§ 4.20   Other U.S. Antidumping Law Issues

Congress ratified and implemented the Uruguay Round accords of 1994 under the Uruguay Round Agreements Act (URAA).[123] For present purposes, the most significant aspect of the URAA was the amendment of the Tariff Act to conform to the WTO Antidumping Agreement. In nearly all respects, therefore, the important rules on dumping determinations as described in the Sections above conform to the requirements of the Antidumping Agreement. Nonetheless, the URAA brought about a few more specific changes that are worthy of emphasis here.

De Minimis Dumping

First, the URAA amended the Tariff Act to address "*de minimis*" dumping.[124] In specific, the Tariff Act now requires that, in making its preliminary determination, the administrating authority (the Secretary of Commerce/ITA) disregard any weighted average dumping margin less than two percent ad valorem or the equivalent specific rate for the subject merchandise. Any weighted average dumping margin that is *de minimis* must also be disregarded by the administrating authority when making its final determinations.[125]

Statutory Time Limits

A significant new effect from the adoption of the URAA is the imposition of strict new statutory timelines for dumping determinations by the ITA. In the case of an antidumping petition, the ITA must make an initial determination within twenty days after the date on which a petition is filed. This time limit may be extended to forty days in any case where the ITA is required to poll or otherwise determine support for the petition by the industry and exceptional circumstances exist.[126] Time limits are also imposed on the ITC in its determination of whether there is a reasonable indication of injury.[127] Separately, the ITC must conduct a review no

---

[120]   *See* Section 4.18.

[121]   19 U.S.C. § 1677(24)(A)(ii).

[122]   19 U.S.C. § 1677(24)(C).

[123]   Public Law No. 103–465, 108 Stat. 4809.

[124]   19 U.S.C. § 1673b(b)(3).

[125]   19 U.S.C. § 1673d(a).

[126]   19 U.S.C. § 1673a(c).

[127]   19 U.S.C. § 1673b(a).

later than five years after an antidumping duty order is issued to determine whether revoking the order would likely lead to continuation or recurrence of dumping and material injury. Known as the "sunset provision," this new requirement will result in periodic reviews of antidumping (and countervailing duty) orders.

Notice and Comment

The URAA requires that the ITC provide all parties to a proceeding with an opportunity to comment, prior to a formal decision, on *all* information collected in the investigation.

Other Issues

The URAA requires the ITC to consider the magnitude of the dumping margin (although not the magnitude of the margin of subsidization) in making material injury determinations. It also authorizes an adjustment to sales-below-cost calculations to accommodate start-up costs,[128] a new rule thought to be particularly beneficial to high-tech products. It also adds a new "captive production" section intended to remove such internal sales from ITC injury determinations.[129]

§ 4.21 U.S. Antidumping Procedures—Petition and Response

In an antidumping proceeding, the ITA determines whether the imports are being sold at less than fair value (LTFV), and the ITC makes a separate determination concerning injury to the domestic industry making like or similar products.

United States antidumping proceedings may be initiated by a petition of the Commerce Department itself or by a union or aggrieved business (or by a group association of aggrieved workers or businesses).[130] The petition requirements are set forth by regulation.[131] In general, antidumping proceedings involve the ITA first making a determination that a petition adequately alleges the relevant statutory requirements. But before initiating an investigation, the ITA must find that a sufficient percentage of the affected domestic industry supports the petition—for Tariff Act requires that a petition be filed "by or on behalf of" the entire domestic industry.[132] Generally, this requires that the industry or workers who support the petition account for (a) at least twenty-five

---

[128]   19 U.S.C. § 1677b(f)(1)(c).
[129]   19 U.S.C. § 1677b(f)(1)(c)(iii).
[130]   19 U.S.C. § 1673a.
[131]   *See* 19 C.F.R. § 351.202.
[132]   19 U.S.C. § 1673a(b).

percent of the total industry, and (b) at least fifty percent of those that have actually expressed an opinion for or against the petition.[133]

After an initial investigation, the ITA then makes a "preliminary determination"—based on the "best information available at the time"—on whether there is "a reasonable basis to believe" that the relevant standard is met.[134] Such information cannot include any information furnished by respondents or a respondent's government. In other words, the ITA accepts or rejects the petition almost entirely on the basis of the information supplied by the petitioner.

Once the petition is accepted, the proceeding becomes genuinely adversarial if (as is commonly the case) the parties alleged to be dumping respond to the questionnaires on sales volumes and prices that the ITA creates and later verifies through on-site investigations. It is rare for the "defense" to have more than one month to respond. Any failure to respond or permit verification risks an ITA dumping decision on the "best information available," *i.e.* most likely the petitioner's or other respondent's submissions.[135] Because this obviously is an undesirable result, the best information available rule functions much like a subpoena. Most respondents answer the ITA's questionnaires. Protective orders preserve the confidentiality of the often strategically valuable information submitted to the ITA and ITC in dumping proceedings.[136] Such orders ordinarily preclude release to corporate counsel engaged in competitive decision-making, but permit release to outside counsel and outside experts.

§ 4.22 U.S. Antidumping Administrative Determinations

Antidumping proceedings under U.S. law involve four stages. The ITC first makes a "preliminary determination" that, again "based on the best information available to it" at that time, there is "a reasonable indication" that the challenged practice presents a real or threatened material injury to the affected domestic industry.[137] Use of the best information available test encourages responses to DOJ dumping questionnaires by opponents. If the ITC makes such a finding, the ITA then makes a preliminary determination whether there is "a reasonable basis to believe" that goods are being sold at

---

[133]   19 U.S.C. § 1673a(c)(4).

[134]   19 U.S.C. § 1673a(c).

[135]   *See* 19 U.S.C. § 1677e(b). *See Maverick Tube Corp. v. U.S.*, 857 F.3d 1353 (May 30, 2017) (U.S. authorities may use "adverse facts available" against non-cooperative parties).

[136]   19 U.S.C. § 1677f.

[137]   19 U.S.C. § 1673b(a).

LTFV.[138] If the ITA makes such a preliminary determination, it proceeds to make a "final determination" concerning sales at LTFV.[139] If the ITA finds sales at LTFV as a final determination, the ITC then must make a final determination concerning injury.[140] Thus the chain of decision-making in antidumping proceedings runs as follows:

ITC Preliminary Injury Determination

ITA Preliminary Dumping Determination

ITA Final Dumping Determination

ITC Final Injury Determination

Congress has repeatedly amended U.S. antidumping law so as to accelerate the rate at which these determinations are made. At this point, it is common for the proceeding to be completed within one year. U.S. antidumping duties are then and in the future assessed retrospectively for each importation such that the amount payable varies for each importer and transaction.

Any goods imported after an ITA preliminary determination of sales at LTFV (Stage Two) will be subject to any antidumping duties imposed later, after final determinations are made.[141] In customs law parlance, liquidation of the goods is suspended. In "critical circumstances," the antidumping duties will also be imposed on goods entered 90 days *before* suspension of liquidation.[142] Critical circumstances exist when there is a prior history of dumping or the importer knew or should have known that the sales were below fair value, and there have been massive imports over a relatively short period of time.[143] Because the ITA has demonstrated a willingness to order retroactive antidumping duties and need not find injury as a result of the massive imports, the importer's risks in such a case may be substantial.

§ 4.23 The Importance of the ITA Preliminary Dumping Determination

As a practical matter, the ITA's *preliminary* determination that dumping has occurred will place significant, often overwhelming, pressure on the importers of the covered goods. This is so because at that point any covered goods become subject to antidumping duties

---

[138]   19 U.S.C. § 1673b(b).

[139]   19 U.S.C. § 1673d(a).

[140]   19 U.S.C. § 1673d(b).

[141]   19 U.S.C. § 1673b(d).

[142]   19 U.S.C. § 1673b(e).

[143]   19 U.S.C. § 1673b(e)(1).

that are ultimately determined once the ITA and ITC complete their investigations and make any affirmative final determinations. The preliminary determination, therefore, tends to discourage or even cut off the imports, because at that point importers generally must post cash or bonds to cover any duties as determined by the ITA in its preliminary determination. At a minimum, they likely will have to raise their import prices—unless and until either the ITA or the ITC makes a contrary final determination once the agencies have completed their respective administrative proceedings.

Thus, once a petition is filed, importers will not know what their liabilities for duties will be and must post an expensive bond in the meantime to gain entry. Foreign exporters frequently raise their "United States prices" to the level of home market prices soon after such a preliminary determination. If they do, antidumping law will have accomplished its essential purpose. However, the U.S. Tariff Act disfavors termination of the proceeding on the basis of voluntary undertakings of compliance.[144]

United States antidumping proceedings may be settled by the ITA if the respondents formally agree to cease exporting to the United States within six months or agree to revise their prices so as to eliminate the margin of the dumping.[145] Because price revision agreements are hard to monitor, they are disfavored by the ITA. But an agreement to cease exports also cancels any outstanding suspension of liquidation. The total time secured in this manner may allow foreigners a window of opportunity to establish market presence prior to shifting production to the United States. If requested, the ITA and ITC may proceed to their final determinations after a settlement is agreed. If the respondents prevail, normal trading will resume; but if the petitioners prevail, the settlement agreement will remain in effect. The ITA monitors all settlement agreements and may assess civil penalties (in addition to antidumping duties) in the event of a breach.[146]

§ 4.24 U.S. Antidumping Duty Reviews

The ITA final determination of sales at LTFV establishes the amount of any antidumping duties. Because duties are not imposed to support any specific domestic price, they are set at the "margin of dumping" (the amount the "normal value" exceeds the United States price).[147] In the ordinary case, antidumping duties are retroactive to the date of the suspension of liquidation that occurred when the ITA

---

[144] 19 U.S.C. § 1673c.

[145] 19 U.S.C. § 1673c(b).

[146] 19 U.S.C. § 1673c(i).

[147] 19 U.S.C. § 1677(35).

preliminarily found dumping. However, if the ITC final determination is one of threatened (not actual) domestic injury, the duties usually apply as from the ITC's final decision and not retroactively to the suspension date.

The antidumping duty remains in force only as long as the dumping occurs. Upon request, annual ITA reviews are conducted.[148] The ITA also may review and revoke or modify any antidumping order if changed circumstances warrant such an action, but the burden of proof is on the proponent.[149] In accordance with the WTO Antidumping Agreement, the ITA must also conduct a review of finial antidumping determinations every five years.[150]

Problems in assessing and collecting antidumping duties may arise because the antidumping duty order applies to goods that do not exactly correspond to normal U.S. Harmonized Tariff Schedule (HTS) classifications. While the ITA is given some leeway to modify an antidumping order to accommodate such problems, it may not use them as an excuse to exclude merchandise falling within the scope of the order. Where, on the other hand, merchandise was deliberately excluded from the original antidumping order, the ITA may not subsequently include that merchandise in an anti-circumvention order (see immediately Section 4.26 below).[151]

§ 4.25 U.S. Anti-Circumvention Rules

In 1988, Congress enacted important amendments to Tariff Act to address the "circumvention" of antidumping duties. These "anti-circumvention" rules entered into force while the subject was under discussion in the GATT Uruguay Round negotiations. Ultimately, the WTO Antidumping Agreement included no substantive rules on anti-circumvention, but also did not forbid the practice.

The Tariff Act addresses circumvention in a variety of ways. First, it allows the ITA to ignore fictitious markets in the source country when calculating the foreign market "normal value."[152] Moreover, the ITA may include within the scope of an antidumping order merchandise "completed or assembled" in the United States if such merchandise includes "parts or components produced in the foreign country" that is the original subject of the order.[153] The principal requirements are that the process of completion or assembly in the United States is "minor or insignificant" and the

---

[148] 19 U.S.C. § 1675(a).
[149] 19 U.S.C. § 1675(b).
[150] 19 U.S.C. § 1675(c).
[151] *See, e.g., Wheatland Tube Co. v. United States*, 161 F.3d 1365 (Fed.Cir.1998).
[152] 19 U.S.C. § 1677b(a)(5).
[153] 19 U.S.C. § 1677j(a).

value of the components themselves is a "significant portion of the total value of the merchandise.[154]

Similarly, when the exporter ships the components to a third country for assembly and subsequent exportation to the United States, such circumvention efforts can be defeated by extending an antidumping order to those goods as well.[155] Again, such an action is appropriate if the assembly in the third country is "minor or insignificant" and the components themselves represent the principal value of the merchandise.[156]

§ 4.26 Appeals—United States Courts

A party to an administrative antidumping proceeding may appeal an adverse final determination of the ITA or ITC to the U.S. Court of International Trade (CIT). The CIT was established in 1980 as the successor to the U.S. Court of Customs. The CIT is an Article III court, and its nine judges are appointed by the President with the Advice and Consent of the Senate. The CIT possesses all the powers in law and equity of a U.S. District Court, including the authority to enter money judgments against the United States, but with three general limitations. These limitations (a) prohibit its issuance of injunctions or writs of mandamus in challenges to trade adjustment rulings, (b) allow it to issue only declaratory relief in suits for accelerated review of pre-importation administrative actions, and (c) limit its power to order disclosure of confidential information to a narrowly defined class of cases.

The CIT has "exclusive" subject matter jurisdiction over suits against the United States, its agencies, or its officers arising from any law pertaining to revenue from imports, tariffs, duties or embargoes, or the enforcement of such laws and certain related regulations. The court's exclusive jurisdiction also includes any civil action commenced by the United States that arises out of an import transaction, as well as the authority to review final agency decisions concerning antidumping duties and countervailing duties as well as eligibility for trade adjustment assistance.

CIT decisions may be appealed first to the Court of Appeals for the Federal Circuit (formerly the Court of Customs and Patent Appeals), and ultimately to the U.S. Supreme Court.

---

[154] 19 U.S.C. § 1677j(a)(2).
[155] 19 U.S.C. § 1677j(b).
[156] *Id.*

§ 4.27   WTO and NAFTA Appeals

International institutions also play an increasingly significant role in the resolution of trade disputes. The most important of these is the WTO's Dispute Settlement Body ("DSB"). Dissatisfied parties in domestic administrative proceedings may convince their government to challenge an adverse antidumping before the DSB based on alleged violations of the WTO Antidumping Agreement. As Chapter 1 examines in detail, proceedings before the DSB are governed by a separate WTO Agreement, the Dispute Settlement Understanding (DSU). The DSU generally provides that the involved member states first must pursue consultations. If those consultations are not successful, either party may request that the DSB establish a panel to investigate the dispute and issue a written report. Panel decisions are appealable on issues of law to the WTO's Appellate Body.

Three points are worthy of emphasis concerning proceedings before the DSB. First, since the WTO came into being in 1994, dispute settlement before the DSB, once initiated, is compulsory and binding.[157] Second, this dispute settlement option is not open to private litigants, only member state governments may file an action before the DSB. Finally, although formally binding, the WTO has no direct power to compel compliance with its decisions. Nonetheless, it may order compensation for the aggrieved state(s) or authorize retaliatory trade sanctions, and these may provide a significant incentive for an offending state to bring its domestic law into compliance.

Separately, a special international institution exists for trade disputes involving the three member states of the North American Free Trade Agreement (NAFTA)—the U.S., Canada, and Mexico. NAFTA uniquely provides for resolution of antidumping disputes through "bi-national panels." Such panels apply the domestic law of the importing country, and provide a substitute for judicial review of the decisions of administrative agencies of the importing country. Indeed, the initiation of a review under NAFTA divests the CIT of jurisdiction over the same dispute. Although the decisions of such bi-national panels are not formally binding in U.S. law, the ITA or ITC may decide to review any administrative action to conform to an adverse panel decision, including through a revocation or reduction of antidumping duties. Subsequent U.S. FTAs do not include the NAFTA binational panel system of review of national AD and CVD decisions.

---

[157]   For more detail, *see* Section 1.14.

§ 4.28 WTO Rulings on U.S. Antidumping Law, Zeroing, the Byrd Amendment

The WTO Appellate Body (AB) has taken a restrictive view of what constitutes permissible antidumping duties and in fact has repeatedly ruled against the United States in disputes with other countries. In the *Thai-steel from Poland* dispute, for example, the WTO rejected a cursory material injury determination by the ITC, stressing that all relevant economic factors must be considered. Similarly, in the *United States-Hot-Rolled Steel from Japan* dispute, the AB found bias in the determination of normal value when low-priced sales from a respondent to an exporter were automatically excluded. The AB also indicated that injury determinations must include an analysis of captive production markets in addition to merchant markets. It thus observed that causation in such determinations must be rigorously scrutinized.

Separately, a WTO panel ruled that the Commerce Department's refusal to revoke an antidumping order against South Korean DRAMS was inconsistent with Article 11.2 of the Antidumping Agreement. Hence, U.S. regulations regarding the likelihood of continued dumping after a three-year hiatus are suspect under the Antidumping Agreement. The Court of International Trade, on the other hand, has found that the U.S. regulations in question are consistent with the WTO Antidumping Agreement. The Court took the position that the WTO panel ruling was not binding precedent, merely persuasive.

The Zeroing Controversy

In a series of decisions that ran through 2006, the WTO's Appellate Body also repeatedly ruled against "zeroing," a methodology used in dumping margin calculations by the United States, the EU and other WTO members. To understand this practice, first note that a foreign producer likely will have numerous sales in its home country. As a result, in order to calculate the "home market price," the ITA must use the *average* price from all such sales.[158] This average price is then compared to the "export price" to yield the dumping margin. Under zeroing, however, the ITA in effect considered only those home market sales that were *above* the export price; for sales *below* the export price, it simply assigned a "zero" (*i.e.*, not a negative number). Because on average this meant a higher home country comparison price, it also resulted in a higher average dumping margin.

---

[158] *See* 19 U.S.C. § 1677(35).

In a series of decisions, WTO panels declared that this practice violates United States' obligations under the Article 2.4 of the Antidumping Agreement.[159] Notwithstanding these decisions, the Federal Circuit has repeatedly upheld the methodology as a reasonable interpretation of the actual language in the Tariff Act.[160] In response to the repeated adverse rulings by the WTO, and the 2013 Federal Circuit judgment in *Union Steel,* the ITA has discontinued the practice of zeroing in antidumping investigations but maintained it in antidumping duty reviews.[161]

The "Byrd Amendment" Controversy

The WTO Appellate Body also ruled against the United States with respect to the Continued Dumping and Subsidy Offset Act of 2000 (CDSOA, also known as the "Byrd Amendment"). The controversial aspect of that Act was a mechanism under which the U.S. government funneled the antidumping duties that it collected back to the members of the affected domestic industry. As a result, CDSOA in effect subsidized domestic industries through antidumping procedures, because it made those industries the financial beneficiaries of any duties ultimately assessed.

Nine other member states of the WTO promptly challenged CDSOA pursuant to the procedures set forth in the WTO's Dispute Settlement Understanding (DSU). *See* Chapter 1. Following unsuccessful negotiations, a WTO panel concluded that CDSOA was inconsistent with Articles 5.4, 18.1, and 18.4 of the antidumping Agreement (as well as various provisions of other WTO Agreements). The United States then appealed to the WTO's Appellate Body (AB).

In its ruling, the AB first observed that CDSOA was subject to the obligations in the Antidumping Agreement because it was a "specific action against" dumping. It also found that the only permitted responses to dumping under the Antidumping Agreement are "definitive antidumping duties, provisional measures and price undertakings." The AB ultimately concluded that, because CDSOA did not fall into any of these allowed responses to dumping, it was

---

[159]   *See, e.g.,* Appellate Body Report, *United States—Laws, Regulations and Methodology for Calculating Dumping Margins ("Zeroing"),* ¶ 222, WT/DS294/AB/R, adopted May 9, 2006.

[160]   *See, e.g., Corus Staal BV v. U.S. Dep't of Commerce,* 395 F.3d 1343 (Fed. Cir. 2005); *Union Steel v. United States,* 713 F.3d 1101 (Fed. Cir. 2013) (use of zeroing permissible in administrative reviews but not antidumping investigations).

[161]   *See Antidumping Proceedings: Calculation of the Weighted Average Dumping Margin and Assessment Rate in Certain Antidumping Proceedings,* 75 Fed. Reg. 81533 (Dep't Commerce Dec. 28, 2010); *Union Steel, supra* note 160.

inconsistent with U.S. obligations under the Antidumping Agreement.[162]

When the United State failed to comply with this decision, the WTO authorized the claimant countries to retaliate in their domestic trade laws as permitted under Article 22 of the DSU.[163] Congress then bowed to the pressure created by the WTO decisions and repealed CDSOA effective October 1, 2007.

§ 4.29   Text of WTO Antidumping Agreement

(Agreement on Implementation of Article VI of the General Agreement on Tariffs and Trade 1994)

(Selected Provisions)

PART I

Article 1

Principles

An anti-dumping measure shall be applied only under the circumstances provided for in Article VI of GATT 1994 and pursuant to investigations initiated[1] and conducted in accordance with the provisions of this Agreement. The following provisions govern the application of Article VI of GATT 1994 in so far as action is taken under anti-dumping legislation or regulations.

Article 2

Determination of Dumping

2.1   For the purpose of this Agreement, a product is to be considered as being dumped, i.e. introduced into the commerce of another country at less than its normal value, if the export price of the product exported from one country to another is less than the comparable price, in the ordinary course of trade, for the like product when destined for consumption in the exporting country.

2.2   When there are no sales of the like product in the ordinary course of trade in the domestic market of the exporting country or when, because of the particular market situation or the low volume of the sales in the domestic market of the exporting country,[2] such sales do not permit a proper

---

[162]   *See Appellate Body Report, United States—Continued Dumping and Subsidy Offset Act of 2000,* WT/DS217/R, WT/DS234/R, Jan. 16, 2003.

[163]   *See, e.g., United States—Continued Dumping and Subsidy Offset Act of 2000, Original Complaint by Canada—Recourse to Arbitration by the United States under Article 22.6 of the DSU,* WT/DS234/ARB/CAN, 31 August 2004.

[1]   The term "initiated" as used in this Agreement means the procedural action by which a Member formally commences an investigation as provided in Article 5.

[2]   Sales of the like product destined for consumption in the domestic market of the exporting country shall normally be considered a sufficient quantity for the determination of the normal value if such sales constitute 5 per cent or more of the sales of the product under consideration to the importing Member, provided that a

comparison, the margin of dumping shall be determined by comparison with a comparable price of the like product when exported to an appropriate third country, provided that this price is representative, or with the cost of production in the country of origin plus a reasonable amount for administrative, selling and general costs and for profits.

2.2.1   Sales of the like product in the domestic market of the exporting country or sales to a third country at prices below per unit (fixed and variable) costs of production plus administrative, selling and general costs may be treated as not being in the ordinary course of trade by reason of price and may be disregarded in determining normal value only if the authorities[3] determine that such sales are made within an extended period of time[4] in substantial quantities[5] and are at prices which do not provide for the recovery of all costs within a reasonable period of time. If prices which are below per unit costs at the time of sale are above weighted average per unit costs for the period of investigation, such prices shall be considered to provide for recovery of costs within a reasonable period of time.

2.2.1.1   For the purpose of paragraph 2, costs shall normally be calculated on the basis of records kept by the exporter or producer under investigation, provided that such records are in accordance with the generally accepted accounting principles of the exporting country and reasonably reflect the costs associated with the production and sale of the product under consideration. Authorities shall consider all available evidence on the proper allocation of costs, including that which is made available by the exporter or producer in the course of the investigation provided that such allocations have been historically utilized by the exporter or producer, in particular in relation to establishing appropriate amortization and depreciation periods and allowances for capital expenditures and other development costs. Unless already reflected in the cost allocations under this sub-paragraph, costs shall be adjusted appropriately for those non-recurring items of cost which benefit future and/or current production, or for circumstances in which costs

---

lower ratio should be acceptable where the evidence demonstrates that domestic sales at such lower ratio are nonetheless of sufficient magnitude to provide for a proper comparison.

[3]   When in this Agreement the term "authorities" is used, it shall be interpreted as meaning authorities at an appropriate senior level.

[4]   The extended period of time should normally be one year but shall in no case be less than six months.

[5]   Sales below per unit costs are made in substantial quantities when the authorities establish that the weighted average selling price of the transactions under consideration for the determination of the normal value is below the weighted average per unit costs, or that the volume of sales below per unit costs represents not less than 20 per cent of the volume sold in transactions under consideration for the determination of the normal value.

during the period of investigation are affected by start-up operations.[6]

2.2.2 For the purpose of paragraph 2, the amounts for administrative, selling and general costs and for profits shall be based on actual data pertaining to production and sales in the ordinary course of trade of the like product by the exporter or producer under investigation. When such amounts cannot be determined on this basis, the amounts may be determined on the basis of:

(i) the actual amounts incurred and realized by the exporter or producer in question in respect of production and sales in the domestic market of the country of origin of the same general category of products;

(ii) the weighted average of the actual amounts incurred and realized by other exporters or producers subject to investigation in respect of production and sales of the like product in the domestic market of the country of origin;

(iii) any other reasonable method, provided that the amount for profit so established shall not exceed the profit normally realized by other exporters or producers on sales of products of the same general category in the domestic market of the country of origin.

2.3 In cases where there is no export price or where it appears to the authorities concerned that the export price is unreliable because of association or a compensatory arrangement between the exporter and the importer or a third party, the export price may be constructed on the basis of the price at which the imported products are first resold to an independent buyer, or if the products are not resold to an independent buyer, or not resold in the condition as imported, on such reasonable basis as the authorities may determine.

2.4 A fair comparison shall be made between the export price and the normal value. This comparison shall be made at the same level of trade, normally at the ex-factory level, and in respect of sales made at as nearly as possible the same time. Due allowance shall be made in each case, on its merits, for differences which affect price comparability, including differences in conditions and terms of sale, taxation, levels of trade, quantities, physical characteristics, and any other differences which are also demonstrated to affect price comparability.[7] In the cases referred to in paragraph 3, allowances for costs, including duties and taxes, incurred between importation and resale, and for profits accruing, should also be made. If in

---

[6]   The adjustment made for start-up operations shall reflect the costs at the end of the start-up period or, if that period extends beyond the period of investigation, the most recent costs which can reasonably be taken into account by the authorities during the investigation.

[7]   It is understood that some of the above factors may overlap, and authorities shall ensure that they do not duplicate adjustments that have been already made under this provision.

these cases price comparability has been affected, the authorities shall establish the normal value at a level of trade equivalent to the level of trade of the constructed export price, or shall make due allowance as warranted under this paragraph. The authorities shall indicate to the parties in question what information is necessary to ensure a fair comparison and shall not impose an unreasonable burden of proof on those parties.

2.4.1   When the comparison under paragraph 4 requires a conversion of currencies, such conversion should be made using the rate of exchange on the date of sale,[8] provided that when a sale of foreign currency on forward markets is directly linked to the export sale involved, the rate of exchange in the forward sale shall be used. Fluctuations in exchange rates shall be ignored and in an investigation the authorities shall allow exporters at least 60 days to have adjusted their export prices to reflect sustained movements in exchange rates during the period of investigation.

2.4.2   Subject to the provisions governing fair comparison in paragraph 4, the existence of margins of dumping during the investigation phase shall normally be established on the basis of a comparison of a weighted average normal value with a weighted average of prices of all comparable export transactions or by a comparison of normal value and export prices on a transaction-to-transaction basis. A normal value established on a weighted average basis may be compared to prices of individual export transactions if the authorities find a pattern of export prices which differ significantly among different purchasers, regions or time periods, and if an explanation is provided as to why such differences cannot be taken into account appropriately by the use of a weighted average-to-weighted average or transaction-to-transaction comparison.

2.5   In the case where products are not imported directly from the country of origin but are exported to the importing Member from an intermediate country, the price at which the products are sold from the country of export to the importing Member shall normally be compared with the comparable price in the country of export. However, comparison may be made with the price in the country of origin, if, for example, the products are merely transshipped through the country of export, or such products are not produced in the country of export, or there is no comparable price for them in the country of export.

2.6   Throughout this Agreement the term "like product" ("produit similaire") shall be interpreted to mean a product which is identical, i.e. alike in all respects to the product under consideration, or in the absence of such a product, another product which, although not alike in all respects, has characteristics closely resembling those of the product under consideration.

---

[8]   Normally, the date of sale would be the date of contract, purchase order, order confirmation, or invoice, whichever establishes the material terms of sale.

2.7 This Article is without prejudice to the second Supplementary Provision to paragraph 1 of Article VI in Annex I to GATT 1994.

Article 3

Determination of Injury[9]

3.1 A determination of injury for purposes of Article VI of GATT 1994 shall be based on positive evidence and involve an objective examination of both *(a)* the volume of the dumped imports and the effect of the dumped imports on prices in the domestic market for like products, and *(b)* the consequent impact of these imports on domestic producers of such products.

3.2 With regard to the volume of the dumped imports, the investigating authorities shall consider whether there has been a significant increase in dumped imports, either in absolute terms or relative to production or consumption in the importing Member. With regard to the effect of the dumped imports on prices, the investigating authorities shall consider whether there has been a significant price undercutting by the dumped imports as compared with the price of a like product of the importing Member, or whether the effect of such imports is otherwise to depress prices to a significant degree or prevent price increases, which otherwise would have occurred, to a significant degree. No one or several of these factors can necessarily give decisive guidance.

3.3 Where imports of a product from more than one country are simultaneously subject to anti-dumping investigations, the investigating authorities may cumulatively assess the effects of such imports only if they determine that *(a)* the margin of dumping established in relation to the imports from each country is more than *de minimis* as defined in paragraph 8 of Article 5 and the volume of imports from each country is not negligible and *(b)* a cumulative assessment of the effects of the imports is appropriate in light of the conditions of competition between the imported products and the conditions of competition between the imported products and the like domestic product.

3.4 The examination of the impact of the dumped imports on the domestic industry concerned shall include an evaluation of all relevant economic factors and indices having a bearing on the state of the industry, including actual and potential decline in sales, profits, output, market share, productivity, return on investments, or utilization of capacity; factors affecting domestic prices; the magnitude of the margin of dumping; actual and potential negative effects on cash flow, inventories, employment, wages, growth, ability to raise capital or investments. This list is not exhaustive, nor can one or several of these factors necessarily give decisive guidance.

3.5 It must be demonstrated that the dumped imports are, through the effects of dumping, as set forth in paragraphs 2 and 4, causing injury within the meaning of this Agreement. The demonstration of a causal

---

[9] Under this Agreement the term "injury" shall, unless otherwise specified, be taken to mean material injury to a domestic industry, threat of material injury to a domestic industry or material retardation of the establishment of such an industry and shall be interpreted in accordance with the provisions of this Article.

relationship between the dumped imports and the injury to the domestic industry shall be based on an examination of all relevant evidence before the authorities. The authorities shall also examine any known factors other than the dumped imports which at the same time are injuring the domestic industry, and the injuries caused by these other factors must not be attributed to the dumped imports. Factors which may be relevant in this respect include, *inter alia,* the volume and prices of imports not sold at dumping prices, contraction in demand or changes in the patterns of consumption, trade restrictive practices of and competition between the foreign and domestic producers, developments in technology and the export performance and productivity of the domestic industry.

3.6   The effect of the dumped imports shall be assessed in relation to the domestic production of the like product when available data permit the separate identification of that production on the basis of such criteria as the production process, producers' sales and profits. If such separate identification of that production is not possible, the effects of the dumped imports shall be assessed by the examination of the production of the narrowest group or range of products, which includes the like product, for which the necessary information can be provided.

3.7   A determination of a threat of material injury shall be based on facts and not merely on allegation, conjecture or remote possibility. The change in circumstances which would create a situation in which the dumping would cause injury must be clearly foreseen and imminent.[10] In making a determination regarding the existence of a threat of material injury, the authorities should consider, *inter alia,* such factors as:

(i)   a significant rate of increase of dumped imports into the domestic market indicating the likelihood of substantially increased importation;

(ii)   sufficient freely disposable, or an imminent, substantial increase in, capacity of the exporter indicating the likelihood of substantially increased dumped exports to the importing Member's market, taking into account the availability of other export markets to absorb any additional exports;

(iii)   whether imports are entering at prices that will have a significant depressing or suppressing effect on domestic prices, and would likely increase demand for further imports; and

(iv)   inventories of the product being investigated.

No one of these factors by itself can necessarily give decisive guidance but the totality of the factors considered must lead to the conclusion that further dumped exports are imminent and that, unless protective action is taken, material injury would occur.

---

[10]   One example, though not an exclusive one, is that there is convincing reason to believe that there will be, in the near future, substantially increased importation of the product at dumped prices.

3.8 With respect to cases where injury is threatened by dumped imports, the application of anti-dumping measures shall be considered and decided with special care.

Article 4

Definition of Domestic Industry

4.1 For the purposes of this Agreement, the term "domestic industry" shall be interpreted as referring to the domestic producers as a whole of the like products or to those of them whose collective output of the products constitutes a major proportion of the total domestic production of those products, except that:

> (i) when producers are related[11] to the exporters or importers or are themselves importers of the allegedly dumped product, the term "domestic industry" may be interpreted as referring to the rest of the producers;

> (ii) in exceptional circumstances the territory of a Member may, for the production in question, be divided into two or more competitive markets and the producers within each market may be regarded as a separate industry if *(a)* the producers within such market sell all or almost all of their production of the product in question in that market, and *(b)* the demand in that market is not to any substantial degree supplied by producers of the product in question located elsewhere in the territory. * * *

4.2 When the domestic industry has been interpreted as referring to the producers in a certain area, i.e. a market as defined in paragraph 1(ii), anti-dumping duties shall be levied only on the products in question consigned for final consumption to that area. When the constitutional law of the importing Member does not permit the levying of anti-dumping duties on such a basis, the importing Member may levy the anti-dumping duties without limitation only if *(a)* the exporters shall have been given an opportunity to cease exporting at dumped prices to the area concerned or otherwise give assurances pursuant to Article 8 and adequate assurances in this regard have not been promptly given, and *(b)* such duties cannot be levied only on products of specific producers which supply the area in question.

4.3 Where two or more countries have reached under the provisions of paragraph 8(a) of Article XXIV of GATT 1994 such a level of integration that they have the characteristics of a single, unified market, the industry in the

---

[11] For the purpose of this paragraph, producers shall be deemed to be related to exporters or importers only if *(a)* one of them directly or indirectly controls the other; or *(b)* both of them are directly or indirectly controlled by a third person; or *(c)* together they directly or indirectly control a third person, provided that there are grounds for believing or suspecting that the effect of the relationship is such as to cause the producer concerned to behave differently from non-related producers. For the purpose of this paragraph, one shall be deemed to control another when the former is legally or operationally in a position to exercise restraint or direction over the latter.

entire area of integration shall be taken to be the domestic industry referred to in paragraph 1.

4.4   The provisions of paragraph 6 of Article 3 shall be applicable to this Article.

Article 5

Initiation and Subsequent Investigation

5.1   Except as provided for in paragraph 6, an investigation to determine the existence, degree and effect of any alleged dumping shall be initiated upon a written application by or on behalf of the domestic industry.

5.2   An application under paragraph 1 shall include evidence of *(a)* dumping, *(b)* injury within the meaning of Article VI of GATT 1994 as interpreted by this Agreement and *(c)* a causal link between the dumped imports and the alleged injury. Simple assertion, unsubstantiated by relevant evidence, cannot be considered sufficient to meet the requirements of this paragraph. The application shall contain such information as is reasonably available to the applicant on the following:

(i)   the identity of the applicant and a description of the volume and value of the domestic production of the like product by the applicant. Where a written application is made on behalf of the domestic industry, the application shall identify the industry on behalf of which the application is made by a list of all known domestic producers of the like product (or associations of domestic producers of the like product) and, to the extent possible, a description of the volume and value of domestic production of the like product accounted for by such producers;

(ii)   a complete description of the allegedly dumped product, the names of the country or countries of origin or export in question, the identity of each known exporter or foreign producer and a list of known persons importing the product in question;

(iii)   information on prices at which the product in question is sold when destined for consumption in the domestic markets of the country or countries of origin or export (or, where appropriate, information on the prices at which the product is sold from the country or countries of origin or export to a third country or countries, or on the constructed value of the product) and information on export prices or, where appropriate, on the prices at which the product is first resold to an independent buyer in the territory of the importing Member;

(iv)   information on the evolution of the volume of the allegedly dumped imports, the effect of these imports on prices of the like product in the domestic market and the consequent impact of the imports on the domestic industry, as demonstrated by relevant factors and indices having a bearing on the state of the domestic industry, such as those listed in paragraphs 2 and 4 of Article 3.

5.3   The authorities shall examine the accuracy and adequacy of the evidence provided in the application to determine whether there is sufficient evidence to justify the initiation of an investigation.

5.4   An investigation shall not be initiated pursuant to paragraph 1 unless the authorities have determined, on the basis of an examination of the degree of support for, or opposition to, the application expressed by domestic producers of the like product, that the application has been made by or on behalf of the domestic industry.[12] The application shall be considered to have been made "by or on behalf of the domestic industry" if it is supported by those domestic producers whose collective output constitutes more than 50 per cent of the total production of the like product produced by that portion of the domestic industry expressing either support for or opposition to the application. However, no investigation shall be initiated when domestic producers expressly supporting the application account for less than 25 per cent of total production of the like product produced by the domestic industry.

* * *

5.6   If, in special circumstances, the authorities concerned decide to initiate an investigation without having received a written application by or on behalf of a domestic industry for the initiation of such investigation, they shall proceed only if they have sufficient evidence of dumping, injury and a causal link, as described in paragraph 2, to justify the initiation of an investigation.

* * *

Article 6

Evidence

6.1   All interested parties in an anti-dumping investigation shall be given notice of the information which the authorities require and ample opportunity to present in writing all evidence which they consider relevant in respect of the investigation in question.

6.1.1   Exporters   or   foreign   producers   receiving questionnaires used in an anti-dumping investigation shall be given at least 30 days for reply. Due consideration should be given to any request for an extension of the 30-day period and, upon cause shown, such an extension should be granted whenever practicable.

6.1.2   Subject to the requirement to protect confidential information, evidence presented in writing by one interested party shall be made available promptly to other interested parties participating in the investigation.

6.1.3   As soon as an investigation has been initiated, the authorities shall provide the full text of the written application

---

[12]   Members are aware that in the territory of certain Members employees of domestic producers of the like product or representatives of those employees may make or support an application for an investigation under paragraph 1.

received under paragraph 1 of Article 5 to the known exporters and to the authorities of the exporting Member and shall make it available, upon request, to other interested parties involved. Due regard shall be paid to the requirement for the protection of confidential information, as provided for in paragraph 5.

6.2   Throughout the anti-dumping investigation all interested parties shall have a full opportunity for the defence of their interests. To this end, the authorities shall, on request, provide opportunities for all interested parties to meet those parties with adverse interests, so that opposing views may be presented and rebuttal arguments offered. Provision of such opportunities must take account of the need to preserve confidentiality and of the convenience to the parties. There shall be no obligation on any party to attend a meeting, and failure to do so shall not be prejudicial to that party's case. Interested parties shall also have the right, on justification, to present other information orally.

* * *

6.5   Any information which is by nature confidential (for example, because its disclosure would be of significant competitive advantage to a competitor or because its disclosure would have a significantly adverse effect upon a person supplying the information or upon a person from whom that person acquired the information), or which is provided on a confidential basis by parties to an investigation shall, upon good cause shown, be treated as such by the authorities. Such information shall not be disclosed without specific permission of the party submitting it.

6.5.1   The authorities shall require interested parties providing confidential information to furnish non-confidential summaries thereof. These summaries shall be in sufficient detail to permit a reasonable understanding of the substance of the information submitted in confidence. In exceptional circumstances, such parties may indicate that such information is not susceptible of summary. In such exceptional circumstances, a statement of the reasons why summarization is not possible must be provided.

6.5.2   If the authorities find that a request for confidentiality is not warranted and if the supplier of the information is either unwilling to make the information public or to authorize its disclosure in generalized or summary form, the authorities may disregard such information unless it can be demonstrated to their satisfaction from appropriate sources that the information is correct.

6.6   Except in circumstances provided for in paragraph 8, the authorities shall during the course of an investigation satisfy themselves as to the accuracy of the information supplied by interested parties upon which their findings are based.

6.7   In order to verify information provided or to obtain further details, the authorities may carry out investigations in the territory of other

Members as required, provided they obtain the agreement of the firms concerned and notify the representatives of the government of the Member in question, and unless that Member objects to the investigation. * * *

6.8 In cases in which any interested party refuses access to, or otherwise does not provide, necessary information within a reasonable period or significantly impedes the investigation, preliminary and final determinations, affirmative or negative, may be made on the basis of the facts available. The provisions of Annex II shall be observed in the application of this paragraph.

* * *

6.10 The authorities shall, as a rule, determine an individual margin of dumping for each known exporter or producer concerned of the product under investigation. In cases where the number of exporters, producers, importers or types of products involved is so large as to make such a determination impracticable, the authorities may limit their examination either to a reasonable number of interested parties or products by using samples which are statistically valid on the basis of information available to the authorities at the time of the selection, or to the largest percentage of the volume of the exports from the country in question which can reasonably be investigated.

6.10.1   Any selection of exporters, producers, importers or types of products made under this paragraph shall preferably be chosen in consultation with and with the consent of the exporters, producers or importers concerned.

6.10.2   In cases where the authorities have limited their examination, as provided for in this paragraph, they shall nevertheless determine an individual margin of dumping for any exporter or producer not initially selected who submits the necessary information in time for that information to be considered during the course of the investigation, except where the number of exporters or producers is so large that individual examinations would be unduly burdensome to the authorities and prevent the timely completion of the investigation. Voluntary responses shall not be discouraged.

* * *

6.12 The authorities shall provide opportunities for industrial users of the product under investigation, and for representative consumer organizations in cases where the product is commonly sold at the retail level, to provide information which is relevant to the investigation regarding dumping, injury and causality.

6.13 The authorities shall take due account of any difficulties experienced by interested parties, in particular small companies, in supplying information requested, and shall provide any assistance practicable.

* * *

Article 7

Provisional Measures

7.1   Provisional measures may be applied only if:

(i)   an investigation has been initiated in accordance with the provisions of Article 5, a public notice has been given to that effect and interested parties have been given adequate opportunities to submit information and make comments;

(ii)   a preliminary affirmative determination has been made of dumping and consequent injury to a domestic industry; and

(iii)   the authorities concerned judge such measures necessary to prevent injury being caused during the investigation.

7.2   Provisional measures may take the form of a provisional duty or, preferably, a security—by cash deposit or bond—equal to the amount of the anti-dumping duty provisionally estimated, being not greater than the provisionally estimated margin of dumping. Withholding of appraisement is an appropriate provisional measure, provided that the normal duty and the estimated amount of the anti-dumping duty be indicated and as long as the withholding of appraisement is subject to the same conditions as other provisional measures.

7.3   Provisional measures shall not be applied sooner than 60 days from the date of initiation of the investigation.

7.4   The application of provisional measures shall be limited to as short a period as possible, not exceeding four months or, on decision of the authorities concerned, upon request by exporters representing a significant percentage of the trade involved, to a period not exceeding six months. When authorities, in the course of an investigation, examine whether a duty lower than the margin of dumping would be sufficient to remove injury, these periods may be six and nine months, respectively.

7.5   The relevant provisions of Article 9 shall be followed in the application of provisional measures.

Article 8

Price Undertakings

8.1   Proceedings may[19] be suspended or terminated without the imposition of provisional measures or anti-dumping duties upon receipt of satisfactory voluntary undertakings from any exporter to revise its prices or to cease exports to the area in question at dumped prices so that the authorities are satisfied that the injurious effect of the dumping is eliminated. Price increases under such undertakings shall not be higher than necessary to eliminate the margin of dumping. It is desirable that the price

---

[19]   The word "may" shall not be interpreted to allow the simultaneous continuation of proceedings with the implementation of price undertakings except as provided in paragraph 4.

increases be less than the margin of dumping if such increases would be adequate to remove the injury to the domestic industry.

8.2   Price undertakings shall not be sought or accepted from exporters unless the authorities of the importing Member have made a preliminary affirmative determination of dumping and injury caused by such dumping.

8.3   Undertakings offered need not be accepted if the authorities consider their acceptance impractical, for example, if the number of actual or potential exporters is too great, or for other reasons, including reasons of general policy. Should the case arise and where practicable, the authorities shall provide to the exporter the reasons which have led them to consider acceptance of an undertaking as inappropriate, and shall, to the extent possible, give the exporter an opportunity to make comments thereon.

8.4   If an undertaking is accepted, the investigation of dumping and injury shall nevertheless be completed if the exporter so desires or the authorities so decide. In such a case, if a negative determination of dumping or injury is made, the undertaking shall automatically lapse, except in cases where such a determination is due in large part to the existence of a price undertaking. In such cases, the authorities may require that an undertaking be maintained for a reasonable period consistent with the provisions of this Agreement. In the event that an affirmative determination of dumping and injury is made, the undertaking shall continue consistent with its terms and the provisions of this Agreement.

8.5   Price undertakings may be suggested by the authorities of the importing Member, but no exporter shall be forced to enter into such undertakings. The fact that exporters do not offer such undertakings, or do not accept an invitation to do so, shall in no way prejudice the consideration of the case. However, the authorities are free to determine that a threat of injury is more likely to be realized if the dumped imports continue.

8.6   Authorities of an importing Member may require any exporter from whom an undertaking has been accepted to provide periodically information relevant to the fulfilment of such an undertaking and to permit verification of pertinent data. In case of violation of an undertaking, the authorities of the importing Member may take, under this Agreement in conformity with its provisions, expeditious actions which may constitute immediate application of provisional measures using the best information available. In such cases, definitive duties may be levied in accordance with this Agreement on products entered for consumption not more than 90 days before the application of such provisional measures, except that any such retroactive assessment shall not apply to imports entered before the violation of the undertaking.

Article 9

Imposition and Collection of Anti-Dumping Duties

9.1   The decision whether or not to impose an anti-dumping duty in cases where all requirements for the imposition have been fulfilled, and the decision whether the amount of the anti-dumping duty to be imposed shall be the full margin of dumping or less, are decisions to be made by the authorities of the importing Member. It is desirable that the imposition be permissive in the territory of all Members, and that the duty be less than the margin if such lesser duty would be adequate to remove the injury to the domestic industry.

9.2   When an anti-dumping duty is imposed in respect of any product, such anti-dumping duty shall be collected in the appropriate amounts in each case, on a non-discriminatory basis on imports of such product from all sources found to be dumped and causing injury, except as to imports from those sources from which price undertakings under the terms of this Agreement have been accepted. The authorities shall name the supplier or suppliers of the product concerned. If, however, several suppliers from the same country are involved, and it is impracticable to name all these suppliers, the authorities may name the supplying country concerned. If several suppliers from more than one country are involved, the authorities may name either all the suppliers involved, or, if this is impracticable, all the supplying countries involved.

9.3   The amount of the anti-dumping duty shall not exceed the margin of dumping as established under Article 2.

* * *

Article 10

Retroactivity

10.1 Provisional measures and anti-dumping duties shall only be applied to products which enter for consumption after the time when the decision taken under paragraph 1 of Article 7 and paragraph 1 of Article 9, respectively, enters into force, subject to the exceptions set out in this Article.

* * *

Article 11

Duration and Review of Anti-Dumping Duties and Price Undertakings

11.1 An anti-dumping duty shall remain in force only as long as and to the extent necessary to counteract dumping which is causing injury.

11.2 The authorities shall review the need for the continued imposition of the duty, where warranted, on their own initiative or, provided that a reasonable period of time has elapsed since the imposition of the definitive anti-dumping duty, upon request by any interested party which submits positive information substantiating the need for a review. Interested parties shall have the right to request the authorities to examine whether the continued imposition of the duty is necessary to offset dumping, whether the injury would be likely to continue or recur if the duty were removed or varied, or both. If, as a result of the review under this paragraph, the authorities determine that the anti-dumping duty is no longer warranted, it shall be terminated immediately.

11.3 Notwithstanding the provisions of paragraphs 1 and 2, any definitive anti-dumping duty shall be terminated on a date not later than five years from its imposition (or from the date of the most recent review under paragraph 2 if that review has covered both dumping and injury, or under this paragraph), unless the authorities determine, in a review initiated before that date on their own initiative or upon a duly substantiated request made by or on behalf of the domestic industry within a reasonable period of time prior to that date, that the expiry of the duty would be likely to lead to continuation or recurrence of dumping and injury. The duty may remain in force pending the outcome of such a review.

11.4 The provisions of Article 6 regarding evidence and procedure shall apply to any review carried out under this Article. Any such review shall be carried out expeditiously and shall normally be concluded within 12 months of the date of initiation of the review.

11.5 The provisions of this Article shall apply *mutatis mutandis* to price undertakings accepted under Article 8.

Article 12

Public Notice and Explanation of Determinations

12.1 When the authorities are satisfied that there is sufficient evidence to justify the initiation of an anti-dumping investigation pursuant to Article 5, the Member or Members the products of which are subject to such investigation and other interested parties known to the investigating authorities to have an interest therein shall be notified and a public notice shall be given.

12.1.1   A public notice of the initiation of an investigation shall contain, or otherwise make available through a separate report, adequate information on the following:

(i)   the name of the exporting country or countries and the product involved;

(ii)   the date of initiation of the investigation;

(iii) the basis on which dumping is alleged in the application;

(iv) a summary of the factors on which the allegation of injury is based;

(v)   the address to which representations by interested parties should be directed;

(vi) the time-limits allowed to interested parties for making their views known.

12.2 Public notice shall be given of any preliminary or final determination, whether affirmative or negative, of any decision to accept an undertaking pursuant to Article 8, of the termination of such an undertaking, and of the termination of a definitive anti-dumping duty. * * *

12.2.1   A public notice of the imposition of provisional measures shall set forth, or otherwise make available through a separate report, sufficiently detailed explanations for the preliminary determinations on dumping and injury and shall refer to the matters of fact and law which have led to arguments being accepted or rejected. Such a notice or report shall, due regard being paid to the requirement for the protection of confidential information, contain in particular:

(i)   the names of the suppliers, or when this is impracticable, the supplying countries involved;

(ii)   a description of the product which is sufficient for customs purposes;

(iii)   the margins of dumping established and a full explanation of the reasons for the methodology used in the establishment and comparison of the export price and the normal value under Article 2;

(iv)   considerations   relevant   to   the   injury determination as set out in Article 3;

(v)   the main reasons leading to the determination.

12.2.2   A public notice of conclusion or suspension of an investigation in the case of an affirmative determination providing for the imposition of a definitive duty or the acceptance of a price undertaking shall contain, or otherwise make available through a separate report, all relevant information on the matters of fact and law and reasons which have led to the imposition of final measures or the acceptance of a price undertaking, due regard being paid to the requirement for the protection of confidential information. In particular, the notice or report shall contain the information described in subparagraph 2.1, as well as the reasons for the acceptance or rejection of relevant arguments or claims made by the exporters and importers, and the basis for any decision made under subparagraph 10.2 of Article 6.

12.2.3   A public notice of the termination or suspension of an investigation following the acceptance of an undertaking pursuant to Article 8 shall include, or otherwise make available through a separate report, the non-confidential part of this undertaking.

12.3 The provisions of this Article shall apply *mutatis mutandis* to the initiation and completion of reviews pursuant to Article 11 and to decisions under Article 10 to apply duties retroactively.

Article 13

Judicial Review

Each Member whose national legislation contains provisions on anti-dumping measures shall maintain judicial, arbitral or administrative tribunals or procedures for the purpose, *inter alia,* of the prompt review of administrative actions relating to final determinations and reviews of determinations within the meaning of Article 11. Such tribunals or procedures shall be independent of the authorities responsible for the determination or review in question.

Article 14

Anti-Dumping Action on Behalf of a Third Country

14.1 An application for anti-dumping action on behalf of a third country shall be made by the authorities of the third country requesting action.

14.2 Such an application shall be supported by price information to show that the imports are being dumped and by detailed information to show that the alleged dumping is causing injury to the domestic industry concerned in the third country. The government of the third country shall afford all assistance to the authorities of the importing country to obtain any further information which the latter may require.

14.3 In considering such an application, the authorities of the importing country shall consider the effects of the alleged dumping on the industry concerned as a whole in the third country; that is to say, the injury shall not be assessed in relation only to the effect of the alleged dumping on the industry's exports to the importing country or even on the industry's total exports.

14.4 The decision whether or not to proceed with a case shall rest with the importing country. If the importing country decides that it is prepared to take action, the initiation of the approach to the Council for Trade in Goods seeking its approval for such action shall rest with the importing country.

Article 15

Developing Country Members

It is recognized that special regard must be given by developed country Members to the special situation of developing country Members when considering the application of anti-dumping measures under this Agreement. Possibilities of constructive remedies provided for by this Agreement shall be explored before applying anti-dumping duties where they would affect the essential interests of developing country Members.

PART II

* * *

Article 17

Consultation and Dispute Settlement

17.1 Except as otherwise provided herein, the Dispute Settlement Understanding is applicable to consultations and the settlement of disputes under this Agreement.

17.2 Each Member shall afford sympathetic consideration to, and shall afford adequate opportunity for consultation regarding, representations made by another Member with respect to any matter affecting the operation of this Agreement.

17.3 If any Member considers that any benefit accruing to it, directly or indirectly, under this Agreement is being nullified or impaired, or that the achievement of any objective is being impeded, by another Member or Members, it may, with a view to reaching a mutually satisfactory resolution of the matter, request in writing consultations with the Member or Members in question. Each Member shall afford sympathetic consideration to any request from another Member for consultation.

17.4 If the Member that requested consultations considers that the consultations pursuant to paragraph 3 have failed to achieve a mutually agreed solution, and if final action has been taken by the administering authorities of the importing Member to levy definitive anti-dumping duties or to accept price undertakings, it may refer the matter to the Dispute Settlement Body ("DSB"). When a provisional measure has a significant impact and the Member that requested consultations considers that the measure was taken contrary to the provisions of paragraph 1 of Article 7, that Member may also refer such matter to the DSB.

17.5 The DSB shall, at the request of the complaining party, establish a panel to examine the matter based upon:

(i) a written statement of the Member making the request indicating how a benefit accruing to it, directly or indirectly, under this Agreement has been nullified or impaired, or that the achieving of the objectives of the Agreement is being impeded, and

(ii) the facts made available in conformity with appropriate domestic procedures to the authorities of the importing Member.

17.6 In examining the matter referred to in paragraph 5:

(i) in its assessment of the facts of the matter, the panel shall determine whether the authorities' establishment of the facts was proper and whether their evaluation of those facts was unbiased and objective. If the establishment of the facts was proper and the evaluation was unbiased and objective, even though the panel might have reached a different conclusion, the evaluation shall not be overturned;

(ii) the panel shall interpret the relevant provisions of the Agreement in accordance with customary rules of interpretation of public international law. Where the panel finds that a relevant provision of the Agreement admits of more than one permissible interpretation, the panel shall find the authorities' measure to be in conformity with the Agreement if it rests upon one of those permissible interpretations.

* * *

ANNEX II

BEST INFORMATION AVAILABLE IN TERMS OF PARAGRAPH 8 OF ARTICLE 6

1.   As soon as possible after the initiation of the investigation, the investigating authorities should specify in detail the information required from any interested party, and the manner in which that information should be structured by the interested party in its response. The authorities should also ensure that the party is aware that if information is not supplied within a reasonable time, the authorities will be free to make determinations on the

basis of the facts available, including those contained in the application for the initiation of the investigation by the domestic industry.

2.   The authorities may also request that an interested party provide its response in a particular medium (e.g. computer tape) or computer language. * * *

3.   All information which is verifiable, which is appropriately submitted so that it can be used in the investigation without undue difficulties, which is supplied in a timely fashion, and, where applicable, which is supplied in a medium or computer language requested by the authorities, should be taken into account when determinations are made. If a party does not respond in the preferred medium or computer language but the authorities find that the circumstances set out in paragraph 2 have been satisfied, the failure to respond in the preferred medium or computer language should not be considered to significantly impede the investigation.

4.   Where the authorities do not have the ability to process information if provided in a particular medium (e.g. computer tape), the information should be supplied in the form of written material or any other form acceptable to the authorities.

5.   Even though the information provided may not be ideal in all respects, this should not justify the authorities from disregarding it, provided the interested party has acted to the best of its ability.

6.   If evidence or information is not accepted, the supplying party should be informed forthwith of the reasons therefor, and should have an opportunity to provide further explanations within a reasonable period, due account being taken of the time-limits of the investigation. If the explanations are considered by the authorities as not being satisfactory, the reasons for the rejection of such evidence or information should be given in any published determinations.

7.   If the authorities have to base their findings, including those with respect to normal value, on information from a secondary source, including the information supplied in the application for the initiation of the investigation, they should do so with special circumspection. In such cases, the authorities should, where practicable, check the information from other independent sources at their disposal, such as published price lists, official import statistics and customs returns, and from the information obtained from other interested parties during the investigation. It is clear, however, that if an interested party does not cooperate and thus relevant information is being withheld from the authorities, this situation could lead to a result which is less favorable to the party than if the party did cooperate.

Chapter 5

SUBSIDIES AND COUNTERVAILING DUTIES

Table of Sections

§ 5.1   Subsidies and International Trade

Unfair international trade practices can arise either through practices of producers or exporters, or through unfair practices of foreign governments. The former are subject to antidumping (AD) law; the latter are subject to countervailing duty (CVD) law, both generating tariffs that are additional to normal WTO tariffs. Either can be equally harmful to domestic industries, which often simultaneously pursue both "trade remedies."

In theory, a countervailing duty offsets exactly an unfair export or other subsidy benefiting internationally traded goods. Proponents of countervailing duties argue that they are necessary to keep imports from being unfairly competitive based on foreign government support. Proponents rarely mention comparable home country subsidies. Opponents argue that there is no coherent standard of "fairness" to justify a rational assessment of such duties. Such opponents also point out that it is often difficult to identify precisely when a subsidy exists as compared to governmental actions to support beneficial commercial activity.

A member state of the World Trade Organization (WTO) may impose an increased tariff on an imported item beyond the regular tariff schedule as a "countervailing duty." Such duties are an authorized response to a foreign government providing a "prohibited" or "actionable" subsidy that permits their exporters to sell at lower prices in other countries. Government subsidies come in many forms, including tax reductions or rebates, tax credits, loan guarantees, below market financing, equity infusions and outright monetary grants. Rapidly developing countries routinely offer subsidies to foreign investors designed to generate exports.

But subsidies are not just a phenomenon in developing countries. The Internal Revenue Code is littered with subsidies that lower the cost of U.S. made goods. The Export-Import Bank (EXIMBANK) traditionally offers low cost loans to overseas buyers of U.S. products. Other developed countries have similar subsidy programs. In all cases, the critical legal issue is which subsidies may be countervailed by CVD duties under the rules of the WTO Agreement on Subsidies and Countervailing Measures (SCM).

In 2017, a major subsidy and dumping dispute split the U.S. business community. Solar panels from China had caused dozens of U.S. producers to go bankrupt, leaving only two insolvent U.S. producers, one China-owned. U.S. authorities ruled that solar panels from China and solar cells from Taiwan had unfairly been subsidized abroad and dumped in the USA, imposing high tariffs on those products. A substantial U.S. industry had emerged to install solar panels, often with U.S. tax incentives. The installers strongly opposed the imposition of the high tariffs and predicted job losses. The outcome of this dispute, with its alternative energy implications, is pending.

§ 5.2   The WTO Agreement on Subsidies and Countervailing Measures (SCM)

International concern with unfair subsidies and countervailing duties is reflected in Articles VI, XVI, and XXIII of the General Agreement on Tariffs and Trade (GATT) 1947 and 1994. An optional Subsidies Code was created under the Tokyo Round of GATT multilateral negotiations. In 1995, the mandatory WTO "Agreement on Subsidies and Countervailing Measures" (SCM Agreement) took effect. Like the WTO Antidumping Agreement, Congress approved and implemented the SCM Agreement through the Uruguay Round Agreements Act of 1994 (URAA).[1]

Under the SCM Agreement, government authorities in an importing member state may impose a CVD in the amount of the subsidy for as long as the subsidy continues. The SCM Agreement also provides substantive rules governing when, and under what circumstances, a member state may impose CVDs to offset a claimed governmental or "public body" subsidy. State-owned-enterprises (SOEs) are not generally treated as public bodies unless performing governmental functions. See U.S.-AD and CVD Duties (tires), WT/DS 379/AB/R (2011) (commercial finance by SOE banks in China). The CVD may only be imposed after an investigation, begun on the request of an affected industry, has demonstrated the existence of a prohibited or actionable "specific" subsidy that has adverse trade effects, such as injury to a domestic industry or "serious prejudice" to the interests of the importing state. See U.S.-Cotton, WT/DS 267/AB/RW (2008) (adverse price suppression trade effects constitute serious prejudice). Finally, there must be a causal link between the subsidy and the alleged injury.

Disputes over subsidies may occur either before national administrative authorities (according to prescribed procedures), or before the WTO's Dispute Settlement Body, or both.[2] In addition, a special WTO "Committee on Subsidies and Countervailing Measures" supervises the implementation of the SCM Agreement by the WTO member states.

---

[1]   Public Law No. 103–465, 108 Stat. 4809.

[2]   See Sections 5.20 and 5.25.

The SCM Agreement generally defines a subsidy as a financial contribution provided by a government that confers a benefit on an exporter. The Agreement establishes three classes of subsidies:

(1)   Prohibited subsidies (e.g., export subsidies, also known as "red light" subsidies, and always deemed specific);

(2) Actionable subsidies, *i.e.*, those that are permissible unless they cause adverse trade effects ("yellow light" subsidies); and

(3)   Non-actionable and non-countervailable subsidies ("green light" subsidies). Under the terms of the SCM Agreement, however, the "green light" category expired in 2000.

The SCM Agreement also granted special exemptions for developing countries that permitted them to phase out their export subsidies and local content rules on a gradual basis. These exemptions were to have expired by 2003, but as of 2014, eighteen countries—principally in the Caribbean and Central America— continue to operate under an extension of this deadline granted by the WTO's Committee on Subsidies and Countervailing Measures.

The SCM Agreement also prescribes procedural rules for the investigation and imposition of CVDs by domestic authorities. These rules address, among other things, the initiation of CVD proceedings, the conduct of investigations, the calculation of the amount of the subsidy, and the right of all interested parties to present information. The Agreement also has special rules relating to subsidies that cause a "serious prejudice" to the interests of another member state, though some of these rules have lapsed. Finally, the SCM has rules on the gathering of evidence in CVD proceedings, on the imposition and collection of CVDs, on provisional measures, and on the permitted length of any allowed CVDs, typically five years. Agricultural subsidies that are not exempted by the WTO Agreement on Agriculture (see Section 1.8) can be challenged under the SCM Agreement.

§ 5.3   Historical Introduction to U.S. CVD Law

United States law has long considered the grant of a subsidy by a foreign government to aid its exporters to be an unfair trade practice. Laws granting a right to impose countervailing duties to counter unfair subsidies have existed since 1897, long before the creation of the GATT. The origin of U.S. laws against export "bounties" or "grants" can be traced to Section 5 of the Tariff Act of

1897.[3] For many years, this law vested almost complete discretion in the Treasury Department to levy CVDs as it saw fit. Several early CVD tariffs targeted tax subsidies on sugar exports.[4] And the U.S. Supreme Court essentially gave the Treasury Department *carte blanche* to impose CVDs whenever foreign government regulations favored exports reaching the United States.[5] Prior to the Trade Act of 1974, U.S. law on CVDs was largely administered as a branch of U.S. foreign policy, not as a private international trade remedy.[6] Indeed, it was not until 1974 that negative bounty or grant determinations by the Treasury Department became subject to judicial review. The Trade Act of 1974 also gave private parties a number of procedural rights, notably time limits for Treasury decisions on their petitions for CVD relief and mandatory publication of Treasury rulings. It is from this point, therefore, that a systematic body of case law interpreting and applying U.S. bounty, grant, and CVD provisions began to develop.

The next major development in the U.S. statutes governing this field arrived in the Trade Agreements Act of 1979. This Act, *inter alia,* codified the rules on the use of CVDs to counteract unfair "export subsidies" as agreed in the Tokyo Round GATT Subsidies Code. In addition, the 1979 Act authorized limited use of CVDs against foreign *domestic* subsidies, a subject the GATT Subsidies Code did not address. Furthermore, the 1979 Act adopted the GATT requirement of proof of an actual injury to a domestic industry.

The Uruguay Round Agreements Act of 1994 implemented the numerous changes of the WTO SCM Agreement into U.S. law. Most important, the URAA amended the Tariff Act of 1930 to reflect a rough arrangement similar to the "red light," "yellow light," and "green light" (now lapsed) categories of the SCM Agreement. The requirements of the Tokyo Round Subsidies Code relating to material injury continued in substantially the same form.

§ 5.4   Two U.S. Statutory Tests

The United States currently has two statutory structures on countervailing duties: Section 1671 of the Tariff Act of 1930 provides a test for products imported from countries that participate in the

---

[3]   30 Stat. 205.

[4]   *See Downs v. United States,* 187 U.S. 496 (1903)(relating to Russia); *United States v. Hills Bros.,* 107 Fed. 107 (2nd Cir. 1901)(relating to the Netherlands).

[5]   *See G.S. Nicholas & Co. v. United States,* 249 U.S. 34 (1919).

[6]   *See Energetic Worsted Corp. v. United States,* 53 C.C.P.A. 36 (1966)(relating to wool from Uruguay); *United States v. Hammond Lead Products,* 440 F.2d 1024 (C.C.P.A. 1971), *cert. denied* 404 U.S. 1005 (1971) (relating to Mexican lead).

WTO SCM Agreement (or its equivalent)[7], as compared to products imported from other countries.[8]

The most important difference between the two is that for imports from a "Subsidies Agreement Country,"[9] CVDs may be imposed only upon an affirmative determination that a U.S. industry is "materially" injured, or threatened with such injury, or its development is materially retarded. For the relatively few other countries, CVDs may be imposed *without* any finding of injury to a domestic industry. In most other significant respects, the two tests are the same.[10] Nonetheless, with the continuing growth in the membership of the WTO (roughly now 160 member states), the possibility of imposing CVDs without a showing of material injury is rapidly decreasing in significance.

§ 5.5   U.S. Implementation of the WTO SCM Agreement

The U.S. statutory provisions on countervailing duties are set forth principally in Section 1671 of the Tariff Act of 1930.[11] As derived from the SCM Agreement, Section 1671 imposes two general conditions on the imposition of countervailing duties. First, the International Trade Administration (ITA) in the Department of Commerce must determine that a foreign state is providing a prohibited or actionable subsidy to its exporters. Second, the International Trade Commission (ITC) must determine that imports benefiting from the subsidy injure, threaten to injure, or retard the establishment of a domestic industry.[12] This second condition embraces proof of causation, a difficult CVD and AD issue. If these conditions are met, a duty equal to the net subsidy "shall be imposed" upon the imports.

Like antidumping duties, countervailing duties are a statutory remedy, one which the President cannot veto or in general otherwise affect. If an injured U.S. industry believes that a countervailable subsidy exists, it may pursue CVD proceedings to their conclusion over the President's objection simply by refusing to withdraw a petition once filed.[13] The President nonetheless may have substantial

---

   [7]   19 U.S.C. § 1671(a)(2).

   [8]   19 U.S.C. § 1671(a)(1).

   [9]   19 U.S.C. § 1671(b)(defining a "Subsidies Agreement Country" as a WTO member state or a country the President has determined has laws that are "substantially equivalent" to the SCM Agreement).

   [10]   *But see* § 1671(c)(stating the other general requirements for the imposition of CVDs that do not apply for countries that are not "Subsidies Agreement Countries").

   [11]   19 U.S.C. § 1671 et seq.

   [12]   19 U.S.C. § 1671(a).

   [13]   19 U.S.C. § 1671c(a).

influence in bringing a CVD proceeding to a positive end. Section 1671 allows the suspension of a proceeding if the subsidizing foreign government or exporters accounting for substantially all of the exports agree to cease exporting to the United States, or to eliminate the subsidy within six months.[14]

The subsidy may be eliminated by imposition of either an export tax or a price increase amounting to the net subsidy. In "extraordinary circumstances" benefiting the domestic industry, the ITA may also suspend a proceeding in the case of a settlement agreement reducing the subsidy by at least eighty-five percent and preventing price cutting in the United States.[15] These approaches, which are increasingly common, may effectively give exporters a brief window of opportunity to enter the U.S. market at subsidized price levels prior to shifting production to the United States.

Although the subsidy may arise from public or private sources, all U.S. determinations to date have involved foreign governmental subsidies. Thus, these cases are usually determined on a country-wide basis (for instance, solar panels from China). CVD orders usually apply to all imported goods of a particular tariff classification from a particular country—including indirect imports shipped via other countries. This is one of the few instances in which the GATT/WTO allows an importing country to engage in discriminatory conduct against one or a few member states.

The United States amended its rules on countervailing duties in 1994 to conform to the SCM Agreement. The amendments changed many concepts under U.S. law and, although with a slightly different structure, the U.S. rules on CVDs in large measure are consistent with the substance of the SCM Agreement. In nearly all respects, the important rules on the imposition of CVDs under U.S. law as described in the Sections below conform to the substance of the WTO SCM Agreement.

In general, the U.S. rules state that "there shall be imposed. . . a countervailing duty" if the ITA determines that an exporting country is providing, "directly or indirectly," a disallowed subsidy, and the ITC makes an affirmative injury determination.[16] Thus, U.S. law defines essentially three elements for the imposition of a CVD: (1) a "countervailable subsidy," (2) that is "specific," and (3) that causes or threatens to cause a material injury to a domestic

---

14   19 U.S.C. § 1671c(b).
15   19 U.S.C. § 1671c(c)(4).
16   19 U.S.C. § 1671(a).

industry.[17] If all three elements are satisfied, the ITA must impose a CVD "equal to the amount of the net countervailable subsidy."[18]

The following sections analyze in detail each of the three required elements for the imposition of a CVD.

§ 5.6   The U.S. Subsidy Requirement

The first step in the analysis for the imposition of a CVD is a finding of a "subsidy." This term is defined as a "financial contribution" by a governmental entity that confers a "benefit" on the producer or exporter of the subsidized product.[19] It includes governmental grants, loans, equity infusions, and loan guarantees, as well as tax credits and the failure to collect taxes. *See* U.S.-FSCs, WT/DS 108/AB/R (2000) (foregone taxes are subsidies). It can also include the governmental purchase or providing of goods or services on advantageous terms.[20] Further, direct governmental action is not required. A subsidy may also arise if a government provides any of the above through a private body.

A financial contribution provides a "benefit" if it grants an exporter a better deal than would be available through normal market mechanisms. The Tariff Act states that this "normally" occurs: (1) in the case of an equity infusion, "if the investment decision is inconsistent with the usual investment practice of private investors"; (2) in the case of a loan, if the recipient gains an advantage as against a "comparable commercial loan"; (3) in the case of a loan guarantee, if there is a difference between the fee the recipient paid as compared to the fee for "a comparable commercial loan"; (4) in the case of governmental goods or services, if they "are provided for less than adequate remuneration"; and (5) in the case of goods purchased from the exporter, if the goods are purchased "for more than adequate remuneration."[21]

§ 5.7   The U.S. Specificity Requirement

In addition to a financial contribution that confers a benefit, the Tariff Act requires that the resulting subsidy be "specific" to a particular industry or enterprise. This is where U.S. law uses a slightly different structure as compared to the SCM Agreement (although, again, the substance is largely the same). U.S. law thus refers to "export subsidies" (see § 5.8 below) to correspond to the "prohibited" (red light) subsidies under the SCM Agreement. These

---

[17]   19 U.S.C. § 1671(2).

[18]   *Id.*

[19]   19 U.S.C. § 1677(5).

[20]   19 U.S.C. § 1677(5)(D).

[21]   19 U.S.C. § 1677(5)(E).

are deemed to be specific as a matter of law. Similarly, U.S. law refers to "domestic subsidies" (see § 5.9 below) to correspond to "actionable" (yellow light) subsidies under the SCM Agreement. These may be subject to CVDs if they cause "adverse trade effects" based on a variety of further factual considerations.

Two other categories originally recognized under the SCM Agreement, and incorporated into U.S. law, have lapsed.[22] A so-called "dark amber" subsidy was one that exceeded five percent of the cost basis of the product, or provided debt forgiveness, or covered the operating losses of a specific enterprise industry more than once. The dark amber provisions lapsed in 2000. The "green light" category of allowed subsidies—for industrial research and development, regional development, and adaptation of existing facilities to new environmental standards—also lapsed after five years and was not renewed.[23]

§ 5.8   Export Subsidies

The clearest example of a specific subsidy is a direct export incentive provided by a foreign government, such as an export credit on taxes or export loan guarantees at less than commercial rates. U.S. CVD law provides that a subsidy is an "export subsidy," and thus is specific as a matter of law, if "in law or in fact" it is "contingent upon export performance," even where that condition is only one of several.[24] The same applies for a subsidy that is "conditioned upon the use of domestic goods over imported goods" ("import substitution subsidy").[25]

These rules correspond to the "prohibited" (red light) subsidies under the SCM Agreement. Annex I to the SCM Agreement also provides an "Illustrative List of Export Subsidies." A footnote to the SCM Agreement explains that a subsidy also is contingent on exports if it is "in fact tied to actual or anticipated exportation or export earnings."[26] A 2011 WTO Appellate Body decision in the long-running dispute between the European Union and the United States over aircraft subsidies explained that this concept applies, "[w]here the evidence shows, all other things being equal, that the granting of the subsidy provides an incentive to skew anticipated sales towards exports."[27] Although U.S. law does not expressly incorporate the

---

22   *See* 19 U.S.C. § 1677(5B)(A)–(E).

23   *See* Section 5.2.

24   19 U.S.C. § 1677(5A)(B).

25   19 U.S.C. § 1677(5A)(C).

26   *See* SCM Agreement, art. 3.1(a), footnote 4.

27   *See Report, European Communities and Certain Member States—Measures Affecting Trade in Large Civil Aircraft,* ¶ 1047, WT/DS316/AB/ (May 18, 2011).

language of the SCM Agreement footnote, a fair interpretation of the definition of an "export subsidy" would seem to capture it.

Other examples of an export subsidy might include governmental loans at below market interest rates or with uncompensated deferrals of payments of the principal. If these benefits are used to induce the building of a plant with a capacity too large for the local market, an export subsidy may exist. Outright cash payments to exporters, export tax credits, and accelerated depreciation benefits for exporters provide additional examples of clearly countervailable export subsidies.

More difficulties arise in analyzing whether tax rebates confer the type of benefits that would equate with an export subsidy. Remission or deferral of, or exemption from, a direct tax on exports is a countervailable subsidy. But the remission of an indirect tax (sales tax, value added tax, etc.) is not a "specific" subsidy, as long as it is not excessive. However, a foreign government that makes payments to exporters must show a clear link between the amount, eligibility, and purpose of the payments and the actual payment of indirect taxes, and then document the link.

At one time, the amount of a U.S. CVD would be reduced by the "non-excessive" amount of the remission of an indirect tax. The Tariff Act now provides, however, a definition of "net subsidy" that allows certain subtractions. These include (1) application fees to qualify for the subsidy, (2) any reduction in the value of the subsidy due to a governmentally mandated deferral in payment, and (3) export taxes intended to offset the subsidy.[28]

§ 5.9   Domestic U.S. Subsidies

The Tariff Act as amended by the URAA in 1994 generally covers the SCM Agreement category of "actionable" (yellow light) subsidies under the concept of a "domestic subsidy." Under the SCM Agreement such subsidies are permissible (and thus may not be subject to CVDs), but only if they do not cause "adverse trade effects."[29]

Under the Tariff Act, a domestic subsidy exists if as a matter of law or fact it is provided to a specific enterprise or industry, even if not linked to export performance.[30] The law lists four "guidelines" for determining whether a subsidy so qualifies as a domestic subsidy:

---

[28]   19 U.S.C. § 1677(6).

[29]   SCM Agreement, art. 5.

[30]   19 U.S.C. § 1677(5A)(D).

(1)   If the subsidizing country "expressly limits access" to the subsidy to an enterprise or industry, then it is "specific as a matter of law."

(2)   If the subsidy is in fact automatically granted to all enterprises or industries that meet written and objective criteria or conditions, it is "not specific as a matter of law."

(3)   But a subsidy may be "specific as a matter of fact" where the actual recipients are limited in number; one enterprise or industry is the predominant user or receives a "disproportionately large amount" of the subsidy; or the manner in which the granting authority exercises its discretion indicates that one enterprise or industry is favored over others.

(4)   Finally, a subsidy is specific if it is limited to an enterprise or industry in a "designated geographic region" and is granted by the governmental authority of that region.[31]

For purposes of each of these guidelines, the Tariff Act makes clear that a reference to an enterprise or industry includes "a group of such enterprises or industries."[32]

§ 5.10   Upstream Subsidies

A foreign government may subsidize component parts or raw materials that are incorporated into a final exported product. The latter are called "upstream subsidies" and are subject to CVDs if they both bestow a competitive benefit on the product exported to the United States and have a significant effect on its cost of production.[33] A competitive benefit arises if the price of the subsidized "input product" (the component or raw material) to the producer of the final product is less than it would have been "in an arms-length transaction."[34] Upstream subsidies then become "countervailable subsidies" if this competitive benefit functions to create or support an import substitution subsidy or a domestic subsidy.[35]

The amount of the benefit from an upstream subsidy is determined by calculating the subsidy rate on the input and then

---

[31]   19 U.S.C. § 1677(5A)(D)(i)–(iv).

[32]   19 U.S.C. § 1677(5A)(D), last paragraph.

[33]   19 U.S.C. § 1677–1(a). *See also* 19 U.S.C. § 1671(e)(providing for the inclusion of upstream subsidies in CVDs).

[34]   19 U.S.C. § 1677–1(b).

[35]   19 U.S.C. § 1677–1(a)(stating that an upstream subsidy is one "other than an export subsidy"); 19 U.S.C. §§ 1677(5)(C)(referring to import substitution subsidies), and 1677(5)(D)(referring to domestic subsidies).

determining what percentage of the cost of the final product is represented by the subsidized input. By regulation the ITA has stated that, if the subsidy so calculated represents more than five percent of the total cost, it will presume that there is a "significant effect;" and if it is less than one percent, it will presume no significant effect.[36] However, both presumptions are rebuttable, and the ITA also will consider the importance of price in the competitiveness of the final product.[37]

The Tariff Act has specialized rules for processed agricultural products. A subsidy provided to producers of a "raw agricultural product" is deemed to be provided to the producer of the processed agricultural product if (1) the demand for the "raw" product is substantially dependent upon the demand for the processed product, and (2) the processing adds only limited value to the raw product.[38]

§ 5.11   *De Minimis* Subsidies

De minimis subsidies, defined in U.S. law as subsidies of "less than 0.5 percent *ad valorem*," are disregarded and no CVD is imposed.[39] However, when the ITA calculates country-wide CVD rates, it uses a fair average of aggregate subsidy benefits to exports of all firms from that country. In making such calculations, the ITA must include not only sales by exporters who receive substantial subsidy benefits, but also sales by exporters who receive zero or *de minimis* subsidies, when calculating the weighted average benefit conferred.[40] Thus, in such circumstances, the CVD imposed may not exceed the weighted average benefit received by all exporters of the goods subject to the CVD proceeding. The *de minimis* 0.5 percent rule need not be utilized in sunset reviews of CVDs every five years.[41]

§ 5.12   U.S. CVDs and Nonmarket Economies

The subject of subsidies is particularly difficult with respect to non-market economies (NMEs). The longstanding view was that CVDs for products from NMEs were not appropriate because the NME government in effect is responsible for the entire economy. In accordance with this view, the Federal Circuit Court of Appeals ruled in 1986 that economic incentives given to encourage exportation by

---

[36]   19 CFR § 351.523(d)(1) (2013).

[37]   19 CFR § 351.523(d)(2) (2013).

[38]   19 U.S.C. § 1677–2.

[39]   Although the Tariff Act generally refers to one percent, *see* 19 U.S.C. § 1671b(b)(4), the ITA has refined the standard to .05 percent. *See* 19 CFR § 351.106(c)(1) (2013).

[40]   *See Ipsco, Inc. v. United States*, 899 F.2d 1192 (Fed.Cir.1990).

[41]   *See* Report of the Appellate Body, U.S. *CVD on Certain Corrosion—Resistant Steel Flat Products from Germany*, WT/DS213/AB/R (Dec. 19, 2002).

the government of an NME cannot create a "countervailable subsidy."[42] The court's rationale was that, even though an NME government provides export-oriented benefits, the NME can direct sales to be at any price, so the benefits themselves do not distort competition. The court also suggested that imports from NMEs with unreasonably low prices should be analyzed under the rules for antidumping duties.

For some time one strong view was that Congress implicitly approved of this reasoning when it enacted important amendments to the Tariff Act in 1988, and again in 1994. Those amendments addressed *dumping* from NMEs, but did not address *subsidies* for exports from NMEs.[43] Thus, for many years it was assumed that unfair trade practices by NMEs would only be subject to antidumping reviews and not CVD reviews. But in a major reversal, the Commerce Department in 2007 started pursuing CVD cases against China despite its NME status under U.S. trade law. In 2008, it then imposed CVD duties of up to 616% on steel pipe from China.[44] It did the same in 2010 for certain imports from Vietnam.[45]

In 2011 the Federal Circuit rejected this effort based on its reading of congressional intent in the substantial amendments of CVD law in 1994.[46] In March 2012, however, Congress annulled that decision by special legislation (Public Act 112–99). As a result, countervailing duties may be imposed retroactively to 2006 on goods from non-market economies such as China and Vietnam. China has challenged this legislation before the WTO. Many WTO members have recognized China as a market economy, and the accession provision allowing treatment of China as a nonmarket economy expires in 2016.

The criteria used to determine whether a country has a nonmarket economy in antidumping proceedings[47] will apply for U.S. countervailing duty law as well. These criteria focus principally upon government involvement in setting prices or production levels, private versus collective ownership, and market pricing of inputs.[48] Public Act 112–99 prohibits dual application of CVD and AD duties, a practice China successfully challenged before the WTO. *See* Section 4.0.

---

[42]   *Georgetown Steel Corp. v. United States*, 801 F.2d 1308 (Fed. Cir. 1986).

[43]   *See, e.g.,* 19 U.S.C. §§ 1677b(c) and 1677(18).

[44]   *See* 73 Fed. Reg. 40,480 (July 15, 2008).

[45]   *See* 75 Fed. Reg. 23,670 (May 4, 2010).

[46]   *See GPX Intern. Tire Corp. v. United States*, 666 F.3d 732, 745 (Fed. Cir. 2011).

[47]   *See* Chapter 4.

[48]   *See id.*

§ 5.13   The U.S. Injury Determination

CVD proceedings in the United States for Subsidies Agreement Countries (and only such countries[49]), are conducted in two stages. The ITA is responsible for assessing the substantive grounds for the imposition of a CVD.[50] In the second stage, the International Trade Commission (ITC) must determine whether the subsidization of the imported merchandise has caused or threatens material injury to a domestic industry.[51] The following sections review the material injury determination under U.S. law, including market definition, injury factors, and causation. Injury determinations in CVD proceedings are almost identical to hose the ITC undertakes in AD proceedings. *See* Chapter 4.

The injury determination by the ITC involves three separate inquiries:

(1)   First, the ITC must define the relevant "domestic like product" and relevant domestic industry;

(2)   Second, the ITC must determine whether that industry is suffering or threatened with a sufficiently serious injury; and

(3)   Third, the ITC must determine whether a causal link exists between the injury and the "countervailable subsidy."

The most important of these steps is the determination of whether a countervailable subsidy causes a sufficient injury to a domestic industry. The Tariff Act provides that an affirmative injury determination is required when an industry in the United States is materially injured or is threatened with material injury by reason of dumped imports, or the establishment of an industry in the United States is materially retarded.[52] Both the "material injury"[53] and the "threat of material injury"[54] standards apply to established industries, and substantial overlap exists between the two. Nonetheless, the Act makes clear that they are independent grounds for a sufficient injury to justify a CVD.[55]

---

[49]   *See* Section 5.2 (noting that an injury determination is required only for "Subsidies Agreement Countries").

[50]   *See* generally 19 U.S.C. § 1671(a)(1).

[51]   19 U.S.C. § 1671(a)(2).

[52]   *Id.*

[53]   19 U.S.C. § 1677(7).

[54]   19 U.S.C. § 1677(7)(F).

[55]   19 U.S.C. § 1671(a)(2).

The law governing the injury determination for the imposition of CVDs in nearly all significant respects is the same as that for imposing antidumping duties. Indeed, the definitions of the relevant product market, the relevant industry, and the three alternatives for an affirmative injury determination are essentially identical for CVDs and ADs. Thus, the analysis of the injury determination for CVDs below will often be the same as, or will liberally refer to, the injury analysis for ADs in Chapter 4.

§ 5.14 "Like Product" and Relevant U.S. Industry Determinations

In order to assess "material injury," the ITC must first identify the relevant products and relevant domestic industry affected by a countervailable subsidy.

With regard to the product market, the Tariff Act uses the term "domestic like product." This term is defined, for both CVDs and ADs, as one that is "like, or in the absence of like, most similar in characteristics and uses with" to the foreign product under investigation. The "like product" determination is a factual issue for which the ITC weighs six relevant factors: "(1) physical characteristics and uses; (2) common manufacturing facilities and production employees; (3) interchangeability; (4) customer perceptions; (5) channels of distribution; and, where appropriate, (6) price."[56]

In a CVD proceeding, the ITC must define the relevant product and industry for an assessment of the harm caused by a subsidized product upon importation. The ITA will undertake a similar analysis in AD proceedings in order to determine the foreign market value ("normal value") for the imported merchandise.[57] Since the concept of "like product" is used for a different purpose, its definition need not necessarily be the same as that used by the ITA in determining whether dumping has occurred.[58]

Separately, the ITC in a CVD proceeding must define the relevant domestic industry potentially affected by a proscribed subsidy practice. The Tariff Act defines the relevant "domestic industry" as those domestic producers, "as a whole," of a "domestic like product" or as those producers "whose collective output of a domestic like product constitutes a major proportion" of the total

---

[56]   *Cleo Inc. v. U.S.*, 501 F.3d 1291, 11294–1295 (Fed. Cir. 2007).

[57]   *See* Section 4.6.

[58]   *Cleo Inc. v. U.S.*, 501 F.3d 1291, 1295 (Fed. Cir. 2007); *Mitsubishi Elec. Corp. v. U.S.*, 898 F.2d 1577 (Fed.Cir.1990).

domestic production.[59] Again, although these definitions apply to both the ITA and the ITC, they do not always agree on the outcome.

In addition, the ITC may create regional geographic product markets if the local producers sell most of their production in the regional market, and the demand in the regional market is not supplied by other U.S. producers outside that region.[60] If the relevant domestic injury in such a region is harmed, then there is material injury to a domestic industry.

§ 5.15   Material U.S. Injury

The Tariff Act defines material injury as "harm which is not inconsequential, immaterial, or unimportant."[61] (The same standard applies in AD proceedings,[62] and again much of the law in the area is therefore interchangeable.) In assessing this essential "material injury" standard, the Act *requires* the ITC to consider three factors:

> (1)   The volume of imports of the merchandise subject to investigation;

> (2)   The effect of these imports on prices in the United States for like products; and

> (3)   The impact of these imports on domestic producers of like products, but only in the context of domestic United States production operations.[63]

The Act also *permits* the ITC to consider "such other economic factors as are relevant to the determination regarding whether there is material injury by reason of imports."[64]

The ITC is required to explain its analysis of each factor considered and the relevance of each to its determination.[65] The Tariff Act nonetheless provides that the "presence or absence" of any of the three mandatory factors should "not necessarily give decisive guidance" to the ITC in its material injury determination, and the ITC is not required to assign any particular weight to any one factor.[66] The factors are examined through extensive statistical analyses. This analysis occurs on industry-wide basis and not on a

---

[59]   19 U.S.C. § 1677(4)(A).

[60]   19 U.S.C. § 1677(4)(C).

[61]   19 U.S.C. § 1677(7)(A).

[62]   *See* Section 4.14.

[63]   19 U.S.C. § 1677(7)(B)(i). *See also Angus Chemical Co. v. United States*, 140 F.3d 1478 (Fed.Cir.1998)(holding that consideration of these three factors is mandatory).

[64]   19 U.S.C. § 1677(7)(B)(ii).

[65]   19 U.S.C. § 1677(7)(B).

[66]   19 U.S.C. § 1677(7)(E)(ii).

company-by-company basis. The ITC may select whatever time period best represents the business cycle and competitive conditions in the industry and most reasonably allows it to determine whether an injury exists.[67]

The Tariff Act also gives detailed guidance for the ITC's assessment of each of the three mandatory considerations for a material injury determination. This guidance applies to both CVD and AD proceedings.

Volume of Imports

The Tariff Act requires the ITC to consider the absolute volume of imports or any increases in volume in evaluating the volume of imports subject to investigation. This assessment may be made in relation to production or consumption in the United States. The standard in this evaluation is whether the volume of imports, viewed in any of the above ways, is significant.[68]

Price Effects

Under the Tariff Act, the ITC must consider the effect of the subsidized imports on prices for like products in the domestic market. This is done to the extent that such a consideration assists in evaluating whether (1) there is significant price underselling by the imported merchandise as compared with the price of like products of the United States,[69] and (2) whether the effect of the imported merchandise is otherwise to depress domestic prices to a significant degree or to prevent price increases that otherwise would have occurred to a significant degree.[70]

Domestic Industry Impact

Similar to AD proceedings, the impact on a domestic industry of an allegedly subsidized product commonly is the most important consideration in the ITC's injury analysis. Because of this, the Tariff Act provides supplemental factors for the ITC to consider. These include: (1) actual and potential decline in "output, sales, market share, profits, productivity, return on investments, and utilization of capacity"; (2) impact on domestic prices; (3) actual and potential "negative effects on cash flow, inventories, employment, wages, growth, ability to raise capital, and investment"; and (4) actual and

---

[67]   19 U.S.C. § 1677(7)(C).

[68]   19 U.S.C. § 1677(7)(C)(i).

[69]   19 U.S.C. § 1677(7)(C)(ii)(I).

[70]   19 U.S.C. § 1677(7)(C)(ii)(II). For more detail on the role of "price underselling" in the ITC's determination of injury *see* Section 4.14.

potential negative effects "on the existing development and production efforts of the domestic industry."[71]

The ITC must evaluate all these relevant economic factors within the context of the business cycle and conditions of competition in the affected industry.[72] But traditionally the ITC has relied primarily on two of the factors in making this determination. First, the industry must be in a distressed or a stagnant condition. Second, the low domestic price levels must be a factor in the industry's difficulties (*e.g.*, high unemployment or low capacity utilization rate), and these low prices must have a serious negative effect on profits.

The ITC will often base an affirmative determination of material injury on severe downward trends in profitability among domestic producers. But even in a case of declining profitability, increasing production, shipments, capacity, and market share may demonstrate to the ITC that the affected industry is in a healthy state.[73] Thus, the ITC may make a negative determination concerning material injury even if the industry is experiencing decreases in profitability.

Like AD proceedings, the effect of subsidized imports on employment in the relevant domestic industry may also be significant. Again, employment data are not dispositive due to the broad spectrum of economic factors that may affect such data, many of which may not be attributable to foreign subsidization. However, changes in domestic employment during the period under investigation are one factor to be considered. A decrease in employment during the period of investigation may be an indication of injury, whereas increasing employment commonly is a fact that supports a negative injury determination.

Finally, and again as in AD proceedings, plant capacity utilization can be an important factor. Falling capacity utilization may indicate material injury if no other explanation exists, but the ITC can make negative injury determinations despite falling capacity utilization, if the decline is caused by other factors, such as frequent equipment breakdowns and quality control disruptions.

§ 5.16 Threat of U.S. Material Injury

The ITC may also make an affirmative determination of injury if it finds that a proscribed subsidy practice represents a "threat of material injury" to a domestic industry. The Tariff Act lists a variety

---

[71]   19 U.S.C. § 1677(7)(C)(iii).

[72]   19 U.S.C. § 1677(7)(C), last paragraph.

[73]   *See, e.g., Nucor Corp. v. U.S.*, 675 F. Supp. 2d 1340 (C.I.T. 2010)(relating to a revocation of CVDs after a review); *American Spring Wire Corp. v. U.S.*, 590 F. Supp. 1273 (C.I.T. 1984), *affirmed sub nom. Armco, Inc. v. U.S.*, 760 F.2d 249 (Fed. Cir. 1985).

of "economic factors" that the ITC "shall consider" in making such a determination in an antidumping proceeding. Again, these factors apply for AD proceedings as well, and Chapter 4 analyzes them in detail.[74]

The Tariff Act nonetheless adds one "economic factor" that is relevant only for CVD proceedings. For such proceedings the ITC must also consider "the nature of the subsidy . . . and whether imports of the subject merchandise are likely to increase."[75]

§ 5.17   Material Retardation

For a CVD proceeding as well, the Tariff Act recognizes as an independent ground for an affirmative injury determination by the ITC that a dumped import product has "materially retarded" the establishment of an industry in the United States. This standard of its nature is relevant to new or nascent domestic industries. Like AD proceedings,[76] this ground for an affirmative injury determination has not been a significant one in CVD cases.

§ 5.18   Causation

In addition to sufficient injury to a domestic industry, the ITC must also find causation. As with AD proceedings, however, when the subsidization and material injury already exist, there is a natural tendency to make an affirmative determination for a CVD without a lengthy analysis of the causal link between the two. In a negative injury determination, on the other hand, the ITC may engage in a rather detailed analysis of causation.

The Tariff Act sets out a simple causation standard: that material injury must occur "by reason of" the subsidization of the imports.[77] The same standard applies in AD proceedings and once again the law in this area is largely interchangeable.[78] The Tariff Act does not require that the ITC use any particular methodology in making such a determination, and it "need not isolate the injury caused by other factors from injury caused by unfair imports."[79] Thus the causation requirement is not a high one. Imports need only be a cause of material injury, and need not be the most substantial or even primary cause.

---

[74]   *See* Section 4.15.

[75]   19 U.S.C. § 1677(7)(F)(i)(I).

[76]   *See* Section 4.16.

[77]   19 U.S.C. § 1671(a)(2).

[78]   *See* Section 4.17.

[79]   *Bratsk Aluminium Smelter v. U.S.*, 444 F.3d 1369, 1373 (Fed. Cir. 2006) (*quoting Taiwan Semiconductors Industry Ass'n v. Int'l Trade Comm.*, 266 F.3d 1339, 1345 (Fed. Cir. 2001)).

The causation standard may be satisfied if the subsidized imports simply contribute to the conditions of the domestic injury. Under this "contributing cause" standard, causation may exist despite the absence of a correlation between subsidized imports and the alleged injuries, if substantial evidence exists that the volume of subsidized imports was a contributing factor in the price depression experienced by the domestic injury. Nonetheless, the Federal Circuit has made clear that "causation is not shown if the subject imports contributed only 'minimally or tangentially to the material harm.' "[80]

As in AD proceedings, the ITC must consider causal factors other than subsidies in CVD cases.[81] An industry that is prospering during times of greater import penetration will find it difficult to persuade the ITC that subsidized imports are the cause of any material injury to it. The existence of extraneous injury factors will not, however, necessarily preclude an affirmative finding of material injury for purposes of the Tariff Act, as long as the subsidies are a contributing cause to the material injury of the domestic industry. The ITC is not required to weigh the effects from the subsidized imports against the effects associated with other factors, if the subsidization is a contributing cause of the injury. Nonetheless, the ITC may uncover other major causes for the problems of the domestic industry. These may include huge unnecessary expenses, chronic excess capacity, inefficiency, poor quality, price sensitivity or increased domestic competition.

§ 5.19 Cumulative Causation

Similar to an AD proceeding,[82] the Tariff Act requires that the ITC cumulatively assess the impact of reasonably coincident subsidized imports from two or more countries if the imports compete with "like products" in the United States. In specific, the Act requires the ITC to "cumulatively assess the volume and price effects of imports of the subject merchandise from all countries" with respect to which CVD proceedings were initiated on the same day, "if such imports compete with each other and with domestic like products in the United States market."[83] The reasoning for this approach, again, is that the injury caused by "many nibbles" is just as harmful as that caused by "one large bite."

---

[80]   *Id.*, 444 F.3d at 1373 (*quoting Gerald Metals, Inc. v. U.S.*, 132 F.3d 716, 722 (Fed. Cir. 1997)).

[81]   *Taiwan Semiconductors Industry Ass'n v. International Trade Comm.*, 266 F.3d 1339, 1345 (Fed. Cir. 2001) (so holding with respect to an AD proceeding).

[82]   *See* Section 4.18.

[83]   19 U.S.C. § 1677(7)(G)(i).

The Court of International Trade has observed that to support a cumulation decision, the ITC "must find a reasonable overlap of competition between imports from the subject countries and the domestic like product."[84] In applying this "reasonable overlap" test, the ITC traditionally has applied a four factor test: (1) the degree of fungibility; (2) the presence of sales or offers in the same geographic markets; (3) the existence of common or similar channels of distribution; and (4) whether there is a simultaneous presence in the relevant market.[85] However, neither the "reasonable overlap" test nor the four factors test is "singularly dispositive or the sole factors the ITC may consider."[86]

When cumulating, it is not necessary to find, for each country, a separate causal link between imports and U.S. material injury. Such multiple country cumulation should be distinguished from the "cross cumulation," which is also allowed by the Tariff Act. Cross cumulation involves consideration by the ITC of both dumped and subsidized imports into the United States. The net effect of U.S. rules on cumulation of import injury is to encourage petitioners to name as many countries as possible as the source of their problems and combine these in a single proceeding.

§ 5.20   U.S. Countervailing Duty Procedures

As noted above, the Tariff Act applies different rules for the imposition of CVDs depending on whether the source country is or is not a "Subsidies Agreement Country."[87] The major difference between the two is that for a "Subsidies Agreement Country" a determination of both a countervailable subsidy and an injury is required; for other countries, only a finding of a countervailable subsidy is necessary.[88] Thus, the administrative procedure for deciding whether to impose CVDs for a Subsidies Agreement Country is the same as that for antidumping duties[89] and involves the ITA and ITC (see below) making both preliminary and final determinations. But for subsidized products from other countries, a decision by the ITA will alone be sufficient to impose CVDs.

---

[84]   *Nucor Corp. v. U.S.*, 594 F. Supp. 2d 1320, 1347 (C.I.T. 2008)(*quoting Noviant OY v. United States*, 451 F. Supp. 2d 1367, 1379 (C.I.T. 2006), *aff'd, Nucor Corp. v. U.S.*, 601 F.3d 1291 (Fed. Cir. 2010).

[85]   *Id.*, at 1347.

[86]   *Id.*

[87]   *See* Section 5.4.

[88]   19 U.S.C. § 1671(a)(1), (2).

[89]   *See* Sections 4.21–4.23.

§ 5.21 U.S. Administrative Determinations

Two different governmental agencies are involved in administering U.S. CVD law: The International Trade Administration (ITA), which is part of the Commerce Department and thus the Executive Branch, and the International Trade Commission (ITC), which is an independent agency created by Congress.

The chain of decision-making in CVD proceedings depends on whether a Subsidies Agreement Country is involved. If not, the proceeding is totally before the ITA. This will be a two-stage proceeding:

ITA Preliminary Countervailable Subsidy Determination.

ITA Final Countervailable Subsidy Determination.

If, in contrast, a Subsidies Agreement Country is the source of the challenged goods, then a four-stage proceeding will apply:

ITC Preliminary Injury Determination.

ITA Preliminary Countervailable Subsidy Determination.

ITA Final Countervailable Subsidy Determination.

ITC Final Injury Determination.

The CVD process may be initiated by either the Department of Commerce or by a union or business (or group or association of aggrieved workers or businesses).[90] The petition requirements are set forth by regulation.[91] Pre-filing contact with the ITA and (if necessary) the ITC can often resolve any problems regarding the contents of the petition. Petitioners may also access the ITA's library of information on foreign subsidy practices.

The ITA then first determines whether the petition alleges the elements necessary for the imposition of a duty, based on the best information available at the time.[92] In other words, the ITA essentially accepts or rejects the petition.

Once the petition is accepted, the ITC makes a preliminary determination as to a real or threatened material injury within forty-five days of the filing of the petition based on the best information available to it at that time.[93] If the ITC makes such a finding, the ITA must then make a preliminary determination on whether there is "a reasonable basis to believe" based on the best information available

---

[90]   19 U.S.C. § 1671a(a), (b).

[91]   *See* 19 C.F.R. § 351.102.

[92]   19 U.S.C. § 1671a(b).

[93]   19 U.S.C. § 1671b(a).

that there is a countervailable subsidy with respect to the covered merchandise.[94] The time for making this decision may be extended if the petitioner so requests, or if the ITA determines both that the parties are cooperating and that the case is extraordinarily complicated.[95] The time period may also be extended for "upstream subsidy" investigations.[96]

If the ITA makes a preliminary determination that a countervailable subsidy exists, it must, within seventy-five days, both make a "final determination" on the existence of a countervailable subsidy and calculate the amount of the proposed CVD.[97] If the ITA makes a positive finding on a countervailable subsidy, the ITC then must make a final determination on material injury within 120 days after the ITA's preliminary determination or forty-five days after the ITA's final determination.[98] If the ITA makes a negative preliminary determination, but then an affirmative final determination, the ITC must thereafter make its final determination within seventy-five days.[99]

In reaching their determinations, both the ITA and the ITC frequently circulate questionnaires to interested parties, including foreign governments and exporters. Since any failure to respond risks a determination on the "best information available," this results in the flow of significant and often strategically valuable business information to the government.

§ 5.22 The Importance of the ITA Preliminary Subsidy Determination

An ITA preliminary determination that a countervailable subsidy exists places great pressure on the importers of the foreign goods. Liquidation (entry at a determined rate of tariff) of all such merchandise is suspended by order of customs. Goods imported after an ITA preliminary determination of a countervailable subsidy will be subject to any CVD imposed later, after final determinations are made.[100] Such a preliminary determination, although subject to final determinations by the ITA and the ITC and appealable to the CIT, will effectively cut off further importation of the disputed goods unless an expensive bond is posted pending completion of the process.

---

[94]   19 U.S.C. § 1671b(b).

[95]   19 U.S.C. § 1671b(c).

[96]   19 U.S.C. § 1671b(h).

[97]   19 U.S.C. § 1671d(a).

[98]   19 U.S.C. § 1671d(b)(2).

[99]   19 U.S.C. § 1671d(b)(3).

[100]   19 U.S.C. § 1671b(d).

The respondent importer thus will want a speedy resolution, as its total costs for the imports will have become uncertain. It is for this reason that the Tariff Act is replete with time provisions designed to protect the importer by requiring decisions within specified time limits (see § 5.21 above). As with antidumping proceedings, most CVD proceedings are completed within one year.

At one level, then, a useful intermediate goal in representing a petitioner is to obtain an ITA preliminary determination concerning a "subsidy" that meets the statutory requirements. The respondent's "defense" to such efforts must be organized quickly, usually within thirty days of the filing of a CVD petition. The importer's ability to present a defense is handicapped by the nature of CVD proceedings— the actual target of the petition is the subsidy practices of foreign governments.

Unlike most foreign exporters whose pricing decisions are the focus in AD proceedings, many foreign governments are loath to provide information necessary for an adequate response to a CVD complaint. Because the ITA and ITC are authorized to make decisions on the basis of the "best information available," any failure to adequately respond to a CVD complaint can contribute to adverse rulings. Moreover, responses by foreign governments and exporters to ITA questionnaires that cannot be verified by on-the-spot investigations are ignored and thus removed from the best information available for decision-making. This may leave only the petitioner's or other respondents' submissions for review—one-sided proceeding almost sure to result in affirmative determinations.

The respondent-importer's uncertainties over the amount of duty owed after a preliminary ITA determination that a countervailable subsidy exists can increase for Subsidies Agreement Countries if the ITA decides that "critical circumstances" are present. In such cases, the suspension of liquidation of the goods applies not only prospectively from the date of such determination, but also retrospectively for ninety days.[101] For other countries, moreover, there is *no* time limit on retroactively and no need for a "critical circumstances" determination.

§ 5.23 CVDs and Anti-Circumvention

The ITA final determination of the existence of a subsidy establishes the amount of any CVDs. Because duties are not imposed to support any specific domestic price, they are set only to equal the

---

[101]   19 U.S.C. § 1671b(e).

amount of the net subsidy.[102] The CVDs remain in force as long as the subsidization continues.

Like antidumping duties,[103] the Tariff Act also has rules that address the "circumvention" of CVDs. First, the ITA may include within the scope of a CVD order merchandise "completed or assembled" in the United States if such merchandise includes "parts or components produced in the foreign country" that are the original subject of the order.[104] The principal requirements are that the process of completion or assembly in the United States is "minor or insignificant" and the value of the components themselves is a "significant portion of the total value of the merchandise.[105] Second, when the exporter ships components to a third country for assembly and subsequent exportation to the United States, such circumvention efforts can be defeated by extending an antidumping order to those goods as well.[106] Again, such an action is appropriate if the assembly in the third country is "minor or insignificant" and the value of the components represents a "significant portion" of the total value.

Many petitioners in countervailing duty cases also seek antidumping duties[107] and other relief through safeguard or market disruption proceedings.[108] Thus, domestic producers seeking relief from import competition will often use a "shotgun" approach to obtain protective relief.

§ 5.24   U.S. Court Appeals, Binational NAFTA Panels

Judicial review "on the record" of final (not preliminary) decisions by the ITA and the ITC in both CVD and AD proceedings may be sought before the Court of International Trade (CIT). In turn, CIT decisions may be appealed first to the Court of Appeals for the Federal Circuit, and ultimately to the U.S. Supreme Court.

For proceedings arising out of exports from Canada and Mexico, however, NAFTA provides for resolution of antidumping and countervailing duty disputes through binational panels.[109] Such panels apply the domestic law of the importing country, and provide a substitute for judicial review of the decisions of administrative

---

[102] 19 U.S.C. § 1671e.

[103] *See* Section 4.25.

[104] 19 U.S.C. § 1677j(a).

[105] 19 U.S.C. § 1677j(a)(2).

[106] 19 U.S.C. § 1677j(b).

[107] *See* Chapter 4.

[108] *See* Chapter 6.

[109] Canada-United States Free Trade Agreement (1989), Chapter 19; NAFTA (1994), Chapter 19.

agencies of the importing country. Indeed, the initiation of a review under NAFTA divests the CIT of jurisdiction over the same dispute. Although the decisions of such bi-national panels are not formally binding in U.S. law, the ITA or ITC may decide to review any administrative action to conform to an adverse panel decision, including through a revocation or reduction of countervailing duties. No subsequent U.S. free trade agreements substitute binational panels for national judicial review of CVD decisions. See R. Folsom, *Principles of Free Trade Agreements* (forthcoming).

§ 5.25 WTO SCM Proceedings

International institutions also play an increasingly significant role in the resolution of trade disputes. The most important of these is the WTO's Dispute Settlement Body (DSB). Dissatisfied parties in domestic administrative proceedings may convince their government to challenge an adverse CVD determination before the DSB based on alleged violations of the WTO SCM Agreement. As Chapter 1 examines in detail, proceedings before the DSB are governed by a separate WTO Agreement, the Dispute Settlement Understanding (DSU).

The SCM Agreement also has special rules regarding the resolution of subsidy disputes. The multilateral procedure under WTO first provides for consultations between the complaining state and the subsidizing state. If these do not resolve the dispute within thirty days for a "red light" subsidy, or sixty days for a "yellow light" subsidy, either party is entitled to request that the DSB establish a panel to investigate the dispute and issue a written decision and report. The DSB panel will have ninety days (red light), or 120 days (yellow light), to investigate and prepare its report. The panel report is appealable on issues of law to the Appellate Body. The Appellate Body has thirty days (red light), or sixty days (yellow light), to decide the appeal. Panel and Appellate Body decisions are adopted without modification by the DSB unless rejected by an "inverted consensus."

If a prohibited or actionable subsidy is found to exist, the subsidizing state is obligated under the WTO to withdraw the subsidy. If the subsidy is not withdrawn within a six month period, the AB may authorize the complaining state to take countermeasures. Such countermeasures need not be in the form of countervailing duties, but may instead comprise increased tariffs by the complaining state on exports from the subsidizing state.

A classic, longstanding pair of subsidy disputes concerning Boeing and Airbus aircraft have been decided by the Appellate Body. In 2011, the European Union and various member states were found to have illegally subsidized Airbus, mainly through "launch aid", by

$22 billion (WT/DS316/AB/R (May 18, 2011). In 2012, the Appellate Body determined that the U.S. and various state governments had subsidized Boeing by about $4.3 billion under procurement contracts and tax loopholes (WT/DS353/AB/R (March 12, 2012). In 2017, this decision was reversed in part by the Appellate Body regarding Washington state tax reductions granted Boeing to build its 777X jetliner in that state. At this writing, neither side seems inclined to comply with these rulings, no settlement is in sight, and hence mutual trade retaliation could occur.

§ 5.26   Text of WTO Agreement on Subsidies and Countervailing Measures (SCM)

(Selected Provisions)

PART I: GENERAL PROVISIONS

Article 1

Definition of a Subsidy

1.1   For the purpose of this Agreement, a subsidy shall be deemed to exist if:

(a)(1)   there is a financial contribution by a government or any public body within the territory of a Member (referred to in this Agreement as "government"), i.e. where:

(i)   a government practice involves a direct transfer of funds (e.g. grants, loans, and equity infusion), potential direct transfers of funds or liabilities (e.g. loan guarantees);

(ii)   government revenue that is otherwise due is foregone or not collected (e.g. fiscal incentives such as tax credits)[1];

(iii)   a government provides goods or services other than general infrastructure, or purchases goods;

(iv)   a government makes payments to a funding mechanism, or entrusts or directs a private body to carry out one or more of the type of functions illustrated in (i) to (iii) above which would normally be vested in the government and the practice, in no real sense, differs from practices normally followed by governments;

or

---

[1]   In accordance with the provisions of Article XVI of GATT 1994 (Note to Article XVI) and the provisions of Annexes I through III of this Agreement, the exemption of an exported product from duties or taxes borne by the like product when destined for domestic consumption, or the remission of such duties or taxes in amounts not in excess of those which have accrued, shall not be deemed to be a subsidy.

(a)(2)   there is any form of income or price support in the sense of Article XVI of GATT 1994;

and

(b)   a benefit is thereby conferred.

1.2   A subsidy as defined in paragraph 1 shall be subject to the provisions of Part II or shall be subject to the provisions of Part III or V only if such a subsidy is specific in accordance with the provisions of Article 2.

Article 2

Specificity

2.1   In order to determine whether a subsidy, as defined in paragraph 1 of Article 1, is specific to an enterprise or industry or group of enterprises or industries (referred to in this Agreement as "certain enterprises") within the jurisdiction of the granting authority, the following principles shall apply:

(a)   Where the granting authority, or the legislation pursuant to which the granting authority operates, explicitly limits access to a subsidy to certain enterprises, such subsidy shall be specific.

(b)   Where the granting authority, or the legislation pursuant to which the granting authority operates, establishes objective criteria or conditions[2] governing the eligibility for, and the amount of, a subsidy, specificity shall not exist, provided that the eligibility is automatic and that such criteria and conditions are strictly adhered to. The criteria or conditions must be clearly spelled out in law, regulation, or other official document, so as to be capable of verification.

(c)   If, notwithstanding any appearance of non-specificity resulting from the application of the principles laid down in subparagraphs (a) and (b), there are reasons to believe that the subsidy may in fact be specific, other factors may be considered. Such factors are: use of a subsidy programme by a limited number of certain enterprises, predominant use by certain enterprises, the granting of disproportionately large amounts of subsidy to certain enterprises, and the manner in which discretion has been exercised by the granting authority in the decision to grant a subsidy.[3] In applying this subparagraph, account shall be taken of the extent of diversification of economic activities within the

---

[2]   Objective criteria or conditions, as used herein, mean criteria or conditions which are neutral, which do not favour certain enterprises over others, and which are economic in nature and horizontal in application, such as number of employees or size of enterprise.

[3]   In this regard, in particular, information on the frequency with which applications for a subsidy are refused or approved and the reasons for such decisions shall be considered.

jurisdiction of the granting authority, as well as of the length of time during which the subsidy programme has been in operation.

2.2 A subsidy which is limited to certain enterprises located within a designated geographical region within the jurisdiction of the granting authority shall be specific. It is understood that the setting or change of generally applicable tax rates by all levels of government entitled to do so shall not be deemed to be a specific subsidy for the purposes of this Agreement.

2.3 Any subsidy falling under the provisions of Article 3 shall be deemed to be specific.

2.4 Any determination of specificity under the provisions of this Article shall be clearly substantiated on the basis of positive evidence.

PART II: PROHIBITED SUBSIDIES

Article 3

Prohibition

3.1 Except as provided in the Agreement on Agriculture, the following subsidies, within the meaning of Article 1, shall be prohibited:

(a)   subsidies contingent, in law or in fact,[4] whether solely or as one of several other conditions, upon export performance, including those illustrated in Annex I[5];

(b)   subsidies contingent, whether solely or as one of several other conditions, upon the use of domestic over imported goods.

3.2 A Member shall neither grant nor maintain subsidies referred to in paragraph 1.

Article 4

Remedies

4.1 Whenever a Member has reason to believe that a prohibited subsidy is being granted or maintained by another Member, such Member may request consultations with such other Member.

* * *

4.4 If no mutually agreed solution has been reached within 30 days[6] of the request for consultations, any Member party to such consultations may refer the matter to the Dispute Settlement Body ("DSB") for the immediate

---

[4]   This standard is met when the facts demonstrate that the granting of a subsidy, without having been made legally contingent upon export performance, is in fact tied to actual or anticipated exportation or export earnings. The mere fact that a subsidy is granted to enterprises which export shall not for that reason alone be considered to be an export subsidy within the meaning of this provision.

[5]   Measures referred to in Annex I as not constituting export subsidies shall not be prohibited under this or any other provision of this Agreement.

[6]   Any time-periods mentioned in this Article may be extended by mutual agreement.

establishment of a panel, unless the DSB decides by consensus not to establish a panel.

4.5   Upon its establishment, the panel may request the assistance of the Permanent Group of Experts (referred to in this Agreement as the "PGE") with regard to whether the measure in question is a prohibited subsidy. If so requested, the PGE shall immediately review the evidence with regard to the existence and nature of the measure in question and shall provide an opportunity for the Member applying or maintaining the measure to demonstrate that the measure in question is not a prohibited subsidy. The PGE shall report its conclusions to the panel within a time-limit determined by the panel. The PGE's conclusions on the issue of whether or not the measure in question is a prohibited subsidy shall be accepted by the panel without modification.

4.6   The panel shall submit its final report to the parties to the dispute. The report shall be circulated to all Members within 90 days of the date of the composition and the establishment of the panel's terms of reference.

4.7   If the measure in question is found to be a prohibited subsidy, the panel shall recommend that the subsidizing Member withdraw the subsidy without delay. In this regard, the panel shall specify in its recommendation the time-period within which the measure must be withdrawn.

4.8   Within 30 days of the issuance of the panel's report to all Members, the report shall be adopted by the DSB unless one of the parties to the dispute formally notifies the DSB of its decision to appeal or the DSB decides by consensus not to adopt the report.

4.9   Where a panel report is appealed, the Appellate Body shall issue its decision within 30 days from the date when the party to the dispute formally notifies its intention to appeal. When the Appellate Body considers that it cannot provide its report within 30 days, it shall inform the DSB in writing of the reasons for the delay together with an estimate of the period within which it will submit its report. In no case shall the proceedings exceed 60 days. The appellate report shall be adopted by the DSB and unconditionally accepted by the parties to the dispute unless the DSB decides by consensus not to adopt the appellate report within 20 days following its issuance to the Members.

4.10   In the event the recommendation of the DSB is not followed within the time-period specified by the panel, which shall commence from the date of adoption of the panel's report or the Appellate Body's report, the DSB shall grant authorization to the complaining Member to take appropriate countermeasures, unless the DSB decides by consensus to reject the request.

4.11   In the event a party to the dispute requests arbitration under paragraph 6 of Article 22 of the Dispute Settlement Understanding ("DSU"), the arbitrator shall determine whether the countermeasures are appropriate.

4.12   For purposes of disputes conducted pursuant to this Article, except for time-periods specifically prescribed in this Article, time-periods applicable under the DSU for the conduct of such disputes shall be half the time prescribed therein.

PART III: ACTIONABLE SUBSIDIES

Article 5

Adverse Effects

No Member should cause, through the use of any subsidy referred to in paragraphs 1 and 2 of Article 1, adverse effects to the interests of other Members, i.e.:

(a)   injury to the domestic industry of another Member;

(b)   nullification or impairment of benefits accruing directly or indirectly to other Members under GATT 1994 in particular the benefits of concessions bound under Article II of GATT 1994;

(c)   serious prejudice to the interests of another Member.

This Article does not apply to subsidies maintained on agricultural products as provided in Article 13 of the Agreement on Agriculture.

Article 6

Serious Prejudice

[Note: The provisions of Art. 6(1) have "sunset" under Art. 31, and have not been renewed.]

6.2   Notwithstanding the provisions of paragraph 1, serious prejudice shall not be found if the subsidizing Member demonstrates that the subsidy in question has not resulted in any of the effects enumerated in paragraph 3.

6.3   Serious prejudice in the sense of paragraph (c) of Article 5 may arise in any case where one or several of the following apply:

(a)   the effect of the subsidy is to displace or impede the imports of a like product of another Member into the market of the subsidizing Member;

(b)   the effect of the subsidy is to displace or impede the exports of a like product of another Member from a third country market;

(c)   the effect of the subsidy is a significant price undercutting by the subsidized product as compared with the price of a like product of another Member in the same market or significant price suppression, price depression or lost sales in the same market;

(d)   the effect of the subsidy is an increase in the world market share of the subsidizing Member in a particular subsidized primary product or commodity[17] as compared to the average share

---

[17]   Unless other multilaterally agreed specific rules apply to the trade in the product or commodity in question.

it had during the previous period of three years and this increase follows a consistent trend over a period when subsidies have been granted.

6.4   For the purpose of paragraph 3(b), the displacement or impeding of exports shall include any case in which, subject to the provisions of paragraph 7, it has been demonstrated that there has been a change in relative shares of the market to the disadvantage of the non-subsidized like product (over an appropriately representative period sufficient to demonstrate clear trends in the development of the market for the product concerned, which, in normal circumstances, shall be at least one year). "Change in relative shares of the market" shall include any of the following situations: (*a*) there is an increase in the market share of the subsidized product; (*b*) the market share of the subsidized product remains constant in circumstances in which, in the absence of the subsidy, it would have declined; (*c*) the market share of the subsidized product declines, but at a slower rate than would have been the case in the absence of the subsidy.

6.5   For the purpose of paragraph 3(c), price undercutting shall include any case in which such price undercutting has been demonstrated through a comparison of prices of the subsidized product with prices of a non-subsidized like product supplied to the same market. The comparison shall be made at the same level of trade and at comparable times, due account being taken of any other factor affecting price comparability. However, if such a direct comparison is not possible, the existence of price undercutting may be demonstrated on the basis of export unit values.

6.6   Each Member in the market of which serious prejudice is alleged to have arisen shall, subject to the provisions of paragraph 3 of Annex V, make available to the parties to a dispute arising under Article 7, and to the panel established pursuant to paragraph 4 of Article 7, all relevant information that can be obtained as to the changes in market shares of the parties to the dispute as well as concerning prices of the products involved.

6.7   Displacement or impediment resulting in serious prejudice shall not arise under paragraph 3 where any of the following circumstances exist[18] during the relevant period:

(a)   prohibition or restriction on exports of the like product from the complaining Member or on imports from the complaining Member into the third country market concerned;

(b)   decision by an importing government operating a monopoly of trade or state trading in the product concerned to shift, for non-commercial reasons, imports from the complaining Member to another country or countries;

(c)   natural disasters, strikes, transport disruptions or other *force majeure* substantially affecting production, qualities,

---

[18]   The fact that certain circumstances are referred to in this paragraph does not, in itself, confer upon them any legal status in terms of either GATT 1994 or this Agreement. These circumstances must not be isolated, sporadic or otherwise insignificant.

quantities or prices of the product available for export from the complaining Member;

(d)   existence of arrangements limiting exports from the complaining Member;

(e)   voluntary decrease in the availability for export of the product concerned from the complaining Member (including, *inter alia,* a situation where firms in the complaining Member have been autonomously reallocating exports of this product to new markets);

(f)   failure to conform to standards and other regulatory requirements in the importing country.

6.8   In the absence of circumstances referred to in paragraph 7, the existence of serious prejudice should be determined on the basis of the information submitted to or obtained by the panel, including information submitted in accordance with the provisions of Annex V.

6.9   This Article does not apply to subsidies maintained on agricultural products as provided in Article 13 of the Agreement on Agriculture.

Article 7

Remedies

7.1   Except as provided in Article 13 of the Agreement on Agriculture, whenever a Member has reason to believe that any subsidy referred to in Article 1, granted or maintained by another Member, results in injury to its domestic industry, nullification or impairment or serious prejudice, such Member may request consultations with such other Member.

* * *

7.4   If consultations do not result in a mutually agreed solution within 60 days, any Member party to such consultations may refer the matter to the DSB for the establishment of a panel, unless the DSB decides by consensus not to establish a panel. The composition of the panel and its terms of reference shall be established within 15 days from the date when it is established.

7.5   The panel shall review the matter and shall submit its final report to the parties to the dispute. The report shall be circulated to all Members within 120 days of the date of the composition and establishment of the panel's terms of reference.

7.6   Within 30 days of the issuance of the panel's report to all Members, the report shall be adopted by the DSB unless one of the parties to the dispute formally notifies the DSB of its decision to appeal or the DSB decides by consensus not to adopt the report.

* * *

7.9   In the event the Member has not taken appropriate steps to remove the adverse effects of the subsidy or withdraw the subsidy within six months from the date when the DSB adopts the panel report or the Appellate

Body report, and in the absence of agreement on compensation, the DSB shall grant authorization to the complaining Member to take countermeasures, commensurate with the degree and nature of the adverse effects determined to exist, unless the DSB decides by consensus to reject the request.

* * *

PART IV: NON-ACTIONABLE SUBSIDIES

Article 8

Identification of Non-actionable Subsidies

[Note: The provisions of Arts. 8 and 9 have "sunset" under Art. 31, and have not been renewed.]

* * *

Article 9

Consultations and Authorized Remedies

[Note: The provisions of Art. 8 and 9 have "sunset" under Art. 31, and have not been renewed.]

PART V: COUNTERVAILING MEASURES

Article 10

Application of Article VI of GATT 1994[35]

Members shall take all necessary steps to ensure that the imposition of a countervailing duty[36] on any product of the territory of any Member imported into the territory of another Member is in accordance with the provisions of Article VI of GATT 1994 and the terms of this Agreement. Countervailing duties may only be imposed pursuant to investigations initiated and conducted in accordance with the provisions of this Agreement and the Agreement on Agriculture.

---

[35]   The provisions of Part II or III may be invoked in parallel with the provisions of Part V; however, with regard to the effects of a particular subsidy in the domestic market of the importing Member, only one form of relief (either a countervailing duty, if the requirements of Part V are met, or a countermeasure under Articles 4 or 7) shall be available. The provisions of Parts III and V shall not be invoked regarding measures considered non-actionable in accordance with the provisions of Part IV. However, measures referred to in paragraph 1(a) of Article 8 may be investigated in order to determine whether or not they are specific within the meaning of Article 2. In addition, in the case of a subsidy referred to in paragraph 2 of Article 8 conferred pursuant to a programme which has not been notified in accordance with paragraph 3 of Article 8, the provisions of Part III or V may be invoked, but such subsidy shall be treated as non-actionable if it is found to conform to the standards set forth in paragraph 2 of Article 8.

[36]   The term "countervailing duty" shall be understood to mean a special duty levied for the purpose of offsetting any subsidy bestowed directly or indirectly upon the manufacture, production or export of any merchandise, as provided for in paragraph 3 of Article VI of GATT 1994.

Article 11

Initiation and Subsequent Investigation

11.1 Except as provided in paragraph 6, an investigation to determine the existence, degree and effect of any alleged subsidy shall be initiated upon a written application by or on behalf of the domestic industry.

11.2 An application under paragraph 1 shall include sufficient evidence of the existence of *(a)* a subsidy and, if possible, its amount, (b) injury within the meaning of Article VI of GATT 1994 as interpreted by this Agreement, and *(c)* a causal link between the subsidized imports and the alleged injury. Simple assertion, unsubstantiated by relevant evidence, cannot be considered sufficient to meet the requirements of this paragraph. The application shall contain such information as is reasonably available to the applicant on the following:

(i) the identity of the applicant and a description of the volume and value of the domestic production of the like product by the applicant. Where a written application is made on behalf of the domestic industry, the application shall identify the industry on behalf of which the application is made by a list of all known domestic producers of the like product (or associations of domestic producers of the like product) and, to the extent possible, a description of the volume and value of domestic production of the like product accounted for by such producers;

(ii) a complete description of the allegedly subsidized product, the names of the country or countries of origin or export in question, the identity of each known exporter or foreign producer and a list of known persons importing the product in question;

(iii) evidence with regard to the existence, amount and nature of the subsidy in question;

(iv) evidence that alleged injury to a domestic industry is caused by subsidized imports through the effects of the subsidies; this evidence includes information on the evolution of the volume of the allegedly subsidized imports, the effect of these imports on prices of the like product in the domestic market and the consequent impact of the imports on the domestic industry, as demonstrated by relevant factors and indices having a bearing on the state of the domestic industry, such as those listed in paragraphs 2 and 4 of Article 15.

11.3 The authorities shall review the accuracy and adequacy of the evidence provided in the application to determine whether the evidence is sufficient to justify the initiation of an investigation.

11.4 An investigation shall not be initiated pursuant to paragraph 1 unless the authorities have determined, on the basis of an examination of the degree of support for, or opposition to, the application expressed[38] by domestic producers of the like product, that the application has been made by or on behalf of the domestic industry.[39] The application shall be considered to have been made "by or on behalf of the domestic industry" if it is supported by those domestic producers whose collective output constitutes more than 50 per cent of the total production of the like product produced by that portion of the domestic industry expressing either support for or opposition to the application. However, no investigation shall be initiated when domestic producers expressly supporting the application account for less than 25 per cent of total production of the like product produced by the domestic industry.

* * *

11.6 If, in special circumstances, the authorities concerned decide to initiate an investigation without having received a written application by or on behalf of a domestic industry for the initiation of such investigation, they shall proceed only if they have sufficient evidence of the existence of a subsidy, injury and causal link, as described in paragraph 2, to justify the initiation of an investigation.

* * *

11.9 An application under paragraph 1 shall be rejected and an investigation shall be terminated promptly as soon as the authorities concerned are satisfied that there is not sufficient evidence of either subsidization or of injury to justify proceeding with the case. There shall be immediate termination in cases where the amount of a subsidy is *de minimis*, or where the volume of subsidized imports, actual or potential, or the injury, is negligible. For the purpose of this paragraph, the amount of the subsidy shall be considered to be *de minimis* if the subsidy is less than 1 per cent ad valorem.

* * *

Article 12

Evidence

12.1 Interested Members and all interested parties in a countervailing duty investigation shall be given notice of the information which the authorities require and ample opportunity to present in writing all evidence which they consider relevant in respect of the investigation in question.

12.1.1   Exporters,   foreign   producers   or   interested Members receiving questionnaires used in a countervailing duty investigation shall be given at least 30 days for reply. Due consideration should be given to any request for an extension of

---

[38]   In the case of fragmented industries involving an exceptionally large number of producers, authorities may determine support and opposition by using statistically valid sampling techniques.

[39]   Members are aware that in the territory of certain Members employees of domestic producers of the like product or representatives of those employees may make or support an application for an investigation under paragraph 1.

the 30-day period and, upon cause shown, such an extension should be granted whenever practicable.

12.1.2   Subject to the requirement to protect confidential information, evidence presented in writing by one interested Member or interested party shall be made available promptly to other interested Members or interested parties participating in the investigation.

* * *

12.4 Any information which is by nature confidential (for example, because its disclosure would be of significant competitive advantage to a competitor or because its disclosure would have a significantly adverse effect upon a person supplying the information or upon a person from whom the supplier acquired the information), or which is provided on a confidential basis by parties to an investigation shall, upon good cause shown, be treated as such by the authorities. Such information shall not be disclosed without specific permission of the party submitting it.

12.4.1   The authorities shall require interested Members or interested parties providing confidential information to furnish non-confidential summaries thereof. These summaries shall be in sufficient detail to permit a reasonable understanding of the substance of the information submitted in confidence. In exceptional circumstances, such Members or parties may indicate that such information is not susceptible of summary.

In such exceptional circumstances, a statement of the reasons why summarization is not possible must be provided.

12.4.2   If the authorities find that a request for confidentiality is not warranted and if the supplier of the information is either unwilling to make the information public or to authorize its disclosure in generalized or summary form, the authorities may disregard such information unless it can be demonstrated to their satisfaction from appropriate sources that the information is correct.

12.5 Except in circumstances provided for in paragraph 7, the authorities shall during the course of an investigation satisfy themselves as to the accuracy of the information supplied by interested Members or interested parties upon which their findings are based.

12.6 The investigating authorities may carry out investigations in the territory of other Members as required, provided that they have notified in good time the Member in question and unless that Member objects to the investigation. Further, the investigating authorities may carry out investigations on the premises of a firm and may examine the records of a firm if (a) the firm so agrees and (b) the Member in question is notified and does not object. * * *

12.7 In cases in which any interested Member or interested party refuses access to, or otherwise does not provide, necessary information within a reasonable period or significantly impedes the investigation, preliminary and final determinations, affirmative or negative, may be made on the basis of the facts available.

* * *

12.10 The authorities shall provide opportunities for industrial users of the product under investigation, and for representative consumer organizations in cases where the product is commonly sold at the retail level, to provide information which is relevant to the investigation regarding subsidization, injury and causality.

12.11 The authorities shall take due account of any difficulties experienced by interested parties, in particular small companies, in supplying information requested, and shall provide any assistance practicable.

* * *

Article 13

Consultations

13.1 As soon as possible after an application under Article 11 is accepted, and in any event before the initiation of any investigation, Members the products of which may be subject to such investigation shall be invited for consultations with the aim of clarifying the situation as to the matters referred to in paragraph 2 of Article 11 and arriving at a mutually agreed solution.

13.2 Furthermore, throughout the period of investigation, Members the products of which are the subject of the investigation shall be afforded a reasonable opportunity to continue consultations, with a view to clarify the factual situation and to arriving at a mutually agreed solution.[44]

* * *

Article 14

Calculation of the Amount of a Subsidy in Terms of the Benefit to the Recipient

For the purpose of Part V, any method used by the investigating authority to calculate the benefit to the recipient conferred pursuant to paragraph 1 of Article 1 shall be provided for in the national legislation or implementing regulations of the Member concerned and its application to each particular case shall be transparent and adequately explained. Furthermore, any such method shall be consistent with the following guidelines:

(a) government provision of equity capital shall not be considered as conferring a benefit, unless the investment decision

---

[44] It is particularly important, in accordance with the provisions of this paragraph that no affirmative determination whether preliminary or final be made without reasonable opportunity for consultations having been given. Such consultation may establish the basis for proceeding under the provisions of Part II, III, or X.

can be regarded as inconsistent with the usual investment practice (including for the provision of risk capital) of private investors in the territory of that Member;

(b) a loan by a government shall not be considered as conferring a benefit, unless there is a difference between the amount that the firm receiving the loan pays on the government loan and the amount the firm would pay on a comparable commercial loan which the firm could actually obtain on the market. In this case the benefit shall be the difference between these two amounts;

(c) a loan guarantee by a government shall not be considered as conferring a benefit, unless there is a difference between the amount that the firm receiving the guarantee pays on a loan guaranteed by the government and the amount that the firm would pay on a comparable commercial loan absent the government guarantee. In this case the benefit shall be the difference between these two amounts adjusted for any differences in fees;

(d) the provision of goods or services or purchase of goods by a government shall not be considered as conferring a benefit unless the provision is made for less than adequate remuneration, or the purchase is made for more than adequate remuneration. The adequacy of remuneration shall be determined in relation to prevailing market conditions for the good or service in question in the country of provision or purchase (including price, quality, availability, marketability, transportation and other conditions of purchase or sale).

Article 15

Determination of Injury[45]

15.1 A determination of injury for purposes of Article VI of GATT 1994 shall be based on positive evidence and involve an objective examination of both *(a)* the volume of the subsidized imports and the effect of the subsidized imports on prices in the domestic market for like products[46] and *(b)* the consequent impact of these imports on the domestic producers of such products.

15.2 With regard to the volume of the subsidized imports, the investigating authorities shall consider whether there has been a significant increase in subsidized imports, either in absolute terms or relative to

---

[45] Under this Agreement the term "injury" shall, unless otherwise specified, be taken to mean material injury to a domestic industry, threat of material injury to a domestic industry or material retardation of the establishment of such an industry and shall be interpreted in accordance with the provisions of this Article.

[46] Throughout this Agreement the term "like product" ("produit similaire") shall be interpreted to mean a product which is identical, i.e. alike in all respects to the product under consideration, or in the absence of such a product, another product which, although not alike in all respects, has characteristics closely resembling those of the product under consideration.

production or consumption in the importing Member. With regard to the effect of the subsidized imports on prices, the investigating authorities shall consider whether there has been a significant price undercutting by the subsidized imports as compared with the price of a like product of the importing Member, or whether the effect of such imports is otherwise to depress prices to a significant degree or to prevent price increases, which otherwise would have occurred, to a significant degree. No one or several of these factors can necessarily give decisive guidance.

15.3 Where imports of a product from more than one country are simultaneously subject to countervailing duty investigations, the investigating authorities may cumulatively assess the effects of such imports only if they determine that *(a)* the amount of subsidization established in relation to the imports from each country is more than *de minimis* as defined in paragraph 9 of Article 11 and the volume of imports from each country is not negligible and *(b)* a cumulative assessment of the effects of the imports is appropriate in light of the conditions of competition between the imported products and the conditions of competition between the imported products and the like domestic product.

15.4 The examination of the impact of the subsidized imports on the domestic industry shall include an evaluation of all relevant economic factors and indices having a bearing on the state of the industry, including actual and potential decline in output, sales, market share, profits, productivity, return on investments, or utilization of capacity; factors affecting domestic prices; actual and potential negative effects on cash flow, inventories, employment, wages, growth, ability to raise capital or investments and, in the case of agriculture, whether there has been an increased burden on government support programmes. This list is not exhaustive, nor can one or several of these factors necessarily give decisive guidance.

15.5 It must be demonstrated that the subsidized imports are, through the effects[47] of subsidies, causing injury within the meaning of this Agreement. The demonstration of a causal relationship between the subsidized imports and the injury to the domestic industry shall be based on an examination of all relevant evidence before the authorities. The authorities shall also examine any known factors other than the subsidized imports which at the same time are injuring the domestic industry, and the injuries caused by these other factors must not be attributed to the subsidized imports. Factors which may be relevant in this respect include, *inter alia,* the volumes and prices of non-subsidized imports of the product in question, contraction in demand or changes in the patterns of consumption, trade restrictive practices of and competition between the foreign and domestic producers, developments in technology and the export performance and productivity of the domestic industry.

15.6 The effect of the subsidized imports shall be assessed in relation to the domestic production of the like product when available data permit the separate identification of that production on the basis of such criteria as the production process, producers' sales and profits. If such separate

---

47   As set forth in paragraphs 2 and 4.

identification of that production is not possible, the effects of the subsidized imports shall be assessed by the examination of the production of the narrowest group or range of products, which includes the like product, for which the necessary information can be provided.

15.7 A determination of a threat of material injury shall be based on facts and not merely on allegation, conjecture or remote possibility. The change in circumstances which would create a situation in which the subsidy would cause injury must be clearly foreseen and imminent. In making a determination regarding the existence of a threat of material injury, the investigating authorities should consider, *inter alia,* such factors as:

(i) nature of the subsidy or subsidies in question and the trade effects likely to arise therefrom;

(ii) a significant rate of increase of subsidized imports into the domestic market indicating the likelihood of substantially increased importation;

(iii) sufficient freely disposable, or an imminent, substantial increase in, capacity of the exporter indicating the likelihood of substantially increased subsidized exports to the importing Member's market, taking into account the availability of other export markets to absorb any additional exports;

(iv) whether imports are entering at prices that will have a significant depressing or suppressing effect on domestic prices, and would likely increase demand for further imports; and

(v) inventories of the product being investigated.

No one of these factors by itself can necessarily give decisive guidance but the totality of the factors considered must lead to the conclusion that further subsidized exports are imminent and that, unless protective action is taken, material injury would occur.

15.8 With respect to cases where injury is threatened by subsidized imports, the application of countervailing measures shall be considered and decided with special care.

Article 16

Definition of Domestic Industry

16.1 For the purposes of this Agreement, the term "domestic industry" shall, except as provided in paragraph 2, be interpreted as referring to the domestic producers as a whole of the like products or to those of them whose collective output of the products constitutes a major proportion of the total domestic production of those products, except that when producers are related[48] to the exporters or importers or are themselves importers of the

---

[48] For the purpose of this paragraph, producers shall be deemed to be related to exporters or importers only if (a) one of them directly or indirectly controls the other; or (b) both of them are directly or indirectly controlled by a third person; or (c) together they directly or indirectly control a third person, provided that there are grounds for believing or suspecting that the effect of the relationship is such as to cause the producer concerned to behave differently from non-related producers. For the purpose

allegedly subsidized product or a like product from other countries, the term "domestic industry" may be interpreted as referring to the rest of the producers.

16.2 In exceptional circumstances, the territory of a Member may, for the production in question, be divided into two or more competitive markets and the producers within each market may be regarded as a separate industry if *(a)* the producers within such market sell all or almost all of their production of the product in question in that market, and *(b)* the demand in that market is not to any substantial degree supplied by producers of the product in question located elsewhere in the territory. In such circumstances, injury may be found to exist even where a major portion of the total domestic industry is not injured, provided there is a concentration of subsidized imports into such an isolated market and provided further that the subsidized imports are causing injury to the producers of all or almost all of the production within such market.

16.3 When the domestic industry has been interpreted as referring to the producers in a certain area, i.e. a market as defined in paragraph 2, countervailing duties shall be levied only on the products in question consigned for final consumption to that area. When the constitutional law of the importing Member does not permit the levying of countervailing duties without limitation only if *(a)* the exporters shall have been given an opportunity to cease exporting at subsidized prices to the area concerned or otherwise give assurances pursuant to Article 18, and adequate assurances in this regard have not been promptly given, and *(b)* such duties cannot be levied only on products of specific producers which supply the area in question.

16.4 Where two or more countries have reached under the provisions of paragraph 8(a) of Article XXIV of GATT 1994 such a level of integration that they have the characteristics of a single, unified market, the industry in the entire area of integration shall be taken to be the domestic industry referred to in paragraphs 1 and 2.

16.5 The provisions of paragraph 6 of Article 15 shall be applicable to this Article.

Article 17

Provisional Measures

17.1 Provisional measures may be applied only if:

(a) an investigation has been initiated in accordance with the provisions of Article 11, a public notice has been given to that effect and interested Members and interested parties have been given adequate opportunities to submit information and make comments;

---

of this paragraph, one shall be deemed to control another when the former is legally or operationally in a position to exercise restraint or direction over the latter.

(b)   a preliminary affirmative determination has been made that a subsidy exists and that there is injury to a domestic industry caused by subsidized imports; and

(c)   the authorities concerned judge such measures necessary to prevent injury being caused during the investigation.

17.2 Provisional measures may take the form of provisional countervailing duties guaranteed by cash deposits or bonds equal to the amount of the provisionally calculated amount of subsidization.

17.3 Provisional measures shall not be applied sooner than 60 days from the date of initiation of the investigation.

17.4 The application of provisional measures shall be limited to as short a period as possible, not exceeding four months.

17.5 The relevant provisions of Article 19 shall be followed in the application of provisional measures.

Article 18

Undertakings

18.1 Proceedings may[49] be suspended or terminated without the imposition of provisional measures or countervailing duties upon receipt of satisfactory voluntary undertakings under which:

(a)   the government of the exporting Member agrees to eliminate or limit the subsidy or take other measures concerning its effects; or

(b)   the exporter agrees to revise its prices so that the investigating authorities are satisfied that the injurious effect of the subsidy is eliminated. Price increases under such undertakings shall not be higher than necessary to eliminate the amount of the subsidy. It is desirable that the price increases be less than the amount of the subsidy if such increases would be adequate to remove the injury to the domestic industry.

18.2 Undertakings shall not be sought or accepted unless the authorities of the importing Member have made a preliminary affirmative determination of subsidization and injury caused by such subsidization and, in case of undertakings from exporters, have obtained the consent of the exporting Member.

18.3 Undertakings offered need not be accepted if the authorities of the importing Member consider their acceptance impractical, for example if the number of actual or potential exporters is too great, or for other reasons, including reasons of general policy. Should the case arise and where practicable, the authorities shall provide to the exporter the reasons which have led them to consider acceptance of an undertaking as inappropriate,

---

49   The word "may" shall not be interpreted to allow the simultaneous continuation of proceedings with the implementation of undertakings, except as provided in paragraph 4.

and shall, to the extent possible, give the exporter an opportunity to make comments thereon.

18.4 If an undertaking is accepted, the investigation of subsidization and injury shall nevertheless be completed if the exporting Member so desires or the importing Member so decides. In such a case, if a negative determination of subsidization or injury is made, the undertaking shall automatically lapse, except in cases where such a determination is due in large part to the existence of an undertaking. In such cases, the authorities concerned may require that an undertaking be maintained for a reasonable period consistent with the provisions of this Agreement. In the event that an affirmative determination of subsidization and injury is made, the undertaking shall continue consistent with its terms and the provisions of this Agreement.

18.5 Price undertakings may be suggested by the authorities of the importing Member, but no exporter shall be forced to enter into such undertakings. The fact that governments or exporters do not offer such undertakings, or do not accept an invitation to do so, shall in no way prejudice the consideration of the case. However, the authorities are free to determine that a threat of injury is more likely to be realized if the subsidized imports continue.

18.6 Authorities of an importing Member may require any government or exporter from whom an undertaking has been accepted to provide periodically information relevant to the fulfilment of such an undertaking, and to permit verification of pertinent data. In case of violation of an undertaking, the authorities of the importing Member may take, under this Agreement in conformity with its provisions, expeditious actions which may constitute immediate application of provisional measures using the best information available. In such cases, definitive duties may be levied in accordance with this Agreement on products entered for consumption not more than 90 days before the application of such provisional measures, except that any such retroactive assessment shall not apply to imports entered before the violation of the undertaking.

Article 19

Imposition and Collection of Countervailing Duties

19.1 If, after reasonable efforts have been made to complete consultations, a Member makes a final determination of the existence and amount of the subsidy and that, through the effects of the subsidy, the subsidized imports are causing injury, it may impose a countervailing duty in accordance with the provisions of this Article unless the subsidy or subsidies are withdrawn.

19.2 The decision whether or not to impose a countervailing duty in cases where all requirements for the imposition have been fulfilled, and the decision whether the amount of the countervailing duty to be imposed shall be the full amount of the subsidy or less, are decisions to be made by the authorities of the importing Member. It is desirable that the imposition should be permissive in the territory of all Members, that the duty should be less than the total amount of the subsidy if such lesser duty would be adequate to remove the injury to the domestic industry, and that procedures should be established which would allow the authorities concerned to take due account of representations made by domestic interested parties[50] whose interests might be adversely affected by the imposition of a countervailing duty.

19.3 When a countervailing duty is imposed in respect of any product, such countervailing duty shall be levied, in the appropriate amounts in each case, on a non-discriminatory basis on imports of such product from all sources found to be subsidized and causing injury, except as to imports from those sources which have renounced any subsidies in question or from which undertakings under the terms of this Agreement have been accepted. Any exporter whose exports are subject to a definitive countervailing duty but who was not actually investigated for reasons other than a refusal to cooperate, shall be entitled to an expedited review in order that the investigating authorities promptly establish an individual countervailing duty rate for that exporter.

19.4 No countervailing duty shall be levied on any imported product in excess of the amount of the subsidy found to exist, calculated in terms of subsidization per unit of the subsidized and exported product.

Article 20

Retroactivity

20.1 Provisional measures and countervailing duties shall only be applied to products which enter for consumption after the time when the decision under paragraph 1 of Article 17 and paragraph 1 of Article 19, respectively, enters into force, subject to the exceptions set out in this Article.

* * *

Article 21

Duration and Review of Countervailing Duties and Undertakings

21.1 A countervailing duty shall remain in force only as long as and to the extent necessary to counteract subsidization which is causing injury.

21.2 The authorities shall review the need for the continued imposition of the duty, where warranted, on their own initiative or, provided that a reasonable period of time has elapsed since the imposition of the definitive countervailing duty, upon request by any interested party which submits positive information substantiating the need for a review. Interested parties shall have the right to request the authorities to examine whether the continued imposition of the duty is necessary to offset subsidization, whether the injury would be likely to continue or recur if the duty were removed or varied, or both. If, as a result of the review under this paragraph, the

---

[50]   For the purpose of this paragraph, the term "domestic interested parties" shall include consumers and industrial users of the imported product subject to investigation.

authorities determine that the countervailing duty is no longer warranted, it shall be terminated immediately.

21.3 Notwithstanding the provisions of paragraphs 1 and 2, any definitive countervailing duty shall be terminated on a date not later than five years from its imposition (or from the date of the most recent review under paragraph 2 if that review has covered both subsidization and injury, or under this paragraph), unless the authorities determine, in a review initiated before that date on their own initiative or upon a duly substantiated request made by or on behalf of the domestic industry within a reasonable period of time prior to that date, that the expiry of the duty would be likely to lead to continuation or recurrence of subsidization and injury. The duty may remain in force pending the outcome of such a review.

21.4 The provisions of Article 12 regarding evidence and procedure shall apply to any review carried out under this Article. Any such review shall be carried out expeditiously and shall normally be concluded within 12 months of the date of initiation of the review.

21.5 The provisions of this Article shall apply *mutatis mutandis* to undertakings accepted under Article 18.

Article 22

Public Notice and Explanation of Determinations

22.1 When the authorities are satisfied that there is sufficient evidence to justify the initiation of an investigation pursuant to Article 11, the Member or Members the products of which are subject to such investigation and other interested parties known to the investigating authorities to have an interest therein shall be notified and a public notice shall be given.

22.2 A public notice of the initiation of an investigation shall contain, or otherwise make available through a separate report, adequate information on the following:

(i)   the name of the exporting country or countries and the product involved;

(ii)   the date of initiation of the investigation;

(iii) a description of the subsidy practice or practices to be investigated;

(iv)   a summary of the factors on which the allegation of injury is based;

(v)   the address to which representations by interested Members and interested parties should be directed; and

(vi)   the time-limits allowed to interested Members and interested parties for making their views known.

22.3 Public notice shall be given of any preliminary or final determination, whether affirmative or negative, of any decision to accept an undertaking pursuant to Article 18, of the termination of such an undertaking, and of the termination of a definitive countervailing duty. * * *

22.4 A public notice of the imposition of provisional measures shall set forth, or otherwise make available through a separate report, sufficiently detailed explanations for the preliminary determinations on the existence of a subsidy and injury and shall refer to the matters of fact and law which have led to arguments being accepted or rejected. Such a notice or report shall, due regard being paid to the requirement for the protection of confidential information, contain in particular:

(i)   the names of the suppliers or, when this is impracticable, the supplying countries involved;

(ii)   a description of the product which is sufficient for customs purposes;

(iii)   the amount of subsidy established and the basis on which the existence of a subsidy has been determined;

(iv)   considerations relevant to the injury determination as set out in Article 15;

(v)   the main reasons leading to the determination.

22.5 A public notice of conclusion or suspension of an investigation in the case of an affirmative determination providing for the imposition of a definitive duty or the acceptance of an undertaking shall contain, or otherwise make available through a separate report, all relevant information on the matters of fact and law and reasons which have led to the imposition of final measures or the acceptance of an undertaking, due regard being paid to the requirement for the protection of confidential information. In particular, the notice or report shall contain the information described in paragraph 4, as well as the reasons for the acceptance or rejection of relevant arguments or claims made by interested Members and by the exporters and importers.

22.6 A public notice of the termination or suspension of an investigation following the acceptance of an undertaking pursuant to Article 18 shall include, or otherwise make available through a separate report, the non-confidential part of this undertaking.

22.7 The provisions of this Article shall apply *mutatis mutandis* to the initiation and completion of reviews pursuant to Article 21 and to decisions under Article 20 to apply duties retroactively.

Article 23

Judicial Review

Each Member whose national legislation contains provisions on countervailing duty measures shall maintain judicial, arbitral or administrative tribunals or procedures for the purpose, *inter alia,* of the prompt review of administrative actions relating to final determinations and reviews of determinations within the meaning of Article 21. Such tribunals or procedures shall be independent of the authorities responsible for the determination or review in question, and shall provide all interested parties who participated in the administrative proceeding and are directly and individually affected by the administrative actions with access to review.

* * *

PART VII: NOTIFICATION AND SURVEILLANCE

Article 25

Notifications

25.1 Members agree that, without prejudice to the provisions of paragraph 1 of Article XVI of GATT 1994, their notifications of subsidies shall be submitted not later than 30 June of each year and shall conform to the provisions of paragraphs 2 through 6.

25.2 Members shall notify any subsidy as defined in paragraph 1 of Article 1, which is specific within the meaning of Article 2, granted or maintained within their territories.

25.3 The content of notifications should be sufficiently specific to enable other Members to evaluate the trade effects and to understand the operation of notified subsidy programmes. * * *

25.6 Members which consider that there are no measures in their territories requiring notification under paragraph 1 of Article XVI of GATT 1994 and this Agreement shall so inform the Secretariat in writing.

* * *

25.10 Any Member which considers that any measure of another Member having the effects of a subsidy has not been notified in accordance with the provisions of paragraph 1 of Article XVI of GATT 1994 and this Article may bring the matter to the attention of such other Member. If the alleged subsidy is not thereafter notified promptly, such Member may itself bring the alleged subsidy in question to the notice of the Committee.

25.11 Members shall report without delay to the Committee all preliminary or final actions taken with respect to countervailing duties. Such reports shall be available in the Secretariat for inspection by other Members. Members shall also submit, on a semi-annual basis, reports on any countervailing duty actions taken within the preceding six months. The semi-annual reports shall be submitted on an agreed standard form.

* * *

PART VIII: DEVELOPING COUNTRY MEMBERS

Article 27

Special and Differential Treatment of Developing Country Members

27.1 Members recognize that subsidies may play an important role in economic development programmes of developing country Members.

27.2 The prohibition of paragraph 1(a) of Article 3 shall not apply to:

(a)   developing country Members referred to in Annex VII.

(b)   other developing country Members for a period of eight years from the date of entry into force of the WTO Agreement, subject to compliance with the provisions in paragraph 4.

27.3 The prohibition of paragraph 1(b) of Article 3 shall not apply to developing country Members for a period of five years, and shall not apply to least developed country Members for a period of eight years, from the date of entry into force of the WTO Agreement.

27.4 Any developing country Member referred to in paragraph 2(b) shall phase out its export subsidies within the eight-year period, preferably in a progressive manner. * * *

* * *

PART X: DISPUTE SETTLEMENT

Article 30

The provisions of Articles XXII and XXIII of GATT 1994 as elaborated and applied by the Dispute Settlement Understanding shall apply to consultations and the settlement of disputes under this Agreement, except as otherwise specifically provided herein.

PART XI: FINAL PROVISIONS

Article 31

Provisional Application

The provisions of paragraph 1 of Article 6 and the provisions of Article 8 and Article 9 shall apply for a period of five years, beginning with the date of entry into force of the WTO Agreement. Not later than 180 days before the end of this period, the Committee shall review the operation of those provisions, with a view to determining whether to extend their application, either as presently drafted or in a modified form, for a further period.

* * *

ANNEX I

ILLUSTRATIVE LIST OF EXPORT SUBSIDIES

(a)   The provision by governments of direct subsidies to a firm or an industry contingent upon export performance.

(b)   Currency retention schemes or any similar practices which involve a bonus on exports.

(c)   Internal transport and freight charges on export shipments, provided or mandated by governments, on terms more favourable than for domestic shipments.

(d)   The provision by governments or their agencies either directly or indirectly through government-mandated schemes, of imported or domestic products or services for use in the production of exported goods, on terms or conditions more favourable than for provision of like or directly competitive products or services for use in the production of goods for domestic consumption, if (in the case of products) such terms or conditions are more favourable than those commercially available[57] on world markets to their exporters.

(e) The full or partial exemption remission, or deferral specifically related to exports, of direct taxes[58] or social welfare charges paid or payable by industrial or commercial enterprises.[59]

(f) The allowance of special deductions directly related to exports or export performance, over and above those granted in respect to production for domestic consumption, in the calculation of the base on which direct taxes are charged.

(g) The exemption or remission, in respect of the production and distribution of exported products, of indirect taxes in excess of those levied in respect of the production and distribution of like products when sold for domestic consumption.

(h) The exemption, remission or deferral of prior-stage cumulative indirect taxes on goods or services used in the production of exported products in excess of the exemption, remission or deferral of like prior-stage cumulative indirect taxes on goods or services used in the production of like

---

[57] The term "commercially available" means that the choice between domestic and imported products is unrestricted and depends only on commercial considerations.

[58] For the purpose of this Agreement:

The term "direct taxes" shall mean taxes on wages, profits, interests, rents, royalties, and all other forms of income, and taxes on the ownership of real property;

The term "import charges" shall mean tariffs, duties, and other fiscal charges not elsewhere enumerated in this note that are levied on imports;

The term "indirect taxes" shall mean sales, excise, turnover, value added, franchise, stamp, transfer, inventory and equipment taxes, border taxes and all taxes other than direct taxes and import charges;

"Prior-stage" indirect taxes are those levied on goods or services used directly or indirectly in making the product;

"Cumulative" indirect taxes are multi-staged taxes levied where there is no mechanism for subsequent crediting of the tax if the goods or services subject to tax at one stage of production are used in a succeeding stage of production;

"Remission" of taxes includes the refund or rebate of taxes;

"Remission or drawback" includes the full or partial exemption or deferral of import charges.

[59] The Members recognize that deferral need not amount to an export subsidy where, for example, appropriate interest charges are collected. The Members reaffirm the principle that prices for goods in transactions between exporting enterprises and foreign buyers under their or under the same control should for tax purposes be the prices which would be charged between independent enterprises acting at arm's length. Any Member may draw the attention of another Member to administrative or other practices which may contravene this principle and which result in a significant saving of direct taxes in export transactions. In such circumstances the Members shall normally attempt to resolve their differences using the facilities of existing bilateral tax treaties or other specific international mechanisms, without prejudice to the rights and obligations of Members under GATT 1994, including the right of consultation created in the preceding sentence.

Paragraph (e) is not intended to limit a Member from taking measures to avoid the double taxation of foreign-source income earned by its enterprises or the enterprises of another Member.

products when sold for domestic consumption; provided, however, that prior-stage cumulative indirect taxes may be exempted, remitted or deferred on exported products even when not exempted, remitted or deferred on like products when sold for domestic consumption, if the prior-stage cumulative indirect taxes are levied on inputs that are consumed in the production of the exported product (making normal allowance for waste).[60] This item shall be interpreted in accordance with the guidelines on consumption of inputs in the production process contained in Annex II.

(i)   The remission or drawback of import charges in excess of those levied on imported inputs that are consumed in the production of the exported product (making normal allowance for waste); provided, however, that in particular cases a firm may use a quantity of home market inputs equal to, and having the same quality and characteristics as, the imported inputs as a substitute for them in order to benefit from this provision if the import and the corresponding export operations both occur within a reasonable time period, not to exceed two years. This item shall be interpreted in accordance with the guidelines on consumption of inputs in the production process contained in Annex II and the guidelines in the determination of substitution drawback systems as export subsidies contained in Annex III.

(j)   The provision by governments (or special institutions controlled by governments) of export credit guarantee or insurance programmes, of insurance or guarantee programmes against increases in the cost of exported products or of exchange risk programmes, at premium rates which are inadequate to cover the long-term operating costs and losses of the programmes.

(k)   The grant by governments (or special institutions controlled by and/or acting under the authority of governments) of export credits at rates below those which they actually have to pay for the funds so employed (or would have to pay if they borrowed on international capital markets in order to obtain funds of the same maturity and other credit terms and denominated in the same currency as the export credit), or the payment by them of all or part of the costs incurred by exporters or financial institutions in obtaining credits, in so far as they are used to secure a material advantage in the field of export credit terms.

Provided, however, that if a Member is a party to an international undertaking on official export credits to which at least twelve original Members to this Agreement are parties as of 1 January 1979 (or a successor undertaking which has been adopted by those original Members), or if in practice a Member applies the interest rates provisions of the relevant undertaking, an export credit practice which is in conformity with those provisions shall not be considered an export subsidy prohibited by this Agreement.

---

[60]   Paragraph (h) does not apply to value-added tax systems and border-tax adjustment in lieu thereof; the problem of the excessive remission of value-added taxes is exclusively covered by paragraph (g).

(*l*)   Any other charge on the public account constituting an export subsidy in the sense of Article XVI of GATT 1994.

* * *

ANNEX IV

CALCULATION OF THE TOTAL AD VALOREM SUBSIDIZATION (PARAGRAPH 1(A) OF ARTICLE 6)

1.   Any calculation of the amount of a subsidy for the purpose of paragraph 1(a) of Article 6 shall be done in terms of the cost to the granting government.

2.   Except as provided in paragraphs 3 through 5, in determining whether the overall rate of subsidization exceeds 5 per cent of the value of the product, the value of the product shall be calculated as the total value of the recipient firm's sales in the most recent 12-month period, for which sales data is available, preceding the period in which the subsidy is granted.

3.   Where the subsidy is tied to the production or sale of a given product, the value of the product shall be calculated as the total value of the recipient firm's sales of that product in the most recent 12-month period, for which sales data is available, preceding the period in which the subsidy is granted.

4.   Where the recipient firm is in a start-up situation, serious prejudice shall be deemed to exist if the overall rate of subsidization exceeds 15 per cent of the total funds invested. For purposes of this paragraph, a start-up period will not extend beyond the first year of production.

5.   Where the recipient firm is located in an inflationary economy country, the value of the product shall be calculated as the recipient firm's total sales (or sales of the relevant product, if the subsidy is tied) in the preceding calendar year indexed by the rate of inflation experienced in the 12 months preceding the month in which the subsidy is to be given.

6.   In determining the overall rate of subsidization in a given year, subsidies given under different programmes and by different authorities in the territory of a Member shall be aggregated.

7.   Subsidies granted prior to the date of entry into force of the WTO Agreement, the benefits of which are allocated to future production, shall be included in the overall rate of subsidization.

8.   Subsidies which are non-actionable under relevant provisions of this Agreement shall not be included in the calculation of the amount of a subsidy for the purpose of paragraph 1(a) of Article 6.

ANNEX V

PROCEDURES FOR DEVELOPING INFORMATION CONCERNING SERIOUS PREJUDICE

1.   Every Member shall cooperate in the development of evidence to be examined by a panel in procedures under paragraphs 4 through 6 of Article 7. The parties to the dispute and any third-country Member

concerned shall notify to the DSB, as soon as the provisions of paragraph 4 of Article 7 have been invoked, the organization responsible for administration of this provision within its territory and the procedures to be used to comply with requests for information.

2.   In cases where matters are referred to the DSB under paragraph 4 of Article 7, the DSB shall, upon request, initiate the procedure to obtain such information from the government of the subsidizing Member as necessary to establish the existence and amount of subsidization, the value of total sales of the subsidized firms, as well as information necessary to analyze the adverse effects caused by the subsidized product.[66] This process may include, where appropriate, presentation of questions to the government of the subsidizing Member and of the complaining Member to collect information, as well as to clarify and obtain elaboration of information available to the parties to a dispute through the notification procedures set forth in Part VII.[67]

3.   In the case of effects in third-country markets, a party to a dispute may collect information, including through the use of questions to the government of the third-country Member, necessary to analyse adverse effects, which is not otherwise reasonably available from the complaining Member or the subsidizing Member. This requirement should be administered in such a way as not to impose an unreasonable burden on the third-country Member. In particular, such a Member is not expected to make a market or price analysis specially for that purpose. The information to be supplied is that which is already available or can be readily obtained by this Member (e.g. most recent statistics which have already been gathered by relevant statistical services but which have not yet been published, customs data concerning imports and declared values of the products concerned, etc.). However, if a party to a dispute undertakes a detailed market analysis at its own expense, the task of the person or firm conducting such an analysis shall be facilitated by the authorities of the third-country Member and such a person or firm shall be given access to all information which is not normally maintained confidential by the government.

4.   The DSB shall designate a representative to serve the function of facilitating the information-gathering process. The sole purpose of the representative shall be to ensure the timely development of the information necessary to facilitate expeditious subsequent multilateral review of the dispute. In particular, the representative may suggest ways to most efficiently solicit necessary information as well as encourage the cooperation of the parties.

5.   The information-gathering process outlined in paragraphs 2 through 4 shall be completed within 60 days of the date on which the matter has been referred to the DSB under paragraph 4 of Article 7. The information obtained during this process shall be submitted to the panel established by

---

[66]   In cases where the existence of serious prejudice has to be demonstrated.

[67]   The information-gathering process by the DSB shall take into account the need to protect information which is by nature confidential or which is provided on a confidential basis by any Member involved in this process.

the DSB in accordance with the provisions of Part X. This information should include, *inter alia,* data concerning the amount of the subsidy in question (and, where appropriate, the value of total sales of the subsidized firms), prices of the subsidized product, prices of the non-subsidized product, prices of other suppliers to the market, changes in the supply of the subsidized product to the market in question and changes in market shares. It should also include rebuttal evidence, as well as such supplemental information as the panel deems relevant in the course of reaching its conclusions.

6.   If the subsidizing and/or third-country Member fails to cooperate in the information-gathering process, the complaining Member will present its case of serious prejudice, based on evidence available to it, together with facts and circumstances of the non-cooperation of the subsidizing and/or third-country Member. Where information is unavailable due to non-cooperation by the subsidizing and/or third-country Member, the panel may complete the record as necessary relying on best information otherwise available.

7.   In making its determination, the panel should draw adverse inferences from instances of non-cooperation by any party involved in the information-gathering process.

8.   In making a determination to use either best information available or adverse inferences, the panel shall consider the advice of the DSB representative nominated under paragraph 4 as to the reasonableness of any requests for information and the efforts made by parties to comply with these requests in a cooperative and timely manner.

9.   Nothing in the information-gathering process shall limit the ability of the panel to seek such additional information it deems essential to a proper resolution to the dispute, and which was not adequately sought or developed during that process. However, ordinarily the panel should not request additional information to complete the record where the information would support a particular party's position and the absence of that information in the record is the result of unreasonable non-cooperation by that party in the information-gathering process.

* * *

Chapter 6

SAFEGUARD PROCEEDINGS, TRADE ADJUSTMENT ASSISTANCE

Table of Sections

§ 6.1 Temporary Relief from Import Competition

Safeguard ("escape clause") and market disruption proceedings are anticipated by Article XIX of the General Agreement on Tariffs and Trade (GATT). A WTO "Safeguards Agreement" emerged from the Uruguay Round of negotiations.[1] In contrast to the statutory remedies against dumping and countervailable subsidies reviewed in Chapters 4 and 5, safeguard proceedings are not targeted at unfair international trade practices. Rather, the goods are assumed to be fairly traded but imports are in such an unexpected volume that

---

[1] *See* Section 6.3.

temporary protection is appropriate to allow the domestic industry to adjust to the new competitive environment.

In the United States, businesses may seek protection from import competition by initiating what are known as "escape clause" (safeguard) proceedings under the Trade Act of 1974. Escape clause proceedings can involve imports from anywhere in the world, and are authorized by Section 201 of the Trade Act.[2] Escape clause proceedings are also typically found in the free trade agreements of the United States.

In addition, "market disruption proceedings" can also provide temporary relief from import competition. Market disruption proceedings concern imports from communist nations and are authorized by Section 406 of the 1974 Trade Act.[3] They are similar but not identical to escape clause proceedings. Either may result in the imposition of U.S. import restraints, or presidential negotiation of export restraints from the source country.

Import injury relief available under the Trade Act of 1974 is basically of two kinds: (1) Presidential relief designed to temporarily protect domestic producers of like or directly competitive products; and (2) governmental assistance to workers and firms economically displaced by import competition. This assistance is intended to enhance job opportunities and competitiveness. Protective relief tends to be awarded when the President believes that U.S. industry needs time to adjust. Governmental assistance is seen as a means to accommodate the injury caused by import competition. In either case, adjustment to import competition is the longer term goal, hopefully resulting in more competitive U.S. industries and markets.

§ 6.2   The Impact of Limited U.S. Judicial Review

Because of the President's power over escape clause and market disruption remedies, judicial review of these proceedings and remedies is very limited. As the Federal Circuit observed in *Corus Group PLC. v. International Trade Commission*, "under the escape clause provision of the Trade Act of 1974, '[f]or a court to interpose, there has to be a clear misconstruction of the governing statute, a significant procedural violation, or action outside delegated authority."[4] This flows from the President's broad constitutional powers over foreign affairs. Derivatively, the actions of the International Trade Commission (ITC, or Commission) in these

---

2   19 U.S.C. § 2251.

3   19 U.S.C. § 2436.

4   352 F.3d 1351, 1361 (Fed. Cir. 2003)(*quoting Maple Leaf Fish Co. v. United States*, 762 F.2d 86, 89 (Fed. Cir. 1985)).

proceedings are likewise sheltered from extensive judicial review.[5] This means that the decisions of the ITC are critical to obtaining escape clause relief.

GATT/WTO compensation duties, U.S. free trade agreements, presidential prerogatives, and important amendments to Section 201 in 1988 and 1994 have significantly reduced the potential for protective trade relief. During the 1990s, there were very few Section 201 or Section 406 proceedings. Since 2003, the ITC has not instituted any Section 201 proceedings (although it has instituted six under a special rule related to Chinese imports arising from China's accession to the WTO)[6]. The main focus of U.S. escape clause relief has instead become trade adjustment assistance, as Sections 6.14 and 6.15 discuss in detail.

§ 6.3   The WTO Safeguards Agreement

One of the important "Codes" of the Uruguay Round negotiations is the "WTO Agreement on Safeguards." It concerns escape clause and related "gray area" protective measures. Under the Safeguards Agreement, the imposition of temporary protective relief from increased imports (absolutely or relatively) does not require a showing of any unfair trade practice, such as dumping or subsidies. But the injury standard is seemingly higher: Such duties are only permitted only where increased imports cause a "*serious* injury or threat thereof" (emphasis added) to a domestic industry. For antidumping duties and countervailing duties, the standard is merely "material" injury.[7] In addition, reaching back to language found in Article XIX of the GATT, the WTO Appellate Body has ruled that safeguards may be imposed only when the surge of imports is result from "unforeseen developments".[8]

The Safeguards Agreement permits escape clause measures "only to the extent necessary" to prevent or remedy such an injury and to "facilitate adjustment." Such measures are allowed for a maximum of four years, and on a progressively decreasing basis. Upon a further investigation, a member state may extend the measures, but not beyond a total period of eight years.

Perhaps the most important provision of the Safeguards Agreement is that it expressly prohibits a member state from seeking, undertaking, or maintaining voluntary export or import

---

[5] *Id. See also Maple Leaf Fish Co. v. United States*, 762 F.2d 86 (Fed. Cir. 1985).

[6] *See* Section 6.12.

[7] *See* Sections 4.12, 5.13.

[8] *See* Argentina—Footwear (EC), WT/DS56 (1998); U.S. Steel Safeguards, WT/DS248 (2003).

restraint agreements (VERs or OMAs).[9] These were quite common, especially by developed countries to protect against unwanted imports, prior to the adoption of the Safeguards Agreement in 1994.

Protective safeguard remedies are often in the form of tariff increases and tariff rate quotas (TRQs). In general, such remedies must be applied on an MFN-basis to imports regardless of their source. Exporting countries with substantial interests at stake are entitled, absent satisfactory compensation, to suspend trade concessions benefiting the safeguarding country. The duty to compensate can generally be avoided if the safeguard action is for less than three years, responds to absolute import increases, and conforms to the provisions of the Safeguards Code.

Typically, the affected exporters suspend concessions, then de-activate those suspensions while challenging conformity in WTO proceedings. The suspended concessions come back into force after three years, or a WTO ruling of nonconformity with the Safeguards Code, whichever is sooner. Special rules limit the use of safeguard measures against imports from developing countries, and allow such countries to impose safeguard measures to protect domestic industries for up to ten years. The utilization of protective safeguard measures cannot generally be followed by a second usage in the same product market within two years or half the duration of the first use.

Congress implemented the Safeguards Agreement accords in December of 1994 through the Uruguay Round Agreements Act.[10] This Act changed a number of rules of U.S. law relating to escape clause relief. The most notable of these changes were: (1) clarifications of the meaning of significant terms, such as "domestic industry," "serious injury," and "threat of serious injury"; (2) changes to the duration of relief to provide an initial period of up to four years and an overall limit of eight years; (3) a requirement that any relief actions exceeding one year be "phased down at regular intervals" during the relief period; (4)permissible ITC investigations at the request of the President or on petition by industry with respect to continuing a relief measure; (5) certain new rules to protect confidential business information collected as part of a proceeding; and (6) an allowance of expedited proceedings in "critical circumstances."[11]

The more general effect of URAA was to bring U.S. escape clause law into compliance with the Safeguards Agreement. Except as to

---

[9]   *See* Safeguards Agreement, art. 11.

[10]   Public Law No. 103–465, 108 Stat. 4809.

[11]   A summary of these changes is available in the International Trade Commission's "Annual Report".

certain doubts noted below, the standards and procedures for the granting of escape clause relief as described in the Sections below conform to the substance of the WTO's Safeguards Agreement. At this stage, the United States and the European Union almost never invoke safeguards, but developing nations (for example India, Indonesia and Turkey) have frequently done so.

§ 6.4   U.S. Safeguard Proceedings—Petitions

Decisions about the granting of escape clause relief are made by the President upon the recommendation of the ITC. Any entity that is representative of an industry, including a "trade association, firm, certified or recognized union, or group of workers," may file a petition requesting such import relief.[12] The petition must state the "specific purposes" for any requested action "which may include facilitating the orderly transfer of resources to more productive pursuits, enhancing competitiveness, or other means of adjustment to new conditions of competition."[13] The ITC also must initiate an escape clause proceeding at the request of the President, the United States Trade Representative, and certain congressional committees, and may do so "on its own motion."[14]

The Trade Act indicates that the purposes of the safeguards relief is to facilitate the orderly transfer of resources to more productive pursuits, enhance competitiveness, or otherwise assist an industry to adjust to new conditions of competition.[15] The petition may request provisional relief pending the outcome of an escape clause proceeding. Petitions under Section 201 also must show that a substantial number of the companies or workers in the industry support the petition, as the Trade Act requires that the petitioning "entity" be "representative of an industry."[16] In this sense, the petitioner is like a class action representative. While it is not necessary for all companies or workers in the industry to support the petition, a substantial proportion must do so because Section 201 is focused upon industry-wide relief.

The petitioner industry or worker group may—and is well advised to—submit its own specific plan "to facilitate positive adjustment to import competition" during the term of any protective relief.[17] This is often done because the Commission is required in conducting its escape clause investigation to seek information on

---

[12]   19 U.S.C. § 2252(a)(1).
[13]   19 U.S.C. § 2252(a)(2).
[14]   19 U.S.C. § 2252(b)(1)(A).
[15]   19 U.S.C. § 2252(a)(2).
[16]   19 U.S.C. § 2252(a)(1).
[17]   19 U.S.C. § 2252(a)(4).

actions being taken or planned by the firms and workers in the industry to make a positive adjustment to import competition. Moreover, the Commission is authorized to accept "commitments" regarding such action if it affirmatively determines that the statutory criteria of Section 201 are met.[18]

§ 6.5   USITC Investigations

Upon the filing of a petition that meets the statutory requirements, the ITC must then "promptly" begin an investigation to determine whether the import competition meets the statutory standard for temporary escape clause relief.[19] Separately, if the industry is unable to adequately document its case for escape clause relief, it may be possible to convince the Commission to do this on its own under what is known as a general Section 332 investigation.[20] If successful, a Section 332 investigation will shift the burden and the cost of preparing a Section 201 proceeding from the industry or its representatives to the Commission.

As the Commission's investigation proceeds, it will develop an extensive questionnaire to send to domestic producers. This questionnaire focuses on the kinds of information the Commission needs to obtain in order to assess the statutory criteria for escape clause relief. Although industry members typically support escape clause relief, they may not wish to reveal all the information requested in the questionnaire. In this case, the ITC can obtain subpoena enforcement from the U.S. District Court for the District of Columbia.[21]

The hearings held by the ITC in connection with escape clause proceedings involve testimony under oath with the right of cross examination by opposing parties. Thus, for example, importers that do not wish to see restrictive measures imposed may oppose the domestic industry and its witnesses. The various procedures governing escape clause investigations by the ITC defined in 19 C.F.R. Parts 201 and 206. The entire ITC investigation normally takes about six months.

§ 6.6   U.S. Statutory Criteria for Safeguard Relief

Section 201 of the Trade Act of 1974 requires proof of an increase in imports which substantially causes or threaten to causes serious injury to domestic industries producing like or directly competitive

---

[18]   19 U.S.C. § 2252(a)(4)–(7).

[19]   19 U.S.C. § 2252(b)(1)(A).

[20]   19 U.S.C. § 1332.

[21]   19 U.S.C. § 1333(b).

articles.[22] The ITC traditionally has divided this statutory standard for escape clause relief into three separate criteria. In order to make an affirmative determination on an escape clause petition, the ITC must find, as it stated in the famous (or infamous) *Steel Safeguards* determination, that:

"(1) Imports of the subject article are in *increased quantities. . .*;

(2) The domestic industry producing an article that is like or directly competitive with the imported article is *seriously injured or threatened with serious injury*; and

(3) The article is being imported in such increased quantities as to be a *substantial cause* of serious injury or threat of serious injury to the domestic industry."[23]

Of these three, the causation and injury criteria are the most consequential. They are the subject of separate analysis in Sections 6.8 and 6.9 below.

The increased quantity of imports test is comparatively uncontroversial. But for clarity the Trade Act emphasizes that the required "increase" in imports may be "either actual or relative to domestic production," and in consideration of imports from all sources. Relative increases occur when domestic production declines when measured against imports. Imports could thus decline but be relatively increasing if domestic production is declining at an even faster rate.[24]

§ 6.7   Relevant Domestic U.S. Industry

The focus of an escape clause proceeding is the harm to a domestic industry. Thus, the ITC must first identify what the relevant domestic industry is. But this in turn requires an identification of the relevant domestic products affected by the imports. The Trade Act focuses on the domestic industry that "produc[es] an article like or directly competitive with the imported article."[25] In determining what constitutes a "like product," the ITC has traditionally consider a wide variety of factors, including "the physical properties of the product, its customs treatment, its

---

[22]   19 U.S.C. § 2251(a).

[23]   *See* U.S. International Trade Commission—*Steel*, Investigation No. TA–201–73, at 27 (Pub. No. 3479, Dec., 2001).

[24]   *See* 19 U.S.C. § 2252(c)(1)(C).

[25]   19 U.S.C. § 2252(b)(1)(A).

manufacturing process (*i.e.*, where and how it is made), its uses, and the marketing channels through which the product is sold."[26]

Escape clause proceedings nonetheless commonly involve disputes as to the definition of the "competitive" imported article. Typically, domestic producers will want to define the imported article broadly so as to enhance the possibility of proving domestic injury as well as of obtaining broader relief. Importers of the product in question will want to define the imported article narrowly or in terms of separate categories so as to minimize the potential for escape clause remedies.

One issue concerning the definition of the domestic industry is whether it can involve various stages of processing. In other words, the issue is whether the imports must be at the same level of processing as the domestic industry. Once a uncertain area, the Trade Act now specifically states that various stages of processing can be considered in defining the relevant imported product. This has the practical effect of allowing the imported article to be at a different level of process from that which causes injury to the domestic industry.[27]

The next step is to identify the relevant domestic industry with respect to the relevant competitive products. The Trade Act defines the relevant "domestic industry" as either all of the producers of the articles at issue or "those producers whose collective production of the like or directly competitive article constitutes a major proportion of the total domestic production" of those articles.[28]

Having defined the industry, the Commission then must decide which particular companies belong to it. This is not always easy. In the ITC's automobile investigation during the serious economic downturn of the 1970s, for example, the Commission had to decide whether dealers and independent parts suppliers were part of the same domestic industry. It found that neither were part of the domestic industry because the dealers did not produce any article, and the independent suppliers of parts did not produce products that were like or directly competitive with the final product.[29]

To guide this difficult issue, the Trade Act provides specific instructions to the ITC: First, if a domestic company is also an importer, the ITC may only consider that part of the business that

[26]   *See* U.S. International Trade Commission—*Steel*, Investigation No. TA–201–73, at 30 (Pub. No. 3479, Dec., 2001).

[27]   *See* 19 U.S.C. § 2481(5).

[28]   19 U.S.C. § 2252(c)(6)(A).

[29]   *See* U.S. International Trade Commission—*Certain Motor Vehicles and Certain Chassis and Bodies Thereof*, Investigation No. TA–201–44, Publication No. 1110 (Dec. 1980).

relates to domestic production to be in the domestic industry.[30] Second, if a domestic company produces more than one article, the ITC may treat as part of such domestic industry "only that portion or subdivision of the producer which produces the like or directly competitive article."[31] Finally, if the domestic producers are concentrated in one geographic area of the country and the imports also are concentrated in that area, the ITC may treat as the relevant domestic industry "only that segment of the production located in such area."[32]

§ 6.8   Substantial Causation

The issue of causation commonly is among the most controversial in escape clause proceedings. As a general matter, the Trade Act requires that the ITC "investigate any factor which in its judgment may be contributing to increased imports of the article under investigation."[33] But it also provides that the ITC "shall" consider the condition of the domestic industry not only at the specific time of the petition but over "the course of its relevant business cycle."[34]

The Trade Act defines "substantial cause" as "a cause which is important and not less than any other cause."[35] Thus, as the ITC has observed, "increased imports must be both an important cause of the serious injury or threat and a cause that is equal to or greater than any other cause."[36] The Act directs the ITC to consider all relevant economic factors, including "an increase in imports (either actual or relative to domestic production) and a decline in the proportion of the domestic market supplied by domestic producers."[37] As a more general matter, the Trade Act obligates the ITC to "examine factors other than imports" that may be the cause of an injury to a domestic industry.[38] However, the ITC may not aggregate the cause of declining demand associated with a recession or economic downturn into "a single cause" of serious injury or threat of injury.[39]

Of its nature, the adjective "substantial" leaves considerable latitude to the ITC in making its determinations of import injury

---

[30]   19 U.S.C. § 2252(c)(4)(A).

[31]   19 U.S.C. § 2252(c)(4)(B).

[32]   19 U.S.C. § 2252(c)(4)(C).

[33]   19 U.S.C. § 2252(c)(5).

[34]   19 U.S.C. § 2252(c)(2).

[35]   19 U.S.C. § 2252(b)(1)(B).

[36]   *See* U.S. International Trade Commission—*Steel*, Investigation No. TA–201–73, at 34 (Pub. No. 3479, Dec., 2001).

[37]   19 U.S.C. § 2252(c)(1)(C).

[38]   19 U.S.C. § 2252(c)(2)(B).

[39]   19 U.S.C. § 2252(c)(2)(A).

under Section 201. The difficulty with the "substantial cause" element comes in determining whether increased imports are "equal to or greater than" the myriad of other competing factors that may cause harm to an industry. Management may be inept; labor may be underproductive or overly costly; general economic trends may be predominantly negative; and technological innovations may be causing obsolescence. Myriad causes may be at play. Whether one cause is more substantial than another is often very difficult to pinpoint with precision.

The issue of causation also may be affected by political currents at the ITC. For example, the controversial *Steel* decision of 2001 was initiated by the U.S. Trade Representative and clearly unfolded in an atmosphere of political support for the steel industry at the highest levels of government.[40] In another controversial case, ITC refused to consider a general recession as a more substantial cause for a decline in the U.S. motorcycle industry.[41] On this point, Congress was forced to step in to clarify by express language that, also noted above, the ITC may not aggregate the causes of declining production associated with a general economic downturn into a single cause.[42] The point of this rule is that increasing imports may also be a "substantial cause" of a serious injury to a domestic industry even during a serious recession.

Economic Factors

The Trade Act requires that the ITC not only "investigate" other contributing factors, but also that it then "take into account all economic factors which it considers relevant" in making its ultimate determination.[43] In carrying out this obligation, the ITC in fact has considered a wide array of causes in past decisions, including the following alternative causes of injury to domestic industries:

(1)   Consumer cycles that affect product purchases;

(2)   Fundamental changes in consumption;

(3)   Governmental regulation;

(4)   Industry competition;

(5)   Management decision making;

---

[40]   *See* U.S. International Trade Commission—*Steel*, Investigation No. TA–201–73 (Pub. No. 3479, Dec., 2001).

[41]   U.S. International Trade Commission—H*eavy Weight Motorcycles, & Engines & Power Train Subassemblies Therefor*, Investigation No. TA–201–47 (1983).

[42]   *See* 19 U.S.C. § 2252(c).

[43]   19 U.S.C. § 2252(c)(1).

(6) Trends in imports, domestic consumption and production;

(7) Price changes in the product market;

(8) Business cycle changes;

(9) Labor contract negotiations; and

(10) World price and competitive conditions.[44]

Finally, the legislative history of the Trade Act expressly identified other types of causes that may be more important than increased imports, including "changes in technology or in consumer tastes, domestic competition from substitute products, plant obsolescence, or poor management."[45]

§ 6.9   Serious U.S. Domestic Industry Injury

A less developed, but nonetheless also potentially controversial, area of ITC determinations under Section 201 involves the question of what constitutes "serious injury" to the domestic industry. The statutory criteria indicate that loss of production should be the relevant inquiry, whereas loss of market share is relevant primarily to causation.

The Trade Act defines a "serious injury" as "a significant overall impairment in the position of the domestic industry."[46] In making its determinations with reference to a serious injury to a domestic industry, the Trade Act requires the ITC to take into account the following specific "economic factors":

(1) The significant idling of productive facilities;[47]

(2) The inability of a significant number of firms to carry out domestic production at a reasonable level of profit; and

(3) Significant unemployment or underemployment within the domestic industry.[48]

Due to the decline in safeguards proceedings in recent years, most of the ITC authority on the serious injury test comes from some time ago. An exception is the *Steel* safeguards case from 2001, which

---

[44]   For a review of these alternative causation factors, *see* especially U.S. International Trade Commission—*Carbon & Certain Alloy Steel Products*, Publication 1553 (July 1984).

[45]   *See* Sen. Rep. No. 93–1298, at 121 (1974).

[46]   19 U.S.C. § 2252(c)(6)(C).

[47]   The term "significant idling of productive facility" includes the closing of plants or underutilization of production capacity. *See* 19 U.S.C. § 2252(c)(6)(B).

[48]   19 U.S.C. § 2252(c)(1)(A).

is examined in Section 6.13 below. From its earlier cases, the ITC has interpreted the term "serious injury" to mean damage of a grave or important proportion.[49] In a decision denying relief to U.S. cigar producers, the Commission determined that a marked decline in U.S. consumption of large cigars was a more important cause of injury than import competition.[50] Similarly, it found that a decline in housing construction was more important to the injury suffered by door manufacturers than was import competition.[51] In most of its decisions concerning causation and serious injury, the Commission ordinarily reviews the economic trends over the past five years so as to screen out temporary problems.

The Trade Act also states that a mere "threat" of serious injury is sufficient. This means a "serious injury that is clearly imminent."[52] The Act provides further guidelines on this alternative injury standard as well. It directs the ITC to consider:

(1) Declines in sales or market share and higher and growing inventories as well as downward trends in production, profits, wages or employment in the domestic industry;

(2) The extent to which the industry is unable to generate adequate capital to finance modernization or maintain existing levels of research and development; and

(3) The extent to which the United States market is the focal point for the diversion of exports of the article in question by reason of trade restraints in other countries.[53]

In actual practice, however, there may be little difference between evaluating actual and threatened injury in escape clause proceedings.

Whether there is serious injury or threat of serious injury will of course depend upon the definition of the domestic industry. This is a bit like deciding the relevant market in United States antitrust litigation. Sub-markets, including sub-product markets and sub-geographic markets, can clearly be domestic industries for purposes of Section 201. The ITC has in fact used tariff classifications of the United States in order to determine the domestic industry. Using

---

[49]   U.S. International Trade Commission—*Bolts, Nuts & Screws of Iron or Steel*, Publication 747, (Nov. 1975).

[50]   U.S. International Trade Commission—Wrapper Tobacco, Publication 746 (Nov. 1975).

[51]   U.S. International Trade Commission—*Birch Plywood Door Skins*, Publication 743 (Oct. 1975).

[52]   *See* 19 U.S.C. § 2252(c)(6)(D).

[53]   *See* 19 U.S.C. § 2252(c)(1)(A).

such classifications has the practical feature of allowing identifiable tariff relief if that is ultimately granted.

Because the injury determination is closely tied to the definition of the affected domestic industry, the parties typically attempt to promote either a broader or narrower definition depending on whether they are the petitioner or respondent industry. Importers may contest the definition initially offered by the domestic industry so as to decrease the perception that like or directly competitive products are at risk or to reduce the measurement of increase in imports. The definition of the industry will also impact on the question of causation. This was a principal issue in the *Heavy Weight Motorcycles* case. In that highly controversial decision, the Commission ruled that imported sub-assemblies were not directly competitive with domestic sub-assemblies because the imports were captively consumed.[54]

Similar issues were raised in the automobile investigation. The domestic industry argued that passenger cars should be defined as a single industry producing automobiles and light trucks. Importers opposed to the escape clause proceeding sought to subdivide the industry into large automobiles and small automobiles. The Commission ultimate determined that three different industries were involved, passenger automobiles, light trucks, and medium-heavy weight trucks.[55]

§ 6.10   USITC Safeguard Relief Recommendations

The statute requires the ITC to report its findings to the President within 120 days after the petition is filed.[56] If the ITC determines that the case is "extraordinarily complicated," the deadline is extended to 150 days.[57] If the ITC decides that the statutory criteria of Section 201 are met, it "shall" make recommendations to address the serious injury or threat thereof to the domestic industry as well as consider the most effective means to allow that industry to make a positive adjustment to import competition.[58]

The Trade Act authorizes the Commission to choose from a menu of relief options. It may recommend an increase in or the imposition

---

[54]   *See* U.S. International Trade Commission—*Heavy Weight Motorcycles*, Investigation No. TA–201–47, Publication No. 1342 (Feb. 1983).

[55]   *See* U.S. International Trade Commission—*Certain Motor Vehicles and Certain Chassis and Bodies Thereof*, Investigation No. TA–201–44, Publication No. 1110 (Dec. 1980).

[56]   19 U.S.C. § 2252(b)(2)(A).

[57]   19 U.S.C. § 2252(b)(2)(B).

[58]   19 U.S.C. § 2252(e).

of a tariff or a tariff rate quota, modification or imposition of an import quota, various trade adjustment measures including trade adjustment assistance, or any combination of these options.[59] No initial recommended relief may exceed four years and, if renewed, the total may not exceed eight years.[60] In addition, the Commission may recommend that the President initiate international negotiations to address the underlying cause of the increase in imports.[61] Interestingly, only those members of the ITC who voted in affirmatively on the satisfaction of the Section 201 criteria in the first place are eligible to vote on the recommendations to the President. Dissenting members appear to have no input on relief recommendations.[62]

The ITC's report to the President will also include any adjustment plans submitted by the domestic industry in its petition and any commitments made by firms and workers in that industry in order to facilitate positive adjustment to import competition.[63] The Commission's report must also analyze the long and short term economic effects of the relief it recommends. The report to the President is advisory, but if the President decides not to follow any recommended import relief, Congress may pass a joint resolution by majority vote of both houses disapproving of the President's action. The President may veto this joint resolution, but of course Congress may override that veto. If this were to occur, then the Commission's original relief recommendations would be implemented.[64]

§ 6.11 Presidential Relief Decisions

The Trade Act authorizes the President to grant escape clause relief *only if* the ITC has made an affirmative finding that the increased imports have caused or threaten to cause serious injury to a domestic industry.[65] But if the ITC makes an affirmative finding, the Act requires the President to take "all appropriate and feasible action within his power" to facilitate efforts by the industry to make "a positive adjustment to import competition."[66]

Presidential Discretion

Notwithstanding the mandatory nature of this language, the President, as the Federal Circuit has observed, "has broad latitude to

---

[59] 19 U.S.C. § 2252(e)(2).
[60] *See* 19 U.S.C. § 2252(e)(2), § 2253(e).
[61] 19 U.S.C. § 2252(e)(4)(A).
[62] 19 U.S.C. § 2252(e)(6).
[63] 19 U.S.C. § 2252(e)(5)(B).
[64] *See* 19 U.S.C. § 2253(b), (c).
[65] *See* 19 U.S.C. § 2253(a)(1)(A).
[66] *Id.*

determine the type of action to take."[67] The President need not follow the ITC's relief recommendations. Thus, even though the word "shall" is used, the Act leaves substantial discretion to the President in defining the appropriate protective action. In other words, unlike antidumping and countervailing duty proceedings, the President has effective control over whether any relief will be given in a Section 201 proceeding, and what form that relief will take. Indeed, the President need not take any action at all.

If the President decides to provide escape clause relief, the Trade Act gives the President "an expansive, non-exclusive list"[68] of available relief measures. These include tariffs, a tariff rate quota, an import quota, adjustment assistance, orderly marketing agreements with foreign countries,[69] an allocation among importers by auction of import licenses, international negotiations, legislative proposals, or any combination thereof.[70] Duty free treatment under the Generalized System of Tariff Preferences of the United States is automatically suspended if the President decides to impose an escape clause proceeding tariff.

In deciding whether to undertake escape clause relief, the President is directed to take into account the ITC's report, the extent to which the workers and firms in the industry are benefiting from trade adjustment assistance,[71] the efforts being made by the industry to make a positive adjustment to import competition, the likelihood of effectiveness of relief in facilitating such adjustment, and the short and long term economic and social costs of the relief relative to their short and long term economic and social benefits.[72]

The President must also consider other factors related to the national economic interest of the United States, including but not limited to, the economic and social costs if relief is not granted, the impact on consumers and on competition in domestic markets, and the impact on United States industries if other nations were to take retaliatory action.[73] Consumer interests have sometimes been critical of the President's decision to grant escape clause relief. Various presidents have noted that such relief can as a practical matter increase prices to consumers and that this would be adverse to the

---

[67]   *Corus Group PLC. v. International Trade Com.*, 352 F.3d 1351, 1354 (Fed. Cir. 2003).

[68]   *Id.*

[69]   As noted in Section 6.3 above, the WTO Safeguards Agreement expressly prohibits such agreements to limit import competition.

[70]   19 U.S.C. § 2253(a)(3).

[71]   *See* Sections 6.14 and 6.15.

[72]   19 U.S.C. § 2253(a)(2)(A)–(E).

[73]   19 U.S.C. § 2253(a)(2)(F).

national economic interests of the United States. The argument that escape clause relief may cause inflation in the United States is a variation on this theme.

The Trade Act further directs the President to consider the extent to which there is a diversion of foreign exports to the U.S. markets by reason of foreign restraints, the potential for circumvention of any relief taken, the national security interests of the United States, and those factors that the Commission is required to consider in reaching its recommendations.[74]

These considerations have frequently caused Presidents to deny escape clause relief. This is consistent with the President's primary role in the foreign affairs. Thus, for example, the President once decided not to grant escape clause relief regarding imports of copper when doing so might have influenced then-pending negotiations under the auspices of GATT and with UNCTAD about the commodities trade.[75] A similar refusal to grant relief in connection with imports of copper was based on the need for the U.S. exporters of copper to obtain adequate export earnings.[76] In the latter case, the President expressly declared that "granting import relief is not consistent with our national economic interest."[77]

Limits on Escape Clause Relief

Although the President has almost unlimited discretion on the form of escape clause relief, the Trade Act places some outer limits: First, because escape clause relief is intended to be temporary, no relief ordered by the President may exceed four years initially, and eight years in total; second no increase in tariff resulting from escape clause proceedings can exceed fifty percent *ad valorem* of the rate existing at the time of the escape clause proceeding; finally, if the ordered relief exceeds one year, it "shall be phased down at regular intervals during the period in which [it] is in effect."[78]

Petitioners in escape clause proceedings should consider in advance which form of relief they hope to receive. Tariffs may not provide effective relief because of floating currency values. For example, if the dollar declines in value, imports will become cheaper and the negative impact of tariffs might be offset. On the other hand, if dollar values are rising, this will cause tariffs to be an effective form of protection because imports become notably more expensive. Thus, tariff relief may or may not provide the type of protection the

---

[74]   19 U.S.C. § 2253(a)(2)(G)–(J).

[75]   Domestic Copper Industry, 43 Fed. Reg. 49523 (Oct. 24, 1978).

[76]   *See* Copper Import Relief Determination, 49 Fed. Reg. 35609 (1984).

[77]   *Id.*

[78]   19 U.S.C. § 2253(e).

petitioners anticipate. For one thing, the importers may simply pay the increased tariffs if allowed by the economics of the market.

One reason why protective escape clause relief is difficult to obtain is that the WTO Safeguards Agreement entitles most trading partners to seek compensation for the adverse effects of any relief granted by another member state. Formal retaliation through a return suspension of concessions on exports generally is prohibited for three years. But because escape clause proceedings do not concern any unfair trade practice, protective relief measures typically are a source of substantial friction in world trade. This perspective helps explain why the President frequently decides that it is not in the economic interest of the United States to impose escape clause relief or, if granted, decides to terminate the relief earlier than originally ordered.

The President has provided escape clause relief in relatively few instances. Again, Congress can (but never has chosen to) override any presidential denial of escape clause or market disruption relief recommended by the ITC. Congress can do so by adopting a joint resolution of disapproval. Once this is enacted, the President is required to adopt the import relief previously recommended by the Commission. However, the President may veto this joint resolution, in which case an override of the President's veto is required to obtain relief.[79]

Review of Relief

If the President decides to impose protective escape clause relief, the ITC must monitor the granted relief during the period it is in effect.[80] The President also may later decide to reduce, modify, terminate, or extend the relief.[81] The level of the relief granted, however, cannot be increased. In the subsequent proceedings, the Commission's role is advisory, but if the period of relief exceeds three years, it must provide reports to the President and Congress on any continuing injury and on the progress of the domestic industry in adjusting to import competition.[82] The President may alter existing escape clause relief if he or she finds that the domestic industry has failed to make adequate efforts to adjust to import competition, the circumstances have sufficiently changed to warrant a reduction or termination in relief, or upon the request of the domestic industry.[83]

---

[79]   *See* 19 U.S.C. § 2253(b), (c).

[80]   19 U.S.C. § 2254(a).

[81]   19 U.S.C. § 2254(b).

[82]   19 U.S.C. § 2254(a)(2).

[83]   19 U.S.C. § 2254(b)(1).

Amendments to the Trade Act of 1974 adopted in 1988, and reaffirmed in the URAA in 1994, promote the goal of adjustment to import competition instead of trade protection relief. This is accomplished by strongly encouraging the submission of adjustment plans and commitments by petitioners for Section 201 relief, and by expanding the range of remedies the Commission may recommend to the President in escape clause proceedings to *any* action that will facilitate adjustment.

Further, the standards for presidential relief mandate a determination that the relief will facilitate efforts by the domestic industry to make a positive adjustment to import competition. Finally, the Trade Act requires increased monitoring of Section 201 relief plans and imposes time limits on any relief granted by the President. Thus, as compared to the past Section 201 of the Trade Act is now considerably less protectionist and more adjustment-oriented.

§ 6.12 Special U.S. Safeguard Rules for Chinese Imports

In addition to the general rule in Section 201, U.S. law has a special provision—which arose in connection with China's accession to the WTO in 2001—for safeguard measures relating to imports from China. Because of worries over a flood of inexpensive Chinese imports, these "Section 421" safeguard measures require only that increased imports be a "significant cause" of a "material" injury to a domestic industry.[84] These standards are significantly lower than for regular safeguard measures, which (as noted above) require a cause that is "equal to or greater than any other cause" and a real or threatened "serious" injury to a domestic industry.

In recent years, the special Section 421 safeguards rule has played a much more significant role than traditional Section 201 proceedings. Between 2003 and 2013, the ITC initiated six investigations under Section 421, but none under Section 201. A prominent example is President Obama's imposition in June 2009 of protective tariffs of 35% on vehicle tires from China.[85] Pursuant to the special authorization for such actions in China's WTO Accession Protocol, however, the United States has not initiated such China-specific actions since 2013.

---

[84]   19 U.S.C. § 2451(a), (c).

[85]   *See* Proclamation No. 8414, 74 Fed. Reg. 47,861 (Sept. 17, 2009).

§ 6.13   WTO Rulings on U.S. Safeguard Actions

The rulings of the WTO's Appellate Body concerning the Safeguards Agreement have strictly limited the use of escape clause remedies. Indeed, the United States has lost a number of related disputes before the WTO, including in complaints brought by Australia and New Zealand on lamb; by the European Union on wheat gluten; by India and Pakistan on wool shirts and blouses; by South Korea on line pipe; and by Japan and numerous others on steel.

In 2001 alone, the Appellate Body (AB) ruled against the United States in three separate safeguard cases. In *U.S.-Wheat Gluten from the EC*, the AB emphasized the critical issue of causation. The AB found that the ITC's causation analysis lacked clarity and inadequately addressed factors other than imports that may have caused domestic industry injury. It also criticized the U.S. for a failure to give timely notice and to allow for a "meaningful exchange" in the required consultations. In *U.S.-Lamb Meat from New Zealand*, the AB reiterated that all causation factors must be isolated and examined. Further, it rejected the "domestic industry" definition adopted by the ITC because growers were included. Both of these decisions also emphasized the need for the ITC to find "unforeseen developments" in its injury determinations. The third 2001 AB ruling against U.S. safeguard measures concerned cotton yarn from India and Pakistan. In this decision, the AB rejected an exclusion of vertically integrated yarn producers from the definition of "domestic industry."

In its 2002 decision on U.S. safeguards on line pipe from Korea, the WTO similarly criticized the ITC for a "mere assertion" that challenged imports were "an important cause of serious injury and . . . not less than any other cause." More generally, the AB has repeatedly emphasized that the U.S. may not exclude consideration of imports from NAFTA countries (Canada and Mexico) in making safeguard determinations.

The U.S. Steel Safeguards Case

Perhaps the most controversial recent escape clause action by the United States was the imposition of tariffs on steel by President Bush in 2002. The ITC found, following an extensive investigation and numerous hearings, that certain categories of steel imports caused, or threatened to cause, serious injury to the domestic steel industry. President Bush then imposed on the covered steel products annually decreasing tariffs of up to thirty percent, although only for a three year period.[86] This escape clause relief was tempered by exclusions for selected steel from selected countries. Most Australian and Japanese steel products, for example, were not subject to the extra U.S. tariffs. About half of all EU steel imports were exempt. Canada and Mexico, as members of NAFTA, were fully exempt.

Opponents promptly challenged the imposition of the safeguard measures in both U.S. courts and the WTO. The Federal Circuit upheld the action as a matter of domestic law.[87] But numerous WTO member states then challenged the imposition of this safeguard relief before the WTO's Dispute Settlement Body. In 2003, the Appellate Body ultimately ruled that the special U.S. tariffs on steel were illegal under the WTO Safeguards Agreement.[88]

The AB held that the U.S. erred in utilizing the protective tariffs some four years after the surge of steel imports during the Asian economic meltdown of the late 1990s, and in excluding NAFTA partners Canada and Mexico. It also found that the ITC failed properly to address the requirement of "unforeseen developments." Although the AB acknowledged that the term does not appear in the Safeguards Agreement, it reiterated its earlier holdings that the Agreement must be understood against the backdrop of GATT Article XIX, which conspicuously includes such a requirement.

The European Union then threatened over $2 billion annually in retaliatory tariffs on U.S. exports of clothing, citrus, and boats, products thought to be politically damaging to the Bush Administration. But before the WTO could authorize such sanctions, President Bush—pursuant to corresponding authority in the Trade Act[89]—terminated the tariffs in December 2003. He stated that the effectiveness of the tariffs "ha[d] been impaired by changed economic circumstances."[90]

Interestingly, in the meantime domestic interests separately petitioned the ITA and ITC to impose CVDs or ADs on many of the same products. Reasoning that the temporary safeguard measures effectively mitigated the damaging effects of imports, the ITC concluded that there was no material injury to justify responsive duties on either basis.[91]

---

[86]   *See* Proclamation No. 7529, 67 Fed. Reg. 10553 (Mar. 5, 2002).

[87]   *See Corus Group PLC v. ITC*, 352 F.3d 1351 (Fed. Cir. 2003).

[88]   *See* Appellate Body Report, *U.S.-Definitive Safeguard Measures on Imports of Certain Steel Products*, WT/DS248/AB/R, *et al.* (adopted Dec. 10, 2003).

[89]   19 U.S.C. § 2254(b)(1).

[90]   *See* Proclamation No. 7741, 68 Fed. Reg. 68,483, ¶ 6 (Dec. 4, 2003).

[91]   *See Nucor Corp. v. U.S.*, 414 F.3d 1331 (Fed. Cir. 2005).

United States utilization of safeguard remedies has been minimal since the steel safeguards outcome, though the Trump administration has been making noises about invoking safeguard relief.

§ 6.14   U.S. Trade Adjustment Assistance— Individual and Company Assistance Criteria

The idea of trade adjustment assistance has its origins in programs intended to assist people who were dislocated when the European Community (now Union) was established. Its adoption in the United States has had a checkered history, particularly as regards Congressional willingness to fund trade adjustment assistance. The first authority for such assistance was provided in the Trade Expansion Act of 1962. However, no assistance was actually provided until 1969.

The Trade Act of 1974 made trade adjustment assistance a greater possibility. But dramatic increases in payments to workers under the program during the early 1980s caused the Reagan Administration to seek to repeal the Trade Adjustment Assistance Program. During the 1980s, tighter eligibility requirements and shrinking budgetary allocations reduced the scope of the program. It was not until the Omnibus Trade and Competitiveness Act of 1988 that significant funds were committed to trade adjustment assistance and the program was reauthorized through 1993.

Nonetheless, actual payment of adjustment assistance to workers occurred slowly, and assistance to companies was extremely difficult to obtain. Trade adjustment assistance programs of the United States were consolidated and expanded in 2002, including for the first time worker assistance with health insurance, coverage of "secondary workers," a new pilot program on wage insurance for older workers, benefits for family farmers and ranchers, and expanded training and income support.

Trade adjustment assistance is designed to provide financial relief to workers (and, to a lesser extent, firms) for the effects of the increased imports—not to prevent, reduce, or restrict the imports. Escape clause relief is always considered temporary, but adversely affected workers may obtain "adjustment assistance" payments and other displacement benefits for a longer period.

Trade adjustment assistance decisions are made by the U.S. Department of Labor. Such assistance does not require an affirmative determination by the ITC on import injuries (as is required for protective relief, *see* above). Adjustment assistance also is available to workers whose plants relocate to U.S. free trade partners, or GSP, CBI, Andean or African trade preference countries.

Congress expanded the trade adjustment assistance (TAA) programs significantly in 2009 and 2011, and renewed it for six years in 2015. Such expansions and extensions of trade adjustment assistance often are closely connected with the granting of Trade Promotion Authority ("fast track") by Congress to the President for free trade agreements, as well as to actual congressional approval of such agreements once concluded by the President. An example is the extension of the enhanced TAA programs in 2011 in connection with the approval of the free trade agreements with South Korea, Colombia, and Panama.

Among the variety of benefits and services now available for eligible workers are the following: employment counseling and job referrals; job search allowances for travel and related costs; "relocation allowances" to cover moving expenses; retraining assistance; and, perhaps most important, simple income support after state unemployment benefits have run out. The expanded TAA programs also allow financial assistance for health insurance as well as special wage subsidies for workers over fifty.

Petitions and DOL Determinations

U.S. law permits petitions for trade adjustment assistance by a "group of workers," unions, or "employers of such workers."[92] Generally, three groups of workers may be eligible for adjustment assistance: (1) those who have lost their jobs because increased imports caused significant harm to production by their former employer; (2) those who lost their jobs because increased imports caused their former employer to shift production to a foreign country; and (3) "adversely affected secondary workers"—those who lost their jobs with a supplier of a primary firm harmed by increased imports.[93]

Distilled to its essence, the Trade Act requires for a grant of trade adjustment assistance that the Secretary of Labor determine the existence of two elements:

First, there must be *negative employment effects* from trade in the form of the loss or threatened loss of jobs by "a significant number or proportion of the workers" in a firm.

Second, there must be evidence of *causation*. The Secretary may find such causation in one of two ways:

---

[92]   19 U.S.C. § 2271.

[93]   19 U.S.C. §§ 2271(a), 2272(b). For a case analyzing the special requirements for "adversely affected secondary workers" *see Former Employees of Southeast Airlines v. U.S. Secretary of Labor*, 774 F .Supp. 2d 1333 (C.I.T 2011).

- Sales or production by the firm have decreased absolutely, (b) imports of directly competitive goods (or their component parts) or services have increased, *and* (c) the increase in imports "contributed importantly" to the loss or threatened loss of the workers' jobs;

or

- the workers' firm moved production or services to a foreign country or has begun importing its products or services from a foreign country, *and* (b) either of these things "contributed importantly" to the loss or threatened loss of the workers' jobs.[94]

These criteria are related to but not identical with those considered by the ITC in connection with escape clause proceedings. For example, the term "contributed importantly" means a cause which is important but not necessarily more important than any other cause.[95] This is a lesser standard than the required "substantial causation" for Section 201 proceedings.[96] Whether imports are "like or directly competitive" with domestic products is a question of interchangeability or substitutability. The fact that imports are actually decreasing does not *per se* eliminate the possibility of trade adjustment assistance. The critical issue is whether those imports have "contributed importantly" to unemployment.[97]

Adjustment Assistance for Companies

Congress also has authorized a separate, but more limited, program of Trade Adjustment Assistance for Firms (TAAF) which is administered by the Department of Commerce.[98] Assistance to companies is primarily limited to technical aid.[99] Companies may receive adjustment assistance only if the Secretary of Commerce finds that a significant number of their workers have been separated or threatened with separation, that sales or production have decreased absolutely, and that increased importation of like or directly competitive articles contributed importantly to these results.[100] Agricultural firms may apply for adjustment assistance. Although once authorized by statute, Congress has not been willing

---

[94]   19 U.S.C. § 2272(a).

[95]   19 U.S.C. § 2272(c)(1).

[96]   *See* Section 6.8.

[97]   For an analysis of the importance of the "contributed importantly" standard in a long-running disagreement between the Secretary of Labor and the Court of International Trade *see Chen v. Solis*, 2009 WL 2058659 (C.I.T 2009).

[98]   *See* 19 U.S.C. § 2341.

[99]   *See* 19 U.S.C. § 2342(b).

[100]   *See* 19 U.S.C. § 2341(c).

to fund trade adjustment assistance for communities impacted by import competition.

A grant of trade adjustment assistance does not require an affirmative determination by the ITC on import injuries (as is required for protective relief, *see* above). Such separate assistance flows from the separate determinations by the Secretaries of Labor and Commerce under the Trade Act of 1974. One important difference is the fact that in adjustment assistance proceedings the effect of imports on the industry as a whole is not at issue. The focus is instead on specific workers and specific companies. Whenever the ITC commences an investigation for purposes of Section 201 escape clause proceedings, the Secretary of Labor is required to begin a parallel investigation as to the likelihood and number of workers who may be certified as eligible for trade adjustment assistance. The Secretary of Labor then prepares a report which is forwarded to the President along with the report of the ITC concerning the escape clause petition.

§ 6.15   Secretary of Labor Determinations

The Trade Act gives considerable discretion to the Secretary of Labor in making trade adjustment assistance determinations. The Court of International Trade has thus held that it will uphold a grant of such assistance "if it is supported by substantial evidence on the record and is otherwise in accordance with law."[101] Substantial evidence merely means "such relevant evidence as a reasonable mind might accept as adequate to support a conclusion."[102]

In making determinations as to worker eligibility, the Secretary of Labor must obtain from the workers' firm whatever information he or she "determines to be necessary to make the certification."[103] This may be done "through questionnaires and in such other manner as the Secretary determines appropriate."[104] The Secretary may also seek additional information from officials or employees of the workers' firm, officials of customers of the workers' firm, and officials of "certified or recognized unions" for the workers.[105] The Trade Act also expressly gives the Secretary *subpoena* powers.[106] But he or she

---

[101]   *See Former Employees of Western Digital Technologies, Inc. v. U.S. Secretary of Labor*, 2012 WL 7006347, at *3 (C.I.T 2012) and 19 U.S.C. § 2395(b).

[102]   *Former Emps. of Barry Callebaut v. Chao*, 357 F.3d 1377, 1380–81 (Fed. Cir. 2004)(quoting *Universal Camera Corp. v. NLRB*, 340 U.S. 474, 477 (1951)).

[103]   19 U.S.C § 2272(d).

[104]   *Id.*

[105]   *Id.*

[106]   19 U.S.C. § 2272(d)(3)(B).

must ensure confidentiality for any secret business information gathered in the process.[107]

The Secretary of Labor may conduct investigations in any reasonable manner.[108] But he or she must publish notice of the fact that an eligible group of workers has filed a petition for certification for trade adjustment assistance benefits, and must publish a summary of the determinations on that petition in the Federal Register.[109]

Once an investigation is commenced "the Labor Department is vested with considerable discretion in the conduct of its investigation of trade adjustment assistance claims."[110] Nonetheless, "there exists a threshold requirement of reasonable inquiry" by the Secretary.[111] This means, for example, that petitioners do not have a right to a trial-type hearing with cross examination of the witnesses of the Department of Labor as part of the process of determining eligibility for trade adjustment assistance. If, however, the CIT finds that the Department did not conduct a "reasonable inquiry," it may remand the case to require further investigation.[112]

Until recently, services were not covered by worker adjustment assistance programs. Thus, in the 1970s and 1980s courts held that workers engaged in airline services, automobile services, and shipyard maintenance services were not impacted by the importation of "articles" within the meaning of the Trade Act.[113] As amended, the Trade Act now expressly covers workers that have lost their jobs because, among other reasons, their employer either (a) has lost sales or production due to "imports of articles *or services* like or directly competitive with articles produced *or services* supplied by" the employer,[114] or (b) shifted work to a foreign country "in the production of articles or the supply of *services* like or directly

---

[107]   19 U.S.C. § 2272(d)(3)(C).

[108]   *Abbott v. Donovan*, 570 F. Supp. 41 (C.I.T. 1983), *appeal after remand* 588 F. Supp. 1438 (1984).

[109]   19 U.S.C. § 2271(a)(3).

[110]   *Former Employees of Invista, S.A.R.L. v. U.S. Sec'y of Labor*, 714 F. Supp. 2d 1320, 1329 (C.I.T 2010).

[111]   *Id.* (quoting *Former Employees of Hawkins Oil & Gas, Inc. v. U.S. Sec'y of Labor*, 814 F. Supp. 1111, 1115 (1993)).

[112]   *See* 19 U.S.C. § 2395(b) and *Former Employees of Fairchild Semi-Conductor Corp. v. U.S. Sec'y of Labor*, 2008 WL 1765519 (C.I.T 2008).

[113]   *See, e.g., Woodrum v. United States*, 737 F.2d 1575 (Fed. Cir. 1984); *Miller v. Donovan*, 568 F. Supp. 760 (C.I.T. 1983); *Pemberton v. Marshall*, 639 F.2d 798 (D.C. Cir. 1981); *Fortin v. Marshall*, 608 F.2d 525 (1st Cir.1979).

[114]   19 U.S.C. § 2272(a)(2)(A).

competitive with articles which are produced or *services* which are supplied by" the employer.[115]

§ 6.16 Text of WTO Agreement on Safeguards

(Selected Provisions)

Having in mind the overall objective of the Members to improve and strengthen the international trading system based on GATT 1994;

Recognizing the need to clarify and reinforce the disciplines of GATT 1994, and specifically those of its Article XIX (Emergency Action on Imports of Particular Products), to re-establish multilateral control over safeguards and eliminate measures that escape such control;

Recognizing the importance of structural adjustment and the need to enhance rather than limit competition in international markets; and

Recognizing further that, for these purposes, a comprehensive agreement, applicable to all Members and based on the basic principles of GATT 1994, is called for;

Hereby *agree* as follows:

Article 1

General Provision

This Agreement establishes rules for the application of safeguard measures which shall be understood to mean those measures provided for in Article XIX of GATT 1994.

Article 2

Conditions

1.   A Member[1] may apply a safeguard measure to a product only if that Member has determined, pursuant to the provisions set out below, that such product is being imported into its territory in such increased quantities, absolute or relative to domestic production, and under such conditions as to cause or threaten to cause serious injury to the domestic industry that produces like or directly competitive products.

2.   Safeguard measures shall be applied to a product being imported irrespective of its source.

* * *

---

[115]   19 U.S.C. § 2272(a)(2)(B).

[1]   A customs union may apply a safeguard measure as a single unit or on behalf of a member State. When a customs union applies a safeguard measure as a single unit, all the requirements for the determination of serious injury or threat thereof under this Agreement shall be based on the conditions existing in the customs union as a whole. When a safeguard measure is applied on behalf of a member State, all the requirements for the determination of serious injury or threat thereof shall be based on the conditions existing in that member State and the measure shall be limited to that member State. Nothing in this Agreement prejudges the interpretation of the relationship between Article XIX and paragraph 8 of Article XXIV of GATT 1994.

Article 4

Determination of Serious Injury or Threat Thereof

1.   For the purposes of this Agreement:

(a)   "serious injury" shall be understood to mean a significant overall impairment in the position of a domestic industry;

(b)   "threat of serious injury" shall be understood to mean serious injury that is clearly imminent, in accordance with the provisions of paragraph 2. A determination of the existence of a threat of serious injury shall be based on facts and not merely on allegation, conjecture or remote possibility; and

(c)   in determining injury or threat thereof, a "domestic industry" shall be understood to mean the producers as a whole of the like or directly competitive products operating within the territory of a Member, or those whose collective output of the like or directly competitive products constitutes a major proportion of the total domestic production of those products.

2.   (a) In the investigation to determine whether increased imports have caused or are threatening to cause serious injury to a domestic industry under the terms of this Agreement, the competent authorities shall evaluate all relevant factors of an objective and quantifiable nature having a bearing on the situation of that industry, in particular, the rate and amount of the increase in imports of the product concerned in absolute and relative terms, the share of the domestic market taken by increased imports, changes in the level of sales, production, productivity, capacity utilization, profits and losses, and employment.

(b)   The determination referred to in subparagraph (a) shall not be made unless this investigation demonstrates, on the basis of objective evidence, the existence of the causal link between increased imports of the product concerned and serious injury or threat thereof. When factors other than increased imports are causing injury to the domestic industry at the same time, such injury shall not be attributed to increased imports.

(c)   The competent authorities shall publish promptly, in accordance with the provisions of Article 3, a detailed analysis of the case under investigation as well as a demonstration of the relevance of the factors examined.

Article 5

Application of Safeguard Measures

1.   A Member shall apply safeguard measures only to the extent necessary to prevent or remedy serious injury and to facilitate adjustment. If a quantitative restriction is used, such a measure shall not reduce the quantity of imports below the level of a recent period which shall be the average of imports in the last three representative years for which statistics are available, unless clear justification is given that a different level is

necessary to prevent or remedy serious injury. Members should choose measures most suitable for the achievement of these objectives.

2.   (a) In cases in which a quota is allocated among supplying countries, the Member applying the restrictions may seek agreement with respect to the allocation of shares in the quota with all other Members having a substantial interest in supplying the product concerned. In cases in which this method is not reasonably practicable, the Member concerned shall allot to Members having a substantial interest in supplying the product shares based upon the proportions, supplied by such Members during a previous representative period, of the total quantity or value of imports of the product, due account being taken of any special factors which may have affected or may be affecting the trade in the product.

(b) A Member may depart from the provisions in subparagraph (a) provided that consultations under paragraph 3 of Article 12 are conducted under the auspices of the Committee on Safeguards provided for in paragraph 1 of Article 13 and that clear demonstration is provided to the Committee that (*i*) imports from certain Members have increased in disproportionate percentage in relation to the total increase of imports of the product concerned in the representative period, (*ii*) the reasons for the departure from the provisions in subparagraph (a) are justified, and (*iii*) the conditions of such departure are equitable to all suppliers of the product concerned. The duration of any such measure shall not be extended beyond the initial period under paragraph 1 of Article 7. The departure referred to above shall not be permitted in the case of threat of serious injury.

Article 6

Provisional Safeguard Measures

In critical circumstances where delay would cause damage which it would be difficult to repair, a Member may take a provisional safeguard measure pursuant to a preliminary determination that there is clear evidence that increased imports have caused or are threatening to cause serious injury. The duration of the provisional measure shall not exceed 200 days, during which period the pertinent requirements of Articles 2 through 7 and 12 shall be met. Such measures should take the form of tariff increases to be promptly refunded if the subsequent investigation referred to in paragraph 2 of Article 4 does not determine that increased imports have caused or threatened to cause serious injury to a domestic industry. The duration of any such provisional measure shall be counted as a part of the initial period and any extension referred to in paragraphs 1, 2 and 3 of Article 7.

Article 7

Duration and Review of Safeguard Measures

1.   A Member shall apply safeguard measures only for such period of time as may be necessary to prevent or remedy serious injury and to facilitate

adjustment. The period shall not exceed four years, unless it is extended under paragraph 2.

2.   The period mentioned in paragraph 1 may be extended provided that the competent authorities of the importing Member have determined, in conformity with the procedures set out in Articles 2, 3, 4 and 5, that the safeguard measure continues to be necessary to prevent or remedy serious injury and that there is evidence that the industry is adjusting, and provided that the pertinent provisions of Articles 8 and 12 are observed.

3.   The total period of application of a safeguard measure including the period of application of any provisional measure, the period of initial application and any extension thereof, shall not exceed eight years.

4.   In order to facilitate adjustment in a situation where the expected duration of a safeguard measure as notified under the provisions of paragraph 1 of Article 12 is over one year, the Member applying the measure shall progressively liberalize it at regular intervals during the period of application. If the duration of the measure exceeds three years, the Member applying such a measure shall review the situation not later than the mid-term of the measure and, if appropriate, withdraw it or increase the pace of liberalization. A measure extended under paragraph 2 shall not be more restrictive than it was at the end of the initial period, and should continue to be liberalized.

5.   No safeguard measure shall be applied again to the import of a product which has been subject to such a measure, taken after the date of entry into force of the WTO Agreement, for a period of time equal to that during which such measure had been previously applied, provided that the period of non-application is at least two years.

6.   Notwithstanding the provisions of paragraph 5, a safeguard measure with a duration of 180 days or less may be applied again to the import of a product if:

(a)   at least one year has elapsed since the date of introduction of a safeguard measure on the import of that product; and

(b)   such a safeguard measure has not been applied on the same product more than twice in the five-year period immediately preceding the date of introduction of the measure.

Article 8

Level of Concessions and Other Obligations

1.   A Member proposing to apply a safeguard measure or seeking an extension of a safeguard measure shall endeavour to maintain a substantially equivalent level of concessions and other obligations to that existing under GATT 1994 between it and the exporting Members which would be affected by such a measure, in accordance with the provisions of paragraph 3 of Article 12. To achieve this objective, the Members concerned may agree on any adequate means of trade compensation for the adverse effects of the measure on their trade.

2.   If no agreement is reached within 30 days in the consultations under paragraph 3 of Article 12, then the affected exporting Members shall be free, not later than 90 days after the measure is applied, to suspend, upon the expiration of 30 days from the day on which written notice of such suspension is received by the Council for Trade in Goods, the application of substantially equivalent concessions or other obligations under GATT 1994, to the trade of the Member applying the safeguard measure, the suspension of which the Council for Trade in Goods does not disapprove.

3.   The right of suspension referred to in paragraph 2 shall not be exercised for the first three years that a safeguard measure is in effect, provided that the safeguard measure has been taken as a result of an absolute increase in imports and that such a measure conforms to the provisions of this Agreement.

Article 9

Developing Country Members

1.   Safeguard measures shall not be applied against a product originating in a developing country Member as long as its share of imports of the product concerned in the importing Member does not exceed 3 per cent, provided that developing country Members with less than 3 per cent import share collectively account for not more than 9 per cent of total imports of the product concerned.[2]

2.   A developing country Member shall have the right to extend the period of application of a safeguard measure for a period of up to two years beyond the maximum period provided for in paragraph 3 of Article 7. Notwithstanding the provisions of paragraph 5 of Article 7, a developing country Member shall have the right to apply a safeguard measure again to the import of a product which has been subject to such a measure, taken after the date of entry into force of the WTO Agreement, after a period of time equal to half that during which such a measure has been previously applied, provided that the period of non-application is at least two years.

Article 10

Pre-existing Article XIX Measures

Members shall terminate all safeguard measures taken pursuant to Article XIX of GATT 1947 that were in existence on the date of entry into force of the WTO Agreement not later than eight years after the date on which they were first applied or five years after the date of entry into force of the WTO Agreement, whichever comes later.

Article 11

Prohibition and Elimination of Certain Measures

1.   (a) A Member shall not take or seek any emergency action on imports of particular products as set forth in Article XIX of GATT 1994

---

[2]   A Member shall immediately notify an action taken under paragraph 1 of Article 9 to the Committee on Safeguards.

unless such action conforms with the provisions of that Article applied in accordance with this Agreement.

(b)   Furthermore, a Member shall not seek, take or maintain any voluntary export restraints, orderly marketing arrangements or any other similar measures on the export or the import side.[3,4] These include actions taken by a single Member as well as actions under agreements, arrangements and understandings entered into by two or more Members. Any such measure in effect on the date of entry into force of the WTO Agreement shall be brought into conformity with this Agreement or phased out in accordance with paragraph 2.

(c)   This Agreement does not apply to measures sought, taken or maintained by a Member pursuant to provisions of GATT 1994 other than Article XIX, and Multilateral Trade Agreements in Annex 1A other than this Agreement, or pursuant to protocols and agreements or arrangements concluded within the framework of GATT 1994.

2.   The phasing out of measures referred to in paragraph 1(b) shall be carried out according to timetables to be presented to the Committee on Safeguards by the Members concerned not later than 180 days after the date of entry into force of the WTO Agreement. These timetables shall provide for all measures referred to in paragraph 1 to be phased out or brought into conformity with this Agreement within a period not exceeding four years after the date of entry into force of the WTO Agreement, subject to not more than one specific measure per importing Member,[5] the duration of which shall not extend beyond 31 December 1999. Any such exception must be mutually agreed between the Members directly concerned and notified to the Committee on Safeguards for its review and acceptance within 90 days of the entry into force of the WTO Agreement. The Annex to this Agreement indicates a measure which has been agreed as falling under this exception.

3.   Members shall not encourage or support the adoption or maintenance by public and private enterprises of non-governmental measures equivalent to those referred to in paragraph 1.

* * *

---

[3]   An import quota applied as a safeguard measure in conformity with the relevant provisions of GATT 1994 and this Agreement may, by mutual agreement, be administered by the exporting Member.

[4]   Examples of similar measures include export moderation, export-price or import-price monitoring systems, export or import surveillance, compulsory import cartels and discretionary export or import licensing schemes, any of which afford protection.

[5]   The only such exception to which the European Communities is entitled is indicated in the Annex to this Agreement.

Article 14

Dispute Settlement

The provisions of Articles XXII and XXIII of GATT 1994 as elaborated and applied by the Dispute Settlement Understanding shall apply to consultations and the settlement of disputes arising under this Agreement.

ANNEX

EXCEPTION REFERRED TO IN PARAGRAPH 2 OF ARTICLE 11

Members concerned	Product	Termination
EC/Japan	Passenger cars, off road vehicles, light commercial vehicles, light trucks (up to 5 tonnes), and the same vehicles in wholly knocked-down form (CKD sets).	31 December 1999

Chapter 7

U.S. NONTARIFF TRADE BARRIERS AND DISPUTES

Table of Sections

For texts of the WTO TBT and SPS Codes, see the Appendix to this book.

There are numerous nontariff trade barriers (NTBs) applicable to United States imports. Many of these barriers arise out of federal or state safety and health regulations. Others concern the environment, consumer protection, product standards and government procurement. Many of the relevant rules were created for legitimate consumer and public protection reasons. They were often created without extensive consideration of their international impact as potential nontariff trade barriers. Nevertheless, the practical impact of legislation of this type is to ban the importation of nonconforming products from the United States market. Thus, unlike tariffs which can always be paid and unlike quotas which permit a certain amount of goods to enter the United States market, nontariff trade barriers have the potential to totally exclude foreign exports.

§ 7.1   U.S. Import Quotas and Restraints

Goods imported into the United States may have to qualify within numerical quota limitations imposed on that item or upon that kind of item. "Tariff-rate quotas" admit a specified quantity of goods at a preferential rate of duty. Once imports reach that quantity, tariffs are normally increased.

If a quota system is created, a fundamental subsidiary issue is: How will the quotas be allocated? The U.S. Customs Service generally administers quotas on a first-come, first-served basis. This approach creates a race to enter goods into the United States. One potential allocation method is through the use of licenses, which would be the documentation for administration of such quantitative restrictions. Licensing of imports can have trade restrictive effects. International concern about delays which result from cumbersome licensing procedures was manifested in the 1979 Tokyo Round MTN Import Licensing Code (which most developing countries refused to sign). The United States adhered to this Code, as did a reasonable number of other developed nations.

The Uruguay Round made the Agreement on Import Licensing Procedures (1994) binding on all World Trade Organization members. The Agreement's objectives include facilitating the simplification and harmonization of import licensing and licensing renewal procedures, ensuring adequate publication of rules governing licensing procedures, and reducing the practice of refusing importation because of minor variations in quantity, value or weight of the import item under license. *See* Section 1.6.

The President is authorized to sell U.S. import licenses at public auctions.[2] One advantage of an auction system is its revenue raising potential. The U.S. Tariff Act of 1930 also provides that to the extent practicable and consistent with efficient and fair administration, the President is to insure against inequitable sharing of imports by a relatively small number of larger importers.[3] In fact, allocating quotas among U.S. importers rarely happens. Rather, in the past, quotas have been part of a "voluntary restraint" or orderly market agreement between the U.S. and one or more foreign governments, and represent adherence by those governments to U.S. initiatives. These negotiations typically concentrated on obtaining foreign government agreement to limitations on exportation of their products into the U.S. market, and did not pursue limitations on who might use the resulting allocations.

Voluntary export restraints (VERs) and orderly marketing agreements (OMAs) limiting exports into the U.S. market have been applied in the past to textiles, autos, steel, machine tools and semiconductors. Their use is now severely limited by the WTO Agreement on Safeguards. *See* Section 6.3.

---

[2]   19 U.S.C.A. § 2581.

[3]   *Id.*

Agricultural and Meat Import Quotas

Like many nations, the United States has long protected its agricultural base with a variety of trade restraints. To this end, the United States has employed numerous food import quotas. Tariff-rate quotas, for example, have been applied to dairy products, olives, tuna fish, anchovies, brooms, and sugar, syrups and molasses.

Quite a few absolute quotas originate under Section 22 of the Agricultural Adjustment Act.[1] These quotas are undertaken when necessary to United States farm price supports or similar agricultural programs. They have been used on animal feeds, dairy products, chocolate, peanuts, and selected syrups and sugars. The question whether import restraints imposed under Section 22 are lawful under the General Agreement on Tariffs and Trade was settled in 1955 when a waiver was granted by the GATT to the United States for Section 22 purposes.

Sugar Quotas

The United States has periodically imposed import quotas on sugar and sugar products under Section 22 of the Agricultural Adjustment Act. In addition, since 1982, heavily restrictive quotas were imposed on the importation of sugars, syrups and molasses under the authority of Note 3 to Chapter 17 of the Harmonized Tariff System of the United States. This caused the importation of sugar to drop from 4.5 million tons in 1981 to 1.25 million tons in 1989. In 1989, a GATT panel ruled that the U.S. sugar import quotas established through the Harmonized Tariff System were illegal under Article XI of the GATT.[2]

The United States acceded to the 1989 GATT ruling and in 1990 the President announced the conversion of these quotas into tariff-rate quotas.[3] Under this approach, foreign exporters receive a base quota which permits their sugar to enter at either a rate of approximately 6 cents per pound or duty free if eligible under the GSP or CBI programs. Any exports in excess of a nation's base quota are tariffed at approximately 16 cents a pound. The United States Secretary of Agriculture issues certificates to the various supplying countries for their base quotas. In issuing these certificates, the Secretary is to consider traditional shipping patterns, harvesting periods, United States import requirements, and other relevant factors. How the certificate quota is allocated among exporters within foreign nations is left to them to decide.

---

[1]   7 U.S.C.A. § 624.

[2]   *See* GATT 1947 coverage in Section 1.7.

[3]   Presidential Proclamation 6179, 55 Fed. Reg. 38293.

Sugar prices are also supported by quotas on U.S. imports of sugar-containing products. Such quotas apply to blended syrups, edibles with over 65 percent sugar (not in containers), sweetened cocoa, flour mixes and doughs with at least 10 percent sugar (except in containers), and edibles with 10 percent sugar (in containers). All of these import restraints are designed to reinforce the nonrecourse loan/price support program that the U.S. administers for the benefit of its sugar-cane and sugar-beet growers and processors.[4]

U.S. quotas and tariff-rate quotas on sugar and sugar-containing products, designed to reinforce U.S. price support and loan programs, have notably increased domestic costs well above world prices. The average price of U.S. sugar is frequently more than double world-wide average prices. These quotas are administered by the Department of Agriculture by allocating certificates to sugar exporting countries. Only Mexico, under NAFTA, is permitted unlimited sugar exports into the United States, but this privilege has been constrained repeatedly by antidumping suspension order agreements between the two countries. *See* R. Folsom and W. D. Folsom, *NAFTA Re-Negotiated and Its Business Implications* (forthcoming). Some U.S. agricultural quotas have been "tariffied" under the WTO Agreement on Agriculture. *See* Section 1.8.

Meat Quotas

The Meat Import Act of 1979[5] requires the President to impose countercyclical quotas on the importation of meat into the United States. The only countries exempt from this requirement are Canada and Mexico. Beef, mutton (but not lamb) and goat meat, as well as processed beef or veal, are generally subject to a meat import quota. The quota is countercyclical in the sense that the greater the domestic production of meat, the more restrictive the quota. If domestic production declines, the quota is expanded. The net result is stabilization of prices for meat in the United States. The Meat Import Act authorizes the President to suspend the quota whenever natural disasters, disease or major national disruptions to the market occur.

Typically, presidents have proclaimed meat quotas as required by the Act, but later suspended those quotas because of the nation's economic interests. Various statutory trigger levels are established for the imposition of meat quotas. One of these is known as the "minimum access floor", a statutory minimum for certain action. This floor does not guarantee a minimum market access to foreign

---

4   *See* the Food, Agriculture, Conservation and Trade Act of 1990.
5   Public Law No. 96–177.

exporters of meat into the United States market.[6] To avoid meat import quotas, the President has usually negotiated a large number of bilateral agreements with the major meat supplying countries. These agreements are negotiated under the authority of Section 204 of the Agricultural Act of 1956.[7] Such agreements involve "voluntary restraints" by the exporting countries to the effect that they will restrict their shipment of meat into the United States. As a practical matter, the agreements keep the overall meat imports into the United States below the limits permitted by the Meat Import Act. Australia, for example, has entered into successive bilateral agreements with the United States to restrict its export of meat products.

Cotton Quotas

The Agricultural Act of 1949 requires the President to impose global import quotas on Upland Cotton unless the Secretary of Agriculture determines that its average price exceeds certain statutory limits.[8] This provision tends to be countercyclical to market forces for cotton in the United States, meaning the greater the U.S production of cotton, the more restrictive the quota. Brazil successfully challenged parts of this program in a WTO dispute proceeding, but it has largely remained in place under a U.S. settlement that makes payments to Brazilian cotton growers. *See* Section 1.15. A similar countercyclical system applies under the Meat Import Act of 1979. To avoid meat import quotas, the president usually negotiates "voluntary restraint" agreements with major meat exporting countries such as Australia.

Agricultural Marketing Order Import Restraints

The Agricultural Marketing Agreement Act of 1937 authorizes the issuance of marketing orders by the Secretary of Agriculture. These orders typically restrict the grade, size, quality or maturity of fruits and vegetables sold in the United States market. By mandating restrictions of this type, the price for those fruits and vegetables reaching the market is enhanced and the incomes of growers similarly raised. In order for this agricultural support program to work, import restraints must be imposed. The Act automatically prohibits the importation of commodities whenever a marketing order is in effect unless those commodities meet the same requirements that have been established for U.S.-grown produce.[9]

---

[6]   *See Australian Meat and Live-Stock Corp. v. Block*, 590 F. Supp. 1230 (C.I.T. 1984).

[7]   7 U.S.C.A. § 1854.

[8]   7 U.S.C.A. § 1444.

[9]   7 U.S.C.A. § 608(e–1).

The United States has issued a significant number of marketing orders since 1937. These often involve raisins, prunes, avocadoes, limes, lemons, tomatoes, grapefruit, oranges, walnuts, peanuts, plums, peaches, grapes, cranberries, lettuce, almonds, and a variety of other fruits and vegetables. The most current regulations governing imports that are subject to U.S. agricultural marketing orders can be found in 7 C.F.R. Parts 944, 980 and 999. The issuance of these regulations is subject to public notice and comment.[10] Size regulations on tomatoes, even if intended to reduce imports, were a valid import restraint.[11] Inspections of grapes upon arrival in the United States were valid even if more likely to bar importation than inspections at the source as with domestic grapes.[12] U.S. raisin producers successfully challenged marketing order restraints mandating destruction or export of "surplus" raisins.

National Emergency/Security Import Restraints

The United States sometimes imposes import restraints for national security or national emergency reasons. In 1971, for example, President Nixon invoked national emergency powers under Section 5(b) of the Trading with the Enemy Act of 1917 to justify a 10% tariff surcharge on Japanese steel. The U.S. Court of Customs and Patent Appeals upheld this invocation as a matter of Presidential discretion in *United States v. Yoshida International,* 526 F.2d 560 (C.C.P.A. 1975). President Nixon closed the gold exchange window for the U.S. dollar and in the name of "national security" imposed a 10% tariff surcharge on imports in order to reach new currency exchange rate parities with other countries.

Many national security trade restraints originate from Section 232 of the Trade Expansion Act of 1962. This provision broadly authorizes the President to "adjust imports" whenever necessary to the national security of the country. In 2017, President Trump instructed the Secretary of Commerce to investigate whether aluminum imports were a threat to U.S. national security. In his memo, President Trump stated that "core industries" such as steel, aluminum, vehicles, aircraft, shipbuilding and semiconductors were critical elements of the U.S. manufacturing and industrial bases, which "we must defend against unfair trade practices and other abuses." Shortly thereafter, the Trump administration opened a wide-ranging investigation on whether to restrict steel imports in the name of national security.

---

[10]   *See Walter Holm & Co. v. Hardin*, 449 F.2d 1009 (D.C.Cir.1971).
[11]   *Walter Holm & Co. v. Hardin*, 449 F.2d 1009 (D.C.Cir.1971).
[12]   *Cal-Fruit Suma Intern. v. U.S. Dept. of Agriculture*, 698 F. Supp. 80 (E.D.Pa.1988), affirmed 875 F.2d 309 (3d Cir.1989).

Embargoes and Other U.S. Import Restraints

Trade embargoes are sometimes imposed on all the goods from politically incorrect nations (e.g., North Korea). *See* Chapter 11. The Burmese Freedom and Democracy Act of 2003 (Public Law 108–61) banned the importation of Burmese goods, in protest against repression of democracy in that country. Recognizing pro-democracy developments in Myanmar, this ban was lifted in 2012. Trade embargoes have been periodically imposed on all or some imports from other countries, such as Libya, Iraq, Syria, and Iran.

Product-specific import bans also exist for selected goods, e.g., narcotic drugs and books urging insurrection against the United States.[13] The importation of "immoral" goods is generally prohibited[14], even for private use, and the obscenity of such items is decided by reviewing the community standards at the port of entry.[15] Generally, as well, goods produced with forced, convict, indentured or bonded child labor is excluded from the United States.[16] The 1997 Bonded Child Labor Elimination Act amended 19 U.S.C. § 1307 to prohibit the U.S. importation of goods produced by "bonded child labor." Such labor is defined as work or service exacted by confinement against his or her will from persons under age 15 in payment for debts of parents, relatives or guardians, or drawn under false pretexts.

Some quotas imposed by the U.S. are sanctions for unfair trade practices, as against tungsten from China. Other quotas originate in international commodity agreements, and important restraints on textile imports were achieved as a result of the international Multi-Fiber Arrangement. These quotas were phased out under the WTO Textiles Agreement. See Section 1.6.

Jones Act Shipping Controls

Generally speaking, the United States maintains an open market for competitive trade in services. One major exception is maritime transport. In this area, the U.S. protects its domestic industry from import competition under the Merchant Marine Act of

---

[13]   21 U.S.C.A. § 171 and 19 U.S.C.A. § 1305.

[14]   19 U.S.C.A. § 1305.

[15]   *United States v. Various Articles of Obscene Merchandise*, 536 F.Supp. 50 (S.D.N.Y.1981).

[16]   19 U.S.C.A. § 1307. Section 1307 bans products of convict, forced and indentured labor. *See China Diesel Imports, Inc. v. United States*, 870 F.Supp. 347 (C.I.T. 1994) (Chinese government documents referring to factory as "Reform through Labor Facility" probative of convict labor origin of goods; exclusion order affirmed; U.S. consumption demand exception applies only to forced and indentured labor). On standing to sue to block importation of prohibited labor goods, *see McKinney v. United States Department of Treasury*, 799 F.2d 1544 (Fed.Cir.1986) (causal link between imports and clear economic injury must be shown).

1920 ("Jones Act") and other statutes. For example, the shipment of Alaskan oil is reserved for U.S.-flag vessels as is the supply of offshore drill rigs. The Jones Act most notably prohibits foreign vessels from transporting goods or passengers between U.S. ports and on U.S. rivers, lakes and canals. The reservation of goods for U.S.-flag ships (such trade is known as cabotage) is very significant economically, amounting to billions annually, with a heavy concentration in petroleum products.

§ 7.2   U.S. Nontariff Trade Barriers (NTBs)

The diversity of regulatory approaches to products and the environment makes it extremely difficult to generalize about nontariff trade barriers. The material in this Section concerns health restrictions relating to food, safety restrictions relating to consumer products, environmental auto emissions standards and selected other NTBs. These areas have been chosen merely as examples of the types of NTB barriers to the United States market, and are by no means exhaustive.

Food Products

All foods imported into the United States are subject to inspection for their wholesomeness, freedom from contamination, and compliance with labeling requirements (including the 1993 nutritional labeling rules). This examination is conducted by the Food and Drug Administration using samples submitted to it by the United States Customs Service. If these tests result in a finding that the food products cannot be imported into the United States, they must be exported or destroyed.[17] Milk and cream imports are the subject of special permit requirements administered by the Department of Health and Human Services. Basically, the Department certifies that foreign producers operate under sanitary conditions.

There is a broad web of federal rules governing food products, including food imports. These involve, for example, the Federal Insecticide, Fungicide and Rodenticide Act,[18] the Perishable Agricultural Commodities Act,[19] and the Food, Drug and Cosmetic Act.[20] Food which is admitted into the United States under surety bond pending FDA inspection and later found inadmissible must be exported or destroyed. If this does not occur, an action by the Customs Service against the importer and the surety for liquidated

---

17   *See* 21 C.F.R. §§ 1.83 to 1.99.
18   7 U.S.C.A. §§ 136 et seq.
19   7 U.S.C.A. §§ 499a to 499t.
20   21 U.S.C.A. §§ 391 to 393.

damages will typically follow.[21] A strict six-year statute of limitations applies to government complaints seeking liquidated damages running from the importer's breach of the bond.[22]

The Bioterrorism Act of 2002 requires all U.S. and foreign food companies selling in the United States to register with the Food and Drug Administration. Importers must notify the FDA in advance and in detail of food shipments, and keep records of suppliers and customers. The FDA can detain any food deemed a risk, including late or missing notice items.

Seeds, Plants, Animals and Wood

The Customs Service and the Agricultural Marketing Service of the USDA regulate the importation of seeds under the Federal Seed Act of 1939.[23] Seeds that fail to meet the statute's requirements are destroyed unless re-exported within one year of their denial of admission into the United States. Another branch of the USDA called APHIS (Animal and Plant Health Inspection Service) regulates plants, domestic animals, and plant and animal products coming into the U.S. This authority is created in the Plant Quarantine Act,[24] Section 306 of the Tariff Act of 1930,[25] the Federal Plant Pest Act,[26] and other statutes.[27] Basically, an import permit system has been established. Applications to import goods of these types must be made to APHIS.

In 2008, all imports wood products (even toothpicks) were subjected to new Lacey Act criminal rules that inhibit trade. Wood derived from illegal logging, for example, has been denied entry and seized by U.S. Customs. Gibson Guitar Corp. paid about $300,000 to settle alleged violations of the Lacey Act.

Consumer Products

The Consumer Products Safety Act bars the importation of consumer products which do not comply with the standards of the Consumer Products Safety Commission.[28] Exporters of consumer products must certify that their goods conform to applicable United States safety and labeling standards. Any product that has a defect which is determined to constitute a "substantial product hazard" or

---

[21]   *See* Epstein, The Land of Liquidated Damages: Recent Judicial Decisions and Unresolved Issues, 14 Fordham Int'l L.J. 7 (199091).

[22]   *United States v. Cocoa Berkau, Inc.*, 990 F.2d 610 (Fed.Cir.1993).

[23]   7 U.S.C.A. §§ 1581 et seq. *See* 19 C.F.R. § 12.16, 7 C.F.R. §§ 210.208 et seq.

[24]   7 U.S.C.A. §§ 150aa et seq. *See* 7 C.F.R. § 352.

[25]   19 U.S.C.A. § 1306. *See* 9 C.F.R. §§ 92, 94.

[26]   7 U.S.C.A. §§ 150bb et seq. *See* 7 C.F.R. § 330.

[27]   *See* 21 U.S.C.A. § 111.

[28]   15 U.S.C.A. § 2066.

is imminently hazardous may be banned from the United States market. The Customs Service may seize any such nonconforming goods. These goods may be modified in order to conform them to U.S. Consumer Products Safety Commission requirements. Otherwise, such goods must be exported or destroyed, an end result notably applied in 2007 to children's toys from China.

Another example in this area concerns the Flammable Fabrics Act. This Act prohibits the importation of wearing apparel or interior furnishings that fail to meet its flammability standards.[29] The National Energy Conservation Act requires that any imported consumer appliances be labeled to show their energy efficiency as are domestically made products.[30]

Motor Vehicles

All automobiles imported into the United States must comply with the safety standards of the Department of Transportation.[31] The exporters of vehicles to the United States must certify compliance to the standards. In addition, most autos and automobile engines must meet federal air pollution control standards as set by the Environmental Protection Agency before they will be allowed into the United States.[32] The owner or importer may suffer severe penalties if a nonconforming vehicle is brought into the United States and not subsequently brought into conformity. A common scenario involves the posting of a surety bond by the importer of the auto promising payment of liquidated damages if this does not occur.[33]

Trade barrier conflicts also surround U.S. Corporate Average Fuel Economy (CAFE) standards. Whereas United States manufacturers have been able to average fuel efficient cars and gas guzzlers, European firms largely building premium cars in the U.S. have not been able to do so. In 1991, the European Community claimed that 88 percent of the U.S. revenues from CAFE taxes and penalties were disproportionately levied on European carmakers which only had 4 percent of the total U.S. market. The EC pursued a GATT complaint against the U.S. on these grounds. The GATT panel report on this complaint was delivered in 1994 and largely upheld CAFE.[34]

---

[29]   15 U.S.C.A. §§ 1191 et seq.

[30]   31 U.S.C.A. § 316.

[31]   19 C.F.R. §§ 12.73, 12.80. *See* 49 C.F.R. Part 571.

[32]   19 C.F.R. § 12.73.

[33]   *See* Epstein, The Land of Liquidated Damages: Recent Judicial Decisions and Unresolved Issues, 14 Fordham Int'l L.J. 7 (1990–91).

[34]   GATT DOC DS 31/R 5.52 to 5.55 (Sept. 29, 1994).

The European Union and the United States, and (separately) Canada and the U.S., have reached Mutual Recognition Agreements on certain product standards. The Agreements attempt to reduce the trade restraining potential of regulations applicable to telecommunications equipment, medical devices, pharmaceuticals, recreational craft, electrical safety and electromagnetic compatibility. Each side promises to test their exports according to the other's standards. A second test in the country of importation should no longer be necessary.

Environmental Law NTBs

A host of federal and state laws regulating the environment have an impact on international trade. Europeans, for example, have long argued that U.S. auto emissions' requirements amount to a substantial nontariff trade barrier causing them to incur significant costs in producing cars for the United States market. Other environmental controls are more specifically connected to international trade.

The Marine Mammal Protection Act[35] prohibits the importation of fish (tuna) caught with methods that incidentally kill marine mammals (dolphins). Under this law, the U.S. undertakes a review of each exporting country's harvesting procedures to see if they are comparable to United States standards. If not, an import ban on fish from that nation and intermediary nations follows. Environmental activists succeeded in 1990 in obtaining a preliminary injunction against tuna imports from Mexico, Panama, Venezuela, Ecuador and Vanuatu under the Act.[36] In 1991, a GATT dispute settlement panel declared the embargo of Mexican tuna an illegal restraint of trade. However, the U.S. and Mexico subsequently "settled" the dispute (over much protest in the world community) with Mexico agreeing to improve its harvesting procedures. In 1994, acting on a complaint filed by the European Union, a second GATT panel ruled against United States tuna embargoes.[37]

Tuna exporting nations that join the Panama Declaration, a multilateral set of principles to protect dolphins from tuna fishermen, may avoid the U.S. Marine Mammal Protection Act. The Panama Declaration was agreed in October 1995 by the United States and eleven Nations (Belize, Colombia, Costa Rica, Ecuador, France, Honduras, Mexico, Panama, Spain, Vanuatu and Venezuela). The U.S. Congress authorized the lifting of the tuna import ban for

[35]   16 U.S.C.A. § 1367.

[36]   *Earth Island Institute v. Mosbacher*, 929 F.2d 1449 (9th Cir.1991).

[37]   The GATT Tuna I and Tuna II Panel Decisions are reported in the GATT Basic Instruments and Selected Documents (BISD) 39th Supp. 155 (1993) and GATT Doc. DS 29/R (June 16, 1994).

Panama Declaration adherents in 1997. This is exactly the kind of multilateral accord that opponents of U.S. unilateralism and extraterritorial jurisdiction support.

United States environmental or conservation laws notably affecting international trade include:

- The Endangered Species Act of 1973 prohibiting import/export of endangered species.

- The "Pelley Amendment" authorizing import restraints against fish products of nations undermining international fisheries or wildlife conservation agreements.

- The High Seas Driftnet Fisheries Enforcement Act of 1992 banning imports of fish, fish products and sport fishing gear from countries violating the United Nations driftnet moratorium.

- The Sea Turtle Conservation Act prohibiting shrimp imports harvested with adverse effects on sea turtles first used in 1993 against shrimp from several Caribbean nations and now applicable globally to Thailand, India, China and Bangladesh among others.

- The Wild Bird Conservation Act banning imports of tropical wild birds.

- The Antarctic Marine Living Resources Convention Act prohibiting import/export of living resources.

- The African Elephant Conservation Act restricting ivory imports.

- The Lacey Act prohibiting imports of fish, wildlife, plant and wood that violate foreign laws.

Special NTB rules apply in the context of the Canada-U.S. Free Trade Agreement and the NAFTA. *See* R. Folsom, *Principles of Free Trade Agreements* (forthcoming). Sanitary and phytosanitary (SPS) measures dealing with food safety and animal and plant health regulations are the subject of a WTO SPS Code, as are products standards generally (TBT Code). *See* Section 1.7.

§ 7.3   U.S. Public Procurement Preferences as NTBs

Where public procurement is involved, and the taxpayer's money is at issue, virtually every nation has some form of legislation or tradition that favors buying from domestic suppliers. In federal nations like the United States, these rules can also be found in state and local purchasing requirements. Determining which goods are "American" under globalized supply chains produces some unusual results. Finished steel products made from steel slab imported to the U.S., auto panels for example, are not "American" for procurement law purposes.

Buy American Act

The principal United States statute affecting imports in connection with government procurement is the Buy American Act of 1933.[38] This Act requires the government to buy American unless the acquisition is for use outside the U.S.,[39] there are insufficient quantities of satisfactory quality available in the U.S., or domestic purchases would be inconsistent with the public interest or result in unreasonable costs.

As currently applied, the United States Buy American Act requires federal agencies to treat a domestic bid as unreasonable or inconsistent with the public interest only if it exceeds a foreign bid by more than six percent (customs duties included) or ten percent (customs duties and specific costs excluded). Exceptions to this general approach exist for reasons of national interest, certain designated small business purchases, domestic suppliers operating in areas of substantial unemployment and demonstrated national security needs. Bids by small businesses and companies located in labor surplus areas are generally protected by a 12 percent margin of preference. Bids from U.S. companies are considered foreign rather than domestic when the materials used in the products concerned are below 50 percent American in origin. These rules apply to civil purchasing by the United States government,[40] but are suspended for purchasing subject to the GATT/WTO Procurement Codes as implemented by the Trade Agreements Act of 1979 and the Uruguay Round Agreements Act of 1994. *See* Section 1.13.

The Department of Defense has its own Buy American rules. Generally speaking, a 50 percent price preference (customs duties excluded) or a 6 or 12 percent preference (customs duties included) whichever is more protective to domestic suppliers is applied. However, intergovernmental "Memoranda of Understanding" (MOU) on defense procurement provide important exceptions to the

---

[38]   41 U.S.C.A. §§ 10a–10d.

[39]   *See* the U.S. Balance of Payments Program, 48 C.F.R. § 225.302 et seq., creating procurement preferences for materials used outside the U.S. but suspended if the Code on Procurement applies.

[40]   *See* Executive Order No. 10582 (Dec. 17, 1954), 19 Fed.Reg. 8723 *as amended by* Exec. Order No. 11051 (Sept. 27, 1962), 27 Fed.Reg. 9683 and Exec. Order No. 12148, July 20, 1979, 44 Fed.Reg. 43239.

standard Department of Defense procurement rules.[41] Additional procurement preferences are established by the Small Business Act of 1953.[42] Under this Act, federal agencies may set-aside certain procurement exclusively for small U.S. businesses. In practice, the federal government normally sets aside about 30 percent of its procurement needs in this fashion. Special set-aside rules apply to benefit socially and economically disadvantaged minority-owned businesses. These preferences are exempt from U.S. adherence to the GATT/WTO Procurement Codes under a U.S. reservation.

A number of federal statutes also contain specific Buy American requirements. These include various GSA, NASA and TVA appropriations' bills, the AMTRAK Improvement Act of 1978,[43] the Public Works Employment Act of 1977,[44] various highway and transport acts,[45] the Clean Water Act of 1977,[46] and the Rural Electrification Acts of 1936 and 1938.[47] Many of these statutes involve federal funding of state and local procurement. Most are generally excluded from the GATT/WTO Procurement Codes as applied by the United States.

A practice known as "unbalanced bidding" has arisen in connection with the Buy American Act. Unbalanced bidding involves the use of United States labor and parts by foreigners in sufficient degree so as to overcome the bidding preferences established by law for U.S. suppliers. This occurs because the United States value added is *not* included in the calculations of the margin of preference for the U.S. firms. Thus foreign bids minus the value of work done in the U.S. are multiplied by the 6, 12 or 50 percent Buy American Act preference. If the U.S. bids are above the foreign bids but within the margin of preference, the U.S. bidder gets the contract. If the U.S. bids are higher than the foreign bids plus the margin of preference, the foreigners get the contract.[48]

GATT/WTO Procurement Codes

The optional Tokyo Round GATT Procurement Code was not particularly successful at opening up government purchasing. Only Austria, Canada, the twelve European Union states, Finland, Hong Kong, Israel, Japan, Norway, Singapore, Sweden, Switzerland and

[41]   *See Self-Powered Lighting, Ltd. v. United States*, 492 F.Supp. 1267 (S.D.N.Y.1980).

[42]   15 U.S.C.A. §§ 631–648. *See* 48 C.F.R. §§ 19.000–.902.

[43]   Public Law 95–421.

[44]   42 U.S.C.A. § 6705.

[45]   *See, e.g.*, Highway Improvement Act of 1982, Pub.L. 97–424.

[46]   33 U.S.C.A. § 1295.

[47]   7 U.S.C.A. § 903.

[48]   *See Allis-Chalmers Corp. v. Friedkin*, 635 F.2d 248 (3d Cir. 1980).

the United States adhered to the Procurement Code. This was also partly the result of the 1979 Code's many exceptions. For example, the Code did not apply to contracts below its threshold amount of $150,000 SDR (about $171,000 since 1988), service contracts, and procurement by entities on each country's reserve list (including most national defense items). Because procurement in the European Union and Japan is often decentralized, many contracts fall below the SDR threshold and were therefore exempt. By dividing up procurement into smaller contracts national preferences were retained. U.S. government procurement tends to be more centralized and thus more likely covered by the Code. This pattern helps explain why Congress restrictively amended the Buy American Act in 1988.

The Buy American Act generally conformed to the GATT Code on Government Procurement negotiated during the Tokyo Round. However, Congress expressed its displeasure with the degree to which that Code opened up sales opportunities for United States firms abroad. It therefore amended the Buy American Act in 1988 to deny the benefits of the Procurement Code when foreign governments are not in good standing under it. United States government procurement contracts are also denied to suppliers from countries whose governments "maintain. . . a significant and persistent pattern of practice or discrimination against U.S. products or services which results in identifiable harm to U.S. businesses."[49] Presidential waivers of these statutory denials may occur in the public interest, to avoid single supply situations or to assure sufficient bidders to provide supplies of requisite quality and competitive prices.

The European Union was one of the first to be identified as a persistent procurement discriminator by the USTR. This identification concerns longstanding heavy electrical and telecommunications disputes that were partly settled by negotiation. The remaining disputes led to U.S. trade sanctions and European retaliation. This did not occur with Greece, Spain and Portugal (where the EU procurement rules do not apply), and with Germany which broke ranks and negotiated a path breaking bilateral settlement with the U.S. Japan was also identified as a persistent procurement discriminator in the construction, architectural and engineering areas.

The Uruguay Round Procurement Code replaced the Tokyo Round agreement. It is one of very few WTO agreements that is optional. The WTO Code expands coverage to include procurement of services, construction, government-owned utilities, and some state

---

[49]   41 U.S.C.A. § 10d.

and local (sub-central) contracts. Various improvements to the procedural rules surrounding procurement practices and dispute settlement attempt to reduce tensions in this difficult area. For example, an elaborate system for bid protests is established. Bidders who believe the Code's procedural rules have been abused will be able to lodge, litigate and appeal their protests. The United States has agreed, with few exceptions, to bring all procurement by executive agencies subject to the Federal Acquisition Regulations under the Code's coverage (i.e., to suspend application of the normal Buy American preferences to such procurement).

That said, thirteen U.S. states have not conformed to the WTO Procurement Agreement. The United States, amid considerable controversy, adopted "Buy American" steel rules in the Obama administration economic stimulus plan (the American Recovery and Reinvestment Act of 2009), exempting WTO Procurement Code participants and U.S. free trade agreements. Additional Buy American preferences were created by the Obama administration auto bail-out plans and other legislation. In approving oil pipelines moving Canadian tar sands products to the USA, President Trump specifically required use of American-made pipes.

All "Buy American" rules raise questions of what products and services are "American". This question is easier to ask than answer. Typically, Buy American programs have "rules of origin" attached to them. Steel, for example, is deemed American only if foreign raw materials are "substantially transformed" in the USA. *See* Chapter 3. To meet this rule of origin, foreign steel must be melted down into a liquid, then made into a steel product in America. Older U.S. "integrated" steel mills still do this, but modern mills import rough steel slabs then convert them into steel coils using "slab converters". This technique disqualifies their end product under the Buy American rules of origin for steel.

WTO Procurement Code Analysis

Special thanks to Professor Matthew Schaefer of the University of Nebraska Law School for the following analytical framework to assess the applicability of the WTO Procurement Agreement:

(a) Is the country a party to the Agreement?

(b) If so, is the procuring entity listed in the Annex of that country as open to foreign bidders?

(c) Does the contract amount exceed the minimum threshold of the Agreement (roughly 130,000 SDRs or $182,000)?

(d)   Is the good being procured listed by the procuring country as covered by the Agreement?

(e)   Do any general exceptions of the Agreement apply?

State, Local and NAFTA Procurement Preferences

In addition to the Buy American Act, state and local purchasing requirements may inhibit import competition in the procurement field. For example, California once had a law which made it mandatory to purchase American products. This law was declared unconstitutional as an encroachment upon the federal power to conduct foreign affairs.[50] A Massachusetts ban on contracts with companies invested in Burma was preempted by federal sanctions adopted in 1997 against Burma.[51]

State statutes which have copied the federal Buy American Act, on the other hand, and incorporated public interest and unreasonable cost exceptions to procurement preferences, have generally withstood constitutional challenge.[52] A Pennsylvania statute requiring state and local agencies to ensure that contractors do not provide products containing foreign steel was upheld by the Third Circuit Court of Appeals.[53] This case illustrated the inapplicability of the Tokyo Round Procurement Code to state and local purchasing requirements.[54]

Chapter 13 of the 1989 Canada-United States Free Trade Area Agreement opens government procurement to U.S. and Canadian suppliers on contracts as small as $25,000. However, the goods supplied must have at least 50 percent U.S. and Canadian content. The NAFTA also establishes distinct procurement regulations. The thresholds are $50,000 for goods and services provided to federal agencies and $250,000 for government-owned enterprises (notably PEMEX and CFE). These regulations are particularly important because Mexico, unlike Canada, has not traditionally joined in GATT/WTO procurement codes.

---

[50]   *Bethlehem Steel Corp. v. Board of Commissioners of the Department of Water and Power of the City of Los Angeles*, 276 Cal.App.2d 221, 80 Cal.Rptr. 800 (1969).

[51]   *Crosby v. National Foreign Trade Council*, 530 U.S. 363, 120 S.Ct. 2288, 147 L.Ed.2d 352 (2000).

[52]   *See K.S.B. Technical Sales Corp. v. North Jersey District Water Supply Commission of the State of New Jersey*, 75 N.J. 272, 381 A.2d 774 (1977), *appeal dismissed* 435 U.S. 982, 98 S.Ct. 1635, 56 L.Ed.2d 76 (1978).

[53]   *Trojan Technologies, Inc. v. Pennsylvania*, 916 F.2d 903 (3d Cir.1990), *cert. denied* 501 U.S. 1212, 111 S.Ct. 2814, 115 L.Ed.2d 986 (1991).

[54]   *See* Southwick, Binding the States: A Survey of State Law Conformance with Standards of the GATT Procurement Code, 13 U.Pa.J.Int'l Bus.L. 57 (1992).

§ 7.4   U.S. TBT Code Disputes

Widespread use of "standards" requirements as NTB import restraints resulted in 1979 in the optional GATT Agreement on Technical Barriers to Trade (called the "Standards Code").[55] This Code was made operative in the United States by the Trade Agreements Act of 1979,[56] and was followed by a reasonable number of other nations. Its successor is the Uruguay Round Agreement on Technical Barriers to Trade (1994) (TBT). This agreement is binding on all WTO members. In general, this Code deals with the problem of countries' manipulation of product standards, product testing procedures, and product certifications in order to slow or stop imported goods. It is reproduced in the Appendix to this book.

The TBT Code provides, in part and subject to some exceptions, that imported products shall be accorded treatment (including testing treatment and certification) no less favorable than that accorded to like products of national origin or those originating in any other country. It also requires that participating nations establish a central office for standards inquiries, publish advance and reasonable notice of requirements that are applicable to imported goods, and provide an opportunity for commentary by those who may be affected adversely. The Code establishes an international committee to deal with alleged instances of noncompliance.

Under United States law,[57] state and federal agencies may create standards which specify the characteristics of a product, such as levels of quality, safety, performance or dimensions, or its packaging and labeling. However, these "standards-related activities" must not create "unnecessary obstacles to U.S. foreign trade," and must be demonstrably related to "a legitimate domestic objective" such as protection of health and safety, security, environmental or consumer interests. Sometimes there is a conflict between federal and state standards. For example, federal law licensing endangered species' articles preempted California's absolute ban on trade in such goods.[58]

The Office of the USTR is charged with responsibility for implementation of the Standards Code within the United States.[59] The Secretary of Commerce maintains a "standards information center" (National Bureau of Standards, National Center for Standards and Certification Information), in part to "serve as the

---

[55]   *See* 18 Int'l Legal Mat. 1079.

[56]   19 U.S.C.A. § 1531 et seq.

[57]   19 U.S.C.A. § 2531.

[58]   *Man Hing Ivory and Imports, Inc. v. Deukmejian*, 702 F.2d 760 (9th Cir.1983).

[59]   19 U.S.C.A. §§ 2541, 2552.

central national collection facility for information relating to standards, certification systems, and standards-related activities, whether such standards, systems or activities are public or private, domestic or foreign, or international, regional, national, or local [and to] make available to the public at . . . reasonable fee . . . copies of information required to be collected."[60]

U.S. GATT/WTO Product Standards Disputes

United States standards have been attacked in international tribunals as violating international obligations. Sometimes the standards have been upheld, sometimes not. For example, a binational arbitration panel established under Chapter 18 of the Canada-U.S. FTA issued a decision upholding a United States law setting a minimum size on lobsters sold in interstate commerce. The panel found that, since the law applied to both domestic and foreign lobsters, it was not a disguised trade restriction. On the other hand, in 1991, a GATT panel found that United States import restrictions designed to protect dolphin from tuna fishers did violate the GATT. The panel ruled that GATT did not permit any import restrictions based on environmental concerns, whether they were considered disguised trade restrictions or not. This decision suggested repeal of a number of United States laws which concern health, safety and environmental conditions in exporting nations. A 1994 decision by a second GATT panel recognized the legitimacy of extraterritorial environmental regulations, but ruled against the tuna boycott of the U.S. because of its focus on production methods.

In 1998, the WTO Appellate Body ruled against a U.S. ban on shrimp imports from nations that fail to use turtle exclusion devises comparable to those required under U.S. law. The Appellate Body found the U.S. ban "arbitrary" and "unjustifiable". The standards of other nations have also been challenged as violations of GATT obligations. For example, the United States has criticized European Union bans of imports of meat from the United States, first for containing certain hormones, later for unsanitary conditions in U.S. meatpacking facilities. In 1997, and again in 2004, the WTO Appellate Body ruled against the EU hormone-treated beef ban, citing lack of an adequate scientific basis as required under the WTO SPS Code. *See* Section 1.7.

In 2012, the WTO Appellate Body determined that the United States ban on flavored cigarettes, as applied to clove cigarettes from Indonesia, breached the TBT Code national treatment standard. The Appellate Body noted particularly the discriminatory allowance for

---

[60]   19 U.S.C.A. § 2544.

sale in the U.S. of menthol flavored cigarettes. WT/DS 406/AB/R (April 23, 2012).

§ 7.5   U.S. Import Labeling TBT Disputes

The United States requires clear markings of countries of origin on imports. This can be perceived, especially by those abroad, as a nontariff trade barrier intended to promote domestic purchases. Section 304 of the Tariff act of 1930 establishes the basic rules for origin markings.[61] Every imported article of foreign origin (or its container) must be marked conspicuously, legibly, indelibly and as permanently as practical in English so as to indicate to ultimate purchasers its country of origin.[62] Violation of these rules can result in additional tariffs of up to 10 percent. Intentional removal or alteration of markings is a crime.[63]

In 2008, Mexico initiated WTO proceedings against U.S. "dolphin-safe" label rules embodied in the 1990 Dolphin Protection Consumer Information Act, and a Ninth Circuit decision (*Earth Island Institute v. Hogarth*, 494 F.3d 757 (2007)) requiring zero use of purse seine nets for such labels. In 2010, the U.S. commenced NAFTA proceedings seeking to force Mexico to withdraw its WTO complaint and re-file it under NAFTA. "Standards" disputes are supposed to be resolved exclusively under NAFTA Chapter 20 procedures and trade rules that strongly favor national laws. In 2011, a WTO panel held in favor of Mexico's complaint, which Mexico declined to re-file under NAFTA. The WTO Appellate Body affirmed (WT/DS381/AB/R (July13, 2012), ruling that the U.S. dolphin-safe label rules violated the national treatment standard of the WTO TBT Code. *See* Section 1.7.

In 2008, as part of the Farm Bill, new Lacey Act import disclosure and country of origin requirements were broadly created for plants and wood products. *See* Section 7.5. Additional import disclosure and origin "COOL" rules for meat and meat products were also legislated in the 2008 Farm Bill. The COOL rules were successfully challenged by Canada and Mexico before the WTO. The Appellate Body declared them discriminatory, and violations of TBT Code national treatment obligations. WT/DS384 and 386/AB/R (July 23, 2012).

---

[61]   19 U.S.C.A. § 1304.

[62]   *See Precision Specialty Metals, Inc. v. United States*, 116 F.Supp.2d 1350 (C.I.T.2000).

[63]   19 U.S.C. § 1304(c).

Labeling Law Sanctions and Litigation

The principle sanction for failure to properly mark imports is the imposition of statutory tariffs of 10 percent ad valorem, which are imposed in addition to regular duties and even if the goods would ordinarily enter the U.S. duty free. Importers ordinarily receive notice from the Customs Service and an opportunity to comply with marking requirements. Any untimely failure to comply can result in liquidated damages proceedings by Customs against the importer. The amount of damages assessed will vary with the frequency and circumstances of the offense, and will be assessed as a percentage of the appraised value of the merchandise.

In severe cases, U.S. Customs may seek civil penalties under Section 592 of the Tariff Act of 1930.[64] This provision generally sanctions imports under false documents. Furthermore, criminal sanctions are also possible, either for use of false documents[65] or altering a required marking with concealment intended.[66] The latter penalties can rise to $250,000 or one year imprisonment or both. The severity of these sanctions must be measured against the temptation of traders to alter country of origin markings so as to obtain duty free or quota free entry of goods into the United States.

Various exceptions apply to the U.S. country of origin marking requirements.[67] These include goods that are incapable of being marked, goods economically prohibitive to mark (unless the failure to do so was a deliberate attempt at avoiding the law), or goods that will be injured if marked. If the containers will reasonably indicate origin to the ultimate consumer, or the import circumstances or character of the goods necessarily convey knowledge of their source, no marking is required.

Nor is it mandatory to mark goods not intended for resale, goods which when processed will obliterate the mark, goods over twenty years old and goods intended for export without entering U.S. commerce. Certain United States fishery products, products of U.S. possessions and products that originally came from the U.S. and are being imported are likewise exempt. Lastly, there is a "J-list" of specific goods that have been individually ruled exempt by the Secretary of the Treasury.[68] These include items like cordage, buttons, nails, etc., all of which must be marked by container.

---

[64]   19 U.S.C.A. § 1592.

[65]   18 U.S.C.A. § 1001.

[66]   19 U.S.C.A. § 1304.

[67]   *See* 19 C.F.R. § 134.32.

[68]   *See* 19 C.F.R. § 134.33.

Special regulations govern the marking requirements for imported textiles. These are created by the Textile Fiber Products Identification Act.[69] This Act is enforced by the U.S. Federal Trade Commission. It mandates disclosure of country of origin, generic fiber contents and the name or identification number of the manufacturer or marketer. Violation of the Textile Fiber Products Identification Act amounts to a violation of Section 5 of the Federal Trade Commission Act.[70] This means that F.T.C. cease and desist order proceedings, injunction actions, civil penalties and consumer redress relief can follow. Similar but not identical labeling requirements are established by the Wool Products Labeling Act[71] (country of origin required) and the Fur Products Labeling Act[72] (country of origin not required). These laws are also enforced by the Federal Trade Commission.

Significant litigation has ensued under the Tariff Act country of origin requirements regarding when a U.S. manufacturer is to be deemed the "ultimate purchaser" which may render the goods exempt from marking. In a major decision by the Court of Customs and Patent Appeals, wooden brush handles from Japan were processed in the U.S. by inserting bristles which obliterated the marking. The CCPA, adopting a common rationale in U.S. customs law, held that the handles had undergone a "substantial transformation" into a new product in the United States and were thus subject only to container marking obligations.[73]

In contrast, when leather uppers for shoes were imported from Indonesia, the Court of International Trade required individual markings despite the attachment of soles in the U.S. and argument that a "substantial transformation" had taken place.[74] Gifts of products to ordinary consumers (umbrellas to racetrack patrons) may still require origin markings even if the donor would be exempt.[75]

Other litigation has focused on the duty to mark origin "conspicuously." The Court of International Trade initially reversed a "plainly erroneous" Customs Service position that frozen food markings at the rear of the package (Made in Mexico) were

[69]   15 U.S.C.A. § 70–70K.

[70]   15 U.S.C.A. § 45.

[71]   15 U.S.C.A. § 68–68j.

[72]   15 U.S.C.A. § 69–69j.

[73]   *United States v. Gibson-Thomsen Co.*, 27 C.C.P.A. 267 (1940), *superseded by regulation as stated in Cumins Engine Co. v. United States*, 83 F.Supp.2d 1366 (C.I.T.1999).

[74]   *Uniroyal, Inc. v. United States*, 542 F.Supp. 1026 (C.I.T.1982), *affirmed* 702 F.2d 1022 (Fed.Cir.1983).

[75]   *Pabrini, Inc. v. United States*, 630 F.Supp. 360 (C.I.T.1986).

conspicuous.[76] The Court took the position that such markings did not give U.S. consumers realistic choices when shopping and noted the health risks associated with such goods. Subsequently, the Court of International Trade vacated this opinion.

§ 7.6   U.S. Foreign Trade Zones and Bonded Warehouses

Foreign Trade Zones

The United States has authorized the creation of numerous foreign trade zones.[77] These zones are typically established in enclosed areas near ports of entry into the United States. However, foreign trade zones are treated as being outside the customs territory of the United States.[78] They are subject to state and local public health, labor and other laws. But state regulations regarding food, drugs or cosmetics do not apply to goods transshipped through foreign trade zones.[79] Goods that are imported into a United States foreign trade zone receive different treatment depending on their status. Goods treated as "privileged foreign merchandise" are assessed tariffs according to their condition and quantity upon entry into the zone. This means that the tariff in effect at that time will apply.[80] However, although the goods are considered liquidated upon entry into the zone, the actual tariffs are not payable until the merchandise is later removed into the United States customs territory. This status thus has the advantage of securing an advance determination of the U.S. tariffs due. This determination will continue to be binding even if the goods are thereafter manufactured, processed or manipulated in the zone prior to entry into the United States customs territory. This will be true even if the effect of such alterations is to change the ordinary tariff classification of a product.

Another status of goods entering U.S. foreign trade zones is that of "non-privileged foreign merchandise." Goods of this kind are not tariffed until they leave the zone and enter the United States customs territory. Thus their value, condition and classification, as well as the applicable tariff, will be determined only at that later date. However, the value subject to U.S. tariffs as applied to non-privileged

---

[76]   *Norcal/Crosetti Foods, Inc. v. United States Customs Service*, 758 F.Supp. 729 (C.I.T.1991), *opinion vac'd* 790 F.Supp. 302 (C.I.T.1992).

[77]   19 U.S.C.A. §§ 81a to 81u. *See* 15 C.F.R. Part 400 (General regulations and rules of procedure); 19 C.F.R. Part 146 (General provisions); 19 C.F.R. Part 196 (Exportation and removals).

[78]   *See Hawaiian Independent Refinery v. United States*, 460 F.Supp. 1249 (Cust.Ct.1978).

[79]   *3M Health Care, Ltd. v. Grant*, 908 F.2d 918 (11th Cir.1990).

[80]   But *see Inter-Maritime Forwarding Co. v. United States*, 192 F.Supp. 631 (Cust.Ct.1961) (tariff-rate quota merchandise may be subject to higher rates).

merchandise does not include the cost of processing in the foreign trade zone, general expenses and profits attributable to zone operations, incidental expenses incurred in the zone such as packing, and freight, insurance and related costs.[81] Thus, to a very large degree, the value added in the foreign trade zone is exempt from United States tariffs. The privileged foreign merchandise and non-privileged foreign merchandise statuses are the most prevalent in U.S. foreign trade zones. Other possible statuses include privileged domestic merchandise, non-privileged domestic merchandise and zone-restricted merchandise.

Once goods have entered a United States foreign trade zone, they may be held in storage, exhibited, broken up, repackaged, distributed, sorted, graded, cleaned, mixed with foreign or domestic merchandise, assembled, manufactured or otherwise processed. Certain kinds of operations are prohibited in U.S. foreign trade zones. These include those relating to tobacco and liquor as would incur an excise tax in the United States, and retail sales (except with respect to domestic or duty paid or duty free goods).

There has been a substantial growth in the use of United States foreign trade zones. One reason for this is the ability to take advantage of differences in the United States tariff structure. For example, when a finished product is tariffed at a notably lower rate than the raw materials or components from which it is made, it can be quite desirable to bring those materials or components into a foreign trade zone and thereafter manufacture them into finished goods. In one case, for example, Japanese steel plates were brought into a foreign trade zone on a non-privileged basis and manufactured into barges. Had the plates come into the U.S. Customs territory directly they would have been subject to a 7.5 percent tariff. Barges, on the other hand, are not subject to United States tariffs and therefore when they left the foreign trade zone they entered the United States on a duty free basis.[82] However, machinery imported into a foreign trade zone in order to process materials into finished goods is subject to U.S. tariff duties,[83] whereas foreign merchandise (namely oil) that is "consumed" inside an FTZ is not dutiable.[84]

Another advantage of foreign trade zones is that United States import quotas do not apply. Thus, if an import quota is about to be reached, goods can be put into a foreign trade zone for storage until

---

[81]   See 19 C.F.R. § 146.48(e).

[82]   *Armco Steel Corp. v. Stans*, 431 F.2d 779 (2d Cir.1970).

[83]   *Nissan Motor Mfg. Corp., U.S.A. v. United States*, 693 F.Supp. 1183 (C.I.T.1988), affirmed 884 F.2d 1375 (Fed.Cir.1989).

[84]   *Hawaiian Independent Refinery v. United States*, 460 F.Supp. 1249 (Cust.Ct.1978).

the next quota period and thereafter entered into the United States Customs territory. Goods from nonmarket economies ordinarily subject to Column 2 United States tariffs can be brought into a foreign trade zone and if they undergo substantial transformation may emerge in the form of a product that will be tariffed at the lower Column 1 rate.[85]

A very large percentage of the goods processed in United States foreign trade zones are automotive products. This is the case despite the historical intent that foreign trade zones were to benefit exporters rather than importers. Foreign trade zones are established by approval of the Foreign Trade Zones Board, an interagency committee composed of the Secretaries of Commerce, Treasury and the Army or their designees.[86] The Board may prohibit or restrict any FTZ proposal if it is deemed detrimental to the public interest, health or safety.[187] It has done so reasonably often when proposed zones conflict with powerful domestic lobbies (steel, textiles, sugar). In addition to general purpose FTZ, subzones designed specifically for use by a single firm are possible.[88]

Bonded Warehouses

Temporary duty free importation of goods into the U.S. can also be achieved through bonded warehouses for a maximum of five years. The goods may be stored, cleaned, packed, manipulated or manufactured in such warehouses. Customs Service regulations authorize eight varieties of bonded warehouses.[89] Tariffs are paid when the goods are withdrawn for consumption in the United States at the rate then applicable. Manipulation of the goods in a warehouse to achieve a different tariff classification is allowed. No duties need be paid if the goods are exported, supplied to international vessels or aircraft or destroyed under Customs Service supervision. Goods held in customs-bonded warehouses are exempt from state and local personal property taxes.[90] Applications to establish bonded warehouses are processed through district Customs Service directors. Extensive record-keeping requirements apply.[91]

---

[85] *See* Chinese Chemicals, Customs Service Decision 79–41.

[86] *See* 15 C.F.R. Part 400.

[87] 19 U.S.C.A. § 81o.

[88] *See Armco Steel Corp. v. Stans*, 303 F.Supp. 262 (S.D.N.Y.1969), affirmed 431 F.2d 779 (2d Cir.1970).

[89] *See* 19 C.F.R. § 19.1.

[90] *Xerox Corp. v. County of Harris*, 459 U.S. 145, 103 S.Ct. 523, 74 L.Ed.2d 323 (1982).

[91] *See* 19 C.F.R. § 19.12.

Chapter 8

COUNTERFEIT AND IP INFRINGING IMPORTS

Table of Sections

§ 8.1   Trade in Counterfeit Goods

Theft of intellectual property and use of counterfeit goods are rapidly increasing in developing and developed countries. Such theft is not limited to consumer goods (Pierre Cardin clothing, Rolex watches). Industrial products and parts (e.g., automotive brake pads) are now being counterfeited. Some countries see illegal technology transfers as part of their strategy for economic development. They encourage piracy or choose not to oppose it. Since unlicensed producers pay no royalties, they often have lower production costs than the original source. This practice fuels the fires of intellectual property piracy. Unlicensed low-cost reproduction of entire copyrighted books (may it not happen to this book) is said to be rampant in such diverse areas as Nigeria, Saudi Arabia, and South Korea. Apple computers have been inexpensively counterfeited in Hong Kong. General Motors estimates that about 40 percent of its auto parts are counterfeited in the Middle East. Recordings are duplicated almost everywhere without license or fee. The Internet fuels film and TV piracy. . . try a Google search. And the list goes on.

Among the industrialized countries, efforts occur to acquire (even by way of stealing) "leading edge" technology. One example in the 1980s involved attempted theft of IBM computer technology by Japanese companies ultimately caught by the F.B.I. In the United States, the Office of Export Administration uses the export license procedure to control strategic technological "diversions." But falsification of licensing documents by prominent Norwegian and Japanese companies allowed the Soviets to obtain the technology for making vastly quieter submarine propellers. In the ensuing scandal, "anti-Toshiba" trade sanctions were adopted in the United States. Leading Japanese executives resigned, which is considered the highest form of apology in Japanese business circles.

U.S. officials have seized billions in counterfeit goods. Chinese gangs accounted for the bulk of these goods, which are often footwear, consumer electronics, luxury goods and pharmaceuticals. U.S. military and civilian procurement agencies have begun actively targeting counterfeit suppliers. The European Union has likewise seized billions in counterfeit goods, roughly two-thirds of which generally come from China. Cigarettes often comprise the biggest counterfeit seizures.

§ 8.2   Counterfeit Goods, U.S. Remedies

Legal protection against intellectual property theft and counterfeit goods is not very effective. The four principal U.S. remedies are: (1) seizure of goods by Customs; (2) infringement actions in federal courts; (3) criminal prosecutions or treble damages actions under the Trademark Counterfeiting Act of 1984; and (4) Section 337 proceedings. Each of these is discussed below.

The Anti-counterfeiting Consumer Protection Act of 1996, Public Law 104–153 (110 Stat. 1386), made a number of statutory changes intended to combat counterfeiting. Trafficking in counterfeit goods is now an offense under the RICO Act (Racketeer Influenced and Corrupt Organizations Act). Importers must disclose the identity of any trademark on imported merchandise, ex parte seizures by law enforcement officers of counterfeit goods and vehicles used to transport them are widely authorized, damages and civil penalties that can be recovered from counterfeiters and importers were increased, and the Customs Service's authority to return counterfeit merchandise to its source (and potential re-entry into commerce) has been repealed. Customs must now destroy all counterfeit merchandise that it seizes unless the trademark owner otherwise consents and the goods are not a health or safety threat.

In the United States, the Copyright Felony Act of 1992 criminalized all copyright infringements. The No Electronic Theft Act of 1997 (NET) removed the need to prove financial gain as element of copyright infringement law, thus ensuring coverage of copying done with intent to harm copyright owners or copying simply for personal use. The Digital Millennium Copyright Act of 1998 (DMCA) brought the United States into compliance with WIPO treaties and created two new copyright offenses; one for circumventing technological measures used by copyright owners to protect their works ("hacking") and a second for tampering with copyright management information (encryption). The DMCA also made it clear that "webmasters" digitally broadcasting music on the internet must pay performance royalties. Criminal and civil sanctions apply.[1]

§ 8.3   U.S. Customs Service Seizures

United States trademark and copyright holders may register with the Customs Service and seek the blockade of pirated items made abroad. Such exclusions are authorized in the Tariff Act of 1930 and the Copyright Act of 1976.[2] The thrust of these provisions is that unauthorized imports bearing U.S. registered trademarks or copyrights may be seized by the Customs Service. Trade names that have been used for at least six months can also be recorded with the Customs Service.

Such recordation permits those names to receive the same relief accorded registered trademark and copyright holders when imports that counterfeit or simulate those trade names are found.[3] Since the trademark, copyright and trade name remedies are only available to United States citizens, distributors of foreign goods must ordinarily be assigned United States trademark rights held by foreigners. Such assignments would permit the distributor to seek a new registration from the Patent and Trademark Office so as to be able to invoke these trade remedies.

The importation of semiconductor chip products or equipment that contains a semiconductor chip design or "mask work" registered

---

[1]   *See, e.g., Universal City Studios, Inc. v. Shawn C. Reimerdes*, 111 F.Supp.2d 294 (2000) (injunction against anti-encryption software).

[2]   *See* 19 U.S.C.A. § 1526(a) (trademarks) and 17 U.S.C.A. § 602(b) (copyrights). *See also* 19 C.F.R. § 133, Parts A, D.

[3]   *See* 19 C.F.R. § 133, Parts B, C.

with the U.S. Copyright Office is prohibited.[4] As with trademarks, copyrights and trade names, the owner of such a mask work may register it with the U.S. Customs Service or the U.S. International Trade Commission so as to invoke trade remedies which will preclude infringing products and equipment from entering into the United States. The Customs Service also administers a high-tech copyright protection program specially targeted at pirated computer programs.[5] Generally, the Customs Service will seize infringing programs if there is proof of access by the infringer and a "substantial similarity" between the imports and the registered program.[6]

U.S. Customs Seizure Procedures

There are some differences in Customs Service seizure proceedings depending upon whether the product seized is alleged to be a trademark counterfeit or a copyright counterfeit. The Customs Service rules indicate that in administrative hearings the burden is on the importer to demonstrate why allegedly counterfeit trademarked goods should be released, whereas the burden is on the copyright owner to prove that copyrighted goods are being pirated. These burdens are different because of the greater difficulties in proving copyright infringements.

The Second Circuit has ruled that the Customs Service must employ the "average purchaser test" in determining whether imports are counterfeits subject to seizure and forfeiture.[7] In this case, the Service had used experts to determine differences in the trademark such that it was deemed not a counterfeit (merely infringing) and therefore admissible if the confusing mark was obliterated. The consumer test mandated by the Second Circuit should give greater protection from counterfeits.

Attorneys invoking the Customs Service process frequently sense the inadequacy of relief against counterfeit goods. The first problem is knowing when counterfeit goods are likely to enter the United States market. The Customs Service has enormous duties and can only pay limited attention to the possibility that certain goods are pirated. This is understandable. How is the Customs Service officer to know that the goods are pirated? Can the Customs Service do anything more than look at the invoice in a cursory way? Pirates

---

[4]   *See* 17 U.S.C.A. § 601(a).

[5]   *See* 19 C.F.R. § 133.31 et seq.

[6]   *See* Webster and Pryor, Customs Administration of the High-tech Copyright Protection Program, 73 J. Pat. & Trademark Off. Society 538 (1991).

[7]   *Montres Rolex, S.A. v. Snyder,* 718 F.2d 524 (2d Cir.1983), *cert. denied* 465 U.S. 1100, 104 S.Ct. 1594, 80 L.Ed.2d 126 (1984).

often take great pains to imitate the logo and trademarks they are copying. This makes such piracy non-obvious.

Copyright piracy of sound recordings is even more difficult to ascertain. It cannot reasonably be expected of the Customs Service that they will play records and tapes in order to determine that they are counterfeit goods. To make customs relief effective it is necessary for private interests to notify the Customs Service that a suspected shipment of counterfeit goods is about to or has arrived in the United States. Companies are increasingly hiring private detectives in order to assist with this task. Private detectives might also be used to try to locate pirated copies and counterfeiting operations inside the United States.

ROMless Computers Case

A second frustration with Customs Service relief concerns narrow Customs Service interpretations, such as in the *ROMless Computers* case.[8] In that decision, the Customs Service refused to seize ROMless computers alleged to be in violation of Apple Computer Company copyrights. The practical effect of this decision was to permit ROMless computers to enter the U.S. market, and thereafter be altered in rather simple fashion so as to become effective competitors and arguably infringers of copyrights held by the Apple Computer Company. By removing the ROM (Read Only Memory operating system computer program) unit from the computers, the importers eliminated the only copyrighted element in the computer and thereby nullified attempts at blocking importation of these goods:

> "Assuming without deciding that the making of the "ROMless" computers constitutes a contributory infringement against the copyright holder's copyrights, the importation of such merchandise is not prohibited by 17 U.S.C. 602(b). While the phrase "an infringement of copyright" arguably includes contributory copyright infringement, preventing the importation of "ROMless" computers would be inconsistent with other language in the statute. The objects against which the provisions of 17 U.S.C. 602(b) are directed are copies or phonorecords of a work that have been acquired outside the United States.
>
> With regard to the very computer programs in issue, the statutory copyright requirement of fixation has been held to be satisfied through the embodiment of these programs in ROM devices. . . . Furthermore, computer programs contained in ROMs can be perceived, reproduced,

---

[8]   *See* 9 BNA U.S. Import Wkly 1062 (May 30, 1984).

or otherwise communicated therefrom with the aid of other computer equipment. Accordingly, the provisions of 17 U.S.C. 602(b) are operative against ROMs (or diskettes, tapes, or other devices for fixed storage of software) that contain unlawful reproductions of copyrighted computer software, for these items are copies within the meaning of that section. . . . Therefore, inasmuch as "ROMless" computers do not include such copies upon arrival in the United States, they may enter the country without violation of 17 U.S.C. 602(b)."

§ 8.4   Infringement Actions in U.S. Courts

Another alternative available to counsel attempting to assist U.S. firms combating foreign counterfeiting of their products is infringement relief, including temporary restraining orders, injunctions, damages and an award of the defendant's profits. The major problem with infringement relief is the inability of United States trademark, patent and copyright owners to get effective jurisdiction over and relief from foreign counterfeiters.

Infringement and contributory infringement actions can be used more effectively against the importers, distributors or retailers of counterfeit goods. But relief against one such party may merely shift counterfeit sales to another who must then be brought to court, and then another, and another, etc. While such proceedings can result in *ex parte* seizure orders of counterfeit goods already in the United States, they do not represent a long term solution to production of counterfeit goods in foreign jurisdictions.

Most injunctive and damages relief remains illusory, but it can sometimes be useful. For example, it has been held that counterfeit goods seized *ex parte* under the Lanham Trademark Act can be destroyed upon court order.[9] Civil remedies are *not* limited to simply removing the offending trademark.[10] That said, injunction remedies in federal courts for IP infringement have been stiffened by the Supreme Court.[11][3]

Infringement and treble damages actions may be commenced in United States courts against importers and distributors of counterfeit goods, but service of process and jurisdictional barriers often preclude effective relief against foreign pirates. Even if such relief is obtained, counterfeiters and the sellers of counterfeit goods have proven adept at the "shell game," moving across the road or to

---

[9]   *Fendi S.a.s. Di Paola Fendi E Sorelle v. Cosmetic World*, 642 F.Supp. 1143 (S.D.N.Y.1986).

[10]   *Id.*

[11]   *See eBay Inc v. MercExchange LLC*, 547 U.S. 388 (2006).

another country to resume operations. Moreover, the mobility and economic incentives of counterfeiters have rendered the criminal sanctions of the Trademark Counterfeiting Act of 1984 (below) largely a Pyrrhic victory.

§ 8.5   U.S. Criminal Prosecutions

Many states have enacted criminal statutes to combat increased counterfeiting of goods and services in the United States. After much debate, Congress enacted the Trademark Counterfeiting Act of 1984.[12] Criminal penalties are established for anyone who "intentionally traffics or attempts to traffic in goods or services and knowingly uses a counterfeit mark on or in connection with such goods or services." Treble damages or profits (whichever is greater) and attorney fees may be recovered in civil actions unless there are "extenuating circumstances."

Ex parte seizure orders for counterfeit goods may be issued by the federal courts. Parallel imports of genuine or "gray market goods" (goods legitimately produced overseas but imported into the United States via unauthorized distribution channels, infra) and "overruns" (goods produced without authorization by a licensee) are expressly *excluded* from the Act's coverage. *See* Chapter 9. The real problem with criminal sanctions as a remedy for counterfeiting is to persuade public prosecutors to take these crimes seriously and to allocate law enforcement resources to them. However, in recent years, the Justice Department has significantly increased prosecutions of cyber-attacks and industrial espionage thefts of U.S. owned technology.

§ 8.6   International Solutions to Counterfeiting

International solutions to the problem of intellectual property piracy have been no less elusive. A draft "Anti-Counterfeiting Code" received close scrutiny in the Uruguay Round of negotiations. Although the TRIPs accord incorporates some coverage of counterfeiting (see Section 1.11), it is not the encompassing anti-counterfeiting code that the developed world sought. The TRIPs agreement does mandate border measures to block the release of counterfeit goods into domestic circulation. It also requires criminal penalties for willful trademark counterfeiting or copyright piracy undertaken on a commercial scale. However, the TRIPs agreement does not reject the practice of re-exportation of counterfeit merchandise. Re-exportation has the practical effect of pushing the problem on some other jurisdiction and does not represent a final solution from the point of view of the infringed party.

---

[12]   18 U.S.C.A. § 2320 et seq.

France and Italy have made it illegal to knowingly purchase counterfeit goods. For example, if a student buys a "Louis Vuitton" bag for $15 in a Paris or Florence flea market, he or she may be arrested, fined and imprisoned. Until recently, France went a step further. A government agency monitored Internet piracy. French offenders were subject to a "three strikes" rule: Two warnings were issued before Net access could be terminated and fines imposed by court order. South Korea and Taiwan also employ warnings and penalties against illegal downloading.

Various United States statutes authorize the President to withhold trade benefits from or apply trade sanctions to nations inadequately protecting the intellectual property rights of U.S. citizens. This is true of the Caribbean Basin Economic Recovery Act of 1983, the Generalized System of Preferences Renewal Act of 1984, the Trade and Tariff Act of 1984 (amending Section 301 of the 1974 Trade Act), and Title IV of the 1974 Trade Act as it applies to most-favored-nation tariffs. *See* Chapter 2.

Slowly this carrot and stick approach has borne fruit. Under these pressures for example, Singapore drafted a new copyright law, Korea new patent and copyright laws, and Taiwan a new copyright, patent, fair trade and an amended trademark law. Brazil introduced legislation intended to allow copyrights on computer programs. Though changes have been made, there is some doubt as to the rigor with which these laws will be enforced when local jobs and national revenues are lost.

§ 8.7   U.S. Section 337 Proceedings

Section 337 of the Tariff Act of 1930[13] provides exclusionary Customs Service remedies against the importation of counterfeit and infringing goods into the United States. Section 337 proceedings are administered. by the U.S. International Trade Commission, which makes remedy recommendations (often "general exclusion orders") that are subject to veto by the President.

Statutory Provisions

Section 337 proceedings traditionally have involved some relatively complicated statutory provisions. Prior to 1988, the basic prohibition was against: (1) unfair methods of competition and unfair acts in the importation of goods (2) the effect or tendency of which is to destroy or substantially injure (3) an industry efficiently and economically operated in the U.S. Such importation was also prohibited when it prevented the establishment of an industry, or restrained or monopolized trade and commerce in the U.S. Section

---

[13]   19 U.S.C.A. § 1337.

337 proceedings are *in rem* which explains why they are preferable to a series of *in personam* actions for infringement in the federal courts.

The Omnibus Trade and Competitiveness Act of 1988 revised Section 337. The requirement that the U.S. industry be efficiently and economically operated was dropped. Proof of injury to a domestic industry is *not* required in intellectual property infringement cases. The importation of articles infringing U.S. patents, copyrights, trademarks or semiconductor chip mask works[14] is specifically prohibited provided a U.S. industry relating to such articles exists or is in the process of being established. Such an industry exists if there is significant plant and equipment investment, significant employment of labor or capital, or **substantial** investment in exploitation of the intellectual property rights (including research and development or licensing).

Licensing by itself has been held a sufficient basis for finding the existence of a domestic industry.[15] The substantial IP investment requirement (along with the public interest remedy rule, see Section 8.13) is thought by some to exclude use of Section 337 by patent trolls. This test has origins in prior ITC case law.[16] There is also prior case law on the question of whether an American industry is "in the process of being established."[17]

Determination of violations and the recommendation of remedies to the President under Section 337 is the exclusive province of the International Trade Commission (ITC). Most of the case law under Section 337 concerns the infringement of patents. Trademark, copyright and mask work infringements may also be pursued under

---

[14]　The Semiconductor Chip Protection Act of 1984 (17 U.S.C.A. §§ 901–914) provides a national system for the registration of original mask works. Only a mask work that was first commercially exploited in the United States, or which was owned by a national or domiciliary of the United States or a national, domiciliary, or sovereign authority of a foreign nation that is a party to a treaty affording protection to mask works to which the United States is also a party or a stateless person at the time of its first commercial exploitation outside the United States, is entitled to registration. The owner of a registered mask work has exclusive rights to reproduce the work by optical, electronic, or any other means and to import or distribute a semiconductor chip product in which the mask work is embodied. The violation of any of these exclusive rights would amount to infringement. However, the owner of a particular semiconductor chip product made by the owner of the mask work, or by any person authorized by the owner of the mask work, may import, distribute, or otherwise dispose of or use, but not reproduce, that particular semiconductor chip product without the authority of the owner of the mask work. Reverse engineering of the mask work is permitted for the purpose of teaching, analysis or evaluation or for the purpose of making another original mask work.

[15]　*Interdigital Communications v. I.T.C.*, 690 F.3d 1318 (Fed.Cir.2012).

[16]　*See* Airtight Cast-Iron Stoves, 3 ITRD 1158, U.S.I.T.C. Pub. No. 1126 (1980).

[17]　*See* Caulking Guns, 6 ITRD 1432, U.S.I.T.C. Pub. No. 1507 (1984).

Section 337.[18] In copyright cases, the petitioner must prove ownership of the copyright and the fact of copying.[19]

A 1989 GATT Panel ruled that Section 337 violated the national treatment provision of Article III (4) of the GATT 1947 agreement. The Panel was persuaded that goods imported into the United States were treated less favorably (i.e., more severely) under Section 337 in terms of patent infringement remedies than domestic goods in federal courts. Under the Uruguay Round Agreements Act, the U.S. made procedural changes, such as the allowance of counterclaims in Section 337y proceedings, intended to address the imbalance in patent infringement remedies. Federal district courts must stay infringement proceedings at the request of the respondent to a Section 337 action.

§ 8.8   Section 337 Proceedings—Complaint and Response

Section 337 complaints may be filed by domestic producers with the International Trade Commission in Washington, D.C., provided the complainants have not agreed by contract to litigate all disputes elsewhere.[20] The complainant must be a representative of the industry. The complaint itself must contain a statement of the facts alleged to constitute unfair import methods or acts. The complaint must also specify instances when unlawful importations occurred, the names and addresses of respondents, and if they exist, a description of any related court proceeding. The complaint must describe the domestic industry that is affected by the import practices and the petitioner's interest in that industry.

If the case involves intellectual property rights, detailed information regarding the patent, copyright, trademark or mask work must be provided. Lastly, the complaint must indicate what relief is sought.[21] Section 337 complainants are subject to the "duty of candor" recognized in *Convertible Rowing Exercisers*.[22] This duty is violated by (1) a failure to disclose material information or a submission of false material information and (2) an intent to mislead.

Once a complaint is filed, or the Commission decides to start a Section 337 proceeding on its own initiative, an investigation is

---

[18]   19 U.S.C.A. § 1337(a).

[19]   *See* Coin-Operated Audio-Visual Games and Components, 1981 WL 50518, U.S.I.T.C. Pub. No. 1160 (June 1981).

[20]   *See Texas Instruments Inc. v. Tessera, Inc.*, 231 F.3d 1325 (Fed.Cir.2000) (agreement that all litigation must take place in California precludes Section 337 complaint).

[21]   C.F.R. § 210.20 (1990).

[22]   Inv. No. 337–TA–212, U.S.I.T.C. Pub. No. 2111 (1988).

normally commenced. The Commission takes the position that it is not obliged to commence an investigation after the filing of a private complaint. Its Office of Unfair Imports (OUI) takes 30 days to examine the sufficiency of the complaint. This Office is an independent party in Section 337 proceedings charged with representing the public interest. Pre-filing review of draft complaints by the OUI is possible, and counsel for the respondents may also seek to have the OUI recommend against proceeding with a Section 337 complaint.

Although it is a rare event, the Commission occasionally has declined to pursue a Section 337 investigation. If this happens, the complaint is dismissed.[23] The Commission has maintained its discretionary authority to review Section 337 complaints despite statutory language which would appear to be mandatory.[24] Thus, it has dismissed complaints where there is insufficient data to support the allegations, or the allegations themselves are insufficient to prove a Section 337 violation.[25] The complainant may of course amend and refile its complaint. Furthermore, a rejection of Section 337 complaints by the Commission can be appealed to the Federal Circuit Court of Appeals.[26] The Commission serves the complaint on foreign parties, thus avoiding the delay of international service of process. Parties who fail to appear default, and can have exclusion orders automatically entered against them.

The respondents in Section 337 proceedings are given an opportunity to submit written briefs regarding the complaint. Such briefs should respond to each allegation in the complaint and set forth any defenses. Failure to provide a response to the complaint can result in a determination that the facts alleged in the complaint are deemed admitted.[27] For example, if the complaint is based upon patent infringement, the respondent would typically allege non-infringement by suggesting that the product is not covered by the patent and/or the invalidity of the patent. An unusual aspect of Section 337 proceedings is the appointment of an investigative attorney by the ITC to represent the public interest. This attorney is a party to the investigation and may participate in discovery and hearings to the full extent of the complainant and respondent.[28]

---

[23] *See* 19 C.F.R. § 210.12.

[24] *See* 19 U.S.C.A. § 1337(b)(1).

[25] *See* Certain Fruit Preserves in Containers Having Lids With Gingham Cloth Design, Docket 1056 (May 21, 1984); Certain Architectural Panels, Docket 1122 (November 30, 1984).

[26] *See Syntex Agribusiness, Inc. v. U.S. International Trade Commission*, 617 F.2d 290 (C.C.P.A.1980) and 659 F.2d 1038 (C.C.P.A.1981).

[27] 19 C.F.R. § 210.21.

[28] 19 C.F.R. § 210.4.

§ 8.9   Section 337 Proceedings—Temporary Relief

If the Commission decides, in the process of its investigation, that there is reason to believe that a violation of Section 337 has occurred, it may order the goods to be excluded from entry into the United States or permit entry only under a bond as a temporary remedy.[29] Such remedies require proof not only of the reasons to believe in the violation, but also of an immediate and substantial injury to the domestic industry in the absence of a temporary remedy.[30]

The statute requires that the Commission consider the public interest in making temporary remedial decisions in connection with Section 337. Thus, the Commission ends up balancing the probability of the complainant's success on the merits, the prospect for immediate and substantial harm to the domestic industry if no relief is granted, the harm to the respondent if such relief is granted, and the effect that temporary remedies would have on the public interest.[31] If the Commission is concerned that the complainant may possibly have filed a frivolous claim or that the harm to the respondent is particularly large, it can require the complainant to post a bond in order to get temporary relief. Decisions about temporary relief are made by the administrative law judge in the case, although they may be modified or vacated by the Commission upon review.[32]

§ 8.10   Section 337 Proceedings—Administrative Process

Section 337 investigations normally last one year but may be extended to eighteen months in complicated cases. This relatively short period has been described as "due process with dispatch." Section 337 investigations are the only investigations conducted by the International Trade Commission that are governed by the Administrative Procedure Act. Thus, the investigation will follow the established procedures for discovery under the Federal Rules of Civil Procedure, pre-hearing conferences, an initial determination of the issues by an administrative judge, and final review by the Commission.[33]

---

[29]   19 U.S.C.A. § 1337(e).

[30]   *See* Certain Apparatus, 12 ITRD 1841, U.S.I.T.C. Pub. No. 1132 (April 1981).

[31]   19 U.S.C.A. § 1337(e).

[32]   19 C.F.R. § 210.24(17).

[33]   *See* 19 C.F.R. §§ 2210.1–2210.71.

One problem is the frequent need for extraterritorial discovery in Section 337 cases. Another issue is sanctions for abuse of discovery,[34] although findings of default can be made. Section 337 discovery responses are typically due in 10 days, much more rapidly than in civil litigation. Although the Commission is authorized to promulgate rules allowing costs and attorneys' fees as sanctions, it has not yet done so. In contrast, the Commission has aggressively enforced its protective orders against disclosure of confidential and business information of a proprietary character.[35] At any point during its investigation, the Commission may decide to settle the proceedings by consent order or by agreement of the parties. This happens reasonably often, especially when the parties to an intellectual property case agree to a licensing arrangement. In either case, the Commission will review the motion to terminate or a proposed consent order from the standpoint of the public interest in the proceeding. An arbitration agreement between parties who are contesting a Section 337 proceeding is no grounds for terminating the ITC investigation.[36]

When the International Trade Commission reviews the advisory decision of the administrative law judge in Section 337 proceedings, it need not undertake a review of that entire determination. It is sufficient for purposes of appeal that the Commission decides the case on the basis of a single dispositive issue. For example, in patent infringement litigation, if the Commission decides that there was no infringement, it need not render decisions concerning any other issues in the Section 337 proceeding.[37] Thus it was only this issue that could be appealed to the Federal Circuit Court of Appeals. Put another way, the only issues that can be appealed are those upon which the Commission has decided, and this is true even in cases concerning temporary relief under Section 337.[38]

§ 8.11 Section 337 Proceedings—Sanctions

If the Commission ultimately decides that an unfair import method or act has been committed, it is authorized to issue a cease and desist order or an exclusion order barring the goods from entering the United States. Any violation of those orders is

---

[34] *See* Certain Concealed Cabinet Hinges and Mounting Plates, 12 ITRD 1841 (Jan. 8, 1990).

[35] *See* Certain Electrically Resistive Monocomponent Toner, 10 ITRD 1672 (1988).

[36] *Farrel Corp. v. U.S. ITC*, 949 F.2d 1147 (Fed.Cir.1991), *cert. denied* 504 U.S. 913, 112 S.Ct. 1947, 118 L.Ed.2d 551 (1992).

[37] *Beloit Corp. v. Valmet Oy*, 742 F.2d 1421 (Fed.Cir.1984), *cert. denied* 472 U.S. 1009, 105 S.Ct. 2706, 86 L.Ed.2d 721 (1985).

[38] *See Warner Bros., Inc. v. U.S. International Trade Commission*, 787 F.2d 562 (Fed.Cir.1986).

punishable by civil penalties up to $100,000 per day or twice the value of the merchandise in question. Final ITC determinations under Section 337 are appealed directly to the Federal Circuit Court of Appeals.

The Federal Circuit Court of Appeals has ruled that the ITC may impose civil penalties for violation of consent orders (as well as cease and desist orders) that terminate patent infringement investigations under Section 337.[39]

§ 8.12   Section 337 Proceedings—Settlements

As the Section 337 investigation proceeds, the complainant may move for a summary determination by the ITC. This is analogous to summary judgment under the Federal Rules of Civil Procedure.[40] If the complaint concerns patent infringement, one solution is for the parties to enter into a licensing agreement. However, the parties must give the Commission a copy of their complete agreement. The Commission's investigative attorney then comments on the settlement and the administrative law judge makes an initial decision as to whether to terminate the investigation on the basis of the settlement. This determination is sent to the Commission for final approval.[41] The purpose of these procedures is to insure that the public interest is preserved as part of the patent infringement dispute settlement.

In non-patent cases, the typical route for settlement is by consent order. To do this, a joint motion is filed by all of the complainants, the Commission's investigative attorney, and one or more of the respondents.[42] This typically occurs before the commencement of the hearing before the administrative law judge. Consent settlements of this type must contain admissions of all jurisdictional facts, waivers of rights to seek judicial review or other means of challenging the consent order, and an agreement that the enforcement, modification and revocation of the order will be undertaken pursuant to ITC rules. The consent order typically is not deemed to constitute an admission of a violation of Section 337 and usually states that it is undertaken solely for settlement purposes.[43] There is a ten-day notice period which allows any interested party to comment on the proposed termination of a Section 337 proceeding on the basis of a consent order.[44]

---

[39]   *San Huan New Materials High Tech, Inc. v. ITC*, 161 F.3d 1347 (Fed.Cir.1998).
[40]   19 C.F.R. § 210.50.
[41]   19 C.F.R. § 210.51.
[42]   19 C.F.R. § 211.20.
[43]   19 C.F.R. § 211.22.
[44]   19 C.F.R. § 211.20.

§ 8.13 Section 337 Proceedings—ITC Public Interest Review

The International Trade Commission is not required to impose a Section 337 remedy if it finds a violation. Its remedial powers are discretionary. In deciding whether to accept proposed consent orders or to impose any remedy, the Commission is required to consider all of the public comments that have been received, the effect upon the public health and welfare of the United States, the effect upon competitive conditions in the U.S. economy, the effect on production of like or directly competitive articles in the United States, and its effect upon U.S. consumers.[45]

The Commission has rarely invoked the public interest exception to Section 337 relief. When it has, the domestic industry typically was unable to supply critically needed items[46] or the public's strong interest in the research overrode patent rights.[47] President Obama cited the public interest exception in vetoing a prominent exclusion order won by Samsung against Apple involving essential industry standard patents. *See* Section 8.15.

§ 8.14 Section 337 Proceedings—ITC General Exclusion and Cease and Desist Orders

The International Trade Commission may issue three different kinds of remedies under Section 337. The first is an exclusion order of a limited or general nature, and this type of relief predominates in intellectual property cases. The second is a cease and desist order, and this type of relief is often issued if there are significant inventories of the offending product already imported into the United States. The effect of such a cease and desist order is to prevent further distribution within the country. The Commission is expressly authorized to issue exclusion orders and cease and desist orders together.[48] Unlike general exclusion orders, ITC cease and desist orders can lead to significant civil penalties.

In either case, the Commission may authorize entry of the goods under bond pending the President's final determination in the proceeding. The amount of the bond varies from case to case, but is generally intended to offset the competitive advantages that are perceived to exist. Such bonds have ranged upwards to 600 percent

---

[45] 19 U.S.C.A. § 1337(d), (e), (f).

[46] *See* Automatic Crankpin Grinders, 2 ITRD 5121, U.S.I.T.C. Pub. No. 1022 (1979) (engine parts needed to meet fuel efficiency standards); Certain Fluidized Supporting Apparatus reported at 7 I.T.R.D. 1089 (1984).

[47] Certain Inclined-Field Acceleration Tubes, 2 ITRD 5572 (1980).

[48] 19 U.S.C.A. § 1337(f).

of the value of the imports.[49] Many Section 337 bonds have been determined by measuring the difference between the complainant's prices in the U.S. and the customs value of the imports. Forfeiture orders are relatively uncommon and typically follow notice by the Secretary of the Treasury that forfeiture would result from further importation of goods that offend Section 337.

Plaintiffs usually wish to obtain general exclusion orders in intellectual property cases. Such orders will keep out all infringing products. The problem with this approach is that it may unfairly bar the importation of goods that resemble but do not infringe the patented product. This is a generally undesirable result that the Commission will try to avoid.[50]

Consequently, the Commission requires those seeking general exclusion orders to prove a widespread pattern of unauthorized use of the patented invention and reasonable inferences that foreign manufacturers other than the respondents may attempt to enter the United States market with infringing goods.[51] A widespread pattern of unauthorized use can be demonstrated by the importation of the infringing goods by numerous companies, by pending foreign infringement suits based upon foreign patents which correspond to the United States patent at issue, or by other evidence which demonstrates a history of unauthorized foreign use of the invention.[52]

In providing evidence that it is reasonable to infer that other foreign manufacturers may attempt to enter the U.S. market, plaintiffs may offer proof of the established demand for the product, the existence of a distribution system in the United States for its marketing, the cost to foreigners of manufacturing or creating a facility capable of manufacturing the goods, the ease and number of foreign manufacturers who could retool so as to produce the offending article, and the cost of such retooling.[53] As these criteria suggest, obtaining a general exclusion order is not always easy, and certainly not automatic.

§ 8.15   Section 337 Proceedings—Presidential Veto

Any order issued by the International Trade Commission under Section 337 goes into effect immediately. However, the President

---

[49]   *See* Certain Cube Puzzles, supra.

[50]   *See* Certain Cloisonne Jewelry, 8 ITRD 2028, U.S.I.T.C. Pub. No. 1822 (March 1986).

[51]   *See* Certain Airless Spray Pumps and Components Thereof, 3 ITRD 2041, U.S.I.T.C. Pub. No. 1199 (1981).

[52]   *Id.*

[53]   *Id.*

may veto that order for public policy reasons.[54] Vetoes by the President of Commission orders in Section 337 proceedings are rare and not generally reviewable by the courts.[55] In 2013, however, President Obama vetoed an ITC-recommended general exclusion order sought by Samsung against importation of patent-infringing Apple iPhone and iPad devices. The President determined that the patents owned by Samsung comprised essential industry standards, subject to reasonable licensing requirements, and that it would not be in the public interest to exclude Apple's devices.[56] Not long thereafter, the President declined to veto an exclusion order recommendation that barred imports of Samsung phones found to be infringing Apple patents... no essential industry standards were involved.

The President has sixty days within which to make a decision concerning ITC orders under Section 337. If the President does not take action within this period, then the order becomes final.[57] Final ITC orders under Section 337 remain in effect until the Commission decides that there is no longer reason to continue the order.[58] Any violation of an outstanding ITC order under Section 337 can incur a civil penalty of up to $10,000 per day or twice the domestic value of the goods sold, whichever is greater.[59]

§ 8.16 Section 337 Proceedings—ITC Opinion Letters

The ITC follows the practice of issuing informal or formal opinion letters in connection with Section 337 matters. Requests for informal opinions from the ITC staff should be addressed to the Assistant General Counsel of the Commission. Formal opinions actually issued by the Commission itself may be obtained if the staff opinion letter is adverse or a formal opinion is just simply necessary. Requests for such opinions are filed with the Secretary of the Commission.[60]

---

[54]   19 U.S.C.A. § 1337(j).

[55]   *Duracell, Inc. v. U.S. International Trade Commission,* 778 F.2d 1578 (Fed.Cir.1985).

[56]   Certain Electronic Digital Media Devices and Components, ITC, 337–TA–796 (Aug. 9, 2013).

[57]   *Id.*

[58]   19 U.S.C.A. § 1337(k).

[59]   19 U.S.C.A. § 1337(j).

[60]   19 C.F.R. § 211.54.

§ 8.17   Section 337 Proceedings—General Exclusion of IP Infringing Imports

This section focuses on the application of Section 337 of the Tariff Act of 1930 to imports that infringe U.S. intellectual property rights. A 1989 decision by a General Agreement on Tariffs and Trade (GATT) panel ruled that Section 337 violates the national treatment provisions of Article III:4 of the GATT. The panel was persuaded that imported goods are treated less favorably (i.e., more severely) under Section 337 in terms of patent infringement remedies than domestic goods which are remedied in the federal courts. The panel's decision was ultimately adopted by the GATT Council and the U.S. indicated that it would consider ways to reach compliance after the TRIPs accord was finalized.

The Uruguay Round Agreements Act of 1994 did not alter the substance of Section 337 law. It did make procedural changes (such as allowance of counterclaims in Section 337 proceedings) intended to address the issue of an imbalance in patent infringement remedies. The federal district courts must stay infringement proceedings at the request of the respondent to Section 337 actions.

Patent Infringing Imports

While not quite a per se rule, it is nearly axiomatic that any infringement of United States patent rights amounts to an unfair import practice for purposes of Section 337.[61] Both product and process patents are entitled to protection under Section 337. In a major decision affecting biotechnology firms, the Federal Circuit Court of Appeals refused Section 337 relief when the U.S. patent owner had no claim either to the final product or the process used to create it even though the foreign party had to use the patented product to create the product being imported into the United States.[62] Had the same activity been undertaken in the U.S., an infringement would most probably have been found. Section 337 can be used to obtain exclusionary orders based upon misappropriation abroad of trade secrets of U.S. companies. Such complaints are governed by federal common law (not state law).[63]

All legal and equitable defenses (but not counterclaims) may be presented, including attacks upon the validity or enforceability of the

---

[61]   *See* Synthetic Star Sapphires, § 316, No. 13 (Sept. 1954), *aff'd sub nom. In re Von Clemm*, 229 F.2d 441 (C.C.P.A.1955).

[62]   *Amgen, Inc. v. U.S. Int'l Trade Comm.*, 902 F.2d 1532 (Fed.Cir.1990).

[63]   *See TianRui Group v. Int'l Trade Commission*, 661 F.3d 1322 (2011) (misappropriation in China from licensees of wheel production trade secrets of U.S. manufacturer).

patent.[64] A patent license that required all "litigation" to take place in California barred pursuit of Section 337 relief.[65] The ITC's refusal to entertain a Section 337 proceeding because the complainant's patent was unenforceable due to prior inequitable conduct was upheld by the Federal Circuit Court of Appeals.[66] This decision illustrates the power of the ITC, as a practical matter, to rule on patent validity.

International Trade Commission decisions on patent validity, and Federal Circuit Court of Appeals opinions on appeal from the ITC, can be treated as preclusive fact findings under collateral estoppel principles in ordinary federal court proceedings.[67] Res judicata effect is ordinarily denied given the fundamental differences between ITC administrative and federal judicial proceedings concerning patent validity.[68]

Patent-based Section 337 proceedings are multiplying. ITC decisions take about 12 to 15 months, versus three to five years for federal court lawsuits. General exclusion orders are typically sought. Hearings are held before one of four administrative law judges specializing in patent law, with final decisions taken by the ITC. Infringing products are excluded from importation during the appeals process. About one-fourth of all 337 proceedings find infringements.

In 2007, in a major decision, the ITC excluded the importation of cell phones containing Qualcomm microchips found to infringe Broadcom patents. In 2012, Samsung succeeded before the ITC in alleging patent infringement by imported Apple cellphones, but the President denied a general exclusion order because the patents in question were part of an industry standard and thus he determined it was against the public interest to exclude the imports on the basis of such patent infringement. This was the first denial of ITC-recommended Section 337 relief since President Reagan. Apple's subsequent attempt to bar Samsung cellphones on patent infringement grounds were upheld by the ITC. Absent involvement of industry standards, no Presidential veto was forthcoming.

Invocation of Section 337 in patent disputes will be influenced by the U.S. Supreme Court's ruling in *KSR International Co. v. Teleflex, Inc.* (April 30, 2007) where it unanimously held that a patent combining pre-existing elements is invalid if the combination is no

---

[64]   19 U.S.C.A. § 1337(c).

[65]   *Texas Instruments Inc. v. Tessera, Inc.*, 231 F.3d 1325 (Fed.Cir.2000).

[66]   *LaBounty Manufacturing, Inc. v. U.S. ITC*, 958 F.2d 1066 (Fed.Cir.1992).

[67]   *In re Convertible Rowing Exerciser Patent Litigation*, 814 F.Supp. 1197 (D.Del.1993).

[68]   *Id.*

"more than the predictable use of prior art elements according to their established functions" (obvious). Likewise, the Supreme Court's cautious consideration of business method patents in *Bilski v. Kappos* (June 28, 2010), as well as *KSR International Co. v. Teleflex Inc.*, 550 U.S. 398, 127 S.Ct. 1727, 167 L.Ed.2d 705 (2007) (raising patentability standards for non-obviousness), *Ass'n of Molecular Pathology v. Myriad Genetics*, 569 U.S. 12–398 (2013) (isolated human genes not patentable), and *Alice Corp. Pty v. CLS Bank Int'l*, 134 S.Ct. 2347 (June 19, 2014) (software limiting risk in currency transactions not patentable), will influence Section 337 disputes.

An increasing number of foreign owners of U.S. patents are invoking 337 procedures. About half of all such complaints are settled, often using cross-licensing among the parties. Section 337 proceedings can result in general exclusion orders permitting seizure of patent counterfeits at any U.S. point of entry. Apple Computer, for example, was able to get such an order against computers sold under the label "Orange" that contained infringing programs and color display circuits.[14] However, as previously noted, the Customs Service finds it extremely difficult when inspecting invoices and occasionally opening boxes to ascertain which goods are counterfeit or infringing. Many counterfeits do look like "the real thing." For most seizure remedies to work, the holder must notify the Customs Service of an incoming shipment of patent offending goods. Such advance notice is hard to obtain.

§ 8.18   Text of Section 337 (19 U.S.C.A. § 1337)

Unlawful activities; covered industries; definitions

(1) Subject to paragraph (2), the following are unlawful, and when found by the Commission to exist shall be dealt with, in addition to any other provision of law, as provided in this section:

(A) Unfair methods of competition and unfair acts in the importation of articles (other than articles provided for in subparagraphs (B), (C), (D), and (E)) into the United States, or in the sale of such articles by the owner, importer, or consignee, the threat or effect of which is—

(i) to destroy or substantially injure an industry in the United States;

(ii) to prevent the establishment of such an industry; or

(iii) to restrain or monopolize trade and commerce in the United States.

---

[14]   In Re Certain Personal Computers and Components Thereof, 6 ITRD 1140, 1984 Copr.L.Dec. p 25651, U.S.I.T.C. Pub. No. 1504.

(B) The importation into the United States, the sale for importation, or the sale within the United States after importation by the owner, importer, or consignee, of articles that—

  (i) infringe a valid and enforceable United States patent or a valid and enforceable United States copyright registered under title 17; or

  (ii) are made, produced, processed, or mined under, or by means of, a process covered by the claims of a valid and enforceable United States patent.

(C) The importation into the United States, the sale for importation, or the sale within the United States after importation by the owner, importer, or consignee, of articles that infringe a valid and enforceable United States trademark registered under the Trademark Act of 1946 [15 U.S.C. § 1051 et seq.].

(D) The importation into the United States, the sale for importation, or the sale within the United States after importation by the owner, importer, or consignee, of a semiconductor chip product in a manner that constitutes infringement of a mask work registered under chapter 9 of title 17.

(E) The importation into the United States, the sale for importation, or the sale within the United States after importation by the owner, importer, or consigner, of an article that constitutes infringement of the exclusive rights in a design protected under chapter 13 of title 17.

(2) Subparagraphs (B), (C), (D), and (E) of paragraph (1) apply only if an industry in the United States, relating to the articles protected by the patent, copyright, trademark, mask work, or design concerned, exists or is in the process of being established.

(3) For purposes of paragraph (2), an industry in the United States shall be considered to exist if there is in the United States, with respect to the articles protected by the patent, copyright, trademark, mask work, or design concerned—

  (A) significant investment in plant and equipment;

  (B) significant employment of labor or capital; or

  (C) substantial investment in its exploitation, including engineering, research and development, or licensing.

(4) For the purposes of this section, the phrase "owner, importer, or consignee" includes any agent of the owner, importer, or consignee.

(b) Investigation of violations by Commission

(1) The Commission shall investigate any alleged violation of this section on complaint under oath or upon its initiative. Upon commencing any such investigation, the Commission shall publish notice thereof in the Federal Register. The Commission shall conclude any such investigation and make its determination under this section at the earliest practicable time after the date of publication of notice of such investigation. To promote expeditious adjudication, the Commission shall, within 45 days after an investigation is initiated, establish a target date for its final determination.

(2) During the course of each investigation under this section, the Commission shall consult with, and seek advice and information from, the Department of Health and Human Services, the Department of Justice, the Federal Trade Commission, and such other departments and agencies as it considers appropriate.

(3) Whenever, in the course of an investigation under this section, the Commission has reason to believe, based on information before it, that a matter, in whole or in part, may come within the purview of part II of subtitle IV of this chapter, it shall promptly notify the Secretary of Commerce so that such action may be taken as is otherwise authorized by such part II. If the Commission has reason to believe that the matter before it

    (A) is based solely on alleged acts and effects which are within the purview of section 1671 or 1673 of this title, or

    (B) relates to an alleged copyright infringement with respect to which action is prohibited by section 1008 of title 17, the Commission shall terminate, or not institute, any investigation into the matter. If the Commission has reason to believe the matter before it is based in part on alleged acts and effects which are within the purview of section 1671 or 1673 of this title, and in part on alleged acts and effects which may, independently from or in conjunction with those within the purview of such section, establish a basis for relief under this section, then it may institute or continue an investigation into the matter. If the Commission notifies the Secretary or the administering authority (as defined in section 1677(1) of this title) with respect to a matter under this paragraph, the Commission may suspend its investigation during the time the matter is before the Secretary or administering authority for final decision. Any final decision by the administering authority under section 1671 or 1673 of this title with respect to the matter within such section 1671 or 1673 of this title of which the Commission has notified the Secretary or administering authority shall be conclusive upon the Commission with respect to the issue of less-than-fair-value sales or subsidization and the matters necessary for such decision.

(c) Determinations; review

The Commission shall determine, with respect to each investigation conducted by it under this section, whether or not there is a violation of this section, except that the Commission may, by issuing a consent order or on the basis of an agreement between the private parties to the investigation, including an agreement to present the matter for arbitration, terminate any such investigation, in whole or in part, without making such a determination. Each determination under subsection (d) or (e) of this section shall be made on the record after notice and opportunity for a hearing in conformity with the provisions of subchapter II of chapter 5 of title 5. All legal and equitable defenses may be presented in all cases. A respondent may raise any counterclaim in a manner prescribed by the Commission. Immediately after a counterclaim is received by the Commission, the respondent raising such counterclaim shall file a notice of removal with a

United States district court in which venue for any of the counterclaims raised by the party would exist under section 1391 of title 28. Any counterclaim raised pursuant to this section shall relate back to the date of the original complaint in the proceeding before the Commission. Action on such counterclaim shall not delay or affect the proceeding under this section, including the legal and equitable defenses that may be raised under this subsection. Any person adversely affected by a final determination of the Commission under subsection (d), (e), (f), or (g) of this section may appeal such determination, within 60 days after the determination becomes final, to the United States Court of Appeals for the Federal Circuit for review in accordance with chapter 7 of title 5. Notwithstanding the foregoing provisions of this subsection, Commission determinations under subsections (d), (e), (f), and (g) of this section with respect to its findings on the public health and welfare, competitive conditions in the United States economy, the production of like or directly competitive articles in the United States, and United States consumers, the amount and nature of bond, or the appropriate remedy shall be reviewable in accordance with section 706 of title 5. Determinations by the Commission under subsections (e), (f), and (j) of this section with respect to forfeiture of bonds and under subsection (h) of this section with respect to the imposition of sanctions for abuse of discovery or abuse of process shall also be reviewable in accordance with section 706 of title 5.

(d) Exclusion of articles from entry

(1) If the Commission determines, as a result of an investigation under this section, that there is a violation of this section, it shall direct that the articles concerned, imported by any person violating the provision of this section, be excluded from entry into the United States, unless, after considering the effect of such exclusion upon the public health and welfare, competitive conditions in the United States economy, the production of like or directly competitive articles in the United States, and United States consumers, it finds that such articles should not be excluded from entry. The Commission shall notify the Secretary of the Treasury of its action under this subsection directing such exclusion from entry, and upon receipt of such notice, the Secretary shall, through the proper officers, refuse such entry.

(2) The authority of the Commission to order an exclusion from entry of articles shall be limited to persons determined by the Commission to be violating this section unless the Commission determines that—

(A) a general exclusion from entry of articles is necessary to prevent circumvention of an exclusion order limited to products of named persons; or

(B) there is a pattern of violation of this section and it is difficult to identify the source of infringing products.

(e) Exclusion of articles from entry during investigation except under bond; procedures applicable; preliminary relief

(1) If, during the course of an investigation under this section, the Commission determines that there is reason to believe that there is a violation of this section, it may direct that the articles concerned, imported by any person with respect to whom there is reason to believe that such person is violating this section, be excluded from entry into the United States, unless, after considering the effect of such exclusion upon the public health and welfare, competitive conditions in the United States economy, the production of like or directly competitive articles in the United States, and United States consumers, it finds that such articles should not be excluded from entry. The Commission shall notify the Secretary of the Treasury of its action under this subsection directing such exclusion from entry, and upon receipt of such notice, the Secretary shall, through the proper officers, refuse such entry, except that such articles shall be entitled to entry under bond prescribed by the Secretary in an amount determined by the Commission to be sufficient to protect the complainant from any injury. If the Commission later determines that the respondent has violated the provisions of this section, the bond may be forfeited to the complainant.

(2) A complainant may petition the Commission for the issuance of an order under this subsection. The Commission shall make a determination with regard to such petition by no later than the 90th day after the date on which the Commission's notice of investigation is published in the Federal Register. The Commission may extend the 90-day period for an additional 60 days in a case it designates as a more complicated case. The Commission shall publish in the Federal Register its reasons why it designated the case as being more complicated. The Commission may require the complainant to post a bond as a prerequisite to the issuance of an order under this subsection. If the Commission later determines that the respondent has not violated the provisions of this section, the bond may be forfeited to the respondent.

(3) The Commission may grant preliminary relief under this subsection or subsection (f) of this section to the same extent as preliminary injunctions and temporary restraining orders may be granted under the Federal Rules of Civil Procedure.

(4) The Commission shall prescribe the terms and conditions under which bonds may be forfeited under paragraphs (1) and (2).

(f) Cease and desist orders; civil penalty for violation of orders

(1) In addition to, or in lieu of, taking action under subsection (d) or (e) of this section, the Commission may issue and cause to be served on any person violating this section, or believed to be violating this section, as the case may be, an order directing such person to cease and desist from engaging in the unfair methods or acts involved, unless after considering the effect of such order upon the public health and welfare, competitive conditions in the United States economy, the production of like or directly competitive articles in the United States, and United States consumers, it finds that such order should not be issued. The Commission may at any time, upon such notice and in such manner as it deems proper, modify or revoke any such order, and, in the case of a revocation, may take action under subsection (d) or (e) of this section, as the case may be. If a temporary cease and desist order is issued in addition to, or in lieu of, an exclusion order under subsection (e) of this section, the Commission may require the complainant to post a bond, in an amount determined by the Commission to be sufficient to protect the respondent from any injury, as a prerequisite to the issuance of an order under this subsection. If the Commission later determines that the respondent has not violated the provisions of this section, the bond may be forfeited to the respondent. The Commission shall prescribe the terms and conditions under which the bonds may be forfeited under this paragraph.

(2) Any person who violates an order issued by the Commission under paragraph (1) after it has become final shall forfeit and pay to the United States a civil penalty for each day on which an importation of articles, or their sale, occurs in violation of the order of not more than the greater of $100,000 or twice the domestic value of the articles entered or sold on such day in violation of the order. Such penalty shall accrue to the United States and may be recovered for the United States in a civil action brought by the Commission in the Federal District Court for the District of Columbia or for the district in which the violation occurs. In such actions, the United States district courts may issue mandatory injunctions incorporating the relief sought by the Commission as they deem appropriate in the enforcement of such final orders of the Commission.

(g) Exclusion from entry or cease and desist order; conditions and procedures applicable

(1)   If—

   (A)   a complaint is filed against a person under this section;

   (B)   the complaint and a notice of investigation are served on the person;

   (C)   the person fails to respond to the complaint and notice or otherwise fails to appear to answer the complaint and notice;

   (D)   the person fails to show good cause why the person should not be found in default; and

   (E)   the complainant seeks relief limited solely to that person;

the Commission shall presume the facts alleged in the complaint to be true and shall, upon request, issue an exclusion from entry or a cease and desist order, or both, limited to that person unless, after considering the effect of such exclusion or order upon the public health and welfare, competitive conditions in the United States economy, the production of like or directly competitive articles in the United States, and United States consumers, the Commission finds that such exclusion or order should not be issued.

(2)   In addition to the authority of the Commission to issue a general exclusion from entry of articles when a respondent appears to contest an investigation concerning a violation of the provisions of this section, a general exclusion from entry of articles, regardless of the source or importer of the articles, may be issued if—

   (A)   no person appears to contest an investigation concerning a violation of the provisions of this section,

(B) such a violation is established by substantial, reliable, and probative evidence, and

(C) the requirements of subsection (d)(2) of this section are met.

(h) Sanctions for abuse of discovery and abuse of process

The Commission may by rule prescribe sanctions for abuse of discovery and abuse of process to the extent authorized by Rule 11 and Rule 37 of the Federal Rules of Civil Procedure.

(i) Forfeiture

(1) In addition to taking action under subsection (d) of this section, the Commission may issue an order providing that any article imported in violation of the provisions of this section be seized and forfeited to the United States if—

(A) the owner, importer, or consignee of the article previously attempted to import the article into the United States;

(B) the article was previously denied entry into the United States by reason of an order issued under subsection (d) of this section; and

(C) upon such previous denial of entry, the Secretary of the Treasury provided the owner, importer, or consignee of the article written notice of—

(i) such order, and

(ii) the seizure and forfeiture that would result from any further attempt to import the article into the United States.

(2) The Commission shall notify the Secretary of the Treasury of any order issued under this subsection and, upon receipt of such notice, the Secretary of the Treasury shall enforce such order in accordance with the provisions of this section.

(3) Upon the attempted entry of articles subject to an order issued under this subsection, the Secretary of the Treasury shall immediately notify all ports of entry of the attempted importation and shall identify the persons notified under paragraph (1)(C).

(4) The Secretary of the Treasury shall provide—

(A) the written notice described in paragraph (1)(C) to the owner, importer, or consignee of any article that is denied entry into the United States by reason of an order issued under subsection (d) of this section; and

(B) a copy of such written notice to the Commission.

(j) Referral to President

(1) If the Commission determines that there is a violation of this section, or that, for purposes of subsection (e) of this section, there is reason to believe that there is such a violation, it shall—

(A) publish such determination in the Federal Register, and

(B) transmit to the President a copy of such determination and the action taken under subsection (d), (e), (f), (g), or (i) of this section, with respect thereto, together with the record upon which such determination is based.

(2) If, before the close of the 60-day period beginning on the day after the day on which he receives a copy of such determination, the President, for policy reasons, disapproves such determination and notifies the Commission of his disapproval, then, effective on the date of such notice, such determination and the action taken under subsection (d), (e), (f), (g), or (i) of this section with respect thereto shall have no force or effect.

(3) Subject to the provisions of paragraph (2), such determination shall, except for purposes of subsection (c) of this section, be effective upon publication thereof in the Federal Register, and the action taken under subsection (d), (e), (f), (g), or (i) of this section, with respect thereto shall be effective as provided in such subsections, except that articles directed to be excluded from entry under subsection (d) of this section or subject to a cease and desist order under subsection (f) of this section shall, until such determination becomes final, be entitled to entry under bond prescribed by the Secretary in an amount determined by the Commission to be sufficient to protect the complainant from any injury. If the determination becomes final, the bond may be forfeited to the complainant. The Commission shall prescribe the terms and conditions under which bonds may be forfeited under this paragraph.

(4) If the President does not disapprove such determination within such 60-day period, or if he notifies the Commission before the close of such period that he approves such determination, then, for purposes of paragraph (3) and subsection (c) of this section such determination shall become final on the day after the close of such period or the day on which the President notifies the Commission of his approval, as the case may be.

(k) Period of effectiveness; termination of violation or modification or rescission of exclusion or order

(1) Except as provided in subsections (f) and (j) of this section, any exclusion from entry or order under this section shall continue in effect until the Commission finds, and in the case of exclusion from entry notifies the Secretary of the Treasury, that the conditions which led to such exclusion from entry or order no longer exist.

(2) If any person who has previously been found by the Commission to be in violation of this section petitions the Commission for a determination that the petitioner is no longer in violation of this section or for a modification or rescission of an exclusion from entry or order under subsection (d), (e), (f), (g), or (i) of this section—

(A) the burden of proof in any proceeding before the Commission regarding such petition shall be on the petitioner; and

(B) relief may be granted by the Commission with respect to such petition—

(i) on the basis of new evidence or evidence that could not have been presented at the prior proceeding, or

(ii) on grounds which would permit relief from a judgment or order under the Federal Rules of Civil Procedure.

(*l*)   Importation by or for United States

Any exclusion from entry or order under subsection (d), (e), (f), (g), or (i) of this section, in cases based on a proceeding involving a patent, copyright, mask work, or design under subsection (a)(1) of this section, shall not apply to any articles imported by and for the use of the United States, or imported for, and to be used for, the United States with the authorization or consent of the Government. Whenever any article would have been excluded from entry or would not have been entered pursuant to the provisions of such subsections but for the operation of this subsection, an owner of the patent, copyright, mask work, or design adversely affected shall be entitled to reasonable and entire compensation in an action before the United States Court of Federal Claims pursuant to the procedures of section 1498 of title 28.

(m) "United States" defined

For purposes of this section and sections 1338 and 1340 of this title, the term "United States" means the customs territory of the United States as defined in general note 2 of the Harmonized Tariff Schedule of the United States.

(n) Disclosure of confidential information

(1) Information submitted to the Commission or exchanged among the parties in connection with proceedings under this section which is properly designated as confidential pursuant to Commission rules may not be disclosed (except under a protective order issued under regulations of the Commission which authorizes limited disclosure of such information) to any person (other than a person described in paragraph (2)) without the consent of the person submitting it.

(2) Notwithstanding the prohibition contained in paragraph (1), information referred to in that paragraph may be disclosed to—

(A) an officer or employee of the Commission who is directly concerned with—

(i)   carrying out the investigation or related proceeding in connection with which the information is submitted,

(ii) the administration of a bond posted pursuant to subsection (e), (f), or (j) of this section,

(iii) the administration or enforcement of an exclusion order issued pursuant to subsection (d), (e), or (g) of this section, a cease and desist order issued pursuant to subsection (f) of this section, or a consent order issued pursuant to subsection (c) of this section,

(iv) proceedings for the modification or rescission of a temporary or permanent order issued under subsection (d), (e), (f), (g), or (i) of this section, or a consent order issued under this section, or

(v) maintaining the administrative record of the investigation or related proceeding,

(B) an officer or employee of the United States Government who is directly involved in the review under subsection (j) of this section, or

(C) an officer or employee of the United States Customs Service who is directly involved in administering an exclusion from entry under subsection (d), (e), or (g) of this section resulting from the investigation or related proceeding in connection with which the information is submitted.

Chapter 9

GRAY MARKET IMPORTS

Table of Sections

§ 9.1   Trade in Gray Market Goods

One of the most controversial areas of customs law concerns "gray market goods," goods produced abroad with authorization and payment but which are imported into unauthorized markets. Trade in gray market goods has dramatically increased in recent years, in part because fluctuating currency exchange rates create opportunities to import and sell such goods at a discount from local price levels. Licensors and their distributors suddenly find themselves competing in their home or other "reserved" markets with products made abroad by their own licensees.

Or, in the reverse, startled licensees find their licensor's products intruding on their local market shares. In either case, third party importers and exporters are often the immediate source of the gray market goods, and they have little respect for who agreed to what in the licensing agreement. When pressed, such third parties will undoubtedly argue that any attempt through licensing at allocating markets or customers is an antitrust or competition law violation.

In times of floating exchange rates, importers have found that by shopping around the world for gray market goods they can undercut local prices with "parallel imports." This explains in large part the dramatic growth in trade in gray market goods in recent years. Gray market goods have become an important source of price competition in the United States marketplace, particularly in years when the U.S. dollar is strong. Some retail firms, like K-Mart, are major traders of gray market goods.

A decline of the dollar against the Japanese yen or EURO would reduce the flow of gray market *imports* from those sources, but perhaps increase the flow of gray market *exports* from the U.S. to those countries. For example, assume a Cadillac sells in the U.S. for $30,000 and a Mercedes in Germany for 30,000 EUROs. At exchange rate of .75 EUROs to the dollar, the dollar is very strong. Mercedes sells in Germany for $22,500, Cadillac sells in the U.S. for 40,000 EUROs. This encourages importing cars bought in Germany to the U.S. The cars are converted to U.S. specifications for $2,000 and sold for $24,500 by non-authorized companies, often independent Mercedes repair shops. Then the dollar drops in value to 1.50 EUROs. Now you must pay $45,000 in Germany to buy a Mercedes, but need only 20,000 EUROs to buy a Cadillac. This encourages exporting cars bought in the U.S. to Germany.

There is no international agreement, WTO or otherwise, concerning trade in gray market goods. Hence each jurisdiction is free to adopt its own rules. United Sates, European Union, Japanese and treatment of gray market goods in other jurisdictions are examined in this Chapter.

§ 9.2   U.S. Genuine Goods Exclusion Act

In the early part of the century, gray market litigation provoked a Supreme Court decision blocking French cosmetics from entering the United States.[1] A United States firm was assigned the U.S. trademark rights for French cosmetics as part of the sale of the United States business interests of the French producer. The assignee successfully obtained infringement relief in federal district court against Katzel, an importer of the French product benefiting from exchange rate fluctuations. On appeal, the Second Circuit vacated this relief in a holding which followed a line of cases allowing "genuine goods" to enter the U.S. market in competition with established sources. The Supreme Court ultimately reversed the Second Circuit emphasizing the trademark ownership (not license) and independent public good will of the assignee as reasons for its reversal.

Genuine Goods Exclusion Act

Congress, before the Supreme Court reversal, passed the Genuine Goods Exclusion Act, now appearing as Section 526 of the Tariff Act of 1930.[2] This Act bars *unauthorized importation* of goods bearing trademarks of U.S. citizens. Registration of such marks with the Customs Service can result in the seizure of unauthorized

---

[1]   *A. Bourjois & Co. v. Katzel*, 260 U.S. 689, 43 S.Ct. 244, 67 L.Ed. 464 (1923).
[2]   19 U.S.C.A. § 1526.

imports. Persons dealing in such imports may be enjoined, required to export the goods, destroy them or obliterate the offending mark, as well as pay damages. The Act has had a checkered history in the courts and Customs Service.

The Customs Service view (influenced by antitrust policy) was that genuine (gray market) goods may be excluded only when the foreign and U.S. trademark rights are not under common ownership or control, or those rights have been used without authorization. The practical effect of this position was to admit most gray market goods into the U.S., thereby providing substantial price competition, but uncertain coverage under manufacturers' warranty, service and rebate programs. Some firms, like K-Mart, excel at gray market importing and may provide independent warranty and repair service contracts. Since 1986, New York and California require disclosure that manufacturers' programs may not apply to sellers of gray market goods.

K Mart Decision

A split in the federal Courts of Appeal as to the legitimacy in light of the Genuine Goods Exclusion Act of the Customs Service position on gray market imports resulted in a U.S. Supreme Court ruling.[3] In an extremely technical, not very policy-oriented decision, the Supreme Court arrived at a compromise. The Customs Service can continue to permit entry of genuine goods when there is common ownership or control of the trademarks. The Service must seize such goods only when they were authorized (licensed), but the marks are not subject to common ownership or control. For these purposes, "common ownership or control" is defined as a 50 percent shareholding or the effective control of policy and operations. Gray market goods originating from such "affiliated companies" will still be allowed to enter the United States.[4]

However, a Fifth Circuit decision indicates that close and profitable business ties between a foreign trademark owner and the foreign owner of U.S. trademark rights do not amount to "common control." Rolex was thus able to obtain a Customs Service forfeiture ruling against gray market imports of its watches by Wal-Mart. The court applied a strict common ownership test to Section 526.[5] The Tenth Circuit affirmed summary judgment in favor of an Oklahoma company owning U.S. trademark rights to "Vittoria" for bicycle tires. The rights were transferred by an Italian company, the maker of the

---

[3]   *K Mart Corp. v. Cartier, Inc.*, 486 U.S. 281, 108 S.Ct. 1811, 100 L.Ed.2d 313 (1988).

[4]   *See* 19 C.F.R. §§ 133.21(c), 133.2(d).

[5]   *United States v. Eighty-Three Rolex Watches*, 992 F.2d 508 (5th Cir.1993)., *cert. denied* 510 U.S. 991, 114 S.Ct. 547, 126 L.Ed.2d 449 (1993).

tires. The "common control" exception to gray market trademark protection did not apply because there was at most "a close business relationship" between the two companies.[6]

Many believe that the bulk of U.S. imports of gray market goods have continued under the Supreme Court's *K Mart* ruling. However, this perspective is somewhat undermined by treatment of gray market imports under other statutory regimes.

§ 9.3   U.S. Section 337 Remedies

An attempt in 1985 by Duracell to exclude gray market batteries alternatively under Section 337 of the Tariff Act of 1930 as an unfair import practice was upheld by the U.S. International Trade Commission, but denied relief by President Reagan in deference to the Customs Service position.[7]

Absent veto by the president, Section 337 exclusion orders can be used against gray market imports. In one decision, the Federal Circuit Court of Appeals upheld the ITC's order against used Kubota-brand tractors.[8] This decision relies heavily on the existence of material differences between the gray market tractors and those distributed by authorized Kubota dealers in the U.S. These differences included parts and the absence of English-language labels and instructions.

§ 9.4   U.S. Trademark, Copyright and Patent Remedies

Section 42 of the Lanham Trademark Act prohibits the importation of goods that copy or simulate a registered U.S. trademark.[9] In *K Mart,* the U.S. Supreme Court specifically declined

---

[6]   *Vittoria North America, LLC v. Euro-Asia Imports, Inc.*, 278 F.3d 1076 (10th Cir.2001).

[7]   *See Duracell, Inc. v. U.S. International Trade Commission*, 778 F.2d 1578 (Fed.Cir.1985). Compare *Bourdeau Bros. Inc. v. Int'l Trade Comm.*, 444 F.3d 1317 (2006) (goods produced in U.S., exported to Europe, importation can be blocked if materially different from goods sold in USA).

[8]   *Gamut Trading Co. v. U.S. I.T.C.*, 200 F.3d 775 (Fed.Cir.1999).

[9]   **Genuine Goods Exclusion Act, 15 U.S.C.A. § 1124:**

(a)   Importation prohibited

Except as provided in subsection (d) of this section, it shall be unlawful to import into the United States any merchandise of foreign manufacture if such merchandise, or the label, sign, print, package, wrapper, or receptacle, bears a trademark owned by a citizen of, or by a corporation or association created or organized within, the United States, and registered in the Patent and Trademark Office by a person domiciled in the United States, under the provisions of sections 81 to 109 of title 15, and if a copy of the certificate of registration of such trademark is filed with the Secretary of the Treasury, in the manner provided in section 106 of said title 15, unless written consent of the owner of such trademark is produced at the time of making entry.

(b) Seizure and forfeiture

Any such merchandise imported into the United States in violation of the provisions of this section shall be subject to seizure and forfeiture for violation of the customs laws.

(c) Injunction and damages

Any person dealing in any such merchandise may be enjoined from dealing therein within the United States or may be required to export or destroy such merchandise or to remove or obliterate such trademark and shall be liable for the same damages and profits provided for wrongful use of a trade-mark, under the provisions of sections 81 to 109 of title 15.

(d) Exemptions; publication in Federal Register; forfeitures; rules and regulations

(1)   The trademark provisions of this section and section 1124 of title 15, do not apply to the importation of articles accompanying any person arriving in the United States when such articles are for his personal use and not for sale if

(A)   such articles are within the limits of types and quantities determined by the Secretary pursuant to paragraph (2) of this subsection, and

(B)   such person has not been granted an exemption under this subsection within thirty days immediately preceding his arrival.

(2)   The Secretary shall determine and publish in the Federal Register lists of the types of articles and the quantities of each which shall be entitled to the exemption provided by this subsection. In determining such quantities of particular types of trade-marked articles, the Secretary shall give such consideration as he deems necessary to the numbers of such articles usually purchased at retail for personal use.

(3)   If any article which has been exempted from the restrictions on importation of the trade-mark laws under this subsection is sold within one year after the date of importation, such article, or its value (to be recovered from the importer), is subject to forfeiture. A sale pursuant to a judicial order or in liquidation of the estate of a decedent is not subject to the provisions of this paragraph.

(4)   The Secretary may prescribe such rules and regulations as may be necessary to carry out the provisions of this subsection.

(e) Merchandise bearing counterfeit mark; seizure and forfeiture; disposition of seized goods

Any such merchandise bearing a counterfeit mark (within the meaning of section 1127 of title 15) imported into the United States in violation of the provisions of section 1124 of title 15, shall be seized and, in the absence of the written consent of the trademark owner, forfeited for violations of the customs laws. Upon seizure of such merchandise, the Secretary shall notify the owner of the trademark, and shall, after forfeiture, destroy the merchandise. Alternatively, if the merchandise is not unsafe or a hazard to health, and the Secretary has the consent of the trademark owner, the Secretary may obliterate the trademark where feasible and dispose of the goods seized—

(1)   by delivery to such Federal, State, and local government agencies as in the opinion of the Secretary have a need for such merchandise,

(2)   by gift to such eleemosynary institutions as in the opinion of the Secretary have a need for such merchandise, or

(3)   more than 90 days after the date of forfeiture, by sale by the Customs Service at public auction under such regulations as the Secretary prescribes, except that before making any such sale the Secretary shall determine that no Federal, State, or local government agency or eleemosynary institution has established a need for such merchandise under paragraph (1) or (2).

to review the legality of barring gray market goods under this provision. Some courts have denied relief under Section 42 against gray market imports. These cases stress the absence of consumer confusion when genuine goods are involved.[10] Other courts have reached conclusions that in the absence of adequate disclosure Section 42 is actionable against gray market goods that materially differ in physical content from those sold in the U.S.A.[11] When there are material differences, labeling suffices to avoid Section 42.[12]

A Second Circuit decision relying upon Section 32 of the Lanham Act also supports blocking imports of materially different gray market goods.[13] In this case, Cabbage Patch dolls produced in Spain under license came with birth certificates, adoption papers and instructions in Spanish, but were otherwise the same product. The U.S. manufacturer refused to register these dolls, leading to numerous complaints by parents and children. These complaints supported the court's injunction against importation of the dolls from Spain under Section 32. Section 32 provides trademark owners with remedies against persons who, without consent by the owner, use a "reproduction, counterfeit, copy or colorable imitation" of a mark so as to cause confusion, mistake or deception.[14] However, a Ninth Circuit decision relying of Sections 32 and 43(a) (country of origin markings) of the Lanham Act leads to the opposite conclusion,

---

(f) Civil penalties

(1) Any person who directs, assists financially or otherwise, or aids and abets the importation of merchandise for sale or public distribution that is seized under subsection (e) of this section shall be subject to a civil fine.

(2) For the first such seizure, the fine shall be not more than the value that the merchandise would have had if it were genuine, according to the manufacturer's suggested retail price, determined under regulations promulgated by the Secretary.

(3) For the second seizure and thereafter, the fine shall be not more than twice the value that the merchandise would have had if it were genuine, as determined under regulations promulgated by the Secretary.

(4) The imposition of a fine under this subsection shall be within the discretion of the Customs Service, and shall be in addition to any other civil or criminal penalty or other remedy authorized by law.

[10] *See, e.g., Monte Carlo Shirt v. Daewoo International (America) Corp.*, 707 F.2d 1054 (9th Cir.1983); *Bell & Howell: Mamiya Co. v. Masel Supply Co., Corp.*, 719 F.2d 42 (2d Cir.1983).

[11] *See Lever Bros. Co. v. United States*, 877 F.2d 101 (D.C.Cir.1989); *Ferrero U.S.A., Inc. v. Ozak Trading, Inc.*, 753 F.Supp. 1240 (D.N.J.1991), *affirmed* 935 F.2d 1281 (3d Cir.1991); *Société Des Produits Nestle, S.A. v. Casa Helvetia, Inc.*, 982 F.2d 633 (1st Cir.1992); *Lever Bros. Co. v. United States*, 981 F.2d 1330 (D.C.Cir.1993).

[12] *See* the U.S. Customs Service Regulation at 19 C.F.R. § 133.23.

[13] *Original Appalachian Artworks v. Granada Electronics, Inc.*, 816 F.2d 68 (2d Cir.1987), *cert. denied* 484 U.S. 847, 108 S.Ct. 143, 98 L.Ed.2d 99 (1987). Accord, *Société Des Produits Nestle, S.A. v. Casa Helvetia, Inc.*, 982 F.2d 633 (1st Cir.1992).

[14] 15 U.S.C.A. § 1114.

finding no support for the argument that gray market imports can be remedied under those provisions.[15]

Sections 103 and 602 of the Copyright Act provide that importing goods into the U.S. without the consent of copyright owners is an infringement.[16] But Section 109 limits the distribution rights of copyright owners under what is known as the "first sale doctrine."[17] This doctrine limits the owner's control over copies to their first sale or transfer. Two Third Circuit decisions split on the use of copyright law against gray market imports in spite of the first sale doctrine.[18] In *Sebastian,* the Third Circuit held that a U.S. manufacturer who sells goods with copyrighted labels to foreign distributors is barred by the first sale doctrine from obtaining import infringement relief. In *Scorpio,* where the goods were manufactured abroad under license by the U.S. copyright holder, such relief was granted.

The Supreme Court subsequently held that the first sale doctrine bars injunctive relief under the Copyright Act[19] against goods previously exported from the USA, even if the goods are foreign made.[20]

Citing the longstanding precedent of "exhaustion" of patents after sale of the products to which they attach, the U.S. Supreme Court ruled in *Impression Products Inc. v. Lexmark Int'l Inc* (May 30, 2017) that patent rights cannot be invoked to bar importation of those products, in this case refilled Lexmark printer ink cartridges, regardless of whether they were made in the USA or abroad.

§ 9.5   Treatment of Gray Market Imports in Non-U.S. Jurisdictions

An excellent review of the treatment of gray market goods in other jurisdictions is presented in an article by Takamatsu.[21] This review is of particular interest to U.S. *exporters* of gray market goods.

---

[15]   *NEC Electronics v. CAL Circuit Abco, Inc.*, 810 F.2d 1506 (9th Cir.1987), *cert. denied* 484 U.S. 851, 108 S.Ct. 152, 98 L.Ed.2d 108 (1987).

[16]   17 U.S.C.A. § 106.

[17]   17 U.S.C.A. § 109.

[18]   *Columbia Broadcasting System v. Scorpio Music Distributors*, 569 F.Supp. 47 (E.D.Pa.1983), *affirmed* 738 F.2d 424 (3d Cir.1984) (relief granted); *Sebastian Int'l, Inc. v. Consumer Contacts (PTY), Ltd.*, 847 F.2d 1093 (3d Cir.1988) (relief denied).

[19]   *Quality King Distributors, Inc. v. L'ANZA Research International, Inc.*, 523 U.S. 135, 118 S.Ct. 1125, 140 L.Ed.2d 254 (1998).

[20]   *See Kirtsaeng v. John Wiley & Sons*, 133 S.Ct. 1351 (March 19, 2013) *reversing Parfums Givenchy, Inc v. Drug Emporium*, 38 F.3d 477 (9th Cir.1994)., *cert. denied* 514 U.S. 1004, 115 S.Ct. 1315, 131 L.Ed.2d 197 (1995).

[21]   Takamatsu, Parallel Importation of Trademarked Goods: A Comparative Analysis, 57 Wash.L.Rev. 433 (1982).

For the most part, his review indicates that other jurisdictions permit gray market goods to enter. This is true of the *Parker Pen* cases under Japanese law,[22] the *Maja* case under German law[23] and the *Agfa-Gevaert* case in Austria,[24] all of which are reviewed by Takamatsu. Canadian Superior Court law strongly supports free trade in gray market goods.[25]

The legal analysis contained in these opinions has been very influential in European Union law.[26] EU law basically posits that once goods subject to intellectual property rights of common origin have been sold on the market with authorization, the holders can no longer block importation of those goods ("parallel imports") through the use of national property rights. Such use is not thought to have been intended as part of the original grant of rights and is said to have been "exhausted" upon sale. An extensive body of law permits parallel imports (even of qualitatively different goods) as part of the promotion of the Common Market and rejects attempts to divide the market territorially along the lines of national property rights. Product labeling as to source and contents is thought sufficient notice to consumers that qualitatively different goods are involved.

In a major decision, the European Court of Justice ruled that trademark rights can be used to block gray market imports into the Common Market. These rights are not exhausted once the goods are voluntarily put into the stream of international commerce. An Austrian maker of high-quality sunglasses was therefore entitled to bar imports from Bulgaria.[27] In *Zino Davidoff, SA*, and *Levi Strauss* the European Court of Justice affirmed the right of trademark owners to block gray market sales of their goods sold at prices below those they utilize in the EU. No "implied consent" to gray market imports was found via the sale of goods outside the EU.[28]

Gray market car imports into China, traditionally illegal or of dubious legality, are now legal in the Shanghai Free Trade Zone,

---

[22]   *NMC Co. v. Schulyro Trading Co.*, Feb. 20, 1970 (Osaka Dist. Ct., 234 Hanrei Taimuzu 57) reprinted in English at 16 Japanese Annual of Int'l Law 113 (1972) affirmed by Osaka High Court. *See Nestle Nihon K.K. v. Sanhi Shoten* (unreported Tokyo Dist.Ct. May 29, 1965) summarized in T. Doi, Digest of Japanese Court Decisions in Trademarks and Unfair Competition Cases (1971).

[23]   Fed.Sup.Ct. (W.Ger.) Jan. 22, 1964, 41 Bundesgerichtshof 84 summarized in 54 Trademark Rep. 452 (1964).

[24]   *Agfa-Gevaert GmbH v. Schark*, Sup.Ct. (Aus.), Nov. 30, 1970.

[25]   *Consumers Distributing Co., Ltd. v. Seiko Time Canada Ltd.*, 1 Sup.Ct. 583 (1984). But *see Mattel Canada Inc. v. GTS Acquisitions*, 27 C.P.R.(3d) 358 (1989) (preliminary injunction against identical gray market goods).

[26]   *See* R. Folsom, *Principles of European Union Law.*

[27]   *Silhouette International v. Hartlauer*, 1998 WL 1043033 (July 16, 1998).

[28]   Cases C–414–99, 415/99 and 416/99, 2001 WL 1347061 (Levi jeans sold by supermarket in Britain) (Nov. 20, 2001).

subject to the same warranty and recall rules as for authorized distributors. Other Chinese free trade zones are expected to adopt similar policies.

Part Three

EXPORT LAW

Chapter 10

UNITED STATES
EXPORT CONTROLS

Table of Sections

§ 10.0   International Trade Law on Exports

Parts One and Two of this book explore the law of international trade, especially that of the World Trade Organization (WTO), as applied almost entirely to **imports**.

Why does the World Trade Organization fail to have equally extensive legal disciplines regarding **exports**?

The answer is less than clear. National export controls have certainly been less numerous, and therefore less on the international trade radar screen. Restricting exports is often counterintuitive to trade policy. Exports represent local production, employment and earnings, whereas imports may disrupt domestic companies, jobs and economic growth. Governments are therefore inclined to promote exports, not inhibit them. In the developing world, there has been a major policy shift away from import substitution in favor of export enhancement. Yet, apart from the law of export subsidies and countervailing duties (see Chapter 5) and to a degree the law of export quotas (see Section 1.6), the WTO package of agreements marginally touches upon export issues.

In the absence of WTO rules on export controls, member states have pursued different policies. The United States, one of the world's top exporters, shipping trillions of dollars of exports each year, has nevertheless maintained an extensive system of export controls. This system is the focus of this Chapter.

§ 10.1   U.S. Governance of Exports, Deemed Technology Exports, Sanctions

United States export controls involve three primary laws and government agencies. The U.S. Dept. of Commerce, Bureau of Industry and Security (BIS), administers the Export Administration Act Regulations (EAR, 22 C.F.R. Parts 730–774), discussed in this chapter, and the U.S. anti-boycott laws, discussed in Chapter 12. The U.S. Dept. of the Treasury, Office of Foreign Asset Controls (OFAC), administers U.S. boycott laws, discussed in Chapter 11. Lastly, the U.S. Dept. of State administers the International Traffic in Arms Regulations (ITAR, 22 C.F.R. Parts 120–130). The United States also supports various non-proliferation treaties, and U.N. Security Council Resolution 1540 calling on all nations to enforce effective laws against non-state actors' possession and use of weapons of mass destruction, particularly for terrorist purposes.

Unlike the control of imports, U.S. laws regulating exports are briefer and rely on the issuance of extensive administrative regulations. For example, the *statutes* prohibiting U.S. persons from assisting boycotts against friendly nations fill only a few pages. But the *regulations* and examples of prohibited and permissible conduct fill dozens of pages in the Code of Federal Regulations. The statement of policy in the Export Administration Act, the primary source of U.S. export controls, indicates that it is only after consideration of the impact of restrictions on the economy that restrictive export regulations restrictions are to be adopted, and only to the extent necessary.[1]

U.S. exports are controlled for three reasons stated in the governing rules—(1) to protect against the drain of scarce materials and reduce inflation from foreign demand, (2) to further U.S. foreign policy and (3) to assure national security.[2] These goals are expressed in the principal export enactment, the Export Administration Act (EAA), and are implemented by means of licensing requirements.[3] But the EAA does not contain many substantive provisions regulating exports. They are contained in the Export Administration Regulations (EAR). These regulations constitute an extensive set of provisions detailing the governance of U.S. exports, and re-exports. Following the "nationality of the goods", the EAR are primarily focused on the "end-use" or "end-user" of U.S. exports, including technology. The EAR rely heavily on "know your customer" determinations by exporters. Sanctions for violating the EAR are potentially severe (see Section 10.19). This leads to preventative lawyering under ongoing compliance programs.

Control of U.S. exports is principally done by The Department of Commerce's Bureau of Industry and Security (BIS). But other departments also have some regulatory authority, especially the Department of State where the goods are "dual-use" items, meaning that they have both commercial and military application. Application

---

[1]   50 U.S.C.A.App. § 2402.

[2]   15 C.F.R. § 730.6.

[3]   The EAA of 1979 has been amended several times. It expired in 1994 but has been kept in force ever since by the President declaring a state of emergency under the International Emergency Economic Powers Act (IEEPA). 50 U.S.C.A. §§ 1701–1706. The President is required to report to Congress every six months on the national emergency. The report is more an outline of changes in export rules and actions taken than a disclosure of any conditions which any "reasonable man" might conclude constitute a national emergency. The Congress and the President have allowed the EAA to expire because of the continuing conflict between the Congress and the President regarding control over export trade. Unhappy with what Congress presents as a new framework for regulating exports, usually granting little discretion to the President to curtail exports to countries for U.S. foreign policy reasons, the President threatens a veto, the act is not passed, and the provisions of the old act remain in force under the International Emergency Economic Powers Act. Waiting for a "better" new law from Congress which does not so severely limit discretionary power of the President, with legislators annually predicting that it will be passed "this year", decades have passed without any expectation that a new law will be forthcoming "this year or next."

for a license may be done electronically under the Simplified Network Application Process Redesign (SNAP-R), but only if the exporter has a BIS Company Identification Number (CIN). The BIS processes tens of thousands of export licenses annually, affecting billions of dollars of U.S. exports. In recent years, for example, high-tech goods involving encryption software and advance semiconductor chips with military applications have been a focus of these licenses.

Technology and "Deemed" Exports

The EAR controls apply to exports and re-exports of U.S.-origin technology and technical data. The term "technology," which can take the form of either technical data or technical assistance, is broadly defined to include "[s]pecific information necessary for the 'development,' 'production,' or 'use' of a product." "Technical data" includes "blueprints, plans, diagrams, models, formulae, tables, engineering designs and specifications, manuals and instructions written or recorded on other media or devices such as disk, tape, read-only memories." For purposes of the national security controls, "technology" is generally controlled if it is related to the development, production, or use of items that are subject to a license requirement.

Exports of technology, or technical data, can occur by any means of communication. The regulations define an export of technical data as any of the following:

(i)   An actual shipment or transmission of technical data out of the United States;

(ii)   Any release of technical data in the United States with the knowledge or intent that the data will be shipped or transmitted from the United States to a foreign country; or

(iii) Any release of technical data of U.S.-origin in a foreign country; or

(iv) Any release of technical data to a foreign national in the United States, if that foreign national is not a permanent resident of the United States (the so-called **"deemed export" rule**).

Thus, virtually any exchange of information—including telephone conversations, fax communications, the sharing of computer data bases, briefings, training sessions, and even question and answer exchanges—can involve an export of technical data. Visits to U.S. plants by foreign nationals raise export control issues because plant tours may visually convey technical data, such as manufacturing know-how, even without the exchange of written information. In addition, exports of technical data can occur through licensing or joint venture arrangements, technical assistance or training, or a U.S. person's use of his or her own technical expertise abroad if the information was acquired in the United States.

Export and Boycott Sanctions

A range of sanctions may apply to violations of the EAR, ITAR and U.S. boycott rules. Some sanctions may derive from the United Nations (e.g. North Korea) or be undertaken with others (e.g. U.S.-EU sanctions on Russia). Individual and/or business sanctions may be imposed, and may apply extraterritorially to persons, activities and businesses located outside the United States.

Individual sanctions typically result in U.S. visa denials, the seizure of U.S.-based individual assets, and/or prohibitions against U.S firms doing business with the sanctioned individuals (Blacklists, *see* Section 10.21). In 2017, prominent individual sanctions were outstanding against foreign leaders Kim Jong Un of North Korea, Robert Mugabe of Zimbabwe, Bashar al-Assad of Syria and Nicolas Maduro of Venezuela. High ranking officials in Russia, Iran, Venezuela, Syria and North Korea were also named in the U.S. sanctions lists.

Business sanctions can involve U.S. asset seizures, denial of U.S. financing, credit lines and bank or other financial services, imposition of internal control systems, prohibitions against doing business with sanctioned entities, and/or extension of sanctions to third parties not directly named on sanctions lists. For example, in 2017 U.S. sanctions were applied to: (1) Revolutionary Guard businesses in Iran; (2) Russian oil, gas, defense, bank, and intelligence companies; (3) Chinese firms said to be enabling North Korean missile and nuclear efforts, (4) Cuban resorts and hotels owned by its military forces; and (5) any company assisting new Venezuelan debt financing.

Some of the Russian sanctions adopted in the Countering America's Adversaries through Sanctions Act (2017) (CAATSA) were particularly notable because they barred repeal by Executive Order of the President.

§ 10.2 The Meaning of a "License" to Export

Prior to 1996, exporters sent items abroad under either a "general" license or a "validated" license. The general license was used for most exports and did not require prior approval by the Department of Commerce. When most goods were shipped and a "Shipper's Export Declaration (SED)" was filled out, the SED constituted a general license. Validated licenses were issued only upon application to and approval by the Department of Commerce.

The current regulations eliminate the terms "general license" and "validated license". "License" refers to an authorization to export granted by the Department of Commerce. The change is to some degree a matter of semantics. General licenses, which were in a sense "self-granted", are abolished in favor of referring to such exports as exports permitted without any license. The new export "license" replaces the old "validated license." In 2012, the BIS processed over 23,000 export licenses for transactions valued at approximately $204 billion. Encryption-enabling goods and advanced semiconductor chips were high on the list of BIS export license concerns.

But much more was accomplished in the rearrangement of the regulations. The myriad of "special" licenses has been redone. There are now ten general prohibitions making up Part 736 of the C.F.R., rather than the previous scattering of the prohibitions throughout the regulations. These prohibitions indicate the circumstances where a license must be obtained. Note particularly that disclosure of controlled technology to a foreign national located *in the United States* constitutes a "deemed export". Transfers to foreign affiliates or subsidiaries within a corporate family are also treated as exports, as are electronic transmissions, donations and hand-carried items.

§ 10.3   U.S. Export Administration Regulations (EAR), Enhanced Proliferation Control Initiative (EPIC)

U.S. Export Administration Regulations[4] govern most export activity, including the issuance of licenses. The regulations are implemented and enforced by the Bureau of Industry and Security (BIS). The regulations include helpful provisions for exporters, which attempt to explain the regulations in simple terms. The regulations introduce the exporter to considerable new terminology.[5] The export of some commodities and technical data is absolutely prohibited, while other commodities are permitted to be exported under a range of lenient to severe restrictions.

Special provisions of the EAA apply to further control the proliferation of missiles, and chemical and biological weapons.[6] The EAR has integrated the role of the former Coordinating Committee for Multilateral Export Controls (COCOM), a group of nations which sought to keep sensitive material from communist dominated

---

[4]   15 C.F.R. §§ 730–774.

[5]   Terms are defined in 50 U.S.C.A.App. § 2415, and in 15 C.F.R. § 772.

[6]   50 U.S.C.A.App. §§ 2410b and c.

nations. COCOM was abolished soon after the Soviet Union was dismantled.[7]

The United States enacted the Enhanced Proliferation Control Initiative (EPCI), motivated by the Iraq conflict. This enactment seeks to establish greater control where commodities or technical data are destined for a prohibited nuclear, chemical or biological weapons or missile development use or end user. Considerable emphasis is placed on making the exporter aware of the nature of the buyer and where the items are going. The EPIC consists of Sections 744.1–744.6 of the C.F.R. EPIC addresses how technology and goods are *used* rather than by their *description*. They include essentially the "design, development, production, stockpiling, or use" of nuclear explosive devices, missiles, or chemical or biological weapons. The end result is that a license is required where otherwise it might not be. Exporters are thus given the responsibility to know more about their dual-use goods. The use of the EPCI in the control of weapons of mass destruction, especially after September 11, 2001, is clear.

The Department of Commerce has considerable discretion to allow or block exports when they are subject to licensing. In addition, certain *items* may be subject to mandatory controls, just as certain *destinations* may be subject to mandatory controls (e.g., a boycott that disallows most or all exports, such as with Cuba or North Korea). Actually, these mandatory controls allow some deviation, usually by the President rather than an agency exercising discretion. Some examples of mandatory controls include the Nuclear Non-Proliferation Act regulations governing exports that have nuclear explosive capability, unprocessed timber under the Forest Resources Conservation and Shortage Relief Act (FRCSRA 1990), oil for purposes of conservation or to establish reserves, and oil from certain locations such as the North Slope of Alaska. Exports are thus subject to a mix of regulations *by* different persons or agencies, *of* different products, *for* different purposes, and *to* different places.

§ 10.4 Steps for Using the U.S. EAR

Part 730 provides a general introduction to the EAR. It outlines the scope of the regulations, statutory authority, defines "dual use" exports (generally civil versus military), other agencies which participate in the regulation of exports, extraterritorial application of regulations, purposes of control, and limited situations requiring licenses. Part 732 includes the 29 steps for using the EAR. They include an overview, steps regarding the scope of the EAR, the ten general prohibitions, License Exceptions, Shipper's Export

---

[7]   COCOM expired in 1994. It has been replaced by the Wassenaar Arrangement, discussed below in § 10.34.

Declaration and other documents and records, and other requirements.

The overview notes some important questions to which the exporter must give thought, such as:

What is the item?

Where is it going?

Who will actually receive and use it?

What will the item be used for?[8]

Answers to these questions will help the exporter determine whether the EAR are applicable. The BIS maintains a list of "Red Flags" to assist with compliance and signal the need for further inquiries by exporter.

The first six steps regarding the scope of the EAR cover: (1) items subject to the exclusive jurisdiction of another federal agency; (2) publicly available technology and software; (3) re-export of U.S. origin items; (4) foreign made items incorporating less than a *de minimis* level of U.S. parts, components and materials; (5) foreign made items incorporating more than a *de minimis* level of U.S. parts, components and materials, and (6) foreign made items produced with certain U.S. technology for export to specified destinations.

§ 10.5 EAR—General Prohibitions[9]

If an export is subject to the EAR, the general prohibitions, as well as the License Exceptions, must be reviewed to determine if a license is necessary. This part informs the exporter of both the facts that make the proposed transaction subject to the general prohibitions, and the nature of the general prohibitions.

§ 10.6 EAR—Determination of the Applicability of the General Prohibitions, Re-Exports

Five factors help determine the obligations of the exporter under the ten general prohibitions.[10] They are:

1.   Classification of the item using the Country Control List (CCL).

2.   Destination of the item using the CCL and Country Chart.

---

8   15 C.F.R. § 732.1.

9.   15 C.F.R. Part 736.

10   15 C.F.R. § 736.2.

    3.   End-user referring to a list of persons the exporter may not deal with.

    4.   End-use.

    5.   Conduct such as contracting, financing and freight forwarding in support of a proliferation project.

General Export Prohibitions

The ten general prohibitions follow, with commentary under the following headings:

    1.   General Prohibition One—Export and re-export of controlled items to listed countries (Exports and Re-exports).

    2.   General Prohibition Two—Re-export and export from abroad of foreign-made items incorporating more than a *de minimis* amount of controlled U.S. content (Parts and Components Re-exports).

    3.   General Prohibition Three—Re-export and export from abroad of the foreign-produced direct product of U.S. technology and software (Foreign-Produced Direct Product Re-exports).

    4.   General Prohibition Four—Engaging in actions prohibited by a denial order (Denial Orders).

    5.   General Prohibition Five—Export or re-export to prohibited end-uses or end-users (End-Use End-User).

    6.   General Prohibition Six—Export or re-export to embargoed destinations (Embargo).

    7.   General Prohibition Seven—Support of Proliferation Activities (U.S. Person Proliferation Activity).

    8.   General Prohibition Eight—In transit shipments and items to be removed from vessels or aircraft (In transit).

    9.   General Prohibition Nine—Violation of any order, terms, and conditions (Orders, Terms, and Conditions).

    10. General Prohibition Ten—Proceeding with transactions with knowledge that a violation has occurred or is about to occur (Knowledge Violation to Occur).

In preparing these prohibitions, the Commerce Department rejected a number of suggestions to liberalize existing re-export controls, such as to create a separate part for re-exports. Re-exports create a problem with the nation from which the item may be re-exported. That nation may object to any extraterritorial application of the U.S. rules. Indeed, foreign made products that include more than *de minimis* controlled U.S. content are also subject to the EAR.

§ 10.7   Overview of BIS Export Controls

The Commerce Control List (CCL—Part 774 of the EAR) is maintained by the BIS. The CCL includes all items (i.e., commodities, software, and technology) subject to BIS controls. The CCL does not include items exclusively governed by other agencies. But where there is shared governance, the CCL will note other agency participation. Knowing the Harmonized Code (customs classification for tariff purposes) Schedule B number does not help to determine whether or not an export license is required. That number is used by the Census Bureau for trade statistics. It is only the five-character Export Control Classification Number (ECCN) that will indicate whether or not an export license is required.

§ 10.8   The U.S. Commerce Control List (CCL)

The CCL is contained in Supplement No. 1 to Part 774. Supplement No. 2 to Part 774 contains the General Technology and Software Notes relevant to entries in the CCL. **The CCL basic structure includes the following ten general categories:**

> 0.   Nuclear Materials, Facilities and Equipment (and Miscellaneous Items)

> 1.   Materials, Chemicals, "Microorganisms," and Toxins

> 2.   Materials Processing

> 3.   Electronics

> 4.   Computers

> 5.   Telecommunications and Information Security

> 6.   Sensors and Lasers

> 7.   Navigation and Avionics

> 8.   Marine

> 9.   Propulsion Systems, Space Vehicles, and Related Equipment

Within each of the above ten categories are five different groups of items, identified by the letters A through E, as follows:

> A.   Systems, Equipment and Components

> B.   Test, Inspection and Production Equipment

    C.   Material

    D.   Software

    E.   Technology

To classify an item the exporter determines the general characteristics that will usually be expressed by one of the categories. Having the appropriate category, the next step is to match the characteristics and functions with one of the groups. For example, electronics equipment would be in category 3 and group A. The first digit and letter of the five-character ECCN would thus be 3A.

This pairing is followed by a number that signals the types of controls involved. The Reasons for Control are as follows:

    0.   National Security reasons (including Dual Use and International Munitions List) and Items on the NSG Dual Use Annex and Trigger List

    1.   Missile Technology reasons

    2.   Nuclear Nonproliferation reasons

    3.   Chemical & Biological Weapons reasons. . .

    9.   Anti-terrorism, Crime Control, Regional Stability, Firearms Convention, Short Supply, Encryption, Computers and Significant Items

§ 10.9 U.S. License Requirements and Exceptions

Next to each ECCN is a brief description, followed by "License Requirements", "License Exceptions", and "List of Items Controlled" sections.

"License Requirements" identifies all possible Reasons for Control in order of precedence. Items within a particular ECCN number may be controlled for more than one reason. All the possible Reasons for Control are as follows:[11]

AT Anti-Terrorism

CB Chemical & Biological Weapons

CC Crime Control

EI Encryption Items

FC Firearms Convention

MT Missile Technology

---

[11]   15 C.F.R. § 738.2(d)(2)(i).

NS National Security

NP Nuclear Nonproliferation

RS Regional Stability

SS Short Supply

XP Computers

SI Significant Items

The applicable reasons appear in one of two columns in the License Requirements, entitled "Control(s)". The second column, entitled "Country Chart", identifies a column name and number for each applicable Reason for Control (e.g., CB Column 1). Once the exporter has determined that the item is controlled by a specific ECCN, information contained in the "License Requirements" section of the ECCN in combination with the Country Chart will allow a decision regarding the need for a license.

"License Exceptions" is used after it is determined that a license is required. It provides a brief eligibility statement for each ECCN-driven License Exception that may be applicable to the transaction. This is intended to help the exporter decide which ECCN-driven License Exception should be considered before submitting an application.[12] License Exceptions, the subject of Part 740, includes numerous categories. In the regulations, several exceptions were "bundled" under the grouping symbol LST (limited value shipments (LVS), shipments to group B countries (GBS), civil end-users (CIV), technology and software under restriction (TSR) and computers (APP)).

But objections by exporters with automated processes, who complained that an additional step was created, resulted in 1996 changes which dropped the LST, "de-bundled" the process, putting each exception into its own section. This makes them similar to other separated exceptions (i.e., temporary imports and exports (TMP), servicing and parts replacement (RPL), governments and international organizations (GOV), gift parcels and humanitarian donations (GFT), some technology and software (TSU), baggage (BAG), aircraft and vessels (AVS) and additional permissive re-exports (APR)). Part 740 is an extensive and important part of the EAR. It is followed by three supplements to Part 740, including (1) Country Groups, (2) meeting basic human needs, and (3) favorable treatment countries (ENC).

---

[12]   15 C.F.R. § 738.2(d)(2)(ii).

§ 10.10   The U.S. Commerce Country Chart (CCC)

Consulting the Country Chart is an essential step in determining the need for a license. It is useful in all cases except where short-supply reasons apply, or where there are unique entries.[13] The Country Chart is Supplement No. 1 to Part 738 of the EAR, and over several pages lists countries alphabetically. Territories, possessions, and departments are not listed, but are subject to the same rules as the governing country. On the right of the listed countries are the numerous columns identifying the various Reasons for Control. There may be one, two or three columns under a particular Reason for Control. They correlate to references in the License Requirements section of the applicable ECCN. There may be an "x" in one or more of the cells. Where it appears in more than one cell, there will be multiple reviews.

§ 10.11   Determining the Need for a License[14]

Having determined that the item to be exported is controlled by a specific ECCN number, the exporter uses information in the "License Requirements" section of the ECCN entry in combination with the Country Chart. The need for a license is thus determined. Using the CCL "Controls" the exporter learns the reasons for control. Turning to the Country Chart and finding the appropriate country and the heading(s) for the reason(s), and with the column identifiers from the ECCN, the exporter looks for an "x". If an "x" is found in the cell on the Country Chart, the exporter knows a license is required.

A license application must be submitted unless a License Exception applies. Turning to the License Exceptions in the ECCN entry list, if a "yes" appears a further search of Part 740 will disclose whether an exception is available. Where there is no "x" in the cell on the Country Chart, a license is not required for control and destination, but one or more of General Prohibitions Four through Ten (see Section 10.6) may prohibit the export. One can thus go to Parts 758 and 762 for information on export clearance procedures and record keeping.

§ 10.12   U.S. Export Licenses—Advisory Opinions

A party who wishes to know whether a license is required may obtain an Advisory Opinion from the BIS.[15] Receipt of an opinion does not mean the subsequent application will be granted, opinions are not binding. But the BIS is likely to help the applicant in the

---

[13]   15 C.F.R. § 738.3.
[14]   15 C.F.R. § 738.4.
[15]   15 C.F.R. § 748.3.

preparation of an application which will meet the Advisory Opinion's requirements. An applicant may wish to avoid asking for an Advisory Opinion for fear that the opinion will be unfavorable. But if an export is made without an opinion and is in violation of the law, the sanctions may be severe.[16] Certainly, obtaining an unfavorable opinion and then exporting without a license creates a rather clear case of intent to disregard the law. But the Advisory Opinion is a good route to follow. If an unfavorable opinion is received, the BIS may explain what is required to obtain permission, unless the case is a clear one where no exports are permitted.

Support documents may be required along with an application.[17] Numerous countries are exempt from the need of support documents, mostly (1) any exports or re-exports in the Western Hemisphere, (2) sales to government purchasers, and licenses submitted under special procedures, such as by A.I.D., or under the Special Comprehensive License procedure. When support documentation is required, the required data is to gain information about the disposition of the items, and to answer questions about national security controls and certain destinations. The transaction may require an End-User Certificate, or a Statement of Ultimate Consignee and Purchaser.[18]

§ 10.13   Issuance and/or Denial of U.S. Export Applications[19]

Part 750 of the EAR describes the BIS's process for reviewing a license application, including processing times, denials, revocations, issuance, duplicates, transfers, and shipping tolerances on approved licenses. The part also includes information on processing Advisory Opinion requests.

The BIS undertakes a complete review of the application, including an analysis of the license and support documentation, plus a consideration of the reliability of each party to the transaction, including any intelligence information. The Departments of Defense, Energy, State and the Arms Control and Disarmament Agency may also have review authority. Furthermore, the BIS may request review by other departments or agencies, which may agree to review, or waive review.

There has been a continuing dispute between Commerce and State over control of technology that seems to fall within the

---

[16]   Persons convicted of a violation of any statute specified in § 11(h) of the EAA may not apply for any export license for ten years. 15 C.F.R. § 748.4(c).

[17]   15 C.F.R. § 748.9.

[18]   *See also* 15 C.F.R. § 748.10–13, and Supplements.

[19]   15 C.F.R. Part 750.

jurisdiction of each department. While the Arms Export Control Act gives State exclusive authority to issue jurisdiction determinations, Commerce has attempted to obtain concurrent authority to issue commodity jurisdiction determinations. Hearings were held in 1995 by the Senate Armed Services Committee after complaints that Commerce had issued export licenses for stealth technology that was under the jurisdiction of State. State intervened to stop the shipments, determined that they had jurisdiction, and denied the license. This kind of dispute has made it difficult to reach agreement on a new Export Administration Act. With proposals to abolish Commerce and transfer much of its export jurisdiction to State, the issue could become moot. There is little likelihood that State will agree to the transfer of any authority to Commerce.

Delay has been used by the government, especially by the Department of Defense, as a means of discouraging exports which might be permissible, but to which the Department objects. The *Daedalus Enterprises, Inc. v. Baldrige* case is an example.[20] Twenty-nine months after the filing of an application, the Department of Commerce had not reached a decision. The company had to seek a court order that the Secretary comply with the statutory timetable. There is little a company can do. It may not export the goods when the time period has expired if no response has been made by the government. It must go to court at each stage when the government fails to comply with the statute. Fortunately, the *Daedalus* case is an exception, and this kind of delay has been much diminished. The filing process is considerably improved. Furthermore, the President in 1996 made a major transfer of authority over encryption devices from the Department of State to the Department of Commerce.

§ 10.14   Timetable for Application Review

The BIS is required to resolve all applications, or refer them to the President, within 90 calendar days from the date of registration by the BIS. That is the date the BIS enters the application into the electronic license processing system.[21] Where there are deficiencies, the BIS tries to contact the applicant to obtain needed information. If no contact is made, the license is returned with notations of the deficiencies. This may cause a suspension in the processing time. If another department or agency is involved, or if government-to-government assurances or consultations are involved, there are additional time requirements for making requests and analyzing their results. When certain countries are involved, such as

---

[20]   563 F.Supp. 1345 (D.D.C.1983).

[21]   15 C.F.R. § 750.4.

Congressional designated terrorist supporting nations, Congress may have to be notified, delaying the application for another 60 days.

§ 10.15   Issuance of a U.S. Export License[22]

A license is issued for a transaction, or series of transactions. The application may be approved in whole or in part. A license number is issued and a validation date. The license number must be used when discussing the license with the Department of Commerce. Nonmaterial changes may be made without obtaining a "Replacement" license.

§ 10.16   Revocation or Suspension of a License[23]

All licenses may be revised, suspended, or revoked. This may occur without notice when the BIS learns that the EAR have been violated or are about to be violated. The exporter may have to stop a shipment about to be made, or if possible one that is already en route. When revocation or suspension occurs, the exporter is required to return the license to the BIS. Appeals from actions taken under the EAA or the EAR by the BIS are allowed for most actions.[24] There is an internal appeal process prior to appealing to the federal courts.

§ 10.17   Review of Export Applications by International Agencies

In December, 1995, 28 nations,[25] including the United States, agreed to establish a new export control regime that would assume some of the functions of the expired COCOM. The Wassenaar Arrangement on Export Controls for Conventional Arms and Dual-Use Goods and Technologies (the organizational meeting was in Wassenaar, the Netherlands; the secretariat was established in Vienna) fell short of U.S. expectations, not containing a requirement of prior notification of sales by one country to other countries in the group. A second concern is the lack of agreement on prohibiting dual-use goods and conventional weapons to civilian as well as military end-users in such nations as Iran, Iraq, Libya and North Korea. An additional concern is the lack of transparency in exchanging information on exports of dual use goods and conventional arms.

---

[22]   15 C.F.R. § 750.7.

[23]   15 C.F.R. § 750.8.

[24]   15 C.F.R. § 756.1.

[25]   Australia, Austria, Belgium, Canada, the Czech Republic, Denmark, Finland, France, Germany, Greece, Hungary, Iceland, Italy, Japan, Luxembourg, the Netherlands, New Zealand, Norway, Poland, Portugal, the Russian Federation, the Slovak Republic, Spain, Sweden, Switzerland, Turkey, the United Kingdom, and the United States. Several other nations have since joined.

There are other multilateral export regimes, including the Nuclear Suppliers group (NSG), the Australia Group (AG), the Missile Technology Control Regime (MTCR), and the Technical Advisory Committees (TACs). It is reasonably safe to assume that the goals of these groups govern products carefully controlled under U.S. law.

§ 10.18   Shipper's U.S. Export Declaration (SED)

The exporter is responsible for following the regulations that govern carrying out the export.[26] This is so whether a license is issued or the exporter relies on a License Exception. The most important responsibility is the proper preparation of the Shipper's Export Declaration (SED), or Automated Export System (AES) record. They are primarily statements to the U.S. government used for gathering information to prepare trade statistics. There are numerous exemptions, such as gift parcels, aircraft and vessels, governments and international organizations, technology and software, and tools of trade.

As many as one-half the filings contain errors of omission or commission, according to the Bureau of Census and U.S. Customs Service. The two organizations have compared SEDs with outboard vessel manifests and discovered numerous inaccuracies in the vessel manifests as well as the SEDs. Cargo is often manifested not on the vessel actually carrying the goods, but on the manifest of a later departing vessel. The reason is the failure of exporters (and forwarders) to supply SEDs with complete and accurate information when the goods are shipped. This causes difficulties for Customs in detecting export law violations, and creates inaccurate trade statistics. Unless voluntary compliance improves, Customs may delay or detain an increasing number of shipments unless filings are presented with complete and accurate information.

§ 10.19   U.S. Sanctions—Fines, Suspensions and Revocation of Export Authority

Violation of laws and regulations governing U.S. exports brings into play both the basic law and the regulations. The EAA contains provisions governing violations of both the EAA and EAR.[27] The Export Administrative Regulations contain supplementary provisions, applying strict liability standards.[28] The general sanction for violations of the export laws, where the conduct was entered into

---

[26]   15 C.F.R. § 758.3.

[27]   50 U.S.C.A.App. § 2410. *See* www.bis.doc.gov, for considerable information concerning enforcement.

[28]   15 C.F.R. Part 764.

knowingly, is a fine of the higher of $250,000 or twice the value of the exports.[29] This can obviously be *very* substantial.[30] In 2017, Exxon was fined $2 million for "reckless disregard" of U.S. export sanctions against Russia, imposed after its annexation of Crimea.

Willful violations, with knowledge that the commodities or technology will be used to benefit, or are destined for, a controlled country, may result in a fine for business entities of the higher of $1 million per violation.[31] For individuals who engage in such willful violations the fine is $1,000,000 and/or 20 years imprisonment. This provision covers misuse of licenses.

Cases involving violations of the licensing requirements tend to be quite complex.[32] If the party exported to a controlled country commodities or technology under a license with knowledge that the commodities or technology were being used for military or intelligence gathering purposes, and willfully fails to report this use, the business entity fine is the same as above, the higher of $1 million or five times the value of the exports, but for the individual the imprisonment drops to five years, with the fine remaining the same, $250,000.[33] Even possession of goods or technology either with the intent to export in violation of the law, or knowing that the goods might be so exported, can result in a fine.

Perhaps the most severe statutory penalty in the EAA is in the civil penalty section. The Department of Commerce may impose a fine of $10,000 for violations (in certain cases up to $100,000), and they may *suspend or revoke the authority to export.*[34] This is a most severe sanction, used only in extreme cases. It was used in the Toshiba dispute, where Toshiba (Japan) and Köngsberg (Norway) enterprises sold to the Soviet Union technology allegedly useful for developing submarine propellers which would be sufficiently silent to avoid detection.[35] Debarment Lists can effectively "blacklist" foreign violators, barring U.S. firms from dealing with named parties, such as Dresser France in the Reagan-era Russian pipeline dispute. Temporary Denial Orders can also be employed against "related

[29]   50 U.S.C.A. App. § 2410(a).

[30]   *See United States v. Ortiz de Zevallos,* 748 F.Supp. 1569, 1573 (S.D.Fla.1990), *judgment reversed* in *United States v. Macko,* 994 F.2d 1526 (11th Cir.1993). *See also United States v. Brodie,* 403 F.3d 123 (3d Cir. 2005).

[31]   50 U.S.C.A. App. § 2410(b)(1).

[32]   *United States v. Pervez,* 871 F.2d 310 (3d Cir.1989); *cert. denied* 492 U.S. 925, 109 S.Ct. 3258, 106 L.Ed.2d 603 (1989).

[33]   50 U.S.C.A. App. § 2410(b)(2).

[34]   50 U.S.C.A. § 2410(c).

[35]   *See* Robert van den Hoven van Genderen, Cooperation on Export Control Between the United States and Europe: A Cradle of Conflict in Technology Transfer? 14 N.C.J.Int'l L. & Com.Reg. 391 (1989).

parties", as they were against Delft Instruments concerning the illegal export of munitions and night-vision devices. At one point, the Denial Order was extended to all 47 Delft companies located in 13 countries![36]

The result was enactment of the Multilateral Export Control Enhancements Act in 1988,[37] amending the EAA and providing trade prohibition sanctions for two to five years.[38] These sanctions are applied whether or not the other nations take action against their companies. The EAR repeat and expand upon these statutory sanctions. They further add provisions dealing with actions including "causing, aiding, or abetting" a violation,[39] and "solicitation and attempt", and "conspiracy."[40] More details are provided addressing misrepresentation and concealment of facts, or evasion,[41] failing to comply with reporting and record keeping requirements',[42] alterations of documents,[43] and acting contrary to the terms of a denial order.[44]

The political nature of export controls is emphasized by judicial refusal to agree to a settlement negotiated between a company accused of violations of the export laws and the Justice Department. In one instance a bargained $1 million fine was rejected by the court, which imposed a $3 million fine.[45]

§ 10.20 U.S. Administrative Proceedings and Denial Orders

Administrative procedures which supplement the U.S. Administrative Procedures Act, are the subject of a separate Part of the EAA and EAR.[46] They provide the framework for proceedings dealing largely with denial of export privileges and civil penalties.

---

[36] *See* Fitzgerald, Pierre Goes Online: Blacklisting and Secondary Boycotts in U.S. Trade Policy, 31 Vand. J. Trans. L. 1 (1998).

[37] It was part of the 1988 Omnibus Trade and Competitiveness Act. *See* 50 U.S.C.A.App. § 2410a.

[38] 50 U.S.C.A.App. § 2410a.

[39] 15 C.F.R. § 764(2)(b).

[40] 15 C.F.R. § 764(2)(c) & (d).

[41] 15 C.F.R. § 764.2(g) & (h).

[42] 15 C.F.R. § 764.2(i).

[43] 15 C.F.R. § 764.2(j).

[44] 15 C.F.R. § 764.2(k).

[45] *United States v. Datasaab Contracting A.B.*, (D.D.C.Criminal No. § 84–00130, 4–27–84).

[46] 50 U.S.C.A.App. § 2412; 15 C.F.R. Parts 756, 764, and 766. One court has held that attorneys' fees of a prevailing defendant are not allowable under § 2412, because Congress did not make the equal Access to Justice Act part of the EAA. *See Dart v. United States*, 961 F.2d 284 (D.C.Cir.1992).

Appeals are the subject of several parts of the regulations.[47] The denial of export rights occurs principally either as an administrative sanction for violation of the EAR; or as a temporary measure when there is evidence of an imminent violation of the EAR. A denial order prohibits the party from any exports, unless there are exceptions in the order. The denial order states the extent to which exports are restricted. Because all denial orders are not the same, it is important to read carefully any specific denial order to determine the extent of the denial.

The denial order also affects persons dealing with the denied party.[48] The denied party may not be part of a transaction nor receive any benefit from a transaction. What are subject to regulation are essentially items of U.S. origin, or foreign items which require re-export permission. A person who deals with a denied party is not innocent if there is no knowledge of the denial status; everyone is responsible for knowing that any person with whom they engage in transactions is *not* on the denial list.

Licensed items to be shipped to a denied party may place the exporter at risk. The denial order must be checked to determine the extent of the loss of export privileges *if* the sale to the denied party is a product to be re-exported, or it releases controlled technical data to a denied foreign national. A person may buy products from a denied party in the United States, however, unless the intention is to subsequently export the product, which would give a "benefit" to the denied party. A transaction within a foreign country may be prohibited, as the foreign recipient of U.S. origin items may not sell them to a denied party even if the sale occurs within the foreign nation.[49] This purportedly applies whether the foreign firm is a U.S. subsidiary or not.

§ 10.21   U.S. Sanctions Against Designated Foreign Nationals and Entities, "Blacklists"

Although it is part of sanctions, being designated a foreign national merits separate consideration because it is so potentially restrictive. The Office of Foreign Assets Control (OFAC) in the Department of the Treasury may designate individuals and companies owned or controlled by, or acting for or on behalf of, targeted companies. They become so-called "specially designated

---

[47]   15 C.F.R. Part 764. *See Iran Air v. Kugelman*, 996 F.2d 1253 (D.C.Cir.1993).

[48]   It could even limit employment of a denied party, to the extent that the party could not engage in transactions subject to the EAR.

[49]   This is not likely to be acceptable to the foreign country, which is apt to consider the prohibition an unreasonable extension of U.S. laws into its territory. A foreign court might order the transaction to take place.

nationals" or "SDNs." Their assets are blocked and U.S. persons are for the most part prohibited in dealing with them. The list of such designated nationals and entities exceeds 550 pages. It can be a devastating designation and effectively end trade with the United States, an outcome not lost on the U.S. when it blacklisted 271 workers at Syrian agencies involved with chemical weapons.

The blacklist designation in 2017 of Rosneft, the state-owned Russian oil company, made it unlikely that Rosneft could obtain via a loan collateral agreement control of Citgo, a U.S. subsidiary of Venezuela's state-owned oil company PdVSA which owns refineries, pipelines and storage tanks in the USA. The blacklisting in 2017 of various Venezuelan officials caused a number of global bond traders to halt buying or selling secondary market bonds of PdVSA, even though U.S. export sanctions covered only *new* Venezuelan bonds.

§ 10.22 International Traffic in Arms Regulations (ITAR)*

In 1976 Congress enacted the Arms Export Control Act (AECA) (22 U.S.C. § 2778) "[i]n furtherance of world peace and the security and foreign policy of the United States." The AECA provides the President with authority to control the export of defense articles and services. Executive Order 11958, as amended, delegated the President's statutory authority to the Secretary of State. The Secretary of State promulgated regulations, the International Traffic in Arms Regulations (ITAR) (22 C.F.R. §§ 120–130), to implement the AECA.

ITAR controls the export of defense-related articles and services by requiring approval for the exportation and temporary importation of items it designates as defense articles or services. In general, as discussed in more detail below, ITAR prohibits sharing or disclosing any defense related articles or technology with anyone who is not a U.S. citizen or permanent resident without authorization from the Secretary of State.

Structure of ITAR

ITAR is divided into eleven (11) parts, numbered 120 through 130.[50] Part 120 consists of 45 sections that contain the purpose, general authority for the regulations, and definitions of the key terms used throughout the regulations.[51] Some of the key terms defined in

---

*   Courtesy of Joshua Summers, Esq.

[50]   *See* 22 C.F.R. §§ 120–130.

[51]   22 C.F.R. § 120.

this part include "defense article,"[52] "defense service,"[53] "technical data,"[54] "export,"[55] and "foreign person,"[56] among various others. Part 121 contains the United States Munitions List ("Munitions List") and related provisions.[57] As discussed further below, the Munitions List is a categorized list containing in-depth descriptions of items, services, and related technical data ITAR defines as "defense articles" and "defense services" within the meaning of the AECA.

Part 122 covers registration of manufacturers, exporters, and temporary importers of defense articles.[58] In general, with a few narrow exceptions, anyone within the United States who manufactures a defense article or provides a defense service as defined by ITAR is required to register with the Directorate of Defense Trade Controls ("DDTC"), a division of the U.S. Department of State.[59] This part also prescribes the requirements for the registration statement, fees, notification of changes, and the maintenance of records of registrants. Although registration does not confer any right or privilege under ITAR, it is often a precondition to the issuance of any license or other approval under ITAR.[60]

Parts 123 through 125 contain the major licensing and authorization requirements under ITAR. Generally, Part 123 governs the licensing requirements for the export and temporary import of "defense articles."[61] This part also contains various special licensing provisions, shipment requirements, procedural rules, and records keeping requirements. Part 124 regulates agreements to provide defense services.[62] It provides that any U.S. person who furnishes defense services must obtain written approval from the DDTC before providing any of the proposed services.[63] Part 125 governs the licensing, as well as licensing exemptions, for the exportation of "technical data" and "classified defense articles" as those terms are defined by ITAR.[64] Part 125 also contains such provisions as procedural and documentation requirements.

---

[52]   22 C.F.R. § 120.6.

[53]   22 C.F.R. § 120.9.

[54]   22 C.F.R. § 120.10.

[55]   22 C.F.R. § 120.17.

[56]   22 C.F.R. § 120.16.

[57]   22 C.F.R. § 121.

[58]   22 C.F.R. § 122.

[59]   22 C.F.R. § 122.1.

[60]   22 C.F.R. § 122.1(c).

[61]   22 C.F.R. § 123.

[62]   22 C.F.R. § 124.

[63]   22 C.F.R. § 124.1.

[64]   22 C.F.R. § 125.

Part 126 contains the rather robust "General Policies and Provisions."[65] This part contains various substantive rules, as well as procedural rules and certain expedited processing provisions. Specifically, Part 126 contains provisions that prohibit the export, import, or sale of defense articles and/or services to or from certain specified countries;[66] grants the Deputy Assistant Secretary for Defense Trade Controls with authority to temporarily suspend or modify any or all of the provisions of ITAR, and to grant exceptions to the provisions of ITAR;[67] provides the methods and reasons the DDTC may deny, revoke, suspend, or amend a license or other approval;[68] permits special comprehensive authorizations with respect to NATO members, Australia, Japan, and Sweden;[69] and provides for the expedited processing of license applications for the export of defense articles and defense services to Australia or the United Kingdom.[70]

The general provisions also provide for various exemptions, most of which are tied to trade with specific countries or the U.S. government.[71] In addition, Part 126 covers the following: procedural provisions, including authorizing any person to request an advisory opinion or related export authorizations from the DDTC;[72] the disclosure of information subject to the Freedom of Information Act;[73] ITAR's relation to other laws;[74] provides that all determinations, licenses and authorizations issued or made by the Department of State continue in full force and effect unless modified, revoked, or superseded by the Department of State;[75] and specifies the information that must be submitted to the DDTC for any license, authorization, or approval.[76]

---

[65]   22 C.F.R. § 126.

[66]   22 C.F.R. § 126.1.

[67]   22 C.F.R. §§ 126.2 & 126.3.

[68]   22 C.F.R. § 126.7.

[69]   22 C.F.R. § 126.14.

[70]   22 C.F.R. § 126.15.

[71]   *See* 22 C.F.R. § 126.4 (exempts certain shipments by or on behalf of agencies of the United States government); 22 C.F.R. § 126.5 (Canadian exemptions); 22 C.F.R. § 126.6 (Foreign-owned military aircraft and naval vessels, and the Foreign Military Sales program); 22 C.F.R. § 126.16 (Exemption pursuant to the Defense Trade Cooperation Treaty between the United States and Australia); 22 C.F.R. § 126.17 (Exemption pursuant to the Defense Trade Cooperation Treaty between the United States and the United Kingdom); and 22 C.F.R. § 126.18 (Exemptions regarding intra-company, intra-organization, and intra-governmental transfers to employees who are dual nationals or third-country nationals).

[72]   22 C.F.R. § 126.9.

[73]   22 C.F.R. § 126.10.

[74]   22 C.F.R. § 126.11.

[75]   22 C.F.R. § 126.12.

[76]   22 C.F.R. § 126.13.

Part 127 covers violations of ITAR and various penalties.[77] Part 128 covers administrative procedures, including the procedures relating to an administrative hearing, proceedings before an administrative law judge, re-hearings, appeals, orders, etc.[78] Part 129 governs the registration and licensing requirements of brokers.[79] Generally, anyone who takes action on behalf of another to facilitate any manufacture, export, permanent import, transfer, re-export, or retransfer of a U.S. or foreign defense article or defense service is required to register with the DDTC.[80] Also, anyone who brokers certain types of defense articles or services, such as weapons, explosives, vessels of war, tanks or military vehicles, manned and unmanned aircrafts, night vision-related articles, chemical agents, and submersible vessels, must be approved by the DDTC to act as a broker for such defense articles or services.[81] Part 129 also contains such provisions as procedures for obtaining approval, registrations statements, registration fees, notification requirements, and records requirements. Part 130 concludes ITAR with provisions relating to payment of fees, commissions, political contributions, reporting and information requirements, and defines additional terms not defined in Part 120.[82]

In 2017, removal of guns and ammunition from ITAR controls was proposed, to be replaced largely by EAR Commerce Control List rules. See Section 10.8. If implemented, this change would presumably expand opportunities for U.S. exports of guns and ammunition.

---

[77]   22 C.F.R. § 127.
[78]   22 C.F.R. § 128.
[79]   22 C.F.R. § 129.
[80]   22 C.F.R. § 129.3; 22 C.F.R. § 129.2.
[81]   22 C.F.R. § 129.4.
[82]   22 C.F.R. § 130.

Chapter 11

UNITED STATES
BOYCOTT LAWS*

Table of Sections

§ 11.1   U.S. Boycotts

U.S. boycott (embargo) laws deny or restrict import and export transactions by United States and other parties. As such, they represent a kind of ultimate import and export control system.

In the past few decades the United States has boycotted or embargoed goods from or to such countries as Cuba, Iran, Sudan, Burma, Syria, Iraq, Libya, Nicaragua, North Korea, South Africa, Rhodesia and Vietnam. The effectiveness of these boycotts in achieving political goals has been widely debated.[1] The U.S. boycotts have not all been unilateral. It has engaged in collective sanctions when many others have joined, such as the U.N. trade boycott against Iraq after the invasion of Kuwait,[2] or against Serbia and Montenegro after the Serbian-promoted invasion of Bosnia.[3] Less "collective" were the trade sanctions imposed on Argentina by the United States and the European Union after the Argentine invasion of the Falklands/Malvinas Islands.[4]

The United States has sometimes stood nearly alone among major nations in implementing boycotts, such as that directed against Cuba. Additionally, the United States has engaged in long term boycotts, notably against Cuba, and very brief boycotts, such as

---

*   I am indebted to Prof. Michael Gordon for his work on a prior version of this chapter.

[1]   *See* Gary C. Hufbauer, Jeffrey J. Schott & Kimberly Ann Elliot, Economic Sanctions Reconsidered (1990).

[2]   *See* United Nations Security Council Resolution 661 (1990).

[3]   *See* United Nations Security Council Resolution 757 (1992).

[4]   *See* Domingo E. Acevedo, The U.S. Measures Against Argentina Resulting from the Malvinas Conflict, 78 Am.J.Int'l L. 323 (1984).

limits on exports to Europe which might be used in the construction of a gas pipeline from the USSR after the Soviet invasion of Poland. The 2000 Trade Sanctions Reform and Export Enhancement Act prevents, except in extraordinary circumstances, use of unilateral agricultural and medical sector trade sanctions, provided only cash sales are involved. Despite doubts about their utility, there is little doubt that in the future unilateral or collective boycotts will continue to be part of U.S. foreign policy.

§ 11.2   U.S. Boycott Law, OFAC Regulations

With whom the United States does not trade tends to be the decision of the President, although the Congress may act in special situations to deny trade benefits. Trade embargoes or other sanctions are often imposed quickly following some act which the U.S. President finds politically unacceptable. The Department of Commerce participates in the process of enforcing trade sanctions by controls on exports to various nations. Although Congress governs foreign commerce and specifically *exports* by means of the Export Administration Act, Congress tends to leave to presidential discretion the imposition of sanctions against specific countries.

This is not always the case, however. Congress may enact specific laws targeting particular nations. An example is the Cuban Democracy Act of 1992, which placed severe limitations on trade with Cuba, including trade by U.S. controlled subsidiaries abroad.[5] When Congress does act, it usually provides that its law will be carried out with additional regulations. The Export Administration Act (EEA) has substantial regulations that are enforced largely by the Department of Commerce.

OFAC

When Congress prohibits trade, or delegates such authority to the President, there is a shift of much of the enforcement (and enactment of regulations) responsibility from the Department of Commerce to the Department of the Treasury. Part of the reason is that Treasury has an extensive framework of regulations governing the control of foreign assets.[6] The Office of Foreign Assets Control (OFAC) of Treasury has jurisdiction over a broad range of controls on transactions between U.S. persons and persons in foreign countries.[7] When those latter persons are in certain foreign countries, the

---

[5]   Public Law No. 102–484, §§ 1706–12, 106 Stat. 2315, 2578–81 (1992).

[6]   31 C.F.R. Parts 500–585.

[7]   For a clash of OFAC and the Constitution *see Looper v. Morgan*, 1995 WL 499816 (S.D.Tex.1995) (regarding the search of an attorney's briefcase upon entry to the United States in search of documents supporting violations of the Libyan sanctions).

controls may prohibit nearly any form of "transaction" or "transfer". A transaction or transfer may involve money or goods or services. Certain transactions or transfers may be absolutely prohibited, others may be subject to special licensing.[8] The OFAC regulations extend to U.S. persons and permanent resident aliens no matter where located, to all persons and entities (including foreign branches and subsidiaries), and foreign branches of U.S. companies, but generally not foreign subsidiaries of U.S. firms (except Cuba).

The general regulations governing foreign assets control are followed by a series of mostly country-specific regulations.[9] These regulations vary in intensity of restrictiveness, but follow a general format including: (1) the relation of the regulations to other laws and regulations; (2) what transactions are prohibited; (3) definitions; (4) interpretations; (5) licensing process; (6) reports; (7) penalties; and (8) procedures. Some of the provisions are brief, others extensive. OFAC sanction programs target designated foreign countries, designated foreign entities and designated foreign individuals. To give an idea of how these restrictions function, the experience of Cuba is outlined in the following section.

OFAC Sanctions

The Office of Foreign Assets Control has two forms of sanctions. One is financial sanctions and asset freezes. Criminal sanctions generally range up to $1,000,000 per violation and up to 10 years in prison. Civil sanctions generally range between $12,000 and $250,000 per violation. The second form of sanction is trade and commercial embargoes. They may be used selectively or quite comprehensively. Selective sanctions may include blocking assets held in the United States, limitations on engaging in contracts, in travel, in transportation or even in exporting any goods or services. These sanctions can reach foreign companies that violate U.S. boycott law. In 2017, for example, the Chinese smartphone firm of ZTE Corp. paid $892 million after pleading guilty to violating the U.S. boycott of Iran and obstructing a federal investigation into its activities. ZTE was particularly concerned with the threat that the U.S. would prohibit the export of processors and other goods to it.

Selective U.S. sanctions have been used against various countries, including former "communist bloc" nations, South Africa, Iran, Russia and Angola. Comprehensive sanctions usually involve

---

[8]   Licensing is in 31 C.F.R. Part 500, subpart E.

[9]   The consolidation of regulations as of July 1, 2009, included specific regulations for Burma, Cuba, Iran, Iraq, Sudan, Syria, Taliban (Afghanistan), Zimbabwe, the former Liberian Regime of Charles Taylor, and parts of the former Yugoslavia (Bosnian Serb-controlled areas of that Republic, Milosevic, and Kosovo).

all the available options, and have been used against Cuba, Iran, Syria, Iraq, Libya, North Korea and parts of the former Yugoslavia.

The Cuban sanctions discussed immediately below represent the most severe sanctions yet adopted. They were partly used as a model for the 1996 Iran and Libya Sanctions Act, often referred to as the D'Amato Act.[10] This Act, following the Libertad Act, requires the President to impose sanctions against *foreign* companies that invest more than $20 million a year in the development of petroleum resource production in Iran, or more than $40 million in Libya. The proposed $2 billion investment in Iran by the French Total company in the late 1990s generated a conflict between France and the United States over possible sanctions, which the U.S. President did not impose although he was under pressure to do so. If sanctions had been imposed, this matter quickly would have been taken to the WTO by the European Union on behalf of France.

The U.S.-Iran accord under the Obama administration on nuclear development and trade is said to have been strongly influenced by effective boycotts of Iran, notably the denial by SWIFT (the Society for Worldwide Interbank Financial Communications) of interbank payments' settlements by Iranian banks. The accord resulted in a relaxation of the U.S. led boycott of Iran. Indeed, a large number of Boeing and Airbus aircraft have been sold to Iran, and U.S., Japanese and European investors have arrived in force in that country, especially in the oil and gas sector. That said, U.S. banks remain wary of financing Iranian deals. Whether the relaxation of the U.S. boycott will continue under the Trump administration is not at all clear.

Russia's annexation of Crimea and divisive foment in western Ukraine have triggered strong U.S. and European boycott sanctions in recent years, though not as yet a SWIFT denial.

State and Local Boycotts

Although the focus of this chapter is on federal law, in the past few years a number of state and local governments have adopted international boycott provisions. The provisions for the most part limit government procurement for reasons of perceived violations of human rights (a principal target has been Burma (Myanmar)), religious freedom (many countries), and the failure to deal with the return of Holocaust assets (Switzerland). These laws have created additional opposition among some foreign nations.

For example, the EU initiated a challenge under the WTO government procurement rules against a 1996 Massachusetts law

---

[10] Public Law No. 104–172, 110 Stat. 1541 (1996).

addressed to Burma. Federal sanctions were authorized against Burma in 1997,[11] but the law did not discuss preemption. In a case against the Massachusetts law brought by the National Foreign Trade Council (NFTC), the federal district court, the federal circuit court and the U.S. Supreme Court all held for the NFTC.[12] The federal ruling caused the EU to withdraw its action under the WTO dispute resolution procedures.

§ 11.3   The Boycott of Cuba, Normalization

The trade boycott of Cuba illustrates how the United States carries out a unilateral boycott. The Cuban boycott has endured longer than current sanctions against other nations. Furthermore, Cuba has received attention by Congress and the U.S. President of varying levels of forcefulness over the past three decades, often in direct relation to political campaigns.

Nationalization and the Start of the U.S. Boycott

The boycott of Cuba began as a response to the Cuban nationalization of all U.S. citizens' properties in 1959 and 1960,[13] and to the trade agreement concluded by Cuba with the USSR in February, 1960. The U.S. Congress amended the Sugar Act of 1948 giving the President authority to alter the Cuban sugar quota. The President used this authority during the height of the July, 1960, bitterness to nearly totally remove the extensive quotas, leaving Cuba with no access to the U.S. sugar market. In October, 1960, the President imposed an extensive embargo on shipments of goods to Cuba, except for nonsubsidized food, medicines and medical supplies.

With the cessation of diplomatic relations, the United States has continued the boycott without a break, but the intensity of the boycott has varied. The boycott provisions were amended in 1975 to allow foreign subsidiaries of U.S. companies to trade with Cuba. These amendments followed U.S. threats to tighten controls on foreign subsidiaries that caused several foreign governments to angrily denounce the policy, and even threaten nationalization of the companies. After 1975, U.S. subsidiaries abroad developed

---

[11]   Omnibus Consolidated Appropriations Act, Public Law No. 104–208, § 570, 110 Stat. 3009, 3009–166–167, on September 30, 1996.

[12]   *National Foreign Trade Council v. Baker*, 26 F.Supp.2d 287 (D.Mass.1998), *aff'd, National Foreign Trade Council v. Natsios*, 181 F.3d 38 (1st Cir.1999), *aff'd sub nom., Crosby v. National Foreign Trade Council*, 530 U.S. 363, 120 S.Ct. 2288, 147 L.Ed.2d 352 (2000) (holding Massachusetts' Burma law invalid under the Supremacy Clause because it threatens to frustrate federal statutory objectives).

[13]   The expropriations effectively commenced under the Agrarian Reform Law on June 1, 1959, but did not reach their zenith until the resolutions issued under the authority of the major nationalization law of July, 1960. *See* Michael Wallace Gordon, The Cuban Nationalizations: The Demise of Foreign Private Property (1976).

significant trade with Cuba. This trade angered anti-Castro groups in the United States, and led to the enactment of the Cuban Democracy Act in 1992. The Cuban Assets Control Regulations were amended to reflect the Act's strict provisions.

The Libertad Act

Proponents of the Cuban Democracy Act kept urging adoption of a much harsher act, which would allow litigation by current U.S. citizens who were Cuban nationals at the time of the Castro expropriations, seeking compensation from persons currently using expropriated properties. This became the Cuban Liberty and Democratic Solidarity (Libertad) Act (more commonly known as Helms-Burton), enacted in March, 1996,[14] primarily because of the emotions aroused due to the shooting down of two U.S. civilian aircraft by Cuba near Cuban territory.

The Libertad Act included two very controversial sections. The first, Title III, created a right of action in U.S. courts for a U.S. national with a claim that Cuba expropriated property after January 1, 1959, against any person who is "trafficking" in such property. Trafficking is quite broadly defined, including not only such actions as selling, buying, leasing or transferring, but also engaging in a "commercial activity using or otherwise benefitting from confiscated property."[15]

The Libertad Act authorizes the President to suspend the effectiveness of Title III actions for successive periods of six months. President Clinton issued such suspension every six months beginning in August, 1996, throughout his term, and each president elected since has continued that practice. These suspensions were the only reason the European Union deferred its request for a panel under the WTO to challenge the extraterritorial effects of the Libertad Act. The United States has stated that it would use the national security defense under the WTO, and also in response to any similar challenge brought by Canada or Mexico under the NAFTA.[16]

The second important part of the Libertad Act, Title IV, requires that the Secretary of State deny visas for entry into the United States to corporate officers, principals, shareholders and even the spouse, minor children or agents of such persons, if they are trafficking in or have confiscated property.[17] This authority has been used against officials of Canadian, Israeli, and Mexican companies.

---

[14]   Public Law No. 104–114, 110 Stat. 785 (Mar. 12, 1996).

[15]   Libertad Act § 4(13).

[16]   The use of the national security defense was strongly criticized in such a case, where there was no foreseeable security threat.

[17]   *Id.* at § 401.

Other nations and organizations have responded in very strong terms against the Libertad Act by adopting blocking laws and enacting resolutions.[18] Cuba enacted its own response to the Libertad Act, which, *inter alia*, denies any possible compensation in a future settlement with the government of Cuba to anyone attempting to take advantage of the Libertad Act by using the U.S. courts under Title III.[19]

Finally, the Florida legislature largely deferred to the Miami Cuban-American groups and passed a state version of Helms-Burton, essentially a "feel good" action since the federal government had pre-empted governance of trade with Cuba. Florida later passed a law attempting to ban any Florida university researchers from traveling to Cuba using private funds, even if licensed by the federal government, and another, the 2008 Sellers of Travel Act, setting huge fees on federally authorized travel agencies in Florida that booked flights to Cuba. Both were quickly overturned by a federal district court.

Cuban Asset Control Regulations (CACR)

The Cuban Assets Control Regulations (CACR), approximately four dozen pages and nearly 150 separate provisions, are the principal regulations which govern trade with Cuba.[20] The application of the Regulations is limited by the Cuban Democracy Act, which removed administrative discretion in allowing some trade with Cuba from foreign subsidiaries. Furthermore, the Regulations may not conflict with the Trading with the Enemy Act,[21] or the Foreign Assistance Act of 1961, both as amended.[22] The administration of the Regulations is delegated to the Office of Foreign Assets Control (OFAC) of the Department of the Treasury.

---

[18]   *See, e.g.*, Peter Glossop, Canada's Foreign Extraterritorial Measures Act and U.S. Restrictions on Trade with Cuba, 32 Int'l Lawyer 93 (1998); Mexico: Act to Protect Trade and Investment from Foreign Statutes which Contravene International Law, with Introductory note by Jorge Vargas, 36 Int'l Legal Materials 133 (1997); Douglas H. Forsythe, Introductory Note, Canada: Foreign Extraterritorial Measures Act Incorporating the Amendments Countering the U.S. Helms-Burton Act, 36 Int'l Legal Materials 111 (1997); Protecting Against the Effects of the Extraterritorial Application of Legislation Adopted by the Third Country, E.U. Council Regulation 2271/96, 1996 O.J. (L 309), reprinted in 36 Int'l Legal Materials 127 (1997).

[19]   Ley de Reafirmacion de la Dignidad y Soberania Cubana (Ley No. 80), Dec. 24, 1996.

[20]   OFAC publishes a useful overview of the regulations. *See* www.treasury.gov.

[21]   The original powers of the President were in the Trading With the Enemy Act (TWEA) of 1917. The President delegated authority to Treasury in accordance with the TWEA. The International Emergency Economic Powers Act (IEEPA) was enacted in 1988 and substantially replaced the TWEA. The authority of the President continues under the IEEPA.

[22]   31 C.F.R. § 515.101.

The Regulations prohibit certain transactions and transfers, where Cuba or a Cuban national is involved. The scope is very wide, including various transfers involving (1) currency, securities, and gold or silver coin or bullion; (2) property or indebtedness; and (3) any form where the transfer is one which attempts to evade or avoid the first two prohibitions.[23] But the Secretary of the Treasury is given authority to authorize such transfers. Imports are prohibited if (1) Cuban in origin,[24] (2) the goods have been in Cuba (including transported through), or (3) made from any Cuban parts.[25]

CACR Exceptions

There are few exceptions to the Cuban trade restrictions. One is a limited exception allowing trade in informational materials, such as some books.[26] More recently cash sales of certain agricultural products have been allowed. The trade prohibitions conclude with a restriction that disallows (1) any vessel which has entered a Cuban port for trade purposes from entering a U.S. port for 180 days after the departure from Cuba, or (2) any vessel carrying goods or passengers to or from Cuba (or goods in which a Cuban has any interest) from entering any U.S. port with such goods or passengers on board.[27]

The Regulations were modified in September, 2009, to increase allowed family visits and remittances, and increase permitted telecommunications. Additionally legislation in 2009 created a new *general* license to allow travel related transactions linked to commercial marketing of agricultural commodities, medicine, or medical devices. While general tourist travel is permitted, almost any U.S. national can find a group to travel with, especially church groups. The addition of the general license covering considerable travel has opened travel to many U.S. persons without Cuban relatives. The U.S. administration under President Obama seemed less inclined to source U.S. foreign policy towards Cuba in Miami, but there has been no major step toward removing the trade embargo. What has become important is an apparent relaxation by OFAC of zealous control demanded by a decreasing number of Cuban exiles.

---

[23]   31 C.F.R. § 515.201.

[24]   *See, e.g., United States v. Plummer*, 221 F.3d 1298 (11th Cir.2000).

[25]   31 C.F.R. § 515.204.

[26]   31 C.F.R. § 515.206. But no cigars or rum. The regulations even prohibit a U.S. citizen or legal resident alien from smoking a Cuban cigar or drinking Cuban rum while in a third country. One might think that OFAC has more important things to do than produce and publish Cuban Cigar Updates.

[27]   31 C.F.R. § 515.207. These vessel restrictions were added to comply with § 1706(b) of the Cuban Democracy Act.

U.S. Foreign Subsidiaries

The CACR prohibitions are followed by quite extensive definitions.[28] While nearly all of the definitions create little problem, one is of considerable importance to U.S. businesses with subsidiaries. A "person subject to the jurisdiction of the United States," upon whom the Regulations impose trade restrictions, includes, "any corporation, partnership, or association, wherever organized or doing business, that is owned or controlled by persons" citizen or resident of the United States or where an entity is organized under the laws of the United States.[29] The meaning of "owned" or "controlled" is not included in the Regulations. The focus of the Cuban Democracy Act is to limit trade with Cuba from foreign subsidiaries of U.S. corporations. It has brought negative responses from the European Union (and separately from member states of the EU), Canada, Argentina, Mexico and the U.N. General Assembly. It is one more example of the extraterritorial application of U.S. laws, and one more example of foreign rejection of such application.

Until this point, the Regulations are mostly prohibitory. But the next section contains important provisions covering "licenses, authorizations, and statements of licensing policy."[30] These provisions authorize the Secretary of the Treasury to issue licenses in a wide variety of circumstances, including (1) for certain judicial proceedings to take place, (2) to determine persons to be unblocked nationals, (3) and to allow transfers by operations of law. The provisions of most importance for U.S. business interests allow some limited trade with Cuba by U.S. owned or controlled firms.[31]

But it was this provision which was the principal focus of the Cuban Democracy Act, which reversed a decade old policy allowing Treasury to license foreign subsidiaries to trade with Cuba.[32] The current law prohibits the issuance of any such licenses to contracts entered into after the enactment of the Cuban Democracy Act. The governments of the foreign nations in which many U.S. subsidiaries are located, however, have enacted laws which mandate that the subsidiaries disregard the U.S. restrictions. It must be assumed that some trade continues, without any attempt to obtain a license.

The subsequent subpart governs reports, and requires reports by any person engaging in any transaction subject to the

---

[28]   31 C.F.R. Subpart C.
[29]   31 C.F.R. § 515.329(d).
[30]   31 C.F.R. Subpart E.
[31]   31 C.F.R. § 515.559.
[32]   Cuban Democracy Act § 1706(a).

Regulations.[33] Thus, a U.S. company trading through a subsidiary may twice violate the law, first by trading and second by failing to report the trade. Penalties are contained in the next provisions,[34] and are severe. Fines may reach $1 million for willful violations, with a maximum of $500,000 as civil penalties.[35] A U.S. firm in violation of some of the CACR provisions may have a mitigating argument not present in the antiboycott situation—to comply with the U.S. law means violation of the law of the nation in which the U.S. subsidiary is incorporated and operating.

Normalization

In 2015, Presidents Obama and Raul Castro normalized U.S.-Cuba relations after a 54 year hiatus. The restoration of diplomatic ties and the opening of a U.S. Embassy in Havana occurred on July 20, 2015. Prisoners were swapped and the U.S. has moved to take Cuba off the list of state sponsors of terrorism. The easing of travel restrictions under 12 existing categories allows many more Americans to visit Cuba, but travel generally is still not authorized. The United States has licensed ferries and cruises to Cuba, both awaiting expanded Cuban approval. A major agreement was reached allowing extensive, regular U.S. flights to Cuba to commence in the Fall of 2016.

U.S. export restrictions on agricultural and telecommunications gear, and health and medical goods and services, will be reduced, and liberalization of U.S. banking rules are expected to permit increased family remittances, trade financing and use of U.S.-based credit cards in Cuba. Cuba has begun to expand Internet access.

President Trump has reversed some of the Obama era normalization of relations with Cuba. There will be less freedom for Americans to travel independently under self-certifications to Cuba, and no business may be done with Cuba's military and intelligence affiliated companies. The latter restriction bans American use of numerous Cuban hotels, resorts and retail chains affiliated with the Cuban military.

No change in the U.S. boycott of Cuba has occurred, which President Castro stated was the "main issue" from Cuba's perspective. That would require an act of Congress, where opposition

---

[33]   31 C.F.R. § 515.601.

[34]   31 C.F.R. Subpart F.

[35]   *See United States v. Brodie*, 403 F.3d 123 (3d Cir. 2005); *United States v. Plummer*, 221 F.3d 1298 (11th Cir. 2000); *United States v. Macko*, 994 F.2d 1526 (11th Cir. 1993); and *United States v. Ortiz de Zevallos*, 748 F.Supp. 1569 (S.D.Fla. 1990), all dealing with violations of the Cuban boycott rules.

is significant. The first U.S. investment in Cuba, to make small tractors in the Mariel Special Development Zone, has been approved.

Some $1.9 billion ($8 billion with interest) in expropriation claims have been certified by the U.S. Foreign Claims Settlement Commission against Cuba. Cuba has raised extensive counterclaims against the United States for damages flowing from the U.S. boycott. The two governments are in negotiations over these issues.

Chapter 12

UNITED STATES ANTI-BOYCOTT LAW*

Table of Sections

§ 12.1   The Arab Boycott of Israel

United States import and export controls[1] are generated under legislation intended to counteract the longstanding, though not terribly effective, Arab boycott of Israel. U.S. "anti-boycott" law attempts to restrict trading by individuals and firms that are deemed to support that boycott. Federal U.S. law was adopted exclusively because of the Arab boycott of Israel. But nowhere does the law specifically mention either Arabs or Israel. Instead, the law is directed to prohibiting U.S. persons from participating in or supporting boycotts by foreign nations against other foreign nations friendly to the United States. U.S. anti-boycott law is likely to remain on the books well after the Arab boycott expires.

---

*   I am indebted to Prof. Michael Gordon for his work on a prior version of this chapter.

[1]   *See generally* Chapters 7 and 10.

The Arab nations employ an international primary, secondary and tertiary boycott of Israel. A primary boycott is where one nation, for example, Oman, refuses to deal with another, for example, Israel. The boycott is secondary when the boycotting nation (Oman) refuses to deal with any third party nation, such as the United States, if that nation deals with the boycotted nation, Israel. The tertiary boycott arises when the boycotting nation (Oman) refuses to deal with the third party nation (the United States), if any of the elements of its products are from a fourth party nation company (e.g., The Netherlands) which trades with the boycotted nation (e.g., Israel).

The boycott has been inconsistently applied by the Arab nations. Where the product or project is of high priority, the Arab nations either ignore their own boycott or grant a waiver.[2]

§ 12.2 U.S. Federal Anti-Boycott Law

The Arab boycott of Israel led to the adoption of U.S. laws and regulations essentially prohibiting U.S. persons from complying with or supporting any boycott by a foreign nation against a nation friendly to the United States.[3] Nowhere in the law is there any direct reference to either Israel or any specific Arab nation. Nevertheless, of 376 boycott requests notified to the Office of Anti-boycott Compliance in 2011, 369 involved an Arab League member. These provisions owe their existence to a long and bitter struggle within Congress, and between Congress and the administration, over the creation of rules that would prohibit U.S. companies from assisting the Arab nations in their attempts to harm Israel.[4]

Prior to the enactment of federal export laws dealing with the Arab boycott of Israel, several states enacted similar laws, and the federal tax and antitrust laws were used to deter U.S. companies from compliance with boycott requests. Although the boycott of Israel by the Arab nations is the reason the federal law exists, there has been some question raised about the applicability of the law to foreign boycotts against South Africa. The Department of Commerce interpreted the law as not applicable to the (since terminated) boycotts against South Africa. The law does affect many commercial relationships between U.S. persons and Middle Eastern governments, private individuals and banks.

---

[2]   See Abrams v. Baylor College of Medicine, 581 F.Supp. 1570, 1576 n. 3 (S.D.Tex.1984) for an example of a waiver of the boycott regarding medical equipment from a blacklisted company.

[3]   Export Administration Act of 1979, 50 App.U.S.C.A. § 2407; Export Administrative Regulations, 15 C.F.R. Part 769.

[4]   The history of the boycott provisions is contained in Trane Co. v. Baldrige, 552 F.Supp. 1378 (W.D.Wis.1983). There are numerous references to Arab nations in the Supplements to 15 C.F.R. Part 769, which include interpretations of the regulations.

§ 12.3   U.S. Export Administration Act (EAA)

Enforcement of the federal anti-boycott laws lies largely within the Department of Commerce Bureau of Industry and Security. The Export Administration Act (EAA) governs the export of goods from the United States, including the anti-boycott provisions. These antiboycott provisions, and the regulations, prohibit U.S. persons from participating in boycotts by a foreign nation against third nations that are friendly towards the United States. The statutory language is very broad, not unlike the concept of the U.S. antitrust laws. The EAA structure requires the President to issue regulations that prohibit any U.S. person from engaging principally in two different areas of activity, *refusals to deal* and *furnishing information*, if such actions further or support a boycott by one foreign nation against another foreign nation that is friendly to the United States.[5]

There is a further provision that applies particularly to banks, that prohibits certain actions with regard to letters of credit which also may further or support a boycott. These prohibitions are included in six sections of the law.[6] The law subsequently states that the regulations should provide exceptions governing some six classes of activity.[7] Reporting to the Secretary of Commerce is required of any request to furnish information.[8] Violations of these provisions are subject to the same statutes that govern other violations of the U.S. export laws. *See* Chapter 10.

§ 12.4   Export Administration Regulations (EAR)

The Export Administration Regulations (EAR) supplement the EEA.[9] They include very extensive examples of conduct which provide guidance in determining whether specific conduct may constitute an anti-boycott violation of the EAA and EAR. Many of the examples are of common occurrences where companies are in jeopardy of refusing to deal, or furnishing prohibited information. Use of these examples is essential to determining both the sense of the administration in interpreting the law, and the likelihood that the conduct in question may be challenged.

The examples in the regulations follow the pattern of the principal statute. Thus, the regulations begin (after a section with

---

5   50 App.U.S.C.A. § 2407(a)(1).
6   50 App.U.S.C.A. § 2407(a)(1)(A)–(F).
7   50 App.U.S.C.A. § 2407(a)(2)(A)–(F).
8   50 App.U.S.C.A. § 2407(b)(2).
9   15 C.F.R. Part 769.

definitions[10]) with examples of six classes of prohibited conduct,[11] and are followed by examples of six classes of exceptions.[12] Following the regulations are a series of 16 Supplements that include Department of Commerce interpretations of various provisions, with some suggested contractual provisions that may avoid challenges by the Department.

§ 12.5 Prohibited Intentional Actions

The purpose of the anti-boycott provisions is to prohibit any U.S. person "from taking or knowingly agreeing to take [certain actions] with intent to comply with, further, or support any boycott" against a country friendly to the United States.[13] It specifically exempts boycotts pursuant to U.S. law. The requirement of intent is essential, but what constitutes intent may seem marginal.

In *United States v. Meyer,*[14] the defendant Meyer was held to have knowledge that a form required by Saudi Arabia to have a trademark registered in that country was not used to obtain information needed for the registration, but to further the boycott of Israel. Meyer claimed that his actions were inadvertent and not intentional. But Meyer's knowledge and intention were rather clearly illustrated by his receipt of information from the Department of State that it could not notarize the form because of the boycott, and his subsequent acquisition of a notarization through the U.S.-Arab Chamber of Commerce. The *Meyer* decision involves a clear attempt to find a way past the law. It is thus not very helpful for a case where the intent is based on less apparent criteria.

§ 12.6 Refusals to Deal

The first prohibition in the EAA is against directly refusing to do business with or in the boycotted country (i.e. Israel), or with a national or resident of that country. Also prohibited is any refusal to do business with the boycotted country by agreement with or response to requests from any other person.[15] This means a U.S. company may not refuse to do business with Israel at the request of the central boycott office of the Arab nations in Damascus. Intent to refuse to do business is not established by the absence of any business relationship with the boycotted country.

---

[10]   15 C.F.R. § 769.1.
[11]   15 C.F.R. § 769.2.
[12]   15 C.F.R. § 769.3.
[13]   50 App.U.S.C.A. § 2407(a)(1).
[14]   864 F.2d 214 (1st Cir.1988).
[15]   50 App.U.S.C.A. § 2407(a)(1)(A).

The Export Administration Regulations, which include ten subsections further defining the meaning of refusing to do business, expand upon this prohibition.[16] The regulations make it clear that a refusal to do business may be established by a course of conduct as well as a specific refusal, or by a use of any "blacklist" or "whitelist". They emphasize, nevertheless, that intent to comply with or support a boycott is required.

Prior to 1985–86, the focus of the Department of Commerce was on reporting violations. But in 1986 the Department, concerned with its limited resources, began to concentrate on blacklists, religious discrimination and refusals to deal. These are viewed by the Department as the most serious violations.

The regulations attempt to cover many variations, but obviously cannot offer an example for each possible situation. Refusals to deal arise for reasons both directly related and totally unrelated to the boycott. When normally justified business reasons for refusing to deal begin to show a pattern of not dealing for reasons consistent with a boycott, the party is in some danger of a challenge from Commerce. But the law does include language of intent, which is most difficult to show from a pattern of conduct that indicates good business reasons for refusing to deal.

The regulations also suggest what does *not* constitute a refusal to do business, such as an agreement to comply generally with the laws of the boycotting country. There does not have to be an agreement not to do business. Compliance with a request, or a unilateral decision, if for boycott reasons, will suffice. These regulations raise one especially difficult issue—the use of a list of suppliers. The regulations give a specific example, although specific examples are usually left for the "examples" section.[3] A U.S. person under contract to provide management services for a construction contract may provide a list of qualified bidders for the client if the service is customary, and if qualified persons are not excluded because they are blacklisted.

Examples of Refusals to Deal

The regulations and especially the examples disclose the nearly unlimited possible configurations of fact situations that may give rise to problems. Consider only a few possible variations, from which numerous additional variations may be easily constructed:

Example 1. A U.S. company is doing business in Israel, but wants to do business in Arab nations while retaining the Israel

---

[16]   15 C.F.R. § 769.2(a). *See also* Supplements No. 6(a), 7, and 15(a) to Part 769.

[3]   15 C.F.R. § 769.2(a)(6).

business. This creates a problem if the Arab nations have alternative sources for the goods, especially from companies in nations which do not have anti-boycott laws, meaning essentially all other nations in the world.

Example 2. Same as above but the company would like to terminate the business in Israel because:

(a)   It believes in or doesn't really care about the boycott. The company is in danger of challenge by the Department of Commerce. But is a business likely to state that it believes in or doesn't care about the boycott?

(b)   The Israel business is not as large as the potential Arab nation's business and the company does not have the capacity to do business in both. As long as the decision is not boycott based, it is proper to drop the Israel business. But it may have to prove that its motives were business and not boycott based.

(c)   The company had planned to close the Israel business because it has been losing money. It had best be able to prove that loss.

Example 3. The company trades with Arab nations and would also like to do business with Israel. It knows if it does do business with Israel it may lose the business with the Arab nations.

Example 4. The same but the company is willing to drop the business with the Arab nations. It may do so without violating the boycott rules because Israel is not boycotting the Arab nations.

Example 5. The company is doing business in both Israel and Arab nations. The Arabs do not know this. The company wants to drop the Israel business because it fears that the Arabs will learn of that business and terminate very profitable Arab business.

§ 12.7   Discriminatory Actions

The second statutorily prohibited conduct is refusing to employ or otherwise discriminating against any U.S. person on the basis of race, religion, sex or national origin, where such conduct is intentional and in furtherance of an unlawful boycott.[17] This section addresses the Arab nations' attempts to injure Jewish people wherever they may live, rather than to harm Israel as a nation. Thus, a company may not refuse to employ Jewish persons so that it may gain favor with Arab clients. In one of the few court decisions

---

[17]   50 App.U.S.C.A. § 2407(a)(B). Even if employment discrimination is not boycott based, and thus not a violation of the EAA, it may violate other laws, such as civil rights legislation.

involving the antiboycott provisions, Baylor College of Medicine was found to have persistently appointed non-Jewish persons for a project with Saudi Arabia.[18]

The antidiscrimination section of the EAA includes both refusals to employ and *other discrimination*. For example, a requirement that a U.S. company not use a six-pointed star on its packaging of products to be sent to the Arab nation would be a violation because it is part of the enforcement effort of the boycott. But it is not a violation if the demand is that no symbol of Israel be included on the packaging. The former is a religious symbol generally, the latter an acceptable request which does not include reference to any person's religion.[19] This illustrates a general attempt to acknowledge that the boycotting nations are entitled to have *some* control over what comes into their nation. They are entitled to say no imports may be stamped "Products of Israel", but they may not attack the Jewish religion more broadly by requiring certification that no religious symbols appear on any packages. The United States is attempting to say that Arab nations may have a right to engage in a primary boycott against Israel, but they may not draw U.S. persons into supporting that boycott.

The regulations governing discriminatory actions make it clear that such actions must involve "intent to comply with, further or support an unsanctioned foreign boycott."[20] The regulations further state that the boycott provisions do not supersede or limit U.S. civil rights laws.[21]

§ 12.8   Furnishing Information Regarding Race, Religion, Sex or National Origin

The third specific prohibition relates to the refusal to hire for reasons of race, religion, sex or national origin, discussed immediately above. This provision prohibits furnishing information with respect to race, religion, sex or national origin.[22] This brief provision is supplemented by regulations that state that it shall apply whether the information is specifically requested or offered voluntarily and whether stated in the affirmative or negative.[23] Furthermore, prohibited information includes place of birth or

---

[18]   *Abrams v. Baylor College of Medicine*, 581 F.Supp. 1570 (S.D.Tex.1984), *aff'd*, 805 F.2d 528 (5th Cir.1986). The case also deals with the issue of the right to bring a private action. Using the *Cort v. Ash* factors test, the court held that there is an implied right under the EAA.

[19]   These are examples included in 15 C.F.R. § 769.2(b), examples (viii) and (ix). *See* Supplement No. 6(b) & (c) to Part 769.

[20]   15 C.F.R. § 769.2(b)(2).

[21]   15 C.F.R. § 769.2(b)(3).

[22]   50 App.U.S.C.A. § 2407(a)(C).

[23]   15 C.F.R. § 769.2(c)(2).

nationality of the parents, and information in code words or symbols that would identify a person's race, religion, sex or national origin.[24] The regulations also reaffirm the element of intent.[25]

The examples in the regulations illustrate the difficulty of clearly defining "prohibited information". If the boycotting nation requests a U.S. company to give all employees who will work in the boycotting nation visa forms, and these visa forms request otherwise prohibited information, the company is not in violation for giving the forms to its employees or for sending the forms back to the boycotting country party. This is considered a ministerial function and not support of the boycott. But the company may not itself provide the information on race, religion, sex or nationality of its employees, if it meets the intent requirement. The company might certify that none of its employees to be sent to the boycotting nation are women, where the laws of the boycotting country prohibit women from working. The reason for the submission has nothing to do with the boycott.

§ 12.9 Furnishing Information Regarding Business Relationships—"Blacklists"

The fourth prohibition is one that is often at issue. It involves the use of blacklists. The Arab nations maintain a blacklist of persons and companies with whom they will not do business. Arab nations often ask a prospective commercial agreement party to certify that none of the goods will include components obtained from any companies on the blacklist.

Persons are prohibited from furnishing information about an extensive list of business activities ("including a relationship by way of sale, purchase, legal or commercial representation, shipping or other transport, insurance, investment, or supply"[26]), with an equally extensive list of business relationships ("with or in the boycotted country, with any business concern organized under the laws of the boycotted country, with any national or resident of the boycotted country, or with any other person which is known or believed to be restricted from having any business relationship with or in the boycotting country"[27]). At the end is a statement that the section does not prohibit furnishing "normal business information in a commercial context as defined by the Secretary." Thus, clients are very extensively governed with regard to the flow of information between the company and the boycotting country.

---

[24]   15 C.F.R. § 769.2(c)(3).

[25]   15 C.F.R. § 769.2(c)(4).

[26]   50 App.U.S.C.A. § 2407(a)(D).

[27]   *Id.*

The regulations develop this already expansive section.[28] The prohibited information may not be given whether directly or indirectly requested or furnished on the initiative of the U.S. person.[29] The Secretary's definition of normal business in a commercial context is that related "to factors such as financial fitness, technical competence, or professional experience" as might be normally found in documents available to the public, such as "annual reports, disclosure statements concerning securities, catalogues, promotional brochures, and trade and business handbooks."[30] Such public information may not be supplied if in response to a boycott request.[31]

But it may be supplied if it could be used by the boycotting country to further the boycott—knowledge and intent on the part of the U.S. person is the key to making the furnishing of the information unlawful. There are numerous examples of this prohibition, many referring to use of blacklists. For example, a person may not certify that its suppliers are not on a furnished blacklist.[32] If a company is on the blacklist, or if it wishes to know whether it is on the blacklist, it may request such information.[33] That is not furnishing information. But if it furnishes information in order to be removed, it may be in violation. If a company believes it is on the blacklist but no longer would be listed were the Arab nations to know the true facts, supplying those facts may constitute a violation.[34] The same may occur when a company believes it is mistakenly listed, and wishes to make this known to the Arab nations. Companies have removed their names, but it must be done with great care.

The most publicized blacklist case involved Baxter International Inc., a large U.S. medical supply company.[35] As a result of an informant's disclosure, Baxter was investigated and charged with violating the EAA because of the way in which it attempted to have its name removed from the Arab blacklist.[36] Commerce was prepared to charge Baxter and a senior officer with providing over 300 items of prohibited information to Syrian authorities and a Saudi Arabian

---

[28]   15 C.F.R. § 769.2(d).

[29]   15 C.F.R. § 769.2(d)(2)(ii).

[30]   15 C.F.R. § 769.2(d)(3).

[31]   15 C.F.R. § 769.2(d)(4).

[32]   15 C.F.R. § 769.2(d) example (x).

[33]   15 C.F.R. § 769.2(d) example (xv).

[34]   A U.S. subsidiary of the French cosmetics company L'Oreal provided the parent information to assist in removal from the blacklist. Providing this information and failing to report to the Commerce department led to L'Oreal agreeing to pay $1.4 million in civil penalties. *See, e.g.,* Los Angeles Times, August 30, 1995, at Part D.

[35]   *See, e.g.,* The Case Against Baxter International, Business Week, Oct. 7, 1991, pg. 106.

[36]   *See* 5 OEL Insider 7 (Dec. 1993).

firm. The company and the officer admitted civil and criminal violations and were assessed total civil penalties of $6,060,600—the highest at the time. The case would not have succeeded without the informant providing substantial documentation of the violations.

§ 12.10   Prohibition of Intentional Evasion

The EAA and the EAR regulations each include a section that states that no U.S. person may take any action with intent to evade the law.[37] Permitted activities are not to be considered an evasion of the law. An example of an evasion is placing a person at a commercial disadvantage or imposing on that person special burdens because that person is blacklisted or otherwise restricted from business relations for boycott reasons.[38] Another evasion may be use of risk-of-loss provisions that expressly impose a financial risk on another because of the import laws of a boycotting country, unless customarily used.[39] Two final suggested evasions are the use of dummy corporations or other devices to mask prohibited activities, or diverting boycotting country orders to a foreign subsidiary.[40]

§ 12.11   Reporting Requirements for Requests

Under the title "Foreign policy controls," the EAA includes very important provisions that require the reporting of the receipt of any request for the "furnishing of information, the entering into or implementing of agreements, or the taking of any other action" outlined in the policy section[41] of the EAA.[42] The receipt of any such request must be reported to the Secretary of Commerce. Failure to report boycott-associated requests is perhaps the most frequent violation of the EAA. The report must include any information the Secretary deems appropriate and must state whether the person intends to comply or has complied with the request. These reports are public records, except to the extent that certain confidential information is included that would cause a competitive disadvantage to the reporting person.

The regulations include quite extensive provisions, covering (a) the scope of reporting requirements, (b) the manner of reporting, and (c) the disclosure of information.

---

[37]   50 App. U.S.C.A. § 2407(a)(5); 15 C.F.R. § 769.4; *see also* Supplement No. 12 to Part 769 for an interpretation dealing with use of an agent.

[38]   15 C.F.R. § 769.4(c).

[39]   15 C.F.R. § 769.4(d).

[40]   15 C.F.R. § 769.4(e).

[41]   50 App. U.S.C.A. § 2402(5).

[42]   50 App. U.S.C.A. § 2407(b).

Reporting Requirements

Whenever a person receives a written or oral request to take any action in furtherance or support of a boycott against a friendly foreign country it must be reported. The request may be to enter into or implement an agreement. It may involve a solicitation, directive, legend or instruction asking for information or action (or inaction). The request must be reported whether or not the action requested is prohibited, except as the regulations provide.[43] That essentially means reporting is required if the person knows or has reason to know that the purpose of the request is to enforce, implement or otherwise support, further or secure compliance with the boycott.[44]

When a request is received by a U.S. person located outside the United States (subsidiary, branch, partnership, affiliate, office or other controlled permanent foreign establishment), it is reportable if received in connection with a transaction in interstate or foreign commerce.[45] A general boycott questionnaire, unrelated to any specific transaction, must be reported when that person has or anticipates a business relationship with or in the boycotting country, also in interstate or foreign commerce.

The reporting requirements apply whether the U.S. person is an exporter, bank or other financial institution, insurer, freight forwarder, manufacturer, or other person.[46] If the information about a country's boycotting requirements is learned by means of the receipt or review of books, pamphlets, legal texts, exporter's guidebooks and other similar publications, it is not considered a reportable request. The same is true of receipt of an unsolicited bid where there is no intention to respond.[47]

Reporting Exemptions

The EAR regulations include ten specific requests that are not reportable. They were added because of the customary use of certain terms for boycott and non-boycott purposes, Congressional mandates for clear guidelines in uncertain areas, and the Department of Commerce's desire to reduce paperwork and costs. The non-reportable requests are:[48]

---

[43]   15 C.F.R. § 769.6(a)(1).

[44]   15 C.F.R. § 769.6(a)(2).

[45]   *Id.*, citing 15 C.F.R. §§ 769.1(c) and (d). The definition of "interstate or foreign commerce" is the subject of a Department of Commerce interpretation in Supplement No. 8 to Part 769.

[46]   15 C.F.R. § 769.6(a)(3).

[47]   15 C.F.R. § 769.6(a)(4). A definition of "unsolicited invitation to bid" is included in Supplement No. 11 to Part 769.

[48]   15 C.F.R. § 769.6(a)(5); *see also* Supplement No. 10(b) to Part 769.

(i)   Request to refrain from shipping goods on a carrier flying the flag of a particular country, or that is owned, chartered, leased or operated by a particular country or its nationals or residents; or a request for certification to such effect;

(ii)   Request to ship goods, or refrain from shipping goods, on a prescribed route, or a certification request of either;

(iii)   Request for an affirmative statement or certification regarding the country of origin of goods;

(iv)   Request for an affirmative statement or certification of supplier's or manufacturer's or service provider's name;

(v)   Request to comply with laws of another country except where it requires compliance with that country's boycott laws;

(vi)   Request to individual for personal information about himself or family for immigration, passport, visa or employment requirements;

(vii)   Request for an affirmative statement or certification stating destination of exports or confirming or indicating the cargo will be unloaded at a particular destination;

(viii) Request for certification from owner, master, charterer, or any employee thereof, that a vessel, aircraft, truck or other transport is eligible, permitted, nor restricted from or allowed to enter, a particular port, country or group of countries under the laws, rules, or regulations of that port, country or countries;

(ix)   Request for certification from insurance company stating the issuing company has an agent or representative (plus name and address) in a boycotting country; or

(x)   Request to comply with term or condition that vendor bears the risk of loss and indemnify the purchaser if goods are denied entry for any reason if this clause was in use by the purchaser prior to January 18, 1978.

The Department of Commerce periodically surveys domestic concerns to determine the worldwide scope of boycott requests received by U.S. subsidiaries and controlled affiliates regarding activities outside U.S. commerce.[49] This is intended to cover requests that would be required to be reported, but for the fact that they involve commerce outside the United States. Information collected from U.S. persons will include the number and nature of non-reportable requests received, action requested, action taken, and countries making such requests.

Manner of Reporting Requests

Every request must be reported; however, only the first need be reported when the same request is received in several forms.[50] But each different request regarding the same transaction must be reported. Each U.S. person receiving a request must report the request, but one person may designate another to make the report, such as a parent reporting on behalf of a subsidiary.[51]

Disclosure of Information

The third part of the regulations applying to reporting states that the reports shall become public records, except for "certain proprietary information."[52] The reporting party may certify that the disclosure of information relating to the (1) quantity, (2) description, or (3) value of any articles, materials or supplies (including technical data and other information), may place the company at a competitive disadvantage. In such case the information will not be made public.

But the reporting party must edit the public inspection copy of the accompanying documents as noted below, and the Secretary may reject the request for confidentiality for reasons either of disagreement regarding the competitive disadvantage, or of national interest in not withholding the information.[53] If such decision is made, the party must be given an opportunity to comment.

Because the report is made public, one copy must be submitted intact and the other may be edited in accordance with the above limitations. Any additional material considered confidential may also be deleted, as may be any material not required to be reported.[54] The copy is to be marked "Public Inspection Copy."

---

[49]   15 C.F.R. § 769.6(a)(7).
[50]   15 C.F.R. § 769.6(b)(1).
[51]   15 C.F.R. § 769.6(b)(2).
[52]   15 C.F.R. § 769.6(c)(1).
[53]   *Id.*
[54]   15 C.F.R. § 769.6(c)(2).

§ 12.12   U.S. Anti-Boycott Violations and Enforcement

Violations and enforcement of the antiboycott laws are subject to the same provisions as violations and enforcement of the export laws.[55] The enforcement of the antiboycott laws has generated few court decisions. Most have involved issues of constitutionality, creation of private rights of action, or the statute of limitations.[56]

Several persons have had licenses suspended and fines exceeding $5 million have been levied. Most of these cases involved the receipt of requests for information from Arab countries. In instances where the companies had complied with the request, the Department of Commerce and the company usually agreed on a fine as part of a consent decree. The procedures were dealt with administratively, and the decisions are found only in some private reporters.[57] One of the largest civil penalties was imposed in a settlement with Baxter International Inc., in 1993. Baxter, a Swiss subsidiary, and an officer paid a penalty totaling $6,060,600. For all of 2011, eight companies paid penalties totaling only $129,300.

U.S. subsidiaries that carry out boycott activities of foreign parents are within the reach of the provisions. The French L'Oreal, S.A. cosmetics company requested information from two U.S. subsidiaries, Parbel of Florida, Inc. (formerly Helena Rubenstein, Inc.) and Cosmair, Inc., about their business relationships in or with Israel. More than 100 items of information were provided, and no report of the request was made to Commerce. The two subsidiaries (and individual corporate counsel for Cosmair) agreed to fines exceeding $1.4 million in 1995.

§ 12.13   U.S. Private Rights of Action

There is no clear indication whether the EAA includes a private right of action. A Texas federal district court, in *Abrams v. Baylor College of Medicine,*[58] addressed a claim by two Jewish medical students that Baylor University denied them opportunities when it excluded Jews from medical teams it sent to Saudi Arabia. The court

---

[55]   50 App.U.S.C.A. §§ 2410, 2411 and 2412. *See* supra, chapter 17. Considerable information on the boycotts is at www.bis.doc.gov, including major cases.

[56]   *See United States v. Core Laboratories, Inc.*, 759 F.2d 480 (5th Cir.1985) (EAA and the statute of limitations); *Abrams v. Baylor College of Medicine*, 581 F.Supp. 1570 (S.D.Tex.1984), *aff'd* 805 F.2d 528 (5th Cir.1986) (EAA and affirming private right of action); *Bulk Oil (ZUG) A.G. v. Sun Co., Inc.*, 583 F.Supp. 1134 (S.D.N.Y.1983), *aff'd* 742 F.2d 1431 (2d Cir.1984), *cert. denied* 469 U.S. 835, 105 S.Ct. 129, 83 L.Ed.2d 70 (1984) (EAA and rejecting private right).

[57]   *See* Int'l Boycotts (Business Law Inc.); Boycott L. Bull.

[58]   581 F.Supp. 1570 (S.D.Tex.1984), *aff'd* 805 F.2d 528 (5th Cir.1986).

found an implied right of action by applying the factors in the *Cort v. Ash* decision of the U.S. Supreme Court.[59] The Fifth Circuit upheld the decision. But in *Bulk Oil (ZUG) A.G. v. Sun Co.,* the Second Circuit rejected the existence of a private right of action, affirming a New York federal district court decision involving an accusation of violation of the anti-boycott provisions by failing to deliver oil to Israel.[60] The Seventh Circuit has also rejected private causes of action under U.S. anti-boycott law.[61]

---

[59]   422 U.S. 66, 95 S.Ct. 2080, 45 L.Ed.2d 26 (1975).

[60]   583 F.Supp. 1134 (S.D.N.Y.1983), *aff'd* 742 F.2d 1431 (2d Cir.1984), *cert. denied* 469 U.S. 835, 105 S.Ct. 129, 83 L.Ed.2d 70 (1984).

[61]   *Israel Aircraft Ind. v. Sanwa Business Credit Corp.,* 16 F.3d 198 (7th Cir. 1994).

Chapter 13

FOREIGN CORRUPT PRACTICES

Table of Sections

Bribery in some nations has reached epidemic proportions. Visit the Transparency International website for their global maps graphically displaying a Corruption Index of the world. A UK organization, Control Risks, suggests three classes of corruption. First is the payment of bribes to officials and businesses for favorable treatment. Second is nepotism carried to a level of domination of business by family clans. And third is the evolution of corruption into organized crime, with the participation of officials at the highest

401

levels of government. This last class seems the case with Russia, for example, creating a potentially serious risk of extortion and kidnaping to all persons transacting business in the country.

Disclosures of corruption in China frequently appear to involve government officials and officers of state-controlled corporations. For example, the Chinese People's Procuratorate, a government department, reported in one year 34,070 cases of economic crimes (bribes, embezzlement, graft, etc.) involving more than 7,000 officials, including 3,017 managers of state owned industries and 2,141 involved with banking and negotiable securities. The current, vigorous anti-corruption campaign of President Xi Jinping has netted an unprecedented number of high-ranking government and military officials, many of whom as members are subject to Chinese Communist Party (CCP) discipline. The CCP Central Commission for Disciplinary Inspection (CCDI) is opaque. It appears able to cause CCP members to "disappear", often returning several months later accompanied by publicly revealed confessions. Woe unto foreign investors in China who are named in such confessions as the source of unlawful payments. In extreme cases, corruption can result in capital punishment.

The regulated nature of procurement contracts and foreign investments, and the frequently large sums involved, invite business-driven corruption. Suggestions and sometimes even extortion by government officials can result in payments made to obtain, maintain or influence business interests. Laws against bribery, starting prominently with the U.S. Foreign Corrupt Practices Act in 1977 (FCPA), have proliferated. Individual and corporate sanctions are almost always severe, and sanctioning under several legal regimes for the same practices is not infrequent. Rolls-Royce, for example, agreed in 2017 to pay combined bribery penalties amounting to over $800 million to British, Brazilian and U.S. authorities.

§ 13.0 The U.S. Foreign Corrupt Practices Act (FCPA)

The Foreign Corrupt Practices Act of 1977 (FCPA) was enacted to reduce U.S. business participation in making payments or giving of items of value to foreign officials in an attempt to favorably influence government decisions.[1] The FCPA has been strongly enforced. Some 150 U.S. investigations are pending at this writing, encouraged by Dodd-Frank whistleblower rewards. While it has mostly concerned foreign investment practices, it has also been

---

[1]   Public Law 95–213, 91 Stat. 1494, Dec.19, 1977.

applied where corrupt practices favor U.S. exports. Anyone dealing with the FCPA should read the Department of Justice Resource Guide to the U.S. Foreign Corrupt Practices Act.

One difficulty with the FCPA is defining what constitutes a wrongful payment. Because the payment is made to a foreign official, cultural standards of that official's nation may affect the payment. Conflicts of interest by government officials may be governed by very different notions. While apparently no foreign country has written laws permitting foreign officials to accept bribes to influence their conduct, the "operational code" or unwritten law of many countries makes such conduct commonplace.

The FCPA imposes a U.S. ethic on conduct in the United States and abroad by U.S. persons, and to conduct within the United States by foreign persons. For 20 years, except for Sweden, the United States stood almost alone in the global community on foreign corrupt practices law. Finally, in 1997, the Organization for Economic Cooperation and Development (OECD), comprised about 35 of the world's most developed nations, adopted a Convention on Combatting Bribery of Foreign officials in International Business Transactions. In 2004, the United Nations promulgated a widely ratified Convention against Corruption. Neither of these Conventions is a clone of the FCPA (see Section 13.4), but the lonely U.S. position on corrupt practices now has many allies.

§ 13.1   History of the FCPA

Back in the 1970s, as a spin-off of Watergate, secret slush funds used by over 400 U.S. companies to pay foreign officials to advance business interests were revealed. There was an outcry by the press within the United States and abroad about the disclosed payments, especially by U.S. aircraft corporations to Japanese and Dutch officials. Names of alleged recipients were disclosed, causing considerable embarrassment (Prince Bernard of the Netherlands), and even withdrawal or removal from office (Prime Minister Tanaka of Japan[2]) of national leaders.

There was almost no legislative response from other nations, and only a very modest response internationally. Many foreign observers, especially from other major exporting nations, did not object to the proposed legislation. Preventing U.S. persons from making such payments would give foreign businesses a competitive

---

[2]   Lockheed was alleged to have paid $1.4 million to Prime Minister Tanaka, which led to his removal and imprisonment. *See* 134 Cong. Rec. S9617–18 (July 14, 1988) (quoting statement of Senator Proxmire).

advantage. Some foreign observers wondered why Americans needed to make such public disclosure of their moments of transgression.

The United States thus stood nearly alone for decades in responding to the general condemnation of payments to foreign officials. Many U.S. businesses objected to the United States adopting a law prohibiting foreign payments. These businesses had to compete abroad for contractors and investors from nations which had no such laws, and which in some cases, even allowed foreign bribes to be considered tax deductible ordinary and necessary business expenses.

The Foreign Corrupt Practices Act of 1977 (FCPA) was enacted under the Carter Administration to reduce United States participation in making payments or giving of items of value to foreign government officials, or to agents who would pass them on to such officials, when done in an attempt to influence government decisions. The Act also sought to achieve political goals by preventing U.S. persons from making payments to officials abroad that might destabilize foreign policy relationships between the foreign nation and the United States.

§ 13.2   FCPA Amendments in 1988 and 1998

FCPA amendments in 1988 removed some of the strictness of the initial Act.[3] The level of conduct required to violate the FCPA was altered in favor of U.S. business by substantial elimination of the "reason to know" standard when payments made to agents might be passed on to foreign officials. The amendment requires that payments to agents must have been knowingly made, and includes a definition of such knowledge. One leading proponent of the original provision in the Senate was so incensed at the change that he suggested that the new loophole established by the amendment was "big enough to fly a Lockheed through." This author does not agree. *See* Section 13.12.

The FCPA was amended in 1998 to comply with U.S. obligations under the 1997 OECD Convention on Combating Bribery of Foreign Officials in International Business Transactions.[4] The Convention included language, added to the FCPA, making it unlawful to make payments to gain "any improper advantage" in order to obtain or renew business. The FCPA was further amended to expand its scope to cover prohibited acts by "any person." Domestic concerns other than issuers and "other" persons are now covered. This makes the

---

[3]   15 U.S.C.A. §§ 78q(b), 78dd, 78ff(a).

[4]   Public Law 105–366, Nov. 10, 1998 (International Anti-bribery & Fair Competition Act).

FCPA cover all *foreign* natural and legal persons who commit acts while in the United States.[5]

The amendments also reach payments by U.S. businesses and persons taking place wholly outside the United States, and payments to officials of international agencies. Finally, penalties for non-U.S. citizen employees and agents of U.S. employers and principals, previously limited to civil sanctions, now include the same criminal sanctions as for U.S. citizen employees and agents.

§ 13.3   Summary of FCPA Prohibitions and Sanctions

The current, twice-amended FCPA remains relatively concise. It establishes stringent accounting, internal control and disclosure standards for U.S. issuers supervised by the SEC, including for example a specific 2016 SEC disclosure rule for "resource extraction issuers". The FCPA prohibits payments by "any person" to foreign officials, designated public international organizations, or political parties directly, or "while knowing" by way of third persons or subsidiaries, when such payments are for the purpose of influencing or inducing any act, inaction or decision of the official of a foreign government *or an instrumentality* of that government (interpreted as including state-owned or state-controlled enterprises) to secure "any improper advantage" in order to obtain or maintain business. For example, procurement contracts, tax benefits, customs preferences, and foreign investment privileges fall within its scope.

Since many FCPA investigations involve payments made via third parties (often consultants), the meaning of "knowing" is critical. There is a convoluted definition in the Act which stresses "awareness" of either a "substantial certainty" or a "high probability" that some of the payments will end up in the hands of public officials. In the many countries where corruption is systemic, such awareness cannot easily be avoided by sticking your head in the sands of bribery. The courts have consistently rejected "willful blindness", "conscious ignorance" or "conscious avoidance" defenses.

The FCPA can apply to extraterritorial activities of foreign as well as U.S. firms. For FCPA purposes, there must generally have been some use of the mails or any means or instrumentality of U.S. interstate commerce, or acts committed in the USA. These jurisdictional requirements embrace the constitutional concept of minimum contacts. Foreign issuers on U.S. financial exchanges, including those with "American Depository Receipts", easily fall under the FCPA umbrella.

---

[5]   15 U.S.C.A. §§ 78dd–2, 78dd–3.

The Justice Department enforces the illegal payments prohibitions, and may reward whistleblowers under the Dodd-Frank or Sarbanes Oxley Acts, such sums typically falling between 10 to 30% of the monies Justice and SEC recover. Sanctions can include felony criminal penalties for willful violations, civil penalties, non-deductible disgorgement of profits (subject to a Supreme Court dispute as to whether a five year statute of limitations applies), and jail terms, and even the threat of being denied contracting rights with the U.S. government. Any criminal fine imposed on a person under the FCPA may not be paid or indemnified by the company directly or indirectly. There is an important exception for routine government action (small "grease payments"), which is further defined in a separate section. The Act also establishes affirmative defenses cases where the payment was lawful under the *written* laws of the foreign country (this defense has never successfully been invoked), or was a "reasonable and bona fide expenditure" for business purposes.

Anyone interested in or dealing with the FCPA and its exemptions should read the 2012 Department of Justice/SEC Resource Guide to the U.S. Foreign Corrupt Practices Act. The Guide contains some excellent examples drawn from DOJ/SEC enforcement practice. The law firm of Sherman & Sterling produced in 2010 a 400 page FCPA Digest of Cases and Review Releases Relating to Bribes to Foreign Officials under the Foreign Corrupt Practices Act of 1977 that is also an excellent resource. These resources make it clear that voluntary disclosure, cooperation with the DOJ and SEC, and robust compliance programs can reduce or even eliminate FCPA sanctions.

Other "sanctions" are less formal, but potentially no less severe. Reputational damage, stock market declines, foreign procurement exclusion, shareholder and RICO lawsuits, wrongful termination actions, and higher capital costs may follow. For example, the in-house counsel for 25 years at Bio-Rad Laboratories finally blew the whistle on bribes allegedly paid in China, was fired, and filed a wrongful termination suit in 2016. An initial ruling allows memos and otherwise privileged information to be entered into evidence on behalf of the former counsel.

FCPA settlements typically also impose ongoing compliance costs. For example, in 2015 a small Florida company (IAP) paid over $7 million to settle criminal charges regarding procurement payments to Kuwaiti officials made via a consultant. In addition, IAP promised high-level commitment against corruption, a clear corporate policy against corruption and regular corruption risk reviews, assignment of compliance responsibilities to a senior executive reporting to independent monitoring bodies, extensive training, reporting and investigation systems, disciplinary procedures, and corruption due diligence in mergers and acquisitions.

§ 13.4 FCPA—Who Is Covered?

In addition to limiting prohibited practices to certain kinds of payments, the drafters of the Act also had to consider the scope of coverage regarding who would fall within its prohibitions. That meant both which persons would be subject to an action for making prohibited payments, and which persons abroad had to be the recipients of the payments for the transaction to be unlawful. The amendments in 1998 expanded the scope of coverage of payors, extending to "any person", natural or legal, United States or foreign, acting within United States territory. Omitted are foreign persons acting outside the United States. Payments to officials, political parties, party officials, or candidates (except in some one-party states) are covered under the FCPA.

§ 13.5 FCPA—Prohibited and Exempted Payments, Sanctions

The FCPA makes it unlawful for an issuer of registered securities under § 12 of the Securities Exchange Act (SEA), or an issuer required to file reports under § 15(d) of the SEA, to make certain payments to foreign officials or other persons. The FCPA also requires those issuers to maintain accurate financial records which would disclose such payments. The Act additionally extends the scope of prohibited payments to any issuer *or domestic concern* making use of the mails or any means or instrumentality of interstate commerce.[6] This effectively extends liability to all corporations, in a manner not unlike the insider trading provisions of § 10 of the SEA. These rules focus on a shareholder's right to know if its corporation books are inaccurate, if management used corporate money to violate U.S. or foreign laws, if bribes were paid with corporate funds, or if payments were made to consultants with no accountability as to their disbursements.

The current FCPA remains relatively concise. After establishing accounting standards,[7] it prohibits payments by any person to foreign government or international organization officials directly, or by way of third persons, when such payments are for the purpose of influencing any act or decision of the foreign official,[8] inducing the foreign official to act or refrain from acting in violation of the official's

---

[6] 15 U.S.C.A. §§ 78dd–1(a), 78dd–2(a). The latter part also defines both "domestic concern" and "interstate commerce." *See* § 78dd–2(h)(1) and (5).

[7] 15 U.S.C.A. § 78m(b).

[8] 15 U.S.C.A. § 78dd–1(a)(1)(A)(i).

duty,[9] inducing the foreign official to use influence with a foreign government or instrumentality to influence that government's or instrumentality's act or decision,[10] or to secure any improper advantage.[11] The beneficiary of the business obtained or retained need not be the person making the corrupt payment.

There is an important exception for routine government action,[12] which is further defined in a separate section.[13] The Act then establishes as an affirmative defense, cases where the payment was lawful under the *written* laws of the foreign country, or was a "reasonable and bona fide expenditure."[14] The Act defines of "foreign official", "public international organization", "knowing" and "routine governmental action."[15]

Section 78dd–1 and § 78dd–2 violations for making illegal payments are governed in these two different provisions, for issuers and domestic concerns, respectively, and their officers, directors, agents and shareholders acting on behalf of the entity. Each section leads to the same levels of penalties.[16]

The entities are subject to fines of not more than $2 million or double the intended benefit. The officers, directors, employees, agents, and shareholders acting on behalf of the concerns are subject to fines up to $250,000, or five years' imprisonment, or both, if the violation was willful.[17] Any fine imposed on a person under these provisions may not be paid or indemnified by the company directly or indirectly. These penalties illustrate that the U.S. government is serious about violations of the FCPA.[18] Individual and corporate civil penalties may also be assessed, along with disgorgement of corruptly obtained proceeds. See Section 13.16 for examples of major fines and penalties secured by the federal government under the FCPA.

---

[9]   15 U.S.C.A. § 78dd–1(a)(1)(A)(ii).

[10]   15 U.S.C.A. § 78dd–1(a)(1)(B).

[11]   15 U.S.C.A. §§ 78dd–1(a)(1)(A)(iii), 78dd–1(a)(2)(A)(iii), 78dd–1(a)(3)(A)(iii). The content of these provisions is essentially repeated in sections 78dd–2 and 78dd–3.

[12]   15 U.S.C.A. § 78dd–1(b).

[13]   15 U.S.C.A. § 78dd–1(f)(2).

[14]   15 U.S.C.A. § 78dd–1(c).

[15]   15 U.S.C.A. §§ 78dd–1(f), 78dd–2(h). Section 78dd–2(h) also defines "domestic concern" and "interstate commerce."

[16]   15 U.S.C.A. §§ 78ff(c) and 78dd–2(g).

[17]   Only willful violations are subject to criminal penalties. *See Trane Co. v. O'Connor Securities*, 718 F.2d 26 (2d Cir.1983).

[18]   Two units of Litton Industries pleaded guilty in 1999 to fraud and conspiracy in making payments to obtain defense business in Greece and Taiwan. Litton agreed to pay $18.5 million to settle the matter (including an amount to reimburse the Department of Justice for the costs of the investigation).

§ 13.6   FCPA—Accounting Standards

One approach used in the FCPA to discourage illegal payments is to require issuers subject to the SEA to maintain accounting records that assist in disclosing payments that might violate the substantive sections of the FCPA. The original law generated considerable criticism about standards that threatened harsh penalties for even slight, incorrect accounting entries. The standards further required considerable documentation of foreign transactions. The 1988 amendments addressed what was a concern for "reasonable detail" and "reasonable assurances" in internal accounting controls, and indicate that the Act does not cover technical or insignificant errors in record keeping. But records must be "accurately and fairly". . . . in other words a bribe must recorded as a bribe. Liability is to be imposed on persons who "knowingly circumvent or knowingly fail to implement a system of internal controls or knowingly falsify any book, record or account."[19]

The proof of accounting violations is mostly available in the United States, where the corporate books are located. But the books often disclose little to auditors, since payments may be made to persons who appear to be legitimate foreign consultants, and thus are listed only as payments made to consultants, not to foreign officials.

Section 78m(b) violations, the record-keeping and internal accounting-control standards section, may lead where there is a willful violation, or a willful and knowing making of a false or misleading statement in filed applications, statements or reports, to a criminal penalty for individuals of not more than $5,000,000 and not more than 20 years imprisonment, or both.[20] Corporate criminal violations can result in up to $25 million fines or double the intended benefit. Individual and corporate civil penalties may also be assessed, along with disgorgement of corruptly obtained proceeds. See Section 13.16 for examples of major fines and penalties secured by the federal government under the FCPA.

§ 13.7   FCPA—What Is Given?

Persons who are subject to the Act may not "make use of the mails or any means or instrumentality of interstate commerce *corruptly*" where the act is "in furtherance of" any one of several actions, including an:

---

[19]   15 U.S.C.A. § 78m(b)5.

[20]   15 U.S.C.A. § 78ff(a). An exchange may be fined up to $2,500,000. Proof of no knowledge of the rule or regulation will avoid imprisonment. *Id.*

1. Offer,

2. Payment,

3. Promise to pay, or

4. Authorization of the payment

"of any money".

Or an:

1. Offer,

2. Gift,

3. Promise to give, or

4. Authorization of the giving

"of anything of value."[21]

Thus, the Act divides numerous "giving" actions between giving either money or anything of value. The fact that something offered, promised or given has a very small value does not remove it from the Act. There is no *de minimis* exemption. The exemptions exist in *to whom* the item is offered, promised or given, or *for what purpose* the item is offered, promised or given.

§ 13.8 FCPA—Acting "Corruptly"

The act of offering, promising or giving must be done *corruptly*. "Corruptly" is not defined in the FCPA. If all of the provisions are met, i.e., a payment is made to a defined foreign official and there is no statutory affirmative defense, does the government nevertheless have to prove that the act was done corruptly? Or does the giving to a foreign official where there is no statutory defense constitute a corrupt act?

The word "corruptly" seems unnecessary. The FCPA prohibits certain conduct, about which persons might debate endlessly regarding whether it is corrupt conduct. One decision suggests that the word "corruptly" means that the court or jury determines whether the conduct violates the provisions of the Act, rather than meeting some external definition of "corrupt".[22] The party charged must be the one who acts corruptly. Carrying out an employer's instructions might not be acting corruptly.[23] Thus, an employee of a U.S. aircraft-maintenance contractor who made a "gesture" to the chief of maintenance for Nigerian Air Force cargo planes, in the form of purchasing airline tickets for the official's honeymoon, after the

---

[21]   15 U.S.C.A. §§ 78dd–1(a), 78dd–2(a).

[22]   *See United States v. Liebo*, 923 F.2d 1308 (8th Cir.1991).

[23]   *Id.*

contract was awarded, was entitled to a new trial to determine whether the employee met the "corrupt" standard.[24]

An unusual comment in the Senate Committee Report on the 1977 Act stated:

> That the payment may have been first proposed by the recipient rather than the U.S. company does not alter the corrupt purpose on the part of the person paying the bribe. On the other hand true extortion situations would not be covered by this provision since a payment to an official to keep an oil rig from being dynamited should not be held to be made with the requisite corrupt purpose.[25]

This would be a useful defense where there is clearly an attempt to extort money from the company or individual. But it may be very difficult to prove, and may require the kind of dramatic case noted in the Senate Report.

§ 13.9   FCPA—Foreign Officials

The definition of a foreign official has long been debated. Defendants have argued that employees of state-owned or state-controlled companies are not foreign officials under the FCPA. Justice and the SEC disagree.

The offer, promise or gift may not be made to any person in any one of three classes. One class is a payment to any *foreign official* if the offer, promise or gift is either (1) to influence an official act or decision, induce an act or omission in violation of lawful duty, or secure any advantage, or (2) to induce the use of the official's influence with a foreign government or instrumentality in order to "affect or influence" any act thereof, and where the ultimate purpose is assisting the issuer in either obtaining or retaining business, or directing business to any person.[26]

The "obtaining or retaining" business language was discussed in *United States v. Liebo,* where the court held the standard had been met.[27] It later came before the court in *United States v. Kay,* where the Fifth Circuit found the "obtaining or retaining" business to mean more than bribes beyond payments sufficient only to "obtain or retain government contracts."[28] But it also held that bribes did not have to rise to the level of influencing awarding contracts to violate the Act.

---

[24]   *Id.*

[25]   Senate Report No. 114, 95th Cong. 10 (1977).

[26]   15 U.S.C.A. §§ 78dd–1(a)(1), 78dd–2(a)(1).

[27]   923 F.2d 1308 (8th Cir.1991).

[28]   359 F.3d 738 (5th Cir.2004).

In addition to defining "knowing", the Act offers some help in defining the term "foreign official."[29] A foreign official is any "officer or employee" of any foreign government, or department, agency or **instrumentality** thereof. "Official" is thus very broadly defined to include the lowest-level employee.[30] Also included are persons acting in an *official capacity* for or on behalf of a government.

Corrupt payments to international organizations and officers or employees of international organizations, including NGOs, were added in 1988. The addition of international organizations substantially expands the scope of the FCPA. When payments to only foreign *government* officials were covered, it was necessary to define "government." That is not always easy. Some entities, such as the Vatican, the PLO, or a territory over which there is some government control, may or may not be considered governments.

Case law suggests that foreign officials cannot be prosecuted under the FCPA.[31] But foreign nationals, otherwise subject to U.S. jurisdiction, fall under its scope.[32]

§ 13.10 FCPA—Foreign Political Party, Official or Candidate

An offer, promise or gift may not be made to any *foreign political party* or *official of that party* or *candidate for political office,* if it is (1) to influence such party in an official act or decision, induce an act or omission in violation of lawful duty, or secure any improper advantage, or (2) to induce the use of that party's influence with a foreign government or instrumentality to "affect or influence" any act thereof. The ultimate purpose must be to assist in either obtaining or retaining business, or directing business to any person.[33] "Candidate" may be difficult to define, since it may not be clear that a person is a candidate at the time of making a payment. The act does not specifically cover a person intending to become a candidate.

§ 13.11 FCPA—Any Person "While Knowing"

An offer, promise or gift may not be made to *any person,* while *knowing* it will be offered, promised or given to (1) a foreign official, (2) a foreign political party, (3) an official of a foreign political party, or (4) a candidate for foreign political office, where the purpose is the

[29] 15 U.S.C.A. §§ 78dd–1(f)(1), 78dd–2(h)(2).

[30] But the exceptions for routine government actions are most likely to apply to payments to relatively low-level employees.

[31] *United States v. Castle,* 925 F.2d 831 (5th Cir. 1991).

[32] *Dooley v. United Technologies Corp.,* 803 F.Supp. 428 (D.D.C. 1992).

[33] 15 U.S.C.A. §§ 78dd–1(a)(3), 78dd–2(a)(3).

same as in the first two sections above.[34] This third category of persons to whom payments are prohibited governs payments to persons hired as agents or consultants, but adds the very important requirement that a payment to such third party be made "while knowing" that the money or item of value will be passed on to a prohibited person.

In the original Act, the language was "knowing or having reason to know."[35] The "having reason to know" language was the subject of continual criticism by business persons, who believed it created an unfair and ambiguous standard that placed the burden on the business to prove that its conduct was proper. Although proponents of the original language lost the fight to retain it in the 1988 amendments, a broad definition of "knowing" was added to the Act.

The definition of "knowing" states that knowing conduct is where either (1) the person is *aware* of the conduct, that "such circumstance" exists, or the result is "substantially certain" to occur, or (2) the person has a "firm belief" that such circumstance exists or the result is substantially certain to occur.[36] The provision then adds that the knowing standard is met if the person is "aware of a high probability" of the existence of such circumstance, *unless* the person "actually believes" that such circumstance does not exist.[37] The "high probability" language seems to carry the knowing standard into the territory of a reason to know standard. . . . and in any event hardly creates a loophole "big enough to fly a Lockheed through."

§ 13.12   FCPA—"Grease" Payments

Probably many business persons have paid a small amount to a customs official to expedite the processing of goods in danger of spoilage or needed for an impatient customer. Congress did not wish to label as corrupt the myriad of minor "grease" payments made to government officials to do what they are supposed to do, but in a shorter period of time. The result is that corruption has a *de minimis* element, but it is not defined by a dollar amount. But even *de minimis* payments may be subject to the accounting requirements of the Act.

The original Act exempted payments for acts that were ministerial, using language that exempted payments to foreign government employees "whose duties are essentially ministerial or clerical."[38] The 1988 amendments changed that language to create an exception for "facilitating or expediting" payments when the

---

[34]   15 U.S.C.A. §§ 78dd–1(a)(3), 78dd–2(a)(3).

[35]   15 U.S.C.A. §§ 78dd–1(a)(3), 78dd–2(a)(3) (1977).

[36]   15 U.S.C.A. §§ 78dd–1(f)(2)(A), 78dd–2(h)(3)(A).

[37]   15 U.S.C.A. §§ 78dd–1(f)(2)(B), 78dd–2(h)(3)(B).

[38]   15 U.S.C.A. § 77dd–1(b) (1977).

purpose is to "expedite or to secure the performance of a routine governmental action."[39] A "routine governmental action" is defined in the Act,[40] in four specific sections and one general subsection. Payments are specifically allowed made when:

1.   Obtaining permits, licenses or other official documents which are part of the process of qualifying to do business in the country,

2.   Processing papers such as visas and work orders,

3.   Providing police protection, mail pick-up and delivery, or scheduling inspections which are associated with the performance of a contract or related to transit of goods across country, and

4.   Providing telephone service, power and water supply, loading and unloading cargo, or protecting perishables from deterioration.

A final, fifth class encompasses "actions of a similar nature."

Any decision by a foreign official about the terms of a new contract, the awarding of such contract, continuing business, or any action by any official involved in the process of new or renewal business is specifically **not** exempted.[41]

There is a very large gap between what is specifically allowed and what is specifically disallowed. One of the least clear areas involves the extent to which foreign officials may be entertained. Entertaining is not always motivated solely by courtesy. Foreign officials are usually entertained as part of the process of receiving the award of a contract, or establishing or continuing a business. The line of legitimacy must fall somewhere between reasonable expenses associated with normal business, and unreasonable expenses associated with unreasonable influence. Finding that line is helped by the special provisions providing affirmative defenses.[42]

§ 13.13   FCPA—Payments Lawful Under "Written" Laws

The FCPA establishes two basic classes of affirmative defenses. The first is when the payment, gift, offer or promise is lawful under the *written* laws and regulations of the foreign country.[43] Since nations rarely enact laws giving legitimacy to what may be common

---

[39]   15 U.S.C.A. §§ 78dd–1(b), 78dd–2(b).

[40]   15 U.S.C.A. §§ 78dd–1(f)(3), 78dd–2(h)(4).

[41]   15 U.S.C.A. §§ 78dd–1(f)(3)(B), 78dd–2(h)(4)(B).

[42]   15 U.S.C.A. §§ 78dd–1(c), 78dd–2(c).

[43]   15 U.S.C.A. § 77dd–1(c)(1).

but corrupt practices of its officials, this section is likely to be of little use. Were it to allow payments where the *unwritten* laws, i.e., the expected and common practice, mandate payments, the loophole would be considerably wider than merely enough to fly a Lockheed through.

To be safe, counsel should obtain an opinion in writing from foreign local counsel that identifies the written law or regulation that allows a payment. It is of course possible that payments may be allowed to political campaigns under local written law, but not personally to serving officials to influence their official decisions.

§ 13.14   FCPA—"Reasonable and Bona Fide Expenditures"

The second specific affirmative defense is when the payment, gift, offer or promise is a "reasonable and bona fide expenditure, such as travel and lodging expenses" that a foreign official incurs, and which is *directly* related to either (1) the promotion, demonstration or explanation of products or services, or (2) the execution or performance of a contract.[44] While the first part of this section broadens the permissible payments, the second part narrows it. Noticeably excluded are payments when the contract is being considered, either initially or for renewal. But a carefully crafted corporate policy might provide that even in the advance of obtaining a contract or having it renewed, payments to foreign officials are exclusively based on promotions, demonstrations and/or explanations relating to the performance of the contract if granted or renewed.

The Department of Justice issued an Opinion approving some planned paid travel for Chinese journalists to a Trace International event in China[45]. This DOJ procedure may be the best process to follow for travel expenses about which a corporation has some doubt.

§ 13.15   FCPA—U.S. Enforcement Actions

The severity of penalties for violations of the FCPA (see Sections 13.6 and 7) mandates close consideration of its provisions by all persons doing business abroad. Subsidiaries owned or controlled by publicly-traded U.S. companies fall within its jurisdictional scope. Violations of the FCPA are dealt with principally by the SEC (which monitors the record keeping) and the Department of Justice (which enforces the antibribery provisions). In the past decade, there has been a substantial increase in FCPA prosecutions. In 2010, the DOJ

---

[44]   15 U.S.C.A. § 77dd–1(c)(2).

[45]   *See* 43 Int'l Lawyer 783 (2009). U.S. Dep't of Justice, Foreign Corrupt Practices Act Review, Opinion Procedure Release No. 08–03 (July 11, 2008).

and SEC collected over $1.8 billion in FCPA fines and penalties. Comparatively few actions brought by the Department of Justice have reached the appellate courts. One example, involving the International Harvester Company, alleged participation in a series of charges relating to dealings with officials of Petroleos Mexicanos (PEMEX), the national oil company.[46]

But it is not only the largest U.S. corporations which have been the subject of actions. Another action involved an individual who owned a postage stamp concession for a Caribbean island and who paid for flights for citizens to return to the island to vote for the reelection of the president, allegedly to influence the government to renew the concession.[47]

Investigations are often reported in the news, suggesting that U.S. persons and companies have not ceased making payments to foreign officials.[48] Some of the most controversial allegations have involved IBM and Mexico in 1993, during the sensitive negotiations for the North American Free Trade Agreement.[49] An Iranian-born British businessman was retained by IBM to be its agent in a tender bid for a new air-control system in Mexico City. The agent alleged that soon after a meeting with several Mexican officials at which they tried to obtain a $1 million bribe, IBM's bid was rejected and the contract given to the French Thomson Company. The agents' subsequent public disclosure and numerous newspaper articles led nowhere, but caused a sensation in Mexico. The Minister of Communications was ousted in a cabinet reorganization. The agent alleged that the Mexican government later tried to buy him off. IBM did not support the agent in his claims, and settled with the agent out of court.

The whole episode illustrates many problems. The U.S. government showed no inclination to become involved or investigate the matter. There were foreign policy problems, NAFTA priorities, perhaps a sense that the whole story was not implausible, but a realization that this is how things work. Aliases or no names, secret meetings, finger pointing, and leaks to the press are all part of the

---

[46]   The company pleaded guilty to conspiracy to violate the FCPA. *See McLean v. International Harvester Co.*, 902 F.2d 372 (5th Cir.1990); *McLean v. International Harvester Co.*, 817 F.2d 1214 (5th Cir.1987); Executive Legal Summary No. 5, Business Laws, Inc. 100.03 (Hancock ed., Oct. 1988).

[47]   Executive Legal Summary No. 5, Business Laws, Inc., 100.03, 100.04 (Hancock ed., Oct. 1988).

[48]   *See, e.g.*, Some Weapons Makers Are Said To Continue Illicit Foreign Outlays, Wall St.J., Nov. 5, 1993, at 1, discussing GE, Teledyne Inc., Litton Industries, Inc., Loral Corp., and United Technologies Corp. problems.

[49]   *See* The Independent, August 29, 1993, Sunday Review at 2; The Financial Post, Oct. 27, 1993, at 13.

game. No one seems to have asked how the French Thomson Company got the bid so quickly after IBM was rejected.

IBM was later again in the news regarding an investigation of bribes in Argentina to obtain a $250 million contract to modernize the computer system for the Banco de la Nación.[50] IBM allegedly paid bribes to CCR, a computer systems company, in connection with obtaining a contract with Nación, money which soon found its way into Swiss accounts.[51]

The Rise in FCPA Enforcement

FCPA prosecutions rose dramatically under the George W. Bush and Barack Obama presidencies. Most FCPA investigations are settled under deferred or non-prosecution agreements. This explains the relative absence of FCPA case law and reinforces the wide discretion to the SEC and DOJ to interpret the Act as they see fit. For example, the DOJ asserted J. P. Morgan's hiring of relatives of influential Chinese officials was covered by the FCPA. The firm maintained spread sheets showing the cost of "Sons and Daughters" hires and their value in terms of increased business. In 2016, J.P. Morgan settled the investigation for roughly $264 million.

Here are some additional FCPA settlement examples:

Siemens AG paid bribes in numerous countries and an agreed in 2008 to an FCPA fine of $800 million. The Siemens' FCPA settlement remains the largest to date. German and 20 other anti-bribery law enforcement authorities also pursued Siemens, which is reported to have spent over $1 billion in legal and accounting fees. The Siemens cases involved the Oil-for-Food program, which resulted in four other settlements against Akzo Nobel of the Netherlands for $3 million in penalties, against Flowserve Corporation for $10.55 million of criminal and civil penalties, against AB Volvo resulting in $12.6 million in penalties, and against Fiat for $17.8 million civil and criminal penalties.

The French engineering giant, Alstom, pleaded guilty in 2014 and agreed to pay $772 million in record FCPA criminal fines. Alstom failed to disclose its misconduct or cooperate with U.S. authorities concerning its corrupt payments via consultants in Indonesia, Egypt, Saudi Arabia and the Bahamas. The total fines amounted to over 2.5 times Alstom's profits from its corrupt activities and delayed GE's due diligence leading to acquisition of Alstom for several years pending settlement. Alstom also faces criminal charges before Britain's Serious Fraud Office.

---

[50]   National Law Journal, Mar. 3, 1997, at B16.
[51]   Financial Times, Oct. 19, 1995, at 5.

In 2016, Teva Pharmaceutical paid $519 million, the hedge fund, Och-Ziff settled for over $400 million, VimpelCom $398 million (notably in part for payments to a charity affiliated with an Uzbek official). Odebrecht/Braskem of Brazil paid $632 million in FCPA fines along with additional sums to Switzerland and Brazil in the "Car Wash" investigation focusing on Petrobras and corrupt practices throughout Latin America involving construction contract work order addenda. In 2015, Hitachi of Japan agreed to pay $19 million to settle FCPA charges concerning payments made to South Africa's ruling political party regarding power station construction contracts.

In prior years, Lucent Technologies paid settlement penalties of $137 million, KBR/Halliburton settled for $579 million, BAE for $400 million, Johnson & Johnson for $70 million, and Daimler for $185 million. Avon voluntarily reported itself concerning illegal payments in China leading to a "moderate" FCPA settlement of $135 million in 2014, along with the placement of an independent FCPA "monitor" inside the company. And the list of corporate FCPA settlements goes on: Embraer, Novartis, Nordion, AB InBev, SciClone Pharmaceuticals, Bilfinger, Parker Drilling, Diebold, Pfizer, Eli Lilly, Alcoa, Total, Stryker, Hewlett-Packard, Philips, Weatherford, and Ralph Lauren.

A New York Times feature article in December 2012 described bribes allegedly made by Wal-Mart in Mexico. The payments led to a Department of Justice investigation that is still ongoing, an expensive *global* in-house review of payments' practices by Wal-Mart (reportedly costing over a million dollars a day!), and a dramatic drop in the value of Wal-Mart stock. Wal-Mart is said to be afraid of a settlement ban on participation in the Food Stamp SNAP program, treated as a U.S. procurement contract. Wal-Mart's SNAP sales run close to $13 billion a year. Wal-Mart has already instituted extensive FCPA compliance programs (*see* Section 13.22).

Towards the end of the Obama administration, the DOJ commenced a one year pilot program (ending, unless renewed, April 2017) reducing corporate fines if companies voluntarily disclosed violations, fully cooperated, and demonstrated remediation in exchange for approximately 20 to 50% reductions in financial penalties under the U.S. Sentencing Guidelines. The SEC has followed similar policies, continuing to focus on China and misconduct generally in the pharmaceutical and financial services industries. During 2016, roughly $2.5 billion in FCPA fines were collected, the highest in the history of the statute.

There have also been individual prosecutions, often following corporate settlements, assuming personal jurisdiction can be had. Individual prosecutions have for example, included some high profile persons. Albert Stanley, CEO of KBR, a subsidiary of Halliburton, agreed to serve seven years in prison and pay $10.8 million in restitution. In 2010, the FBI conducted its first FCPA sting operation ("Shot Show"), resulting in the arrest of 22 executives from military and law enforcement products companies. The government has also seized personal assets (pensions, cars and homes) of "willful" violators as forfeited proceeds of bribery.

§ 13.16　FCPA—Consent Decrees

Few of the FCPA cases investigated ever come to court.[52] Most cases are resolved by consent decrees. Corporations prefer to accept a negotiated fine rather than litigate in the federal courts.[53] Furthermore, corporations usually prefer to avoid the publicity accompanying charges of making foreign payments corruptly. There is also the problem that the payment usually occurs in a foreign country and proof of the payment is difficult to establish. The foreign country is not likely to assist in allowing discovery or taking depositions.

§ 13.17　FCPA—DOJ Review Process

The FCPA requires the Department of Justice to establish a procedure allowing persons to request an opinion about proposed activity that might create some FPCA concern.[54] The first step is for the person or company to present to the Department of Justice details of the proposed transaction. The person or company may only rely upon a review letter signed by the Assistant Attorney General (or delegate) in charge of the criminal division. The procedure has not been used very often, possibly because of concern about identifying foreign officials and the consequences if the review request information is not held confidential.[55]

The 1988 amendments provide more definitional information of what may be allowed, and may lead to even less use of the review procedure. The DOJ has however rejuvenated the opinion procedure,

---

[52]　*See United States v. McLean*, 738 F.2d 655 (5th Cir.1984), *cert. denied* 470 U.S. 1050, 105 S.Ct. 1748, 84 L.Ed.2d 813 (1985).

[53]　The FCPA Reporter includes information regarding consent decrees and guilty pleas. The names of corporations charged are well known, including such companies as Ashland Oil, General Electric, Goodyear International, International Harvester, and Lockheed Martin.

[54]　15 U.S.C.A. §§ 78dd–1(e), 78dd–2(f). The review procedure is contained in 28 C.F.R. § 50.18.

[55]　Furthermore, information provided in a review request might be used against the person in a criminal prosecution. *See* John W. Bagby, Enforcement of the Accounting Standards in the Foreign Corrupt Practices Act, 21 Am.Bus.L.J. 213 (1983).

and issued several opinions addressing disclosures, takeovers, acquisitions by auction, and payment of some travel expenses.[56]

§ 13.18   U.S. Private Rights of Action

There have not been many suits charging violations of the FCPA initiated by private individuals or companies against other private parties. One federal circuit court has held that there is no private right of action under the FCPA.[57] The case involved donations Philip Morris allegedly promised a Venezuelan Children's Foundation (the wife of the President of Venezuela was the president of the Foundation) for benefits to Philip Morris in obtaining Venezuelan tobacco. Two U.S. tobacco producers sued Philip Morris for harm caused by the alleged violation of the FCPA (and antitrust law).

The *Lamb* decision is influential and law in the Sixth Circuit, but may not be the last word on the issue. With the recent substantial increase in enforcement by several governments, there may be a significant increase in bribery related private civil litigation. Shareholder derivative suits have become common once a FCPA investigation becomes public. Breach of fiduciary duty lawsuits under ERISA have also been pursued by pensioners.

§ 13.19   U.S. Employee Suits

The original 1977 Act included what was known as the Eckhardt provision, which did not allow government actions to be brought against employees without first going against the employer. The amendments in 1988 reversed this and allow such actions. An employer may now urge the government to bring suit directly against the employee who made the payment, even if the payment was authorized by other higher-level officers. The possibility of a scapegoat is back. But the scapegoat employee may not be without a remedy. That employee is likely to be or soon become a *former* employee, and may have an action against the company. Employees who are dismissed for refusing to comply with orders to make foreign payments may bring unlawful discharge suits, usually in the form of

---

[56]   *See* 43 Int'l Lawyer 782–784 (2009).

[57]   *Lamb v. Phillip Morris, Inc.*, 915 F.2d 1024 (6th Cir.1990), *cert. denied* 498 U.S. 1086, 111 S.Ct. 961, 112 L.Ed.2d 1048 (1991). *See also Citicorp Int'l Trading Co., Inc. v. Western Oil & Refining Co.*, 771 F.Supp. 600 (S.D.N.Y.1991) (applying the well established four-part Cort v. Ash test to determine that there is no private cause of action); *Shields on Behalf of Sundstrand Corp. v. Erickson*, 710 F.Supp. 686 (N.D.Ill.1989) (violations of financial and accounting controls do not give rise to private right); *Lewis v. Sporck*, 612 F.Supp. 1316 (N.D.Cal.1985) (same conclusion).

a breach of contract action, or become whistle-blowers and tell all to the government.[58]

Ashland Oil Inc., learned that firing an employee for refusing to make an illegal payment abroad is costly.[59] Ashland's vice-president William McKay was instructed but refused to make an illegal payment to an official in Oman. McKay later cooperated with SEC and IRS investigations of the payment. Another executive, Harry Williams, was sympathetic to McKay's attempt to change the corporate policy at Ashland. Both were soon no longer employed. They sued Ashland for wrongful discharge and received a verdict of nearly $70 million, later settled for $25 million.

A key to the settlement was a provision in McKay's employment contract that he would not be compelled to make unlawful payments. It is an appropriate employment contract provision for an officer, because many states do not allow suits for termination in the absence of a contractual provision. Any suit commenced under such a contract provision would be based on the contract and not the FCPA. It would therefore not face the uncertain issue noted above of bringing private suits under the Act. Because it is a suit based on breach of the employment contract, it requires inquiry only regarding the company's act of demanding a payment that, if made, would be a violation.[60]

The FCPA itself does not provide any basis for a corporate employee to bring a claim against the corporation where the corporation appears to have made the employee the scapegoat for allegedly unlawful payments.[61] Nevertheless, Teledyne Systems faced another possible use of the FCPA: Whistle-blower suits. A significant military contractor, Teledyne became involved in several whistle-blower suits in the early 1990s. One filed by a former program manager for Teledyne in the Middle East alleged a payment to an Egyptian general to help obtain Air Force contracts.[62] Whistleblower awards under the Dodd-Frank Act are possible.

---

[58]   A whistle-blower's experience at GE is described in Some Weapons Makers Are Said To Continue Illicit Foreign Outlays, Wall St.J., Nov. 5, 1993, at 1.

[59]   See Marshall Sella, More Big Bucks in Jury Verdicts, 75 A.B.A. Journal 69 (July 1989). See also Williams v. Hall, 683 F.Supp. 639 (E.D.Ky.1988).

[60]   See also Pratt v. Caterpillar Tractor Co., 149 Ill.App.3d 588, 102 Ill.Dec. 900, 500 N.E.2d 1001 (1986), appeal denied 114 Ill.2d 556, 107 Ill.Dec. 68, 506 N.E.2d 959 (1987), holding that the FCPA did not create a basis for a state claim of retaliatory discharge.

[61]   McLean v. International Harvester Co., 817 F.2d 1214 (5th Cir.1987), appeal after remand 902 F.2d 372 (5th Cir.1990).

[62]   See At Teledyne, A Chorus of Whistle-Blowers, Business Week, Dec. 14, 1992, at 40.

§ 13.20   U.S. Suits Charging Competitor with Violation of FCPA

A person or company believing that a competitor violated the FCPA and obtained business at the company's expense has several choices. First, a direct suit charging a violation of the FCPA may fail as in the case of the Philip Morris experience discussed above, because it is an attempt to bring a private cause of action.[63] Second, a suit might be based on violations of antitrust laws. A third choice is a violation of the Racketeer Influenced and Corrupt Organizations Act (RICO).[64] In each of the latter two actions, the corrupt payment would be *evidence* of the wrong alleged, but not used as the basis of the suit, and thus the suit would not fail as a disallowed private right of action. A fourth possible cause of action would be for tortious interference with a current or prospective business relationship.[65]

A RICO action was brought in *W.S. Kirkpatrick & Co., Inc. v. Environmental Tectonics Corp., Int'l.*[66] Environmental Tectonics was an unsuccessful bidder for a contract with the Nigerian Air Force. The company complained that Kirkpatrick had paid unlawful bribes to Nigerian officials. The company sued under the federal RICO statute. The court ruled that the act of state doctrine did not apply because the lawfulness of acts of a foreign government in its own territory were not at issue, but only the motives of foreign officials in accepting payments. The case was remanded. RICO thus may be an effective method for private suits involving violations of the FCPA.

Facing litigation by dismissed employees who refused to make illegal payments, and by competitors injured by such payments, not to mention multiple government prosecutions, companies may find it better to stop such payments rather than attempt to hide them. Many firms have developed serious internal policies and training programs which are intended both to prevent company officials from making such payments abroad, and to assure that they are in fact not made.

---

[63]   *Lamb v. Phillip Morris, Inc.*, 915 F.2d 1024 (6th Cir.1990), *cert. denied* 498 U.S. 1086, 111 S.Ct. 961, 112 L.Ed.2d 1048 (1991).

[64]   18 U.S.C.A. §§ 1961–1968.

[65]   *See* discussion in *Citicorp Int'l Trading Co., Inc. v. Western Oil & Refining Co., Inc.*, 771 F.Supp. 600 (S.D.N.Y.1991).

[66]   493 U.S. 400, 110 S.Ct. 701, 107 L.Ed.2d 816 (1990) (antitrust laws). *See Town of Kearny v. Hudson Meadows Urban Renewal Corp.*, 829 F.2d 1263 (3d Cir. 1987) (civil RICO) and *United States v. Rubicam*, 741 F.Supp. 334 (D.Conn. 1990) (Travel Act).

§ 13.21   OECD and United Nations Conventions, British Bribery Act

Transparency International, a European-based NGO, maintains a highly regarded global corruption perception index. *See* www.transparency.org. Every country is rated from very clean (e.g., Denmark) to highly corrupt (e.g., Somalia). Perhaps the most difficult "corruption" to address is that which is culturally ingrained, for example "ttokkap" (rice cake expenses) in Korea and "guanxi" in China. Both the industrial nations of the OECD and the United Nations have attempted to address corruption.

The 1997 OECD Convention

There was an outcry in the 1970s by the press within the United States and abroad about the disclosed payments made by U.S. corporations. Except for Sweden, there was almost no legislative response from other nations. The United States thus stood nearly alone for two decades in responding to the general condemnation of payments to foreign officials by enacting the FCPA.

Pushed hard by the United States, the 35 industrial nations of the Organization for Economic Cooperation and Development (OECD) addressed corruption by adopting in 1997 the OECD Convention on Combatting Bribery of Foreign Officials in International Business Transactions, some 20 years after the FCPA. The OECD Convention obligates signatories to criminalize bribery of foreign officials and sanction inaccurate accounts. It is a floor not a ceiling. Japan, for example, moved quickly to take the bribery issue seriously. Japan's Ministry of International Trade and Industry (MITI) adopted measures consistent with the OECD guidelines. The OECD also recommended prohibiting tax deductions for bribes, a recommendation that Canada, France and others have followed.

Enactment of laws in some OECD countries followed slowly, indeed Britain's Bribery Act did not arrive until 2010 (see below). Though not members of the OECD, Russia, Bulgaria, Colombia, Argentina, South Africa and Brazil officially subscribe to its principles. China (not an OECD member) has since 2011 criminalized bribes to foreign officials and international public organizations. It has also been undertaking a massive internal anti-corruption campaign, principally targeting CCP members and state-owned enterprises.

Adoption and enforcement of anti-bribery policies often differ, but some foreign enforcement actions have gained attention in Brazil, Russia, Finland, France, Germany, India, Ireland and South Korea. Guatemala has obtained considerable prosecutorial assistance and expertise via the United Nations, while the IMF continues to push Ukraine along the anti-corruption curve by slowing down release of its loans to that country.

One of the overlooked features of the OECD Convention is the agreement to provide Mutual Assistance to enable government enforcement. Such assistance has led, for example, to cooperative anti-corruption investigations, and to the extradition of individual violators.

The 2005 UN Convention

The United Nations finally came into the game in 2005, after years of inability to agree and failure to acknowledge that perhaps some governments were responsible for their officials' actions in receiving bribes from foreign entities. The U.N. Convention against Corruption went beyond the scope of the FCPA and OECD enactments to focus on making bribery and receipt of bribes illegal under national laws. It also notably included procedures for recouping bribes "hidden" abroad by the officials who received them. Some 170 nations have subscribed to the U.N. Convention, but many of the worst offending nations have acted to make it just so many words. Some $20 to $40 billion a year are reportedly lost by developing nations to corruption.

The U.N. and World Bank are collaborating on a Stolen Assets Recovery Initiative. They are joined by the U.S. Department of Justice's Kleptocracy Initiative. Recoveries of corruptly derived assets are few and far between, and in some countries graft has become openly brazen. While the UN Convention against Corruption is welcome, the OECD appears to have largely preempted the field with respect to serious attention.

The British Bribery Act of 2010

The British Bribery Act of 2010 (BBA) may have been late in arriving, but is now widely perceived to be one of the most rigorous. It extends not just to payments to foreign officials, but also to private parties. The Act applies to solicitation as well as receipt of bribes, and appears to have no statute of limitations. Its coverage is broad in scope (for example, "grease payments" are not exempted) and its criminal and civil liability is strict with no need to prove corrupt intent. Formal criminal charges were commenced for the first time by the Serious Fraud Office in 2013 against individuals associated with a bio fuel investment fund, and the first criminal corporate conviction secured in 2016. It is also a crime under the BBA to fail to prevent bribery. Deferred prosecution agreements (DPA) with corporate offenders have been authorized and undertaken with cooperating parties since 2014. A record fine of nearly 500 Pounds Sterling was paid by Rolls Royce under a DPA in 2017.

The BBA extends to essentially all firms doing business in the U.K. Hypothetically, therefore, the BBA reaches U.S. firms with U.K. stock listings or sales offices, and perhaps those processing illegal payments via British banks. The BBA governs the activities of such firms around the world, say bribes in India. It is tempered by a defense (as yet undefined) if "adequate procedures" to prevent offenses were in place. It can be argued that a serious, effective anti-bribery compliance system (see Section 13.22) may constitute "adequate procedures".

§ 13.22 Corrupt Practices Compliance Programs, Warning Signs

Compliance Programs

The dramatic increase in FCPA proceedings during recent years, combined with minimal jurisdictional requirements and major reputational and corrective action costs (not to mention share price declines), have caused widespread adoption of company compliance policies and programs. In France, a 2017 law (Sapin II) requires companies to implement a compliance policy. Corruption risk reviews, appointment of FCPA compliance officers, reporting and investigation systems, disciplinary actions and lots of due diligence on persons and firms having contact with foreign public officials and state-controlled companies add to risk reduction. Hiring independent third parties, often law firms, to assess FCPA risks helps prove good faith compliance goals. Training of all employees, especially foreign employees, in contact with foreign officials has become routine. Such training should be repeated regularly, and recorded in personnel files.

A corporate policy will not assure that illegal payments are not made in an investment or procurement context. But even if illegal payments are later found to have been made, a written policy, acknowledged by employees' signatures, will to establish the company's good intentions and should help in minimizing penalties. Morgan Stanley is thought to have avoided FCPA penalties completely when one of their Chinese employees "went rogue" despite repeated training and compliance efforts. DOJ and SEC declinations to prosecute under the FCPA increase when credible, robust comprehensive compliance programs are found to exist and disgorgement of profits takes place.

Vendors, customs brokers, transport carriers, construction and other service providers of U.S. corporations are frequently being required to undergo FCPA training. Such third parties must also complete FCPA audits, and sign contract clauses and affidavits as to compliance and awareness of FCPA risks. Some firms decline absolutely to make any grease payments.

Dealing with distributors, agents and consultants creates special vetting problems. They should be asked for details about the existence of any relatives or business associates who are in the government. The company should contact various persons in the U.S. government, Chambers of Commerce, local counsel, and the like to check on their reputation, and conduct Google and social media searches. All this "due diligence" might help to later establish that the company did not act "while knowing" (the FCPA standard) that payments to third parties would end up going corruptly to officials. A common method to create additional margin for corrupt payments is through excessive discounts or rebates, a risk that necessitates transaction-specific due diligence. Finally, the agreement with the agent or consultant should contain a clause that none of the funds paid to the agent will be used in any manner which might violate the FCPA.

FCPA due diligence in connection with international mergers and acquisitions has become the norm. The resulting business assumes FCPA liabilities, though it may seek indemnification. Record keeping and internal control compliance programs are mandatory and critical to adhering to the strict FCPA accounting and disclosure rules, which require a bribe to be declared a bribe.

Warning Signs

Warning signs of FCPA violations should be taken extremely seriously. Some such signs include:

1.   Previous company history of FCPA violations.

2.   Previous history of FCPA violations by officers and directors.

3.   Previous industry history of FCPA violations.

4.   Doing business in a nation with a reputation for corruption, and for FCPA violations.

5.   Transactions where local distributor or agent is related to, or has business links with, or is recommended by, government officials.

6.   Transactions where local distributor or agent wishes commissions to be paid to third-nation account, especially a numbered account in a nation known as a safe haven.

7. Transactions with local distributor or agent who suggests irregular procedures, such as incorrect dates on invoices, double invoicing for customs, checks for more than the invoice amount, different check dates, cash or bearer instrument payments, excessive credit line, advance payments, etc.

8. Transactions with local distributor or agent which call for excessive commissions.

9. Transactions with local distributor or agent with poor reputation.

10. Transactions with local distributor or agent without any experience in the field of business.

11. Transactions with local distributor or agent who insists on anonymity.

12. Transactions with local distributor or agent who refuses to sign company policy that the FCPA not be violated.

13. Transactions with local distributor or agent who appears not to have adequate facilities and staff to undertake task by effort versus by bribes.

§ 13.23   Text of the Foreign Corrupt Practices Act

(Selected Provisions)

Public Law 95–213, 91 Stat. 1494, Dec. 19, 1977 (amending The Securities Exchange Act of 1934, 15 U.S.C.A. §§ 78q(b), 78dd, 78ff(a) (1976)); as amended by Public Law 100–418, 102 Stat. 1107, Aug. 23, 1988; as amended by Public Law 105–366, Nov. 10, 1998 (International Anti-Bribery & Fair Competition Act)

15 U.S.C. § 78m(b)

Accounting Standards

* * *

(2)   Every issuer which has a class of securities registered pursuant to section 78*l* of this title and every issuer which is required to file reports pursuant to section 78o(d) of this title shall—

(A)   make and keep books, records, and accounts, which, in reasonable detail, accurately and fairly reflect the transactions and dispositions of the assets of the issuer; and

(B)   devise and maintain a system of internal accounting controls sufficient to provide reasonable assurances that—

(i)   transactions are executed in accordance with management's general or specific authorization;

(ii)   transactions are recorded as necessary (I) to permit preparation of financial statements in conformity with generally accepted accounting principles or any other criteria applicable to such statements, and (II) to maintain accountability for assets;

(iii)   access to assets is permitted only in accordance with management's general or specific authorization; and

(iv)   the recorded accountability for assets is compared with the existing assets at reasonable intervals and appropriate action is taken with respect to any differences.

* * *

15 U.S.C. § 78dd–1

Prohibited foreign trade practices by issuers

(a)   Prohibition. It shall be unlawful for any issuer which has a class of securities registered pursuant to section 78*l* of this title or which is required to file reports under section 78*o*(d) of this title, or for any officer, director, employee, or agent of such issuer or any stockholder thereof acting on behalf of such issuer, to make use of the mails or any means or instrumentality of interstate commerce corruptly in furtherance of an offer, payment, promise to pay, or authorization of the payment of any money, or offer, gift, promise to give, or authorization of the giving of anything of value to—

(1)   any foreign official for purposes of—

(A)(i)   influencing any act or decision of such foreign official in his official capacity, (ii) inducing such foreign official to do or omit to do any act in violation of the lawful duty of such official, or (iii) securing any improper advantage; or

(B)   inducing such foreign official to use his influence with a foreign government or instrumentality thereof to affect or influence any act or decision of such government or instrumentality,

in order to assist such issuer in obtaining or retaining business for or with, or directing business to, any person;

* * *

(3)   any person, while knowing that all or a portion of such money or thing of value will be offered, given, or promised, directly or indirectly, to any foreign official, to any foreign political party or official thereof, or to any candidate for foreign political office, for purposes of—

(A)(i)   influencing any act or decision of such foreign official, * * * in his or its official capacity, (ii) inducing such foreign official, * * * to do or omit to do any act in violation of the lawful duty of such foreign official, * * *, or (iii) securing any improper advantage; or

(B) inducing such foreign official * * * to use his or its influence with a foreign government or instrumentality thereof to affect or influence any act or decision of such government or instrumentality,

in order to assist such issuer in obtaining or retaining business for or with, or directing business to, any person.

(b) Exception for routine governmental action. Subsections (a) and (g) shall not apply to any facilitating or expediting payment to a foreign official, political party, or party official the purpose of which is to expedite or to secure the performance of a routine governmental action by a foreign official, political party, or party official.

(c) Affirmative defenses. It shall be an affirmative defense to actions under subsection (a) or (g) that—

(1) the payment, gift, offer, or promise of anything of value that was made, was lawful under the written laws and regulations of the foreign official's * * * country; or

(2) the payment, gift, offer, or promise of anything of value that was made, was a reasonable and bona fide expenditure, such as travel and lodging expenses, incurred by or on behalf of a foreign official * * * and was directly related to—

(A) the promotion, demonstration, or explanation of products or services; or

(B) the execution or performance of a contract with a foreign government or agency thereof.

(d) Guidelines by the Attorney General. Not later than one year after August 23, 1988, the Attorney General, after consultation with the Commission, the Secretary of Commerce, the United States Trade Representative, the Secretary of State, and the Secretary of the Treasury, and after obtaining the views of all interested persons through public notice and comment procedures, shall determine to what extent compliance with this section would be enhanced and the business community would be assisted by further clarification of the preceding provisions of this section and may, based on such determination and to the extent necessary and appropriate, issue—

(1) guidelines describing specific types of conduct, associated with common types of export sales arrangements and business contracts, which for purposes of the Department of Justice's present enforcement policy, the Attorney General determines would be in conformance with the preceding provisions of this section; and

(2) general precautionary procedures which issuers may use on a voluntary basis to conform their conduct to the Department of Justice's present enforcement policy regarding the preceding provisions of this section.

* * *

(e) Opinions of the Attorney General. (1) The Attorney General, after consultation with appropriate departments and agencies of the United States and after obtaining the views of all interested persons through public notice and comment procedures, shall establish a procedure to provide responses to specific inquiries by issuers concerning conformance of their conduct with the Department of Justice's present enforcement policy regarding the preceding provisions of this section. * * *

(f) Definitions. For purposes of this section:

(1)(A) The term "foreign official" means any officer or employee of a foreign government or any department, agency, or instrumentality thereof, or of a public international organization, or any person acting in an official capacity for or on behalf of any such government or department, agency, or instrumentality, or for or on behalf of any such public international organization.

(B) For purposes of subparagraph (A), the term "public international organization" means—

(i) an organization that is designated by Executive Order pursuant to section 1 of the International Organizations Immunities Act (22 U.S.C. § 288); or

(ii) any other international organization that is designated by the President by Executive order for the purposes of this section, effective as of the date of publication of such order in the Federal Register.

(2)(A) A person's state of mind is "knowing" with respect to conduct, a circumstance, or a result if—

(i) such person is aware that such person is engaging in such conduct, that such circumstance exists, or that such result is substantially certain to occur; or

(ii) such person has a firm belief that such circumstance exists or that such result is substantially certain to occur.

(B) When knowledge of the existence of a particular circumstance is required for an offense, such knowledge is established if a person is aware of a high probability of the existence of such circumstance, unless the person actually believes that such circumstance does not exist.

(3)(A) The term "routine governmental action" means only an action which is ordinarily and commonly performed by a foreign official in—

(i) obtaining permits, licenses, or other official documents to qualify a person to do business in a foreign country;

(ii) processing governmental papers, such as visas and work orders;

(iii) providing police protection, mail pick-up and delivery, or scheduling inspections associated with contract performance or inspections related to transit of goods across country;

(iv) providing phone service, power and water supply, loading and unloading cargo, or protecting perishable products or commodities from deterioration; or

(v) actions of a similar nature.

(B) The term "routine governmental action" does not include any decision by a foreign official whether, or on what terms, to award new business to or to continue business with a particular party, or any action taken by a foreign official involved in the decisionmaking process to encourage a decision to award new business to or continue business with a particular party.

(g) Alternative Jurisdiction

(1) It shall also be unlawful for any issuer organized under the laws of the United States, or a State, territory, possession, or commonwealth of the United States or a political subdivision thereof and which has a class of securities registered pursuant to section 12 of this title or which is required to file reports under section 15(d) of this title, or for any United States person that is an officer, director, employee, or agent of such issuer or a stockholder thereof acting on behalf of such issuer, to corruptly do any act outside the United States in furtherance of an offer, payment, promise to pay, or authorization of the payment of any money, or offer, gift, promise to give, or authorization of the giving of anything of value to any of the persons or entities set forth in paragraphs (1), (2), and (3) of this subsection (a) of this section for the purposes set forth therein, irrespective of whether such issuer or such officer, director, employee, agent, or stockholder makes use of the mails or any means or instrumentality of interstate commerce in furtherance of such offer, gift, payment, promise, or authorization.

(2) As used in this subsection, the term "United States person" means a national of the United States (as defined in section 101 of the Immigration and Nationality Act (8 U.S.C. § 1101)) or any corporation, partnership, association, joint-stock company, business trust, unincorporated organization, or sole proprietorship organized under the laws of the United States or any State, territory, possession, or commonwealth of the United States, or any political subdivision thereof.

15 U.S.C. § 78dd–2

Prohibited foreign trade practices by domestic concerns

(a) Prohibition. It shall be unlawful for any domestic concern, other than an issuer which is subject to section 78dd–1 of this title. [At this point, the language for the most part follows that of section 77dd–1, except injunctive relief is specifically allowed. Domestic concerns include individuals who are citizens, nationals or residents of the United States, or essentially any form of business with a principal place of business in the

United States, or organized in one of the United States, or a territory, possession or commonwealth of the United States.]

* * *

(g) Penalties

(1)(A) Any domestic concern that is not a natural person and that violates subsection (a) or (i) [alternative jurisdiction] of this section shall be fined not more than $2,000,000.

(B) Any domestic concern that is not a natural person and that violates subsection (a) or (i) of this section shall be subject to a civil penalty of not more than $10,000 imposed in an action brought by the Attorney General.

(2)(A) Any natural person that is an officer, director, employee, or agent of a domestic concern, or stockholder acting on behalf of such domestic concern, who willfully violates subsection (a) or (i) of this section shall be fined not more than $100,000 or imprisoned not more than 5 years, or both.

(B) Any natural person that is an officer, director, employee, or agent of a domestic concern, or stockholder acting on behalf of such domestic concern, who violates subsection (a) or (i) of this section shall be subject to a civil penalty of not more than $10,000 imposed in an action brought by the Attorney General.

(3) Whenever a fine is imposed under paragraph (2) upon any officer, director, employee, agent, or stockholder of a domestic concern, such fine may not be paid, directly or indirectly, by such domestic concern.

* * *

15 U.S.C. § 78dd–3

Prohibited foreign trade practices by persons other than issuers or domestic concerns

(a) Prohibition. It shall be unlawful for any person other than an issuer that is subject to section 30A of the Securities Exchange Act of 1934 or a domestic concern, (as defined in section 104 of this Act), or for any officer, director, employee, or agent of such person or any stockholder thereof acting on behalf of such person, while in the territory of the United States, corruptly to make use of the mails or any means or instrumentality of interstate commerce or to do any other act in furtherance of an offer, payment, promise to pay, or authorization of the payment of any money, or offer, gift, promise to give, or authorization of the giving of anything of value to—[At this point, the language follows that of active 78dd–1, except injunctive relief similar to that in section 78dd–2.]

* * *

(e) Penalties

(1)(A) Any juridical person that violates subsection (a) of this section shall be fined not more than $2,000,000.

(B)   Any juridical person that violates subsection (a) of this section shall be subject to a civil penalty of not more than $10,000 imposed in an action brought by the Attorney General.

(2)(A)   Any natural person who willfully violates subsection (a) of this section shall be fined not more than $100,000 or imprisoned not more than 5 years, or both.

(B)   Any natural person who violates subsection (a) of this section shall be subject to a civil penalty of not more than $10,000 imposed in an action brought by the Attorney General.

(3)   Whenever a fine is imposed under paragraph (2) upon any officer, director, employee, agent, or stockholder of a person, such fine may not be paid, directly or indirectly, by such person.

(f)   Definitions. For purposes of this section:

(1)   The term "person," when referring to an offender, means any natural person other than a. national of the United States (as defined in 8 U.S.C. § 1101) or any corporation, partnership, association, joint-stock company, business trust, unincorporated organization, or sole proprietorship organized under the law of a foreign nation or a political subdivision thereof.

* * *

15 U.S.C. § 78ff

Penalties

(a)   Willful violations; false and misleading statements. Any person who willfully violates any provision of this chapter (other than section 78dd–1 of this title), or any rule or regulation thereunder the violation of which is made unlawful or the observance of which is required under the terms of this chapter, or any person who willfully and knowingly makes, or causes to be made, any statement in any application, report, or document required to be filed under this chapter or any rule or regulation thereunder or any undertaking contained in a registration statement as provided in subsection (d) of section 78o of this title, or by any self-regulatory organization in connection with an application for membership or participation therein or to become associated with a member thereof, which statement was false or misleading with respect to any material fact, shall upon conviction be fined not more than $1,000,000, or imprisoned not more than 10 years, or both, except that when such person is a person other than a natural person, a fine not exceeding $2,500,000 may be imposed; but no person shall be subject to imprisonment under this section for the violation of any rule or regulation if he proves that he had no knowledge of such rule or regulation.

* * *

(c)   Violations by issuers, officers, directors, stockholders, employees, or agents of issuers

(1)(A)   Any issuer that violates subsection (a) or (g) of Section 30A of this title shall be fined not more than $2,000,000.

(B)   Any issuer that violates subsection (a) or (g) of Section 30A of this title shall be subject to a civil penalty of not more than $10,000 imposed in an action brought by the Commission.

(2)(A)   Any officer, director, employee, or agent of an issuer, or stockholder acting on behalf of such issuer, who willfully violates subsection (a) or (g) of Section 30A of this title shall be fined not more than $10,000, or imprisoned not more than 5 years, or both.

(B)   Any officer, director, employee, or agent of an issuer, or stockholder action on behalf of such issuer, who violates subsection (a) or (g) of Section 30A of this title shall be subject to a civil penalty of not more than $10,000 imposed in an action brought by the Commission.

(3)   Whenever a fine is imposed under paragraph (2) upon any officer, director, employee, agent or stockholder of an issuer, such fine may not be paid, directly or indirectly, by such issuer.

Chapter 14

UNILATERAL U.S. SECTION 301 TRADE SANCTIONS

Table of Sections

§ 14.1 Foreign Country Practices and U.S. Export Access

Although the U.S. was a strong supporter of the GATT from its inception in 1947, Section 301 reflects U.S. frustration with the multilateral methods and procedures of GATT 1947. It received hostile responses from United States trade partners, especially after the amendments to Section 301 implemented in 1988 through the Omnibus Trade and Competitiveness Act. It certainly created a bargaining chip as the U.S. pushed hard for the creation of the World Trade Organization, a goal it realized in 1995.

Section 301 of the Trade Act of 1974 (19 U.S.C. § 2411) is one of the most highly political remedies concerning United States trade relations. Basically, this section applies when United States rights or benefits under international trade agreements are at risk or when foreign nations engage in unjustifiable, unreasonable or discriminatory conduct. Thus Section 301 is primarily focused on the activities of foreign governments. Although it has been used to protect United States markets from foreign imports, Section 301 has been most notably applied to open up foreign markets to United States exports, investments and intellectual property rights. The focus has been on foreign market access for U.S. goods and services.

Most Section 301 proceedings have been resolved through negotiations leading to alteration of foreign country practices. Ultimately, if the President or United States Trade Representative (USTR) is not satisfied with any negotiated result in connection with a Section 301 complaint, the United States may undertake unilateral retaliatory trade measures. Unlike subsidy, dumping, and safeguard proceedings (see Chapters 4, 5 and 6), Section 301 of the Trade Act of 1974 has no origins in or other imprimatur of legitimacy from the GATT/WTO. The offenses under Section 301 are primarily subject to the authority of the United States Trade Representative as opposed to the President. The 1988 Act also introduced the concept of mandatory versus discretionary retaliation. Offenses for which retaliation is mandatory involve the breach of international agreements to which the United States is a party, and unjustifiable trade practices. The USTR has discretionary authority to retaliate under Section 301 regarding unreasonable or discriminatory practices of foreign countries.

The **unilateral** nature of Section 301 is thought by many to run counter to the multilateral approach to trade relations. Brazil lodged but did not actively pursue a GATT 1947 complaint about Section 301 during the Uruguay Round negotiations. Late in 1999, a panel of the World Trade Commission concluded that Section 301 was NOT inconsistent with U.S. obligations under the WTO (WTO/DS 152/1). The panel relied heavily on President Clinton's Congressionally approved statement that the U.S. would refrain from Section 301 retaliation until the WTO has ruled on disputes falling within its domain. Should some future U.S. administration fail to adhere to this policy (for example the Trump administration), the WTO panel indicated that Section 301 would violate the WTO Dispute Settlement Understanding.

§ 14.2 The Evolution of Section 301

The origins of Section 301 can be traced to a trade dispute between the United States and the European Community (now Union) during the 1960s. This dispute became known as "the Chicken War." Basically, United States chicken producers had mechanized and developed a large export market in the European Union. The Union sought to protect its smaller chicken producers and did so by establishing a minimum price for imported chicken. This had the effect of drastically curtailing United States exports into the European market.

At that time, there was no vehicle through which the United States growers could express their complaints over this practice. Nevertheless, the United States government sought to resolve the dispute through the nullification and impairment provisions of Article XXIII of the GATT 1947. These attempts failed and ultimately the United States imposed unilateral trade restraints upon European Union exports as a matter of compensation for the minimum import price program. In the Chicken War, the retaliatory tariffs concerned brandy, trucks and potato starch, including pick-up truck tariffs of 25% that endure to this day. These trade restraints, while arguably compensating the United States as a nation, did little to satisfy the chicken exporters. In other words, the remedy was not linked to the source of the complaint, a reality that remains in Section 301 law.

As the Chicken War was in progress, the Trade Expansion Act of 1962 was adopted. Section 252 of that Act specifically authorized the President to retaliate against foreign import restrictions imposed in breach of GATT obligations. Furthermore, the President was authorized to impose higher tariffs or other import restraints on the products of countries that established burdensome restraints upon U.S. exports of agricultural goods. The latter could be imposed regardless of whether the import restraints of the foreign country constituted a breach of the GATT. Section 252 of the Trade Expansion Act of 1962 thus preceded and anticipated Section 301 of the Trade Act of 1974.

The President exercised retaliatory authority under Section 252 only twice. Both cases involved the imposition of import restraints because of agricultural disputes. Between 1974 and 1979, the first of the private petitions for Section 301 action were considered. However the typical result was to refer the dispute to the GATT organization, which deliberated at length and effectively turned the disputes into issues for review during the Tokyo Round of GATT negotiations concluded in 1979. Congress was not happy with these results, and in the Trade Agreements Act of 1979 imposed a variety of time limitations in connection with Section 301 complaints. Congress also expanded the range of complaints that could be filed, and on balance sought to rejuvenate Section 301.

From 1979 through the 1980s, the number of Section 301 investigations initiated by private complaints increased considerably. Through the Trade and Tariff Act of 1984, Congress continued to seek to make Section 301 an effective trade remedy. Its availability for complaints in the field of intellectual property rights and trade involving services was made clear. Nevertheless, a significant number of these complaints were still being referred to the GATT and its remarkably slow dispute settlement procedures. Through the Omnibus Trade and Competitiveness Act of 1988, Congress expressed its displeasure with GATT 1947 as a dispute settlement forum. Congress amended the law to indicate that under appropriate circumstances Section 301 investigations and remedies could proceed notwithstanding the fact that GATT dispute settlement had not run its full course. At the same time, Congress switched the ultimate authority for determining Section 301 offenses and Section 301 remedies from the President to the United States Trade Representative.

The bottom line after all of these legislative efforts on the part of Congress to invigorate Section 301 is that it became a significant forum for opening up foreign markets to United States exports (see Section 14.8 below). This forum can be accessed by private initiative, as well as governmental action.

§ 14.3   The Impact of the WTO Dispute Settlement Understanding

United States membership in the World Trade Organization since 1995 has committed it to multilateral dispute settlement of disputes arising out of the numerous WTO agreements. If the dispute is covered by a WTO agreement, the United States is obliged to pursue remedies under the WTO Dispute Settlement Understanding (DSU), and almost always has done so. *See* Chapter 1.

Section 301 petitions falling within the scope of the WTO routinely trigger USTR complaints with the multilateral Dispute Settlement Body. The United States has been involved in more WTO disputes (as a complaining and responding party) than any other member country. The DSU creates procedures under which unilateral retaliation is restrained until the offending nation has failed to conform to a WTO panel or Appellate Body ruling. Retaliation is then authorized by the WTO in an amount equal to the damages incurred. *See* Section 1.14.

When a petition concerns subject matter not covered by a WTO agreement (media goods) or a country that is not a WTO member (Iran), Section 301 and its unilateral remedies remain in full force and effect.

In 2017 the Trump Administration self-initiated a broad Section 301 investigation of China's IP practices, including mandatory technology transfers (*see* Chapter 16), theft of IP and cybersecurity. Whether this investigation will trigger WTO dispute settlement will depend on an analysis of the coverage of these topics under TRIPs and related WTO law.

§ 14.4   Section 301—Mandatory versus Discretionary Offenses and Remedies

Section 301 of the Trade Act of 1974 vests in the United States Trade Representative the power to determine when the *rights* of the United States under any trade agreement are being denied, when foreign country practices are inconsistent with or otherwise denying the *benefits* to the United States of trade agreements, or foreign countries are engaged in unjustifiable practices that burden or restrict United States commerce. An affirmative finding by the USTR in connection with any of the above requires **mandatory** retaliation on the part of the United States "subject to Presidential direction."[1]

The USTR is not required to take action whenever the dispute has been adjudicated within the GATT/WTO and there has been a finding that United States rights under a trade agreement are not being denied, or that the foreign country practices under dispute are not in violation of nor impair the benefits of the United States under any trade agreement. In addition, the USTR does not have to take retaliatory action if he or she determines that the foreign country in question is taking satisfactory measures to grant the rights of the United States under a trade agreement, or has agreed to eliminate or phase out the practices that are in dispute. If this is not possible, but the foreign country agrees to provide the United States with compensatory trade benefits satisfactory to the USTR, no mandatory retaliation will take place. In extraordinary cases, the USTR need not undertake retaliatory action if that would have an adverse impact on the United States economy substantially out of proportion to the benefits of that, or would cause serious harm to the national security of the United States.[2]

Section 301 also authorizes the USTR to determine when foreign countries are engaged in unreasonable or discriminatory practices that burden or restrict United States commerce. If such findings are reached, the Trade Representative (subject to directives from the President) may decide to undertake retaliatory action.[3] Hence, these offenses do not require mandatory retaliation; they are **discretionary**.

With reference to both mandatory and discretionary actions under Section 301, the USTR is authorized to withdraw the benefits of trade agreements enjoyed by the foreign country engaging in the offending activities, impose tariffs or other import restrictions upon the goods of those nations, and enter into binding international

---

[1]   19 U.S.C.A. § 2411.

[2]   19 U.S.C.A. § 2411(a)(2).

[3]   19 U.S.C.A. § 2411(b).

agreements to eliminate or phase out the unfair practices or to provide the United States with compensatory trade benefits. If the dispute concerns services, and many Section 301 disputes have been focused upon services, the USTR may restrict any "service sector access authorization" under United States law. Presumably, for example, the USTR subject to presidential directives could deny access to foreign banks by withholding licenses from federal authorities. It is less clear, but appears possible, that the USTR could order state authorities to deny similar access to the services sector.[4]

One problem with Section 301 remedies is that they need not necessarily benefit those who have been injured by foreign country practices. Thus, for example, if the complaint concerns European Union export subsidies on wheat, the ultimate retaliatory action taken by the United States may involve the imposition of tariffs upon European wine. Similarly, if the dispute concerns the intellectual property rights afforded pharmaceuticals in Brazil, the ultimate Section 301 remedy may impose quotas or other trade restraints upon Brazilian hardwoods.

§ 14.5   Section 301—Statutory Definitions

The provisions of Section 301 are remarkably broad and open-ended in language. The statute therefore seeks to define with greater specificity some of the important terms involved. These definitions are found in Section 301(d) of the Trade Act of 1974.[5] One important definition provides an expansive interpretation of the appropriate international commerce to which Section 301 applies. For these purposes, commerce includes trade in goods and services, and foreign direct investment by United States persons with implications for trade in goods or services.

The statutory definitions of unreasonableness reviewed above were greatly expanded in 1988. This suggests that the most likely avenue of success under Section 301 is in pleading unreasonable practices. Foreign country practices are *"unreasonable"* if they are unfair and inequitable, regardless of whether they are in violation of or inconsistent with the international legal rights of the United States. Unreasonable practices include those which deny fair and equitable opportunities for the establishment of a business abroad, those which provide inadequate or ineffective protection of intellectual property rights, those which deny market opportunities as a result of systematic anticompetitive activities of private firms, and those which constitute export targeting (defined to mean any government scheme designed to assist its exporters in becoming more

---

4   19 U.S.C.A. § 2411(c)(2).

5   19 U.S.C.A. § 2411(d).

competitive). Unreasonable practices include those which constitute a persistent pattern of conduct that denies workers the right to associate, organize or bargain collectively. They also include practices which tolerate forced or compulsory labor, fail to provide a minimum working age for children, or fail to provide general standards on minimum wages, hours of work and occupational safety and health requirements.

However, Section 301(d) indicates that foreign country practices are not to be treated as unreasonable if the USTR determines that nation is taking action which demonstrates a significant and tangible advancement towards providing the rights and standards discussed above or that the practices in question are not inconsistent with the level of economic development of the foreign country. Where appropriate, the absence or presence of reciprocal opportunities in the United States for foreign nationals shall be taken into account in determining whether any particular practice is unreasonable.

It is important to bear in mind that this lengthy definition of unreasonable foreign country practices coincides with discretionary USTR action if such practices are found. The other discretionary category under Section 301 includes foreign country practices which are *"discriminatory."* Section 301(d) defines discriminatory as any practice which denies national or most favored nation treatment to United States goods, services or investment. The prohibition against *"unjustifiable"* foreign country practices is expanded by a definition which indicates that such practices must violate or be inconsistent with the international legal rights of the United States. These include those which deny national or most favored nation treatment, the right of establishment or the protection of intellectual property rights. Unjustifiable practices, if determined to exist by the USTR, mandate retaliatory action by the United States.

Perhaps the most critical difference in the Section 301(d) definitions of Section 301 offenses concerns "international legal rights". This is part of the definition of unjustifiable practices, but not found in connection with unreasonable or discriminatory practices. There is no requirement that unreasonable, discriminatory or unjustifiable practices violate or contradict any international agreement to which the United States is a party. Thus the international legal rights which must be breached in order to find an unjustifiable practice may turn upon the customary international law of trade.

§ 14.6 Section 301—Petitioning and Procedures

Section 302 of the Trade Act of 1974 permits any interested person to file a petition with the United States Trade Representative requesting action under Section 301. Complaints from U.S. industries have in fact driven most Section 301 proceedings, and they can be screened by the USTR before filing. The USTR is given 45 days within which to determine whether to initiate an investigation. Interested parties may include but are not limited to domestic companies and workers, representatives of consumer interests, U.S. exporters, and any industrial users of goods or services potentially affected by Section 301 actions.[6]

The Trade Representative's powers to initiate investigations under Section 301 appear to be completely discretionary. That is to say, if the USTR is not persuaded by the petition and supporting documents, no Section 301 procedures will be commenced. This is true for both mandatory and discretionary action under Section 301. However, if the USTR decides not to initiate an investigation, he or she must inform the petitioner of the reasons why and publish notice of that determination together with its reasons in the Federal Register.[7]

If the USTR decides to initiate an investigation under Section 301, he or she then publishes a summary of the petition and is required to provide an opportunity for the presentation of views including a public hearing. The USTR may self-initiate Section 301 investigations.[8] The USTR is not required to initiate any investigation if he or she determines that to do so would be detrimental to United States economic interests.[9]

Once an investigation under Section 301 is launched, either by petition or self-initiation, the USTR must consult with the foreign country alleged to have engaged in unfair trade practices. If a mutually acceptable solution is not reached, and the complaint concerns a breach of an international agreement to which the United States is a party, the USTR is obliged to commence dispute settlement procedures as provided for in that agreement.[10] WTO dispute settlement procedures are frequently invoked as a consequence.

The regulations which detail the procedures and conduct of investigations in connection with Section 301 are found at 15 C.F.R. § 2006 et seq. An interagency committee composed of staff from the Departments of State, Treasury, Commerce, Justice, Agriculture, Labor and the Council of Economic Advisors is involved in the

---

[6]   19 U.S.C.A. § 2411(d)(9).

[7]   19 U.S.C.A. § 2412(a).

[8]   19 U.S.C.A. § 2412(b).

[9]   19 U.S.C.A. § 2412(b).

[10]   19 U.S.C.A. § 2413(a).

decisionmaking under Section 301. This Committee is sometimes called the "Section 301 Committee" and its report and advice will be considered by the USTR in making Section 301 determinations. The input of this Committee does not diminish the discretion of the USTR in deciding whether to commence a Section 301 investigation.

Private Sector Petitions

When a petition is received from the private sector alleging a Section 301 offense, the USTR typically notifies the country that is the object of the complaint. That country may supply any relevant information it chooses. In the absence of such a response, the USTR is entitled to proceed on the basis of the "best information available."[11] This will often as a practical matter be the information submitted by the petitioner or otherwise derived from the Section 301 Committee or other independent sources. Thus the procedures utilized in Section 301 make it imperative that private petitioners properly document the nature of their complaint.

The rules require that a private petition for Section 301 action describe the petitioner's interest that is allegedly impacted by the foreign country practice about which the petitioner is complaining. If the complaint is based upon international agreements to which the United States is a party and the denial of rights thereunder, this must be clearly cited and documented. The petition must specifically identify the foreign country alleged to be engaging in a Section 301 offense. It must identify the specific product or service which is the subject of the complaint. Most importantly, the petition must show exactly how the practice in question is inconsistent with a trade agreement or is otherwise unjustifiable, unreasonable or discriminatory and that it burdens or restricts United States commerce. Lastly, the petitioner must indicate whether any other requests for relief under the Trade Act of 1974 or other United States law have been filed.

Once the USTR determines to initiate an investigation under Section 301, the petitioner has 30 days to submit a written request for a public hearing.[12] Any other interested person can also submit an application for such a hearing. Section 305 of the Trade Act of 1974 allows U.S. companies and other interested persons to essentially request of the USTR information necessary to substantiate a Section 301 complaint. Such requests have the practical effect of obliging the USTR to provide any such available information, and perhaps even to require the USTR to contact foreign governments in order to satisfy this request for information. Such

---

[11]   15 C.F.R. § 2006.4.

[12]   19 U.S.C.A. § 2414(b).

requests can amount to a kind of preliminary Section 301 investigation before formal investigations are initiated.[13]

§ 14.7   Section 301—USTR Determinations

Since the amendments of 1988, the USTR is required to make a determination of whether foreign country practices are actionable under Section 301 regardless of whether any retaliatory action is taken. For many years disputes concerning export subsidies, particularly export subsidies of the European Union, dominated Section 301 proceedings.[14] Whenever Section 301 complaints involve an alleged breach of United States benefits under an existing international agreement, such as the package of WTO agreements, the USTR must initiate the dispute settlement procedures of that agreement. This commitment has significantly reduced the number of unilateral trade remedies imposed since 1995 by the United States under Section 301.

The USTR is required to determine whether unfair practices have occurred under Section 301 within certain time limits. These are 12 months in cases involving export subsidies and practices not covered by trade agreements, 18 months in trade agreement cases other than subsidies unless the dispute settlement procedures of the relevant agreement are concluded earlier. Generally speaking, the USTR must determine whether a Section 301 offense has occurred in all instances where an investigation has been commenced within a 12-month deadline. These time limits could pressure the USTR into making a determination before the international dispute settlement procedures of the WTO or other trade agreements are concluded.[15]

§ 14.8   Section 301 in Action

Prior to the arrival of the WTO in 1995, there were a large number of complaints, investigations and unilateral U.S. remedies undertaken via Section 301 of the Trade Act of 1974. In some instances, complaints under Section 301 were dismissed by the President or USTR as without merit. In other instances, the complaints led to a GATT 1947 dispute settlement panel which decided against the position of the United States. This had the effect of terminating the Section 301 proceeding. Since 1995, many private

---

[13]   *See* 19 U.S.C.A. § 2411(d)(2).

[14]   *See* Bishop, The Multilateral Trade Negotiations, Subsidies and the Great Plains Wheat Case, 16 International Lawyer 339 (1982).

[15]   *See generally* Bliss, The Amendments to Section 301: An Overview and Suggested Strategies for Foreign Response, 20 Law & Policy of International Business 501 (1989).

Section 301 complaints to the USTR alleging trade agreement violations have triggered WTO dispute settlement proceedings.

Section 301 complaints are sometimes resolved to the satisfaction of those concerned through international negotiations. For example, in the early 1970s, a shipping company complained about the discriminatory practices of the government of Guatemala. The United States undertook negotiations with that government and reached an agreement satisfactory to the complainant.[16] In the same year, Canada had been imposing a quota on the importation of eggs from the United States. A trade association complaint to the USTR led to negotiations and an increase in this quota.[17] An exporter of thrown silk to Japan complained about the difficulties in obtaining import licenses for such silk. This complaint led to the threat of retaliatory action against Japanese-made silk products. However, subsequent negotiations resulted in an agreement which caused the Japanese to remove their import licensing restraints.[18]

A lengthy Section 301 complaint concerned European Union tariff restraints in connection with the export of Florida citrus products. In this case, the GATT (pre-WTO) did not provide an adequate dispute resolution forum, and the United States decided to retaliate by imposing substantial tariffs on European pasta products. Europe in turn retaliated with tariff increases on U.S. walnuts and lemons. Ultimately the United States and the European Union agreed to mutual elimination of the tariffs in question. This result did not really resolve the underlying dispute concerning the export of citrus products from the United States to Europe.[19]

One Section 301 complaint involved the Cigar Association of America. This complaint was against Japanese practices which had the effect of raising the price on U.S. cigars and making them difficult to market in Japan. International negotiations led to the formation of a GATT dispute settlement panel. However, this panel did not need to complete its task because the Japanese government agreed to substantial reductions in the relevant tariffs and retail requirements.[20]

While many Section 301 complaints have concerned export opportunities for United States firms, some have involved import competition. For example, a complaint was filed against Taiwanese subsidies of rice exports. International negotiations led to an

---

[16]   *See* 41 Fed.Reg. 26758 (1976).

[17]   41 Fed.Reg. 9430 (1976).

[18]   43 Fed.Reg. 8876 (1978).

[19]   *See* 50 Fed.Reg. 26143 (1985).

[20]   *See* 44 Fed.Reg. 19083 (1979), 44 Fed.Reg. 64938 (1979) and 46 Fed.Reg. 1388, 1389 (1981).

agreement limiting these subsidized exports such that the Section 301 complaint was withdrawn.[21]

The United States Trade Representative has occasionally commenced Section 301 proceedings on its own initiative. For example, the Brazilian "informatics policy" was challenged in this manner. This policy discriminated against foreign computer and high technology imports principally through local content requirements and the grant of exclusive monopolies. International negotiations, backed up by a threat by the United States to suspend the benefits for Brazil under the U.S. Generalized System of Tariff Preferences, eventually resulted in an opening of the Brazilian informatics market.[22]

Another self-initiated Section 301 proceeding concerned Korea's restraints on foreign insurance companies. Korean law was discriminatory and failed to give foreign companies the same benefits that domestic firms obtained. An international settlement was reached between the United States and Korea which gave access to that market for life and non-life insurance.[23] Korea was also the object of another Section 301 investigation concerning its intellectual property rights. These were thought to be inadequate, particularly in the copyright area. International negotiations led to the creation of a comprehensive copyright system for Korea, including coverage of computer software. Amendments were also made to the Korean patent laws and the country joined the Universal Copyright Convention.[24]

Several Section 301 disputes were resolved with Thailand. Following Section 301 success at opening the Japanese, Taiwanese and South Korean markets to United States cigarettes, the first dispute concerned Thai tariffs on U.S. cigarettes. United States producers petitioned under Section 301, and a lengthy investigation resulted in the formation of a GATT dispute settlement panel. This panel ruled against the tariffs and Thailand removed them.[25] A second Section 301 complaint by the International Intellectual Property Alliance and others led to an investigation focused on Thai piracy of audio and video cassettes. A substantial Thai industry had developed around such activities. The USTR threatened removal of Thailand's GSP duty free tariff entry benefits and the imposition of

---

[21]   See 48 Fed.Reg. 56289 (1983), 49 Fed.Reg. 10761 (1984).

[22]   See 51 Fed.Reg. 35993.

[23]   See 51 Fed.Reg. 29443.

[24]   See 51 Fed.Reg. 29445.

[25]   55 Fed.Reg. 49724 (USTR 1990).

a total U.S. barrier to Thai imports. Thailand capitulated and announced copyright reforms targeted at cassette piracy.[26]

A longstanding dispute between the United States and Japan concerning semiconductor products resulted in a Section 301 complaint in the late 1980s. The essence of the complaint was that a prior agreement concerning trade in such products between the two nations had been breached and therefore the United States intended to impose tariffs on certain imports from Japan.[27] The United States argued that Japan had not opened up its market sufficiently to foreign semiconductor manufacturers and had not avoided dumping of Japanese-made semiconductors in various markets around the world. Thus the heart of this complaint was that the benefits of an international agreement previously made were being denied to the United States and that this constituted a burden or restraint on U.S. commerce. The United States did impose additional duties on Japanese data processing machines, rotary drills and color television sets. However, these duties were suspended when the USTR found improved compliance by the Japanese with the semiconductor agreement.[28]

Section 307 of the Trade and Tariff Act of 1984 focuses specifically on export performance requirements created by foreign countries. Such requirements are thought by many United States investors to be unreasonable. Section 307 requires the USTR to enter into consultations with any foreign country imposing export performance requirements in an effort to seek to alleviate them when they adversely the economic interests of the United States. If such consultations do not result in a settlement, the USTR is authorized to impose import restraints on the products or services of the country in question.[29] In one instance, for example, the USTR was able to successfully negotiate away export performance requirements maintained by the Taiwanese relative to automobiles.[30]

The Telecommunications Trade Act of 1988[31] focuses upon foreign market opportunities in the telecommunication field. It is integrated into Section 301 procedures and administrative determinations. In undertaking retaliation, however, the USTR is directed to target telecommunications industry exports to the U.S. unless other action would be more effective in opening up foreign export markets. Section 1374 of the 1988 Act requires the USTR to

---

[26]   56 Fed.Reg. 67114 (USTR 1991).
[27]   See 52 Fed.Reg. 13412 (1987).
[28]   See 52 Fed.Reg. 22693 (1987).
[29]   See 19 U.S.C.A. § 2112(g)(3).
[30]   See 51 Fed.Reg. 41558.
[31]   Pub.L. 100–418.

identify priority countries whose practices cause the greatest telecommunications trade barriers. South Korea and the European Union were so identified in 1989. Ensuing negotiations resulted in a market-opening telecommunications agreement with South Korea and the European Union.

In the fall of 1991, the USTR initiated a prominent investigation of restrictive trade practices of the People's Republic of China. This investigation was undertaken in part to mitigate Congressional frustration over President Bush's continued willingness to grant most-favored-nation tariff status to Chinese goods despite record U.S. trade deficits with the PRC (then second only to Japan). The Section 301 investigation focused upon PRC import quotas, prohibitions and licensing procedures, and PRC technical barriers to trade (e.g., standards, testing and certification requirements). It also challenged the failure to publish PRC laws, regulations, judicial decisions and administrative rulings relating to import restraints. Additional discussions regarding PRC tariffs (ranging up to 200 percent) and import taxes were held. The main thrust of the proceeding was to open up China's markets to U.S. exports.

Since China was not a member of the GATT 1947, and in spite of U.S. bilateral trade agreements with the PRC, the USTR proceeded with this investigation on an unfair practices' basis. This meant that no trade agreement dispute settlement procedures were triggered. In October of 1992 the United States and China signed a memorandum of understanding that narrowly avoided massive, unilateral Section 301 trade sanctions. The People's Republic agreed to phase out by the end of 1977 numerous nontariff trade barriers, including import licenses, quotas and bans as well as regulatory restraints. The removal of these barriers improved U.S. export possibilities for telecommunications equipment, airplanes, machinery, agricultural goods, electrical appliances, computers, auto parts and pharmaceuticals. Furthermore, China promised to undertake a series of significant tariff cuts.

China's import-substitution regulations and policies were eliminated. In particular, the PRC may not condition entry into its market upon technology transfers. All laws, regulations, policies and decrees dealing with China's import and export system will be published on a regular basis and no such rules can be enforced unless they have been made readily available to foreign traders and governments. The goal is complete "transparency" of PRC trade law and an end to the use of secret internal directives. For its part, the United States committed itself to full GATT/WTO membership for the PRC, which was finally realized in 2001.

§ 14.9   Text of Section 301 (19 U.S.C. § 2411)

(a)   Mandatory action

(1)   If the United States Trade Representative determines under section 2414(a)(1) of this title that—

(A)   the rights of the United States under any trade agreement are being denied; or

(B)   an act, policy, or practice of a foreign country—

(i)   violates, or is inconsistent with, the provisions of, or otherwise denies benefits to the United States under, any trade agreement, or

(ii)   is unjustifiable and burdens or restricts United States commerce;

the Trade Representative shall take action authorized in subsection (c) of this section, subject to the specific direction, if any, of the President regarding any such action, and shall take all other appropriate and feasible action within the power of the President that the President may direct the Trade Representative to take under this subsection, to enforce such rights or to obtain the elimination of such act, policy, or practice. Actions may be taken that are within the power of the President with respect to trade in any goods or services, or with respect to any other area of pertinent relations with the foreign country.

(2)   The Trade Representative is not required to take action under paragraph (1) in any case in which—

(A)   the Dispute Settlement Body (as defined in section 3531(5) of this title) has adopted a report, or a ruling issued under the formal dispute settlement proceeding provided under any other trade agreement finds, that—

(i)   the rights of the United States under a trade agreement are not being denied, or

(ii)   the act, policy, or practice—

(I)   is not a violation of, or inconsistent with, the rights of the United States, or

(II)   does not deny, nullify, or impair benefits to the United States under any trade agreement; or

(B)   the Trade Representative finds that—

(i)   the foreign country is taking satisfactory measures to grant the rights of the United States under a trade agreement,

(ii)   the foreign country has—

(I)   agreed to eliminate or phase out the act, policy, or practice, or

(II) agreed to an imminent solution to the burden or restriction on United States commerce that is satisfactory to the Trade Representative,

(iii) it is impossible for the foreign country to achieve the results described in clause (i) or (ii), as appropriate, but the foreign country agrees to provide to the United States compensatory trade benefits that are satisfactory to the Trade Representative,

(iv) in extraordinary cases, where the taking of action under this subsection would have an adverse impact on the United States economy substantially out of proportion to the benefits of such action, taking into account the impact of not taking such action on the credibility of the provisions of this subchapter, or

(v) the taking of action under this subsection would cause serious harm to the national security of the United States.

(3) Any action taken under paragraph (1) to eliminate an act, policy, or practice shall be devised so as to affect goods or services of the foreign country in an amount that is equivalent in value to the burden or restriction being imposed by that country on United States commerce.

(b) Discretionary action

If the Trade Representative determines under section 2414(a)(1) of this title that—

(1) an act, policy, or practice of a foreign country is unreasonable or discriminatory and burdens or restricts United States commerce, and

(2) action by the United States is appropriate, the Trade Representative shall take all appropriate and feasible action authorized under subsection (c) of this section, subject to the specific direction, if any, of the President regarding any such action, and all other appropriate and feasible action within the power of the President that the President may direct the Trade Representative to take under this subsection, to obtain the elimination of that act, policy, or practice. Actions may be taken that are within the power of the President with respect to trade in any goods or services, or with respect to any other area of pertinent relations with the foreign country.

(c) Scope of authority

(1) For purposes of carrying out the provisions of subsection (a) or (b) of this section, the Trade Representative is authorized to—

(A) suspend, withdraw, or prevent the application of, benefits of trade agreement concessions to carry out a trade agreement with the foreign country referred to in such subsection;

(B) impose duties or other import restrictions on the goods of, and, notwithstanding any other provision of law, fees or restrictions on the services of, such foreign country for such time as the Trade Representative determines appropriate;

(C) in a case in which the act, policy, or practice also fails to meet the eligibility criteria for receiving duty-free treatment under subsections (b) and

(c) of section 2462 of this title, subsections (b) and (c) of section 2702 of this title, or subsections (c) and (d) of section 3202 of this title, withdraw, limit, or suspend such treatment under such provisions, notwithstanding the provisions of subsection (a)(3) of this section; or

(D) enter into binding agreements with such foreign country that commit such foreign country to—

    (i) eliminate, or phase out, the act, policy, or practice that is the subject of the action to be taken under subsection (a) or (b) of this section,

    (ii) eliminate any burden or restriction on United States commerce resulting from such act, policy, or practice, or

    (iii) provide the United States with compensatory trade benefits that—

        (I) are satisfactory to the Trade Representative, and

        (II) meet the requirements of paragraph (4).

(2)

(A) Notwithstanding any other provision of law governing any service sector access authorization, and in addition to the authority conferred in paragraph (1), the Trade Representative may, for purposes of carrying out the provisions of subsection (a) or (b) of this section—

    (i) restrict, in the manner and to the extent the Trade Representative determines appropriate, the terms and conditions of any such authorization, or

    (ii) deny the issuance of any such authorization.

(B) Actions described in subparagraph (A) may only be taken under this section with respect to service sector access authorizations granted, or applications therefor pending, on or after the date on which—

    (i) a petition is filed under section 2412(a) of this title, or

    (ii) a determination to initiate an investigation is made by the Trade Representative under section 2412(b) of this title.

(C) Before the Trade Representative takes any action under this section involving the imposition of fees or other restrictions on the services of a foreign country, the Trade Representative shall, if the services involved are subject to regulation by any agency of the Federal Government or of any State, consult, as appropriate, with the head of the agency concerned.

(3) The actions the Trade Representative is authorized to take under subsection (a) or (b) of this section may be taken against any goods or economic sector—

(A) on a nondiscriminatory basis or solely against the foreign country described in such subsection, and

(B) without regard to whether or not such goods or economic sector were involved in the act, policy, or practice that is the subject of such action.

(4) Any trade agreement described in paragraph (1)(D)(iii) shall provide compensatory trade benefits that benefit the economic sector which includes the domestic industry that would benefit from the elimination of the act, policy, or practice that is the subject of the action to be taken under subsection (a) or (b) of this section, or benefit the economic sector as closely related as possible to such economic sector, unless—

(A) the provision of such trade benefits is not feasible, or

(B) trade benefits that benefit any other economic sector would be more satisfactory than such trade benefits.

(5) If the Trade Representative determines that actions to be taken under subsection (a) or (b) of this section are to be in the form of import restrictions, the Trade Representative shall—

(A) give preference to the imposition of duties over the imposition of other import restrictions, and

(B) if an import restriction other than a duty is imposed, consider substituting, on an incremental basis, an equivalent duty for such other import restriction.

(6) Any action taken by the Trade Representative under this section with respect to export targeting shall, to the extent possible, reflect the full benefit level of the export targeting to the beneficiary over the period during which the action taken has an effect.

(d) Definitions and special rules

For purposes of this subchapter—

(1) The term "commerce" includes, but is not limited to—

(A) services (including transfers of information) associated with international trade, whether or not such services are related to specific goods, and

(B) foreign direct investment by United States persons with implications for trade in goods or services.

(2) An act, policy, or practice of a foreign country that burdens or restricts United States commerce may include the provision, directly or indirectly, by that foreign country of subsidies for the construction of vessels used in the commercial transportation by water of goods between foreign countries and the United States.

(3)

(A) An act, policy, or practice is unreasonable if the act, policy, or practice, while not necessarily in violation of, or inconsistent with, the international legal rights of the United States, is otherwise unfair and inequitable.

(B) Acts, policies, and practices that are unreasonable include, but are not limited to, any act, policy, or practice, or any combination of acts, policies, or practices, which—

(i)   denies fair and equitable—

(I) opportunities for the establishment of an enterprise,

(II) provision of adequate and effective protection of intellectual property rights notwithstanding the fact that the foreign country may be in compliance with the specific obligations of the Agreement on Trade-Related Aspects of Intellectual Property Rights referred to in section 3511(d)(15) of this title,

(III) nondiscriminatory market access opportunities for United States persons that rely upon intellectual property protection, or

(IV) market opportunities, including the toleration by a foreign government of systematic anticompetitive activities by enterprises or among enterprises in the foreign country that have the effect of restricting, on a basis that is inconsistent with commercial considerations, access of United States goods or services to a foreign market,

(ii)   constitutes export targeting, or

(iii)   constitutes a persistent pattern of conduct that—

(I)   denies workers the right of association,

(II)   denies workers the right to organize and bargain collectively,

(III) permits any form of forced or compulsory labor,

(IV) fails to provide a minimum age for the employment of children, or

(V) fails to provide standards for minimum wages, hours of work, and occupational safety and health of workers.

(C)

(i) Acts, policies, and practices of a foreign country described in subparagraph (B)(iii) shall not be treated as being unreasonable if the Trade Representative determines that—

(I) the foreign country has taken, or is taking, actions that demonstrate a significant and tangible overall advancement in providing throughout the foreign country (including any designated zone within the foreign country) the rights and other standards described in the subclauses of subparagraph (B)(iii), or

(II) such acts, policies, and practices are not inconsistent with the level of economic development of the foreign country.

(ii) The Trade Representative shall publish in the Federal Register any determination made under clause (i), together with a description of the facts on which such determination is based.

(D) For purposes of determining whether any act, policy, or practice is unreasonable, reciprocal opportunities in the United States for foreign nationals and firms shall be taken into account, to the extent appropriate.

(E) The term "export targeting" means any government plan or scheme consisting of a combination of coordinated actions (whether carried out severally or jointly) that are bestowed on a specific enterprise, industry, or group thereof, the effect of which is to assist the enterprise, industry, or group to become more competitive in the export of a class or kind of merchandise.

(F)

(i) For the purposes of subparagraph (B)(i)(II), adequate and effective protection of intellectual property rights includes adequate and effective means under the laws of the foreign country for persons who are not citizens or nationals of such country to secure, exercise, and enforce rights and enjoy commercial benefits relating to patents, trademarks, copyrights and related rights, mask works, trade secrets, and plant breeder's rights.

(ii) For purposes of subparagraph (B)(i)(IV), the denial of fair and equitable nondiscriminatory market access opportunities includes restrictions on market access related to the use, exploitation, or enjoyment of commercial benefits derived from exercising intellectual property rights in protected works or fixations or products embodying protected works.

(4)

(A) An act, policy, or practice is unjustifiable if the act, policy, or practice is in violation of, or inconsistent with, the international legal rights of the United States.

(B) Acts, policies, and practices that are unjustifiable include, but are not limited to, any act, policy, or practice described in subparagraph (A) which denies national or most-favored-nation treatment or the right of establishment or protection of intellectual property rights.

(5) Acts, policies, and practices that are discriminatory include, when appropriate, any act, policy, and practice which denies national or most-favored-nation treatment to United States goods, services, or investment.

(6) The term "service sector access authorization" means any license, permit, order, or other authorization, issued under the authority of Federal law, that permits a foreign supplier of services access to the United States market in a service sector concerned.

(7) The term "foreign country" includes any foreign instrumentality. Any possession or territory of a foreign country that is administered separately for customs purposes shall be treated as a separate foreign country.

(8) The term "Trade Representative" means the United States Trade Representative.

(9) The term "interested persons", only for purposes of sections 2412(a)(4)(B), 2414(b)(1)(A), 2416(c)(2), and 2417(a)(2) of this title, includes, but is not limited to, domestic firms and workers, representatives of consumer interests, United States product exporters, and any industrial user of any goods or services that may be affected by actions taken under subsection (a) or (b) of this section.

Part Four

TECHNOLOGY TRANSFERS ACROSS BORDERS

Chapter 15

TECHNOLOGY TRANSFERS ACROSS BORDERS

Table of Sections

This chapter focuses on lawful technology transfers, including a summary of the acquisition of intellectual property rights around the globe. Transfers of IP rights via franchising, and patent and know-how licensing, are reviewed, along with the regulation of such transfers. Such transfers are massive. In a recent year, the United States paid over $33 billion in technology royalties and license fees, receiving that year over $89 billion. Japan is the only other country to have received more than it paid in technology transfer monies. Singapore, Canada, South Korea and China typically pay substantially more for technology than they receive.

Issues surrounding the transfer of knowledge across national borders have provoked intense discussions that continue unabated. At the core is the desire of third world countries (often advanced developing countries like Brazil, South Korea, China and India) to obtain protected information quickly and affordably irrespective of the proprietary rights and profit motives of current holders (usually persons from the most developed countries). Capital intensive production processes (e.g., robot production of automobiles) are increasingly of interest. Smaller developing countries often want production processes which maximize uses of abundant, inexpensive labor but which result in products that are competitive in the international marketplace.

MNEs may be willing to share (by way of license or sale) a good deal of proprietary information, but are reluctant to part with their "core or leading edge technologies." This reluctance is understandable. A vast amount of technology is transferred illegally around the world by pirates and counterfeiters. That subject is covered in Chapter 8.

Among the industrialized countries, efforts often occur to acquire (even by way of stealing or hacking) "leading edge" technology. One example involved attempted theft of IBM computer technology by Japanese companies ultimately caught by the F.B.I. In the United States, the Office of Export Administration uses the export license procedure to control strategic technological "diversions." But falsification of licensing documents by prominent Norwegian and Japanese companies allowed the Soviets to obtain the technology for making vastly quieter submarine propellers. In the ensuing scandal, "anti-Toshiba" trade sanctions were adopted in the U.S. Leading Japanese executives resigned their positions, which is considered the highest form of apology in Japanese business circles.

The predominant vehicle for controlling technology transfers across national borders is the "license" or "franchise" contract. Some $180 billion in licensing royalties flow annually across borders. The holder of a patent, copyright or trademark in one country first acquires the legally protected right to the same in another country. With few exceptions, IP rights are national in origin, products of territorial domestic regimes. This makes the acquisition of IP rights around the globe remarkably expensive.

Once acquired, the holder then licenses that right, usually for a fee known as royalty, to a person in the other country. Thus, the licensor typically conveys to the licensee rights to make, use or sell the technology. The very sharing of intellectual property rights across borders raises a risk that proprietary control of the technology may be lost or, at a minimum, that a competitor will be created. For these reasons, international licensing agreements are complex legal documents that need to be carefully negotiated and drafted.

PART A

TRADEMARKS AND FRANCHISING

§ 15.1   Franchising Abroad

Franchising constitutes a rapidly expanding form of doing business abroad. Most franchisors have established fairly standard contracts and business formulae which are utilized in their home markets, and receive counsel on the myriad of laws relevant to their domestic business operations. Approaches to developing, defining and managing franchise relationships that have worked domestically may not work abroad. For example, agreements authorizing development of multiple locations within a given territory and, possibly, sub-franchising by a master franchisee are often used overseas while infrequent in the United States.

International franchising confronts the attorney with the need to research and evaluate a broad range of foreign laws which may apply in any particular jurisdiction. Such laws tend to focus on placing equity and control in the hands of local individuals and on regulating the franchise agreement to benefit the franchisees. In addition, counsel should be sensitive to the cultural impact of foreign franchising. For example, the appearance of a franchise building or trademark symbol may conflict in a foreign setting with traditional architectural forms (such as in European cities) or nationalist feelings hostile to the appearance of foreign trademarks on franchised products (such as in India or Mexico). Cultural conflicts can diminish the value of international franchises. To anticipate and solve legal and cultural problems, foreign counsel is often chosen to assist in the task of franchising abroad.

This chapter explores some of the concerns a franchisor or prospective franchisee may encounter in opting for, negotiating, drafting or enforcing an international franchise agreement. Although patents, copyrights and trademarks may all be involved in international franchising, trademark licensing is at the core of most international franchise agreements. Many rightly consider franchising to be a U.S. invention, but foreigners have rapidly been developing international franchising systems. Thus, while the primary focus in this chapter is on the problems of United States franchisors who intend to go abroad, additional coverage is given to United States law relevant to franchising.

§ 15.2   International Trademark Protection

Virtually all countries offer some legal protection to trademarks, even when they do not have trademark registration systems. Trademark rights derived from the use of marks on goods in commerce have long been recognized at common law and remain so today in countries as diverse as the United States and the United Arab Emirates. The latter nation, for example, had no trademark registration law in 1986, but this did not prevent McDonald's from obtaining an injunction against a local business using its famous name and golden arches without authorization.[1] However, obtaining international trademark protection normally involves separate registration under the law of each nation. Over three million trademarks are registered around the globe each year.

In the United States, trademarks are protected at common law and by state and federal registrations. Federal registration is permitted by the U.S. Trademark Office for all marks capable of distinguishing the goods on which they appear from other goods.[2] Unless the mark falls within a category of forbidden registrations (e.g., those that offend socialist morality in the People's Republic of China), a mark becomes valid for a term of years following registration.

In some countries (like the U.S. prior to 1989), marks must be used on goods before registration. In others, use is not required and speculative registration of marks can occur. It is said that ESSO was obliged to purchase trademark rights from such a speculator when it switched to EXXON in its search for the perfect global trademark. Since 1989, United States law has allowed applications when there is a bona fide intent to use a trademark within 12 months and, if there is good cause for the delay in actual usage, up to 24 additional months.[3] Such filings in effect reserve the mark for the applicant. The

---

[1]   Case No. 823/85. *See* 76 Trademark Reports 356 (1986).

[2]   15 U.S.C.A. § 1052.

[3]   15 U.S.C.A. § 1051(b).

emphasis on bona fide intent and good cause represent an attempt to control any speculative use of U.S. trademark registrations.

The scope of trademark protection may differ substantially from country to country. Under U.S. federal trademark law, injunctions, damages and seizures of goods by customs officials may follow infringement. Other jurisdictions may provide similar remedies on their law books, but offer little practical enforcement. Thus, trademark registration is no guarantee against trademark piracy. A pair of blue jeans labeled "Levi Strauss made in San Francisco" may have been counterfeited in Israel or Paraguay without the knowledge or consent of Levi Strauss and in spite of its trademark registrations in those countries. Trademark counterfeiting is not just a third world problem, as any visitor to a United States "flea market" can tell. Congress created criminal offenses and private treble damages remedies for the first time in the Trademark Counterfeiting Act of 1984.

In many countries trademarks (appearing on goods) may be distinguished from "service marks" used by providers of services (e.g., the Law Store), "trade names" (business names), "collective marks" (marks used by a group or organization), and "certificate marks" (marks which certify a certain quality, origin, or other fact). Although national trademark schemes differ, it can be said generally that a valid trademark (e.g., a mark not "canceled," "renounced," "abandoned," "waived" or "generic") will be protected against infringing use. A trademark can be valid in one country (ASPIRIN brand tablets in Canada), but invalid because generic in another (BAYER brand aspirin in the United States).

Unlike patents and copyrights, trademarks may be renewed in perpetuity. A valid mark may be licensed, perhaps to a "registered user" or it may be assigned, in some cases only with the sale of the goodwill of a business. A growing example of international licensing of trademarks can be found in franchise agreements taken abroad. And national trademark law sometimes accompanies international licensing. The principal U.S. trademark law, the Lanham Act of 1946, has been construed to apply extraterritorially (much like the Sherman Antitrust Act) to foreign licensees engaging in deceptive practices.[4] Foreigners who seek a registration may be required to prove a prior and valid "home registration," and a new registration in another country may not have an existence "independent" of the continuing validity of the home country registration. Foreigners are

---

[4]   *See especially Scotch Whiskey Association v. Barton Distilling Co.*, 489 F.2d 809 (7th Cir.1973).

often assisted in their registration efforts by international and regional trademark treaties.

The WTO TRIPs Agreement (see Section 1.11) supports common approaches to trademark rights, including recognition of service marks, a ban on linking foreign marks with local marks, a prohibition of compulsory trademark licensing, and general re-affirmation of the Paris Convention (see Section 15.8).

§ 15.3   Quality Controls in Franchising

Because franchising links trademarks with business attributes, there is a broad duty in the law for the franchisor to maintain quality controls over the franchisee, particularly in the business format franchise system. Any failure of the franchisor to maintain such quality controls could cause the trademark in question to be abandoned and lost to the franchisor.[5] In order to maintain adequate quality controls, the franchisor must typically police the operations of the franchisee.[6]

Broadly speaking, the duty to maintain quality controls arises because a trademark is a source symbol. The public is entitled to rely upon that source symbol in making its purchasing decisions so as to obtain consistent product quality and attributes. International franchisors operating at a distance from their franchisees must be especially concerned with quality controls. On the other hand, excessive control or the public appearance of such control may give rise to an agency relationship between the franchisor and the franchisee. Such a relationship could be used to establish franchisor liability for franchisee conduct, including international product and other tort liabilities.[7] It may be possible to minimize these risks through disclaimer or indemnification clauses in the franchise agreement.

§ 15.4   Copyright Protection in Franchising

Although franchising primarily focuses upon trademarks and trademark licensing, the use of copyrights frequently parallels such activity. For example, the designs and logos of the franchisor may be copyrighted, and certainly its instruction manual and other such written communications to franchisees should be copyrighted. These copyrights benefit in many countries from the Universal Copyright Convention (UCC) of 1952 and the Berne Convention of 1886. The

---

[5]   *See, e.g., Yamamoto & Co. v. Victor United, Inc.,* 219 U.S.P.Q. 968 (C.D.Cal.1982).

[6]   *See Dawn Donut Co. v. Hart's Food Stores, Inc.,* 267 F.2d 358 (2d Cir.1959).

[7]   *See* Hanson, The Franchising Dilemma: Franchisor Liability for Actions of a Local Franchisee, 19 N.C.Central L.J. 190 (1991).

United States now adheres to both of these conventions. Under the UCC, copyright holders receive national treatment, translation rights (subject to compulsory license) and other benefits. This convention will excuse any national registration requirement provided a notice of a claim of copyright is adequately given. However, in the United States, a reservation was made such that registration of foreign copyrights is required if the only convention under which foreigners are seeking such protection is the Universal Copyright Convention of 1952.

If the foreigner comes from a nation which adheres to the Berne Convention, national treatment and a release from U.S. registration formalities is obtained. The Berne Convention permits local copyright protection independent of protection granted in the country of origin and does not require copyright notice. Prior to 1987, most United States copyright holders acquired Berne Convention benefits by simultaneously publishing their works in Canada, a member country. Since 1987 the United States has ratified the Berne Convention, including an ambiguous adherence to its provisions on "moral rights" (rights of "integrity" and "paternity") for artists and authors. This has the practical effect of eliminating registration requirements for foreign copyright holders. It also extends United States copyright relations to approximately 25 new nations.

§ 15.5   Protection of Franchise Trade Secrets

Franchise formulae often involve utilization of trade secrets. This may range from recipes and cooking techniques to customer lists, pricing formulas, market data or bookkeeping procedures. It is extremely difficult to protect such trade secrets under United States law. The first problem arises from the concept of what is a trade secret. Generally speaking, abstract ideas or business practices which do not involve an element of novelty are not considered trade secrets.[8] Even if franchise trade secrets are involved, maintaining such secrets can be difficult given the wide number of persons who may have access to the confidential information. Even though the franchisees may promise to maintain such secrets, once released into the business public there may not be an effective way to recapture the secret or remedy the harm.[9]

The duty not to disclose trade secrets should be extended to employees of the franchisee. This can be done by permitting dissemination only on a need-to-know basis. However, it may be impossible not to permit certain employees from the knowledge of

---

[8]   *See Kewanee Oil Co. v. Bicron Corp.*, 416 U.S. 470, 94 S.Ct. 1879, 40 L.Ed.2d 315 (1974).

[9]   *See Smith v. Dravo Corp.*, 203 F.2d 369 (7th Cir.1953).

cooking procedures or recipes, for example. Once again the remedies and efforts to recapture the secret are likely to be inadequate.[10] Terminated employees and terminated franchisees are another fertile source of the loss of trade secrets. Tort remedies employing misappropriation theories may prevent the utilization or disclosure by such persons of trade secrets where there is a possibility of competition with the franchisor.[11] Damages are generally viewed as an inadequate remedy in the trade secret field because the harm of the loss of the secret is irreparable. *See* Section 15.16.

§ 15.6 The Franchise Agreement, U.S. Franchising

International franchising raises a host of legal issues under intellectual property, antitrust, tax, licensing and other laws. The significance of these issues is magnified by the rapid growth of international franchising. Hundreds of U.S. companies have, in total, tens of thousands of foreign franchises. Nearly 70 percent of these franchisors started in Canada, with Japan and Britain following. Some United States investors have found franchising the least risky and most popular way to enter Eastern Europe. But franchising is not just a United States export. Many foreign franchisors have entered the U.S. market.

Most franchisors have standard contracts which are used in their home markets and receive counsel on the myriad of laws relevant to their business operations. Such contracts need to be revised and adapted to international franchising without significantly altering the franchisor's successful business formula. Franchise fees and royalties must be specified, the provision of services, training, and control by the franchisor detailed, the term and area of the franchise negotiated ("master franchises" conveying rights in an entire country or region are common in international franchise agreements), accounting procedures agreed upon, business standards and advertising selected, insurance obtained, taxes and other liabilities allocated, default and dispute settlement procedures decided. At the heart of all franchise agreements lies a trademark licensing clause conveying local trademark rights of the franchisor to the franchisee in return for royalty payments.

Franchising in the United States

Franchising is an important sector in the United States economy. Thousands of franchisors have created and administer franchise systems throughout the nation. U.S. franchisees number in

---

[10] *See Shatterproof Glass Corp. v. Guardian Glass Co.*, 322 F.Supp. 854 (E.D.Mich.1970) *affirmed* 462 F.2d 1115 (6th Cir.1972).

[11] *See FMC Corp. v. Taiwan Tainan Giant Industrial Co.*, 730 F.2d 61 (2d Cir.1984).

the hundreds of thousands. These franchisees are typically independent business persons, and their local franchise outlets employ millions of people. It has been estimated that approximately one-third of all retail sales in the United States take place through franchised outlets. Just as U.S. franchisors have found franchising particularly effective for market penetration abroad, Canadian, European and Japanese companies are increasingly penetrating the U.S. market through franchising.

Franchising is a business technique that permits rapid and flexible penetration of markets, growth and capital development. In the United States, there are traditional distinctions between product franchises and business format franchises. Product franchises involve manufacturers who actually produce the goods that are distributed through franchise agreements. For example, ice cream stores, soft drink bottling companies and gasoline retailers are often the subject of product franchises. Business format franchises are more common. These do not involve the manufacture by the franchisor of the product being sold by the franchisee. More typically, the franchisor licenses intellectual property rights in conjunction with a particular "formula for success" of the business. Fast food establishments, hotels, and a variety of service franchises are examples of business format franchising.

U.S. regulation of franchise relationships occurs at both the federal and state levels of government. Such regulation can be as specific as the Federal Trade Commission Franchising Rule and state franchise disclosure duties, or as amorphous as the ever present dangers of state and federal antitrust law. Another variety of state regulation of franchising is more intrusive than disclosure requirements. Approximately half of the states regulate the franchise relationship over its life. Iowa, for example, adopted a notable Franchise Act in 1992.[12] This Act gives franchisees a variety of transfer, renewal and termination only for good cause rights. It also gives them encroachment protection by means of a right of first refusal over new outlets located within an "unreasonable proximity" of existing outlets.

In particular, states have enacted legislation which deals with the termination of franchisees. These laws ordinarily prohibit a franchisor from undertaking termination before the ordinary end of the franchise contract unless there is "good cause." Good cause is frequently defined to mean a breach by the franchisee of a material provision of the franchise agreement that has not been cured. Good cause typically does not include the relevant business needs of the

---

[12]   Iowa Code, Chapter 523 H.

franchisor. Some of these laws also require renewal of the franchise agreement unless there is "good cause" for nonrenewal. In some jurisdictions, this provision may not apply to a franchise which has a fixed term as opposed to a franchise which creates by contract a right of renewal or option for a successor. Special franchise termination rules often apply to automobile and petroleum franchise agreements, including the federal Automobile Dealer Franchise Act and the Federal Petroleum Marketing Practices Act.

There is relatively little case law elaborating upon what constitutes good cause to terminate franchisees. However, the following have been recognized as good cause for such terminations: (1) failure to meet sales goals;[13] (2) health and safety violations by the franchisee;[14] (3) breach of implied covenants;[15] and (4) verbal customer abuse.[16] If there is good cause for franchisee termination, the fact of economic hardship to the franchisee may not override the franchisor's right of termination.[17] Ending franchise relationships can sometimes be tumultuous. Texas franchisees who set up a directly competing business one month before the termination of their muffler franchise even using the same phone number were ultimately held liable for actual and punitive damages of $10,000 plus $560,000 in attorneys' fees on breach of contract and civil conspiracy claims.[18]

A related issue is whether the franchisor owes any fiduciary duties to the franchisee. There is a decision of the Eighth Circuit Court of Appeals which suggests that fiduciary duties are inherent in the franchise relationship.[19] There is a Fifth Circuit Court of Appeals decision which rejects this approach,[20] and a later decision of the Eighth Circuit suggests that there is no fiduciary duty beyond the ordinary implied contractual term of good faith and fair dealing.[21] The general trend in the trial courts is against finding any fiduciary duties as between franchisor and franchisee. But the duty to act in

---

[13]   *Al Bishop Agency, Inc. v. Lithonia-Division of National Service Industries, Inc.*, 474 F.Supp. 828 (E.D.Wis.1979).

[14]   *Dayan v. McDonald's Corp.*, 125 Ill.App.3d 972, 81 Ill.Dec. 156, 466 N.E.2d 958 (1984).

[15]   *Photovest Corp. v. Fotomat Corp.*, 606 F.2d 704 (7th Cir.1979).

[16]   *Aselta v. Radio Shack*, 806 Antitrust & Trade Regulation Reporter (BNA) at P. A–23.

[17]   *See Chia-Hsin Huang v. Holiday Inns, Inc.*, 594 F.Supp. 352 (C.D.Cal.1984).

[18]   *Meineke Discount Muffler v. Jaynes*, 999 F.2d 120 (5th Cir.1993).

[19]   *See Arnott v. American Oil Co.*, 609 F.2d 873 (8th Cir.1979).

[20]   *See Carter Equipment Co. v. John Deere Industrial Equipment Co.*, 681 F.2d 386 (5th Cir.1982).

[21]   *See Bain v. Champlin Petroleum Co.*, 692 F.2d 43 (8th Cir.1982).

good faith in connection with termination of franchisees has been affirmed in a number of leading opinions.[22]

For extensive coverage of U.S. franchising law and sample international franchise agreements, see R. Folsom, *International Business Transactions Practitioner Treatise*, Chapter 22.

§ 15.7   Regulation of International Franchising

If franchising was unaffected by regulation, the attorney's role would be limited to negotiation and drafting of the agreement. But international franchising is increasingly regulated by home and host jurisdictions, including regional groups like the European Union (EU). In third world countries, especially Latin America, technology transfer laws aimed principally at international patent and know-how licensing also regulate franchise agreements. These laws benefit franchisees and further development policies, e.g., the conservation of hard currencies by control of royalty levels. In 1986, the European Court of Justice issued a major opinion on the legality of franchise agreements under EU competition law.[23] This decision indicates that Union law can depart significantly from leading United States antitrust law on market division arrangements for distributors.[24] The EU first implemented a comprehensive regulation on franchise agreements in 1988.[25]

There is often a perception of being invaded culturally that follows franchising. Local laws sometimes respond to the cultural impact of foreign franchises, but this did not stop McDonald's from opening in Moscow with great success. In India and Mexico, nationalist feelings hostile to the appearance of foreign trademarks on franchised products have produced laws intended to remove such usage. For example, the Mexican Law of Inventions and Trademarks (1976) (repealed 1987) anticipated requiring use of culturally Mexican marks in addition to marks of foreign origin. Dual marks are now voluntary in Mexico and prohibited by NAFTA. Other nations require local materials (olive oil in the Mediterranean) to be substituted. This could, for example, alter the formula for success (and value) of fast food franchises. Still others (e.g., Alberta, Canada)

---

[22]   See *Photovest Corp. v. Fotomat Corp.*, 606 F.2d 704 (7th Cir.1979); *Larese v. Creamland Dairies, Inc.*, 767 F.2d 716 (10th Cir.1985); *Conoco, Inc. v. Inman Oil Co.*, 774 F.2d 895 (8th Cir.1985), appeal after remand 815 F.2d 514 (8th Cir.1987).

[23]   *Pronuptia de Paris GmbH v. Pronuptia de Paris Irmgard Schillgallis* (1986) Eur.Comm.Rep. 353.

[24]   Compare *Continental T.V., Inc. v. GTE Sylvania Inc.*, 433 U.S. 36, 97 S.Ct. 2549, 53 L.Ed.2d 568 (1977) (location clauses not per se illegal); *American Motor Inns, Inc. v. Holiday Inns, Inc.*, 521 F.2d 1230 (3d Cir.1975) (allocation of franchisor/franchisee towns and territories *per se* illegal).

[25]   Commission Regulation No. 4087/88, replaced by Regulation 2790/99, and replaced again by Regulation 330/10.

mandate extensive disclosures by franchisors in a registered prospectus before agreements may be completed. Disclosure violations can trigger a range of franchisee remedies: recision, injunctions and damages. Such laws are also found in many of the states of the United States.

Franchise advertising must conform to local law. For example, regulations in the People's Republic of China prohibit ads which "have reactionary . . . content." Antitrust and tax law are important in international franchising. Double taxation treaties, for example, will affect the level of taxation of royalties. Antitrust law will temper purchasing requirements of the franchisor, lest unlawful "tying arrangements" be undertaken. Tying arrangements involve coercion of franchisees to take supplies from the franchisor or designated sources as part of the franchise.

Such arrangements must, by definition, involve two products: the tying and tied products. They are subject to a complex and not entirely consistent body of case law under the U.S. Sherman Antitrust Act, Articles 101 and 102 of the TFEU and other laws. For example, one leading United States antitrust case treats the trademark licenses as a separate tying product and the requirement of the purchase by franchisees of non-essential cooking equipment and paper products unlawful.[26] Another case permits franchisors to require franchisees to purchase "core products" (e.g., chicken) subject to detailed specifications, or from a designated list of approved sources.[27] Sometimes the "core product" and the trademark license are treated as a single product incapable of being tied in violation of the law.[28] Still another leading case suggests that anything comprising the franchisor's "formula for success" may possibly be tied in the franchise contract.[29] This may be notably lawful if there was full pre-contract disclosure by the franchisor.

§ 15.8   The Paris Convention as Applied to Trademarks

The premium placed on priority of use of a trademark is reflected in several international trademark treaties. These include the 1883 Paris Convention for the Protection of Industrial Property, the 1957

---

[26]   *Siegel v. Chicken Delight, Inc.*, 448 F.2d 43 (9th Cir.1971), *cert. denied* 405 U.S. 955, 92 S.Ct. 1172, 31 L.Ed.2d 232 (1972).

[27]   *Kentucky Fried Chicken Corp. v. Diversified Packaging Corp.*, 549 F.2d 368 (5th Cir.1977).

[28]   *Krehl v. Baskin-Robbins Ice Cream Co.*, 664 F.2d 1348 (9th Cir.1982) (franchisees must buy Baskin-Robbins ice cream).

[29]   *Principe v. McDonald's Corp.*, 631 F.2d 303 (4th Cir.1980), *cert. denied* 451 U.S. 970, 101 S.Ct. 2047, 68 L.Ed.2d 349 (1981) (franchisees required to lease land and buildings from McDonald's).

Arrangement of Nice Concerning the International Classification of Goods and Services, and the 1973 Trademark Registration Treaty. The treaties of widest international application are the Paris Convention and the Arrangement of Nice, to which the United States is a signatory. The International Bureau of the World Intellectual Property Organization (WIPO) in Geneva plays a central role in the administration of arrangements contemplated by these agreements.

The Paris Convention reflects an effort to internationalize some trademark rules. In addition to extending the nondiscriminatory principal of national treatment and providing for a right of priority of six months for trademarks, the Convention mitigates the frequent national requirement that foreigners seeking trademark registration prove a pre-existing, valid and continuing home registration. This makes it easier to obtain foreign trademark registration, avoids the possibility that a lapse in registration at home will cause all foreign registrations to become invalid, and allows registration abroad of entirely different (and perhaps culturally adapted) marks. The Paris Convention right of priority eliminates the need to simultaneously file for trademark protection around the globe. Filings abroad that are undertaken within six months of the home country filing for trademark registration will take priority. Paris Convention parties may, however, reject trademark applications if they infringe existing marks, lack distinctive character, offend public morality or order, or may deceive the public.

The Paris Convention has in excess of 170 member nations. Since the Convention provides that any domestic trademark registration filing gives rise to priority in all Paris Convention countries, this means that foreign marks registered in countries that do not require use of the mark on an actual product can be obtained in the United States. In other words, foreign trademarks that are not used are entitled under the Paris Convention to U.S. trademark registration. Since 1988, the foreign applicant must state a bona fide intention to use the mark in commerce, but actual use is not required prior to registration.[30]

The Paris Convention also deals with unregistered trademarks. Article 6bis requires the member nations to refuse to register, to cancel an existing registration or to prohibit the use of a trademark which is considered by the trademark registration authorities of that country to be "well known" and owned by a person entitled to the benefits of the Paris Convention. This provision concerns what are called "famous marks" and prevents their infringement even if there has been no local registration of the mark. This is a remarkable

---

[30].   15 U.S.C.A. § 1126(e).

development because it effectively creates trademark rights without registration. It has, for example, been successfully invoked in the People's Republic of China in order to protect against infringing use of Walt Disney and other well-known trademarks. In protecting such marks, China sided with the interpretation of the Paris Convention that marks that are well-known internationally deserve protection, even if not well known locally.

§ 15.9 The Nice Agreement on Trademark Classification

The Nice Agreement addresses the question of registration by "class" or "classification" of goods. In order to simplify internal administrative procedures relating to marks, many countries classify and thereby identify goods (and sometimes services) which have the same or similar attributes. An applicant seeking registration of a mark often is required to specify the class or classes to which the product mark belongs. However, not all countries have the same classification system and some lack any such system. Article 1 of the Nice Agreement adopts, for the purposes of the registration of marks, a single classification system for goods and services. This has brought order out of chaos in the field.

§ 15.10 International Trademark Registration Treaties

The 1973 Vienna Trademark Registration Treaty (to which the United States is a signatory) contemplates an international filing and examination scheme like that in force for patents under the Patent Cooperation Treaty of 1970. *See* Section 15.15. This treaty has not yet been fully implemented, but holds out the promise of reduced costs and greater uniformity when obtaining international trademark protection. The 1994 Trademark Law Treaty substantially harmonized trademark registration procedures.

Numerous European and Mediterranean countries are parties to the 1891 Madrid Agreement for International Registration of Marks. Since 2002, the United States has joined in the Madrid Protocol of 1989. This agreement permits international filings to obtain national trademark rights and is administered by WIPO. German, French and U.S. filers are the greatest users of the Madrid Protocol, often seeking Chinese, EU or Russian registrations.

A Common Market trademark can now be obtained in the European Union, an alternative to national trademark registrations and the "principle of territoriality" underlying IP laws. *See* R. Folsom, *Principles of European Union Law.*

PART B

COPYRIGHTS

§ 15.11   Protecting Copyrights

Nearly one hundred nations recognize some form of copyright protection for "authors' works." The scope of this coverage and available remedies varies from country to country, with some uniformity established in the roughly 100 nations participating in the Berne and Universal Copyright Conventions. In the United States, for example, the Copyright Act of 1976 protects all original expressions fixed in a tangible medium (now known or later developed), including literary works, musical works, dramatic works, choreographic works, graphic works, audiovisual works, sound recordings, computer programs and selected databases. It is not necessary to publish a work to obtain a U.S. copyright; it is sufficient that the work is original and fixed in a tangible medium of expression. To retain a U.S. copyright, the author must give formal notice of a reservation of rights when publishing the work. Publication of the work without such notice dedicates it to free public usage.

U.S. copyright protection now extends for 70 years after the death of the author (95 years for films, a provision intended to protect Disney's Mickey-Mouse). The author also controls "derivative works," such as movies made from books. Only the author (or her assignees or employer regarding "works for hire") may make copies, display, perform, and first sell the work. Registration with the U.S. Copyright Office is not required to obtain copyright rights, but is essential to federal copyright infringement remedies. Infringers are subject to criminal penalties, injunctive relief and civil damages. Infringing works are impounded pending trial and ultimately destroyed. But educators, critics and news reporters are allowed "fair use" of the work, a traditional common law doctrine now codified in the 1976 Copyright Act.

The marketing of copyrights is sometimes accomplished through agency "clearinghouses." This is especially true of musical compositions because the many authors and potential users are dispersed. In the United States, the American Society of Composers, Authors and Publishers (ASCAP) and Broadcast Music, Inc. (BMI) are the principal clearinghouses for such rights. Thousands of these rights are sold under "blanket licenses" for fees established by the clearinghouses and later distributed to their members. Similar organizations exist in most European states. Their activities have repeatedly been scrutinized under United States and European

Union antitrust law. A Joint International Copyright Information Service run since 1981 by WIPO and UNESCO is designed to promote licensing of copyrights in the third world. This Service does not act as an agency clearinghouse for authors' rights, a deficiency sometimes said to promote copyright piracy.

Copyright protection in other countries may be more or less comprehensive or capable of adaptation to modern technologies. The copyrightability of computer programs, for example, is less certain in many jurisdictions. In some developing countries, "fair use" is a theme which is expansively construed to undermine copyright protection. But these differences seem less significant when contrasted with the worldwide problem of copyright piracy ranging from satellite signal poaching to unlicensed music and books.

In the United States, the Copyright Felony Act of 1992 criminalized all copyright infringements. The No Electronic Theft Act of 1997 (NET) removed the need to prove financial gain as element of copyright infringement law, thus ensuring coverage of copying done with intent to harm copyright owners or copying simply for personal use. The Digital Millennium Copyright Act of 1998 (DMCA) brought the United States into compliance with WIPO treaties and created two new copyright offenses; one for circumventing technological measures used by copyright owners to protect their works ("hacking") and a second for tampering with copyright management information (encryption). The DMCA also made it clear that "webmasters" digitally broadcasting music on the Internet must pay performance royalties.

§ 15.12 International Copyright Protection

Absent an appropriate convention, copyright registrations must be tediously acquired in each country recognizing such rights. However, copyright holders receive national treatment, translation rights and other benefits under the Universal Copyright Convention (UCC) of 1952 (U.S. adheres). Most importantly, the UCC *excuses* foreigners from registration requirements provided notice of a claim of copyright is adequately given (e.g., © R. Folsom 2017). Some countries like the U.S. took advantage of an option *not* to excuse registration requirements. The exercise of this option had the effect at that time of reinforcing the U.S. "manufacturing clause" requiring local printing of U.S. copyrighted books and prohibiting importation of foreign copies. This protectionist clause finally expired under U.S. copyright law in 1986. The UCC establishes a minimum term for copyright protection: 25 years after publication, prior registration or death of the author. It also authorizes compulsory license schemes for translation rights in all states and compulsory reprint rights and instructional usage in developing countries. About 25 nations are UCC but not Berne Convention signatories.

National treatment and a release from registration formalities (subject to copyright notice requirements) can be obtained in Pan-American countries under the Mexico City Convention of 1902 and the Buenos Aires Convention of 1911, the U.S. adhering to both. Various benefits can be had in about 160 countries through the Berne Convention of 1886 (as revised). Like the UCC, the Berne Convention suspends registration requirements for copyright holders from participating states. Unlike the UCC, it allows for local copyright protection independent of protection granted in the country of origin and does not require copyright notice. The Berne Convention establishes a minimum copyright term of the life of the author plus 50 years, a more generous minimum copyright than that of the UCC. It also recognizes the exclusive translation rights of authors. Unlike the UCC, the Berne Convention does not contemplate compulsory licensing of translation rights. Most United States copyright holders previously acquired Berne Convention benefits by simultaneously publishing their works in Canada, a member country.

In 1989, the United States ratified the Berne Convention. U.S. ratification of the Berne Convention creates copyright relations with an additional 25 nations. Ratification has eliminated U.S. registration requirements (reserved under the UCC) for foreign copyright holders and required protection of the "moral rights" of authors, i.e., the rights of integrity and paternity. The right of paternity insures acknowledgement of authorship. The right of integrity conveys the ability to object to distortion, alteration or other derogation of the work. It is generally thought that unfair competition law at the federal and state levels provides the legal basis in U.S. law for these moral rights. Limited rights are conveyed under the federal Visual Artists Rights Act of 1990.

PART C

PATENTS, KNOWHOW AND LICENSING

§ 15.13 Patents and Knowhow

The following sections concern the most common form of lawful international technology transfer—patent and knowhow licensing. Before any patent licensing can take place, patents must be acquired in all countries in which the owner hopes there will be persons interested in purchasing the technology. Even in countries where the owner has no such hope, patent rights may still be obtained so as to foreclose future unlicensed competitors.

Licensing is a middle ground alternative to exporting from the owner's home country and direct investment in host markets. It can often produce, with relatively little cost, immediate positive cash flows. After a brief introduction to patents and knowhow, the main themes of are standard licensing contract terms and the regulation of international licensing agreements.

§ 15.14 Protecting Patents

For the most part, patents are granted to inventors according to national law. Thus, patents represent *territorial* grants of exclusive rights. The inventor receives Canadian patents, United States patents, Mexican patents, and so on. There are relatively few jurisdictions without some form of patent protection. However, legally protected intellectual property in one country may not be protected similarly in another country. For example, third world nations sometimes *refuse* to grant patents on pharmaceuticals. These countries often assert that their public health needs require such a policy. Thailand has been one such country and unlicensed "generics" have been a growth industry there. Similarly, most European countries do not grant patents on medical and surgical therapeutic techniques for reasons of public policy.

Nominal patent protection in some developing nations may lack effective forms of relief—giving the appearance but not the reality of legal rights. Since international patent protection is expensive to obtain, some holders take a chance and limit their applications to those markets where they foresee demand or competition for their product. Nevertheless, U.S. nationals continue to receive tens of thousands of patents in other countries. But the reverse is also increasingly true. Residents of foreign countries now receive over 50 percent of the patents issued under United States law. In many countries, persons who deal with the issuance and protection of patents are called patent agents. In the United States, patent practice is a specialized branch of the legal profession. Obtaining international patent protection often involves retaining the services of specialists in each country.

What constitutes a "patent" and how it is protected in any country depends upon domestic law. In the United States, a patent issued by the U.S. Patent Office grants the right for 20 years to exclude everyone from making, using or selling the patented invention without the permission of the patentee.[31] The United States traditionally granted patents to the "first to invent," not (as in many other countries) the "first to file." The U.S. has switched to first to file rules. Moreover, foreign patent applications are now considered part

---

[31]   35 U.S.C.A. § 154.

of the prior art in reviewing novelty issues regardless of their language. Patent infringement can result in injunctive and damages relief in the U.S. courts. "Exclusion orders" against foreign-made patent infringing goods are also available. Such orders are frequently issued by the International Trade Commission under Section 337 of the Tariff Act of 1930, and are enforced by the U.S. Customs Service. *See* Chapter 8.

A U.S. patent thus provides a short-term legal, but not necessarily economic, monopoly. For example, the exclusive legal rights conveyed by the patents held by Xerox on its photocopying machines did not give it a monopoly in the marketplace. There are many other producers of non-infringing photocopy machines with whom Xerox competes.

There are basically two types of patent systems in the world community, registration and examination. Some countries (e.g., France) grant a patent upon "registration" accompanied by appropriate documents and fees, without making an inquiry about the patentability of the invention. The validity of such a patent grant is most difficult to gauge until a time comes to defend the patent against alleged infringement in an appropriate tribunal. In other countries, the patent grant is made following a careful "examination" of the prior art and statutory criteria on patentability or a "deferred examination" is made following public notice given to permit an "opposition." The odds are increased that the validity of such a patent will be sustained in the face of an alleged infringement.

The United States and Germany have examination systems. To obtain U.S. patents, applicants must demonstrate to the satisfaction of the Patent and Trademark Office that their inventions are novel, useful and nonobvious. Nevertheless, a significant number of U.S. patents have been subsequently held invalid in the courts and the Patent Office has frequently been criticized for a lax approach to issuance of patents. Much of this growth is centered in high-tech industries, including computer software and business methods patents, for example Amazon's "Buy Now with 1-Click" software patent. Most jurisdictions of the world limit or simply refuse to issue such patents. The U.S. has also been criticized for sometimes allowing patents on "traditional knowledge" (e.g., Mexican Enola Beans) found primarily in the developing world.

The terms of a patent grant vary from country to country. For example, local law may provide for "confirmation," "importation," "introduction" or "revalidation" patents (which serve to extend limited protection to patents already existing in another country). "Inventor's certificates" and rewards are granted in some socialist countries where private ownership of the means of production is discouraged. The state owns the invention. This was the case in China, for example, but inventors now may obtain patents and exclusive private rights under the 1984 Patent Law.

India requires pharmaceutical patents to be "more efficacious" than existing drugs, an "anti-evergreening" requirement the Indian Supreme Court applied to deny Novartis a patent for its cancer drug Gleevac. Some countries, such as Britain, require that a patent be "worked" (commercially applied) within a designated period of time. This requirement is so important that the British mandate a "compulsory license" to local persons if a patent is deemed unworked. Many developing nations have similar provisions in their patent laws . . . the owner must use it or lose it.

§ 15.15   International Acquisition of Patents

The principal treaties regarding patents are the 1970 Patent Cooperation Treaty and the 1883 Paris Convention for the Protection of Industrial Property, frequently revised and amended. To some extent, the Paris Convention also deals with trademarks, service marks, trade names, industrial designs, and unfair competition. Other recent treaties dealing with patents are the European Patent Convention (designed to permit offices at Munich and The Hague to issue patents of all countries party to the treaty), the European Union Unitary Patent (designed to create a single patent valid throughout most of the EU). *See* R. Folsom, *Principles of European Union Law.*

Paris Convention

The Paris Convention,[32] to which over 170 countries including the U.S. are parties, remains the basic international agreement dealing with treatment of foreigners under national patent laws. It is administered by the International Bureau of the World Intellectual Property Organization (WIPO) at Geneva. The "right of national treatment" (Article 2) prohibits discrimination against foreign holders of local patents and trademarks. Thus, for example, an American granted a Canadian patent must receive the same legal rights and remedies accorded Canadian nationals. Furthermore, important "rights of priority" are granted to patent holders provided they file in foreign jurisdictions within twelve months of their home country patent applications. But such rights conceivably may not overcome prior filings in "first to file" jurisdictions, now including the United States.

Patent applications in foreign jurisdictions are not dependent upon success in the home country: Patentability criteria vary from

---

[32]   21 U.S.T. 1583, T.I.A.S. No. 6295, 828 U.N.T.S. 305 (Stockholm revision).

country to country. Nevertheless, the Paris Convention obviates the need to file simultaneously in every country where intellectual property protection is sought. If an inventor elects not to obtain patent protection in other countries, anyone may make, use or sell the invention in that territory. The Paris Convention does not attempt to reduce the need for individual patent applications in all jurisdictions where patent protection is sought. Nor does it alter the various domestic criteria on patentability. It does anticipate compulsory licensing of patents that are not "worked" within three years of their grant.

Patent Cooperation Treaty

The Patent Cooperation Treaty (PCT),[33] to which about 140 countries including the U.S. are parties, is designed to achieve greater uniformity and less cost in the international patent filing process, and in the examination of prior art. Instead of filing patent applications individually in each nation, filings under the PCT are done in selected countries. The national patent offices of Japan, Sweden, the former Soviet Union and the United States have been designated International Searching Authorities (ISA), as have the European Patent Offices at Munich and The Hague. The international application, together with the international search report, is communicated by an ISA to each national patent office where protection is sought. Nothing in this Treaty limits the freedom of each nation to establish substantive conditions of patentability and determine infringement remedies.

However, the Patent Cooperation Treaty also provides that the applicant may arrange for an international preliminary examination in order to formulate a nonbinding opinion on whether the claimed invention is novel, involves an inventive step (non-obvious) and is industrially applicable. In a country without sophisticated search facilities, the report of the international preliminary examination may largely determine whether a patent will be granted. For this reason alone, the Patent Cooperation Treaty may generate considerable uniformity in world patent law. In 1986 the United States ratified the PCT provisions on preliminary examination reports, thereby supporting such uniformity. China, Japan and South Korea now account for the largest number of PCT applications, with Germany and the United States declining in utilization.

§ 15.16   Protecting Knowhow and Trade Secrets

Knowhow is commercially valuable knowledge. It may or may not be a trade secret, and may or may not be patentable. Though

---

[33]   28 U.S.T. 7645, T.I.A.S. No. 8733.

often technical or scientific, e.g., engineering services, knowhow can also be more general in character. Marketing and management skills as well as simply business advice can constitute knowhow. If someone is willing to pay for the information, it can be sold or licensed internationally.

Legal protection for knowhow varies from country to country and is, at best, limited. Unlike patents, copyrights and trademarks, you cannot by registration obtain exclusive legal rights to knowhow. Knowledge, like the air we breathe, is a public good. Once released in the community, knowhow can generally be used by anyone and is almost impossible to retrieve. In the absence of exclusive legal rights, preserving the confidentiality of knowhow becomes an important business strategy. If everyone knows it, who will pay for it? If your competitors have access to the knowledge, your market position is at risk. It is for these reasons that only a few people on earth ever know the Coca Cola formula, which is perhaps the world's best kept knowhow.

In the United States, the Economic Espionage Act of 1996 creates *criminal* penalties for misappropriation of trade secrets on goods or services for the benefit of foreign governments or anyone. For these purposes, a "trade secret" is defined as "financial, business, scientific, technical, economic or engineering information" that the owner has taken reasonable measures to keep secret and whose "independent economic value derives from being closely held." In addition to criminal fines, forfeitures and jail terms, the Act authorizes seizure of all proceeds from the theft of trade secrets as well as property used or intended for use in the misappropriation (e.g., buildings and capital equipment). The number of criminal prosecutions under this statute is rising, notably regarding theft of software code, hybrid technologies, military technology, and pharmaceutical and chemical formulae.

Protecting knowhow is mostly a function of contract, tort and trade secrets law. NAFTA was the first international agreement to require recognition and protection of trade secrets. Comparable provisions followed in the WTO TRIPs agreement. *See* Section 1.11. Employers will surround their critical knowhow with employees bound by contract to confidentiality. But some valuable knowledge leaks from or moves with these employees, e.g., when a disgruntled retired or ex-employee sells or goes public with the knowhow. The remedies at law or in equity for breach of contract are unlikely to render the employer whole. Neither is tort relief likely to be sufficient since most employees are essentially judgment proof, although they may be of more use if a competitor induced the breach of contract. Likewise, even though genuine trade secrets are protected by criminal statutes in a few jurisdictions, persuading the prosecutor to take up your business problem is not easy and criminal penalties will not recoup the trade secrets (though they may make the revelation of others less likely in the future).

Despite all of these legal hazards, even when certain knowhow is patentable, a desire to prolong the commercial exploitation of that knowledge may result in no patent registrations. The international chemicals industry, for example, is said to prefer trade secrets to public disclosure and patent rights with time limitations. Licensing or selling such knowhow around the globe is risky, but lucrative.

§ 15.17 International Patent and Knowhow Licensing

This section concerns the most common form of lawful international technology transfer-patent and knowhow licensing. Before any patent licensing can take place, patents must be acquired in all countries in which the owner hopes there will be persons interested in purchasing the technology. Even in countries where the owner has no such hope, patent rights may still be obtained so as to foreclose future unlicensed competitors. Licensing is a middle ground alternative to exporting from the owner's home country and direct investment in host markets. It can often produce, with relatively little cost, immediate positive cash flows.

International patent and knowhow licensing is the most critical form of technology transfer to third world development. From the owner's standpoint, it presents an alternative to and sometimes a first step towards foreign investment. Such licensing involves a transfer of patent rights or knowhow (commercially valuable knowledge, often falling short of a patentable invention) in return for payments, usually termed royalties. Unlike foreign investment, licensing does not have to involve a capital investment in a host jurisdiction and may be tax-advantaged. However, licensing of patents and knowhow is not without legal risks.

From the licensee's standpoint, and the perspective of its government, there is the risk that the licensed technology may be old or obsolete, not "state of the art." Goods produced under old technology will be hard to export and convey a certain "second class" status. On the other hand, older more labor intensive technologies may actually be sought (as sometimes done by the PRC) in the early stages of development. Excessive royalties may threaten the economic viability of the licensee and drain hard currencies from the country. The licensee typically is not in a sufficiently powerful position to bargain away restrictive features of standard international licenses. For all these reasons, and more, third world countries frequently regulate patent and knowhow licensing agreements. Such law is found in the Brazilian Normative Act No. 17 (1976) and the Mexican Technology Transfer Law (1982) (repealed 1991), among others. Royalty levels will be limited, certain clauses prohibited (e.g., export restraints, resale price maintenance, mandatory gran backs to the licensor of improvements), and the desirability of the technology evaluated.

Regulation of licensing is not limited to the developing world. The European Union extensively regulates patent and knowhow licensing under its technology transfer regulations. See Section 15.24. In the United States, there is a less direct form of licensing regulation via antitrust law.

The licensor also faces legal risks. The flow of royalty payments may be stopped, suspended or reduced by currency exchange regulations. The taxation of the royalties, if not governed by double taxation treaties, may be confiscatory. The licensee may abscond with the technology or facilitate "gray market" goods (see Chapter 9) which eventually compete for sales in markets exclusively intended for the licensor. In the end, patents expire and become part of the world domain. At that point, unless the technology is somehow tied to a protected trade secret, the licensee has effectively purchased the technology and becomes an independent competitor (though not necessarily an effective competitor if the licensor has made new technological advances).

Licensing is a kind of partnership. If the licensee succeeds, the licensor's royalties (often based on sales volumes) will increase and a continuing partnership through succeeding generations of technology may evolve. If not, the dispute settlement provisions of the agreement may be called upon as either party withdraws from the partnership. Licensing of patents and knowhow often is combined with, indeed essential to, foreign investments. A foreign subsidiary or joint venture will need technical assistance and knowhow to commence operations. When this occurs, the licensing terms are usually a part of the basic joint venture or investment agreement.

Licensing may also be combined with a trade agreement, as where the licensor ships necessary supplies to the licensee, joint venture partner, or subsidiary. Such supply agreements have sometimes been used to overcome royalty limitations through a form of "transfer pricing," the practice of marking up or down the price of goods so as to allocate revenues to preferred parties and jurisdictions (e.g., tax havens).

PART D

TECHNOLOGY TRANSFER AGREEMENTS AND THEIR REGULATION

§ 15.18   Technology Transfer Agreements

There are many variations of technology transfer agreements. But they all in some way address the transfer of intellectual property. The agreement may be exclusively for that purpose, or the transfer may be part of a larger agreement, such as the creation of a joint venture. What is included within the definition of intellectual property or technology transfers tends to be quite broad. The transfer may involve property which is granted protection under such laws as those protecting and regulating patents, copyrights and trademarks, or the transfer may involve property which is not granted such protection, but where some protection is maintained by controlling who obtains the knowledge.

A comparatively new form of transferring technology is by way of a strategic alliance. It is a kind of joint venture where two firms (or more) from different nations agree to jointly exploit technology. The participants often make different contributions to the alliance-one may contribute technology, another capital, or a distribution network, or service facilities, etc. Perhaps the most important part of a strategic alliance is the technology license agreement. It is not always clear whether the alliance structure also transfers enforcement rights to the licensee of the technology.[34]

The process of transferring technology involves an agreement which outlines the relationship between the transferor and the transferee. The extent to which the agreement is detailed may depend upon the character of the transferee.

Even when the technology is transferred to a wholly owned subsidiary in a foreign nation, there is almost always some agreement, at the very least for tax purposes. The corporate structure using a parent and subsidiary (the latter being an entity incorporated under the laws of the foreign host nation) demands that the separate nature of the two entities be maintained. If not, the parent may be held responsible for the debts of the subsidiary under veil piercing theory. Consequently, the transfer of technology from a parent to a subsidiary should be at arms-length to avoid transfer pricing allegations and represented by a written agreement. But if the parent is convinced that there is little likelihood that the subsidiary's

---

[34]   *See* J. Atik, Technology and Distribution as Organizational Elements Within International Strategic Alliances, 14 U. Pa. J. Int'l Bus. L. 273 (1993).

management will adversely affect the value of the technology, or produce poor quality goods using the technology, there are likely to be fewer provisions in the agreement than where the transferee is an independent entity, unrelated to the transferor.

When the agreement is to transfer technology to an entity which is not part of the transferor's corporate structure, such as a subsidiary or affiliate, there will be a sense that more detail ought to appear in the technology agreement. For example, disputes will not be settled "within" the company, as they may when the transfer of technology is to a subsidiary, but by judicial or arbitral tribunals. A transfer within a corporate structure is usually easily worked out, but a transfer to an independent transferee may involve considerable negotiation of many details.

Transfers may assume other functions or address other matters than noted above. They sometimes apply to a particular area because of the frequent use of licensing for that area.

Computer software. The laws of some nations do not recognize computer software as protectable property by copyright or as a trade secret, thus making a transfer particularly risky. It may be recognized as property protected by copyright or patent law. Even when there is legal recognition of computer software as protectable property, however, it may be best not to transfer it if the risk of loss is high. Where the computer technology is contained in the end product, such as the bar coding process for retail products, the software technology may be protected by retaining it in the home country and only transferring the end use product.

Management contracts. Many enterprises, especially in the hotel industry, function by means of management contracts. The transfer usually involves knowhow, the knowledge of how to operate a facility. Often the most important aspect of the transfer is the experience of the manager of the management company. That experience is reflected in the manager's day to day decisions. It is an experience which has proven that it has value. For example, many Cuban government organizations attempted to manage hotels to develop tourism beginning in the mid-1980s. But the hotels were inefficiently managed until foreign management was obtained.

Training contracts. Knowledge of how to undertake a particular function or functions has value. That knowledge may be transferred as any other knowhow. The management contract noted above may include training of host nation persons in hotel management. Even if the management contract is not also a training contract, there will be a certain amount of transfer of training involved, simply by the other employees viewing how a well-managed unit functions.

For extensive coverage of intellectual property licensing law and sample international licensing agreements, see R. Folsom, *International Business Transactions Practitioner Treatise*, Chapter 23.

§ 15.19 Developing World Regulation of Technology Transfers (TT)

When transfer of technology rules do not exist in the recipient country, the technology transfer agreement is the conclusion of the bargaining of the two parties. The agreement will not be public; it will not be registered. But in some nations, especially developing nations and nonmarket economy nations, the government may be involved in the determination and regulation of the technology transfer agreement. Typically, without approval from a technology transfer commission, the TT agreement is void and unenforceable. In such jurisdictions, the parties end up negotiating terms for their agreement that are acceptable to the TT Commission.

During the 1970s a number of developing nations enacted transfer of technology laws. In Latin America, Decision No. 24 of the ANCOM group pioneered the use of regulatory TT Commissions. The ANCOM approach spread like wildfire throughout Latin America. The laws were adopted both as part of the general attempt to control foreign investment and technology transfers, but also to preserve scarce hard currency at a time of severe balance of payment problems. The developing nations viewed technology transfer agreements as an area where there were serious abuses, and believed that their laws would adequately address these issues.[35] The principal abuses were thought to include the following:

1. Transfer of obsolete technology;

2. Excessive price paid for the technology;

3. Limitations on use of new developments by the transferee by grant back provisions;

4. Little research performed by the transferee;

5. Too much intervention by the transferor in transferee activities;

6. Limitations on where the transferee may market the product;

---

[35] *See* Radway, Antitrust, Technology Transfers and Joint Ventures in Latin American Development, 15 Lawyer Am. 47 (1983).

7.   Requirements for components be purchased from the transferor which are available locally or could be obtained from other foreign sources more cheaply;

8.   Inadequate training of transferee's personnel to do jobs performed by personnel of the transferor;

9.   Transfer of technology which has adequate domestic substitutes and is therefore not needed;

10.   Too long a duration of the agreement; and

11.   Application of foreign law and use of foreign tribunals for dispute resolution.

These do not establish an exclusive list. Some nations had different reasons for wishing to more closely govern technology transfers. But these reasons provide an outline of what areas transfer of technology laws in the 1970s attempted to govern.

The result of these restrictive laws was the transfer of less technology, and of technology less valuable to the source. It was often older technology over which the company was willing to relinquish some control. The bureaucracies established to register and approve or disapprove the agreements were often staffed with persons who knew little about technology, less about international business, but who possessed all of the inefficiency and incompetence of many government agencies. The laws did not bring in more technology, but less. The consequence was that they did not serve the purpose of helping the balance of payments. Furthermore, the nations which adopted strict rules regulating the transfer of technology often did not have laws which protected intellectual property.

In the 1980s and 1990s, some of these restrictive laws were dismantled, whether by formal repeal or replacement by more transfer encouraging and intellectual property protecting laws, or by a relaxed interpretation of the laws and a general automatic approval of what the transferor and transferee agreed upon. Mexico, for example, eliminated its Technology Transfer Commission in 1991. Ironically, some technology agreements which were used in the 1960s before the enactment of the strict laws, and which became unusable after such enactments, are now once again being used in the developing world, but regulated in the European Union. *See* Section 15.24.

That said, a substantial number of "technology transfer" control laws remain in force in Latin America, China (Section 15.23) and elsewhere.

§ 15.20   Technology Transfer Agreements as Part of Foreign Direct Investment

Any foreign direct investment which includes the transfer of some technology may include the transfer in an agreement which also includes the direct investment, quite possibly in a joint venture contract. Whether there is such an agreement will depend on the laws of the host nation. China, for example, regularly requires technology transfers in order to obtain foreign investment permits.

In many nations which restrict foreign investment, there may be an agreement which expresses the total relationship, including the transfer of technology. For example, foreign investments established in Cuba must comply with the broad and often vague provisions of the out-of-date 1982 joint venture law. That law notes the need for foreign technology and that a formal agreement with the government for an investment must also outline the nature of any technology transfers. Little technology is being transferred because there is little protection of technology under Cuban law.

Investment in nations which mandate joint ventures are the most likely situations where the investment agreement will also include the technology transfer provisions. There is nothing wrong with combining transfer of technology provisions in a larger scope agreement, but the agreement ought to be just as detailed regarding technology provisions as it would standing alone as a separate agreement.

Where technology is transferred within the context of a joint venture or other form of investment agreement, the agreement ought to be clear as to the access of the host nation joint venture partner to any sensitive technology. Particularly where there is knowhow transferred, the foreign investor may wish to control the local party's access to the technology. Unless there are restrictions on the transfer of ownership interests, the foreign party may change and bringing in persons less trusted.

India demanded in the 1970s that the Coca-Cola Company alter its structure from a wholly foreign owned investment to a joint venture. While the Indian government did not expressly state that the foreign parent would have to share the secret formula, the government did say that such sharing would be the natural consequence of the partnership sense of the joint venture. Coca-Cola would not disclose the technology, and withdrew from India, not to return until the 1990s, when India had relaxed its previously strict foreign investment rules.

§ 15.21   The Impact of U.S. Antitrust Law on Technology Transfers

United States export controls, covered in Chapter 10, directly regulate the transfer of technology and technical data from the U.S. to the rest of the world. United States antitrust law impacts such exports more obliquely. A good example is U.S antitrust law governing "tying arrangements" in franchising and licensing contracts, discussed in Section 15.7. Likewise, European Union business competition law is also concerned with such arrangements. Microsoft, for example, paid a considerable fine under EU law for "bundling" (tying) a media player with its Windows operating system. For coverage of EU competition law's impact on technology transfers, see R. Folsom, *Principles of European Union Law*.

Antitrust law is a distinctly United States subject. It is a body of law that reflects United States economic history and perspectives. Antitrust is one of the relatively few areas of U.S. law that has been exported to foreign jurisdictions, albeit with many local variations. The European Union, Canada, China, Australia, Germany, Brazil, Japan, Britain and (since 1993) Mexico have notably developed such law. Global, co-operative antitrust enforcement can and frequently does result in multiple liabilities, for example via the U.S.-EU Agreement on Cooperation in Antitrust Matters.

United States antitrust law is often of intense interest to foreigners because of its reputation for severity and incomprehensibility, particularly when applied "extraterritorially" to persons and actions located outside the United States. EU competition law also has an extraterritorial component. Unlike most jurisdictions, the U.S. assesses *criminal* antitrust fines, penalties and jail terms. The U.S., for example, extradited an Italian business executive from Germany to face criminal charges under the Sherman Act. The U.S. used Interpol's red notice system to capture him. Dozens of Japanese executives have voluntarily served prison terms for U.S. antitrust violations.

The vast majority of all U.S. antitrust litigation involves private actions for the punitive remedy of *treble damages*. This remedy is unavailable in any other jurisdiction around the globe. Thus the United States does not principally rely upon public law enforcement in the antitrust field. When the incentive of the automatic treble damages remedy is mixed with the allowance of contingency fee arrangements between U.S. lawyers and their clients (a litigation financing device), the successful plaintiffs' ability to recover attorneys' fees and legal costs from defendants (but not vice-versa), and the extensive array of pre-trial private discovery rights accorded civil litigants in the United States, the intense interest of foreigners in antitrust law usually rises to a high level of fear and disbelief.[36] Dealing with these reactions often falls to U.S. counsel.

A less visible but more pervasive aspect of U.S. antitrust law is its influence upon business practices and the terms of business agreements. For example, most licensing, distributorship and sales representatives' agreements are drafted to minimize the risk of treble damages. This can be done by creating geographic "areas of primary responsibility," a technique specifically approved by the U.S. Supreme Court.[37] Many clauses in typical U.S. agreements will reflect calculated antitrust risk assessments in their design. Clauses governing exclusive dealing, full-line coverage, covenants not to compete, purchase requirements, grant-backs of new patents, resale prices and termination are likely to be subjected to such assessments.

In addition, many U.S. companies employ counsel to conduct antitrust "compliance reviews" of their entire business conduct. Thus it is through the advice of business counsel, drawing upon the myriad of reported antitrust cases, that U.S. antitrust law often has its greatest (and often silent) impact on technology transfers.

For more extensive coverage of U.S. antitrust law, notably its extraterritorial component, see R. Folsom et al, *Principles of International Business Transactions*.

PART E

CHINA AND EU TECHNOLOGY TRANSFERS

§ 15.22   China IP Law*

Intellectual Property under PRC Law

China's legal framework for the protection of intellectual property is comprehensive, but the challenge is for China to enforce the legislation effectively and transparently. The complaints from foreign investors in this area are universal and ongoing. China is a member of the WTO and consequently a party to all major intellectual property conventions of the organization, as well as others, including the Paris Convention, Patent Cooperation Treaty, Berne Convention, Universal Copyright Convention, Geneva

---

[36]   For detailed coverage of extraterritorial U.S. antitrust jurisdiction and procedure, *see* R. Folsom, *Principles of International Business Litigation and Arbitration*, Chapters 5 and 6.

[37]   *See United States v. Topco Associates*, 1973-Trade Cases 74,485 (N.D. Ill. 1973), affirmed per curiam 414 U.S. 801, 94 S. Ct. 116, 38 L. Ed. 2d 39 (1973).

*   Prepared with the assistance of Professor John Rogers.

Convention and Madrid Agreement on International Registration of Marks.

Patents

The Patent Law of the People's Republic of China (the "Patent Law") was amended on December 27, 2008. The revision came into effect on October 1, 2009 and was supplemented in 2010 with revised Implementing Regulations (the "Implementing Regulations"). The Implementing Regulations were published on December 30, 2009 and came into effect on February 1, 2010 and there have been subsequent judicial interpretations.

There are three types of patents: patents for inventions of 20 years duration from the application filing date; patents for utility models of 10 years duration; and design patents of 10 years duration. The system is compliant with the WTO Agreement on Trade-related Aspects of Intellectual Property Rights ("TRIPS Agreement"). China has adopted a "first-to-file" rather than "first-to-invent" system and foreign applicants are required to submit patent applications in China through an officially designated patent agent.

Trademarks

The Trademark Law of the People's Republic of China (the "Trademark Law") was amended for the third time with effect on May 1, 2014. The revisions to the Implementing Regulations of the Trademark Law (the "Implementing Regulations") were published on April 29, 2014 and also came into effect on May 1, 2014. A trademark registration is valid for 10 years from the final date of approval (i.e. upon expiration of the three-month opposition period or, for international trademark registrations extended to the PRC under the Madrid Agreement or the Madrid Protocol, the date of filing), with further 10-year renewal terms available.

The law imposes a strict first-to-file rule for obtaining trademark rights, whereby the first party to file for registration of a mark pre-empts later applicants. Prior use of an unregistered mark is generally irrelevant for trademark registration purposes, unless the prior mark in question is a well-known mark, or the later filing is a bad-faith pre-emption of the prior mark that has achieved a certain degree of fame through use.

Copyright

The Copyright Law of the People's Republic of China (the "Copyright Law") was amended with effect from October 27, 2001, and its Implementing Regulations (the "Implementing Regulations") were amended with effect from September 15, 2002. The Copyright Law was again amended in 2010 with effect from April 1, 2010 (the

"2010 Amendment") and the Implementing Regulations were revised with effect from March 1, 2013. The 2010 Amendment was in response to a 2009 WTO dispute, and attempts to confirm that "illegal" works can obtain copyright protection. In recent years, the PRC National

The current Copyright Law introduces protection for (1) written works, (2) oral works, (3) musical, dramatic, Chinese folk art, choreographic and acrobatic works, (4) works of fine art and architectural works, (5) photographic works, (6) cinematographic works, (7) graphic works, (8) model works and (9) computer software. The Copyright Law does not protect databases, i.e. collections of original information that do not qualify for copyright protection. However, if the means of compilation satisfies the requirement of originality, then such compilation can be protected.

Under the Copyright Law, an author's moral rights of attribution, revision and integrity are perpetual. A citizen's right of publication and the various economic rights are protected for the duration of the life of the author plus 50 years. For works of a legal person or other organization, or works for hire vested in a legal person or other organization, as well as for photographic works and cinematographic works, the right of publication and other economic rights are protected for a period of 50 years from the date of first publication. Registration is not a precondition to copyright enforcement but can provide prima facie evidence of ownership in enforcement actions.

Trade Secrets

A trade secret is defined in both the Law of the PRC against Unfair Competition ("Unfair Competition Law") and the PRC Criminal Code as technical and business information which is private, able to bring economic benefits to the rightful party, is practical, and for which that party has adopted measures to maintain its confidentiality. A non-exhaustive list of measures to maintain confidentiality is set forth in the Several Provisions on the Prohibition of Acts of Infringement of Trade Secrets (the "Trade Secrets Provisions"), effective from November 23, 1995 and amended on December 3, 1998. Such measures include disclosing secrets on a need-to-know basis only, adopting physical preventive measures such as locking, marking information "confidential", requiring access codes and passwords, and requiring confidentiality agreements.

Trade secrets are protected under the Unfair Competition Law. Under the legislation, business operators are prohibited from infringing upon commercial secrets by obtaining the commercial secrets of others by theft, inducement, coercion or other illicit means;

revealing, using or allowing others to use commercial secrets obtained by such means; and revealing, using or allowing others to use commercial secrets of others which are in their possession by violation of agreements or other requests for confidentiality by the owners concerned. If a third party knows or should have known of such acts violating the law, but obtains, uses or reveals commercial secrets of others, this will also constitute infringement.

Under a Supreme People's Court Interpretation on intellectual property crimes issued in 2004, the infringement of a trade secret causing loss in excess of RMB500,000 will be regarded as serious and will trigger criminal prosecution under the PRC Criminal Code.

§ 15.23   Technology Transfers to the PRC*

Major changes have been undertaken in the licensing and intellectual property law of the People's Republic of China since the Cultural Revolution. These changes reflect China's desire to create a modern economy by importing technology and by fostering its development. According to a report issued by central authorities in Beijing, the importation of technology augments China's modernization program in four ways: 1) By decreasing the gap on product quality and standards between China and the developed world; 2) By helping to promote the technological upgrading of Chinese enterprises; 3) By enhancing the ability of Chinese enterprises to independently develop their own new products and technology; and 4) By improving enterprise management.

China's desire to modernize its economy through technological imports is most evident in PRC patent and licensing law. A host of technology import regulations authorizing license agreements with foreign sources has been enacted. These regulations are not a blank check permitting technology importation at any cost. Rather, they are carefully constructed rules intended to promote technology transfers to China under acceptable terms and conditions.

Technology Piracy in the PRC

Despite the adoption of major PRC patent, trademark, copyright and technology transfer laws and their implementing regulations, a dark shadow hangs over much of Chinese intellectual property practice. Counterfeiting of goods and unlicensed use of technology is approaching epidemic proportions. Computer software is perhaps the most prominent victim. The official remedies, however diligently applied, seem inadequate to the task of dealing with this problem. Partly, one suspects, there are cultural forces at work. To copy another's work is traditionally a compliment in China. Partly also,

---

*   Prepared with the assistance of Professor John Rogers.

the economics of development fuel piracy in the PRC. It is simply much less expensive to "borrow" from foreigners and (increasingly) domestic entities whatever can be reverse-engineered and imitated. Even "Beijing Jeeps" are reportedly being knocked off by a large number of township enterprises.

Although there have been advances in protection of intellectual property and foreigners have successfully availed themselves of Chinese courts, there are no quick solutions to an environment that is fundamentally hostile to intellectual property. In this area, Chinese law will take a long time to mature.

PRC Regulation of Technology Import Contracts

As in many developing countries, there is a fear in China of paying excessive royalties for potentially redundant, outdated or inappropriate technology under oppressive contract terms. Likewise, there is a fear of standardized licensing contracts created by attorneys of foreign licensors. The principal objective of China's technology import regulations is to insure that such contracts do not contain restrictive clauses and to increase the bargaining power of Chinese licensees. Although pure licensing agreements are reasonably common, many technology transfers take place in the context of equity or contractual joint venture investments.

The 1985 Regulations for the Administration of Technology Import Contracts, with their detailed 1988 implementing rules (the "Regulations"), now superseded by the 1999 Contract Law, are the most important example of China's modern approach to licensing agreements. Similar regulations exist in some of China's economic development zones and coastal cities, notably Shenzhen, Xiamen and Guangzhou (Canton), which compete for technology transfers. Chinese law governs patent, trademark, knowhow and technical service contracts with foreigners. They also apply to technology transfers in connection with foreign investment. Once the parties have reached agreement, all such contracts must be examined and approved by government authorities before implementation.

Since 1988, in a welcome reform, any technology transfer contract not disapproved after filing is deemed approved. Most Chinese licensing agreements are essentially installment sales. This is achieved by limiting the licensing agreement to a maximum of 10 years followed by the absence of restraints on the licensee's use of the technology after expiration of the agreement. The result is truly a technology transfer.

Chinese law stipulates that the imported technology must be "advanced," "appropriate" and "necessary" to modernization of China's industrial base. To this end, a feasibility study (which can be conducted by foreign experts) precedes the contract. The licensing agreement must contain certain terms, such as a guarantee by the supplier that the technology is "complete, free of error, effective and can achieve the objectives stipulated in the contract." This is an important representation and probably the most common source of lawsuits and arbitrations initiated by the Chinese in the technology transfer area.

Certain terms cannot appear in the agreement. These include restraints on the Chinese recipient's ability to choose the sources of relevant raw materials, spare parts or equipment. Such restraints are generally called "tying arrangements." However, the Chinese licensee can choose to take such supplies from the foreign licensor. In that case, the supplies must be offered at competitive international prices, itemized in the contract and are subject to special approvals. Chinese law also prohibits contract terms that are harmful to the public interest, that violate China's sovereignty, or that are unclear, unequal or unreasonable. In general, these regulations are designed to promote economic modernization in China while protecting it from foreign exploitation.

In other areas, either by law or practice, greater flexibility has been shown. For example, there is no legally stipulated maximum royalty payment. Royalties of 2% to 5% of net sales value have been routinely approved. Higher royalties get close scrutiny by the examining authorities. Given China's shortage of foreign exchange, barter and countertrade are often substituted for cash royalties. Chinese law prohibits unreasonable restraints upon the Chinese recipient's domestic or export sales. Nevertheless, as a matter of practice, contract terms which effectively eliminate sales competition with the foreign licensor's products have often been permitted.

Once approved and executed, PRC technology transfer contracts are subject to ongoing regulatory approvals. The contract will often stipulate that certification of the delivery of the technology and its integration into the existing Chinese facility is required before payment to the licensor is allowed. This can get complicated because most technology importation is done by central or regional trading companies, not the end user. These trading companies often lack sufficient knowledge of the application of the technology by a factory hundreds or thousands of miles from their offices. Yet they are the ones who typically must make the necessary certifications.

The level of Chinese sophistication about licensing agreements is increasing. They have developed model patent and knowhow licensing contracts with which they frequently initiate negotiations. In their negotiations, and in the administration of their technology transfer law, the Chinese have so far successfully walked a fine line between providing sufficient incentives to bring foreign licensors into a bargain and discouraging them altogether.

Made in China 2025

The PRC has a Made in China 2025 program that seeks to make China a global leader in strategic manufacturing industries, including semiconductors, advanced machine tools, medical devices, biopharma, aerospace and aeronautics, advanced information technology, artificial intelligence, green and driverless autos, and robotics. To achieve these goals, local content rules are expected to rise to 70%, state subsidies are upward bound, and protection from foreign competition is anticipated. Part of this program also includes pressuring foreign and Chinese companies to provide their leading technology. The principal pressure is access to China's large, lucrative and growing domestic market. In other words, this is the price to pay in order to make investments and do business in the PRC.

One way to force technology transfers is to mandate use of joint ventures with a Chinese partner. Autos, insurance, and telecommunications are subject to such rules. Another way is mandate research and development inside China, with improvements in licensed technology passing or shared with a Chinese partner. Microsoft, Apple (iCloud) and chip-maker Qualcomm, for example, have "voluntarily" set up joint ventures in China under pressure to make technology transfers.

The United States under the Trump administration has launched a broad Section 301 investigation into China's technology transfer practices. *See* Chapter 14.

§ 15.24   EU Technology Transfer Regulations

The European Union, as befits a major technology center, has a strong intellectual property regime. The EU adheres to the TRIPs agreement (above), and has created regional EU Trademarks and EU Unitary Patents, in addition to traditional national IP rights of the member states. See R. Folsom, *Principles of European Union Law including BREXIT.*

Subsequent to major decisions of the European Court of Justice, the EU adopted separate patent licensing and knowhow licensing regulations in 1984 and 1989, which were later merged into the Transfer of Technology Regulations (TT) outlined immediately below. These regulations are called "group exemptions" under EU business competition law, encouraging parties and their lawyers to draft patent and knowhow license agreements that conform to their contents. Failure to do so, can result in Commission prosecutions, fines and penalties, as well as voiding of the agreement or parts thereof. See R. Folsom, *Principles of European Union Law including BREXIT.*

Transfer of Technology Regulation 240/96

In 1996 the European Commission enacted Regulation 240/96 on the application of Article 101(3) of the Treaty on the Functioning of the European Union (TFEU) to transfer technology agreements. The intention of this Regulation was to combine existing patent and knowhow business competition law exemptions into a single regulation covering technology transfer agreements, and to simplify and harmonize the rules for patent and knowhow licensing. It contained detailed lists of permitted, permissible and prohibited clauses.

Regulation 240/96 stated that Article 101(1) of the Treaty did not apply to "pure patent and knowhow licensing agreements and missed patent and knowhow licensing agreements," as well as to agreements with ancillary provisions relating to intellectual property other than patents, when only two undertakings are parties and when one or more of eight listed obligations were included. These were obligations of limitation, such as not to license other undertakings to exploit the technology. There were time limits (5 years patents/10 years knowhow) for the exemption of these eight obligations in certain situations. Article 1 was known as the White List. Article 2 allowed technology transfers even when certain clauses existed (17 were listed). These clauses were considered generally not restrictive of competition. There were various obligations on the licensee, such as not divulging knowhow communicated by the licensor. Article 2 was known as the Permissible List.

Article 3 of Regulation 240/96 designated that Articles 1 and 2(2) did not apply when any one of seven obligations were present, such as restricting a party in the determination of prices, competition restrictions, limitations on production quantity, licensee improvement grant-back requirements, etc. Article 3 was known as the Black List. Article 4 carried the scope of the exemption provided for in Articles 1 and 2 to certain other restrictive agreements which were notified to the Commission and received no Commission opposition. Article 4 was known as the Gray List. Regulation 240/96, according to Article 5, did not apply to four classes of agreements, such as most agreements within a joint venture. But under Article 5 it did apply to three forms of agreements, including where the licensor is itself a licensee of the technology and was authorized to grant sub-licenses.

The Commission retained power to withdraw benefits of the Regulation 240/96 if in a specific case the exempted agreement was incompatible with the conditions of Article 101(3). Final articles provided some definitions, a list of what were deemed patents, preservation of confidentiality of information, and the repeal of the two regulations combined in this regulation.

Transfer of Technology Regulation 772/2004

The detailed regulation of technology transfer agreement clauses contained in Regulation 240/96 was replaced by Regulation 772/2004, which generally applies to patent, knowhow, production trademark and software copyright licensing. The new Regulation distinguishes agreements between those of "competing" and "noncompeting" parties, the latter being treated less strictly than the former. Parties are deemed "competing" if they compete (without infringing each other's IP rights) in either the relevant technology or product market, determined in each instance by what buyers regard as substitutes.[38] If the competing parties have a *combined* market share of 20 percent or less, their licensing agreements are covered by group exemption under Regulation 772/2004.[39] Noncompeting parties, on the other hand, benefit from the group exemption so long as their *individual* market shares do not exceed 30 percent.[40] Agreements initially covered by Regulation 772/2004 that subsequently exceeded the "safe harbor" thresholds noted above lost their exemption subject to a two-year grace period.[41] Outside these exemptions, a "rule of reason" approach applied.

Inclusion of certain "hardcore restraints" causes license agreement to lose their group exemption. For competing parties, such restraints include price fixing,[42] output limitations on both parties,[43] limits on the licensee's ability to exploit its own technology,[44] and allocation of markets or competitors (subject to exceptions).[45] Specifically, restraints on active and passive selling by the licensee in a territory reserved for the licensor are allowed, as are active (but not passive) selling restraints by licensees in territories of other licensees.[46]

---

[38]   Regulation 772/2004, Article 1(1)j.

[39]   *Id.*, Article 3(1).

[40]   *Id.*, Article 3(2).

[41]   *Id.*, Article 8(2).

[42]   *Id.*, Article 4(1)(a).

[43]   *Id.*, Article 4(1)(b).

[44]   *Id.*, Article 4(1)(d).

[45]   *Id.*, Article 4(1)(c).

[46]   *Id.*, Article 4(1)(c)(iv) and (v).

Licensing agreements between noncompeting parties may not contain the "hardcore" restraint of maximum price fixing.[47] Active selling restrictions on licensees can be utilized, along with passive selling restraints in territories reserved to the licensor or (for two years) another licensee.[48] For these purposes, the competitive status of the parties is decided at the outset of the agreement.[49]

Other license terms deemed "excluded restrictions" also cause a loss of exemption.[50] Such clauses include: (1) mandatory grant-backs or assignments of severable improvements by licensees, excepting nonexclusive license-backs;[51] (2) no-challenges by the licensee of the licensor's intellectual property rights, subject to the licensor's right to terminate upon challenge;[52] and (3) for noncompeting parties, restraints on the licensee's ability to exploit its own technology or either party's ability to carry out research and development (unless indispensable to prevent disclosure of the licensed knowhow).[53]

Transfer of Technology Regulation 316/2014

Regulation 316/2014 replaced Regulation 772/2004, with a one-year transition period to adapt existing TT agreements. Regulation 316/2014 is valid until 2026, and clarifies that it applies to technology transfers only if other EU regulations concerning research and development (Regulation 2659/2000) and/or specialization agreements (Regulation 2658/2000) are inapplicable.

The distinction between competing and noncompeting parties under Regulation 772/2004 is retained, as are their market share thresholds.

Restrictive changes were made to the TT group exemption regulation as follows:

(1) All *exclusive* grant-back licensee obligations require individual assessment, as do termination clauses triggered by licensee challenges to the validity of the technology. Such clauses are no longer covered by the group exemption.

(2) Purchase requirements from licensors of raw material or equipment are group exempt only if directly

---

[47] *Id.*, Article 4(2)(a).
[48] *Id.*, Article 4(2)(b).
[49] *Id.*, Article 4(3).
[50] *Id.*, Article 5.
[51] *Id.*, Article 5(1)(a).
[52] *Id.*, Article 5(1)(b) and (c).
[53] *Id.*, Article 5(2).

related to the production or sale of products made with the licensed technology.

(3) No passive sales restrictions on licensees are group exempt unless objectively necessary for the licensee to penetrate a new market.

(4) Settlement agreements which lead to delayed or limited ability for licensee launch of the product in any market ("pay-for-delay" or "reverse payment" agreements) may be prohibited under certain conditions, as may no-challenge clauses in settlement agreements, particularly if the patent was granted on the basis of incorrect or misleading information.

(5) Technology licensing pools now enjoy a comprehensive, detailed group exemption provided they adhere to Regulation 316/2014.

In all cases, exemption under Regulation 772/2004 or Regulation 316/2014 may be withdrawn where in any particular case an agreement has effects that are incompatible with Treaty Article 101(3).[54]

For more coverage of EU technology protection and transfer law, see R. Folsom, *Principles of European Union Law including BREXIT.*

§ 15.25   Text of EU Technology Transfer Regulation 772/2004

COMMISSION REGULATION (EC) No 772/2004

of 27 April 2004

on the application of Article 81(3) of the Treaty to categories of technology transfer agreements (Text with EEA relevance)

THE COMMISSION OF THE EUROPEAN COMMUNITIES,

Having regard to the Treaty establishing the European Community,

Having regard to Council Regulation No 19/65/EEC of 2 March1965 on application of Article 85(3) of the Treaty to certain categories of agreements and concerted practices (1), and in particular Article 1 thereof,

Having published a draft of this Regulation (2),

After consulting the Advisory Committee on Restrictive Practices and Dominant Positions,

Whereas:

(1) Regulation No 19/65/EEC empowers the Commission to apply Article 81(3) of the Treaty by Regulation to certain categories of technology transfer

---

[54]   *Id.,* Article 6.

agreements and corresponding concerted practices to which only two undertakings are party which fall within Article 81(1).

(2)   Pursuant to Regulation No 19/65/EEC, the Commission has, in particular, adopted Regulation (EC) No 240/96 of 31 January 1996 on the application of Article 85(3) of the Treaty to certain categories of technology transfer agreements (3).

(3)   On 20 December 2001 the Commission published an evaluation report on the transfer of technology block exemption Regulation (EC) No 240/96 (4). This generated a public debate on the application of Regulation (EC) No 240/96 and on the application in general of Article 81(1) and (3) of the Treaty to technology transfer agreements.

The response to the evaluation report from Member States and third parties has been generally in favor of reform of Community competition policy on technology transfer agreements. It is therefore appropriate to repeal Regulation (EC) No 240/96.

(4)   This Regulation should meet the two requirements of ensuring effective competition and providing adequate legal security for undertakings. The pursuit of these objectives should take account of the need to simplify the regulatory framework and its application.

It is appropriate to move away from the approach of listing exempted clauses and to place greater emphasis on defining the categories of agreements which are exempted up to a certain level of market power and on specifying the restrictions or clauses which are not to be contained in such agreements. This is consistent with an economics-based approach which assesses the impact of agreements on the relevant market. It is also consistent with such an approach to make a distinction between agreements between competitors and agreements between non-competitors.

(5)   Technology transfer agreements concern the licensing of technology. Such agreements will usually improve economic efficiency and be pro-competitive as they can reduce duplication of research and development, strengthen the incentive for the initial research and development, spur incremental innovation, facilitate diffusion and generate product market competition.

(6)   The likelihood that such efficiency-enhancing and procompetitive effects will outweigh any anti-competitive effects due to restrictions contained in technology transfer agreements depends on the degree of market power of the undertakings concerned and, therefore, on the extent to which those undertakings face competition from undertakings owning substitute technologies or undertakings producing substitute products.

(7)   This Regulation should only deal with agreements where the licensor permits the licensee to exploit the licensed technology, possibly after further research and development by the licensee, for the production of goods or services. It should not deal with licensing agreements for the purpose of subcontracting research and development. It should also not deal with licensing agreements to set up technology pools, that is to say, agreements

for the pooling of technologies with the purpose of licensing the created package of intellectual property rights to third parties.

NOTES: (1)OJ 36, 6.3.1965, p. 533/65. Regulation as last amended by Regulation (EC) No 1/2003 (OJ L 1, 4.1.2003, p. 1).

(2)   OJ C 235, 1.10.2003, p. 10.

(3)   OJ L 31, 9.2.1996, p. 2. Regulation as amended by the 2003 Act of Accession.

(4)   COM(2001) 786 final.

(8)   For the application of Article 81(3) by regulation, it is not necessary to define those technology transfer agreements that are capable of falling within Article 81(1). In the individual assessment of agreements pursuant to Article 81(1), account has to be taken of several factors, and in particular the structure and the dynamics of the relevant technology and product markets.

(9)   The benefit of the block exemption established by this Regulation should be limited to those agreements which can be assumed with sufficient certainty to satisfy the conditions of Article 81(3). In order to attain the benefits and objectives of technology transfer, the benefit of this Regulation should also apply to provisions contained in technology transfer agreements that do not constitute the primary object of such agreements, but are directly related to the application of the licensed technology.

(10)   For technology transfer agreements between competitors it can be presumed that, where the combined share of the relevant markets accounted for by the parties does not exceed 20 % and the agreements do not contain certain severely anti-competitive restraints, they generally lead to an improvement in production or distribution and allow consumers a fair share of the resulting benefits.

(11)   For technology transfer agreements between non-competitors it can be presumed that, where the individual share of the relevant markets accounted for by each of the parties does not exceed 30 % and the agreements do not contain certain severely anti-competitive restraints, they generally lead to an improvement in production or distribution and allow consumers a fair share of the resulting benefits.

(12)   There can be no presumption that above these market share thresholds technology transfer agreements do fall within the scope of Article 81(1). For instance, an exclusive licensing agreement between non-competing undertakings does often not fall within the scope of Article 81(1). There can also be no presumption that, above these market-share thresholds, technology transfer agreements falling within the scope of Article 81(1) will not satisfy the conditions for exemption. However, it can also not be presumed that they will usually give rise to objective advantages of such a character and size as to compensate for the disadvantages which they create for competition.

(13)   This Regulation should not exempt technology transfer agreements containing restrictions which are not indispensable to the improvement of production or distribution. In particular, technology transfer agreements

containing certain severely anti-competitive restraints such as the fixing of prices charged to third parties should be excluded from the benefit of the block exemption established by this Regulation irrespective of the market shares of the undertakings concerned. In the case of such hardcore restrictions the whole agreement should be excluded from the benefit of the block exemption.

(14) In order to protect incentives to innovate and the appropriate application of intellectual property rights, certain restrictions should be excluded from the block exemption. In particular exclusive grant back obligations for severable improvements should be excluded. Where such a restriction is included in a licence agreement only the restriction in question should be excluded from the benefit of the block exemption.

(15) The market-share thresholds, the non-exemption of technology transfer agreements containing severely anticompetitive restraints and the excluded restrictions provided for in this Regulation will normally ensure that the agreements to which the block exemption applies do not enable the participating undertakings to eliminate competition in respect of a substantial part of the products in question.

(16) In particular cases in which the agreements falling under this Regulation nevertheless have effects incompatible with Article 81(3), the Commission should be able to withdraw the benefit of the block exemption. This may occur in particular where the incentives to innovate are reduced or where access to markets is hindered.

(17) Council Regulation (EC) No 1/2003 of 16 December 2002 on the implementation of the rules on competition laid down in Articles 81 and 82 of the Treaty (1) empowers the competent authorities of Member States to withdraw the benefit of the block exemption in respect of technology transfer agreements having effects incompatible with Article 81(3), where such effects are felt in their respective territory, or in a part thereof, and where such territory has the characteristics of a distinct geographic market. Member States must ensure that the exercise of this power of withdrawal does not prejudice the uniform application throughout the common market of the Community competition rules or the full effect of the measures adopted in implementation of those rules.

(18) In order to strengthen supervision of parallel networks of technology transfer agreements which have similar restrictive effects and which cover more than 50 % of a given market, the Commission should be able to declare this Regulation inapplicable to technology transfer agreements containing specific restraints relating to the market concerned, thereby restoring the full application of Article 81 to such agreements.

(19) This Regulation should cover only technology transfer agreements between a licensor and a licensee. It should cover such agreements even if conditions are stipulated for more than one level of trade, by, for instance, requiring the licensee to set up a particular distribution system and specifying the obligations the licensee must or may impose on resellers of the products produced under the licence. However, such conditions and obligations should comply with the competition rules applicable to supply

and distribution agreements. Supply and distribution agreements concluded between a licensee and its buyers should not be exempted by this Regulation.

(20) This Regulation is without prejudice to the application of Article 82 of the Treaty,

HAS ADOPTED THIS REGULATION:

Article 1

Definitions

1.   For the purposes of this Regulation, the following definitions shall apply:

(a)   'agreement' means an agreement, a decision of an association of undertakings or a concerted practice;

(b)   'technology transfer agreement' means a patent licensing agreement, a know-how licensing agreement, a software copyright licensing agreement or a mixed patent, knowhow or software copyright licensing agreement, including any such agreement containing provisions which relate to the sale and purchase of products or which relate to the licensing of other intellectual property rights or the assignment of intellectual property rights, provided that those provisions do not constitute the primary object of the agreement and are directly related to the production of the contract products; assignments of patents, know-how, software copyright or a combination thereof where part of the risk associated with the exploitation of the technology remains with the assignor, in particular where the sum payable in consideration of the assignment is dependent on the turnover obtained by the assignee in respect of products produced with the assigned technology, the quantity of such products produced or the number of operations carried out employing the technology, shall also be deemed to be technology transfer agreements;

(c)   'reciprocal agreement' means a technology transfer agreement where two undertakings grant each other, in the same or separate contracts, a patent licence, a know-how licence, a software copyright licence or a mixed patent, know-how or software copyright licence and where these licences concern competing technologies or can be used for the production of competing products;

(d)   'non-reciprocal agreement' means a technology transfer agreement where one undertaking grants another undertaking a patent licence, a know-how licence, a software copyright licence or a mixed patent, know-how or software copyright licence, or where two undertakings grant each other such a licence but where these licences do not concern competing technologies and cannot be used for the production of competing products;

(e)   'product' means a good or a service, including both intermediary goods and services and final goods and services;

(f)   'contract products' means products produced with the licensed technology;

(g) 'intellectual property rights' includes industrial property rights, know-how, copyright and neighboring rights;

(h) 'patents' means patents, patent applications, utility models, applications for registration of utility models, designs, topographies of semiconductor products, supplementary protection certificates for medicinal products or other products for which such supplementary protection certificates may be obtained and plant breeder's certificates;

(i) 'know-how' means a package of non-patented practical information, resulting from experience and testing, which is:

    (i) secret, that is to say, not generally known or easily accessible,

    (ii) substantial, that is to say, significant and useful for the production of the contract products, and (iii) identified, that is to say, described in a sufficiently comprehensive manner so as to make it possible to verify that it fulfils the criteria of secrecy and substantiality;

(j) 'competing undertakings' means undertakings which compete on the relevant technology market and/or the relevant product market, that is to say:

    (i) competing undertakings on the relevant technology market, being undertakings which license out competing technologies without infringing each other's intellectual property rights (actual competitors on the technology market); the relevant technology market includes technologies which are regarded by the licensees as interchangeable with or substitutable for the licensed technology, by reason of the technologies' characteristics, their royalties and their intended use,

    (ii) competing undertakings on the relevant product market, being undertakings which, in the absence of the technology transfer agreement, are both active on the relevant product and geographic market(s) on which the contract products are sold without infringing each other's intellectual property rights (actual competitors on the product market) or would, on realistic grounds, undertake the necessary additional investments or other necessary switching costs so that they could timely enter, without infringing each other's intellectual property rights, the(se) relevant product and geographic market(s) in response to a small and permanent increase in relative prices (potential competitors on the product market); the relevant product market comprises products which are regarded by the buyers as interchangeable with or substitutable for the contract products, by reason of the products' characteristics, their prices and their intended use;

(k) 'selective distribution system' means a distribution system where the licensor undertakes to license the production of the contract products only to licensees selected on the basis of specified criteria and where these licensees undertake not to sell the contract products to unauthorized distributors;

(l) 'exclusive territory' means a territory in which only one undertaking is allowed to produce the contract products with the licensed technology, without prejudice to the possibility of allowing within that territory another licensee to produce the contract products only for a particular customer where this second licence was granted in order to create an alternative source of supply for that customer;

(m) 'exclusive customer group' means a group of customers to which only one undertaking is allowed actively to sell the contract products produced with the licensed technology;

(n) 'severable improvement' means an improvement that can be exploited without infringing the licensed technology.

2. The terms 'undertaking', 'licensor' and 'licensee' shall include their respective connected undertakings.

'Connected undertakings' means:

(a) undertakings in which a party to the agreement, directly or indirectly:

(i) has the power to exercise more than half the voting rights, or

(ii) has the power to appoint more than half the members of the supervisory board, board of management or bodies legally representing the undertaking, or

(iii) has the right to manage the undertaking's affairs;

(b) undertakings which directly or indirectly have, over a party to the agreement, the rights or powers listed in (a);

(c) undertakings in which an undertaking referred to in (b) has, directly or indirectly, the rights or powers listed in (a);

(d) undertakings in which a party to the agreement together with one or more of the undertakings referred to in (a), (b) or (c), or in which two or more of the latter undertakings, jointly have the rights or powers listed in (a);

(e) undertakings in which the rights or the powers listed in (a) are jointly held by:

(i) parties to the agreement or their respective connected undertakings referred to in (a) to (d), or

(ii) one or more of the parties to the agreement or one or more of their connected undertakings referred to in (a) to (d) and one or more third parties.

Article 2

Exemption

Pursuant to Article 81(3) of the Treaty and subject to the provisions of this Regulation, it is hereby declared that Article 81(1) of the Treaty shall not apply to technology transfer agreements entered into between two undertakings permitting the production of contract products. This exemption shall apply to the extent that such agreements contain restrictions of competition falling within the scope of Article 81(1). The exemption shall apply for as long as the intellectual property right in the licensed technology has not expired, lapsed or been declared invalid or, in the case of know-how, for as long as the know-how remains secret, except in the event where the know-how becomes publicly known as a result of action by the licensee, in which case the exemption shall apply for the duration of the agreement.

Article 3

Market-share thresholds

1.   Where the undertakings party to the agreement are competing undertakings, the exemption provided for in Article 2 shall apply on condition that the combined market share of the parties does not exceed 20% on the affected relevant technology and product market.

2.   Where the undertakings party to the agreement are not competing undertakings, the exemption provided for in Article 2 shall apply on condition that the market share of each of the parties does not exceed 30% on the affected relevant technology and product market.

3.   For the purposes of paragraphs 1 and 2, the market share of a party on the relevant technology market(s) is defined in terms of the presence of the licensed technology on the relevant product market(s). A licensor's market share on the relevant technology market shall be the combined market share on the relevant product market of the contract products produced by the licensor and its licensees.

Article 4

Hardcore restrictions

1.   Where the undertakings party to the agreement are competing undertakings, the exemption provided for in Article 2 shall not apply to agreements which, directly or indirectly, in isolation or in combination with other factors under the control of the parties, have as their object:

(a)   the restriction of a party's ability to determine its prices when selling products to third parties;

(b)   the limitation of output, except limitations on the output of contract products imposed on the licensee in a non-reciprocal agreement or imposed on only one of the licensees in a reciprocal agreement;

(c)   the allocation of markets or customers except:

(i)   the obligation on the licensee(s) to produce with the licensed technology only within one or more technical fields of use or one or more product markets,

(ii)   the obligation on the licensor and/or the licensee, in a non-reciprocal agreement, not to produce with the licensed technology within one or more technical fields of use or one or more product markets or one or more exclusive territories reserved for the other party,

(iii)   the obligation on the licensor not to license the technology to another licensee in a particular territory,

(iv)   the restriction, in a non-reciprocal agreement, of active and/or passive sales by the licensee and/or the licensor into the exclusive territory or to the exclusive customer group reserved for the other party,

(v)   the restriction, in a non-reciprocal agreement, of active sales by the licensee into the exclusive territory or to the exclusive customer group allocated by the licensor to another licensee provided the latter was not a competing undertaking of the licensor at the time of the conclusion of its own licence,

(vi)   the obligation on the licensee to produce the contract products only for its own use provided that the licensee is not restricted in selling the contract products actively and passively as spare parts for its own products,

(vii)   the obligation on the licensee, in a non-reciprocal agreement, to produce the contract products only for a particular customer, where the licence was granted in order to create an alternative source of supply for that customer;

(d)   the restriction of the licensee's ability to exploit its own technology or the restriction of the ability of any of the parties to the agreement to carry out research and development, unless such latter restriction is indispensable to prevent the disclosure of the licensed know-how to third parties.

2.   Where the undertakings party to the agreement are not competing undertakings, the exemption provided for in Article 2 shall not apply to agreements which, directly or indirectly, in isolation or in combination with other factors under the control of the parties, have as their object:

(a)   the restriction of a party's ability to determine its prices when selling products to third parties, without prejudice to the possibility of imposing a maximum sale price or recommending a sale price, provided that it does not amount to a fixed or minimum sale price as a result of pressure from, or incentives offered by, any of the parties;

(b)   the restriction of the territory into which, or of the customers to whom, the licensee may passively sell the contract products, except:

(i)   the restriction of passive sales into an exclusive territory or to an exclusive customer group reserved for the licensor,

(ii)   the restriction of passive sales into an exclusive territory or to an exclusive customer group allocated by the licensor to another licensee during the first two years that this other licensee is selling the contract products in that territory or to that customer group,

(iii)   the obligation to produce the contract products only for its own use provided that the licensee is not restricted in selling the contract products actively and passively as spare parts for its own products,

(iv)   the obligation to produce the contract products only for a particular customer, where the licence was granted in order to create an alternative source of supply for that customer,

(v)   the restriction of sales to end-users by a licensee operating at the wholesale level of trade,

(vi)   the restriction of sales to unauthorised distributors by the members of a selective distribution system;

(c)   the restriction of active or passive sales to end-users by a licensee which is a member of a selective distribution system and which operates at the retail level, without prejudice to the possibility of prohibiting a member of the system from operating out of an unauthorised place of establishment.

3.   Where the undertakings party to the agreement are not competing undertakings at the time of the conclusion of the agreement but become competing undertakings afterwards, paragraph 2 and not paragraph 1 shall apply for the full life of the agreement unless the agreement is subsequently amended in any material respect.

Article 5

Excluded restrictions

1.   The exemption provided for in Article 2 shall not apply to any of the following obligations contained in technology transfer agreements:

(a)   any direct or indirect obligation on the licensee to grant an exclusive licence to the licensor or to a third party designated by the licensor in respect of its own severable improvements to or its own new applications of the licensed technology;

(b)   any direct or indirect obligation on the licensee to assign, in whole or in part, to the licensor or to a third party designated by the licensor, rights to its own severable improvements to or its own new applications of the licensed technology;

(c)   any direct or indirect obligation on the licensee not to challenge the validity of intellectual property rights which the licensor holds in the common market, without prejudice to the possibility of providing for termination of the technology transfer agreement in the event that the licensee challenges the validity of one or more of the licensed intellectual property rights.

2.   Where the undertakings party to the agreement are not competing undertakings, the exemption provided for in Article 2 shall not apply to any direct or indirect obligation limiting the licensee's ability to exploit its own technology or limiting the ability of any of the parties to the agreement to carry out research and development, unless such latter restriction is indispensable to prevent the disclosure of the licensed know-how to third parties.

Article 6

Withdrawal in individual cases

1.   The Commission may withdraw the benefit of this Regulation, pursuant to Article 29(1) of Regulation (EC) No 1/2003, where it finds in any particular case that a technology transfer agreement to which the exemption provided for in Article 2 applies nevertheless has effects which are incompatible with Article 81(3) of the Treaty, and in particular where:

(a)   access of third parties' technologies to the market is restricted, for instance by the cumulative effect of parallel networks of similar restrictive agreements prohibiting licensees from using third parties' technologies;

(b)   access of potential licensees to the market is restricted, for instance by the cumulative effect of parallel networks of similar restrictive agreements prohibiting licensors from licensing to other licensees;

(c)   without any objectively valid reason, the parties do not exploit the licensed technology.

2.   Where, in any particular case, a technology transfer agreement to which the exemption provided for in Article 2 applies has effects which are incompatible with Article 81(3) of the Treaty in the territory of a Member State, or in a part thereof, which has all the characteristics of a distinct geographic market, the competition authority of that Member State may withdraw the benefit of this Regulation, pursuant to Article 29(2) of Regulation (EC) No 1/2003, in respect of that territory, under the same circumstances as those set out in paragraph 1 of this Article.

Article 7

Non-application of this Regulation

1.   Pursuant to Article 1a of Regulation No 19/65/EEC, the Commission may by regulation declare that, where parallel networks of similar technology transfer agreements cover more than 50 % of a relevant market, this Regulation is not to apply to technology transfer agreements containing specific restraints relating to that market.

2.   A regulation pursuant to paragraph 1 shall not become applicable earlier than six months following its adoption.

Article 8

Application of the market-share thresholds

1.   For the purposes of applying the market-share thresholds provided for in Article 3 the rules set out in this paragraph shall apply. The market share shall be calculated on the basis of market sales value data. If market sales value data are not available, estimates based on other reliable market information, including market sales volumes, may be used to establish the market share of the undertaking concerned. The market share shall be calculated on the basis of data relating to the preceding calendar year. The market share held by the undertakings referred to in point (e) of the second subparagraph of Article 1(2) shall be apportioned equally to each undertaking having the rights or the powers listed in point (a) of the second subparagraph of Article 1(2).

2.   If the market share referred to in Article 3(1) or (2) is initially not more than 20 % respectively 30 % but subsequently rises above those levels, the exemption provided for in Article 2 shall continue to apply for a period of two consecutive calendar years following the year in which the 20 % threshold or 30 % threshold was first exceeded.

Article 9

Repeal

Regulation (EC) No 240/96 is repealed. References to the repealed Regulation shall be construed as references to this Regulation.

Article 10

Transitional period

The prohibition laid down in Article 81(1) of the Treaty shall not apply during the period from 1 May 2004 to 31 March 2006 in respect of agreements already in force on 30 April 2004 which do not satisfy the conditions for exemption provided for in this Regulation but which, on 30 April 2004, satisfied the conditions for exemption provided for in Regulation (EC) No 240/96.

Article 11

Period of validity

This Regulation shall enter into force on 1 May 2004. It shall expire on 30 April 2014.

This Regulation shall be binding in its entirety and directly applicable in all Member States.

Done at Brussels, 27 April 2004.

For the Commission, Mario MONTI

Member of the Commission

§ 15.26   Text of EU Technology Transfer Regulation 316/2014

COMMISSION REGULATION (EU) No 316/2014

of 21 March 2014

on the application of Article 101(3) of the Treaty on the Functioning of the European Union to categories of technology transfer agreements (Text with EEA relevance)

THE EUROPEAN COMMISSION,

Having regard to the Treaty on the Functioning of the European Union,

Having regard to Regulation No 19/65/EEC of the Council of 2 March 1965 on application of Article 85(3) of the Treaty to certain categories of agreements and concerted practices (1), and in particular Article 1 thereof,

Having published a draft of this Regulation,

After consulting the Advisory Committee on Restrictive Practices and Dominant Positions,

Whereas:

(1)   Regulation No 19/65/EEC empowers the Commission to apply Article 101(3) of the Treaty by regulation to certain categories of technology transfer agreements and corresponding concerted practices to which only two undertakings are party which fall within Article 101(1) of the Treaty.

(2)   Pursuant to Regulation No 19/65/EEC, the Commission has, in particular, adopted Commission Regulation (EC) No 772/2004 (2).

Regulation (EC) No 772/2004 defines categories of technology transfer agreements which the Commission regarded as normally satisfying the conditions laid down in Article 101(3) of the Treaty. In view of the overall positive experience with the application of that Regulation, which expires on 30 April 2014, and taking into account further experience acquired since its adoption, it is appropriate to adopt a new block exemption regulation.

(3)   This Regulation should meet the two requirements of ensuring effective protection of competition and providing adequate legal security for undertakings. The pursuit of those objectives should take account of the need to simplify administrative supervision and the legislative framework to as great an extent as possible.

(4)   Technology transfer agreements concern the licensing of technology rights. Such agreements will usually improve economic efficiency and be pro-competitive as they can reduce duplication of research and development, strengthen the incentive for the initial research and development, spur incremental innovation, facilitate diffusion and generate product market competition.

(5)   The likelihood that such efficiency-enhancing and pro-competitive effects will outweigh any anti-competitive effects due to restrictions contained in technology transfer agreements depends on the degree of market power of the undertakings concerned and, therefore, on the extent to which those undertakings face competition from undertakings owning substitute technologies or undertakings producing substitute products.

(6)   This Regulation should cover only technology transfer agreements between a licensor and a licensee. It should cover such agreements even if the agreement contains conditions relating to more than one level of trade, for instance requiring the licensee to set up a particular distribution system and specifying the obligations the licensee must or may impose on resellers of the products produced under the licence. However, such conditions and obligations should comply with the competition rules applicable to supply and distribution agreements set out in Commission Regulation (EU) No 330/2010 (3). Supply and distribution agreements concluded between a licensee and buyers of its contract products should not be exempted by this Regulation. EN 28.3.2014 Official Journal of the European Union L 93/17

NOTES: (1)   OJ 36, 6.3.1965, p. 533/65.

(2)   Commission Regulation (EC) No 772/2004 of 7 April 2004 on the application of Article 81(3) of the Treaty to categories of technology transfer agreements (OJ L 123, 27.4.2004, p. 11).

(3)   Commission Regulation (EU) No 330/2010 of 20 April 2010 on the application of Article 101(3) of the Treaty on the Functioning of the European Union to categories of vertical agreements and concerted practices (OJ L 102, 23.4.2010, p. 1).

(7)   This Regulation should only apply to agreements where the licensor permits the licensee and/or one or more of its sub-contractors to exploit the licensed technology rights, possibly after further research and

development by the licensee and/or its sub-contractors, for the purpose of producing goods or services. It should not apply to licensing in the context of research and development agreements which are covered by Commission Regulation (EU) No 1217/2010 (1) or to licensing in the context of specialization agreements which are covered by Commission Regulation (EU) No 1218/2010 (2). It should also not apply to agreements, the purpose of which is the mere reproduction and distribution of software copyright protected products as such agreements do not concern the licensing of a technology to produce but are more akin to distribution agreements. Nor should it apply to agreements to set up technology pools, that is to say, agreements for the pooling of technologies with the purpose of licensing them to third parties, or to agreements whereby the pooled technology is licensed out to those third parties.

(8)   For the application of Article 101(3) of the Treaty by regulation, it is not necessary to define those technology transfer agreements that are capable of falling within Article 101(1) of the Treaty. In the individual assessment of agreements pursuant to Article 101(1), account has to be taken of several factors, and in particular the structure and the dynamics of the relevant technology and product markets.

(9)   The benefit of the block exemption established by this Regulation should be limited to those agreements which can be assumed with sufficient certainty to satisfy the conditions of Article 101(3) of the Treaty. In order to attain the benefits and objectives of technology transfer, this Regulation should not only cover the transfer of technology as such but also other provisions contained in technology transfer agreements if, and to the extent that, those provisions are directly related to the production or sale of the contract products.

(10)   For technology transfer agreements between competitors it can be presumed that, where the combined share of the relevant markets accounted for by the parties does not exceed 20 % and the agreements do not contain certain severely anti-competitive restrictions, they generally lead to an improvement in production or distribution and allow consumers a fair share of the resulting benefits.

(11)   For technology transfer agreements between non-competitors it can be presumed that, where the individual share of the relevant markets accounted for by each of the parties does not exceed 30 % and the agreements do not contain certain severely anti-competitive restrictions, they generally lead to an improvement in production or distribution and allow consumers a fair share of the resulting benefits.

(12)   If the applicable market-share threshold is exceeded on one or more product or technology markets, the block exemption should not apply to the agreement for the relevant markets concerned.

(13)   There can be no presumption that, above those market-share thresholds, technology transfer agreements fall within the scope of Article 101(1) of the Treaty. For instance, exclusive licensing agreements between non-competing undertakings often fall outside the scope of Article 101(1). There can also be no presumption that, above those market-share thresholds,

technology transfer agreements falling within the scope of Article 101(1) will not satisfy the conditions for exemption. However, it can also not be presumed that they will usually give rise to objective advantages of such a character and size as to compensate for the disadvantages which they create for competition.

(14) This Regulation should not exempt technology transfer agreements containing restrictions which are not indispensable to the improvement of production or distribution. In particular, technology transfer agreements containing certain severely anti-competitive restrictions, such as the fixing of prices charged to third parties, should be excluded from the benefit of the block exemption established by this Regulation irrespective of the market shares of the undertakings concerned. In the case of such hardcore restrictions the whole agreement should be excluded from the benefit of the block exemption.

(15) In order to protect incentives to innovate and the appropriate application of intellectual property rights, certain restrictions should be excluded from the benefit of the block exemption. In particular certain grant back obligations and non-challenge clauses should be excluded. Where such a restriction is included in a licence agreement only the restriction in question should be excluded from the benefit of the block exemption.

NOTES: (1) Commission Regulation (EU) No 1217/2010 of 14 December 2010 on the application of Article 101(3) of the Treaty on the Functioning of the European Union to certain categories of research and development agreements (OJ L 335, 18.12.2010, p. 36).

(2)   Commission Regulation (EU) No 1218/2010 of 14 December 2010 on the application of Article 101(3) of the Treaty on the Functioning of the European Union to certain categories of specialization agreements (OJ L 335, 18.12.2010, p. 43).

(16) The market-share thresholds and the non-exemption of technology transfer agreements containing the severely anti-competitive restrictions and the excluded restrictions provided for in this Regulation will normally ensure that the agreements to which the block exemption applies do not enable the participating undertakings to eliminate competition in respect of a substantial part of the products in question.

(17) The Commission may withdraw the benefit of this Regulation, pursuant to Article 29(1) of Council Regulation (EC) No 1/2003 (1), where it finds in a particular case that an agreement to which the exemption provided for in this Regulation applies nevertheless has effects which are incompatible with Article 101(3) of the Treaty. This may occur in particular where the incentives to innovate are reduced or where access to markets is hindered.

(18) The competition authority of a Member State may withdraw the benefit of this Regulation pursuant to Article 29(2) of Regulation (EC) No 1/2003 in respect of the territory of that Member State, or a part thereof where, in a particular case, an agreement to which the exemption provided for in this Regulation applies nevertheless has effects which are incompatible with Article 101(3) of the Treaty in the territory of that Member State, or in

a part thereof, and where such territory has all the characteristics of a distinct geographic market.

(19) In order to strengthen supervision of parallel networks of technology transfer agreements which have similar restrictive effects and which cover more than 50 % of a given market, the Commission may by regulation declare this Regulation inapplicable to technology transfer agreements containing specific restrictions relating to the market concerned, thereby restoring the full application of Article 101 of the Treaty to such agreements,

HAS ADOPTED THIS REGULATION:

Article 1

Definitions

1.   For the purposes of this Regulation, the following definitions shall apply:

(a)   'agreement' means an agreement, a decision of an association of undertakings or a concerted practice;

(b)   'technology rights' means know-how and the following rights, or a combination thereof, including applications for or applications for registration of those rights:

(i)   patents,

(ii)   utility models,

(iii)   design rights,

(iv)   topographies of semiconductor products,

(v)   supplementary protection certificates for medicinal products or other products for which such supplementary protection certificates may be obtained,

(vi)   plant breeder's certificates and

(vii)   software copyrights;

(c)   'technology transfer agreement' means:

(i)   a technology rights licensing agreement entered into between two undertakings for the purpose of the production of contract products by the licensee and/or its sub-contractor(s),

(ii)   an assignment of technology rights between two undertakings for the purpose of the production of contract products where part of the risk associated with the exploitation of the technology remains with the assignor;

(d)   'reciprocal agreement' means a technology transfer agreement where two undertakings grant each other, in the same or separate contracts, a technology rights licence, and where those licences concern competing technologies or can be used for the production of competing products;

(e)   'non-reciprocal agreement' means a technology transfer agreement where one undertaking grants another undertaking a technology rights licence, or where two undertakings grant each other such a licence but where those licences do not concern competing technologies and cannot be used for the production of competing products;

(f) 'product' means goods or a service, including both intermediary goods and services and final goods and services;

(g) 'contract product' means a product produced, directly or indirectly, on the basis of the licensed technology rights;

(h) 'intellectual property rights' includes industrial property rights, in particular patents and trademarks, copyright and neighbouring rights; EN 28.3.2014 Official Journal of the European Union L 93/19

(i) 'know-how' means a package of practical information, resulting from experience and testing, which is:

(i) secret, that is to say, not generally known or easily accessible,

(ii) substantial, that is to say, significant and useful for the production of the contract products, and

(iii) identified, that is to say, described in a sufficiently comprehensive manner so as to make it possible to verify that it fulfils the criteria of secrecy and substantiality;

(j) 'relevant product market' means the market for the contract products and their substitutes, that is to say all those products which are regarded as interchangeable or substitutable by the buyer, by reason of the products' characteristics, their prices and their intended use;

(k) 'relevant technology market' means the market for the licensed technology rights and their substitutes, that is to say all those technology rights which are regarded as interchangeable or substitutable by the licensee, by reason of the technology rights' characteristics, the royalties payable in respect of those rights and their intended use;

(l) 'relevant geographic market' means the area in which the undertakings concerned are involved in the supply of and demand for products or the licensing of technology rights, in which the conditions of competition are sufficiently homogeneous and which can be distinguished from neighboring areas because the conditions of competition are appreciably different in those areas;

(m) 'relevant market' means the combination of the relevant product or technology market with the relevant geographic market;

(n) 'competing undertakings' means undertakings which compete on the relevant market, that is to say:

(i) competing undertakings on the relevant market where the technology rights are licensed, that is to say, undertakings which license out competing technology rights (actual competitors on the relevant market),

(ii) competing undertakings on the relevant market where the contract products are sold, that is to say, undertakings which, in the absence of the technology transfer agreement, would both be active on the relevant market(s) on which the contract products are sold (actual competitors on the relevant market) or which, in the absence of the technology transfer agreement, would, on realistic grounds and not just as a mere theoretical possibility, in response to a small and permanent increase in relative prices, be likely to undertake, within a short period of time, the necessary additional investments or other necessary switching costs to enter the relevant market(s) (potential competitors on the relevant market);

(o)   'selective distribution system' means a distribution system where the licensor undertakes to license the production of the contract products, either directly or indirectly, only to licensees selected on the basis of specified criteria and where those licensees undertake not to sell the contract products to unauthorised distributors within the territory reserved by the licensor to operate that system;

(p)   'exclusive licence' means a licence under which the licensor itself is not permitted to produce on the basis of the licensed technology rights and is not permitted to license the licensed technology rights to third parties, in general or for a particular use or in a particular territory;

(q)   'exclusive territory' means a given territory within which only one undertaking is allowed to produce the contract products, but where it is nevertheless possible to allow another licensee to produce the contract products within that territory only for a particular customer where the second licence was granted in order to create an alternative source of supply for that customer;

(r)   'exclusive customer group' means a group of customers to which only one party to the technology transfer agreement is allowed to actively sell the contract products produced with the licensed technology.

2.   For the purposes of this Regulation, the terms 'undertaking', 'licensor' and 'licensee' shall include their respective connected undertakings.

'Connected undertakings' means:

(a)   undertakings in which a party to the technology transfer agreement, directly or indirectly:

(i)   has the power to exercise more than half the voting rights, or

(ii)   has the power to appoint more than half the members of the supervisory board, board of management or bodies legally representing the undertaking, or

(iii)   has the right to manage the undertaking's affairs;

(b)   undertakings which directly or indirectly have, over a party to the technology transfer agreement, the rights or powers listed in point (a);

(c)   undertakings in which an undertaking referred to in point (b) has, directly or indirectly, the rights or powers listed in point (a);

(d)   undertakings in which a party to the technology transfer agreement together with one or more of the undertakings referred to in points (a), (b) or (c), or in which two or more of the latter undertakings, jointly have the rights or powers listed in point (a);

(e)   undertakings in which the rights or the powers listed in point (a) are jointly held by:

(i)   parties to the technology transfer agreement or their respective connected undertakings referred to in points (a) to (d), or

(ii)   one or more of the parties to the technology transfer agreement or one or more of their connected undertakings referred to in points (a) to (d) and one or more third parties.

Article 2

Exemption

1.   Pursuant to Article 101(3) of the Treaty and subject to the provisions of this Regulation, Article 101(1) of the Treaty shall not apply to technology transfer agreements.

2.   The exemption provided for in paragraph 1 shall apply to the extent that technology transfer agreements contain restrictions of competition falling within the scope of Article 101(1) of the Treaty. The exemption shall apply for as long as the licensed technology rights have not expired, lapsed or been declared invalid or, in the case of know-how, for as long as the know-how remains secret. However, where know-how becomes publicly known as a result of action by the licensee, the exemption shall apply for the duration of the agreement.

3.   The exemption provided for in paragraph 1 shall also apply to provisions, in technology transfer agreements, which relate to the purchase of products by the licensee or which relate to the licensing or assignment of other intellectual property rights or know-how to the licensee, if, and to the extent that, those provisions are directly related to the production or sale of the contract products.

Article 3

Market-share thresholds

1.   Where the undertakings party to the agreement are competing undertakings, the exemption provided for in Article 2 shall apply on condition that the combined market share of the parties does not exceed 20 % on the relevant market(s).

2.   Where the undertakings party to the agreement are not competing undertakings, the exemption provided for in Article 2 shall apply on condition that the market share of each of the parties does not exceed 30 % on the relevant market(s).

Article 4

Hardcore restrictions

1.   Where the undertakings party to the agreement are competing undertakings, the exemption provided for in Article 2 shall not apply to agreements which, directly or indirectly, in isolation or in combination with other factors under the control of the parties, have as their object any of the following:

(a)   the restriction of a party's ability to determine its prices when selling products to third parties;

(b)   the limitation of output, except limitations on the output of contract products imposed on the licensee in a non-reciprocal agreement or imposed on only one of the licensees in a reciprocal agreement;

(c)   the allocation of markets or customers except:

   (i)   the obligation on the licensor and/or the licensee, in a non-reciprocal agreement, not to produce with the licensed technology rights within the exclusive territory reserved for the other party and/or not to sell actively and/or passively into the exclusive territory or to the exclusive customer group reserved for the other party,

   (ii)   the restriction, in a non-reciprocal agreement, of active sales by the licensee into the exclusive territory or to the exclusive customer group allocated by the licensor to another licensee provided the latter was not a competing undertaking of the licensor at the time of the conclusion of its own licence,

   (iii)   the obligation on the licensee to produce the contract products only for its own use provided that the licensee is not restricted in selling the contract products actively and passively as spare parts for its own products,

   (iv)   the obligation on the licensee, in a non-reciprocal agreement, to produce the contract products only for a particular customer, where the licence was granted in order to create an alternative source of supply for that customer;

(d)   the restriction of the licensee's ability to exploit its own technology rights or the restriction of the ability of any of the parties to the agreement to carry out research and development, unless such latter restriction is indispensable to prevent the disclosure of the licensed know-how to third parties.

   2.   Where the undertakings party to the agreement are not competing undertakings, the exemption provided for in Article 2 shall not apply to agreements which, directly or indirectly, in isolation or in combination with other factors under the control of the parties, have as their object any of the following:

(a)   the restriction of a party's ability to determine its prices when selling products to third parties, without prejudice to the possibility of imposing a maximum sale price or recommending a sale price, provided that it does not amount to a fixed or minimum sale price as a result of pressure from, or incentives offered by, any of the parties;

(b)   the restriction of the territory into which, or of the customers to whom, the licensee may passively sell the contract products, except:

   (i)   the restriction of passive sales into an exclusive territory or to an exclusive customer group reserved for the licensor,

(ii)   the obligation to produce the contract products only for its own use provided that the licensee is not restricted in selling the contract products actively and passively as spare parts for its own products,

(iii)   the obligation to produce the contract products only for a particular customer, where the licence was granted in order to create an alternative source of supply for that customer,

(iv)   the restriction of sales to end-users by a licensee operating at the wholesale level of trade,

(v)   the restriction of sales to unauthorised distributors by the members of a selective distribution system;

(c)   the restriction of active or passive sales to end-users by a licensee which is a member of a selective distribution system and which operates at the retail level, without prejudice to the possibility of prohibiting a member of the system from operating out of an unauthorized place of establishment.

3.   Where the undertakings party to the agreement are not competing undertakings at the time of the conclusion of the agreement but become competing undertakings afterwards, paragraph 2 and not paragraph 1 shall apply for the full life of the agreement unless the agreement is subsequently amended in any material respect. Such an amendment includes the conclusion of a new technology transfer agreement between the parties concerning competing technology rights.

Article 5

Excluded restrictions

1.   The exemption provided for in Article 2 shall not apply to any of the following obligations contained in technology transfer agreements:

(a)   any direct or indirect obligation on the licensee to grant an exclusive licence or to assign rights, in whole or in part, to the licensor or to a third party designated by the licensor in respect of its own improvements to, or its own new applications of, the licensed technology;

(b)   any direct or indirect obligation on a party not to challenge the validity of intellectual property rights which the other party holds in the Union, without prejudice to the possibility, in the case of an exclusive licence, of providing for termination of the technology transfer agreement in the event that the licensee challenges the validity of any of the licensed technology rights.

2.   Where the undertakings party to the agreement are not competing undertakings, the exemption provided for in Article 2 shall not apply to any direct or indirect obligation limiting the licensee's ability to exploit its own technology rights or limiting the ability of any of the parties to the agreement to carry out research and development, unless such latter restriction is indispensable to prevent the disclosure of the licensed know-how to third parties.

Article 6

Withdrawal in individual cases

1.   The Commission may withdraw the benefit of this Regulation, pursuant to Article 29(1) of Regulation (EC) No 1/2003, where it finds in any particular case that a technology transfer agreement to which the exemption provided for in Article 2 of this Regulation applies nevertheless has effects which are incompatible with Article 101(3) of the Treaty, and in particular where:

(a)   access of third parties' technologies to the market is restricted, for instance by the cumulative effect of parallel networks of similar restrictive agreements prohibiting licensees from using third parties' technologies;

(b)   access of potential licensees to the market is restricted, for instance by the cumulative effect of parallel networks of similar restrictive agreements prohibiting licensors from licensing to other licensees or because the only technology owner licensing out relevant technology rights concludes an exclusive license with a licensee who is already active on the product market on the basis of substitutable technology rights.

2.   Where, in any particular case, a technology transfer agreement to which the exemption provided for in Article 2 of this Regulation applies has effects which are incompatible with Article 101(3) of the Treaty in the territory of a Member State, or in a part thereof, which has all the characteristics of a distinct geographic market, the competition authority of that Member State may withdraw the benefit of this Regulation, pursuant to Article 29(2) of Regulation (EC) No 1/2003, in respect of that territory, under the same circumstances as those set out in paragraph 1 of this Article.

Article 7

Non-application of this Regulation

1.   Pursuant to Article 1a of Regulation (EC) No 19/65/EEC, the Commission may by regulation declare that, where parallel networks of similar technology transfer agreements cover more than 50% of a relevant market, this Regulation is not to apply to technology transfer agreements containing specific restrictions relating to that market.

2.   A regulation pursuant to paragraph 1 shall not become applicable earlier than six months following its adoption.

Article 8

Application of the market-share thresholds

For the purposes of applying the market-share thresholds laid down in Article 3 the following rules shall apply:

(a)   the market share shall be calculated on the basis of market sales value data; if market sales value data are not available, estimates based on other reliable market information, including market sales volumes, may be used to establish the market share of the undertaking concerned;

(b)   the market share shall be calculated on the basis of data relating to the preceding calendar year;

(c)   the market share held by the undertakings referred to in point (e) of the second subparagraph of Article 1(2) shall be apportioned equally to each undertaking having the rights or the powers listed in point (a) of the second subparagraph of Article 1(2);

(d)   the market share of a licensor on a relevant market for the licensed technology rights shall be calculated on the basis of the presence of the licensed technology rights on the relevant market(s) (that is the product market(s) and the geographic market(s)) where the contract products are sold, that is on the basis of the sales data relating to the contract products produced by the licensor and its licensees combined;

(e)   if the market share referred to in Article 3(1) or (2) is initially not more than 20% or 30% respectively, but subsequently rises above those levels, the exemption provided for in Article 2 shall continue to apply for a period of two consecutive calendar years following the year in which the 20% threshold or 30% threshold was first exceeded.

Article 9

Relationship with other block exemption regulations

This Regulation shall not apply to licensing arrangements in research and development agreements which fall within the scope of Regulation (EU) No 1217/2010 or in specialization agreements which fall within the scope of Regulation (EU) No 1218/2010.

Article 10

Transitional period

The prohibition laid down in Article 101(1) of the Treaty shall not apply from 1 May 2014 until 30 April 2015 to agreements already in force on 30 April 2014 which do not satisfy the conditions for exemption provided for in this Regulation but which, on 30 April 2014, satisfied the conditions for exemption provided for in Regulation (EC) No 772/2004.

Article 11

Period of validity

This Regulation shall enter into force on 1 May 2014. It shall expire on 30 April 2026.

This Regulation shall be binding in its entirety and directly applicable in all Member States.

Done at Brussels, 21 March 2014.

For the Commission, On behalf of the President,

Joaquín ALMUNIA, *Vice President*

Chapter 16

AN EARLY COMMENTARY ON TRADE POLICY UNDER THE TRUMP ADMINISTRATION

Table of Sections

For the first time in many years, international trade was a major issue in a U.S. Presidential election. In 2016, Donald J. Trump made it so. He campaigned and tweeted against trade deficits, currency manipulation, NAFTA as "the worst trade deal ever", other U.S. multilateral and bilateral trade agreements, and the signed but not ratified twelve-nation Trans-Pacific Partnership (TPP) formulated as part of President Obama's "pivot to Asia". Rallying the oft-forgotten losers under U.S. trade policy, he swept into office in 2017 as the world took a deep breath and wondered what might come.

Here is a list of major U.S. trade policy decisions that have been made to date:

1.   President Trump quickly withdrew from the TPP, essentially making a gift of trade leadership in Asia to China. President Xi Xinping at Davos accepted this gift, noting ongoing negotiations for its competing trade alliance: The Regional Cooperation and Economic Partnership (RCEP) comprised of the ASEAN states, Japan, China and India, but not the United States. Meanwhile, the remaining eleven TPP states are actively considering revival of a TPP agreement minus the USA, and Japan has notably agreed to free trade with the EU. *See* R. Folsom, *Principles of Free Trade Agreements* (forthcoming).

2.   President Trump formally notified Congress of his intent to "re-negotiate" NAFTA with Canada and Mexico. Of course, he had tweeted he was going to tear up the NAFTA agreement, so perhaps something resembling reality was beginning to sink in. By May of 2017, the Trump administration had notified Congress of its intent to re-

negotiate NAFTA under U.S. "fast track" (Trade Promotion Authority) rules that carried over into his Presidency, but are scheduled to die July 1, 2018. Negotiations formally commenced in August of 2017. *See* Section 16.1 for a review of issues raised in the NAFTA re-negotiation, adapted from R. Folsom and W. D. Folsom, *NAFTA Re-Negotiated and Its Business Implications* (forthcoming).

3.   The Trump administration launched an extensive review of U.S. participation in the World Trade Organization (WTO), the ultimate multilateral agreement embraced by approximately 165 countries and customs territories. As with NAFTA, the WTO allows for withdrawal upon six months' notice. Special attention is being given to WTO "most-favored-nation" trade principles, trade remedies and dispute resolution. *See* Chapter 1.

4.   The President has promised a free trade agreement with Britain post-BREXIT, and dialogue along those lines has started. The UK is one a few countries with which the United States runs a sizeable trade surplus. Whether and when BREXIT will occur, and on what terms, is hotly debated. An analysis of BREXIT issues, adapted from R. Folsom, *Principles of European Union Law including BREXIT* (2017), follows in Section 16.2.

Meanwhile the U.S.-EU negotiations for a Transatlantic Trade and Investment Partnership (TTIP) initiated by President Obama are on a back burner. After considerable delay, Canada and the EU implemented their Comprehensive Economic and Trade Partnership (CETA) in 2017, and Mexico is re-negotiating its year 2000 EU free trade deal.

5.   In August of 2017, the Trump Administration commenced re-negotiation of the U.S.-South Korea free trade agreement (KORUS), expressing concerns about the large U.S. trade deficit in goods with Korea, while ignoring a sizeable trade surplus in services. Several major Korean firms announced plans to invest in the United States, and Korea pulled its WTO Appellate Body member back home to negotiate with the Trump Administration. Then North Korea shot a missile over Japan and exploded a thermonuclear bomb. The United States, at a hefty price, promised South Korea major defense armaments and withdrew pressure to re-negotiate the KORUS agreement.

6.   Few countries took more abuse than China in the U.S. Presidential election race of 2016, particularly for its massive trade surplus with the United States, though Mexico was a close second. Roughly 20% of all U.S. imports come from China. Upon taking office, President Trump proceeded to question U.S. adherence to the "One China" policy which suggests that Taiwan is not independent from the PRC. It was only after President Trump reaffirmed this Policy that President Xi Xinping visited him in Florida for what seemed to be an amicable meeting. Subsequently, President Trump withdrew, contrary to numerous prior tweets and pronouncements, assertions that China was a currency manipulator. Perhaps he realized that China had in recent years spent about $1 trillion from its reserves keeping the Yuan *up* in the market.

He then waited for China's support against North Korea, which was mostly limited to U.N.-derived trade sanctions. Relatively minor foreign trade and investment law changes were made by China and its control and "development" of the South China Sea advanced. Chinese investments in the USA, which had been growing rapidly, tightened under national security CFIUS reviews, especially when state-owned enterprises were involved. *See* R. Folsom, *Foreign Investment Law* (2016). The ongoing U.S.-China bilateral investment treaty (BIT) negotiation seemed stalled.

At this writing in August of 2017, China-United States trade relations resemble a darkening cloud with storms on the horizon.

§ 16.1   NAFTA Re-Negotiated

Early in 2017, the Trump administration notified Congress of its intent to re-negotiate NAFTA with Canada and Mexico under "fast track" as authorized in the Trade Promotion Authority Act of 2015. President Trump's prior tweets calling NAFTA the "worst trade deal ever" and threats to withdraw from NAFTA or impose high tariffs on Mexican goods in light of that country's sizeable trade surplus with the United States went by the wayside. On balance, the re-negotiation notice was remarkably moderate, as were the subsequently released U.S. negotiating objectives, which partly borrowed from the Trans-Pacific Partnership (TPP) agreement negotiated by President Obama that President Trump quickly withdrew from. NAFTA it seemed would only undergo a tune-up, though when President Trump in late August kept on threatening to withdraw from NAFTA, Mexico began to articulate a Plan B under which it would withdraw.

Many attribute this outcome to lobbying by major U.S. exporters to Mexico, especially farm products. Under NAFTA, Mexico has become the largest foreign market for U.S. corn, dairy products, poultry and wheat. Manufacturers, fearing disruption and added costs, were quick to point out the high degree of supply chain integration among the NAFTA countries. Some components cross NAFTA borders repeatedly before a final product is finished.

When negotiations commenced in August 2017, the priorities of the three NAFTA partners had changed. Mexico at its own initiative had amended its Constitution and significantly opened oil and gas exploration to foreign investors. Meanwhile, Canada quietly seemed to have accepted the reality that satellite and Internet broadcasts had rendered it cultural industries exclusion meaningless. The United States had become noticeably less dependent on foreign oil imports, but hardly self-sufficient. Mexican and Canadian oil and gas still mattered, as President Trump's approval of the Keystone Pipeline connecting Canada's tar sands oil resources to the U.S. supply matrix suggested. That said, Mexico and Canada were still heavily dependent on the U.S. market for their exports, technology and foreign investment capital.

Under WTO rules, Mexico's average MFN tariff on manufactured goods had fallen to approximately 8%, Canada to 4% and the U.S. to 3.5%. All three countries maintained generally higher tariffs on agricultural goods, and selectively higher tariffs on particular manufactured goods such as the 25% U.S. tariff on pick-up trucks. These tariffs were, of course, not applicable to "North American" goods. But tightening the rules of origin quickly became a focus in the U.S. approach to re-negotiation. Tighter rules of origin, however, could cause manufacturers to move elsewhere, as Ford elected to do in 2017 by producing its Focus cars in China, then paying U.S. tariffs (2.5% for autos) upon entry.

The U.S. also wished to re-think the rules on trade remedies, such as safeguards, that could result in tariffs on Mexican and Canadian goods. The Trump administration rapidly secured a revised antidumping "suspension agreement", reducing the flow of refined sugar to the USA. Removal of the waiver for Buy American preferences enjoyed by Canada and Mexico under NAFTA also surfaced as a goal. Stronger labor and environmental provisions than offered through the NAFTA side agreements were also on the negotiating table.

So too, the U.S. sought to open up its neighbors' duty free rules for cross-border online sales, think Amazon. Canada started with an unbelievably low online tariff exemption of only $20 CDN (compared to $200 per day CDN for shopping in the USA and returning to

Canada with the goods). Mexico had $50 US online limit, while United States buyers could import online up to $800 in duty free goods from either Canada or Mexico.

Other items on the U.S. agenda included improved protection of intellectual property rights, facilitation of cross-border data flows and a ban on forced localization of computer servers, Canadian dairy "supply management" restraints, better customs clearance procedures, expanded coverage of state-owned enterprises, vague references to policing currency manipulation, and dispute settlement, particularly elimination of bilateral panel arbitration of dumping and subsidy disputes (returning appeals to national courts) and a tightening of investor-state arbitrations. In a repeat of the endless "Softwood Lumber" subsidy dispute, the Trump administration quickly slapped new countervailing duty tariffs on Canadian exports, Canada covered the losses to its lumber companies, and expected to win again on appeal.

Mexico and Canada also came to the table seeking change. Mexico, for example, emphasized its desire for coverage of security, narcotics and migration issues. Canada reiterated that continued binational panel arbitration of trade remedy disputes (*see* Chapters 4 and 5) could again be a deal-breaker, noting it had been involved in over 70 such proceedings since 1994. Canada also indicated it would like to see reduced application of Buy American procurement rules, and stronger environmental and labor law protections.

The NAFTA re-negotiations commenced in August of 2017 are being pushed by critical deadlines: The elections for the U.S. House of Representatives (November 2018), the expiration of U.S. "fast track" negotiating authority (July 2018), and the election of a new President of Mexico (July 2018).

§ 16.2 BREXIT

This section concerns BREXIT, the pending withdrawal of the United Kingdom from the European Union. Many provocative issues are on the negotiating table.

Since 2009, Article 50 of the Treaty on European Union (TEU) permits member states to commence withdrawal negotiations from the European Union. After approval by 52% of its voters in a June 2016 national referendum and strong approval by the House of Commons, Britain commenced two-year withdrawal negotiations on March 29, 2017, nearly the same date as the 60th anniversary of the EU.

Seeking to raise her bargaining power with the EU under a clear mandate from the British people, Prime Minister May held a snap election in June of 2017. Much to her surprise and that of the pollsters, the Conservative Party actually lost majority control of the UK Parliament. Many factors were in play during the snap election, but it appears that at least some British voters may be having second thoughts about the wisdom of BREXIT, particularly the "hard" version espoused by the Prime Minister.

The Conservatives were consequently forced to govern in coalition with a small Protestant-dominated Northern Ireland party, the DUP. This coalition is fragile. The DUP wants agricultural subsidies post-BREXIT, continued access to EU development funds for poorer regions, and a "frictionless" border with Ireland... basically the DUP leans toward remaining in the EU.

Nevertheless, Prime Minister May has indicated she will likely continue to pursue a "hard versus soft exit", which corresponds with the intent of the EU to discourage additional member-state exits. Prime Minister May is quoted as saying that "better no deal, than a bad deal," suggesting Britain might walk out of the negotiations, assuming she can muster a majority in Parliament to do so.. Both sides are already talking about the need for a "transition period" to accompany any deal.

Any BREXIT deal will need qualified majority approval by the EU Council, which for these purposes means 20 out of 27 member states constituting at least 65% of the EU population must affirm the deal. The consent of the European Parliament as well as the UK Parliament will also be needed. All these consents mandate a rapid timetable within the two year negotiating period. If no exit deal is reached and no additional time for negotiation unanimously agreed, Britain will cease to be a member of the EU in March of 2019.

Many in the EU feel Britain should "pay a price" to leave. Put another way, to paraphrase one EU leader: "It cannot be the case that Britain ends up better off outside the EU than inside". Overall, the adverse trade consequences of BREXIT for the UK appear more significant than for the EU. The UK, for example, sends nearly 50% of its exports in goods to the EU, while less than 10% of EU exports in goods end up in Britain. That said, Britain is the largest market for EU exports and the fifth biggest economy in the world, considerations which play in the UK's favor.

EU negotiators have insisted that "sufficient progress" must be made on the UK's balance due, the rights of EU and UK residents in the other's territory, and Northern Ireland before any discussion of subsequent relations can take place. These issues are discussed below. Since the adverse 2017 UK snap election results, Prime Minister May has seemingly acquiesced to this approach.

BREXIT negotiations raise a number of major issues:

Residency Rights. Students, retirees and workers and their families currently enjoy residency rights throughout the Union. *See* Chapter 4. What happens to the nearly 1 million Poles, 270,000 French citizens, and the other 2 million or so EU nationals working in Britain? What happens to the 1.2 million British retirees and others on the continent? One could argue that Britain has obtained a younger, more skilled taxpaying workforce under the EU free movement of people regime. The EU in turn has received a goodly number of higher cost UK seniors.

The House of Lords voted in 2017 to allow all EU nationals to remain in the UK with no guarantee of reciprocity, a position backed by a detailed plan of the Prime Minister issued after the 2017 snap election. Does this make sense? The European Parliament immediately called the Prime Minister's plan "second class" treatment. What about EU professionals and restaurant owners who have exercised their EU "right of establishment" to set up shop in the UK, and vice-versa? What about local health care rights that normally come with cross-border residency?

Fearing the worst, a number of British citizens have begun efforts to obtain other EU passports as a means to preserving free movement and other EU rights. Dual nationality in Ireland, Sweden and Germany rank high on this list.

Business Passport Rights. Much of the EU services sector operates on "passport" principles under EU law. Bankers, securities firms, insurance companies and the like need only obtain a license in one EU state, which then basically qualifies them to do business in the other member states. Britain, London and The City comprise the financial center of Europe, using British licenses to springboard throughout the EU.

Without passport rights, British, U.S. and global finance and service companies licensed in the UK may join the BREXIT exodus. This appears to already be happening, to the benefit of Frankfurt, Paris, Luxembourg, Dublin and even New York.

What about the passport rights of EU companies doing business in the UK?

Investment. Many foreign, especially Asian and North American, investors have set up manufacturing and service centers in the UK. For example, Japanese car companies are notably invested in Britain. Japan is sufficiently worried about BREXIT that its government delivered a detailed memo of concern to the UK soon after the vote to leave.

British and foreign manufacturers based in the UK are especially nervous about going from zero tariff entry into the EU to paying tariffs to gain entry to what will remain the world's largest common market. Autos, for example, are subject to 10% EU import tariffs, agricultural goods subject to 30–40% tariffs.

What about nontariff regulatory barriers that will emerge if UK health, safety and environmental rules differ from those of the EU?

If you were a British or foreign investor, would you invest or expand your operations in the UK after BREXIT?

Trade Relations. Britain currently derives its trade relations with the world predominantly via the EU. Absent a post-BREXIT agreement with the EU, Britain may revert to World Trade Organization rules. *See* Chapter 1. How sound is that assumption and what are its implications for the UK, the EU and WTO partners like the United States?

The UK currently trades under WTO tariffs negotiated under the EU umbrella. Might it need to start over as an independent WTO member? Will the EU need to compensate WTO members because its tariffs were negotiated on the premise that the UK was included? Since 25% of all American exports to the EU go to Britain, what should be the U.S. position in this debate?

Britain after BREXIT is hoping for lots of bilateral free trade and foreign investment deals. The United States, Canada, Japan, Australia, New Zealand, South Africa, India, China and others are on this wish list and initial dialogues have commenced, but is that hope realistic?

Britain's trade volume with the EU has been declining, but remains significant. Thus the details of EU-UK trade relations are important to both sides. From the EU perspective, it is less than clear that a deal can be struck within the two-year timeline for BREXIT negotiations, particularly with a weakened Prime Minister May. It took, for example, many years for the EU-Canada bilateral agreement (CETA) to finally come to fruition. Most importantly, any UK trade deal with the EU will require unanimous ratification by the remaining 27 EU members plus regional parliaments (those of Belgium for example), the European Parliament, as well as the UK Parliament.

Some Brexiteers have suggested pursuing the "soft exit" Norwegian or Swiss models for relations with the EU post-exit. But these complicated models for the most part involve acceptance of free movement of people, cash contributions to the EU budget, and deference to EU/EFTA Court decisions. *See* R. Folsom, *Principles of*

European Union Law including BREXIT (2017). To what degree is a soft exit really an exit?

Northern Ireland, Scotland and Gibraltar. Every political district in Scotland voted in 2016 to remain in the EU, but the Conservatives won 12 districts in the June 2017 snap election. The Scotch voted against leaving the UK several years prior. A second referendum could achieve Scottish independence in search of EU membership.

Nearly every district in Northern Ireland voted to remain. Peace and border-free transit has been directly linked under the Good Friday Accords to Irish and UK membership in the EU. After BREXIT, the Ireland/Northern Ireland border will be the only land crossing between Britain and the EU. What then?

Ireland, a low-tax manufacturing center for many U.S. multinationals, ships substantial goods to the EU using Britain as an inexpensive land-bridge. This will be a rat's nest of customs law after BREXIT. In addition, Ireland's food imports and exports from and to the UK are significant. Thus Ireland has a big stake in BREXIT.

Spain, which could veto any BREXIT deal, insists on an agreement that clarifies the future of Gibraltar, that very British and strategic enclave located where the Med and the Atlantic Ocean meet. Ideally, Spain wants Gibraltar back. It is also worried about Scotland joining the EU, perhaps setting a dangerous precedent for Catalonian independence.

Suppose Greece conditions approval of a BREXIT deal on return of the Elgin Marbles?

Money Matters. The EU intends to present Britain with an expensive "bill" for what it perceives the UK will owe the Union upon departure in 2019. The demand for cash will include Britain's liabilities under the generous, entirely unfunded EU pension scheme. It also will cover pre-BREXIT and post-BREXIT EU projects under the current British-approved EU budget running from 2013 to 2020.

Total estimates for "the bill" range from 25 to 75 billion Euros, subject certainly to intense bargaining by both sides. Such a bill will no doubt stun many Leave backers, who were led to believe BREXIT would result in a net savings not loss. In addition, Britain will lose two well-staffed and well-paid EU agencies, one on Medicines (EMA), the other on banking (EBA), along with civil nuclear power benefits associated with EURATOM. On the flip side, the EU will need to rework its budget to make up for the loss of Britain, a net payor.

And the List of Issues Goes On. What about *immigration*, an issue central to the BREXIT vote. Since Britain maintains its own border controls, relatively little impact may occur. But France already has taken steps to reduce its willingness to cooperate on immigrants waiting in Calais to enter the UK.

What about the areas where there has arguably been a positive impact by Britain on the EU: Foreign and defense affairs, governance, spending, and market-driven solutions, for examples. How about the common aviation and fisheries markets created by the EU?

The Pound Sterling has been negatively impacted. Does it matter how markets evaluate BREXIT's future?

What about the EU's voluminous "acquis communautaire", its vast body of legislation, regulations, and case law? Prime Minister May obtained approval for a misnamed "Great Repeal Bill" that incorporates all EU rules (some 19,000 in number) into UK law, to be followed by selective removal, alteration or retention. Why do this? An intense battle between pro- and anti-BREXIT Parliamentarians, including members of her own Conservative Party, is sure to follow this Bill.

Many European Union rules seem inescapable since all goods exported from Britain will need to conform to EU law, and extensive cross-border supply chains compel compliance. For example, all auto imports must under the EU End of Life Vehicles Directive be 95% reusable or recyclable.

The Prime Minister has been outspoken against remaining subject to the jurisdiction of the European Court of Justice (ECJ) and the EU General Court (GC). If the UK retains EU rules, do not interpretations of those rules by the ECJ and GC come along with them?

What about the future of the EU? If Britain can exit, whatever the price, why not others? In 2017, anti-EU political parties made themselves felt in Dutch, French and German elections. Marine Le Pen, leader of the National Front Party in France, openly ran on a platform promising a national referendum on leaving the EU (FREXIT). She was resoundingly defeated by Emmanuel Macron, a strong pro-EU candidate, now President of France.

Does BREXIT signal the end of the Union? Or perhaps expansion of a "multi-speed" Union, built around a core of EURO zone states?

Documents Appendix

Table of Sections

Sec.

---

1. GENERAL AGREEMENT ON TARIFFS AND TRADE (GATT)

(Selected Provisions) (as amended)

The following provisions are selected sections from the General Agreement on Tariffs and Trade as enacted in 1947 and as amended and in force in 1994, when the Uruguay Round proposals were enacted. The original GATT 1947 is reproduced in 55 U.N.T.S. 194. It is also reproduced in the GATT Documents, "Basic Instruments and Selected Documents", also referred to as B.I.S.D. B.I.S.D. also includes the GATT as amended and in force in 1994.

Notes and supplementary provisions have been included at the end of each Article and Paragraph to which they apply.

Table of Contents

THE GENERAL AGREEMENT ON TARIFFS AND TRADE

The Governments of the Commonwealth of Australia, the Kingdom of Belgium, the United States of Brazil, Burma, Canada, Ceylon, the Republic of Chile, the Republic of China, the Republic of Cuba, the Czechoslovak Republic, the French Republic, India, Lebanon, the Grand-Duchy of Luxemburg, the Kingdom of the Netherlands, New Zealand, the Kingdom of Norway, Pakistan, Southern Rhodesia, Syria, the Union of South Africa, the United Kingdom of Great Britain and Northern Ireland, and the United States of America:

Recognizing that their relations in the field of trade and economic endeavour should be conducted with a view to raising standards of living, ensuring full employment and a large and steadily growing volume of real income and effective demand, developing the full use of the resources of the world and expanding the production and exchange of goods,

Being desirous of contributing to these objectives by entering into reciprocal and mutually advantageous arrangements directed to the substantial reduction of tariffs and other barriers to trade and to the elimination of discriminatory treatment in international commerce,

Have through their Representatives agreed as follows:

PART I

ARTICLE I.   GENERAL MOST-FAVOURED-NATION TREATMENT

1.   With respect to customs duties and charges of any kind imposed on or in connection with importation or exportation or imposed on the international transfer of payments for imports or exports, and with respect to the method of levying such duties and charges, and with respect to all rules and formalities in connection with importation and exportation, and with respect to all matters referred to in paragraphs 2 and 4 of Article III, any advantage, favour, privilege or immunity granted by any contracting

party to any product originating in or destined for any other country shall be accorded immediately and unconditionally to the like product originating in or destined for the territories of all other contracting parties.

———————

Ad *Article I*

Paragraph 1

The obligations incorporated in paragraph 1 of Article I by reference to paragraphs 2 and 4 of Article III and those incorporated in paragraph 2(b) of Article II by reference to Article VI shall be considered as falling within Part II for the purposes of the Protocol of Provisional Application.

The cross-references, in the paragraph immediately above and in paragraph 1 of Article I, to paragraphs 2 and 4 of Article III shall only apply after Article III has been modified by the entry into force of the amendment provided for in the Protocol Modifying Part II and Article XXVI of the General Agreement on Tariffs and Trade, dated September 14, 1948.

———————

2.   The provisions of paragraph 1 of this Article shall not require the elimination of any preferences in respect of import duties or charges which do not exceed the levels provided for in paragraph 4 of this Article and which fall within the following descriptions:

(a)   Preferences in force exclusively between two or more of the territories listed in Annex A, subject to the conditions set forth therein;

* * *

———————

ARTICLE II.   SCHEDULES OF CONCESSIONS

1.   (a)   Each contracting party shall accord to the commerce of the other contracting parties treatment no less favourable than that provided for in the appropriate Part of the appropriate Schedule annexed to this Agreement.

(b)   The products described in Part I of the Schedule relating to any contracting party, which are the products of territories of other contracting parties, shall, on their importation into the territory to which the Schedule relates, and subject to the terms, conditions or qualifications set forth in that Schedule, be exempt from ordinary customs duties in excess of those set forth and provided for therein. Such products shall also be exempt from all other duties or charges of any kind imposed on or in connection with importation in excess of those imposed on the date of this Agreement or those directly and mandatorily required to be imposed thereafter by legislation in force in the importing territory on that date.

(c) The products described in Part II of the Schedule relating to any contracting party which are the products of territories entitled under Article I to receive preferential treatment upon importation into the territory to which the Schedule relates shall, on their importation into such territory, and subject to the terms, conditions or qualifications set forth in that Schedule, be exempt from ordinary customs duties in excess of those set forth and provided for in Part II of that Schedule. Such products shall also be exempt from all other duties or charges of any kind imposed on or in connection with importation in excess of those imposed on the date of this Agreement or those directly and mandatorily required to be imposed thereafter by legislation in force in the importing territory on that date. Nothing in this Article shall prevent any contracting party from maintaining its requirements existing on the date of this Agreement as to the eligibility of goods for entry at preferential rates of duty.

2. Nothing in this Article shall prevent any contracting party from imposing at any time on the importation of any product:

(a) a charge equivalent to an internal tax imposed consistently with the provisions of paragraph 2 of Article III in respect of the like domestic product or in respect of an article from which the imported product has been manufactured or produced in whole or in part;

Ad *Article II*

Paragraph 2(a)

The cross-reference, in paragraph 2(a) of Article II, to paragraph 2 of Article III shall only apply after Article III has been modified by the entry into force of the amendment provided for in the Protocol Modifying Part II and Article XXVI of the General Agreement on Tariffs and Trade, dated September 14, 1948.

(b) any anti-dumping or countervailing duty applied consistently with the provisions of Article VI;

Ad *Article II*

Paragraph 2(b)

See the note relating to paragraph 1 of Article I.

    (c)   fees or other charges commensurate with the cost of services rendered.

3.   No contracting party shall alter its method of determining dutiable value or of converting currencies so as to impair the value of any of the concessions provided for in the appropriate Schedule annexed to this Agreement.

4.   If any contracting party establishes, maintains or authorizes, formally or in effect, a monopoly of the importation of any product described in the appropriate Schedule annexed to this Agreement, such monopoly shall not, except as provided for in that Schedule or as otherwise agreed between the parties which initially negotiated the concession, operate so as to afford protection on the average in excess of the amount of protection provided for in that Schedule. The provisions of this paragraph shall not limit the use by contracting parties of any form of assistance to domestic producers permitted by other provisions of this Agreement.

Ad *Article II*

Paragraph 4

Except where otherwise specifically agreed between the contracting parties which initially negotiated the concession, the provisions of this paragraph will be applied in the light of the provisions of Article 31 of the Havana Charter.

---

5.   If any contracting party considers that a product is not receiving from another contracting party the treatment which the first contracting party believes to have been contemplated by a concession provided for in the appropriate Schedule annexed to this Agreement, it shall bring the matter directly to the attention of the other contracting party. If the latter agrees that the treatment contemplated was that claimed by the first contracting party, but declares that such treatment cannot be accorded because a court or other proper authority has ruled to the effect that the product involved cannot be classified under the tariff laws of such contracting party so as to permit the treatment contemplated in this Agreement, the two contracting parties, together with any other contracting parties substantially interested, shall enter promptly into further negotiations with a view to a compensatory adjustment of the matter.

* * *

PART II

ARTICLE III. NATIONAL TREATMENT ON INTERNAL TAXATION AND REGULATION

Ad Article III

Any internal tax or other internal charge, or any law, regulation or requirement of the kind referred to in paragraph 1 which applies to an imported product and to the like domestic product and is collected or enforced in the case of the imported product at the time or point of importation, is nevertheless to be regarded as an internal tax or other internal charge, or a law, regulation or requirement of the kind referred to in paragraph 1, and is accordingly subject to the provisions of Article III.

1.   The contracting parties recognize that internal taxes and other internal charges, and laws, regulations and requirements affecting the internal sale, offering for sale, purchase, transportation, distribution or use of products, and internal quantitative regulations requiring the mixture, processing or use of products in specified amounts or proportions, should not be applied to imported or domestic products so as to afford protection to domestic production.

Ad Article III

Paragraph 1

The application of paragraph 1 to internal taxes imposed by local governments and authorities within the territory of a contracting party is subject to the provisions of the final paragraph of Article XXIV. The term "reasonable measures" in the last-mentioned paragraph would not require, for example, the repeal of existing national legislation authorizing local governments to impose internal taxes which, although technically inconsistent with the letter of Article III, are not in fact inconsistent with its spirit, if such repeal would result in a serious financial hardship for the local governments or authorities concerned. With regard to taxation by local governments or authorities which is inconsistent with both the letter and spirit of Article III, the term "reasonable measures" would permit a contracting party to eliminate the inconsistent taxation gradually over a transition period, if abrupt action would create serious administrative and financial difficulties.

2.   The products of the territory of any contracting party imported into the territory of any other contracting party shall not be subject, directly or indirectly, to internal taxes or other internal charges of any kind in excess of those applied, directly or indirectly, to like domestic products. Moreover, no contracting party shall otherwise apply internal taxes or other internal

charges to imported or domestic products in a manner contrary to the principles set forth in paragraph 1.

Ad *Article III*

Paragraph 2

A tax conforming to the requirements of the first sentence of paragraph 2 would be considered to be inconsistent with the provisions of the second sentence only in cases where competition was involved between, on the one hand, the taxed product and, on the other hand, a directly competitive or substitutable product which was not similarly taxed.

---

3.   With respect to any existing internal tax which is inconsistent with the provisions of paragraph 2, but which is specifically authorized under a trade agreement, in force on April 10, 1947, in which the import duty on the taxed product is bound against increase, the contracting party imposing the tax shall be free to postpone the application of the provisions of paragraph 2 to such tax until such time as it can obtain release from the obligations of such trade agreement in order to permit the increase of such duty to the extent necessary to compensate for the elimination of the protective element of the tax.

4.   The products of the territory of any contracting party imported into the territory of any other contracting party shall be accorded treatment no less favourable than that accorded to like products of national origin in respect of all laws, regulations and requirements affecting their internal sale, offering for sale, purchase, transportation, distribution or use. The provisions of this paragraph shall not prevent the application of differential internal transportation charges which are based exclusively on the economic operation of the means of transport and not on the nationality of the product.

5.   No contracting party shall establish or maintain any internal quantitative regulation relating to the mixture, processing or use of products in specified amounts or proportions which requires, directly or indirectly, that any specified amount or proportion of any product which is the subject of the regulation must be supplied from domestic sources. Moreover, no contracting party shall otherwise apply internal quantitative regulations in a manner contrary to the principles set forth in paragraph 1.

Ad *Article III*

Paragraph 5

Regulations consistent with the provisions of the first sentence of paragraph 5 shall not be considered to be contrary to the provisions of the second sentence in any case in which all of the products subject to the regulations are produced domestically in substantial quantities. A regulation cannot be justified as being consistent with the provisions of the second sentence on the ground that the proportion or amount allocated to each of the products which are the subject of the regulation constitutes an equitable relationship between imported and domestic products.

---

* * *

8.   (a)   The provisions of this Article shall not apply to laws, regulations or requirements governing the procurement by governmental agencies of products purchased for governmental purposes and not with a view to commercial resale or with a view to use in the production of goods for commercial sale.

(b)   The provisions of this Article shall not prevent the payment of subsidies exclusively to domestic producers, including payments to domestic producers derived from the proceeds of internal taxes or charges applied consistently with the provisions of this Article and subsidies effected through governmental purchases of domestic products.

9.   The contracting parties recognize that internal maximum price control measures, even though conforming to the other provisions of this Article, can have effects prejudicial to the interests of contracting parties supplying imported products. Accordingly, contracting parties applying such measures shall take account of the interests of exporting contracting parties with a view to avoiding to the fullest practicable extent such prejudicial effects.

* * *

ARTICLE IV. SPECIAL PROVISIONS RELATING TO CINEMATOGRAPH FILMS

* * *

ARTICLE V.   FREEDOM OF TRANSIT

* * *

ARTICLE VI. ANTI-DUMPING AND COUNTERVAILING DUTIES

1.   The contracting parties recognize that dumping, by which products of one country are introduced into the commerce of another country at less than the normal value of the products, is to be condemned if it causes or threatens material injury to an established industry in the territory of a contracting party or materially retards the establishment of a domestic industry. For the purposes of this Article, a product is to be considered as being introduced into the commerce of an importing country at less than its normal value, if the price of the product exported from one country to another

(a)   is less than the comparable price, in the ordinary course of trade, for the like product when destined for consumption in the exporting country, or,

(b)   in the absence of such domestic price, is less than either

(i)   the highest comparable price for the like product for export to any third country in the ordinary course of trade, or

(ii)   the cost of production of the product in the country of origin plus a reasonable addition for selling cost and profit.

Due allowance shall be made in each case for differences in conditions and terms of sale, for differences in taxation, and for other differences affecting price comparability.

Ad *Article VI*

Paragraph 1

1.   Hidden dumping by associated houses (that is, the sale by an importer at a price below that corresponding to the price invoiced by an exporter with whom the importer is associated, and also below the price in the exporting country) constitutes a form of price dumping with respect to which the margin of dumping may be calculated on the basis of the price at which the goods are resold by the importer.

2.   It is recognized that, in the case of imports from a country which has a complete or substantially complete monopoly of its trade and where all domestic prices are fixed by the State, special difficulties may exist in determining price comparability for the purposes of paragraph 1, and in such cases importing contracting parties may find it necessary to take into account the possibility that a strict comparison with domestic prices in such a country may not always be appropriate.

---

2.   In order to offset or prevent dumping, a contracting party may levy on any dumped product an anti-dumping duty not greater in amount than the margin of dumping in respect of such product. For the purposes of this Article, the margin of dumping is the price difference determined in accordance with the provisions of paragraph 1.

3.   No countervailing duty shall be levied on any product of the territory of any contracting party imported into the territory of another contracting party in excess of an amount equal to the estimated bounty or subsidy determined to have been granted, directly or indirectly, on the manufacture, production or export of such product in the country of origin or exportation, including any special subsidy to the transportation of a particular product. The term "countervailing duty" shall be understood to mean a special duty levied for the purpose of offsetting any bounty or subsidy bestowed, directly or indirectly, upon the manufacture, production or export of any merchandise.

Ad *Article VI*

Paragraphs 2 and 3

1.   As in many other cases in customs administration, a contracting party may require reasonable security (bond or cash deposit) for the payment of anti-dumping or countervailing duty pending final determination of the facts in any case of suspected dumping or subsidization.

2.   Multiple currency practices can in certain circumstances constitute a subsidy to exports which may be met by countervailing duties under paragraph 3 or can constitute a form of dumping by means of a partial depreciation of a country's currency which may be met by action under paragraph 2. By "multiple currency practices" is meant practices by governments or sanctioned by governments.

---

4.   No product of the territory of any contracting party imported into the territory of any other contracting party shall be subject to anti-dumping or countervailing duty by reason of the exemption of such product from duties or taxes borne by the like product when destined for consumption in the country of origin or exportation, or by reason of the refund of such duties or taxes.

5.   No product of the territory of any contracting party imported into the territory of any other contracting party shall be subject to both anti-dumping and countervailing duties to compensate for the same situation of dumping or export subsidization.

6.   (a) No contracting party shall levy any anti-dumping or countervailing duty on the importation of any product of the territory of another contracting party unless it determines that the effect of the dumping or subsidization, as the case may be, is such as to cause or threaten material injury to an established domestic industry, or is such as to retard materially the establishment of a domestic industry.

(b)   The CONTRACTING PARTIES may waive the requirement of subparagraph (a) of this paragraph so as to permit a contracting party to levy an anti-dumping or countervailing duty on the importation of any product for the purpose of offsetting dumping or subsidization which causes or threatens material injury to an industry in the territory of another contracting party exporting the product concerned to the territory of the importing contracting party. The CONTRACTING PARTIES shall waive the requirements of sub-paragraph (a) of this paragraph, so as to permit the levying of a countervailing duty, in cases in which they find that a subsidy is causing or threatening material injury to an industry in the territory of another contracting party exporting the product concerned to the territory of the importing contracting party.

Ad *Article VI*

Paragraph 6(b)

Waivers under the provisions of this sub-paragraph shall be granted only on application by the contracting party proposing to levy an anti-dumping or countervailing duty, as the case may be.

————————

(c)   In exceptional circumstances, however, where delay might cause damage which would be difficult to repair, a contracting party may levy a countervailing duty for the purpose referred to in subparagraph (b) of this paragraph without the prior approval of the CONTRACTING PARTIES; *Provided* that such action shall be reported immediately to the CONTRACTING PARTIES and that the countervailing duty shall be withdrawn promptly if the CONTRACTING PARTIES disapprove.

7.   A system for the stabilization of the domestic price or of the return to domestic producers of a primary commodity, independently of the movements of export prices, which results at times in the sale of the commodity for export at a price lower than the comparable price charged for the like commodity to buyers in the domestic market, shall be presumed not to result in material injury within the meaning of paragraph 6 if it is determined by consultation among the contracting parties substantially interested in the commodity concerned that:

(a)   the system has also resulted in the sale of the commodity for export at a price higher than the comparable price charged for the like commodity to buyers in the domestic market, and

(b)   the system is so operated, either because of the effective regulation of production, or otherwise, as not to stimulate exports unduly or otherwise seriously prejudice the interests of other contracting parties.

ARTICLE VII.   VALUATION FOR CUSTOMS PURPOSES

1.   The contracting parties recognize the validity of the general principles of valuation set forth in the following paragraphs of this Article, and they undertake to give effect to such principles, in respect of all products subject to duties or other charges or restrictions on importation and exportation based upon or regulated in any manner by value. Moreover, they shall, upon a request by another contracting party review the operation of any of their laws or regulations relating to value for customs purposes in the light of these principles. The CONTRACTING PARTIES may request from contracting parties reports on steps taken by them in pursuance of the provisions of this Article.

————————

Ad *Article VII*

Paragraph 1

The expression "or other charges" is not to be regarded as including internal taxes or equivalent charges imposed on or in connexion with imported products.

---

2. (a) The value for customs purposes of imported merchandise should be based on the actual value of the imported merchandise on which duty is assessed, or of like merchandise, and should not be based on the value of merchandise of national origin or on arbitrary or fictitious values.

(b) "Actual value" should be the price at which, at a time and place determined by the legislation of the country of importation, such or like merchandise is sold or offered for sale in the ordinary course of trade under fully competitive conditions. To the extent to which the price of such or like merchandise is governed by the quantity in a particular transaction, the price to be considered should uniformly be related to either (i) comparable quantities, or (ii) quantities not less favourable to importers than those in which the greater volume of the merchandise is sold in the trade between the countries of exportation and importation.

(c) When the actual value is not ascertainable in accordance with sub-paragraph (b) of this paragraph, the value for customs purposes should be based on the nearest ascertainable equivalent of such value.

Ad *Article VII*

Paragraph 2

1. It would be in conformity with Article VII to presume that "actual value" may be represented by the invoice price, plus any non-included charges for legitimate costs which are proper elements of "actual value" and plus any abnormal discount or other reduction from the ordinary competitive price.

2. It would be in conformity with Article VII, paragraph 2(b), for a contracting party to construe the phrase "in the ordinary course of trade * * * under fully competitive conditions", as excluding any transaction wherein the buyer and seller are not independent of each other and price is not the sole consideration.

3. The standard of "fully competitive conditions" permits a contracting party to exclude from consideration prices involving special discounts limited to exclusive agents.

4. The wording of sub-paragraphs (a) and (b) permits a contracting party to determine the value for customs purposes uniformly either (1) on the basis of a particular exporter's prices of the imported merchandise, or (2) on the basis of the general price level of like merchandise.

3. The value for customs purposes of any imported product should not include the amount of any internal tax, applicable within the country of origin or export, from which the imported product has been exempted or has been or will be relieved by means of refund.

4. (a) Except as otherwise provided for in this paragraph, where it is necessary for the purposes of paragraph 2 of this Article for a contracting party to convert into its own currency a price expressed in the currency of another country, the conversion rate of exchange to be used shall be based, for each currency involved, on the par value as established pursuant to the Articles of Agreement of the International Monetary Fund or on the rate of exchange recognized by the Fund, or on the par value established in accordance with a special exchange agreement entered into pursuant to Article XV of this Agreement.

(b) Where no such established par value and no such recognized rate of exchange exist, the conversion rate shall reflect effectively the current value of such currency in commercial transactions.

(c) The CONTRACTING PARTIES, in agreement with the International Monetary Fund, shall formulate rules governing the conversion by contracting parties of any foreign currency in respect of which multiple rates of exchange are maintained consistently with the Articles of Agreement of the International Monetary Fund. Any contracting party may apply such rules in respect of such foreign currencies for the purposes of paragraph 2 of this Article as an alternative to the use of par values. Until such rules are adopted by the CONTRACTING PARTIES, any contracting party may employ, in respect of any such foreign currency, rules of conversion for the purposes of paragraph 2 of this Article which are designed to reflect effectively the value of such foreign currency in commercial transactions.

(d) Nothing in this paragraph shall be construed to require any contracting party to alter the method of converting currencies for customs purposes which is applicable in its territory on the date of this Agreement, if such alteration would have the effect of increasing generally the amounts of duty payable.

5. The bases and methods for determining the value of products subject to duties or other charges or restrictions based upon or regulated in any manner by value should be stable and should be given sufficient publicity to enable traders to estimate, with a reasonable degree of certainty, the value for customs purposes.

ARTICLE VIII. FEES AND FORMALITIES CONNECTED WITH IMPORTATION AND EXPORTATION

1. (a) All fees and charges of whatever character (other than import and export duties and other than taxes within the purview of Article III)

imposed by contracting parties on or in connexion with importation or exportation shall be limited in amount to the approximate cost of services rendered and shall not represent an indirect protection to domestic products or a taxation of imports or exports for fiscal purposes.

* * *

ARTICLE IX. MARKS OF ORIGIN

1.   Each contracting party shall accord to the products of the territories of other contracting parties treatment with regard to marking requirements no less favourable than the treatment accorded to like products of any third country.

2.   The contracting parties recognize that, in adopting and enforcing laws and regulations relating to marks of origin, the difficulties and inconveniences which such measures may cause to the commerce and industry of exporting countries should be reduced to a minimum, due regard being had to the necessity of protecting consumers against fraudulent or misleading indications.

3.   Whenever it is administratively practicable to do so, contracting parties should permit required marks of origin to be affixed at the time of importation.

4.   The laws and regulations of contracting parties relating to the marking of imported products shall be such as to permit compliance without seriously damaging the products, or materially reducing their value, or unreasonably increasing their cost.

5.   As a general rule, no special duty or penalty should be imposed by any contracting party for failure to comply with marking requirements prior to importation unless corrective marking is unreasonably delayed or deceptive marks have been affixed or the required marking has been intentionally omitted.

6.   The contracting parties shall co-operate with each other with a view to preventing the use of trade names in such manner as to misrepresent the true origin of a product, to the detriment of such distinctive regional or geographical names of products of the territory of a contracting party as are protected by its legislation. Each contracting party shall accord full and sympathetic consideration to such requests or representations as may be made by any other contracting party regarding the application of the undertaking set forth in the preceding sentence to names of products which have been communicated to it by the other contracting party.

ARTICLE X.   PUBLICATION AND ADMINISTRATION
OF TRADE REGULATIONS (omitted)

* * *

ARTICLE XI.   GENERAL ELIMINATION OF
QUANTITATIVE RESTRICTIONS

Ad *Articles XI, XII, XIII, XIV and XVIII*

Throughout Articles XI, XII, XIII, XIV and XVIII, the terms "import restrictions" or "export restrictions" include restrictions made effective through state-trading operations.

---

1.   No prohibitions or restrictions other than duties, taxes or other charges, whether made effective through quotas, import or export licenses or other measures, shall be instituted or maintained by any contracting party on the importation of any product of the territory of any other contracting party or on the exportation or sale for export of any product destined for the territory of any other contracting party.

2.   The provisions of paragraph 1 of this Article shall not extend to the following:

(a)   Export prohibitions or restrictions temporarily applied to prevent or relieve critical shortages of foodstuffs or other products essential to the exporting contracting party;

(b)   Import and export prohibitions or restrictions necessary to the application of standards or regulations for the classification, grading or marketing of commodities in international trade;

(c)   Import restrictions on any agricultural or fisheries product, imported in any form, necessary to the enforcement of governmental measures which operate:

(i)   to restrict the quantities of the like domestic product permitted to be marketed or produced, or, if there is no substantial domestic production of the like product, of a domestic product for which the imported product can be directly substituted; or

(ii)   to remove a temporary surplus of the like domestic product, or, if there is no substantial domestic production of the like product, of a domestic product for which the imported product can be directly substituted, by making the surplus available to certain groups of domestic consumers free of charge or at prices below the current market level; or

(iii)   to restrict the quantities permitted to be produced of any animal product the production of which is directly dependent, wholly or mainly, on the imported commodity, if the domestic production of that commodity is relatively negligible.

Ad *Article XI*

Paragraph 2(c)

The term "in any form" in this paragraph covers the same products when in an early stage of processing and still perishable, which compete directly with the fresh product and if freely imported would tend to make the restriction on the fresh product ineffective.

Any contracting party applying restrictions on the importation of any product pursuant to sub-paragraph (c) of this paragraph shall give public notice of the total quantity or value of the product permitted to be imported during a specified future period and of any change in such quantity or value. Moreover, any restrictions applied under (i) above shall not be such as will reduce the total of imports relative to the total of domestic production, as compared with the proportion which might reasonably be expected to rule between the two in the absence of restrictions. In determining this proportion, the contracting party shall pay due regard to the proportion prevailing during a previous representative period and to any special factors which may have affected or may be affecting the trade in the product concerned.

Ad *Article XI*

Paragraph 2, last sub-paragraph

The term "special factors" includes changes in relative productive efficiency as between domestic and foreign producers, or as between different foreign producers, but not changes artificially brought about by means not permitted under the Agreement.

ARTICLE XII. RESTRICTIONS TO SAFEGUARD THE BALANCE OF PAYMENTS

Ad *Articles XI, XII, XIII, XIV and XVIII*

Throughout Articles XI, XII, XIII, XIV and XVIII, the terms "import restrictions" or "export restrictions" include restrictions made effective through state-trading operations.

Ad *Article XII*

The CONTRACTING PARTIES shall make provision for the utmost secrecy in the conduct of any consultation under the provisions of this Article.

---

1.   Notwithstanding the provisions of paragraph 1 of Article XI, any contracting party, in order to safeguard its external financial position and its balance of payments, may restrict the quantity or value of merchandise permitted to be imported, subject to the provisions of the following paragraphs of this Article.

2.   (a)   Import restrictions instituted, maintained or intensified by a contracting party under this Article shall not exceed those necessary:

> (i)   to forestall the imminent threat of, or to stop, a serious decline in its monetary reserves, or

> (ii)   in the case of a contracting party with very low monetary reserves, to achieve a reasonable rate of increase in its reserves.

Due regard shall be paid in either case to any special factors which may be affecting the reserves of such contracting party or its need for reserves, including, where special external credits or other resources are available to it, the need to provide for the appropriate use of such credits or resources.

> (b)   Contracting parties applying restrictions under sub-paragraph (a) of this paragraph shall progressively relax them as such conditions improve, maintaining them only to the extent that the conditions specified in that sub-paragraph still justify their application. They shall eliminate the restrictions when conditions would no longer justify their institution or maintenance under that sub-paragraph.

3.   (a)   Contracting parties undertake, in carrying out their domestic policies, to pay due regard to the need for maintaining or restoring equilibrium in their balance of payments on a sound and lasting basis and to the desirability of avoiding an uneconomic employment of productive resources. They recognize that, in order to achieve these ends, it is desirable so far as possible to adopt measures which expand rather than contract international trade.

> (b)   Contracting parties applying restrictions under this Article may determine the incidence of the restrictions on imports of different products or classes of products in such a way as to give priority to the importation of those products which are more essential.

> (c)   Contracting parties applying restrictions under this Article undertake:

(i)ᵛ   to avoid unnecessary damage to the commercial or economic interests of any other contracting party;

Ad *Article XII*

Paragraph 3(c)(i)

Contracting parties applying restrictions shall endeavour to avoid causing serious prejudice to exports of a commodity on which the economy of a contracting party is largely dependent.

(ii)   not to apply restrictions so as to prevent unreasonably the importation of any description of goods in minimum commercial quantities the exclusion of which would impair regular channels of trade; and

(iii) not to apply restrictions which would prevent the importation of commercial samples or prevent compliance with patent, trade mark, copyright, or similar procedures.

(d)   The contracting parties recognize that, as a result of domestic policies directed towards the achievement and maintenance of full and productive employment or towards the development of economic resources, a contracting party may experience a high level of demand for imports involving a threat to its monetary reserves of the sort referred to in paragraph 2(a) of this Article. Accordingly, a contracting party otherwise complying with the provisions of this Article shall not be required to withdraw or modify restrictions on the ground that a change in those policies would render unnecessary restrictions which it is applying under this Article.

4.   (a)   Any contracting party applying new restrictions or raising the general level of its existing restrictions by a substantial intensification of the measures applied under this Article shall immediately after instituting or intensifying such restrictions (or, in circumstances in which prior consultation is practicable, before doing so) consult with the CONTRACTING PARTIES as to the nature of its balance of payments difficulties, alternative corrective measures which may be available, and the possible effect of the restrictions on the economies of other contracting parties.

(b)   On a date to be determined by them, the CONTRACTING PARTIES shall review all restrictions still applied under this Article on that date. Beginning one year after that date, contracting parties applying import restrictions under this Article shall enter into consultations of the type provided for in sub-paragraph (a) of this paragraph with the CONTRACTING PARTIES annually.

Ad *Article XII*

Paragraph 4(b)

It is agreed that the date shall be within ninety days after the entry into force of the amendments of this Article effected by the Protocol Amending the Preamble and Parts II and III of this Agreement. However, should the CONTRACTING PARTIES find that conditions were not suitable for the application of the provisions of this sub-paragraph at the time envisaged, they may determine a later date; Provided that such date is not more than thirty days after such time as the obligations of Article VIII, Sections 2, 3 and 4, of the Articles of Agreement of the International Monetary Fund become applicable to contracting parties, members of the Fund, the combined foreign trade of which constitutes at least fifty per centum of the aggregate foreign trade of all contracting parties.

(c)(i) If, in the course of consultations with a contracting party under sub-paragraph (a) or (b) above, the CONTRACTING PARTIES find that the restrictions are not consistent with the provisions of this Article or with those of Article XIII (subject to the provisions of Article XIV), they shall indicate the nature of the inconsistency and may advise that the restrictions be suitably modified.

(ii) If, however, as a result of the consultations, the CONTRACTING PARTIES determine that the restrictions are being applied in a manner involving an inconsistency of a serious nature with the provisions of this Article or with those of Article XIII (subject to the provisions of Article XIV) and that damage to the trade of any contracting party is caused or threatened thereby, they shall so inform the contracting party applying the restrictions and shall make appropriate recommendations for securing conformity with such provisions within a specified period of time. If such contracting party does not comply with these recommendations within the specified period, the CONTRACTING PARTIES may release any contracting party the trade of which is adversely affected by the restrictions from such obligations under this Agreement towards the contracting party applying the restrictions as they determine to be appropriate in the circumstances.

(d) The CONTRACTING PARTIES shall invite any contracting party which is applying restrictions under this Article to enter into consultations with them at the request of any contracting party which can establish a *prima facie* case that the restrictions are inconsistent with the provisions of this Article or with those of Article XIII (subject to the provisions of Article XIV) and that its trade is adversely affected thereby. However, no such invitation shall be issued unless the CONTRACTING PARTIES have ascertained that direct discussions between the contracting parties concerned have not been successful. If, as a result of the consultations with the CONTRACTING PARTIES, no agreement is reached and they determine that the restrictions are being applied inconsistently with such provisions, and that damage to the trade of the contracting party initiating the procedure is caused or threatened thereby, they shall recommend the withdrawal or modification of the restrictions. If the restrictions are not withdrawn or modified within such time as the CONTRACTING PARTIES may prescribe, they may release the contracting party initiating the procedure from such obligations under this Agreement towards the contracting party applying the restrictions as they determine to be appropriate in the circumstances.

(e) In proceeding under this paragraph, the CONTRACTING PARTIES shall have due regard to any special external factors adversely affecting the export trade of the contracting party applying restrictions.

Ad *Article XII*

Paragraph 4(e)

It is agreed that paragraph 4(e) does not add any new criteria for the imposition or maintenance of quantitative restrictions for balance of payments reasons. It is solely intended to ensure that all external factors such as changes in the terms of trade, quantitative restrictions, excessive tariffs and subsidies, which may be contributing to the balance of payments difficulties of the contracting party applying restrictions, will be fully taken into account.

(f) Determinations under this paragraph shall be rendered expeditiously and, if possible, within sixty days of the initiation of the consultations.

5. If there is a persistent and widespread application of import restrictions under this Article, indicating the existence of a general disequilibrium which is restricting international trade, the CONTRACTING PARTIES shall initiate discussions to consider whether other measures might be taken, either by those contracting parties the balances of payments of which are under pressure or by those the balances of payments of which are tending to be exceptionally favourable, or by any appropriate intergovernmental organization, to remove the underlying causes of the disequilibrium. On the invitation of the CONTRACTING PARTIES, contracting parties shall participate in such discussions.

ARTICLE XIII.   NON-DISCRIMINATORY ADMINISTRATION OF QUANTITATIVE RESTRICTIONS

———————

Ad *Articles XI, XII, XIII, XIV and XVIII*

Throughout Articles XI, XII, XIII, XIV and XVIII, the terms "import restrictions" or "export restrictions" include restrictions made effective through state-trading operations.

———————

1.   No prohibition or restriction shall be applied by any contracting party on the importation of any product of the territory of any other contracting party or on the exportation of any product destined for the territory of any other contracting party, unless the importation of the like product of all third countries or the exportation of the like product to all third countries is similarly prohibited or restricted.

2.   In applying import restrictions to any product, contracting parties shall aim at a distribution of trade in such product approaching as closely as possible the shares which the various contracting parties might be expected to obtain in the absence of such restrictions, and to this end shall observe the following provisions:

(a)   Wherever practicable, quotas representing the total amount of permitted imports (whether allocated among supplying countries or not) shall be fixed, and notice given of their amount in accordance with paragraph 3(b) of this Article;

(b)   In cases in which quotas are not practicable, the restrictions may be applied by means of import licences or permits without a quota;

(c)   Contracting parties shall not, except for purposes of operating quotas allocated in accordance with sub-paragraph (d) of this paragraph, require that import licences or permits be utilized for the importation of the product concerned from a particular country or source;

(d)   In cases in which a quota is allocated among supplying countries, the contracting party applying the restrictions may seek agreement with respect to the allocation of shares in the quota with all other contracting parties having a substantial interest in supplying the product concerned. In cases in which this method is not reasonably practicable, the contracting party concerned shall allot to contracting parties having a substantial interest in supplying the product shares based upon the proportions, supplied by such contracting parties during a previous representative period, of the total quantity or value of imports of the product, due account being taken of any special factors which may have affected or may be affecting the trade in the product. No conditions or formalities shall be imposed which would prevent any contracting party from utilizing fully the share of any such total quantity or value which has been allotted to it, subject to importation being made without any prescribed period to which the quota may relate.

_____

Ad *Article XIII*

Paragraph 2(d)

No mention was made of "commercial considerations" as a rule for the allocation of quotas because it was considered that its application by governmental authorities might not always be practicable. Moreover, in cases where it is practicable, a contracting party could apply these considerations in the process of seeking agreement, consistently with the general rule laid down in the opening sentence of paragraph 2.

_____

3.   (a)   In cases in which import licences are issued in connection with import restrictions, the contracting party applying the restrictions shall provide, upon the request of any contracting party having an interest in the trade in the product concerned, all relevant information concerning the administration of the restrictions, the import licences granted over a recent period and the distribution of such licences among supplying countries; *Provided* that there shall be no obligation to supply information as to the names of importing or supplying enterprises.

(b)   In the case of import restrictions involving the fixing of quotas, the contracting party applying the restrictions shall give public notice of the total quantity or value of the product or products which will be permitted to be imported during a specified future period and of any change in such quantity or value. Any supplies of the product in question which were *en route* at the time at which public notice was given shall not be excluded from entry; *Provided* that they may be counted so far as practicable, against the quantity permitted to be imported in the period in question, and also, where necessary, against the quantities permitted to be imported in the next following period or periods; and *Provided* further that if any contracting party customarily exempts from such restrictions products entered for consumption or withdrawn from warehouse for consumption during a period of thirty days after the day of such public notice, such practice shall be considered full compliance with this sub-paragraph.

(c)   In the case of quotas allocated among supplying countries, the contracting party applying the restrictions shall promptly inform all other contracting parties having an interest in supplying the product concerned of the shares in the quota currently allocated, by quantity or value, to the various supplying countries and shall give public notice thereof.

4. With regard to restrictions applied in accordance with paragraph 2(d) of this Article or under paragraph 2(c) of Article XI, the selection of a representative period for any product and the appraisal of any special factors affecting the trade in the product shall be made initially by the contracting party applying the restriction; *Provided* that such contracting party shall, upon the request of any other contracting party having a substantial interest in supplying that product or upon the request of the CONTRACTING PARTIES, consult promptly with the other contracting party or the CONTRACTING PARTIES regarding the need for an adjustment of the proportion determined or of the base period selected, or for the reappraisal of the special factors involved, or for the elimination of conditions, formalities or any other provisions established unilaterally relating to the allocation of an adequate quota or its unrestricted utilization.

Ad *Article XIII*

Paragraph 4

See note relating to "special factors" in connexion with the last subparagraph of paragraph 2 of Article XI.

---

5. The provisions of this Article shall apply to any tariff quota instituted or maintained by any contracting party, and, in so far as applicable, the principles of this Article shall also extend to export restrictions.

ARTICLE XIV. EXCEPTIONS TO THE RULE OF NONDISCRIMINATION

Ad *Articles XI, XII, XIII, XIV and XVIII*

Throughout Articles XI, XII, XIII, XIV and XVIII, the terms "import restrictions" or "export restrictions" include restrictions made effective through state-trading operations.

---

1. A contracting party which applies restrictions under Article XII or under Section B of Article XVIII may, in the application of such restrictions, deviate from the provisions of Article XIII in a manner having equivalent

effect to restrictions on payments and transfers for current international transactions which that contracting party may at that time apply under Article VIII or XIV of the Articles of Agreement of the International Monetary Fund, or under analogous provisions of a special exchange agreement entered into pursuant to paragraph 6 of Article XV.

Ad *Article XIV*

Paragraph 1

The provisions of this paragraph shall not be so construed as to preclude full consideration by the CONTRACTING PARTIES, in the consultations provided for in paragraph 4 of Article XII and in paragraph 12 of Article XVIII, of the nature, effects and reasons for discrimination in the field of import restrictions.

---

2.   A contracting party which is applying import restrictions under Article XII or under Section B of Article XVIII may, with the consent of the CONTRACTING PARTIES, temporarily deviate from the provisions of Article XIII in respect of a small part of its external trade where the benefits to the contracting party or contracting parties concerned substantially outweigh any injury which may result to the trade of other contracting parties.

Ad *Article XIV*

Paragraph 2

One of the situations contemplated in paragraph 2 is that of a contracting party holding balances acquired as a result of current transactions which it finds itself unable to use without a measure of discrimination.

---

3.   The provisions of Article XIII shall not preclude a group of territories having a common quota in the International Monetary Fund from applying against imports from other countries, but not among themselves, restrictions in accordance with the provisions of Article XII or of Section B of Article XVIII on condition that such restrictions are in all other respects consistent with the provisions of Article XIII.

4.   A contracting party applying import restrictions under Article XII or under Section B of Article XVIII shall not be precluded by Articles XI to XV or Section B of Article XVIII of this Agreement from applying measures to direct its exports in such a manner as to increase its earnings of currencies which it can use without deviation from the provisions of Article XIII.

5.   A contracting party shall not be precluded by Articles XI to XV, inclusive, or by Section B of Article XVIII, of this Agreement from applying quantitative restrictions:

(a)   having equivalent effect to exchange restrictions authorized under Section 3(*b*) of Article VII of the Articles of Agreement of the International Monetary Fund, or

(b)   under the preferential arrangements provided for in Annex A of this Agreement, pending the outcome of the negotiations referred to therein.

ARTICLE XV.   EXCHANGE ARRANGEMENTS

1.   The CONTRACTING PARTIES shall seek co-operation with the International Monetary Fund to the end that the CONTRACTING PARTIES and the Fund may pursue a co-ordinated policy with regard to exchange questions within the jurisdiction of the Fund and questions of quantitative restrictions and other trade measures within the jurisdiction of the CONTRACTING PARTIES.

* * *

ARTICLE XVI.   SUBSIDIES

Ad *Article XVI*

The exemption of an exported product from duties or taxes borne by the like product when destined for domestic consumption, or the remission of such duties or taxes in amounts not in excess of those which have accrued, shall not be deemed to be a subsidy.

Section A—Subsidies in General

1.   If any contracting party grants or maintains any subsidy, including any form of income or price support, which operates directly or indirectly to increase exports of any product from, or to reduce imports of any product into, its territory, it shall notify the CONTRACTING PARTIES in writing of the extent and nature of the subsidization, of the estimated effect of the subsidization on the quantity of the affected product or products imported into or exported from its territory and of the circumstances making the subsidization necessary. In any case, in which it is determined that serious prejudice to the interests of any other contracting party is caused or threatened by any such subsidization, the contracting party granting the subsidy shall, upon request, discuss with the other contracting party or parties concerned, or with the CONTRACTING PARTIES, the possibility of limiting the subsidization.

Section B—Additional Provisions on Export Subsidies

Ad *Article XVI*

Section B

1.   Nothing in Section B shall preclude the use by a contracting party of multiple rates of exchange in accordance with the Articles of Agreement of the International Monetary Fund.

2.   For the purposes of Section B, a "primary product" is understood to be any product of farm, forest or fishery, or any mineral, in its natural form or which has undergone such processing as is customarily required to prepare it for marketing in substantial volume in international trade.

---

2.   The contracting parties recognize that the granting by a contracting party of a subsidy on the export of any product may have harmful effects for other contracting parties, both importing and exporting, may cause undue disturbance to their normal commercial interests, and may hinder the achievement of the objectives of this Agreement.

3.   Accordingly, contracting parties should seek to avoid the use of subsidies on the export of primary products. If, however, a contracting party grants directly or indirectly any form of subsidy which operates to increase the export of any primary product from its territory, such subsidy shall not be applied in a manner which results in that contracting party having more than an equitable share of world export trade in that product, account being taken of the shares of the contracting parties in such trade in the product during a previous representative period, and any special factors which may have affected or may be affecting such trade in the product.

Ad *Article XVI*

Paragraph 3

1.   The fact that a contracting party has not exported the product in question during the previous representative period would not in itself preclude that contracting party from establishing its right to obtain a share of the trade in the product concerned.

2.   A system for the stabilization of the domestic price or of the return to domestic producers of a primary product independently of the movements of export prices, which results at times in the sale of the product for export at a price lower than the comparable price charged for the like product to buyers in the domestic market, shall be considered not to involve a subsidy on exports within the meaning of paragraph 3 if the CONTRACTING PARTIES determine that:

    (a)   the system has also resulted, or is so designed as to result, in the sale of the product for export at a price higher than the comparable price charged for the like product to buyers in the domestic market; and

    (b)   the system is so operated, or is designed so to operate, either because of the effective regulation of production or otherwise, as not to stipulate exports unduly or otherwise seriously to prejudice the interests of other contracting parties.

Notwithstanding such determination by the CONTRACTING PARTIES, operations under such a system shall be subject to the provisions of paragraph 3 where they are wholly or partly financed out of government funds in addition to the funds collected from producers in respect of the product concerned.

----

4.   Further, as from 1 January 1958 or the earliest practicable date thereafter, contracting parties shall cease to grant either directly or indirectly any form of subsidy on the export of any product other than a primary product which subsidy results in the sale of such product for export at a price lower than the comparable price charged for the like product to buyers in the domestic market. Until 31 December 1957 no contracting party shall extend the scope of any such subsidization beyond that existing on 1 January 1955 by the introduction of new, or the extension of existing, subsidies.

Ad *Article XVI*

Paragraph 4

The intention of paragraph 4 is that the contracting parties should seek before the end of 1957 to reach agreement to abolish all remaining subsidies as from 1 January 1958; or, failing this, to reach agreement to extend the application of the standstill until the earliest date thereafter by which they can expect to reach such agreement.

----

5.   The CONTRACTING PARTIES shall review the operation of the provisions of this Article from time to time with a view to examining its effectiveness, in the light of actual experience, in promoting the objectives of this Agreement and avoiding subsidization seriously prejudicial to the trade or interests of contracting parties.

ARTICLE XVII.   STATE TRADING ENTERPRISES

1.   (a)   Each contracting party undertakes that if it establishes or maintains a State enterprise, wherever located, or grants to any enterprise, formally or in effect, exclusive or special privileges, such enterprise shall, in its purchases or sales involving either imports or exports, act in a manner consistent with the general principles of nondiscriminatory treatment prescribed in this Agreement for governmental measures affecting imports or exports by private traders.

Ad *Article XVII*

Paragraph 1

The operations of Marketing Boards, which are established by contracting parties and are engaged in purchasing or selling, are subject to the provisions of sub-paragraphs (a) and (b).

The activities of Marketing Boards which are established by contracting parties and which do not purchase or sell but lay down regulations covering private trade are governed by the relevant Articles of this Agreement.

The charging by a state enterprise of different prices for its sales of a product in different markets is not precluded by the provisions of this Article, provided that such different prices are charged for commercial reasons, to meet conditions of supply and demand in export markets.

Paragraph 1(a)

Governmental measures imposed to ensure standards of quality and efficiency in the operation of external trade, or privileges granted for the exploitation of national natural resources but which do not empower the government to exercise control over the trading activities of the enterprise in question, do not constitute "exclusive or special privileges".

(b)   The provisions of sub-paragraph (a) of this paragraph shall be understood to require that such enterprises shall, having due regard to the other provisions of this Agreement, make any such purchases or sales solely in accordance with commercial considerations, including price, quality, availability, marketability, transportation and other conditions of purchase or sale, and shall afford the enterprises of the other contracting parties adequate opportunity, in accordance with customary business practice, to compete for participation in such purchases or sales.

Ad *Article XVII*

Paragraph 1(b)

A country receiving a "tied loan" is free to take this loan into account as a "commercial consideration" when purchasing requirements abroad.

(c)   No contracting party shall prevent any enterprise (whether or not an enterprise described in sub-paragraph (a) of this paragraph) under its jurisdiction from acting in accordance with the principles of sub-paragraphs (a) and (b) of this paragraph.

2.   The provisions of paragraph 1 of this Article shall not apply to imports of products for immediate or ultimate consumption in governmental use and not otherwise for resale or use in the production of goods for sale. With respect to such imports, each contracting party shall accord to the trade of the other contracting parties fair and equitable treatment.

Ad *Article XVII*

Paragraph 2

The term "goods" is limited to products as understood in commercial practice, and is not intended to include the purchase or sale of services.

---

3.   The contracting parties recognize that enterprises of the kind described in paragraph 1(a) of this Article might be operated so as to create serious obstacles to trade; thus negotiations on a reciprocal and mutually advantageous basis designed to limit or reduce such obstacles are of importance to the expansion of international trade.

Ad *Article XVII*

Paragraph 3

Negotiations which contracting parties agree to conduct under this paragraph may be directed towards the reduction of duties and other charges on imports and exports or towards the conclusion of any other mutually satisfactory arrangement consistent with the provisions of this Agreement. (See paragraph 4 of Article II and the note to that paragraph.)

---

4.   (a) Contracting parties shall notify the CONTRACTING PARTIES of the products which are imported into or exported from their territories by enterprises of the kind described in paragraph 1(a) of this Article.

(b)   A contracting party establishing, maintaining or authorizing an import monopoly of a product, which is not the subject of a concession under Article II, shall, on the request of another contracting party having a substantial trade in the product concerned, inform the CONTRACTING PARTIES of the import mark-up on the product during a recent representative period, or, when it is not possible to do so, of the price charged on the resale of the product.

Ad *Article XVII*

Paragraph 4(b)

The term "import mark-up" in this paragraph shall represent the margin by which the price charged by the import monopoly for the imported product (exclusive of internal taxes within the purview of Article III, transportation, distribution, and other expenses incident to the purchase, sale or further processing, and a reasonable margin of profit) exceeds the landed cost.

(c)   The CONTRACTING PARTIES may, at the request of a contracting party which has reason to believe that its interests under this Agreement are being adversely affected by the operations of an enterprise of the kind described in paragraph 1(a), request the contracting party establishing, maintaining or authorizing such enterprise to supply information about its operations related to the carrying out of the provisions of this Agreement.

(d)   The provisions of this paragraph shall not require any contracting party to disclose confidential information which would impede law enforcement or otherwise be contrary to the public interest or would prejudice the legitimate commercial interests of particular enterprises.

ARTICLE XVIII. GOVERNMENTAL ASSISTANCE TO ECONOMIC DEVELOPMENT

Ad *Articles XI, XII, XIII, XIV and XVIII*

Throughout Articles XI, XII, XIII, XIV and XVIII, the terms "import restrictions" or "export restrictions" include restrictions made effective through state-trading operations.

Ad *Article XVIII*

The CONTRACTING PARTIES and the contracting parties concerned shall preserve the utmost secrecy in respect of matters arising under this Article.

---

1.   The contracting parties recognize that the attainment of the objectives of this Agreement will be facilitated by the progressive development of their economies, particularly of those contracting parties the economies of which can only support low standards of living and are in the early stages of development.

Ad *Article XVIII*

Paragraphs 1 and 4

1.   When they consider whether the economy of a contracting party "can only support low standards of living", the CONTRACTING PARTIES shall take into consideration the normal position of that economy and shall not base their determination on exceptional circumstances such as those which may result from the temporary existence of exceptionally favourable conditions for the staple export product or products of such contracting party.

2.   The phrase "in the early stages of development" is not meant to apply only to contracting parties which have just started their economic development, but also to contracting parties the economics of which are undergoing a process of industrialization to correct an excessive dependence on primary production.

---

2.   The contracting parties recognize further that it may be necessary for those contracting parties, in order to implement programmes and policies of economic development designed to raise the general standard of living of their people, to take protective or other measures affecting imports, and that such measures are justified in so far as they facilitate the attainment of the objectives of this Agreement. They agree, therefore, that those contracting parties should enjoy additional facilities to enable them (a) to maintain sufficient flexibility in their tariff structure to be able to grant the tariff protection required for the establishment of a particular industry and (b) to apply quantitative restrictions for balance of payments purposes in a manner which takes full account of the continued high level of demand for imports likely to be generated by their programmes of economic development.

Ad *Article XVIII*

Paragraphs 2, 3, 7, 13 and 22

The reference to the establishment of particular industries shall apply not only to the establishment of a new industry, but also to the establishment of a new branch of production in an existing industry and to the substantial transformation of an existing industry, and to the substantial expansion of an existing industry supplying a relatively small proportion of the domestic demand. It shall also cover the reconstruction of an industry destroyed or substantially damaged as a result of hostilities or natural disasters.

---

3.   The contracting parties recognize finally that, with those additional facilities which are provided for in Sections A and B of this Article, the provisions of this Agreement would normally be sufficient to enable

contracting parties to meet the requirements of their economic development. They agree, however, that there may be circumstances where no measure consistent with those provisions is practicable to permit a contracting party in the process of economic development to grant the governmental assistance required to promote the establishment of particular industries with a view to raising the general standard of living of its people. Special procedures are laid down in Sections C and D of this Article to deal with those cases.*

4.　(a)　Consequently, a contracting party the economy of which can only support low standards of living and is in the early stages of development shall be free to deviate temporarily from the provisions of the other Articles of this Agreement, as provided in Sections A, B and C of this Article.**

(b)　A contracting party the economy of which is in the process of development, but which does not come within the scope of subparagraph (a) above, may submit applications to the CONTRACTING PARTIES under Section D of this Article.

5.　The contracting parties recognize that the export earnings of contracting parties, the economies of which are of the type described in paragraph 4(a) and (b) above and which depend on exports of a small number of primary commodities, may be seriously reduced by a decline in the sale of such commodities. Accordingly, when the exports of primary commodities by such a contracting party are seriously affected by measures taken by another contracting party, it may have resort to the consultation provisions of Article XXII of this Agreement.

* * *

ARTICLE XIX.　EMERGENCY ACTION ON IMPORTS OF PARTICULAR PRODUCTS

1.　(a)　If, as a result of unforeseen developments and of the effect of the obligations incurred by a contracting party under this Agreement, including tariff concessions, any product is being imported into the territory of that contracting party in such increased quantities and under such conditions as to cause or threaten serious injury to domestic producers in that territory of like or directly competitive products, the contracting party shall be free, in respect of such product, and to the extent and for such time as may be necessary to prevent or remedy such injury, to suspend the obligation in whole or in part or to withdraw or modify the concession.

(b)　If any product, which is the subject of a concession with respect to a preference, is being imported into the territory of a contracting party in the circumstances set forth in sub-paragraph (a) of this paragraph, so as to cause or threaten serious injury to domestic producers of like or directly competitive products in the territory of a contracting party which receives or received such preference, the importing contracting party shall be free, if that other contracting party so requests, to suspend the relevant obligation in whole or in part or to withdraw or modify the

---

*　*See* addition to Paragraph 2.
**　*See* addition to Paragraph 1.

concession in respect of the product, to the extent and for such time as may be necessary to prevent or remedy such injury.

2.   Before any contracting party shall take action pursuant to the provisions of paragraph 1 of this Article, it shall give notice in writing to the CONTRACTING PARTIES as far in advance as may be practicable and shall afford the CONTRACTING PARTIES and those contracting parties having a substantial interest as exporters of the product concerned an opportunity to consult with it in respect of the proposed action. When such notice is given in relation to a concession with respect to a preference, the notice shall name the contracting party which has requested the action. In critical circumstances, where delay would cause damage which it would be difficult to repair, action under paragraph 1 of this Article may be taken provisionally without prior consultation, on the condition that consultation shall be effected immediately after taking such action.

3.   (a)   If agreement among the interested contracting parties with respect to the action is not reached, the contracting party which proposes to take or continue the action shall, nevertheless, be free to do so, and if such action is taken or continued, the affected contracting parties shall then be free, not later than ninety days after such action is taken, to suspend, upon the expiration of thirty days from the day on which written notice of such suspension is received by the CONTRACTING PARTIES, the application to the trade of the contracting party taking such action, or, in the case envisaged in paragraph 1(b) of this Article, to the trade of the contracting party requesting such action, of such substantially equivalent concessions or other obligations under this Agreement the suspension of which the CONTRACTING PARTIES do not disapprove.

(b)   Notwithstanding the provisions of sub-paragraph (a) of this paragraph, where action is taken under paragraph 2 of this Article without prior consultation and causes or threatens serious injury in the territory of a contracting party to the domestic producers of products affected by the action, that contracting party shall, where delay would cause damage difficult to repair, be free to suspend, upon the taking of the action and throughout the period of consultation, such concessions or other obligations as may be necessary to prevent or remedy the injury.

ARTICLE XX.   GENERAL EXCEPTIONS

Subject to the requirement that such measures are not applied in a manner which would constitute a means of arbitrary or unjustifiable discrimination between countries where the same conditions prevail, or a disguised restriction on international trade, nothing in this Agreement shall be construed to prevent the adoption or enforcement by any contracting party of measures:

(a)   necessary to protect public morals;

(b)   necessary to protect human, animal or plant life or health;

(c)   relating to the importation or exportation of gold or silver;

(d)   necessary to secure compliance with laws or regulations which are not inconsistent with the provisions of this Agreement, including those relating to customs enforcement, the enforcement of monopolies operated under paragraph 4 of Article II and Article XVII, the protection of patents, trade marks and copyrights, and the prevention of deceptive practices;

(e)   relating to the products of prison labour;

(f)   imposed for the protection of national treasures of artistic, historic or archaeological value;

(g)   relating to the conservation of exhaustible natural resources if such measures are made effective in conjunction with restrictions on domestic production or consumption;

(h)   undertaken   in   pursuance   of   obligations   under   any intergovernmental commodity agreement which conforms to criteria submitted to the CONTRACTING PARTIES and not disapproved by them or which is itself so submitted and not so disapproved;

Ad *Article XX*

Sub-paragraph (h)

The exception provided for in this sub-paragraph extends to any commodity agreement which conforms to the principles approved by the Economic and Social Council in its resolution 30(IV) of 28 March 1947.

(i)   involving restrictions on exports of domestic materials necessary to ensure essential quantities of such materials to a domestic processing industry during periods when the domestic price of such materials is held below the world price as part of a governmental stabilization plan; *Provided* that such restrictions shall not operate to increase the exports of or the protection afforded to such domestic industry, and shall not depart from the provisions of this Agreement relating to non-discrimination;

(j)   essential to the acquisition or distribution of products in general or local short supply; *Provided* that any such measures shall be consistent with the principle that all contracting parties are entitled to an equitable share of the international supply of such products, and that any such measures, which are inconsistent with the other provisions of this Agreement shall be discontinued as soon as the conditions giving rise to them have ceased to exist. The CONTRACTING PARTIES shall review the need for this sub-paragraph not later than 30 June 1960.

ARTICLE XXI.   SECURITY EXCEPTIONS

Nothing in this Agreement shall be construed

(a)   to require any contracting party to furnish any information the disclosure of which it considers contrary to its essential security interests; or

(b)   to prevent any contracting party from taking any action which it considers necessary for the protection of its essential security interests

(i)   relating to fissionable materials or the materials from which they are derived;

(ii)   relating to the traffic in arms, ammunition and implements of war and to such traffic in other goods and materials as is carried on directly or indirectly for the purpose of supplying a military establishment;

(iii)   taken in time of war or other emergency in international relations; or

(c)   to prevent any contracting party from taking any action in pursuance of its obligations under the United Nations Charter for the maintenance of international peace and security.

ARTICLE XXII. CONSULTATION

1.   Each contracting party shall accord sympathetic consideration to, and shall afford adequate opportunity for consultation regarding, such representations as may be made by another contracting party with respect to any matter affecting the operation of this Agreement.

2.   The CONTRACTING PARTIES may, at the request of a contracting party, consult with any contracting party or parties in respect of any matter for which it has not been possible to find a satisfactory solution through consultation under paragraph 1.

ARTICLE XXIII. NULLIFICATION OR IMPAIRMENT

1.   If any contracting party should consider that any benefit accruing to it directly or indirectly under this Agreement is being nullified or impaired or that the attainment of any objective of the Agreement is being impeded as the result of

(a)   the failure of another contracting party to carry out its obligations under this Agreement, or

(b)   the application by another contracting party of any measure, whether or not it conflicts with the provisions of this Agreement, or

(c)   the existence of any other situation,

the contracting party may, with a view to the satisfactory adjustment of the matter, make written representations or proposals to the other contracting party or parties which it considers to be concerned. Any contracting party thus approached shall give sympathetic consideration to the representations or proposals made to it.

2.   If no satisfactory adjustment is effected between the contracting parties concerned within a reasonable time, or if the difficulty is of the type described in paragraph 1(c) of this Article, the matter may be referred to the CONTRACTING PARTIES. The CONTRACTING PARTIES shall promptly investigate any matter so referred to them and shall make appropriate

recommendations to the contracting parties which they consider to be concerned, or give a ruling on the matter, as appropriate. The CONTRACTING PARTIES may consult with contracting parties, with the Economic and Social Council of the United Nations and with any appropriate inter-governmental organization in cases where they consider such consultation necessary. If the CONTRACTING PARTIES consider that the circumstances are serious enough to justify such action, they may authorize a contracting party or parties to suspend the application to any other contracting party or parties of such concessions or other obligations under this Agreement as they determine to be appropriate in the circumstances. If the application to any contracting party of any concession or other obligation is in fact suspended, that contracting party shall then be free, not later than sixty days after such action is taken, to give written notice to the Executive Secretary to the CONTRACTING PARTIES of its intention to withdraw from this Agreement and such withdrawal shall take effect upon the sixtieth day following the day on which such notice is received by him.

PART III

ARTICLE XXIV. TERRITORIAL APPLICATION—FRONTIER TRAFFIC—CUSTOMS UNIONS AND FREE-TRADE AREAS

1. The provisions of this Agreement shall apply to the metropolitan customs territories of the contracting parties and to any other customs territories in respect of which this Agreement has been accepted under Article XXVI or is being applied under Article XXXIII or pursuant to the Protocol of Provisional Application. Each such customs territory shall, exclusively for the purposes of the territorial application of this Agreement, be treated as though it were a contracting party; *Provided* that the provisions of this paragraph shall not be construed to create any rights or obligations as between two or more customs territories in respect of which this Agreement has been accepted under Article XXVI or is being applied under Article XXXIII or pursuant to the Protocol of Provisional Application by a single contracting party.

2. For the purposes of this Agreement a customs territory shall be understood to mean any territory with respect to which separate tariffs or other regulations of commerce are maintained for a substantial part of the trade of such territory with other territories.

3. The provisions of this Agreement shall not be construed to prevent:

(a) Advantages accorded by any contracting party to adjacent countries in order to facilitate frontier traffic;

(b) Advantages accorded to the trade with the Free Territory of Trieste by countries contiguous to that territory, provided that such advantages are not in conflict with the Treaties of Peace arising out of the Second World War.

4. The contracting parties recognize the desirability of increasing freedom of trade by the development, through voluntary agreements, of closer integration between the economies of the countries parties to such

agreements. They also recognize that the purpose of a customs union or of a free-trade area should be to facilitate trade between the constituent territories and not to raise barriers to the trade of other contracting parties with such territories.

5.   Accordingly, the provisions of this Agreement shall not prevent, as between the territories of contracting parties, the formation of a customs union or of a free-trade area or the adoption of an interim agreement necessary for the formation of a customs union or of a free-trade area; *Provided* that:

(a) with respect to a customs union, or an interim agreement leading to the formation of a customs union, the duties and other regulations of commerce imposed at the institution of any such union or interim agreement in respect of trade with contracting parties not parties to such union or agreement shall not on the whole be higher or more restrictive than the general incidence of the duties and regulations of commerce applicable in the constituent territories prior to the formation of such union or the adoption of such interim agreement, as the case may be;

(b) with respect to a free-trade area, or an interim agreement leading to the formation of a free-trade area, the duties and other regulations of commerce maintained in each of the constituent territories and applicable at the formation of such free-trade area or the adoption of such interim agreement to the trade of contracting parties not included in such area or not parties to such agreement shall not be higher or more restrictive than the corresponding duties and other regulations of commerce existing in the same constituent territories prior to the formation of the free-trade area, or interim agreement, as the case may be; and

(c) any interim agreement referred to in sub-paragraphs (a) and (b) shall include a plan and schedule for the formation of such a customs union or of such a free-trade area within a reasonable length of time.

6.   If, in fulfilling the requirements of sub-paragraph 5(a), a contracting party proposes to increase any rate of duty inconsistently with the provisions of Article II, the procedure set forth in Article XXXVIII shall apply. In providing for compensatory adjustment, due account shall be taken of the compensation already afforded by the reductions brought about in the corresponding duty of the other constituents of the union.

7.   (a) Any contracting party deciding to enter into a customs union or free-trade area, or an interim agreement leading to the formation of such a union or area, shall promptly notify the CONTRACTING PARTIES and shall make available to them such information regarding the proposed union or area as will enable them to make such reports and recommendations to contracting parties as they may deem appropriate.

(b) If, after having studied the plan and schedule included in an interim agreement referred to in paragraph 5 in consultation with the parties to that agreement and taking due account of the information made available in accordance with the provisions of sub-paragraph (a), the CONTRACTING PARTIES find that such agreement is not likely to result in the formation of a customs union or of a free-trade area within the period contemplated by the parties to the agreement or that such period is not a reasonable one, the CONTRACTING PARTIES shall make recommendations to the parties to the agreement. The parties shall not maintain or put into force, as the case may be, such agreement if they are not prepared to modify it in accordance with these recommendations.

(c)   Any substantial change in the plan or schedule referred to in paragraph 5(c) shall be communicated to the CONTRACTING PARTIES, which may request the contracting parties concerned to consult with them if the change seems likely to jeopardize or delay unduly the formation of the customs union or of the free-trade area.

8.   For the purposes of this Agreement:

(a)   A customs union shall be understood to mean the substitution of a single customs territory for two or more customs territories, so that

(i)   duties and other restrictive regulations of commerce (except, where necessary, those permitted under Articles XI, XII, XIII, XIV, XV and XX) are eliminated with respect to substantially all the trade between the constituent territories of the union or at least with respect to substantially all the trade in products originating in such territories, and,

(ii)   subject to the provisions of paragraph 9, substantially the same duties and other regulations of commerce are applied by each of the members of the union to the trade of territories not included in the union;

(b)   A free-trade area shall be understood to mean a group of two or more customs territories in which the duties and other restrictive regulations of commerce (except, where necessary, those permitted under Articles XI, XII, XIII, XIV, XV and XX) are eliminated on substantially all the trade between the constituent territories in products originating in such territories.

9.   The preferences referred to in paragraph 2 of Article I shall not be affected by the formation of a customs union or of a free-trade area but may be eliminated or adjusted by means of negotiations with contracting parties affected. This procedure of negotiations with affected contracting parties shall, in particular, apply to the elimination of preferences required to conform with the provisions of paragraph 8(a)(i) and paragraph 8(b).

Ad *Article XXIV*

Paragraph 9

It is understood that the provisions of Article I would require that, when a product which has been imported into the territory of a member of a customs union or free-trade area at a preferential rate of duty is re-exported to the territory of another member of such union or area, the latter member should collect a duty equal to the difference between the duty already paid and any higher duty that would be payable if the product were being imported directly into its territory.

_____

10. The CONTRACTING PARTIES may by a two-thirds majority approve proposals which do not fully comply with the requirements of paragraphs 5 to 9 inclusive, provided that such proposals lead to the formation of a customs union or a free-trade area in the sense of this Article.

11. Taking into account the exceptional circumstances arising out of the establishment of India and Pakistan as independent States and recognizing the fact that they have long constituted an economic unit, the contracting parties agree that the provisions of this Agreement shall not prevent the two countries from entering into special arrangements with respect to the trade between them, pending the establishment of their mutual trade relations on a definitive basis.

_____

Ad *Article XXIV*

Paragraph 11

Measures adopted by India and Pakistan in order to carry out definitive trade arrangements between them, once they have been agreed upon, might depart from particular provisions of this Agreement, but these measures would in general be consistent with the objectives of the Agreement.

_____

12. Each contracting party shall take such reasonable measures as may be available to it to ensure observance of the provisions of this Agreement by the regional and local governments and authorities within its territory.

ARTICLE XXV. JOINT ACTION BY THE CONTRACTING PARTIES

Article XXV

Joint Action by the Contracting Parties

1. Representatives of the contracting parties shall meet from time to time for the purpose of giving effect to those provisions of this Agreement which involve joint action and, generally, with a view to facilitating the

operation and furthering the objectives of this Agreement. Wherever reference is made in this Agreement to the contracting parties acting jointly they are designated as the CONTRACTING PARTIES.

2.   The Secretary-General of the United Nations is requested to convene the first meeting of the CONTRACTING PARTIES, which shall take place not later than March 1, 1948.

3.   Each contracting party shall be entitled to have one vote at all meetings of the CONTRACTING PARTIES.

4.   Except as otherwise provided for in this Agreement, decisions of the CONTRACTING PARTIES shall be taken by a majority of the votes cast.

5.   In exceptional circumstances not elsewhere provided for in this Agreement, the CONTRACTING PARTIES may waive an obligation imposed upon a contracting party by this Agreement; *Provided* that any such decision shall be approved by a two-thirds majority of the votes cast and that such majority shall comprise more than half of the contracting parties. The CONTRACTING PARTIES may also by such a vote

(i)   define certain categories of exceptional circumstances to which other voting requirements shall apply for the waiver of obligations, and

(ii)   prescribe such criteria as may be necessary for the application of this paragraph.

* * *

ARTICLE XXVI. ACCEPTANCE, ENTRY INTO FORCE AND REGISTRATION

1.   The date of this Agreement shall be 30 October 1947.

2.   This Agreement shall be open for acceptance by any contracting party which, on 1 March 1955, was a contracting party or was negotiating with a view to accession to this Agreement.

3.   This Agreement, done in a single English original and in a single French original, both texts authentic, shall be deposited with the Secretary-General of the United Nations, who shall furnish certified copies thereof to all interested governments.

* * *

6.   This Agreement shall enter into force, as among the governments which have accepted it, on the thirtieth day following the day on which instruments of acceptance have been deposited with the Executive Secretary* to the CONTRACTING PARTIES on behalf of governments named in Annex H, the territories of which account for 85 per centum of the total external trade of the territories of such governments, computed in accordance with the applicable column of percentages set forth therein. The instrument of

---

*   Now referred to as Director-General.

acceptance of each other government shall take effect on the thirtieth day following the day on which such instrument has been deposited.

7.   The United Nations is authorized to effect registration of this Agreement as soon as it enters into force.

ARTICLE XXVII.   WITHHOLDING OR WITHDRAWAL OF CONCESSIONS

Any contracting party shall at any time be free to withhold or to withdraw in whole or in part any concession, provided for in the appropriate Schedule annexed to this Agreement, in respect of which such contracting party determines that it was initially negotiated with a government which has not become, or has ceased to be, a contracting party. A contracting party taking such action shall notify the CONTRACTING PARTIES and, upon request, consult with contracting parties which have a substantial interest in the product concerned.

ARTICLE XXVIII.   MODIFICATION OF SCHEDULES

Modification of Schedules

1.   On the first day of each three-year period, the first period beginning on 1 January 1958 (or on the first day of any other period* that may be specified by the CONTRACTING PARTIES by two-thirds of the votes cast) a contracting party (hereafter in this Article referred to as the "applicant contracting party") may, by negotiations and agreement with any contracting party with which such concession was initially negotiated and with any other contracting party determined by the CONTRACTING PARTIES to have a principal supplying interest* (which two preceding categories of contracting parties, together with the applicant contracting party, are in this Article hereinafter referred to as the "contracting parties primarily concerned"), and subject to consultation with any other contracting party determined by the CONTRACTING PARTIES to have a substantial interest* in such concession, modify or withdraw a concession* included in the appropriate Schedule annexed to this Agreement.

2.   In such negotiations and agreement, which may include provision for compensatory adjustment with respect to other products, the contracting parties concerned shall endeavour to maintain a general level of reciprocal and mutually advantageous concessions not less favourable to trade than that provided for in this Agreement prior to such negotiations.

3.   (a) If agreement between the contracting parties primarily concerned cannot be reached before 1 January 1958 or before the expiration of a period envisaged in paragraph 1 of this Article, the contracting party which proposes to modify or withdraw the concession shall, nevertheless, be free to do so and if such action is taken any contracting party with which such concession was initially negotiated, any contracting party determined under paragraph 1 to have a principal supplying interest and any contracting party determined under paragraph 1 to have a substantial interest shall then be free not later than six months after such action is taken, to withdraw, upon the expiration of thirty days from the day on which written notice of such withdrawal is received by the CONTRACTING PARTIES, substantially

equivalent concessions initially negotiated with the applicant contracting party.

(b) If agreement between the contracting parties primarily concerned is reached but any other contracting party determined under paragraph 1 of this Article to have a substantial interest is not satisfied, such other contracting party shall be free, not later than six months after action under such agreement is taken, to withdraw, upon the expiration of thirty days from the day on which written notice of such withdrawal is received by the CONTRACTING PARTIES, substantially equivalent concessions initially negotiated with the applicant contracting party.

4.   The CONTRACTING PARTIES may, at any time, in special circumstances, authorize* a contracting party to enter into negotiations for modification or withdrawal of a concession included in the appropriate Schedule annexed to this Agreement subject to the following procedures and conditions:

(a)   Such negotiations* and any related consultations shall be conducted in accordance with the provisions of paragraphs 1 and 2 of this Article.

(b)   If agreement between the contracting parties primarily concerned is reached in the negotiations, the provisions of paragraph 3(b) of this Article shall apply.

(c)   If agreement between the contracting parties primarily concerned is not reached within a period of sixty days* after negotiations have been authorized, or within such longer period as the CONTRACTING PARTIES may have prescribed, the applicant contracting party may refer the matter to the CONTRACTING PARTIES.

(d)   Upon such reference, the CONTRACTING PARTIES shall promptly examine the matter and submit their views to the contracting parties primarily concerned with the aim of achieving a settlement. If a settlement is reached, the provisions of paragraph 3(b) shall apply as if agreement between the contracting parties primarily concerned had been reached. If no settlement is reached between the contracting parties primarily concerned, the applicant contracting party shall be free to modify or withdraw the concession, unless the CONTRACTING PARTIES determine that the applicant contracting party has unreasonably failed to offer adequate compensation.* If such action is taken, any contracting party with which the concession was initially negotiated, any contracting party determined under paragraph 4(a) to have a principal supplying interest and any contracting party determined under paragraph 4(a) to have a substantial interest, shall be free, not later than six months after such action is taken, to modify or withdraw, upon the expiration of thirty days from the day on which written notice of such withdrawal is received by the CONTRACTING PARTIES, substantially equivalent concessions initially negotiated with the applicant contracting party.

5.   Before 1 January 1958 and before the end of any period envisaged in paragraph 1 a contracting party may elect by notifying the CONTRACTING PARTIES to reserve the right, for the duration of the next period, to modify the appropriate Schedule in accordance with the procedures of paragraphs 1 to 3. If a contracting party so elects, other contracting parties shall have the right, during the same period, to modify or withdraw, in accordance with the same procedures, concessions initially negotiated with that contracting party.

ARTICLE XXVIII bis.   TARIFF NEGOTIATIONS

1.   The contracting parties recognize that customs duties often constitute serious obstacles to trade; thus negotiations on a reciprocal and mutually advantageous basis, directed to the substantial reduction of the general level of tariffs and other charges on imports and exports and in particular to the reduction of such high tariffs as discourage the importation even of minimum quantities, and conducted with due regard to the objectives of this Agreement and the varying needs of individual contracting parties, are of great importance to the expansion of international trade. The CONTRACTING PARTIES may therefore sponsor such negotiations from time to time.

2.   (a)   Negotiations under this Article may be carried out on a selective product-by-product basis or by the application of such multilateral procedures as may be accepted by the contracting parties concerned. Such negotiations may be directed towards the reduction of duties, the binding of duties at then existing levels or undertakings that individual duties or the average duties on specified categories of products shall not exceed specified levels. The binding against increase of low duties or of duty-free treatment shall, in principle, be recognized as a concession equivalent in value to the reduction of high duties.

(b)   The contracting parties recognize that in general the success of multilateral negotiations would depend on the participation of all contracting parties which conduct a substantial proportion of their external trade with one another.

3.   Negotiations shall be conducted on a basis which affords adequate opportunity to take into account:

(a)   the needs of individual contracting parties and individual industries;

(b)   the needs of less-developed countries for a more flexible use of tariff protection to assist their economic development and the special needs of these countries to maintain tariffs for revenue purposes; and

(c)   all other relevant circumstances, including the fiscal, developmental, strategic and other needs of the contracting parties concerned.

Ad *Article XXVIII bis*

Paragraph 3

It is understood that the reference to fiscal needs would include the revenue aspect of duties and particularly duties imposed primarily for revenue purposes or duties imposed on products which can be substituted for products subject to revenue duties to prevent the avoidance of such duties.

ARTICLE XXIX.   THE RELATION OF THIS AGREEMENT TO THE HAVANA CHARTER (omitted)

* * *

ARTICLE XXX.   AMENDMENTS

1.   Except where provision for modification is made elsewhere in this Agreement, amendments to the provisions of Part I of this Agreement or to the provisions of Article XXIX or of this Article shall become effective upon acceptance by all the contracting parties, and other amendments to this Agreement shall become effective, in respect of those contracting parties which accept them, upon acceptance by two-thirds of the contracting parties and thereafter for each other contracting party upon acceptance by it.

2.   Any contracting party accepting an amendment to this Agreement shall deposit an instrument of acceptance with the Secretary-General of the United Nations within such period as the CONTRACTING PARTIES may specify. The CONTRACTING PARTIES may decide that any amendment made effective under this Article is of such a nature that any contracting party which has not accepted it within a period specified by the CONTRACTING PARTIES shall be free to withdrawn from this Agreement, or to remain a contracting party with the consent of the CONTRACTING PARTIES.

ARTICLE XXXI.   WITHDRAWAL

Without prejudice to the provisions of paragraph 12 of Article XVIII, of Article XXIII or of paragraph 2 of Article XXX, any contracting party may withdraw from this Agreement, or may separately withdraw on behalf of any of the separate customs territories for which it has international responsibility and which at the time possesses full autonomy in the conduct of its external commercial relations and of the other matters provided for in this Agreement. The withdrawal shall take effect upon the expiration of six months from the day on which written notice of withdrawal is received by the Secretary-General of the United Nations.

ARTICLE XXXII.   CONTRACTING PARTIES

1.   The contracting parties to this Agreement shall be understood to mean those governments which are applying the provisions of this Agreement under Article XXVI or XXXIII or pursuant to the Protocol of Provisional Application.

2.   At any time after the entry into force of this Agreement pursuant to paragraph 6 of Article XXVI, those contracting parties which have accepted this Agreement pursuant to paragraph 4 of Article XXVI may decide that any contracting party which has not so accepted it shall cease to be a contracting party.

ARTICLE XXXIII.   ACCESSION

A government not party to this Agreement, or a government acting on behalf of a separate customs territory possessing full autonomy in the conduct of its external commercial relations and of the other matters provided for in this Agreement, may accede to this Agreement, on its own behalf or on behalf of that territory, on terms to be agreed between such government and the CONTRACTING PARTIES. Decisions of the CONTRACTING PARTIES under this paragraph shall be taken by a two-thirds majority.

ARTICLE XXXIV.   ANNEXES

The annexes to this Agreement are hereby made an integral part of this Agreement.

ARTICLE XXXV.   NON-APPLICATION OF THE AGREEMENT BETWEEN PARTICULAR CONTRACTING PARTIES

1.   This Agreement, or alternatively Article II of this Agreement, shall not apply as between any contracting party and any other contracting party if:

(a)   the two contracting parties have not entered into tariff negotiations with each other, and

(b)   either of the contracting parties, at the time either becomes a contracting party, does not consent to such application.

2.   The CONTRACTING PARTIES may review the operation of this Article in particular cases at the request of any contracting party and make appropriate recommendations.

PART IV.   TRADE AND DEVELOPMENT

Ad *Part IV*

The words "developed contracting parties" and the words "less-developed contracting parties," as used in Part IV are to be understood to refer to developed and less-developed countries which are parties to the General Agreement on Tariffs and Trade.

ARTICLE XXXVI. PRINCIPLES AND OBJECTIVES

1. The contracting parties,

(a) recalling that the basic objectives of this Agreement include the raising of standards of living and the progressive development of the economies of all contracting parties, and considering that the attainment of these objectives is particularly urgent for less-developed contracting parties;

(b) considering that export earnings of the less-developed contracting parties can play a vital part in their economic development and that the extent of this contribution depends on the prices paid by the less-developed contracting parties for essential imports, the volume of their exports, and the prices received for these exports;

(c) noting, that there is a wide gap between standards of living in less-developed countries and in other countries;

(d) recognizing that individual and joint action is essential to further the development of the economies of less-developed contracting parties and to bring about a rapid advance in the standards of living in these countries;

(e) recognizing that international trade as a means of achieving economic and social advancement should be governed by such rules and procedures—and measures in conformity with such rules and procedures—as are consistent with the objectives set forth in this Article;

(f) noting that the CONTRACTING PARTIES may enable less-developed contracting parties to use special measures to promote their trade and development;

agree as follows.

Ad *Article XXXVI*

Paragraph 1

This Article is based upon the objectives set forth in Article I as it will be amended by Section A of paragraph 1 of the Protocol Amending Part I and Articles XXIX and XXX when that Protocol enters into force.[1]

---

[1]   This Protocol was abandoned on January 1, 1968.

2.   There is need for a rapid and sustained expansion of the export earnings of the less-developed contracting parties.

3.   There is need for positive efforts designed to ensure that less-developed contracting parties secure a share in the growth in international trade commensurate with the needs of their economic development.

4.   Given the continued dependence of many less-developed contracting parties on the exportation of a limited range of primary products, there is need to provide in the largest possible measure more favourable and acceptable conditions of access to world markets for these products, and wherever appropriate to devise measures designed to stabilize and improve conditions of world markets in these products, including in particular measures designed to attain stable, equitable and remunerative prices, thus permitting an expansion of world trade and demand and a dynamic and steady growth of the real export earnings of these countries so as to provide them with expanding resources for their economic development.

Ad *Article XXXVI*

Paragraph 4

The term "primary products" includes agricultural products, vide paragraph 2 of the note ad Article XVI, Section B.

---

5.   The rapid expansion of the economies of the less-developed contracting parties will be facilitated by a diversification of the structure of their economies and the avoidance of an excessive dependence on the export of primary products. There is, therefore, need for increased access in the largest possible measure to markets under favourable conditions for processed and manufactured products currently or potentially of particular export interest to less-developed contracting parties.

Ad *Article XXXVI*

Paragraph 5

A diversification programme would generally include the intensification of activities for the processing of primary products and the development of manufacturing industries, taking into account the situation of the particular contracting party and the world outlook for production and consumption of different commodities.

---

6.   Because of the chronic deficiency in the export proceeds and other foreign exchange earnings of less-developed contracting parties, there are important inter-relationships between trade and financial assistance to

development. There is, therefore, need for close and continuing collaboration between the CONTRACTING PARTIES and the international lending agencies so that they can contribute most effectively to alleviating the burdens these less-developed contracting parties assume in the interest of their economic development.

7.   There is need for appropriate collaboration between the CONTRACTING PARTIES, other intergovernmental bodies and the organs and agencies of the United Nations system, whose activities relate to the trade and economic development of less-developed countries.

8.   The developed contracting parties do not expect reciprocity for commitments made by them in trade negotiations to reduce or remove tariffs and other barriers to the trade of less-developed contracting parties.

Ad *Article XXXVI*

Paragraph 8

It is understood that the phrase "do not expect reciprocity" means, in accordance with the objectives set forth in this Article, that the less-developed contracting parties should not be expected, in the course of trade negotiations, to make contributions which are inconsistent with their individual development, financial and trade needs, taking into consideration past trade developments.

This paragraph would apply in the event of action under Section A of Article XVII, Article XXVIII, Article XXVIII bis (Article XXIX after the amendment set forth in Section A of paragraph 1 of the Protocol Amending Part I and Articles XXIX and XXX shall have become effective), Article XXXIII, or any other procedure under this Agreement.

---

9.   The adoption of measures to give effect to these principles and objectives shall be a matter of conscious and purposeful effort on the part of the contracting parties both individually and jointly.

ARTICLE XXXVII.   COMMITMENTS

1.   The developed contracting parties shall to the fullest extent possible—that is, except when compelling reasons, which may include legal reasons, make it impossible—give effect to the following provisions:

(a)   accord high priority to the reduction and elimination of barriers to products currently or potentially of particular export interest to less-developed contracting parties, including customs duties and other restrictions which differentiate unreasonably between such products in their primary and in their processed forms;

Ad *Article XXXVII*

Paragraph 1(a)

This paragraph would apply in the event of negotiations for reduction or elimination of tariffs or other restrictive regulations of commerce under Articles XXVIII, XXVIII bis (XXIX after the amendment set forth in Section A of paragraph 1 of the Protocol Amending Part I and Articles XXIX and XXX shall have become effective[1]), and Article XXXIII, as well as in connexion with other action to effect such reduction or elimination which contracting parties may be able to undertake.

(b)   refrain from introducing, or increasing the incidence of, customs duties or non-tariff import barriers on products currently or potentially of particular export interest to less-developed contracting parties; and

(c)(i)   refrain from imposing new fiscal measures, and

(ii)   in any adjustments of fiscal policy accord high priority to the reduction and elimination of fiscal measures, which would hamper, or which hamper, significantly the growth of consumption of primary products, in raw or processed form, wholly or mainly produced in the territories of less-developed contracting parties, and which are applied specifically to those products.

2.   (a)   Whenever it is considered that effect is not being given to any of the provisions of sub-paragraph (a), (b) or (c) of paragraph 1, the matter shall be reported to the CONTRACTING PARTIES either by the contracting party not so giving effect to the relevant provisions or by any other interested contracting party.

(b)(i)   The CONTRACTING PARTIES shall, if requested so to do by any interested contracting party, and without prejudice to any bilateral consultations that may be undertaken, consult with the contracting party concerned and all interested contracting parties with respect to the matter with a view to reaching solutions satisfactory to all contracting parties concerned in order to further the objectives set forth in Article XXXVI. In the course of these consultations, the reasons given in cases where effect was not being given to the provisions of subparagraph (a), (b) or (c) of paragraph 1 shall be examined.

(ii)   As the implementation of the provisions of sub-paragraph (a), (b) or (c) of paragraph 1 by individual contracting parties may in some cases be more readily achieved where action is taken jointly with other developed contracting parties, such consultation might, where appropriate, be directed towards this end.

---

[1]   This Protocol was abandoned on January 1, 1968.

(iii) The consultations by the CONTRACTING PARTIES might also, in appropriate cases, be directed towards agreement on joint action designed to further the objectives of this Agreement as envisaged in paragraph 1 of Article XXV.

3.   The developed contracting parties shall:

(a)   make every effort, in cases where a government directly or indirectly determines the resale price of products wholly or mainly produced in the territories of less-developed contracting parties, to maintain trade margins at equitable levels;

(b)   give active consideration to the adoption of other measures designed to provide greater scope for the development of imports from less-developed contracting parties and collaborate in appropriate international action to this end;

———————

Ad *Article XXXVII*

Paragraph 3(b)

The other measures referred to in this paragraph might include steps to promote domestic structural changes, to encourage the consumption of particular products, or to introduce measures of trade promotion.

———————

(c)   have special regard to the trade interests of less-developed contracting parties when considering the application of other measures permitted under this Agreement to meet particular problems and explore all possibilities of constructive remedies before applying such measures where they would affect essential interests of those contracting parties.

4.   Less-developed contracting parties agree to take appropriate action in implementation of the provisions of Part IV for the benefit of the trade of other less-developed contracting parties, in so far as such action is consistent with their individual present and future development, financial and trade needs taking into account past trade developments as well as the trade interests of less-developed contracting parties as a whole.

5.   In the implementation of the commitments set forth in paragraphs 1 to 4 each contracting party shall afford to any other interested contracting party or contracting parties full and prompt opportunity for consultations under the normal procedures of this Agreement with respect to any matter or difficulty which may arise.

ARTICLE XXXVIII. JOINT ACTION (omitted)

* * *

ANNEX A

LIST OF TERRITORIES REFERRED TO IN PARAGRAPH 2(A) OF ARTICLE I

United Kingdom of Great Britain and Northern Ireland

Dependent territories of the United Kingdom of Great Britain and Northern Ireland

Canada

Commonwealth of Australia

Dependent territories of the Commonwealth of Australia

New Zealand

Dependent territories of New Zealand

Union of South Africa including South West Africa

Ireland

India (as of April 10, 1947)

Newfoundland

Southern Rhodesia

Burma

Ceylon

Certain of the territories listed above have two or more preferential rates in force for certain products. Any such territory may, by agreement with the other contracting parties which are principal suppliers of such products at the most-favoured-nation rate, substitute for such preferential rates a single preferential rate which shall not on the whole be less favourable to suppliers at the most-favoured-nation rate than the preferences in force prior to such substitution.

The imposition of an equivalent margin of tariff preference to replace a margin of preference in an internal tax existing on April 10, 1947 exclusively between two or more of the territories listed in this Annex or to replace the preferential quantitative arrangements described in the following paragraph, shall not be deemed to constitute an increase in a margin of tariff preference.

The preferential arrangements referred to in paragraph 5(b) of Article XIV are those existing in the United Kingdom on April 10, 1947, under contractual agreements with the Governments of Canada, Australia and New Zealand, in respect of chilled and frozen beef and veal, frozen mutton and lamb, chilled and frozen pork, and bacon. It is the intention, without prejudice to any action taken under subparagraph (h) of Article XX, that these arrangements shall be eliminated or replaced by tariff preferences, and that negotiations to this end shall take place as soon as practicable among the countries substantially concerned or involved.

The film hire tax in force in New Zealand on April 10, 1947, shall, for the purposes of this Agreement, be treated as a customs duty under Article

I. The renters' film quota in force in New Zealand on April 10, 1947, shall, for the purposes of this Agreement, be treated as a screen quota under Article IV.

The Dominions of India and Pakistan have not been mentioned separately in the above list since they had not come into existence as such on the base date of April 10, 1947.

* * *

ANNEX H

Percentage Shares of Total External Trade to be Used for the Purpose of Making the Determination Referred to in Article XXVI

(based on the average of 1949–1953)

If, prior to the accession of the Government of Japan to the General Agreement, the present Agreement has been accepted by contracting parties the external trade of which under column I accounts for the percentage of such trade specified in paragraph 6 of Article XXVI, column I shall be applicable for the purposes of that paragraph. If the present Agreement has not been so accepted prior to the accession of the Government of Japan, column II shall be applicable for the purposes of that paragraph.

	Column I (Contracting parties on 1 March 1955)	*Column II* (Contracting parties on 1 March 1955 and Japan)
Australia	3.1	3.0
Austria	0.9	0.8
Belgium-Luxemburg	4.3	4.2
Brazil	2.5	2.4
Burma	0.3	0.3
Canada	6.7	6.5
Ceylon	0.5	0.5
Chile	0.6	0.6
Cuba	1.1	1.1
Czechoslovakia	1.4	1.4
Denmark	1.4	1.4
Dominican Republic	0.1	0.1
Finland	1.0	1.0
France	8.7	8.5
Germany, Federal Republic of	5.3	5.2
Greece	0.4	0.4

	Column I (Contracting parties on 1 March 1955)	*Column II* (Contracting parties on 1 March 1955 and Japan)
Haiti	0.1	0.1
India	2.4	2.4
Indonesia	1.3	1.3
Italy	2.9	2.8
Netherlands, Kingdom of the	4.7	4.6
New Zealand	1.0	1.0
Nicaragua	0.1	0.1
Norway	1.1	1.1
Pakistan	0.9	0.8
Peru	0.4	0.4
Rhodesia and Nyasaland	0.6	0.6
Sweden	2.5	2.4
Turkey	0.6	0.6
Union of South Africa	1.8	1.8
United Kingdom	20.3	19.8
United States of America	20.6	20.1
Uruguay	0.4	0.4
Japan	—	2.3
	100.0	100.0

Note: These percentages have been computed taking into account the trade of all territories in respect of which the General Agreement on Tariffs and Trade is applied.

2. AGREEMENT ESTABLISHING THE WORLD TRADE ORGANIZATION (WTO)

(Selected Provisions)

The *Parties* to this Agreement,

Recognizing that their relations in the field of trade and economic endeavour should be conducted with a view to raising standards of living, ensuring full employment and a large and steadily growing volume of real income and effective demand, and expanding the production of and trade in goods and services, while allowing for the optimal use of the world's resources in accordance with the objective of sustainable development, seeking both to protect and preserve the environment and to enhance the means for doing so in a manner consistent with their respective needs and concerns at different levels of economic development,

Recognizing further that there is need for positive efforts designed to ensure that developing countries, and especially the least developed among them, secure a share in the growth in international trade commensurate with the needs of their economic development,

Being desirous of contributing to these objectives by entering into reciprocal and mutually advantageous arrangements directed to the substantial reduction of tariffs and other barriers to trade and to the elimination of discriminatory treatment in international trade relations,

Resolved, therefore, to develop an integrated, more viable and durable multilateral trading system encompassing the General Agreement on Tariffs and Trade, the results of past trade liberalization efforts, and all of the results of the Uruguay Round of Multilateral Trade Negotiations,

Determined to preserve the basic principles and to further the objectives underlying this multilateral trading system,

Agree as follows:

Article I

Establishment of the Organization

The World Trade Organization (hereinafter referred to as "the WTO") is hereby established.

Article II

Scope of the WTO

1.   The WTO shall provide the common institutional framework for the conduct of trade relations among its Members in matters related to the agreements and associated legal instruments included in the Annexes to this Agreement.

2.   The agreements and associated legal instruments included in Annexes 1, 2 and 3 (hereinafter referred to as "Multilateral Trade Agreements") are integral parts of this Agreement, binding on all Members.

3.   The agreements and associated legal instruments included in Annex 4 (hereinafter referred to as "Plurilateral Trade Agreements") are also part of this Agreement for those Members that have accepted them, and are binding on those Members. The Plurilateral Trade Agreements do not create either obligations or rights for Members that have not accepted them.

4.   The General Agreement on Tariffs and Trade 1994 as specified in Annex 1A (hereinafter referred to as "GATT 1994") is legally distinct from the General Agreement on Tariffs and Trade, dated 30 October 1947, annexed to the Final Act Adopted at the Conclusion of the Second Session of the Preparatory Committee of the United Nations Conference on Trade and Employment, as subsequently rectified, amended or modified (hereinafter referred to as "GATT 1947").

Article III

Functions of the WTO

1.   The WTO shall facilitate the implementation, administration and operation, and further the objectives, of this Agreement and of the Multilateral Trade Agreements, and shall also provide the framework for the implementation, administration and operation of the Plurilateral Trade Agreements.

2.   The WTO shall provide the forum for negotiations among its Members concerning their multilateral trade relations in matters dealt with under the agreements in the Annexes to this Agreement. The WTO may also provide a forum for further negotiations among its Members concerning their multilateral trade relations, and a framework for the implementation of the results of such negotiations, as may be decided by the Ministerial Conference.

3.   The WTO shall administer the Understanding on Rules and Procedures Governing the Settlement of Disputes (hereinafter referred to as the "Dispute Settlement Understanding" or "DSU") in Annex 2 to this Agreement.

4.   The WTO shall administer the Trade Policy Review Mechanism (hereinafter referred to as the "TPRM") provided for in Annex 3 to this Agreement.

5.   With a view to achieving greater coherence in global economic policymaking, the WTO shall cooperate, as appropriate, with the International Monetary Fund and with the International Bank for Reconstruction and Development and its affiliated agencies.

Article IV

Structure of the WTO

1.   There shall be a Ministerial Conference composed of representatives of all the Members, which shall meet at least once every two years. The Ministerial Conference shall carry out the functions of the WTO and take actions necessary to this effect. The Ministerial Conference shall have the authority to take decisions on all matters under any of the Multilateral Trade Agreements, if so requested by a Member, in accordance

with the specific requirements for decision-making in this Agreement and in the relevant Multilateral Trade Agreement.

2.   There shall be a General Council composed of representatives of all the Members, which shall meet as appropriate. In the intervals between meetings of the Ministerial Conference, its functions shall be conducted by the General Council. The General Council shall also carry out the functions assigned to it by this Agreement. The General Council shall establish its rules of procedure and approve the rules of procedure for the Committees provided for in paragraph 7.

3.   The General Council shall convene as appropriate to discharge the responsibilities of the Dispute Settlement Body provided for in the Dispute Settlement Understanding. The Dispute Settlement Body may have its own chairman and shall establish such rules of procedure as it deems necessary for the fulfilment of those responsibilities.

4.   The General Council shall convene as appropriate to discharge the responsibilities of the Trade Policy Review Body provided for in the TPRM. The Trade Policy Review Body may have its own chairman and shall establish such rules of procedure as it deems necessary for the fulfilment of those responsibilities.

5.   There shall be a Council for Trade in Goods, a Council for Trade in Services and a Council for Trade-Related Aspects of Intellectual Property Rights (hereinafter referred to as the "Council for TRIPS"), which shall operate under the general guidance of the General Council. The Council for Trade in Goods shall oversee the functioning of the Multilateral Trade Agreements in Annex 1A. The Council for Trade in Services shall oversee the functioning of the General Agreement on Trade in Services (hereinafter referred to as "GATS"). The Council for TRIPS shall oversee the functioning of the Agreement on Trade-Related Aspects of Intellectual Property Rights (hereinafter referred to as the "Agreement on TRIPS"). These Councils shall carry out the functions assigned to them by their respective agreements and by the General Council. They shall establish their respective rules of procedure subject to the approval of the General Council. Membership in these Councils shall be open to representatives of all Members. These Councils shall meet as necessary to carry out their functions.

* * *

Article V

Relations With Other Organizations

* * *

Article VI

The Secretariat

* * *

Article VII

Budget and Contributions

* * *

Article VIII

Status of the WTO

* * *

Article IX

Decision-Making

1.   The WTO shall continue the practice of decision-making by consensus followed under GATT 1947.[1] Except as otherwise provided, where a decision cannot be arrived at by consensus, the matter at issue shall be decided by voting. At meetings of the Ministerial Conference and the General Council, each Member of the WTO shall have one vote. Where the European Communities exercise their right to vote, they shall have a number of votes equal to the number of their member States[2] which are Members of the WTO. Decisions of the Ministerial Conference and the General Council shall be taken by a majority of the votes cast, unless otherwise provided in this Agreement or in the relevant Multilateral Trade Agreement.[3]

2.   The Ministerial Conference and the General Council shall have the exclusive authority to adopt interpretations of this Agreement and of the Multilateral Trade Agreements. In the case of an interpretation of a Multilateral Trade Agreement in Annex 1, they shall exercise their authority on the basis of a recommendation by the Council overseeing the functioning of that Agreement. The decision to adopt an interpretation shall be taken by a three-fourths majority of the Members. This paragraph shall not be used in a manner that would undermine the amendment provisions in Article X.

3.   In exceptional circumstances, the Ministerial Conference may decide to waive an obligation imposed on a Member by this Agreement or any of the Multilateral Trade Agreements, provided that any such decision shall be taken by three fourths[4] of the Members unless otherwise provided for in this paragraph.

(a)   A request for a waiver concerning this Agreement shall be submitted to the Ministerial Conference for consideration

---

[1]   The body concerned shall be deemed to have decided by consensus on a matter submitted for its consideration, if no Member, present at the meeting when the decision is taken, formally objects to the proposed decision.

[2]   The number of votes of the European Communities and their member States shall in no case exceed the number of the member States of the European Communities.

[3]   Decisions by the General Council when convened as the Dispute Settlement Body shall be taken only in accordance with the provisions of paragraph 4 of Article 2 of the Dispute Settlement Understanding.

[4]   A decision to grant a waiver in respect of any obligation subject to a transition period or a period for staged implementation that the requesting Member has not performed by the end of the relevant period shall be taken only by consensus.

pursuant to the practice of decision-making by consensus. The Ministerial Conference shall establish a time-period, which shall not exceed 90 days, to consider the request. If consensus is not reached during the time-period, any decision to grant a waiver shall be taken by three fourths of the Members.

(b)   A request for a waiver concerning the Multilateral Trade Agreements in Annexes 1A or 1B or 1C and their annexes shall be submitted initially to the Council for Trade in Goods, the Council for Trade in Services or the Council for TRIPS, respectively, for consideration during a time-period which shall not exceed 90 days. At the end of the time-period, the relevant Council shall submit a report to the Ministerial Conference.

4.   A decision by the Ministerial Conference granting a waiver shall state the exceptional circumstances justifying the decision, the terms and conditions governing the application of the waiver, and the date on which the waiver shall terminate. Any waiver granted for a period of more than one year shall be reviewed by the Ministerial Conference not later than one year after it is granted, and thereafter annually until the waiver terminates. In each review, the Ministerial Conference shall examine whether the exceptional circumstances justifying the waiver still exist and whether the terms and conditions attached to the waiver have been met. The Ministerial Conference, on the basis of the annual review, may extend, modify or terminate the waiver.

5.   Decisions under a Plurilateral Trade Agreement, including any decisions on interpretations and waivers, shall be governed by the provisions of that Agreement.

Article X

Amendment

1.   Any Member of the WTO may initiate a proposal to amend the provisions of this Agreement or the Multilateral Trade Agreements in Annex 1 by submitting such proposal to the Ministerial Conference. The Councils listed in paragraph 5 of Article IV may also submit to the Ministerial Conference proposals to amend the provisions of the corresponding Multilateral Trade Agreements in Annex 1 the functioning of which they oversee. Unless the Ministerial Conference decides on a longer period, for a period of 90 days after the proposal has been tabled formally at the Ministerial Conference any decision by the Ministerial Conference to submit the proposed amendment to the Members for acceptance shall be taken by consensus. Unless the provisions of paragraphs 2, 5 or 6 apply, that decision shall specify whether the provisions of paragraphs 3 or 4 shall apply. If consensus is reached, the Ministerial Conference shall forthwith submit the proposed amendment to the Members for acceptance. If consensus is not reached at a meeting of the Ministerial Conference within the established period, the Ministerial Conference shall decide by a two-thirds majority of the Members whether to submit the proposed amendment to the Members for acceptance. Except as provided in paragraphs 2, 5 and 6, the provisions of paragraph 3 shall apply to the proposed amendment, unless the

Ministerial Conference decides by a three-fourths majority of the Members that the provisions of paragraph 4 shall apply.

2.   Amendments to the provisions of this Article and to the provisions of the following Articles shall take effect only upon acceptance by all Members:

Article IX of this Agreement;

Articles I and II of GATT 1994;

Article II:1 of GATS;

Article 4 of the Agreement on TRIPS.

3.   Amendments to provisions of this Agreement, or of the Multilateral Trade Agreements in Annexes 1A and 1C, other than those listed in paragraphs 2 and 6, of a nature that would alter the rights and obligations of the Members, shall take effect for the Members that have accepted them upon acceptance by two thirds of the Members and thereafter for each other Member upon acceptance by it. The Ministerial Conference may decide by a three-fourths majority of the Members that any amendment made effective under this paragraph is of such a nature that any Member which has not accepted it within a period specified by the Ministerial Conference in each case shall be free to withdraw from the WTO or to remain a Member with the consent of the Ministerial Conference.

4.   Amendments to provisions of this Agreement or of the Multilateral Trade Agreements in Annexes 1A and 1C, other than those listed in paragraphs 2 and 6, of a nature that would not alter the rights and obligations of the Members, shall take effect for all Members upon acceptance by two thirds of the Members.

5.   Except as provided in paragraph 2 above, amendments to Parts I, II and III of GATS and the respective annexes shall take effect for the Members that have accepted them upon acceptance by two thirds of the Members and thereafter for each Member upon acceptance by it. The Ministerial Conference may decide by a three-fourths majority of the Members that any amendment made effective under the preceding provision is of such a nature that any Member which has not accepted it within a period specified by the Ministerial Conference in each case shall be free to withdraw from the WTO or to remain a Member with the consent of the Ministerial Conference. Amendments to Parts IV, V and VI of GATS and the respective annexes shall take effect for all Members upon acceptance by two thirds of the Members.

6.   Notwithstanding the other provisions of this Article, amendments to the Agreement on TRIPS meeting the requirements of paragraph 2 of Article 71 thereof may be adopted by the Ministerial Conference without further formal acceptance process.

7.   Any Member accepting an amendment to this Agreement or to a Multilateral Trade Agreement in Annex 1 shall deposit an instrument of acceptance with the Director-General of the WTO within the period of acceptance specified by the Ministerial Conference.

8.   Any Member of the WTO may initiate a proposal to amend the provisions of the Multilateral Trade Agreements in Annexes 2 and 3 by submitting such proposal to the Ministerial Conference. The decision to approve amendments to the Multilateral Trade Agreement in Annex 2 shall be made by consensus and these amendments shall take effect for all Members upon approval by the Ministerial Conference. Decisions to approve amendments to the Multilateral Trade Agreement in Annex 3 shall take effect for all Members upon approval by the Ministerial Conference.

9.   The Ministerial Conference, upon the request of the Members parties to a trade agreement, may decide exclusively by consensus to add that agreement to Annex 4. The Ministerial Conference, upon the request of the Members parties to a Plurilateral Trade Agreement, may decide to delete that Agreement from Annex 4.

10.   Amendments to a Plurilateral Trade Agreement shall be governed by the provisions of that Agreement.

Article XI

Original Membership

1.   The contracting parties to GATT 1947 as of the date of entry into force of this Agreement, and the European Communities, which accept this Agreement and the Multilateral Trade Agreements and for which Schedules of Concessions and Commitments are annexed to GATT 1994 and for which Schedules of Specific Commitments are annexed to GATS shall become original Members of the WTO.

2.   The least-developed countries recognized as such by the United Nations will only be required to undertake commitments and concessions to the extent consistent with their individual development, financial and trade needs or their administrative and institutional capabilities.

Article XII

Accession

1.   Any State or separate customs territory possessing full autonomy in the conduct of its external commercial relations and of the other matters provided for in this Agreement and the Multilateral Trade Agreements may accede to this Agreement, on terms to be agreed between it and the WTO. Such accession shall apply to this Agreement and the Multilateral Trade Agreements annexed thereto.

2.   Decisions on accession shall be taken by the Ministerial Conference. The Ministerial Conference shall approve the agreement on the terms of accession by a two-thirds majority of the Members of the WTO.

3.   Accession to a Plurilateral Trade Agreement shall be governed by the provisions of that Agreement.

Article XIII

*Non-Application of Multilateral Trade Agreements
Between Particular Members*

1.   This Agreement and the Multilateral Trade Agreements in Annexes 1 and 2 shall not apply as between any Member and any other Member if either of the Members, at the time either becomes a Member, does not consent to such application.

2.   Paragraph 1 may be invoked between original Members of the WTO which were contracting parties to GATT 1947 only where Article XXXV of that Agreement had been invoked earlier and was effective as between those contracting parties at the time of entry into force for them of this Agreement.

3.   Paragraph 1 shall apply between a Member and another Member which has acceded under Article XII only if the Member not consenting to the application has so notified the Ministerial Conference before the approval of the agreement on the terms of accession by the Ministerial Conference.

4.   The Ministerial Conference may review the operation of this Article in particular cases at the request of any Member and make appropriate recommendations.

5.   Non-application of a Plurilateral Trade Agreement between parties to that Agreement shall be governed by the provisions of that Agreement.

Article XIV

Acceptance, Entry into Force and Deposit

1.   This Agreement shall be open for acceptance, by signature or otherwise, by contracting parties to GATT 1947, and the European Communities, which are eligible to become original Members of the WTO in accordance with Article XI of this Agreement. Such acceptance shall apply to this Agreement and the Multilateral Trade Agreements annexed hereto. This Agreement and the Multilateral Trade Agreements annexed hereto shall enter into force on the date determined by Ministers in accordance with paragraph 3 of the Final Act Embodying the Results of the Uruguay Round of Multilateral Trade Negotiations and shall remain open for acceptance for a period of two years following that date unless the Ministers decide otherwise. An acceptance following the entry into force of this Agreement shall enter into force on the 30th day following the date of such acceptance.

2.   A Member which accepts this Agreement after its entry into force shall implement those concessions and obligations in the Multilateral Trade Agreements that are to be implemented over a period of time starting with the entry into force of this Agreement as if it had accepted this Agreement on the date of its entry into force.

3.   Until the entry into force of this Agreement, the text of this Agreement and the Multilateral Trade Agreements shall be deposited with the Director-General to the CONTRACTING PARTIES to GATT 1947. The Director-General shall promptly furnish a certified true copy of this

Agreement and the Multilateral Trade Agreements, and a notification of each acceptance thereof, to each government and the European Communities having accepted this Agreement. This Agreement and the Multilateral Trade Agreements, and any amendments thereto, shall, upon the entry into force of this Agreement, be deposited with the Director-General of the WTO.

4.   The acceptance and entry into force of a Plurilateral Trade Agreement shall be governed by the provisions of that Agreement. Such Agreements shall be deposited with the Director-General to the CONTRACTING PARTIES to GATT 1947. Upon the entry into force of this Agreement, such Agreements shall be deposited with the Director-General of the WTO.

Article XV

Withdrawal

1.   Any Member may withdraw from this Agreement. Such withdrawal shall apply both to this Agreement and the Multilateral Trade Agreements and shall take effect upon the expiration of six months from the date on which written notice of withdrawal is received by the Director-General of the WTO.

2.   Withdrawal from a Plurilateral Trade Agreement shall be governed by the provisions of that Agreement.

Article XVI

Miscellaneous Provisions

1.   Except as otherwise provided under this Agreement or the Multilateral Trade Agreements, the WTO shall be guided by the decisions, procedures and customary practices followed by the CONTRACTING PARTIES to GATT 1947 and the bodies established in the framework of GATT 1947.

2.   To the extent practicable, the Secretariat of GATT 1947 shall become the Secretariat of the WTO, and the Director-General to the CONTRACTING PARTIES to GATT 1947, until such time as the Ministerial Conference has appointed a Director-General in accordance with paragraph 2 of Article VI of this Agreement, shall serve as Director-General of the WTO.

3.   In the event of a conflict between a provision of this Agreement and a provision of any of the Multilateral Trade Agreements, the provision of this Agreement shall prevail to the extent of the conflict.

4.   Each Member shall ensure the conformity of its laws, regulations and administrative procedures with its obligations as provided in the annexed Agreements.

5.   No reservations may be made in respect of any provision of this Agreement. Reservations in respect of any of the provisions of the Multilateral Trade Agreements may only be made to the extent provided for in those Agreements. Reservations in respect of a provision of a Plurilateral Trade Agreement shall be governed by the provisions of that Agreement.

6.   This Agreement shall be registered in accordance with the provisions of Article 102 of the Charter of the United Nations.

DONE at Marrakesh this fifteenth day of April one thousand nine hundred and ninety-four, in a single copy, in the English, French and Spanish languages, each text being authentic.

DONE at Marrakesh this fifteenth day of April one thousand nine hundred and ninety-four, in a single copy, in the English, French and Spanish languages, each text being authentic.

———————

Explanatory Notes:

The terms "country" or "countries" as used in this Agreement and the Multilateral Trade Agreements are to be understood to include any separate customs territory Member of the WTO.

In the case of a separate customs territory Member of the WTO, where an expression in this Agreement and the Multilateral Trade Agreements is qualified by the term "national", such expression shall be read as pertaining to that customs territory, unless otherwise specified.

LIST OF ANNEXES

ANNEX 1

ANNEX 1A: Multilateral Agreements on Trade in Goods

   General Agreement on Tariffs and Trade 1994

   Agreement on Agriculture

   Agreement on the Application of Sanitary and Phytosanitary Measures

   Agreement on Textiles and Clothing

   Agreement on Technical Barriers to Trade

   Agreement on Trade-Related Investment Measures

   Agreement on Implementation of Article VI of the General Agreement on Tariffs and Trade 1994

   Agreement on Implementation of Article VII of the General Agreement on Tariffs and Trade 1994

   Agreement on Preshipment Inspection

   Agreement on Rules of Origin

   Agreement on Import Licensing Procedures

   Agreement on Subsidies and Countervailing Measures

   Agreement on Safeguards

ANNEX 1B: General Agreement on Trade in Services and Annexes

ANNEX 1C: Agreement on Trade-Related Aspects of Intellectual Property Rights

ANNEX 2

Understanding on Rules and Procedures Governing the Settlement of Disputes

ANNEX 3

Trade Policy Review Mechanism

ANNEX 4

Plurilateral Trade Agreements

Agreement on Trade in Civil Aircraft

Agreement on Government Procurement

International Dairy Agreement

International Bovine Meat Agreement

ANNEX 1A

MULTILATERAL AGREEMENTS ON TRADE IN GOODS

General interpretative note to Annex 1A:

In the event of conflict between a provision of the General Agreement on Tariffs and Trade 1994 and a provision of another agreement in Annex 1A to the Agreement Establishing the World Trade Organization (referred to in the agreements in Annex 1A as the "WTO Agreement"), the provision of the other agreement shall prevail to the extent of the conflict.

3. DECISION ON MEASURES IN FAVOUR OF LEAST-DEVELOPED COUNTRIES

(Selected Provisions)

Recognizing the plight of the least-developed countries and the need to ensure their effective participation in the world trading system, and to take further measures to improve their trading opportunities;

Recognizing the specific needs of the least-developed countries in the area of market access where continued preferential access remains an essential means for improving their trading opportunities;

Reaffirming their commitment to implement fully the provisions concerning the least-developed countries contained in paragraphs 2(*d*.), 6 and 8 of the Decision of 28 November 1979 on Differential and More Favourable Treatment, Reciprocity and Fuller Participation of Developing Countries;

Having regard to the commitment of the participants as set out in Section B(vii) of Part I of the Punta del Este Ministerial Declaration;

1.   *Decide* that, if not already provided for in the instruments negotiated in the course of the Uruguay Round, notwithstanding their acceptance of these instruments, the least-developed countries, and for so long as they remain in that category, while complying with the general rules set out in the aforesaid instruments, will only be required to undertake commitments and concessions to the extent consistent with their individual development, financial and trade needs, or their administrative and institutional capabilities. The least-developed countries shall be given additional time of one year from 15 April 1994 to submit their schedules as required in Article XI of the Agreement Establishing the World Trade Organization.

2.   *Agree* that:

(i)   Expeditious implementation of all special and differential measures taken in favour of least-developed countries including those taken within the context of the Uruguay Round shall be ensured through, *inter alia,* regular reviews.

(ii)   To the extent possible, MFN concessions on tariff and non-tariff measures agreed in the Uruguay Round on products of export interest to the least-developed countries may be implemented autonomously, in advance and without staging. Consideration shall be given to further improve GSP and other schemes for products of particular export interest to least-developed countries.

(iii) The rules set out in the various agreements and instruments and the transitional provisions in the Uruguay Round should be applied in a flexible and supportive manner for the least-developed countries. To this effect, sympathetic consideration shall be given to specific and motivated concerns raised by the least-developed countries in the appropriate Councils and Committees.

(iv)   In the application of import relief measures and other measures referred to in paragraph 3(c) of Article XXXVII of GATT 1947 and the corresponding provision of GATT 1994, special consideration shall be given to the export interests of least-developed countries.

(v)   Least-developed countries shall be accorded substantially increased technical assistance in the development, strengthening and diversification of their production and export bases including those of services, as well as in trade promotion, to enable them to maximize the benefits from liberalized access to markets.

3.   *Agree* to keep under review the specific needs of the least-developed countries and to continue to seek the adoption of positive measures which facilitate the expansion of trading opportunities in favour of these countries.

4. WTO UNDERSTANDING ON RULES AND PROCEDURES GOVERNING THE SETTLEMENT OF DISPUTES (DSU)

(Annex 2 to the Agreement Establishing the World Trade Organization)

(Selected Provisions)

Article 1

Coverage and Application

1.   The rules and procedures of this Understanding shall apply to disputes brought pursuant to the consultation and dispute settlement provisions of the agreements listed in Appendix 1 to this Understanding (referred to in this Understanding as the "covered agreements"). The rules and procedures of this Understanding shall also apply to consultations and the settlement of disputes between Members concerning their rights and obligations under the provisions of the Agreement Establishing the World Trade Organization (referred to in this Understanding as the "WTO Agreement") and of this Understanding taken in isolation or in combination with any other covered agreement.

2.   The rules and procedures of this Understanding shall apply subject to such special or additional rules and procedures on dispute settlement contained in the covered agreements as are identified in Appendix 2 to this Understanding. To the extent that there is a difference between the rules and procedures of this Understanding and the special or additional rules and procedures set forth in Appendix 2, the special or additional rules and procedures in Appendix 2 shall prevail. In disputes involving rules and procedures under more than one covered agreement, if there is a conflict between special or additional rules and procedures of such agreements under review, and where the parties to the dispute cannot agree on rules and procedures within 20 days of the establishment of the panel, the Chairman of the Dispute Settlement Body provided for in paragraph 1 of Article 2 (referred to in this Understanding as the "DSB"), in consultation with the parties to the dispute, shall determine the rules and procedures to be followed within 10 days after a request by either Member. The Chairman shall be guided by the principle that special or additional rules and procedures should be used where possible, and the rules and procedures set out in this Understanding should be used to the extent necessary to avoid conflict.

Article 2

Administration

1.   The Dispute Settlement Body is hereby established to administer these rules and procedures and, except as otherwise provided in a covered agreement, the consultation and dispute settlement provisions of the covered agreements. Accordingly, the DSB shall have the authority to establish panels, adopt panel and Appellate Body reports, maintain surveillance of

implementation of rulings and recommendations, and authorize suspension of concessions and other obligations under the covered agreements. With respect to disputes arising under a covered agreement which is a Plurilateral Trade Agreement, the term "Member" as used herein shall refer only to those Members that are parties to the relevant Plurilateral Trade Agreement. Where the DSB administers the dispute settlement provisions of a Plurilateral Trade Agreement, only those Members that are parties to that Agreement may participate in decisions or actions taken by the DSB with respect to that dispute.

2.   The DSB shall inform the relevant WTO Councils and Committees of any developments in disputes related to provisions of the respective covered agreements.

3.   The DSB shall meet as often as necessary to carry out its functions within the time-frames provided in this Understanding.

4.   Where the rules and procedures of this Understanding provide for the DSB to take a decision, it shall do so by consensus.[1]

Article 3

General Provisions

1.   Members affirm their adherence to the principles for the management of disputes heretofore applied under Articles XXII and XXIII of GATT 1947, and the rules and procedures as further elaborated and modified herein.

2.   The dispute settlement system of the WTO is a central element in providing security and predictability to the multilateral trading system. The Members recognize that it serves to preserve the rights and obligations of Members under the covered agreements, and to clarify the existing provisions of those agreements in accordance with customary rules of interpretation of public international law. Recommendations and rulings of the DSB cannot add to or diminish the rights and obligations provided in the covered agreements.

3.   The prompt settlement of situations in which a Member considers that any benefits accruing to it directly or indirectly under the covered agreements are being impaired by measures taken by another Member is essential to the effective functioning of the WTO and the maintenance of a proper balance between the rights and obligations of Members.

4.   Recommendations or rulings made by the DSB shall be aimed at achieving a satisfactory settlement of the matter in accordance with the rights and obligations under this Understanding and under the covered agreements.

5.   All solutions to matters formally raised under the consultation and dispute settlement provisions of the covered agreements, including arbitration awards, shall be consistent with those agreements and shall not

---

[1]   The DSB shall be deemed to have decided by consensus on a matter submitted for its consideration, if no Member, present at the meeting of the DSB when the decision is taken, formally objects to the proposed decision.

nullify or impair benefits accruing to any Member under those agreements, nor impede the attainment of any objective of those agreements.

6.   Mutually agreed solutions to matters formally raised under the consultation and dispute settlement provisions of the covered agreements shall be notified to the DSB and the relevant Councils and Committees, where any Member may raise any point relating thereto.

7.   Before bringing a case, a Member shall exercise its judgment as to whether action under these procedures would be fruitful. The aim of the dispute settlement mechanism is to secure a positive solution to a dispute. A solution mutually acceptable to the parties to a dispute and consistent with the covered agreements is clearly to be preferred. In the absence of a mutually agreed solution, the first objective of the dispute settlement mechanism is usually to secure the withdrawal of the measures concerned if these are found to be inconsistent with the provisions of any of the covered agreements. The provision of compensation should be resorted to only if the immediate withdrawal of the measure is impracticable and as a temporary measure pending the withdrawal of the measure which is inconsistent with a covered agreement. The last resort which this Understanding provides to the Member invoking the dispute settlement procedures is the possibility of suspending the application of concessions or other obligations under the covered agreements on a discriminatory basis vis-á-vis the other Member, subject to authorization by the DSB of such measures.

8.   In cases where there is an infringement of the obligations assumed under a covered agreement, the action is considered *prima facie* to constitute a case of nullification or impairment. This means that there is normally a presumption that a breach of the rules has an adverse impact on other Members parties to that covered agreement, and in such cases, it shall be up to the Member against whom the complaint has been brought to rebut the charge.

9.   The provisions of this Understanding are without prejudice to the rights of Members to seek authoritative interpretation of provisions of a covered agreement through decision-making under the WTO Agreement or a covered agreement which is a Plurilateral Trade Agreement.

10.   It is understood that requests for conciliation and the use of the dispute settlement procedures should not be intended or considered as contentious acts and that, if a dispute arises, all Members will engage in these procedures in good faith in an effort to resolve the dispute. It is also understood that complaints and counter-complaints in regard to distinct matters should not be linked.

11.   This Understanding shall be applied only with respect to new requests for consultations under the consultation provisions of the covered agreements made on or after the date of entry into force of the WTO Agreement. With respect to disputes for which the request for consultations was made under GATT 1947 or under any other predecessor agreement to the covered agreements before the date of entry into force of the WTO Agreement, the relevant dispute settlement rules and procedures in effect

immediately prior to the date of entry into force of the WTO Agreement shall continue to apply.[2]

12.　Notwithstanding paragraph 11, if a complaint based on any of the covered agreements is brought by a developing country Member against a developed country Member, the complaining party shall have the right to invoke, as an alternative to the provisions contained in Articles 4, 5, 6 and 12 of this Understanding, the corresponding provisions of the Decision of 5 April 1966 (BISD 14S/18), except that where the Panel considers that the time-frame provided for in paragraph 7 of that Decision is insufficient to provide its report and with the agreement of the complaining party, that time-frame may be extended. To the extent that there is a difference between the rules and procedures of Articles 4, 5, 6 and 12 and the corresponding rules and procedures of the Decision, the latter shall prevail.

Article 4

Consultations

1.　Members affirm their resolve to strengthen and improve the effectiveness of the consultation procedures employed by Members.

2.　Each Member undertakes to accord sympathetic consideration to and afford adequate opportunity for consultation regarding any representations made by another Member concerning measures affecting the operation of any covered agreement taken within the territory of the former.[3]

3.　If a request for consultations is made pursuant to a covered agreement, the Member to which the request is made shall, unless otherwise mutually agreed, reply to the request within 10 days after the date of its receipt and shall enter into consultations in good faith within a period of no more than 30 days after the date of receipt of the request, with a view to reaching a mutually satisfactory solution. If the Member does not respond within 10 days after the date of receipt of the request, or does not enter into consultations within a period of no more than 30 days, or a period otherwise mutually agreed, after the date of receipt of the request, then the Member that requested the holding of consultations may proceed directly to request the establishment of a panel.

4.　All such requests for consultations shall be notified to the DSB and the relevant Councils and Committees by the Member which requests consultations. Any request for consultations shall be submitted in writing and shall give the reasons for the request, including identification of the measures at issue and an indication of the legal basis for the complaint.

5.　In the course of consultations in accordance with the provisions of a covered agreement, before resorting to further action under this

---

　[2]　This paragraph shall also be applied to disputes on which panel reports have not been adopted or fully implemented.

　[3]　Where the provisions of any other covered agreement concerning measures taken by regional or local governments or authorities within the territory of a Member contain provisions different from the provisions of this paragraph, the provisions of such other covered agreement shall prevail.

Understanding, Members should attempt to obtain satisfactory adjustment of the matter.

6.   Consultations shall be confidential, and without prejudice to the rights of any Member in any further proceedings.

7.   If the consultations fail to settle a dispute within 60 days after the date of receipt of the request for consultations, the complaining party may request the establishment of a panel. The complaining party may request a panel during the 60-day period if the consulting parties jointly consider that consultations have failed to settle the dispute.

8.   In cases of urgency, including those which concern perishable goods, Members shall enter into consultations within a period of no more than 10 days after the date of receipt of the request. If the consultations have failed to settle the dispute within a period of 20 days after the date of receipt of the request, the complaining party may request the establishment of a panel.

9.   In cases of urgency, including those which concern perishable goods, the parties to the dispute, panels and the Appellate Body shall make every effort to accelerate the proceedings to the greatest extent possible.

10.   During consultations Members should give special attention to the particular problems and interests of developing country Members.

11.   Whenever a Member other than the consulting Members considers that it has a substantial trade interest in consultations being held pursuant to paragraph 1 of Article XXII of GATT 1994, paragraph 1 of Article XXII of GATS, or the corresponding provisions in other covered agreements,[4] such Member may notify the consulting Members and the DSB, within 10 days after the date of the circulation of the request for consultations under said Article, of its desire to be joined in the consultations. Such Member shall be joined in the consultations, provided that the Member to which the request for consultations was addressed agrees that the claim of substantial interest is well-founded. In that event they shall so inform the DSB. If the request to be joined in the consultations is not accepted, the applicant Member shall be free to request consultations under paragraph 1 of Article XXII or paragraph 1 of Article XXIII of GATT 1994, paragraph 1 of Article XXII or paragraph 1 of Article XXIII of GATS, or the corresponding provisions in other covered agreements.

---

[4]   The corresponding consultation provisions in the covered agreements are listed hereunder: Agreement on Agriculture, Article 19; Agreement on the Application of Sanitary and Phytosanitary Measures, paragraph 1 of Article 11; Agreement on Textiles and Clothing, paragraph 4 of Article 8; Agreement on Technical Barriers to Trade, paragraph 1 of Article 14; Agreement on Trade-Related Investment Measures, Article 8; Agreement on Implementation of Article VI of GATT 1994, paragraph 2 of Article 17; Agreement on Implementation of Article VII of GATT 1994, paragraph 2 of Article 19; Agreement on Preshipment Inspection, Article 7; Agreement on Rules of Origin, Article 7; Agreement on Import Licensing Procedures, Article 6; Agreement on Subsidies and Countervailing Measures, Article 30; Agreement on Safeguards, Article 14; Agreement on Trade-Related Aspects of Intellectual Property Rights, Article 64.1; and any corresponding consultation provisions in Plurilateral Trade Agreements as determined by the competent bodies of each Agreement and as notified to the DSB.

Article 5

Good Offices, Conciliation and Mediation

1.   Good offices, conciliation and mediation are procedures that are undertaken voluntarily if the parties to the dispute so agree.

2.   Proceedings involving good offices, conciliation and mediation, and in particular positions taken by the parties to the dispute during these proceedings, shall be confidential, and without prejudice to the rights of either party in any further proceedings under these procedures.

3.   Good offices, conciliation or mediation may be requested at any time by any party to a dispute. They may begin at any time and be terminated at any time. Once procedures for good offices, conciliation or mediation are terminated, a complaining party may then proceed with a request for the establishment of a panel.

4.   When good offices, conciliation or mediation are entered into within 60 days after the date of receipt of a request for consultations, the complaining party must allow a period of 60 days after the date of receipt of the request for consultations before requesting the establishment of a panel. The complaining party may request the establishment of a panel during the 60-day period if the parties to the dispute jointly consider that the good offices, conciliation or mediation process has failed to settle the dispute.

5.   If the parties to a dispute agree, procedures for good offices, conciliation or mediation may continue while the panel process proceeds.

6.   The Director-General may, acting in an *ex officio* capacity, offer good offices, conciliation or mediation with the view to assisting Members to settle a dispute.

Article 6

Establishment of Panels

1.   If the complaining party so requests, a panel shall be established at the latest at the DSB meeting following that at which the request first appears as an item on the DSB's agenda, unless at that meeting the DSB decides by consensus not to establish a panel.[5]

2.   The request for the establishment of a panel shall be made in writing. It shall indicate whether consultations were held, identify the specific measures at issue and provide a brief summary of the legal basis of the complaint sufficient to present the problem clearly. In case the applicant requests the establishment of a panel with other than standard terms of reference, the written request shall include the proposed text of special terms of reference.

---

[5]   If the complaining party so requests, a meeting of the DSB shall be convened for this purpose within 15 days of the request, provided that at least 10 days' advance notice of the meeting is given.

Article 7

Terms of Reference of Panels

1.   Panels shall have the following terms of reference unless the parties to the dispute agree otherwise within 20 days from the establishment of the panel:

> "To examine, in the light of the relevant provisions in (name of the covered agreement(s) cited by the parties to the dispute), the matter referred to the DSB by (name of party) in document . . . and to make such findings as will assist the DSB in making the recommendations or in giving the rulings provided for in that/those agreement(s)."

2.   Panels shall address the relevant provisions in any covered agreement or agreements cited by the parties to the dispute.

3.   In establishing a panel, the DSB may authorize its Chairman to draw up the terms of reference of the panel in consultation with the parties to the dispute, subject to the provisions of paragraph 1. The terms of reference thus drawn up shall be circulated to all Members. If other than standard terms of reference are agreed upon, any Member may raise any point relating thereto in the DSB.

Article 8

Composition of Panels

1.   Panels shall be composed of well-qualified governmental and/or non-governmental individuals, including persons who have served on or presented a case to a panel, served as a representative of a Member or of a contracting party to GATT 1947 or as a representative to the Council or Committee of any covered agreement or its predecessor agreement, or in the Secretariat, taught or published on international trade law or policy, or served as a senior trade policy official of a Member.

2.   Panel members should be selected with a view to ensuring the independence of the members, a sufficiently diverse background and a wide spectrum of experience.

3.   Citizens of Members whose governments[6] are parties to the dispute or third parties as defined in paragraph 2 of Article 10 shall not serve on a panel concerned with that dispute, unless the parties to the dispute agree otherwise.

4.   To assist in the selection of panelists, the Secretariat shall maintain an indicative list of governmental and non-governmental individuals possessing the qualifications outlined in paragraph 1, from which panelists may be drawn as appropriate. That list shall include the roster of non-governmental panelists established on 30 November 1984 (BISD 31S/9), and other rosters and indicative lists established under any of the covered

---

[6]   In the case where customs unions or common markets are parties to a dispute, this provision applies to citizens of all member countries of the customs unions or common markets.

agreements, and shall retain the names of persons on those rosters and indicative lists at the time of entry into force of the WTO Agreement. Members may periodically suggest names of governmental and non-governmental individuals for inclusion on the indicative list, providing relevant information on their knowledge of international trade and of the sectors or subject matter of the covered agreements, and those names shall be added to the list upon approval by the DSB. For each of the individuals on the list, the list shall indicate specific areas of experience or expertise of the individuals in the sectors or subject matter of the covered agreements.

5. Panels shall be composed of three panelists unless the parties to the dispute agree, within 10 days from the establishment of the panel, to a panel composed of five panelists. Members shall be informed promptly of the composition of the panel.

6. The Secretariat shall propose nominations for the panel to the parties to the dispute. The parties to the dispute shall not oppose nominations except for compelling reasons.

7. If there is no agreement on the panelists within 20 days after the date of the establishment of a panel, at the request of either party, the Director-General, in consultation with the Chairman of the DSB and the Chairman of the relevant Council or Committee, shall determine the composition of the panel by appointing the panelists whom the Director-General considers most appropriate in accordance with any relevant special or additional rules or procedures of the covered agreement or covered agreements which are at issue in the dispute, after consulting with the parties to the dispute. The Chairman of the DSB shall inform the Members of the composition of the panel thus formed no later than 10 days after the date the Chairman receives such a request.

8. Members shall undertake, as a general rule, to permit their officials to serve as panelists.

9. Panelists shall serve in their individual capacities and not as government representatives, nor as representatives of any organization. Members shall therefore not give them instructions nor seek to influence them as individuals with regard to matters before a panel.

10. When a dispute is between a developing country Member and a developed country Member the panel shall, if the developing country Member so requests, include at least one panelist from a developing country Member.

11. Panelists' expenses, including travel and subsistence allowance, shall be met from the WTO budget in accordance with criteria to be adopted by the General Council, based on recommendations of the Committee on Budget, Finance and Administration.

Article 9

Procedures for Multiple Complainants

1. Where more than one Member requests the establishment of a panel related to the same matter, a single panel may be established to examine these complaints taking into account the rights of all Members

concerned. A single panel should be established to examine such complaints whenever feasible.

2.   The single panel shall organize its examination and present its findings to the DSB in such a manner that the rights which the parties to the dispute would have enjoyed had separate panels examined the complaints are in no way impaired. If one of the parties to the dispute so requests, the panel shall submit separate reports on the dispute concerned. The written submissions by each of the complainants shall be made available to the other complainants, and each complainant shall have the right to be present when any one of the other complainants presents its views to the panel.

3.   If more than one panel is established to examine the complaints related to the same manner, to the greatest extent possible the same persons shall serve as panelists on each of the separate panels and the timetable for the panel process in such disputes shall be harmonized.

Article 10

Third Parties

1.   The interests of the parties to a dispute and those of other Members under a covered agreement at issue in the dispute shall be fully taken into account during the panel process.

2.   Any Member having a substantial interest in a matter before a panel and having notified its interest to the DSB (referred to in this Understanding as a "third party") shall have an opportunity to be heard by the panel and to make written submissions to the panel. These submissions shall also be given to the parties to the dispute and shall be reflected in the panel report.

3.   Third parties shall receive the submissions of the parties to the dispute [at] the first meeting of the panel.

4.   If a third party considers that a measure already the subject of a panel proceeding nullifies or impairs benefits accruing to it under any covered agreement, that Member may have recourse to normal dispute settlement procedures under this Understanding. Such a dispute shall be referred to the original panel wherever possible.

Article 11

Function of Panels

The function of panels is to assist the DSB in discharging its responsibilities under this Understanding and the covered agreements. Accordingly, a panel should make an objective assessment of the matter before it, including an objective assessment of the facts of the case and the applicability of and conformity with the relevant covered agreements, and make such other findings as will assist the DSB in making the recommendations or in giving the rulings provided for in the covered agreements. Panels should consult regularly with the parties to the dispute and give them adequate opportunity to develop a mutually satisfactory solution.

Article 12

Panel Procedures

1.   Panels shall follow the Working Procedures in Appendix 3 unless the panel decides otherwise after consulting the parties to the dispute.

2.   Panel procedures should provide sufficient flexibility so as to ensure high-quality panel reports, while not unduly delaying the panel process.

3.   After consulting the parties to the dispute, the panelists shall, as soon as practicable and whenever possible within one week after the composition and terms of reference of the panel have been agreed upon, fix the timetable for the panel process, taking into account the provisions of paragraph 9 of Article 4, if relevant.

4.   In determining the timetable for the panel process, the panel shall provide sufficient time for the parties to the dispute to prepare their submissions.

5.   Panels should set precise deadlines for written submissions by the parties and the parties should respect those deadlines.

6.   Each party to the dispute shall deposit its written submissions with the Secretariat for immediate transmission to the panel and to the other party or parties to the dispute. The complaining party shall submit its first submission in advance of the responding party's first submission unless the panel decides, in fixing the timetable referred to in paragraph 3 and after consultations with the parties to the dispute, that the parties should submit their first submissions simultaneously. When there are sequential arrangements for the deposit of first submissions, the panel shall establish a firm time-period for receipt of the responding party's submission. Any subsequent written submissions shall be submitted simultaneously.

7.   Where the parties to the dispute have failed to develop a mutually satisfactory solution, the panel shall submit its findings in the form of a written report to the DSB. In such cases, the report of a panel shall set out the findings of fact, the applicability of relevant provisions and the basic rationale behind any findings and recommendations that it makes. Where a settlement of the matter among the parties to the dispute has been found, the report of the panel shall be confined to a brief description of the case and to reporting that a solution has been reached.

8.   In order to make the procedures more efficient, the period in which the panel shall conduct its examination, from the date that the composition and terms of reference of the panel have been agreed upon until the date the final report is issued to the parties to the dispute, shall, as a general rule, not exceed six months. In cases of urgency, including those relating to perishable goods, the panel shall aim to issue its report to the parties to the dispute within three months.

9.   When the panel considers that it cannot issue its report within six months, or within three months in cases of urgency, it shall inform the DSB in writing of the reasons for the delay together with an estimate of the period

within which it will issue its report. In no case should the period from the establishment of the panel to the circulation of the report to the Members exceed nine months.

10. In the context of consultations involving a measure taken by a developing country Member, the parties may agree to extend the periods established in paragraphs 7 and 8 of Article 4. If, after the relevant period has elapsed, the consulting parties cannot agree that the consultations have concluded, the Chairman of the DSB shall decide, after consultation with the parties, whether to extend the relevant period and, if so, for how long. In addition, in examining a complaint against a developing country Member, the panel shall accord sufficient time for the developing country Member to prepare and present its argumentation. The provisions of paragraph 1 of Article 20 and paragraph 4 of Article 21 are not affected by any action pursuant to this paragraph.

11. Where one or more of the parties is a developing country Member, the panel's report shall explicitly indicate the form in which account has been taken of relevant provisions on differential and more-favourable treatment for developing country Members that form part of the covered agreements which have been raised by the developing country Member in the course of the dispute settlement procedures.

12. The panel may suspend its work at any time at the request of the complaining party for a period not to exceed 12 months. In the event of such a suspension, the time-frames set out in paragraphs 8 and 9 of this Article, paragraph 1 of Article 20, and paragraph 4 of Article 21 shall be extended by the amount of time that the work was suspended. If the work of the panel has been suspended for more than 12 months, the authority for establishment of the panel shall lapse.

Article 13

Right to Seek Information

1. Each panel shall have the right to seek information and technical advice from any individual or body which it deems appropriate. However, before a panel seeks such information or advice from any individual or body within the jurisdiction of a Member it shall inform the authorities of that Member. A Member should respond promptly and fully to any request by a panel for such information as the panel considers necessary and appropriate. Confidential information which is provided shall not be revealed without formal authorization from the individual, body, or authorities of the Member providing the information.

2. Panels may seek information from any relevant source and may consult experts to obtain their opinion on certain aspects of the matter. With respect to a factual issue concerning a scientific or other technical matter raised by a party to a dispute, a panel may request an advisory report in writing from an expert review group. Rules for the establishment of such a group and its procedures are set forth in Appendix 4.

Article 14

Confidentiality

1.   Panel deliberations shall be confidential.

2.   The reports of panels shall be drafted without the presence of the parties to the dispute in the light of the information provided and the statements made.

3.   Opinions expressed in the panel report by individual panelists shall be anonymous.

Article 15

Interim Review Stage

1.   Following the consideration of rebuttal submissions and oral arguments, the panel shall issue the descriptive (factual and argument) sections of its draft report to the parties to the dispute. Within a period of time set by the panel, the parties shall submit their comments in writing.

2.   Following the expiration of the set period of time for receipt of comments from the parties to the dispute, the panel shall issue an interim report to the parties, including both the descriptive sections and the panel's findings and conclusions. Within a period of time set by the panel, a party may submit a written request for the panel to review precise aspects of the interim report prior to circulation of the final report to the Members. At the request of a party, the panel shall hold a further meeting with the parties on the issues identified in the written comments. If no comments are received from any party within the comment period, the interim report shall be considered the final panel report and circulated promptly to the Members.

3.   The findings of the final panel report shall include a discussion of the arguments made at the interim review stage. The interim review stage shall be conducted within the time-period set out in paragraph 8 of Article 12.

Article 16

Adoption of Panel Reports

1.   In order to provide sufficient time for the Members to consider panel reports, the reports shall not be considered for adoption by the DSB until 20 days after the date they have been circulated to the Members.

2.   Members having objections to a panel report shall give written reasons to explain their objections for circulation at least 10 days prior to the DSB meeting at which the panel report will be considered.

3.   The parties to a dispute shall have the right to participate fully in the consideration of the panel report by the DSB, and their views shall be fully recorded.

4.   Within 60 days after the date of circulation of a panel report to the Members, the report shall be adopted at a DSB meeting[7] unless a party to the dispute formally notifies the DSB of its decision to appeal or the DSB decides by consensus not to adopt the report. If a party has notified its decision to appeal, the report by the panel shall not be considered for adoption by the DSB until after completion of the appeal. This adoption procedure is without prejudice to the right of Members to express their views on a panel report.

Article 17

Appellate Review

Standing Appellate Body

1.   A standing Appellate Body shall be established by the DSB. The Appellate Body shall hear appeals from panel cases. It shall be composed of seven persons, three of whom shall serve on any one case. Persons serving on the Appellate Body shall serve in rotation. Such rotation shall be determined in the working procedures of the Appellate Body.

2.   The DSB shall appoint persons to serve on the Appellate Body for a four-year term, and each person may be reappointed once. However, the terms of three of the seven persons appointed immediately after the entry into force of the WTO Agreement shall expire at the end of two years, to be determined by lot. Vacancies shall be filled as they arise. A person appointed to replace a person whose term of office has not expired shall hold office for the remainder of the predecessor's term.

3.   The Appellate Body shall comprise persons of recognized authority, with demonstrated expertise in law, international trade and the subject matter of the covered agreements generally. They shall be unaffiliated with any government. The Appellate Body membership shall be broadly representative of membership in the WTO. All persons serving on the Appellate Body shall be available at all times and on short notice, and shall stay abreast of dispute settlement activities and other relevant activities of the WTO. They shall not participate in the consideration of any disputes that would create a direct or indirect conflict of interest.

4.   Only parties to the dispute, not third parties, may appeal a panel report. Third parties which have notified the DSB of a substantial interest in the matter pursuant to paragraph 2 of Article 10 may make written submissions to, and be given an opportunity to be heard by, the Appellate Body.

5.   As a general rule, the proceedings shall not exceed 60 days from the date a party to the dispute formally notifies its decision to appeal to the date the Appellate Body circulates its report. In fixing its timetable the Appellate Body shall take into account the provisions of paragraph 9 of Article 4, if relevant. When the Appellate Body considers that it cannot

---

[7]   If a meeting of the DSB is not scheduled within this period at a time that enables the requirements of paragraphs 1 and 4 of Article 16 to be met, a meeting of the DSB shall be held for this purpose.

provide its report within 60 days, it shall inform the DSB in writing of the reasons for the delay together with an estimate of the period within which it will submit its report. In no case shall the proceedings exceed 90 days.

6.   An appeal shall be limited to issues of law covered in the panel report and legal interpretations developed by the panel.

7.   The Appellate Body shall be provided with appropriate administrative and legal support as it requires.

8.   The expenses of persons serving on the Appellate Body, including travel and subsistence allowance, shall be met from the WTO budget in accordance with criteria to be adopted by the General Council, based on recommendations of the Committee on Budget, Finance and Administration.

Procedures for Appellate Review

9.   Working procedures shall be drawn up by the Appellate Body in consultation with the Chairman of the DSB and the Director-General, and communicated to the Members for their information.

10.   The proceedings of the Appellate Body shall be confidential. The reports of the Appellate Body shall be drafted without the presence of the parties to the dispute and in the light of the information provided and the statements made.

11.   Opinions expressed in the Appellate Body report by individuals serving on the Appellate Body shall be anonymous.

12.   The Appellate Body shall address each of the issues raised in accordance with paragraph 6 during the appellate proceeding.

13.   The Appellate Body may uphold, modify or reverse the legal findings and conclusions of the panel.

Adoption of Appellate Body Reports

14.   An Appellate Body report shall be adopted by the DSB and unconditionally accepted by the parties to the dispute unless the DSB decides by consensus not to adopt the Appellate Body report within 30 days following its circulation to the Members.[8] This adoption procedure is without prejudice to the right of Members to express their views on an Appellate Body report.

Article 18

Communications With the Panel or Appellate Body

1.   There shall be no *ex parte* communications with the panel or Appellate Body concerning matters under consideration by the panel or Appellate Body.

2.   Written submissions to the panel or the Appellate Body shall be treated as confidential, but shall be made available to the parties to the dispute. Nothing in this Understanding shall preclude a party to a dispute from disclosing statements of its own positions to the public. Members shall

---

[8]   If a meeting of the DSB is not scheduled during this period, such a meeting of the DSB shall be held for this purpose.

treat as confidential information submitted by another Member to the panel or the Appellate Body which that Member has designated as confidential. A party to a dispute shall also, upon request of a Member, provide a non-confidential summary of the information contained in its written submissions that could be disclosed to the public.

Article 19

Panel and Appellate Body Recommendations

1.   Where a panel or the Appellate Body concludes that a measure is inconsistent with a covered agreement, it shall recommend that the Member concerned[9] bring the measure into conformity with that agreement.[10] In addition to its recommendations, the panel or Appellate Body may suggest ways in which the Member concerned could implement the recommendations.

2.   In accordance with paragraph 2 of Article 3, in their findings and recommendations, the panel and Appellate Body cannot add to or diminish the rights and obligations provided in the covered agreements.

Article 20

Time-frame for DSB Decisions

Unless otherwise agreed to by the parties to the dispute, the period from the date of establishment of the panel by the DSB until the date the DSB considers the panel or appellate report for adoption shall as a general rule not exceed nine months where the panel report is not appealed or 12 months where the report is appealed. Where either the panel or the Appellate Body has acted, pursuant to paragraph 9 of Article 12 or paragraph 5 of Article 17, to extend the time for providing its report, the additional time taken shall be added to the above periods.

Article 21

Surveillance of Implementation of Recommendations and Rulings

1.   Prompt compliance with recommendations or rulings of the DSB is essential in order to ensure effective resolution of disputes to the benefit of all Members.

2.   Particular attention should be paid to matters affecting the interests of developing country Members with respect to measures which have been subject to dispute settlement.

3.   At a DSB meeting held within 30 days[11] after the date of adoption of the panel or Appellate Body report, the Member concerned shall inform the DSB of its intentions in respect of implementation of the recommendations and rulings of the DSB. If it is impracticable to comply

---

[9]   The "Member concerned" is the party to the dispute to which the panel or Appellate Body recommendations are directed.

[10]   With respect to recommendations in cases not involving a violation of GATT 1994 or any other covered agreement, *see* Article 26.

[11]   If a meeting of the DSB is not scheduled during this period, such a meeting of the DSB shall be held for this purpose.

immediately with the recommendations and rulings, the Member concerned shall have a reasonable period of time in which to do so. The reasonable period of time shall be:

(a) the period of time proposed by the Member concerned, provided that such period is approved by the DSB; or, in the absence of such approval,

(b) a period of time mutually agreed by the parties to the dispute within 45 days after the date of adoption of the recommendations and rulings; or, in the absence of such agreement,

(c) a period of time determined through binding arbitration within 90 days after the date of adoption of the recommendations and rulings.[12] In such arbitration, a guideline for the arbitrator[13] should be that the reasonable period of time to implement panel or Appellate Body recommendations should not exceed 15 months from the date of adoption of a panel or Appellate Body report. However, that time may be shorter or longer, depending upon the particular circumstances.

4. Except where the panel or the Appellate Body has extended, pursuant to paragraph 9 of Article 12 or paragraph 5 of Article 17, the time of providing its report, the period from the date of establishment of the panel by the DSB until the date of determination of the reasonable period of time shall not exceed 15 months unless the parties to the dispute agree otherwise. Where either the panel or the Appellate Body has acted to extend the time of providing its report, the additional time taken shall be added to the 15-month period; provided that unless the parties to the dispute agree that there are exceptional circumstances, the total time shall not exceed 18 months.

5. Where there is disagreement as to the existence or consistency with a covered agreement of measures taken to comply with the recommendations and rulings such dispute shall be decided through recourse to these dispute settlement procedures, including wherever possible resort to the original panel. The panel shall circulate its report within 90 days after the date of referral of the matter to it. When the panel considers that it cannot provide its report within this time frame, it shall inform the DSB in writing of the reasons for the delay together with an estimate of the period within which it will submit its report.

6. The DSB shall keep under surveillance the implementation of adopted recommendations or rulings. The issue of implementation of the recommendations or rulings may be raised at the DSB by any Member at any time following their adoption. Unless the DSB decides otherwise, the issue of implementation of the recommendations or rulings shall be placed on the agenda of the DSB meeting after six months following the date of

---

[12] If the parties cannot agree on an arbitrator within ten days after referring the matter to arbitration, the arbitrator shall be appointed by the Director-General within ten days, after consulting the parties.

[13] The expression "arbitrator" shall be interpreted as referring either to an individual or a group.

establishment of the reasonable period of time pursuant to paragraph 3 and shall remain on the DSB's agenda until the issue is resolved. At least 10 days prior to each such DSB meeting, the Member concerned shall provide the DSB with a status report in writing of its progress in the implementation of the recommendations or rulings.

7.   If the matter is one which has been raised by a developing country Member, the DSB shall consider what further action it might take which would be appropriate to the circumstances.

8.   If the case is one brought by a developing country Member, in considering what appropriate action might be taken, the DSB shall take into account not only the trade coverage of measures complained of, but also their impact on the economy of developing country Members concerned.

Article 22

Compensation and the Suspension of Concessions

1.   Compensation and the suspension of concessions or other obligations are temporary measures available in the event that the recommendations and rulings are not implemented within a reasonable period of time. However, neither compensation nor the suspension of concessions or other obligations is preferred to full implementation of a recommendation to bring a measure into conformity with the covered agreements. Compensation is voluntary and, if granted, shall be consistent with the covered agreements.

2.   If the Member concerned fails to bring the measure found to be inconsistent with a covered agreement into compliance therewith or otherwise comply with the recommendations and rulings within the reasonable period of time determined pursuant to paragraph 3 of Article 21, such Member shall, if so requested, and no later than the expiry of the reasonable period of time, enter into negotiations with any party having invoked the dispute settlement procedures, with a view to developing mutually acceptable compensation. If no satisfactory compensation has been agreed within 20 days after the date of expiry of the reasonable period of time, any party having invoked the dispute settlement procedures may request authorization from the DSB to suspend the application to the Member concerned of concessions or other obligations under the covered agreements.

3.   In considering what concessions or other obligations to suspend, the complaining party shall apply the following principles and procedures:

    (a)   the general principle is that the complaining party should first seek to suspend concessions or other obligations with respect to the same sector(s) as that in which the panel or Appellate Body has found a violation or other nullification or impairment;

    (b)   if that party considers that it is not practicable or effective to suspend concessions or other obligations with respect

to the same sector(s), it may seek to suspend concessions or other obligations in other sectors under the same agreement;

(c) if that party considers that it is not practicable or effective to suspend concessions or other obligations with respect to other sectors under the same agreement, and that the circumstances are serious enough, it may seek to suspend concessions or other obligations under another covered agreement;

(d) in applying the above principles, that party shall take into account:

(i) the trade in the sector or under the agreement under which the panel or Appellate Body has found a violation or other nullification or impairment, and the importance of such trade to that party;

(ii) the broader economic elements related to the nullification or impairment and the broader economic consequences of the suspension of concessions or other obligations;

(e) if that party decides to request authorization to suspend concessions or other obligations pursuant to subparagraphs (b) or (c), it shall state the reasons therefor in its request. At the same time as the request is forwarded to the DSB, it also shall be forwarded to the relevant Councils and also, in the case of a request pursuant to subparagraph (b), the relevant sectoral bodies;

(f) for purposes of this paragraph, "sector" means:

(i) with respect to goods, all goods;

(ii) with respect to services, a principal sector as identified in the current "Services Sectoral Classification List" which identifies such sectors,[14]

(iii) with respect to trade-related intellectual property rights, each of the categories of intellectual property rights covered in Section 1, or Section 2, or Section 3, or Section 4, or Section 5, or Section 6, or Section 7 of Part II, or the obligations under Part III, or Part IV of the Agreement on TRIPS;

(g) for purposes of this paragraph, "agreement" means:

(i) with respect to goods, the agreements listed in Annex 1A of the WTO Agreement, taken as a whole as well as the Plurilateral Trade Agreements in so far as the relevant parties to the dispute are parties to these agreements;

(ii) with respect to services, the GATS;

---

[14] The list in document MTN.GNS/W/120 identifies eleven sectors.

(iii) with respect to intellectual property rights, the Agreement on TRIPS.

4.   The level of the suspension of concessions or other obligations authorized by the DSB shall be equivalent to the level of the nullification or impairment.

5.   The DSB shall not authorize suspension of concessions or other obligations if a covered agreement prohibits such suspension.

6.   When the situation described in paragraph 2 occurs, the DSB, upon request, shall grant authorization to suspend concessions or other obligations within 30 days of the expiry of the reasonable period of time unless the DSB decides by consensus to reject the request. However, if the Member concerned objects to the level of suspension proposed, or claims that the principles and procedures set forth in paragraph 3 have not been followed where a complaining party has requested authorization to suspend concessions or other obligations pursuant to paragraph 3(b) or (c), the matter shall be referred to arbitration. Such arbitration shall be carried out by the original panel, if members are available, or by an arbitrator[15] appointed by the Director-General and shall be completed within 60 days after the date of expiry of the reasonable period of time. Concessions or other obligations shall not be suspended during the course of the arbitration.

7.   The arbitrator[16] acting pursuant to paragraph 6 shall not examine the nature of the concessions or other obligations to be suspended but shall determine whether the level of such suspension is equivalent to the level of nullification or impairment. The arbitrator may also determine if the proposed suspension of concessions or other obligations is allowed under the covered agreement. However, if the matter referred to arbitration includes a claim that the principles and procedures set forth in paragraph 3 have not been followed, the arbitrator shall examine that claim. In the event the arbitrator determines that those principles and procedures have not been followed, the complaining party shall apply them consistent with paragraph 3. The parties shall accept the arbitrator's decision as final and the parties concerned shall not seek a second arbitration. The DSB shall be informed promptly of the decision of the arbitrator and shall upon request, grant authorization to suspend concessions or other obligations where the request is consistent with the decision of the arbitrator, unless the DSB decides by consensus to reject the request.

8.   The suspension of concessions or other obligations shall be temporary and shall only be applied until such time as the measure found to be inconsistent with a covered agreement has been removed, or the Member that must implement recommendations or rulings provides a solution to the nullification or impairment of benefits, or a mutually satisfactory solution is reached. In accordance with paragraph 6 of Article 21, the DSB shall

---

[15]   The expression "arbitrator" shall be interpreted as referring either to an individual or a group.

[16]   The expression "arbitrator" shall be interpreted as referring either to an individual or a group or to the members of the original panel when serving in the capacity of arbitrator.

continue to keep under surveillance the implementation of adopted recommendations or rulings, including those cases where compensation has been provided or concessions or other obligations have been suspended but the recommendations to bring a measure into conformity with the covered agreements have not been implemented.

9.   The dispute settlement provisions of the covered agreements may be invoked in respect of measures affecting their observance taken by regional or local governments or authorities within the territory of a Member. When the DSB has ruled that a provision of a covered agreement has not been observed, the responsible Member shall take such reasonable measures as may be available to it to ensure its observance. The provisions of the covered agreements and this Understanding relating to compensation and suspension of concessions or other obligations apply in cases where it has not been possible to secure such observance.[17]

Article 23

Strengthening of the Multilateral System

1.   When Members seek the redress of a violation of obligations or other nullification or impairment of benefits under the covered agreements or an impediment to the attainment of any objective of the covered agreements, they shall have recourse to, and abide by, the rules and procedures of this Understanding.

2.   In such cases, Members shall:

(a)   not make a determination to the effect that a violation has occurred, that benefits have been nullified or impaired or that the attainment of any objective of the covered agreements has been impeded, except through recourse to dispute settlement in accordance with the rules and procedures of this Understanding, and shall make any such determination consistent with the findings contained in the panel or Appellate Body report adopted by the DSB or an arbitration award rendered under this Understanding;

(b)   follow the procedures set forth in Article 21 to determine the reasonable period of time for the Member concerned to implement the recommendations and rulings; and

(c)   follow the procedures set forth in Article 22 to determine the level of suspension of concessions or other obligations and obtain DSB authorization in accordance with those procedures before suspending concessions or other obligations under the covered agreements in response to the failure of the Member concerned to implement the

---

[17]   Where the provisions of any covered agreement concerning measures taken by regional or local governments or authorities within the territory of a Member contain provisions different from the provisions of this paragraph, the provisions of such covered agreement shall prevail.

recommendations and rulings within that reasonable period of time.

Article 24

Special Procedures Involving Least-Developed Country Members

1.   At all stages of the determination of the causes of a dispute and of dispute settlement procedures involving a least-developed country Member, particular consideration shall be given to the special situation of least-developed country Members. In this regard, Members shall exercise due restraint in raising matters under these procedures involving a least-developed country Member. If nullification or impairment is found to result from a measure taken by a least-developed country Member, complaining parties shall exercise due restraint in asking for compensation or seeking authorization to suspend the application of concessions or other obligations pursuant to these procedures.

2.   In dispute settlement cases involving a least-developed country Member, where a satisfactory solution has not been found in the course of consultations the Director-General or the Chairman of the DSB shall, upon request by a least-developed country Member offer their good offices, conciliation and mediation with a view to assisting the parties to settle the dispute, before a request for a panel is made. The Director-General or the Chairman of the DSB, in providing the above assistance, may consult any source which either deems appropriate.

Article 25

Arbitration

1.   Expeditious arbitration within the WTO as an alternative means of dispute settlement can facilitate the solution of certain disputes that concern issues that are clearly defined by both parties.

2.   Except as otherwise provided in this Understanding, resort to arbitration shall be subject to mutual agreement of the parties which shall agree on the procedures to be followed. Agreements to resort to arbitration shall be notified to all Members sufficiently in advance of the actual commencement of the arbitration process.

3.   Other Members may become party to an arbitration proceeding only upon the agreement of the parties which have agreed to have recourse to arbitration. The parties to the proceeding shall agree to abide by the arbitration award. Arbitration awards shall be notified to the DSB and the Council or Committee of any relevant agreement where any Member may raise any point relating thereto.

4.   Articles 21 and 22 of this Understanding shall apply *mutatis mutandis* to arbitration awards.

Article 26

1.   *Non-Violation Complaints of the Type Described in Paragraph 1(b) of Article XXIII of GATT 1994*

Where the provisions of paragraph 1(b) of Article XXIII of GATT 1994 are applicable to a covered agreement, a panel or the Appellate Body may only make rulings and recommendations where a party to the dispute considers that any benefit accruing to it directly or indirectly under the relevant covered agreement is being nullified or impaired or the attainment of any objective of that Agreement is being impeded as a result of the application by a Member of any measure, whether or not it conflicts with the provisions of that Agreement. Where and to the extent that such party considers and a panel or the Appellate Body determines that a case concerns a measure that does not conflict with the provisions of a covered agreement to which the provisions of paragraph 1(b) of Article XXIII of GATT 1994 are applicable, the procedures in this Understanding shall apply, subject to the following:

(a)   the complaining party shall present a detailed justification in support of any complaint relating to a measure which does not conflict with the relevant covered agreement;

(b)   where a measure has been found to nullify or impair benefits under, or impede the attainment of objectives, of the relevant covered agreement without violation thereof, there is no obligation to withdraw the measure. However, in such cases, the panel or the Appellate Body shall recommend that the Member concerned make a mutually satisfactory adjustment;

(c)   notwithstanding the provisions of Article 21, the arbitration provided for in paragraph 3 of Article 21, upon request of either party, may include a determination of the level of benefits which have been nullified or impaired, and may also suggest ways and means of reaching a mutually satisfactory adjustment; such suggestions shall not be binding upon the parties to the dispute;

(d)   notwithstanding the provisions of paragraph 1 of Article 22, compensation may be part of a mutually satisfactory adjustment as final settlement of the dispute.

2.   *Complaints of the Type Described in Paragraph 1(c) of Article XXIII of GATT 1994*

Where the provisions of paragraph 1(c) of Article XXIII of GATT 1994 are applicable to a covered agreement, a panel may only make rulings and recommendations where a party considers that any benefit accruing to it directly or indirectly under the relevant covered agreement is being nullified or impaired or the attainment of any objective of that Agreement is being impeded as a result of the existence of any situation other than those to which the provisions of paragraphs 1(a) and 1(b) of Article XXIII of GATT 1994 are applicable. Where and to the extent that such party considers and a panel determines that the matter is covered by this paragraph, the procedures of this Understanding shall apply only up to and including the point in the proceedings where the panel report has been circulated to the

Members. The dispute settlement rules and procedures contained in the Decision of 12 April 1989 (BISD 36S/61–67) shall apply to consideration for adoption, and surveillance and implementation of recommendations and rulings. The following shall also apply:

(a) the complaining party shall present a detailed justification in support of any argument made with respect to issues covered under this paragraph;

(b) in cases involving matters covered by this paragraph, if a panel finds that cases also involve dispute settlement matters other than those covered by this paragraph, the panel shall circulate a report to the DSB addressing any such matters and a separate report on matters falling under this paragraph.

Article 27

Responsibilities of the Secretariat

1. The Secretariat shall have the responsibility of assisting panels, especially on the legal, historical and procedural aspects of the matters dealt with, and of providing secretarial and technical support.

2. While the Secretariat assists Members in respect of dispute settlement at their request, there may also be a need to provide additional legal advice and assistance in respect of dispute settlement to developing country Members. To this end, the Secretariat shall make available a qualified legal expert from the WTO technical cooperation services to any developing country Member which so requests. This expert shall assist the developing country Member in a manner ensuring the continued impartiality of the Secretariat.

3. The Secretariat shall conduct special training courses for interested Members concerning these dispute settlement procedures and practices so as to enable Members' experts to be better informed in this regard.

APPENDIX 1

AGREEMENTS COVERED BY THE UNDERSTANDING

(A) Agreement Establishing the World Trade Organization

(B) Multilateral Trade Agreements

Annex 1A: Multilateral Agreements on Trade in Goods

Annex 1B: General Agreement on Trade in Services

Annex 1C: Agreement on Trade-Related Aspects of Intellectual Property Rights

Annex 2:   Understanding on Rules and Procedures Governing the Settlement of Disputes

(C) Plurilateral Trade Agreements

Annex 4:   Agreement on Trade in Civil Aircraft

Agreement on Government Procurement

International Dairy Agreement

International Bovine Meat Agreement

The applicability of this Understanding to the Plurilateral Trade Agreements shall be subject to the adoption of a decision by the parties to each agreement setting out the terms for the application of the Understanding to the individual agreement, including any special or additional rules or procedures for inclusion in Appendix 2, as notified to the DSB.

APPENDIX 2

SPECIAL OR ADDITIONAL RULES AND PROCEDURES CONTAINED IN THE COVERED AGREEMENTS

Agreement	*Rules and Procedures*
Agreement on the Application of Sanitary and Phytosanitary Measures	11.2
Agreement on Textiles and Clothing	2.14, 2.21, 4.4, 5.2, 5.4, 5.6, 6.9, 6.10, 6.11, 8.1 through 8.12
Agreement on Technical Barriers to Trade	14.2 through 14.4, Annex 2
Agreement on Implementation of Article VI of GATT 1994	17.4 through 17.7
Agreement on Implementation of Article VII of GATT 1994	19.3 through 19.5, Annex II.2(f), 3, 9, 21
Agreement on Subsidies and Countervailing Measures	4.2 through 4.12, 6.6, 7.2 through 7.10, 8.5, footnote 35, 24.4, 27.7, Annex V
General Agreement on Trade in Services	XXII:3, XXIII:3
Annex on Financial Services	4
Annex on Air Transport Services	4
Decision on Certain Dispute Settlement Procedures for the GATS	1 through 5

The list of rules and procedures in this Appendix includes provisions where only a part of the provision may be relevant in this context.

Any special or additional rules or procedures in the Plurilateral Trade Agreements as determined by the competent bodies of each agreement and as notified to the DSB.

* * *

5. WTO AGREEMENT ON TECHNICAL BARRIERS TO TRADE (TBT STANDARDS CODE)

(Selected Provisions)

Article 1

General Provisions

1.1 General terms for standardization and procedures for assessment of conformity shall normally have the meaning given to them by definitions adopted within the United Nations system and by international standardizing bodies taking into account their context and in the light of the object and purpose of this Agreement.

1.2 However, for the purposes of this Agreement the meaning of the terms given in Annex 1 applies.

1.3 All products, including industrial and agricultural products, shall be subject to the provisions of this Agreement.

1.4 Purchasing specifications prepared by governmental bodies for production or consumption requirements of governmental bodies are not subject to the provisions of this Agreement but are addressed in the Agreement on Government Procurement, according to its coverage.

1.5 The provisions of this Agreement do not apply to sanitary and phytosanitary measures as defined in Annex A of the Agreement on the Application of Sanitary and Phytosanitary Measures.

1.6 All references in this Agreement to technical regulations, standards and conformity assessment procedures shall be construed to include any amendments thereto and any additions to the rules or the product coverage thereof, except amendments and additions of an insignificant nature.

TECHNICAL REGULATIONS AND STANDARDS

Article 2

Preparation, Adoption and Application of Technical Regulations by Central Government Bodies

With respect to their central government bodies:

2.1 Members shall ensure that in respect of technical regulations, products imported from the territory of any Member shall be accorded treatment no less favourable than that accorded to like products of national origin and to like products originating in any other country.

2.2 Members shall ensure that technical regulations are not prepared, adopted or applied with a view to or with the effect of creating unnecessary obstacles to international trade. For this purpose, technical regulations shall not be more trade-restrictive than necessary to fulfil a legitimate objective, taking account of the risks non-fulfilment would create. Such legitimate objectives are, *inter alia*: national security requirements; the prevention of deceptive practices; protection of human health or safety, animal or plant life or health, or the environment. In assessing such risks, relevant elements of consideration are, *inter alia*: available scientific and technical information, related processing technology or intended end-uses of products.

2.3 Technical regulations shall not be maintained if the circumstances or objectives giving rise to their adoption no longer exist or if the changed circumstances or objectives can be addressed in a less trade-restrictive manner.

2.4 Where technical regulations are required and relevant international standards exist or their completion is imminent, Members shall use them, or the relevant parts of them, as a basis for their technical regulations except when such international standards or relevant parts would be an ineffective or inappropriate means for the fulfilment of the legitimate objectives pursued, for instance because of fundamental climatic or geographical factors or fundamental technological problems.

2.5 A Member preparing, adopting or applying a technical regulation which may have a significant effect on trade of other Members shall, upon the request of another Member, explain the justification for that technical regulation in terms of the provisions of paragraphs 2 to 4. Whenever a technical regulation is prepared, adopted or applied for one of the legitimate objectives explicitly mentioned in paragraph 2, and is in accordance with relevant international standards, it shall be rebuttably presumed not to create an unnecessary obstacle to international trade.

* * *

2.7 Members shall give positive consideration to accepting as equivalent technical regulations of other Members, even if these regulations differ from their own, provided they are satisfied that these regulations adequately fulfil the objectives of their own regulations.

2.8 Wherever appropriate, Members shall specify technical regulations based on product requirements in terms of performance rather than design or descriptive characteristics.

2.9 Whenever a relevant international standard does not exist or the technical content of a proposed technical regulation is not in accordance with the technical content of relevant international standards, and if the technical regulation may have a significant effect on trade of other Members, Members shall:

2.9.1 publish a notice in a publication at an early appropriate stage, in such a manner as to enable interested parties in other Members to become acquainted with it, that they propose to introduce a particular technical regulation;

2.9.2 notify other Members through the Secretariat of the products to be covered by the proposed technical regulation, together with a brief indication of its objective and rationale. Such notifications shall take place at an early appropriate stage, when amendments can still be introduced and comments taken into account;

2.9.3 upon request, provide to other Members particulars or copies of the proposed technical regulation and, whenever possible, identify the parts which in substance deviate from relevant international standards;

2.9.4 without discrimination, allow reasonable time for other Members to make comments in writing, discuss these comments upon request, and take these written comments and the results of these discussions into account.

* * *

Article 3

Preparation, Adoption and Application of Technical Regulations by Local Government Bodies and Non-Governmental Bodies

With respect to their local government and non-governmental bodies within their territories:

3.1 Members shall take such reasonable measures as may be available to them to ensure compliance by such bodies with the provisions of Article 2, with the exception of the obligation to notify as referred to in paragraphs 9.2 and 10.1 of Article 2.

3.2 Members shall ensure that the technical regulations of local governments on the level directly below that of the central government in Members are notified in accordance with the provisions of paragraphs 9.2 and 10.1 of Article 2, noting that notification shall not be required for technical regulations the technical content of which is substantially the same as that of previously notified technical regulations of central government bodies of the Member concerned.

3.3 Members may require contact with other Members, including the notifications, provision of information, comments and discussions referred to in paragraphs 9 and 10 of Article 2, to take place through the central government.

3.4 Members shall not take measures which require or encourage local government bodies or non-governmental bodies within their territories to act in a manner inconsistent with the provisions of Article 2.

3.5 Members are fully responsible under this Agreement for the observance of all provisions of Article 2. Members shall formulate and implement positive measures and mechanisms in support of the observance of the provisions of Article 2 by other than central government bodies.

Article 4

Preparation, Adoption and Application of Standards

4.1 Members shall ensure that their central government standardizing bodies accept and comply with the Code of Good Practice for the Preparation, Adoption and Application of Standards in Annex 3 to this Agreement (referred to in this Agreement as the "Code of Good Practice"). They shall take such reasonable measures as may be available to them to ensure that local government and non-governmental standardizing bodies within their territories, as well as regional standardizing bodies of which they or one or more bodies within their territories are members, accept and comply with this Code of Good Practice. In addition, Members shall not take measures which have the effect of, directly or indirectly, requiring or encouraging such standardizing bodies to act in a manner inconsistent with the Code of Good Practice. The obligations of Members with respect to compliance of standardizing bodies with the provisions of the Code of Good Practice shall apply irrespective of whether or not a standardizing body has accepted the Code of Good Practice.

4.2 Standardizing bodies that have accepted and are complying with the Code of Good Practice shall be acknowledged by the Members as complying with the principles of this Agreement.

CONFORMITY WITH TECHNICAL REGULATIONS AND STANDARDS

Article 5

Procedures for Assessment of Conformity by Central Government Bodies

5.1 Members shall ensure that, in cases where a positive assurance of conformity with technical regulations or standards is required, their central government bodies apply the following provisions to products originating in the territories of other Members:

> 5.1.1 conformity assessment procedures are prepared, adopted and applied so as to grant access for suppliers of like products originating in the territories of other Members under conditions no less favourable than those accorded to suppliers of like products of national origin or originating in any other country, in a comparable situation; access entails suppliers' right to an assessment of conformity under the rules of the procedure, including, when foreseen by this procedure, the possibility to have conformity assessment activities undertaken at the site of facilities and to receive the mark of the system;

> 5.1.2 conformity assessment procedures are not prepared, adopted or applied with a view to or with the effect of creating unnecessary obstacles to international trade. This means, *inter alia,* that conformity assessment procedures shall not be more strict or be applied more strictly than is necessary to give the importing Member adequate confidence that products conform with the applicable technical regulations or standards, taking account of the risks non-conformity would create.

* * *

5.4 In cases where a positive assurance is required that products conform with technical regulations or standards, and relevant guides or recommendations issued by international standardizing bodies exist or their completion is imminent, Members shall ensure that central government bodies use them, or the relevant parts of them, as a basis for their conformity assessment procedures, except where, as duly explained upon request, such guides or recommendations or relevant parts are inappropriate for the Members concerned, for, *inter alia,* such reasons as: national security requirements; the prevention of deceptive practices; protection of human health or safety, animal or plant life or health, or the environment; fundamental climatic or other geographical factors; fundamental technological or infrastructural problems.

* * *

5.6 Whenever a relevant guide or recommendation issued by an international standardizing body does not exist or the technical content of a proposed conformity assessment procedure is not in accordance with relevant guides and recommendations issued by international standardizing bodies, and if the conformity assessment procedure may have a significant effect on trade of other Members, Members shall:

> 5.6.1 publish a notice in a publication at an early appropriate stage, in such a manner as to enable interested parties in other Members to become acquainted with it, that they propose to introduce a particular conformity assessment procedure;

> 5.6.2 notify other Members through the Secretariat of the products to be covered by the proposed conformity assessment procedure, together with a brief indication of its objective and rationale. Such notifications shall take place at an early appropriate stage, when amendments can still be introduced and comments taken into account;

> 5.6.3 upon request, provide to other Members particulars or copies of the proposed procedure and, whenever possible, identify the parts which in substance deviate from relevant guides or recommendations issued by international standardizing bodies;

> 5.6.4 without discrimination, allow reasonable time for other Members to make comments in writing, discuss these comments upon request, and take these written comments and the results of these discussions into account.

* * *

Article 6

Recognition of Conformity Assessment by Central Government Bodies

With respect to their central government bodies:

6.1 Without prejudice to the provisions of paragraphs 3 and 4, Members shall ensure, whenever possible, that results of conformity assessment procedures in other Members are accepted, even when those procedures differ from their own, provided they are satisfied that those procedures offer an assurance of conformity with applicable technical regulations or standards equivalent to their own procedures. It is recognized that prior consultations may be necessary in order to arrive at a mutually satisfactory understanding regarding, in particular:

6.1.1   adequate and enduring technical competence of the relevant conformity assessment bodies in the exporting Member, so that confidence in the continued reliability of their conformity assessment results can exist; in this regard, verified compliance, for instance through accreditation, with relevant guides or recommendations issued by international standardizing bodies shall be taken into account as an indication of adequate technical competence;

6.1.2   limitation of the acceptance of conformity assessment results to those produced by designated bodies in the exporting Member.

* * *

Article 7

Procedures for Assessment of Conformity by Local Government Bodies

With respect to their local government bodies within their territories:

7.1   Members shall take such reasonable measures as may be available to them to ensure compliance by such bodies with the provisions of Articles 5 and 6, with the exception of the obligation to notify as referred to in paragraphs 6.2 and 7.1 of Article 5.

7.2   Members shall ensure that the conformity assessment procedures of local governments on the level directly below that of the central government in Members are notified in accordance with the provisions of paragraphs 6.2 and 7.1 of Article 5, noting that notifications shall not be required for conformity assessment procedures the technical content of which is substantially the same as that of previously notified conformity assessment procedures of central government bodies of the Members concerned.

7.3   Members may require contact with other Members, including the notifications, provision of information, comments and discussions referred to in paragraphs 6 and 7 of Article 5, to take place through the central government.

7.4   Members shall not take measures which require or encourage local government bodies within their territories to act in a manner inconsistent with the provisions of Articles 5 and 6.

7.5   Members are fully responsible under this Agreement for the observance of all provisions of Articles 5 and 6. Members shall formulate and implement positive measures and mechanisms in support of the observance of the provisions of Articles 5 and 6 by other than central government bodies.

Article 12

Special and Differential Treatment of Developing Country Members

12.1 Members shall provide differential and more favourable treatment to developing country Members to this Agreement, through the following provisions as well as through the relevant provisions of other Articles of this Agreement.

12.2 Members shall give particular attention to the provisions of this Agreement concerning developing country Members' rights and obligations and shall take into account the special development, financial and trade needs of developing country Members in the implementation of this Agreement, both nationally and in the operation of this Agreement's institutional arrangements.

12.3 Members shall, in the preparation and application of technical regulations, standards and conformity assessment procedures, take account of the special development, financial and trade needs of developing country Members, with a view to ensuring that such technical regulations, standards and conformity assessment procedures do not create unnecessary obstacles to exports from developing country Members.

12.4 Members recognize that, although international standards, guides or recommendations may exist, in their particular technological and socio-economic conditions, developing country Members adopt certain technical regulations, standards or conformity assessment procedures aimed at preserving indigenous technology and production methods and processes compatible with their development needs. Members therefore recognize that developing country Members should not be expected to use international standards as a basis for their technical regulations or standards, including test methods, which are not appropriate to their development, financial and trade needs.

* * *

Article 14

Consultation and Dispute Settlement

14.1 Consultations and the settlement of disputes with respect to any matter affecting the operation of this Agreement shall take place under the auspices of the Dispute Settlement Body and shall follow, *mutatis mutandis,* the provisions of Articles XXII and XXIII of GATT 1994, as elaborated and applied by the Dispute Settlement Understanding.

* * *

14.4 The dispute settlement provisions set out above can be invoked in cases where a Member considers that another Member has not achieved satisfactory results under Articles 3, 4, 7, 8 and 9 and its trade interests are significantly affected. In this respect, such results shall be equivalent to those as if the body in question were a Member.

FINAL PROVISIONS

Article 15

Final Provisions

Reservations

15.1 Reservations may not be entered in respect of any of the provisions of this Agreement without the consent of the other Members.

Review

15.2 Each Member shall, promptly after the date on which the WTO Agreement enters into force for it, inform the Committee of measures in existence or taken to ensure the implementation and administration of this Agreement. Any changes of such measures thereafter shall also be notified to the Committee.

15.3 The Committee shall review annually the implementation and operation of this Agreement taking into account the objectives thereof.

15.4 Not later than the end of the third year from the date of entry into force of the WTO Agreement and at the end of each three-year period thereafter, the Committee shall review the operation and implementation of this Agreement, including the provisions relating to transparency, with a view to recommending an adjustment of the rights and obligations of this Agreement where necessary to ensure mutual economic advantage and balance of rights and obligations, without prejudice to the provisions of Article 12. Having regard, *inter alia,* to the experience gained in the implementation of the Agreement, the Committee shall, where appropriate, submit proposals for amendments to the text of this Agreement to the Council for Trade in Goods.

Annexes

15.5 The annexes to this Agreement constitute an integral part thereof.

ANNEX 1

TERMS AND THEIR DEFINITIONS FOR THE PURPOSE OF THIS AGREEMENT

The terms presented in the sixth edition of the ISO/IEC Guide 2: 1991, General Terms and Their Definitions Concerning Standardization and Related Activities, shall, when used in this Agreement, have the same meaning as given in the definitions in the said Guide taking into account that services are excluded from the coverage of this Agreement.

For the purpose of this Agreement, however, the following definitions shall apply:

1. *Technical regulation*

Document which lays down product characteristics or their related processes and production methods, including the applicable administrative provisions, with which compliance is mandatory. It may also include or deal exclusively with terminology, symbols, packaging, marking or labelling requirements as they apply to a product, process or production method.

Explanatory note

The definition in ISO/IEC Guide 2 is not self-contained, but based on the so-called "building block" system.

2. *Standard*

Document approved by a recognized body, that provides, for common and repeated use, rules, guidelines or characteristics for products or related processes and production methods, with which compliance is not mandatory. It may also include or deal exclusively with terminology, symbols, packaging, marking or labelling requirements as they apply to a product, process or production method.

Explanatory note

The terms as defined in ISO/IEC Guide 2 cover products, processes and services. This Agreement deals only with technical regulations, standards and conformity assessment procedures related to products or processes and production methods. Standards as defined by ISO/IEC Guide 2 may be mandatory or voluntary. For the purpose of this Agreement standards are defined as voluntary and technical regulations as mandatory documents. Standards prepared by the international standardization community are based on consensus. This Agreement covers also documents that are not based on consensus.

3.   *Conformity assessment procedures*

Any procedure used, directly or indirectly, to determine that relevant requirements in technical regulations or standards are fulfilled.

Explanatory note

Conformity assessment procedures include, *inter alia,* procedures for sampling, testing and inspection; evaluation, verification and assurance of conformity; registration, accreditation and approval as well as their combinations.

4.   *International body or system*

Body or system whose membership is open to the relevant bodies of at least all Members.

5.   *Regional body or system*

Body or system whose membership is open to the relevant bodies of only some of the Members.

6.   *Central government body*

Central government, its ministries and departments or any body subject to the control of the central government in respect of the activity in question.

Explanatory note

In the case of the European Communities the provisions governing central government bodies apply. However, regional bodies or conformity assessment systems may be established within the European Communities, and in such cases would be subject to the provisions of this Agreement on regional bodies or conformity assessment systems.

7. *Local government body*

Government other than a central government (e.g. states, provinces, Länder, cantons, municipalities, etc.), its ministries or departments or any body subject to the control of such a government in respect of the activity in question.

8. *Non-governmental body*

Body other than a central government body or a local government body, including a non-governmental body which has legal power to enforce a technical regulation.

ANNEX 3

CODE OF GOOD PRACTICE FOR THE PREPARATION, ADOPTION AND APPLICATION OF STANDARDS

General Provisions

A.   For the purposes of this Code the definitions in Annex 1 of this Agreement shall apply.

B.   This Code is open to acceptance by any standardizing body within the territory of a Member of the WTO, whether a central government body, a local government body, or a non-governmental body; to any governmental regional standardizing body one or more members of which are Members of the WTO; and to any non-governmental regional standardizing body one or more members of which are situated within the territory of a Member of the WTO (referred to in this Code collectively as "standardizing bodies" and individually as "the standardizing body").

C.   Standardizing bodies that have accepted or withdrawn from this Code shall notify this fact to the ISO/IEC Information Centre in Geneva. The notification shall include the name and address of the body concerned and the scope of its current and expected standardization activities. The notification may be sent either directly to the ISO/IEC Information Centre, or through the national member body of ISO/IEC or, preferably, through the relevant national member or international affiliate of ISONET, as appropriate.

SUBSTANTIVE PROVISIONS

D.   In respect of standards, the standardizing body shall accord treatment to products originating in the territory of any other Member of the WTO no less favourable than that accorded to like products of national origin and to like products originating in any other country.

E.   The standardizing body shall ensure that standards are not prepared, adopted or applied with a view to, or with the effect of, creating unnecessary obstacles to international trade.

F.   Where international standards exist or their completion is imminent, the standardizing body shall use them, or the relevant parts of them, as a basis for the standards it develops, except where such international standards or relevant parts would be ineffective or inappropriate, for instance, because of an insufficient level of protection or fundamental climatic or geographical factors or fundamental technological problems.

G.   With a view to harmonizing standards on as wide a basis as possible, the standardizing body shall, in an appropriate way, play a full part, within the limits of its resources, in the preparation by relevant international standardizing bodies of international standards regarding subject matter for which it either has adopted, or expects to adopt, standards. For standardizing bodies within the territory of a Member, participation in a particular international standardization activity shall, whenever possible, take place through one delegation representing all standardizing bodies in the territory that have adopted, or expect to adopt, standards for the subject matter to which the international standardization activity relates.

H.   The standardizing body within the territory of a Member shall make every effort to avoid duplication of, or overlap with, the work of other standardizing bodies in the national territory or with the work of relevant international or regional standardizing bodies. They shall also make every effort to achieve a national consensus on the standards they develop. Likewise the regional standardizing body shall make every effort to avoid duplication of, or overlap with, the work of relevant international standardizing bodies.

I.   Wherever appropriate, the standardizing body shall specify standards based on product requirements in terms of performance rather than design or descriptive characteristics.

J.   At least once every six months, the standardizing body shall publish a work programme containing its name and address, the standards it is currently preparing and the standards which it has adopted in the preceding period. A standard is under preparation from the moment a decision has been taken to develop a standard until that standard has been adopted. The titles of specific draft standards shall, upon request, be provided in English, French or Spanish. A notice of the existence of the work programme shall be published in a national or, as the case may be, regional publication of standardization activities.

The work programme shall for each standard indicate, in accordance with any ISONET rules, the classification relevant to the subject matter, the stage attained in the standard's development, and the references of any international standards taken as a basis. No later than at the time of publication of its work programme, the standardizing body shall notify the existence thereof to the ISO/IEC Information Centre in Geneva.

* * *

N.   The standardizing body shall take into account, in the further processing of the standard, the comments received during the period for commenting. Comments received through standardizing bodies that have accepted this Code of Good Practice shall, if so requested, be replied to as promptly as possible. The reply shall include an explanation why a deviation from relevant international standards is necessary.

* * *

Q.   The standardizing body shall afford sympathetic consideration to, and adequate opportunity for, consultation regarding representations with respect to the operation of this Code presented by standardizing bodies that have accepted this Code of Good Practice. It shall make an objective effort to solve any complaints.

6. WTO AGREEMENT ON THE APPLICATION OF SANITARY AND PHYTOSANITARY MEASURES (SPS CODE)

(Selected provisions)

Article 1

General Provisions

1.   This Agreement applies to all sanitary and phytosanitary measures which may, directly or indirectly, affect international trade. Such measures shall be developed and applied in accordance with the provisions of this Agreement.

2.   For the purposes of this Agreement, the definitions provided in Annex A shall apply.

3.   The annexes are an integral part of this Agreement.

4.   Nothing in this Agreement shall affect the rights of Members under the Agreement on Technical Barriers to Trade with respect to measures not within the scope of this Agreement.

Article 2

Basic Rights and Obligations

1.   Members have the right to take sanitary and phytosanitary measures necessary for the protection of human, animal or plant life or health, provided that such measures are not inconsistent with the provisions of this Agreement.

2.   Members shall ensure that any sanitary or phytosanitary measure is applied only to the extent necessary to protect human, animal or plant life or health, is based on scientific principles and is not maintained without sufficient scientific evidence, except as provided for in paragraph 7 of Article 5.

3.   Members shall ensure that their sanitary and phytosanitary measures do not arbitrarily or unjustifiably discriminate between Members where identical or similar conditions prevail, including between their own territory and that of other Members. Sanitary and phytosanitary measures shall not be applied in a manner which would constitute a disguised restriction on international trade.

4.   Sanitary or phytosanitary measures which conform to the relevant provisions of this Agreement shall be presumed to be in accordance with the obligations of the Members under the provisions of GATT 1994 which relate to the use of sanitary or phytosanitary measures, in particular the provisions of Article XX(b).

Article 3

Harmonization

1.   To harmonize sanitary and phytosanitary measures on as wide a basis as possible, Members shall base their sanitary or phytosanitary measures on international standards, guidelines or recommendations, where they exist, except as otherwise provided for in this Agreement, and in particular in paragraph 3.

2.   Sanitary or phytosanitary measures which conform to international standards, guidelines or recommendations shall be deemed to be necessary to protect human, animal or plant life or health, and presumed to be consistent with the relevant provisions of this Agreement and of GATT 1994.

3.   Members may introduce or maintain sanitary or phytosanitary measures which result in a higher level of sanitary or phytosanitary protection than would be achieved by measures based on the relevant international standards, guidelines or recommendations, if there is a scientific justification, or as a consequence of the level of sanitary or phytosanitary protection a Member determines to be appropriate in accordance with the relevant provisions of paragraphs 1 through 8 of Article 5.[2] Notwithstanding the above, all measures which result in a level of sanitary or phytosanitary protection different from that which would be achieved by measures based on international standards, guidelines or recommendations shall not be inconsistent with any other provision of this Agreement.

* * *

5.   The Committee on Sanitary and Phytosanitary Measures provided for in paragraphs 1 and 4 of Article 12 (referred to in this Agreement as the "Committee") shall develop a procedure to monitor the process of international harmonization and coordinate efforts in this regard with the relevant international organizations.

Article 4

Equivalence

1.   Members shall accept the sanitary or phytosanitary measures of other Members as equivalent, even if these measures differ from their own or from those used by other Members trading in the same product, if the exporting Member objectively demonstrates to the importing Member that its measures achieve the importing Member's appropriate level of sanitary or phytosanitary protection. For this purpose, reasonable access shall be given, upon request, to the importing Member for inspection, testing and other relevant procedures.

---

[2]   For the purposes of paragraph 3 of Article 3, there is a scientific justification if, on the basis of an examination and evaluation of available scientific information in conformity with the relevant provisions of this Agreement, a Member determines that the relevant international standards, guidelines or recommendations are not sufficient to achieve its appropriate level of sanitary or phytosanitary protection.

* * *

Article 5

Assessment of Risk and Determination of the Appropriate
Level of Sanitary or Phytosanitary Protection

1.   Members shall ensure that their sanitary or phytosanitary measures are based on an assessment, as appropriate to the circumstances, of the risks to human, animal or plant life or health, taking into account risk assessment techniques developed by the relevant international organizations.

2.   In the assessment of risks, Members shall take into account available scientific evidence; relevant processes and production methods; relevant inspection, sampling and testing methods; prevalence of specific diseases or pests; existence of pest- or disease-free areas; relevant ecological and environmental conditions; and quarantine or other treatment.

3.   In assessing the risk to animal or plant life or health and determining the measure to be applied for achieving the appropriate level of sanitary or phytosanitary protection from such risk, Members shall take into account as relevant economic factors: the potential damage in terms of loss of production or sales in the event of the entry, establishment or spread of a pest or disease; the costs of control or eradication in the territory of the importing Member; and the relative cost-effectiveness of alternative approaches to limiting risks.

4.   Members should, when determining the appropriate level of sanitary or phytosanitary protection, take into account the objective of minimizing negative trade effects.

5.   With the objective of achieving consistency in the application of the concept of appropriate level of sanitary or phytosanitary protection against risks to human life or health, or to animal and plant life or health, each Member shall avoid arbitrary or unjustifiable distinctions in the levels it considers to be appropriate in different situations, if such distinctions result in discrimination or a disguised restriction on international trade. Members shall cooperate in the Committee, in accordance with paragraphs 1, 2 and 3 of Article 12, to develop guidelines to further the practical implementation of this provision. In developing the guidelines, the Committee shall take into account all relevant factors, including the exceptional character of human health risks to which people voluntarily expose themselves.

6.   Without prejudice to paragraph 2 of Article 3, when establishing or maintaining sanitary or phytosanitary measures to achieve the appropriate level of sanitary or phytosanitary protection, Members shall ensure that such measures are not more trade-restrictive than required to achieve their appropriate level of sanitary or phytosanitary protection, taking into account technical and economic feasibility.[3]

---

[3]   For purposes of paragraph 6 of Article 5, a measure is not more trade-restrictive than required unless there is another measure, reasonably available taking

7.   In cases where relevant scientific evidence is insufficient, a Member may provisionally adopt sanitary or phytosanitary measures on the basis of available pertinent information, including that from the relevant international organizations as well as from sanitary or phytosanitary measures applied by other Members. In such circumstances, Members shall seek to obtain the additional information necessary for a more objective assessment of risk and review the sanitary or phytosanitary measure accordingly within a reasonable period of time.

8.   When a Member has reason to believe that a specific sanitary or phytosanitary measure introduced or maintained by another Member is constraining, or has the potential to constrain, its exports and the measure is not based on the relevant international standards, guidelines or recommendations, or such standards, guidelines or recommendations do not exist, an explanation of the reasons for such sanitary or phytosanitary measure may be requested and shall be provided by the Member maintaining the measure.

Article 6

Adaptation to Regional Conditions, Including Pest- or Disease-Free Areas and Areas of Low Pest or Disease Prevalence

1.   Members shall ensure that their sanitary or phytosanitary measures are adapted to the sanitary or phytosanitary characteristics of the area—whether all of a country, part of a country, or all or parts of several countries—from which the product originated and to which the product is destined. In assessing the sanitary or phytosanitary characteristics of a region, Members shall take into account, *inter alia,* the level of prevalence of specific diseases or pests, the existence of eradication or control programmes, and appropriate criteria or guidelines which may be developed by the relevant international organizations.

2.   Members shall, in particular, recognize the concepts of pest- or disease-free areas and areas of low pest or disease prevalence. Determination of such areas shall be based on factors such as geography, ecosystems, epidemiological surveillance, and the effectiveness of sanitary or phytosanitary controls.

* * *

Article 7

Transparency

Members shall notify changes in their sanitary or phytosanitary measures and shall provide information on their sanitary or phytosanitary measures in accordance with the provisions of Annex B.

---

into account technical and economic feasibility, that achieves the appropriate level of sanitary or phytosanitary protection and is significantly less restrictive to trade.

Article 8

Control, Inspection and Approval Procedures

Members shall observe the provisions of Annex C in the operation of control, inspection and approval procedures, including national systems for approving the use of additives or for establishing tolerances for contaminants in foods, beverages or feedstuffs, and otherwise ensure that their procedures are not inconsistent with the provisions of this Agreement.

Article 9

Technical Assistance

1.   Members agree to facilitate the provision of technical assistance to other Members, especially developing country Members, either bilaterally or through the appropriate international organizations. Such assistance may be, *inter alia,* in the areas of processing technologies, research and infrastructure, including in the establishment of national regulatory bodies, and may take the form of advice, credits, donations and grants, including for the purpose of seeking technical expertise, training and equipment to allow such countries to adjust to, and comply with, sanitary or phytosanitary measures necessary to achieve the appropriate level of sanitary or phytosanitary protection in their export markets.

2.   Where substantial investments are required in order for an exporting developing country Member to fulfil the sanitary or phytosanitary requirements of an importing Member, the latter shall consider providing such technical assistance as will permit the developing country Member to maintain and expand its market access opportunities for the product involved.

Article 10

Special and Differential Treatment

1.   In the preparation and application of sanitary or phytosanitary measures, Members shall take account of the special needs of developing country Members, and in particular of the least-developed country Members.

2.   Where the appropriate level of sanitary or phytosanitary protection allows scope for the phased introduction of new sanitary or phytosanitary measures, longer time-frames for compliance should be accorded on products of interest to developing country Members so as to maintain opportunities for their exports.

3.   With a view to ensuring that developing country Members are able to comply with the provisions of this Agreement, the Committee is enabled to grant to such countries, upon request, specified, time-limited exceptions in whole or in part from obligations under this Agreement, taking into account their financial, trade and development needs.

* * *

Article 11

Consultations and Dispute Settlement

1.   The provisions of Articles XXII and XXIII of GATT 1994 as elaborated and applied by the Dispute Settlement Understanding shall apply to consultations and the settlement of disputes under this Agreement, except as otherwise specifically provided herein.

* * *

Article 12

Administration

1.   A Committee on Sanitary and Phytosanitary Measures is hereby established to provide a regular forum for consultations. It shall carry out the functions necessary to implement the provisions of this Agreement and the furtherance of its objectives, in particular with respect to harmonization. The Committee shall reach its decisions by consensus.

2.   The Committee shall encourage and facilitate ad hoc consultations or negotiations among Members on specific sanitary or phytosanitary issues. The Committee shall encourage the use of international standards, guidelines or recommendations by all Members and, in this regard, shall sponsor technical consultation and study with the objective of increasing coordination and integration between international and national systems and approaches for approving the use of food additives or for establishing tolerances for contaminants in foods, beverages or feedstuffs.

3.   The Committee shall maintain close contact with the relevant international organizations in the field of sanitary and phytosanitary protection, especially with the Codex Alimentarius Commission, the International Office of Epizootics, and the Secretariat of the International Plant Protection Convention, with the objective of securing the best available scientific and technical advice for the administration of this Agreement and in order to ensure that unnecessary duplication of effort is avoided.

4.   The Committee shall develop a procedure to monitor the process of international harmonization and the use of international standards, guidelines or recommendations. For this purpose, the Committee should, in conjunction with the relevant international organizations, establish a list of international standards, guidelines or recommendations relating to sanitary or phytosanitary measures which the Committee determines to have a major trade impact. The list should include an indication by Members of those international standards, guidelines or recommendations which they apply as conditions for import or on the basis of which imported products conforming to these standards can enjoy access to their markets. For those cases in which a Member does not apply an international standard, guideline or recommendation as a condition for import, the Member should provide an indication of the reason therefor, and, in particular, whether it considers that the standard is not stringent enough to provide the appropriate level of sanitary or phytosanitary protection. If a Member revises its position, following its indication of the use of a standard, guideline or recommendation

as a condition for import, it should provide an explanation for its change and so inform the Secretariat as well as the relevant international organizations, unless such notification and explanation is given according to the procedures of Annex B.

* * *

7.   The Committee shall review the operation and implementation of this Agreement three years after the date of entry into force of the WTO Agreement, and thereafter as the need arises. Where appropriate, the Committee may submit to the Council for Trade in Goods proposals to amend the text of this Agreement having regard, *inter alia,* to the experience gained in its implementation.

Article 13

Implementation

Members are fully responsible under this Agreement for the observance of all obligations set forth herein. Members shall formulate and implement positive measures and mechanisms in support of the observance of the provisions of this Agreement by other than central government bodies. Members shall take such reasonable measures as may be available to them to ensure that non-governmental entities within their territories, as well as regional bodies in which relevant entities within their territories are members, comply with the relevant provisions of this Agreement. In addition, Members shall not take measures which have the effect of, directly or indirectly, requiring or encouraging such regional or non-governmental entities, or local governmental bodies, to act in a manner inconsistent with the provisions of this Agreement. Members shall ensure that they rely on the services of non-governmental entities for implementing sanitary or phytosanitary measures only if these entities comply with the provisions of this Agreement.

Article 14

Final Provisions

The least-developed country Members may delay application of the provisions of this Agreement for a period of five years following the date of entry into force of the WTO Agreement with respect to their sanitary or phytosanitary measures affecting importation or imported products. Other developing country Members may delay application of the provisions of this Agreement, other than paragraph 8 of Article 5 and Article 7, for two years following the date of entry into force of the WTO Agreement with respect to their existing sanitary or phytosanitary measures affecting importation or imported products, where such application is prevented by a lack of technical expertise, technical infrastructure or resources.

ANNEX A

DEFINITIONS

1.   Sanitary or phytosanitary measure—Any measure applied:

(a)   to protect animal or plant life or health within the territory of the Member from risks arising from the entry, establishment or spread of pests, diseases, disease-carrying organisms or disease-causing organisms;

(b)   to protect human or animal life or health within the territory of the Member from risks arising from additives, contaminants, toxins or disease-causing organisms in foods, beverages or feedstuffs;

(c)   to protect human life or health within the territory of the Member from risks arising from diseases carried by animals, plants or products thereof, or from the entry, establishment or spread of pests; or

(d)   to prevent or limit other damage within the territory of the Member from the entry, establishment or spread of pests.

Sanitary or phytosanitary measures include all relevant laws, decrees, regulations, requirements and procedures including, *inter alia,* end product criteria; processes and production methods; testing, inspection, certification and approval procedures; quarantine treatments including relevant requirements associated with the transport of animals or plants, or with the materials necessary for their survival during transport; provisions on relevant statistical methods, sampling procedures and methods of risk assessment; and packaging and labelling requirements directly related to food safety.

2.   *Harmonization*—The establishment, recognition and application of common sanitary and phytosanitary measures by different Members.

3.   *International standards, guidelines and recommendations*

(a)   for food safety, the standards, guidelines and recommendations established by the Codex Alimentarius Commission relating to food additives, veterinary drug and pesticide residues, contaminants, methods of analysis and sampling, and codes and guidelines of hygienic practice;

(b)   for animal health and zoonoses, the standards, guidelines and recommendations developed under the auspices of the International Office of Epizootics;

(c)   for plant health, the international standards, guidelines and recommendations developed under the auspices of the Secretariat of the International Plant Protection Convention in cooperation with regional organizations operating within the framework of the International Plant Protection Convention; and

(d)   for matters not covered by the above organizations, appropriate standards, guidelines and recommendations promulgated by other relevant international organizations open for membership to all Members, as identified by the Committee.

4.   *Risk assessment*—The evaluation of the likelihood of entry, establishment or spread of a pest or disease within the territory of an importing Member according to the sanitary or phytosanitary measures which might be applied, and of the associated potential biological and economic consequences; or the evaluation of the potential for adverse effects on human or animal health arising from the presence of additives, contaminants, toxins or disease-causing organisms in food, beverages or feedstuffs.

5.   *Appropriate level of sanitary or phytosanitary protection*—The level of protection deemed appropriate by the Member establishing a sanitary or phytosanitary measure to protect human, animal or plant life or health within its territory.

NOTE: Many Members otherwise refer to this concept as the "acceptable level of risk".

ANNEX B

TRANSPARENCY OF SANITARY AND PHYTOSANITARY REGULATIONS

Notification procedures

5.   Whenever an international standard, guideline or recommendation does not exist or the content of a proposed sanitary or phytosanitary regulation is not substantially the same as the content of an international standard, guideline or recommendation, and if the regulation may have a significant effect on trade of other Members, Members shall:

(a)   publish a notice at an early stage in such a manner as to enable interested Members to become acquainted with the proposal to introduce a particular regulation;

(b)   notify other Members, through the Secretariat, of the products to be covered by the regulation together with a brief indication of the objective and rationale of the proposed regulation. Such notifications shall take place at an early stage, when amendments can still be introduced and comments taken into account;

(c)   provide upon request to other Members copies of the proposed regulation and, whenever possible, identify the parts which in substance deviate from international standards, guidelines or recommendations;

(d)   without discrimination, allow reasonable time for other Members to make comments in writing, discuss these comments upon request, and take the comments and the results of the discussions into account.

6.   However, where urgent problems of health protection arise or threaten to arise for a Member, that Member may omit such of the steps

enumerated in paragraph 5 of this Annex as it finds necessary, provided that the Member:

    (a)   immediately notifies other Members, through the Secretariat, of the particular regulation and the products covered, with a brief indication of the objective and the rationale of the regulation, including the nature of the urgent problem(s);

    (b)   provides, upon request, copies of the regulation to other Members;

    (c)   allows other Members to make comments in writing, discusses these comments upon request, and takes the comments and the results of the discussions into account.

7. WTO AGREEMENT ON TRADE-RELATED ASPECTS OF INTELLECTUAL PROPERTY RIGHTS (TRIPS)

(Selected Provisions)

Table of Contents

AGREEMENT ON TRADE-RELATED ASPECTS OF INTELLECTUAL PROPERTY RIGHTS

Members,

Desiring to reduce distortions and impediments to international trade, and taking into account the need to promote effective and adequate protection of intellectual property rights, and to ensure that measures and procedures to enforce intellectual property rights do not themselves become barriers to legitimate trade;

Recognizing, to this end, the need for new rules and disciplines concerning:

(a)   the applicability of the basic principles of GATT 1994 and of relevant international intellectual property agreements or conventions;

(b)   the provision of adequate standards and principles concerning the availability, scope and use of trade-related intellectual property rights;

(c)   the provision of effective and appropriate means for the enforcement of trade-related intellectual property rights, taking into account differences in national legal systems;

(d)   the provision of effective and expeditious procedures for the multilateral prevention and settlement of disputes between governments; and

(e)   transitional arrangements aiming at the fullest participation in the results of the negotiations;

Recognizing the need for a multilateral framework of principles, rules and disciplines dealing with international trade in counterfeit goods;

Recognizing that intellectual property rights are private rights;

Recognizing the underlying public policy objectives of national systems for the protection of intellectual property, including developmental and technological objectives;

Recognizing also the special needs of the least-developed country Members in respect of maximum flexibility in the domestic implementation of laws and regulations in order to enable them to create a sound and viable technological base;

Emphasizing the importance of reducing tensions by reaching strengthened commitments to resolve disputes on trade-related intellectual property issues through multilateral procedures;

Desiring to establish a mutually supportive relationship between the WTO and the World Intellectual Property Organization (referred to in this Agreement as "WIPO") as well as other relevant international organizations;

Hereby agree as follows:

PART I

GENERAL PROVISIONS AND BASIC PRINCIPLES

Article 1

Nature and Scope of Obligations

1.   Members shall give effect to the provisions of this Agreement. Members may, but shall not be obliged to, implement in their law more extensive protection than is required by this Agreement, provided that such protection does not contravene the provisions of this Agreement. Members

shall be free to determine the appropriate method of implementing the provisions of this Agreement within their own legal system and practice.

2.   For the purposes of this Agreement, the term "intellectual property" refers to all categories of intellectual property that are the subject of Sections 1 through 7 of Part II.

3.   Members shall accord the treatment provided for in this Agreement to the nationals of other Members.[1] In respect of the relevant intellectual property right, the nationals of other Members shall be understood as those natural or legal persons that would meet the criteria for eligibility for protection provided for in the Paris Convention (1967), the Berne Convention (1971), the Rome Convention and the Treaty on Intellectual Property in Respect of Integrated Circuits, were all Members of the WTO members of those conventions.[2] Any Member availing itself of the possibilities provided in paragraph 3 of Article 5 or paragraph 2 of Article 6 of the Rome Convention shall make a notification as foreseen in those provisions to the Council for Trade-Related Aspects of Intellectual Property Rights (the "Council for TRIPS").

Article 2

Intellectual Property Conventions

1.   In respect of Parts II, III and IV of this Agreement, Members shall comply with Articles 1 through 12, and Article 19, of the Paris Convention (1967).

2.   Nothing in Parts I to IV of this Agreement shall derogate from existing obligations that Members may have to each other under the Paris Convention, the Berne Convention, the Rome Convention and the Treaty on Intellectual Property in Respect of Integrated Circuits.

Article 3

National Treatment

1.   Each Member shall accord to the nationals of other Members treatment no less favourable than that it accords to its own nationals with

---

[1]   When "nationals" are referred to in this Agreement, they shall be deemed, in the case of a separate customs territory Member of the WTO, to mean persons, natural or legal, who are domiciled or who have a real and effective industrial or commercial establishment in that customs territory.

[2]   In this Agreement, "Paris Convention" refers to the Paris Convention for the Protection of Industrial Property; "Paris Convention (1967)" refers to the Stockholm Act of this Convention of 14 July 1967. "Berne Convention" refers to the Berne Convention for the Protection of Literary and Artistic Works; "Berne Convention (1971)" refers to the Paris Act of this Convention of 24 July 1971. "Rome Convention" refers to the International Convention for the Protection of Performers, Producers of Phonograms and Broadcasting Organizations, adopted at Rome on 26 October 1961. "Treaty on Intellectual Property in Respect of Integrated Circuits" (IPIC Treaty) refers to the Treaty on Intellectual Property in Respect of Integrated Circuits, adopted at Washington on 26 May 1989. "WTO Agreement" refers to the Agreement Establishing the WTO.

regard to the protection[3] of intellectual property, subject to the exceptions already provided in, respectively, the Paris Convention (1967), the Berne Convention (1971), the Rome Convention or the Treaty on Intellectual Property in Respect of Integrated Circuits. In respect of performers, producers of phonograms and broadcasting organizations, this obligation only applies in respect of the rights provided under this Agreement. Any Member availing itself of the possibilities provided in Article 6 of the Berne Convention (1971) or paragraph 1(b) of Article 16 of the Rome Convention shall make a notification as foreseen in those provisions to the Council for TRIPS.

2.   Members may avail themselves of the exceptions permitted under paragraph 1 in relation to judicial and administrative procedures, including the designation of an address for service or the appointment of an agent within the jurisdiction of a Member, only where such exceptions are necessary to secure compliance with laws and regulations which are not inconsistent with the provisions of this Agreement and where such practices are not applied in a manner which would constitute a disguised restriction on trade.

Article 4

Most-Favoured-Nation Treatment

With regard to the protection of intellectual property, any advantage, favour, privilege or immunity granted by a Member to the nationals of any other country shall be accorded immediately and unconditionally to the nationals of all other Members. Exempted from this obligation are any advantage, favour, privilege or immunity accorded by a Member:

(a)   deriving from international agreements on judicial assistance or law enforcement of a general nature and not particularly confined to the protection of intellectual property;

(b)   granted in accordance with the provisions of the Berne Convention (1971) or the Rome Convention authorizing that the treatment accorded be a function not of national treatment but of the treatment accorded in another country;

(c)   in respect of the rights of performers, producers of phonograms and broadcasting organizations not provided under this Agreement;

(d)   deriving from international agreements related to the protection of intellectual property which entered into force prior to the entry into force of the WTO Agreement, provided that such agreements are notified to the Council for TRIPS and do not constitute an arbitrary or unjustifiable discrimination against nationals of other Members.

---

[3]   For the purposes of Articles 3 and 4, "protection" shall include matters affecting the availability, acquisition, scope, maintenance and enforcement of intellectual property rights as well as those matters affecting the use of intellectual property rights specifically addressed in this Agreement.

Article 5

Multilateral Agreements on Acquisition or Maintenance of Protection

The obligations under Articles 3 and 4 do not apply to procedures provided in multilateral agreements concluded under the auspices of WIPO relating to the acquisition or maintenance of intellectual property rights.

Article 6

Exhaustion

For the purposes of dispute settlement under this Agreement, subject to the provisions of Articles 3 and 4 nothing in this Agreement shall be used to address the issue of the exhaustion of intellectual property rights.

Article 7

Objectives

The protection and enforcement of intellectual property rights should contribute to the promotion of technological innovation and to the transfer and dissemination of technology, to the mutual advantage of producers and users of technological knowledge and in a manner conducive to social and economic welfare, and to a balance of rights and obligations.

Article 8

Principles

1.   Members may, in formulating or amending their laws and regulations, adopt measures necessary to protect public health and nutrition, and to promote the public interest in sectors of vital importance to their socio-economic and technological development, provided that such measures are consistent with the provisions of this Agreement.

2.   Appropriate measures, provided that they are consistent with the provisions of this Agreement, may be needed to prevent the abuse of intellectual property rights by right holders or the resort to practices which unreasonably restrain trade or adversely affect the international transfer of technology.

PART II

STANDARDS CONCERNING THE AVAILABILITY, SCOPE AND USE OF INTELLECTUAL PROPERTY RIGHTS

SECTION 1: COPYRIGHT AND RELATED RIGHTS

Article 9

Relation to the Berne Convention

1.   Members shall comply with Articles 1 through 21 of the Berne Convention (1971) and the Appendix thereto. However, Members shall not have rights or obligations under this Agreement in respect of the rights conferred under Article 6 *bis* of that Convention or of the rights derived therefrom.

2.   Copyright protection shall extend to expressions and not to ideas, procedures, methods of operation or mathematical concepts as such.

Article 10

Computer Programs and Compilations of Data

1.   Computer programs, whether in source or object code, shall be protected as literary works under the Berne Convention (1971).

2.   Compilations of data or other material, whether in machine readable or other form, which by reason of the selection or arrangement of their contents constitute intellectual creations shall be protected as such. Such protection, which shall not extend to the data or material itself, shall be without prejudice to any copyright subsisting in the data or material itself.

Article 11

Rental Rights

In respect of at least computer programs and cinematographic works, a Member shall provide authors and their successors in title the right to authorize or to prohibit the commercial rental to the public of originals or copies of their copyright works. A Member shall be excepted from this obligation in respect of cinematographic works unless such rental has led to widespread copying of such works which is materially impairing the exclusive right of reproduction conferred in that Member on authors and their successors in title. In respect of computer programs, this obligation does not apply to rentals where the program itself is not the essential object of the rental.

Article 12

Term of Protection

Whenever the term of protection of a work, other than a photographic work or a work of applied art, is calculated on a basis other than the life of a natural person, such term shall be no less than 50 years from the end of the calendar year of authorized publication, or, failing such authorized publication within 50 years from the making of the work, 50 years from the end of the calendar year of making.

Article 13

Limitations and Exceptions

Members shall confine limitations or exceptions to exclusive rights to certain special cases which do not conflict with a normal exploitation of the work and do not unreasonably prejudice the legitimate interests of the right holder.

Article 14

Protection of Performers, Producers of Phonograms (Sound Recordings) and Broadcasting Organizations

1.   In respect of a fixation of their performance on a phonogram, performers shall have the possibility of preventing the following acts when

undertaken without their authorization: the fixation of their unfixed performance and the reproduction of such fixation. Performers shall also have the possibility of preventing the following acts when undertaken without their authorization: the broadcasting by wireless means and the communication to the public of their live performance.

2.   Producers of phonograms shall enjoy the right to authorize or prohibit the direct or indirect reproduction of their phonograms.

3.   Broadcasting organizations shall have the right to prohibit the following acts when undertaken without their authorization: the fixation, the reproduction of fixations, and the rebroadcasting by wireless means of broadcasts, as well as the communication to the public of television broadcasts of the same. Where Members do not grant such rights to broadcasting organizations, they shall provide owners of copyright in the subject matter of broadcasts with the possibility of preventing the above acts, subject to the provisions of the Berne Convention (1971).

4.   The provisions of Article 11 in respect of computer programs shall apply *mutatis mutandis* to producers of phonograms and any other right holders in phonograms as determined in a Member's law. If on 15 April 1994 a Member has in force a system of equitable remuneration of right holders in respect of the rental of phonograms, it may maintain such system provided that the commercial rental of phonograms is not giving rise to the material impairment of the exclusive rights of reproduction of right holders.

5.   The term of the protection available under this Agreement to performers and producers of phonograms shall last at least until the end of a period of 50 years computed from the end of the calendar year in which the fixation was made or the performance took place. The term of protection granted pursuant to paragraph 3 shall last for at least 20 years from the end of the calendar year in which the broadcast took place.

6.   Any Member may, in relation to the rights conferred under paragraphs 1, 2 and 3, provide for conditions, limitations, exceptions and reservations to the extent permitted by the Rome Convention. However, the provisions of Article 18 of the Berne Convention (1971) shall also apply, *mutatis mutandis,* to the rights of performers and producers of phonograms in phonograms.

SECTION 2: TRADEMARKS

Article 15

Protectable Subject Matter

1.   Any sign, or any combination of signs, capable of distinguishing the goods or services of one undertaking from those of other undertakings, shall be capable of constituting a trademark. Such signs, in particular words including personal names, letters, numerals, figurative elements and combinations of colours as well as any combination of such signs, shall be eligible for registration as trademarks. Where signs are not inherently capable of distinguishing the relevant goods or services, Members may make

registrability depend on distinctiveness acquired through use. Members may require, as a condition of registration, that signs be visually perceptible.

2. Paragraph 1 shall not be understood to prevent a Member from denying registration of a trademark on other grounds, provided that they do not derogate from the provisions of the Paris Convention (1967).

3. Members may make registrability depend on use. However, actual use of a trademark shall not be a condition for filing an application for registration. An application shall not be refused solely on the ground that intended use has not taken place before the expiry of a period of three years from the date of application.

4. The nature of the goods or services to which a trademark is to be applied shall in no case form an obstacle to registration of the trademark.

5. Members shall publish each trademark either before it is registered or promptly after it is registered and shall afford a reasonable opportunity for petitions to cancel the registration. In addition, Members may afford an opportunity for the registration of a trademark to be opposed.

Article 16

Rights Conferred

1. The owner of a registered trademark shall have the exclusive right to prevent all third parties not having the owner's consent from using in the course of trade identical or similar signs for goods or services which are identical or similar to those in respect of which the trademark is registered where such use would result in a likelihood of confusion. In case of the use of an identical sign for identical goods or services, a likelihood of confusion shall be presumed. The rights described above shall not prejudice any existing prior rights, nor shall they affect the possibility of Members making rights available on the basis of use.

2. Article 6 *bis* of the Paris Convention (1967) shall apply, *mutatis mutandis,* to services. In determining whether a trademark is well-known, Members shall take account of the knowledge of the trademark in the relevant sector of the public, including knowledge in the Member concerned which has been obtained as a result of the promotion of the trademark.

3. Article 6 *bis* of the Paris Convention (1967) shall apply, *mutatis mutandis,* to goods or services which are not similar to those in respect of which a trademark is registered, provided that use of that trademark in relation to those goods or services would indicate a connection between those goods or services and the owner of the registered trademark and provided that the interests of the owner of the registered trademark are likely to be damaged by such use.

Article 17

Exceptions

Members may provide limited exceptions to the rights conferred by a trademark, such as fair use of descriptive terms, provided that such exceptions take account of the legitimate interests of the owner of the trademark and of third parties.

Article 18

Term of Protection

Initial registration, and each renewal of registration, of a trademark shall be for a term of no less than seven years. The registration of a trademark shall be renewable indefinitely.

Article 19

Requirement of Use

1.   If use is required to maintain a registration, the registration may be cancelled only after an uninterrupted period of at least three years of non-use, unless valid reasons based on the existence of obstacles to such use are shown by the trademark owner. Circumstances arising independently of the will of the owner of the trademark which constitute an obstacle to the use of the trademark, such as import restrictions on or other government requirements for goods or services protected by the trademark, shall be recognized as valid reasons for non-use.

2.   When subject to the control of its owner, use of a trademark by another person shall be recognized as use of the trademark for the purpose of maintaining the registration.

Article 20

Other Requirements

The use of a trademark in the course of trade shall not be unjustifiably encumbered by special requirements, such as use with another trademark, use in a special form or use in a manner detrimental to its capability to distinguish the goods or services of one undertaking from those of other undertakings. This will not preclude a requirement prescribing the use of the trademark identifying the undertaking producing the goods or services along with, but without linking it to, the trademark distinguishing the specific goods or services in question of that undertaking.

Article 21

Licensing and Assignment

Members may determine conditions on the licensing and assignment of trademarks, it being understood that the compulsory licensing of trademarks shall not be permitted and that the owner of a registered trademark shall have the right to assign the trademark with or without the transfer of the business to which the trademark belongs.

SECTION 3: GEOGRAPHICAL INDICATIONS (omitted)

* * *

SECTION 4: INDUSTRIAL DESIGNS (omitted)

* * *

SECTION 5: PATENTS

Article 27

Patentable Subject Matter

1.   Subject to the provisions of paragraphs 2 and 3, patents shall be available for any inventions, whether products or processes, in all fields of technology, provided that they are new, involve an inventive step and are capable of industrial application.[5] Subject to paragraph 4 of Article 65, paragraph 8 of Article 70 and paragraph 3 of this Article, patents shall be available and patent rights enjoyable without discrimination as to the place of invention, the field of technology and whether products are imported or locally produced.

2.   Members may exclude from patentability inventions, the prevention within their territory of the commercial exploitation of which is necessary to protect *ordre public* or morality, including to protect human, animal or plant life or health or to avoid serious prejudice to the environment, provided that such exclusion is not made merely because the exploitation is prohibited by their law.

3.   Members may also exclude from patentability:

(a)   diagnostic, therapeutic and surgical methods for the treatment of humans or animals;

(b)   plants and animals other than micro-organisms, and essentially biological processes for the production of plants or animals other than non-biological and microbiological processes. However, Members shall provide for the protection of plant varieties either by patents or by an effective *sui generis* system or by any combination thereof. The provisions of this subparagraph shall be reviewed four years after the date of entry into force of the WTO Agreement.

Article 28

Rights Conferred

1.   A patent shall confer on its owner the following exclusive rights:

(a)   where the subject matter of a patent is a product, to prevent third parties not having the owner's consent from the acts of: making, using, offering for sale, selling, or importing[6] for these purposes that product;

(b)   where the subject matter of a patent is a process, to prevent third parties not having the owner's consent from the act of using the process, and from the acts of: using, offering for sale,

---

[5]   For the purposes of this Article, the terms "inventive step" and "capable of industrial application" may be deemed by a Member to be synonymous with the terms "non-obvious" and "useful" respectively.

[6]   This right, like all other rights conferred under this Agreement in respect of the use, sale, importation or other distribution of goods, is subject to the provisions of Article 6.

selling, or importing for these purposes at least the product obtained directly by that process.

2.   Patent owners shall also have the right to assign, or transfer by succession, the patent and to conclude licensing contracts.

Article 29

Conditions on Patent Applicants

1.   Members shall require that an applicant for a patent shall disclose the invention in a manner sufficiently clear and complete for the invention to be carried out by a person skilled in the art and may require the applicant to indicate the best mode for carrying out the invention known to the inventor at the filing date or, where priority is claimed, at the priority date of the application.

2.   Members may require an applicant for a patent to provide information concerning the applicant's corresponding foreign applications and grants.

Article 30

Exceptions to Rights Conferred

Members may provide limited exceptions to the exclusive rights conferred by a patent, provided that such exceptions do not unreasonably conflict with a normal exploitation of the patent and do not unreasonably prejudice the legitimate interests of the patent owner, taking account of the legitimate interests of third parties.

Article 31

Other Use Without Authorization of the Right Holder

Where the law of a Member allows for other use[7] of the subject matter of a patent without the authorization of the right holder, including use by the government or third parties authorized by the government, the following provisions shall be respected:

(a)   authorization of such use shall be considered on its individual merits;

(b)   such use may only be permitted if, prior to such use, the proposed user has made efforts to obtain authorization from the right holder on reasonable commercial terms and conditions and that such efforts have not been successful within a reasonable period of time. This requirement may be waived by a Member in the case of a national emergency or other circumstances of extreme urgency or in cases of public non-commercial use. In situations of national emergency or other circumstances of extreme urgency, the right holder shall, nevertheless, be notified as soon as reasonably practicable. In the case of public non-commercial use, where the government or contractor, without making a patent search, knows or has demonstrable grounds to know that a valid

---

[7]   "Other use" refers to other than that allowed under Article 30.

patent is or will be used by or for the government, the right holder shall be informed promptly;

(c)   the scope and duration of such use shall be limited to the purpose for which it was authorized, and in the case of semi-conductor technology shall only be for public non-commercial use or to remedy a practice determined after judicial or administrative process to be anti-competitive;

(d)   such use shall be non-exclusive;

(e)   such use shall be non-assignable, except with that part of the enterprise or goodwill which enjoys such use;

(f)   any such use shall be authorized predominantly for the supply of the domestic market of the Member authorizing such use;

(g)   authorization for such use shall be liable, subject to adequate protection of the legitimate interests of the persons so authorized, to be terminated if and when the circumstances which led to it cease to exist and are unlikely to recur. The competent authority shall have the authority to review, upon motivated request, the continued existence of these circumstances;

(h)   the right holder shall be paid adequate remuneration in the circumstances of each case, taking into account the economic value of the authorization;

(i)   the legal validity of any decision relating to the authorization of such use shall be subject to judicial review or other independent review by a distinct higher authority in that Member;

(j)   any decision relating to the remuneration provided in respect of such use shall be subject to judicial review or other independent review by a distinct higher authority in that Member;

(k)   Members are not obliged to apply the conditions set forth in subparagraphs (b) and (f) where such use is permitted to remedy a practice determined after judicial or administrative process to be anti-competitive. The need to correct anti-competitive practices may be taken into account in determining the amount of remuneration in such cases. Competent authorities shall have the authority to refuse termination of authorization if and when the conditions which led to such authorization are likely to recur;

(l)   where such use is authorized to permit the exploitation of a patent ("the second patent") which cannot be exploited without infringing another patent ("the first patent"), the following additional conditions shall apply:

(i)   the invention claimed in the second patent shall involve an important technical advance of considerable economic significance in relation to the invention claimed in the first patent;

(ii)   the owner of the first patent shall be entitled to a cross-licence on reasonable terms to use the invention claimed in the second patent; and

(iii)   the use authorized in respect of the first patent shall be non-assignable except with the assignment of the second patent.

Article 32

Revocation / Forfeiture

An opportunity for judicial review of any decision to revoke or forfeit a patent shall be available.

Article 33

Term of Protection

The term of protection available shall not end before the expiration of a period of twenty years counted from the filing date.[8]

Article 34

Process Patents: Burden of Proof

1.   For the purposes of civil proceedings in respect of the infringement of the rights of the owner referred to in paragraph 1(b) of Article 28, if the subject matter of a patent is a process for obtaining a product, the judicial authorities shall have the authority to order the defendant to prove that the process to obtain an identical product is different from the patented process. Therefore, Members shall provide, in at least one of the following circumstances, that any identical product when produced without the consent of the patent owner shall, in the absence of proof to the contrary, be deemed to have been obtained by the patented process:

(a)   if the product obtained by the patented process is new;

(b)   if there is a substantial likelihood that the identical product was made by the process and the owner of the patent has been unable through reasonable efforts to determine the process actually used.

2.   Any Member shall be free to provide that the burden of proof indicated in paragraph 1 shall be on the alleged infringer only if the condition referred to in subparagraph (a) is fulfilled or only if the condition referred to in subparagraph (b) is fulfilled.

3.   In the adduction of proof to the contrary, the legitimate interests of defendants in protecting their manufacturing and business secrets shall be taken into account.

---

[8]   It is understood that those Members which do not have a system of original grant may provide that the term of protection shall be computed from the filing date in the system of original grant.

SECTION 6: LAYOUT-DESIGNS (TOPOGRAPHIES)
OF INTEGRATED CIRCUITS (omitted)

* * *

SECTION 7: PROTECTION OF UNDISCLOSED INFORMATION

Article 39

1.   In the course of ensuring effective protection against unfair competition as provided in Article 10 *bis* of the Paris Convention (1967), Members shall protect undisclosed information in accordance with paragraph 2 and data submitted to governments or governmental agencies in accordance with paragraph 3.

2.   Natural and legal persons shall have the possibility of preventing information lawfully within their control from being disclosed to, acquired by, or used by others without their consent in a manner contrary to honest commercial practices[10] so long as such information:

(a)   is secret in the sense that it is not, as a body or in the precise configuration and assembly of its components, generally known among or readily accessible to persons within the circles that normally deal with the kind of information in question;

(b)   has commercial value because it is secret; and

(c)   has been subject to reasonable steps under the circumstances, by the person lawfully in control of the information, to keep it secret.

3.   Members, when requiring, as a condition of approving the marketing of pharmaceutical or of agricultural chemical products which utilize new chemical entities, the submission of undisclosed test or other data, the origination of which involves a considerable effort, shall protect such data against unfair commercial use. In addition, Members shall protect such data against disclosure, except where necessary to protect the public, or unless steps are taken to ensure that the data are protected against unfair commercial use.

SECTION 8: CONTROL OF ANTI-COMPETITIVE
PRACTICES IN CONTRACTUAL LICENSES

Article 40

1.   Members agree that some licensing practices or conditions pertaining to intellectual property rights which restrain competition may have adverse effects on trade and may impede the transfer and dissemination of technology.

2.   Nothing in this Agreement shall prevent Members from specifying in their legislation licensing practices or conditions that may in particular

---

[10]   For the purpose of this provision, "a manner contrary to honest commercial practices" shall mean at least practices such as breach of contract, breach of confidence and inducement to breach, and includes the acquisition of undisclosed information by third parties who knew, or were grossly negligent in failing to know, that such practices were involved in the acquisition.

cases constitute an abuse of intellectual property rights having an adverse effect on competition in the relevant market. As provided above, a Member may adopt, consistently with the other provisions of this Agreement, appropriate measures to prevent or control such practices, which may include for example exclusive grantback conditions, conditions preventing challenges to validity and coercive package licensing, in the light of the relevant laws and regulations of that Member.

3.   Each Member shall enter, upon request, into consultations with any other Member which has cause to believe that an intellectual property right owner that is a national or domiciliary of the Member to which the request for consultations has been addressed is undertaking practices in violation of the requesting Member's laws and regulations on the subject matter of this Section, and which wishes to secure compliance with such legislation, without prejudice to any action under the law and to the full freedom of an ultimate decision of either Member. The Member addressed shall accord full and sympathetic consideration to, and shall afford adequate opportunity for, consultations with the requesting Member, and shall cooperate through supply of publicly available non-confidential information of relevance to the matter in question and of other information available to the Member, subject to domestic law and to the conclusion of mutually satisfactory agreements concerning the safeguarding of its confidentiality by the requesting Member.

4.   A Member whose nationals or domiciliaries are subject to proceedings in another Member concerning alleged violation of that other Member's laws and regulations on the subject matter of this Section shall, upon request, be granted an opportunity for consultations by the other Member under the same conditions as those foreseen in paragraph 3.

PART III

ENFORCEMENT OF INTELLECTUAL PROPERTY RIGHTS

SECTION 1: GENERAL OBLIGATIONS

Article 41

1.   Members shall ensure that enforcement procedures as specified in this Part are available under their law so as to permit effective action against any act of infringement of intellectual property rights covered by this Agreement, including expeditious remedies to prevent infringements and remedies which constitute a deterrent to further infringements. These procedures shall be applied in such a manner as to avoid the creation of barriers to legitimate trade and to provide for safeguards against their abuse.

2.   Procedures concerning the enforcement of intellectual property rights shall be fair and equitable. They shall not be unnecessarily complicated or costly, or entail unreasonable time-limits or unwarranted delays.

3.   Decisions on the merits of a case shall preferably be in writing and reasoned. They shall be made available at least to the parties to the proceeding without undue delay. Decisions on the merits of a case shall be

based only on evidence in respect of which parties were offered the opportunity to be heard.

4.   Parties to a proceeding shall have an opportunity for review by a judicial authority of final administrative decisions and, subject to jurisdictional provisions in a Member's law concerning the importance of a case, of at least the legal aspects of initial judicial decisions on the merits of a case. However, there shall be no obligation to provide an opportunity for review of acquittals in criminal cases.

5.   It is understood that this Part does not create any obligation to put in place a judicial system for the enforcement of intellectual property rights distinct from that for the enforcement of law in general, nor does it affect the capacity of Members to enforce their law in general. Nothing in this Part creates any obligation with respect to the distribution of resources as between enforcement of intellectual property rights and the enforcement of law in general.

SECTION 2: CIVIL AND ADMINISTRATIVE PROCEDURES AND REMEDIES

Article 42

Fair and Equitable Procedures

Members shall make available to right holders[11] civil judicial procedures concerning the enforcement of any intellectual property right covered by this Agreement. Defendants shall have the right to written notice which is timely and contains sufficient detail, including the basis of the claims. Parties shall be allowed to be represented by independent legal counsel, and procedures shall not impose overly burdensome requirements concerning mandatory personal appearances. All parties to such procedures shall be duly entitled to substantiate their claims and to present all relevant evidence. The procedure shall provide a means to identify and protect confidential information, unless this would be contrary to existing constitutional requirements.

Article 43

Evidence

1.   The judicial authorities shall have the authority, where a party has presented reasonably available evidence sufficient to support its claims and has specified evidence relevant to substantiation of its claims which lies in the control of the opposing party, to order that this evidence be produced by the opposing party, subject in appropriate cases to conditions which ensure the protection of confidential information.

2.   In cases in which a party to a proceeding voluntarily and without good reason refuses access to, or otherwise does not provide necessary information within a reasonable period, or significantly impedes a procedure relating to an enforcement action, a Member may accord judicial authorities

---

[11]   For the purpose of this Part, the term "right holder" includes federations and associations having legal standing to assert such rights.

the authority to make preliminary and final determinations, affirmative or negative, on the basis of the information presented to them, including the complaint or the allegation presented by the party adversely affected by the denial of access to information, subject to providing the parties an opportunity to be heard on the allegations or evidence.

Article 44

Injunctions

1.   The judicial authorities shall have the authority to order a party to desist from an infringement, *inter alia* to prevent the entry into the channels of commerce in their jurisdiction of imported goods that involve the infringement of an intellectual property right, immediately after customs clearance of such goods. Members are not obliged to accord such authority in respect of protected subject matter acquired or ordered by a person prior to knowing or having reasonable grounds to know that dealing in such subject matter would entail the infringement of an intellectual property right.

2.   Notwithstanding the other provisions of this Part and provided that the provisions of Part II specifically addressing use by governments, or by third parties authorized by a government, without the authorization of the right holder are complied with, Members may limit the remedies available against such use to payment of remuneration in accordance with subparagraph (h) of Article 31. In other cases, the remedies under this Part shall apply or, where these remedies are inconsistent with a Member's law, declaratory judgments and adequate compensation shall be available.

Article 45

Damages

1.   The judicial authorities shall have the authority to order the infringer to pay the right holder damages adequate to compensate for the injury the right holder has suffered because of an infringement of that person's intellectual property right by an infringer who knowingly, or with reasonable grounds to know, engaged in infringing activity.

2.   The judicial authorities shall also have the authority to order the infringer to pay the right holder expenses, which may include appropriate attorney's fees. In appropriate cases, Members may authorize the judicial authorities to order recovery of profits and/or payment of pre-established damages even where the infringer did not knowingly, or with reasonable grounds to know, engage in infringing activity.

Article 46

Other Remedies

In order to create an effective deterrent to infringement, the judicial authorities shall have the authority to order that goods that they have found to be infringing be, without compensation of any sort, disposed of outside the channels of commerce in such a manner as to avoid any harm caused to the right holder, or, unless this would be contrary to existing constitutional requirements, destroyed. The judicial authorities shall also have the authority to order that materials and implements the predominant use of which has been in the creation of the infringing goods be, without compensation of any sort, disposed of outside the channels of commerce in such a manner as to minimize the risks of further infringements. In considering such requests, the need for proportionality between the seriousness of the infringement and the remedies ordered as well as the interests of third parties shall be taken into account. In regard to counterfeit trademark goods, the simple removal of the trademark unlawfully affixed shall not be sufficient, other than in exceptional cases, to permit release of the goods into the channels of commerce.

Article 47

Right of Information

Members may provide that the judicial authorities shall have the authority, unless this would be out of proportion to the seriousness of the infringement, to order the infringer to inform the right holder of the identity of third persons involved in the production and distribution of the infringing goods or services and of their channels of distribution.

Article 48

Indemnification of the Defendant

1.   The judicial authorities shall have the authority to order a party at whose request measures were taken and who has abused enforcement procedures to provide to a party wrongfully enjoined or restrained adequate compensation for the injury suffered because of such abuse. The judicial authorities shall also have the authority to order the applicant to pay the defendant expenses, which may include appropriate attorney's fees.

2.   In respect of the administration of any law pertaining to the protection or enforcement of intellectual property rights, Members shall only exempt both public authorities and officials from liability to appropriate remedial measures where actions are taken or intended in good faith in the course of the administration of that law.

Article 49

Administrative Procedures

To the extent that any civil remedy can be ordered as a result of administrative procedures on the merits of a case, such procedures shall conform to principles equivalent in substance to those set forth in this Section.

SECTION 3: PROVISIONAL MEASURES

Article 50

1.   The judicial authorities shall have the authority to order prompt and effective provisional measures:

(a)   to prevent an infringement of any intellectual property right from occurring, and in particular to prevent the entry into the channels of commerce in their jurisdiction of goods, including imported goods immediately after customs clearance;

(b)   to preserve relevant evidence in regard to the alleged infringement.

2.   The judicial authorities shall have the authority to adopt provisional measures *inaudita altera parte* where appropriate, in particular where any delay is likely to cause irreparable harm to the right holder, or where there is a demonstrable risk of evidence being destroyed.

3.   The judicial authorities shall have the authority to require the applicant to provide any reasonably available evidence in order to satisfy themselves with a sufficient degree of certainty that the applicant is the right holder and that the applicant's right is being infringed or that such infringement is imminent, and to order the applicant to provide a security or equivalent assurance sufficient to protect the defendant and to prevent abuse.

4.   Where provisional measures have been adopted *inaudita altera parte,* the parties affected shall be given notice, without delay after the execution of the measures at the latest. A review, including a right to be heard, shall take place upon request of the defendant with a view to deciding, within a reasonable period after the notification of the measures, whether these measures shall be modified, revoked or confirmed.

5.   The applicant may be required to supply other information necessary for the identification of the goods concerned by the authority that will execute the provisional measures.

6.   Without prejudice to paragraph 4, provisional measures taken on the basis of paragraphs 1 and 2 shall, upon request by the defendant, be revoked or otherwise cease to have effect, if proceedings leading to a decision on the merits of the case are not initiated within a reasonable period, to be determined by the judicial authority ordering the measures where a Member's law so permits or, in the absence of such a determination, not to exceed 20 working days or 31 calendar days, whichever is the longer.

7.   Where the provisional measures are revoked or where they lapse due to any act or omission by the applicant, or where it is subsequently found that there has been no infringement or threat of infringement of an intellectual property right, the judicial authorities shall have the authority to order the applicant, upon request of the defendant, to provide the defendant appropriate compensation for any injury caused by these measures.

8.   To the extent that any provisional measure can be ordered as a result of administrative procedures, such procedures shall conform to principles equivalent in substance to those set forth in this Section.

SECTION 4: SPECIAL REQUIREMENTS
RELATED TO BORDER MEASURES[12]

Article 51

Suspension of Release by Customs Authorities

Members shall, in conformity with the provisions set out below, adopt procedures[13] to enable a right holder, who has valid grounds for suspecting that the importation of counterfeit trademark or pirated copyright goods[14] may take place, to lodge an application in writing with competent authorities, administrative or judicial, for the suspension by the customs authorities of the release into free circulation of such goods. Members may enable such an application to be made in respect of goods which involve other infringements of intellectual property rights, provided that the requirements of this Section are met. Members may also provide for corresponding procedures concerning the suspension by the customs authorities of the release of infringing goods destined for exportation from their territories.

Article 52

Application

Any right holder initiating the procedures under Article 51 shall be required to provide adequate evidence to satisfy the competent authorities that, under the laws of the country of importation, there is *prima facie* an infringement of the right holder's intellectual property right and to supply a sufficiently detailed description of the goods to make them readily recognizable by the customs authorities. The competent authorities shall inform the applicant within a reasonable period whether they have accepted the application and, where determined by the competent authorities, the period for which the customs authorities will take action.

---

[12] Where a Member has dismantled substantially all controls over movement of goods across its border with another Member with which it forms part of a customs union, it shall not be required to apply the provisions of this Section at that border.

[13] It is understood that there shall be no obligation to apply such procedures to imports of goods put on the market in another country by or with the consent of the right holder, or to goods in transit.

[14] For the purposes of this Agreement:

(a) "counterfeit trademark goods" shall mean any goods, including packaging, bearing without authorization a trademark which is identical to the trademark validly registered in respect of such goods, or which cannot be distinguished in its essential aspects from such a trademark, and which thereby infringes the rights of the owner of the trademark in question under the law of the country of importation;

(b) "pirated copyright goods" shall mean any goods which are copies made without the consent of the right holder or person duly authorized by the right holder in the country of production and which are made directly or indirectly from an article where the making of that copy would have constituted an infringement of a copyright or a related right under the law of the country of importation.

Article 53

Security or Equivalent Assurance

1.   The competent authorities shall have the authority to require an applicant to provide a security or equivalent assurance sufficient to protect the defendant and the competent authorities and to prevent abuse. Such security or equivalent assurance shall not unreasonably deter recourse to these procedures.

2.   Where pursuant to an application under this Section the release of goods involving industrial designs, patents, layout-designs or undisclosed information into free circulation has been suspended by customs authorities on the basis of a decision other than by a judicial or other independent authority, and the period provided for in Article 55 has expired without the granting of provisional relief by the duly empowered authority, and provided that all other conditions for importation have been complied with, the owner, importer, or consignee of such goods shall be entitled to their release on the posting of a security in an amount sufficient to protect the right holder for any infringement. Payment of such security shall not prejudice any other remedy available to the right holder, it being understood that the security shall be released if the right holder fails to pursue the right of action within a reasonable period of time.

Article 54

Notice of Suspension

The importer and the applicant shall be promptly notified of the suspension of the release of goods according to Article 51.

Article 55

Duration of Suspension

If, within a period not exceeding 10 working days after the applicant has been served notice of the suspension, the customs authorities have not been informed that proceedings leading to a decision on the merits of the case have been initiated by a party other than the defendant, or that the duly empowered authority has taken provisional measures prolonging the suspension of the release of the goods, the goods shall be released, provided that all other conditions for importation or exportation have been complied with; in appropriate cases, this time-limit may be extended by another 10 working days. If proceedings leading to a decision on the merits of the case have been initiated, a review, including a right to be heard, shall take place upon request of the defendant with a view to deciding, within a reasonable period, whether these measures shall be modified, revoked or confirmed. Notwithstanding the above, where the suspension of the release of goods is carried out or continued in accordance with a provisional judicial measure, the provisions of paragraph 6 of Article 50 shall apply.

Article 56

Indemnification of the Importer and of the Owner of the Goods

Relevant authorities shall have the authority to order the applicant to pay the importer, the consignee and the owner of the goods appropriate compensation for any injury caused to them through the wrongful detention of goods or through the detention of goods released pursuant to Article 55.

Article 57

Right of Inspection and Information

Without prejudice to the protection of confidential information, Members shall provide the competent authorities the authority to give the right holder sufficient opportunity to have any goods detained by the customs authorities inspected in order to substantiate the right holder's claims. The competent authorities shall also have authority to give the importer an equivalent opportunity to have any such goods inspected. Where a positive determination has been made on the merits of a case, Members may provide the competent authorities the authority to inform the right holder of the names and addresses of the consignor, the importer and the consignee and of the quantity of the goods in question.

Article 58

Ex Officio Action

Where Members require competent authorities to act upon their own initiative and to suspend the release of goods in respect of which they have acquired *prima facie* evidence that an intellectual property right is being infringed:

(a)   the competent authorities may at any time seek from the right holder any information that may assist them to exercise these powers;

(b)   the importer and the right holder shall be promptly notified of the suspension. Where the importer has lodged an appeal against the suspension with the competent authorities, the suspension shall be subject to the conditions, *mutatis mutandis,* set out at Article 55;

(c)   Members shall only exempt both public authorities and officials from liability to appropriate remedial measures where actions are taken or intended in good faith.

Article 59

Remedies

Without prejudice to other rights of action open to the right holder and subject to the right of the defendant to seek review by a judicial authority, competent authorities shall have the authority to order the destruction or disposal of infringing goods in accordance with the principles set out in Article 46. In regard to counterfeit trademark goods, the authorities shall not allow the re-exportation of the infringing goods in an unaltered state or subject them to a different customs procedure, other than in exceptional circumstances.

Article 60

De Minimis Imports

Members may exclude from the application of the above provisions small quantities of goods of a non-commercial nature contained in travellers' personal luggage or sent in small consignments.

SECTION 5: CRIMINAL PROCEDURES

Article 61

Members shall provide for criminal procedures and penalties to be applied at least in cases of wilful trademark counterfeiting or copyright piracy on a commercial scale. Remedies available shall include imprisonment and/or monetary fines sufficient to provide a deterrent, consistently with the level of penalties applied for crimes of a corresponding gravity. In appropriate cases, remedies available shall also include the seizure, forfeiture and destruction of the infringing goods and of any materials and implements the predominant use of which has been in the commission of the offence. Members may provide for criminal procedures and penalties to be applied in other cases of infringement of intellectual property rights, in particular where they are committed wilfully and on a commercial scale.

PART IV

ACQUISITION AND MAINTENANCE OF INTELLECTUAL PROPERTY RIGHTS AND RELATED *INTER-PARTES* PROCEDURES

Article 62

1.   Members may require, as a condition of the acquisition or maintenance of the intellectual property rights provided for under Sections 2 through 6 of Part II, compliance with reasonable procedures and formalities. Such procedures and formalities shall be consistent with the provisions of this Agreement.

2.   Where the acquisition of an intellectual property right is subject to the right being granted or registered, Members shall ensure that the procedures for grant or registration, subject to compliance with the substantive conditions for acquisition of the right, permit the granting or registration of the right within a reasonable period of time so as to avoid unwarranted curtailment of the period of protection.

3.   Article 4 of the Paris Convention (1967) shall apply *mutatis mutandis* to service marks.

4.   Procedures concerning the acquisition or maintenance of intellectual property rights and, where a Member's law provides for such procedures, administrative revocation and *inter partes* procedures such as opposition, revocation and cancellation, shall be governed by the general principles set out in paragraphs 2 and 3 of Article 41.

5.   Final administrative decisions in any of the procedures referred to under paragraph 4 shall be subject to review by a judicial or quasi-judicial authority. However, there shall be no obligation to provide an opportunity for such review of decisions in cases of unsuccessful opposition or administrative revocation, provided that the grounds for such procedures can be the subject of invalidation procedures.

PART V

DISPUTE PREVENTION AND SETTLEMENT

Article 63

Transparency

1.   Laws and regulations, and final judicial decisions and administrative rulings of general application, made effective by a Member pertaining to the subject matter of this Agreement (the availability, scope, acquisition, enforcement and prevention of the abuse of intellectual property rights) shall be published, or where such publication is not practicable made publicly available, in a national language, in such a manner as to enable governments and right holders to become acquainted with them. Agreements concerning the subject matter of this Agreement which are in force between the government or a governmental agency of a Member and the government or a governmental agency of another Member shall also be published.

2.   Members shall notify the laws and regulations referred to in paragraph 1 to the Council for TRIPS in order to assist that Council in its review of the operation of this Agreement. The Council shall attempt to minimize the burden on Members in carrying out this obligation and may decide to waive the obligation to notify such laws and regulations directly to the Council if consultations with WIPO on the establishment of a common register containing these laws and regulations are successful. The Council shall also consider in this connection any action required regarding notifications pursuant to the obligations under this Agreement stemming from the provisions of Article 6 *ter* of the Paris Convention (1967).

3.   Each Member shall be prepared to supply, in response to a written request from another Member, information of the sort referred to in paragraph 1. A Member, having reason to believe that a specific judicial decision or administrative ruling or bilateral agreement in the area of intellectual property rights affects its rights under this Agreement, may also request in writing to be given access to or be informed in sufficient detail of such specific judicial decisions or administrative rulings or bilateral agreements.

4.   Nothing in paragraphs 1, 2 and 3 shall require Members to disclose confidential information which would impede law enforcement or otherwise be contrary to the public interest or would prejudice the legitimate commercial interests of particular enterprises, public or private.

Article 64

Dispute Settlement

1.   The provisions of Articles XXII and XXIII of GATT 1994 as elaborated and applied by the Dispute Settlement Understanding shall apply to consultations and the settlement of disputes under this Agreement except as otherwise specifically provided herein.

2.   Subparagraphs 1(b) and 1(c) of Article XXIII of GATT 1994 shall not apply to the settlement of disputes under this Agreement for a period of five years from the date of entry into force of the WTO Agreement.

3.   During the time period referred to in paragraph 2, the Council for TRIPS shall examine the scope and modalities for complaints of the type provided for under subparagraphs 1(b) and 1(c) of Article XXIII of GATT 1994 made pursuant to this Agreement, and submit its recommendations to the Ministerial Conference for approval. Any decision of the Ministerial Conference to approve such recommendations or to extend the period in paragraph 2 shall be made only by consensus, and approved recommendations shall be effective for all Members without further formal acceptance process.

PART VI

TRANSITIONAL ARRANGEMENTS

Article 65

Transitional Arrangements

1.   Subject to the provisions of paragraphs 2, 3 and 4, no Member shall be obliged to apply the provisions of this Agreement before the expiry of a general period of one year following the date of entry into force of the WTO Agreement.

2.   A developing country Member is entitled to delay for a further period of four years the date of application, as defined in paragraph 1, of the provisions of this Agreement other than Articles 3, 4 and 5.

3.   Any other Member which is in the process of transformation from a centrally-planned into a market, free-enterprise economy and which is undertaking structural reform of its intellectual property system and facing special problems in the preparation and implementation of intellectual property laws and regulations, may also benefit from a period of delay as foreseen in paragraph 2.

4.   To the extent that a developing country Member is obliged by this Agreement to extend product patent protection to areas of technology not so protectable in its territory on the general date of application of this Agreement for that Member, as defined in paragraph 2, it may delay the application of the provisions on product patents of Section 5 of Part II to such areas of technology for an additional period of five years.

5.   A Member availing itself of a transitional period under paragraphs 1, 2, 3 or 4 shall ensure that any changes in its laws, regulations and practice

made during that period do not result in a lesser degree of consistency with the provisions of this Agreement.

Article 66

Least-Developed Country Members

1.   In view of the special needs and requirements of least-developed country Members, their economic, financial and administrative constraints, and their need for flexibility to create a viable technological base, such Members shall not be required to apply the provisions of this Agreement, other than Articles 3, 4 and 5, for a period of 10 years from the date of application as defined under paragraph 1 of Article 65. The Council for TRIPS shall, upon duly motivated request by a least-developed country Member, accord extensions of this period.

2.   Developed country Members shall provide incentives to enterprises and institutions in their territories for the purpose of promoting and encouraging technology transfer to least-developed country Members in order to enable them to create a sound and viable technological base.

Article 67

Technical Cooperation

In order to facilitate the implementation of this Agreement, developed country Members shall provide, on request and on mutually agreed terms and conditions, technical and financial cooperation in favour of developing and least-developed country Members. Such cooperation shall include assistance in the preparation of laws and regulations on the protection and enforcement of intellectual property rights as well as on the prevention of their abuse, and shall include support regarding the establishment or reinforcement of domestic offices and agencies relevant to these matters, including the training of personnel.

PART VII

INSTITUTIONAL ARRANGEMENTS; FINAL PROVISIONS
(omitted)

* * *

Table of Cases

Index

References are to Sections